How the Movies Saved Christmas

ALSO BY WILLIAM D. CRUMP

The Christmas Encyclopedia, 3d ed.
(McFarland 2013)

Encyclopedia of New Year's Holidays Worldwide
(McFarland 2008; softcover 2014)

How the Movies Saved Christmas

228 Rescues from Clausnappers, Sleigh Crashes, Lost Presents and Holiday Disasters

WILLIAM D. CRUMP

McFarland & Company, Inc., Publishers
Jefferson, North Carolina

LIBRARY OF CONGRESS CATALOGUING-IN-PUBLICATION DATA

Names: Crump, William D., 1949– author.
Title: How the movies saved Christmas : 228 rescues from Clausnappers, sleigh crashes, lost presents and holiday disasters / William D. Crump.
Description: Jefferson, North Carolina : McFarland & Company, Inc., Publishers, 2017. | Includes bibliographical references and index.
Identifiers: LCCN 2017009577 | ISBN 9781476664880 (softcover : acid free paper) ∞
Subjects: LCSH: Christmas films—Catalogs. | Christmas television programs—Catalogs.
Classification: LCC PN1995.9.C5113 C88 2017 | DDC 016.791436/34—dc23
LC record available at https://lccn.loc.gov/2017009577

BRITISH LIBRARY CATALOGUING DATA ARE AVAILABLE

ISBN (print) 978-1-4766-6488-0
ISBN (ebook) 978-1-4766-2770-0

© 2017 William D. Crump. All rights reserved

No part of this book may be reproduced or transmitted in any form or by any means, electronic or mechanical, including photocopying or recording, or by any information storage and retrieval system, without permission in writing from the publisher.

On the cover: *Rudolph, the Red-Nosed Reindeer*, 1964 (NBC/Photofest); Christmas background decorations © 2017 aykuterdogan/iStock

Printed in the United States of America

*McFarland & Company, Inc., Publishers
Box 611, Jefferson, North Carolina 28640
www.mcfarlandpub.com*

To my Mother
Mary Frances Drake Crump
in whose home
Christmas never had to be saved

Table of Contents

Preface
• 1 •

The Films
• 3 •

*Appendix: Categories of Reasons
for Saving Christmas Matched to the Films*
• 319 •

Index
• 325 •

Preface

While I was writing the first edition of *The Christmas Encyclopedia*, one of my now-late aunts asked, "What can you write about Christmas that's not already in the Bible?" Yes, she was quite serious. Well, how about *Miracle on 34th Street* or *A Christmas Story* or *Dr. Seuss' How the Grinch Stole Christmas* for starters? They're not "biblical," but they and a host of other movies are just as much a beloved part of the Christmas tradition as the biblical account of the birth of Christ. Had my aunt been alive today and had she known of the present work that I had undertaken, she undoubtedly would have asked, "What is there about Christmas that needs to be saved?" Perhaps some feel that Christmas must be saved from all the secularism and materialism that presently surround the holiday; in short, "put Christ back in Christmas." Perhaps others feel that Christmas must be saved from "anti–Christmas-ians" who wage the so-called War on Christmas with political correctness; who, for example, insist on the generic "Happy Holidays" or "Season's Greetings" over "Merry Christmas," "holiday trees" over "Christmas trees," and who stir up legal battles to prohibit the appearance of religious Christmas symbols like Nativity scenes in public places. I happily leave those particularly controversial issues to social, religious, and political analysts.

From the standpoint of the film industry, which is the focus of this book, the reasons for saving Christmas in the movies ("movies" being a generic word that encompasses theatrical releases; TV movies, series, and specials; and animated cartoons) vary widely from the religious and sublime to the ridiculous and comical and even to the macabre and bizarre. After researching more than 3,300 Christmas films, I found 228 with save–Christmas themes to showcase here. It is not the purpose of this book to present every save–Christmas film that's ever been made, principally for three reasons: (1) some are so outrageously blasphemous that they are far beyond serious consideration; (2) some are not available for viewing and lack sufficient details; (3) others are in the pre-production phase and will be released after the manuscript has been submitted for publication. Rather, I include a whole slew of examples that demonstrate a broad spectrum of reasonably tasteful-yet-sometimes-a-bit-spicy reasons for saving Christmas. I note 53 different reasons and group the films accordingly in a list in the back of this book for quick reference. The top five reasons for saving Christmas are, in descending order: Santa Claus or Santa surrogate or elves or reindeer are sick, injured, or incapacitated (36 films, eight of which depict Santa suffering from amnesia); villains sabotage or take over the North Pole (29 films); Santa crashes his sleigh (24 films); Christmas decorations and/or presents are lost or stolen (18 films); protagonists lose the Christmas spirit (17 films). It's not among the top five, but in one interesting group of 10 films, Santa is kidnapped.

Thus, a good percentage of save–Christmas films focus on the materialistic importance of Santa and his delivering the presents to having a successful Christmas. In a typical plot scenario, if a villain or other bogey jeopardizes Santa's delivery, there will be no Christmas unless the villain is vanquished, because in those movies, *Christmas is all about Santa*; the birth of Jesus is rarely ever mentioned (although in *Saving Christmas*, for example, Kirk Cameron attempts to put Christ back in Christmas). Time and again, characters utter typical statements such as, "There won't be a Christmas without Santa" or "Without Santa, Christmas will be ruined." So, when characters exclaim, "We've got to save Christmas!" they usually mean that Santa and gang are in trouble, which means that Christmas is in trouble; no Santa, no Christmas. A completely different sentiment is found in movies like *Dr. Seuss' How the Grinch Stole Christmas* in which the Whos gladly welcome Christmas without material gifts; such idealistic sentiment is lacking in the majority of save-Christmas films, however.

Because Santa is a prime figure here, it's not surprising to note that over half of the films presented are animated and directed at children, especially preschoolers, yet teens and adults will surely find flicks that pique their interest. Although the majority of the films originate in the United States, this book includes a sizeable number produced in foreign countries, either alone or in combination with the United States: Australia, Belgium, Canada, China, Denmark, Finland, France, Germany, India, Ireland, Italy, Japan, Luxembourg, Mexico, Netherlands, New Zealand, South Korea, Spain, Sweden, Switzerland, and the United Kingdom. Most, but not all, of the films are on either DVD, VHS, Amazon Instant Video, Hulu, Hoopla, YouTube, or Netflix. However, just because they are save-Christmas films that often focus on Santa, not all are rated G with fluffy animals and stupidly grinning elves; while many are not rated, the more "spicy" films bear the PG and R brands, so look out!

Despite the focus on saving Christmas, a number of films herein take on a more ecumenical tone by either mentioning Hanukkah in passing or showing a conspicuous menorah. Those save-Christmas films that give a nod to Hanukkah include ***Beauty and the Beast: The Enchanted Christmas; Billy and Mandy Save Christmas; I'm Dreaming of a White Ranger; A Muppets Christmas: Letters to Santa; Olive, the Other Reindeer; Road to the North Pole; Santa Switch; Save the Reindeer; 'Twas the Night Before Bumpy;*** and ***Uncle Grandpa: Christmas Special.*** Kwanzaa and Ramadan receive far less attention, ***Save the Reindeer*** and ***A Tale of Two Santas*** being the only films in this book that mention Kwanzaa, while ***Olive, the Other Reindeer*** is the only film here that mentions Ramadan. And to turn things around a bit, ***The Hebrew Hammer*** focuses on saving Hanukkah from an evil Santa.

All films are presented alphabetically by title. Each film includes the date of release; brief statements about what threatens Christmas and how the holiday is saved; a synopsis and commentary with principal cast members (for live-action movies); principal voices (for animated movies); production credits (writers, producers, directors, production companies, rating, genre, country of origin, run time); and references. Where applicable, each film also includes awards, interesting tidbits and noteworthy information not found in the synopsis, and excerpts of reviews from professional critics. Episodes from television series include brief background information about the series for the benefit of readers who are otherwise unfamiliar with the characters; I leave detailed histories to the Internet. All films are in color unless otherwise indicated. Titles in ***bold italics*** within film entries refer to other films discussed in this book.

A film book would be incomplete without photographs, so I have included several dozen for purposes of illustrating selected, principal characters, should readers not be familiar with them.

Watching Christmas films has done much to help me stay young at heart, even if ole Santa sometimes comes across as a comical yet homicidal maniac. So I sincerely hope that you as readers have as much fun with this book as I did in writing it.

The Films

The Action Elves Save Christmas Eve—December 7, 2009

Episode from the Animated Television Series *The Backyardigans*

THREAT TO CHRISTMAS: The Abominable Brothers steal Santa's magic bag.

HOW CHRISTMAS IS SAVED: A call from Santa convinces the Abominable Brothers to return the magic bag.

SYNOPSIS AND COMMENTARY: Featuring animated bipedal, anthropomorphic animals that appealed to preschool audiences, *The Backyardigans* was a computer-generated, musical adventure series of 80 half-hour episodes that ran on Treehouse TV in Canada from 2004 to 2010. The five preschool protagonists were Uniqua, a pink, high-spirited, unique creature; Pablo, a blue penguin with a yellow beak; Tyrone, a red-headed, orange moose; Tasha, a yellow hippopotamus; and Austin, a purple kangaroo. Possessing tiny hammers, they could build anything necessary at a moment's notice. The Backyardigans lived in houses of corresponding colors, and their back yards served as the settings for their adventures; hence, the word play on "back yard" in the series title. Instead of physically travelling to various destinations, the characters brought on their adventures via their vivid imaginations, whereupon their back yards were transformed into the appropriate settings, complete with musical numbers spanning a variety of genres and with 3-D dance choreography. The back yards returned as before when the adventures ended. The series utilized live-action dancers, the movements of whom were initially filmed and then transported to animation.

Stealing Santa's magic bag is just one of many ways to jeopardize Christmas and is found in other productions such as, for example, an episode of *The Smurfs* titled ***The Magic Sack of Mr. Nicholas***. As the imaginary adventure unfolds in "Action Elves," Uniqua, Pablo, and Tasha assume the secret elf code names of, respectively, Snappy, Mr. Jingles, and Flappy, as they enter Santa's workshop to make toys. Santa, code name Bowl Full of Jelly, is elsewhere, yet he charges the Action Elves by phone with the task of locating the Abominable Brothers and the missing bag, whereupon the Elves commence their search for the culprits on their trusty rocket horse (a play on "rocking horse"). En route, they crash into a snowbank and convert their shattered horse into rocket snow skis. Meanwhile, the Abominable Brothers (portrayed by Austin and Tyrone), have entertained themselves by wishing for items of comfort and pleasure that the bag is able to provide. Confronting the Brothers at their igloo-home, the Action Elves do not retrieve the magic bag until another phone call from Santa convinces the Brothers that the bag is his and that Christmas depends on his dispensing presents from it. Until that time, the Brothers had not realized to whom the bag belonged.

PRINCIPAL VOICES: Conan O'Brien (*Saturday Night Live*) as Santa; LaShawn Tináh Jefferies (*Whitepaddy*) as Uniqua speaking; Avion Baker (*True Blood*) as Uniqua singing; Jake Goldberg (*Grown Ups*) as Pablo speaking; Sean Curley (*Blue Mountain State*) as Pablo singing; Christopher Grant, Jr., as Tyrone speaking; Tyrel Jackson Williams (*Pants on Fire*) as Tyrone singing; Gianna Bruzzesse (*Beating Hearts*) as Tasha speaking; Gabriella Malek (*Henry Hugglemonster*) as Tasha singing; Jonah Bobo (*Crazy, Stupid, Love*) as Austin speaking; Nicholas Barasch (*Mr. Student Body President*) as Austin singing.

AWARDS: *The Backyardigans*—Annie Award

nominations for Best Animated Production for Children and Best Music in an Animated Television Production (2008); Artios nomination for Outstanding Achievement in Television Animation Casting (2011); Daytime Emmy Awards for Outstanding Individual Achievement in Animation (2007) and Outstanding Special Class Animated Program (2008); Daytime Emmy nominations for Outstanding Children's Animated Program (2009, 2010, 2011), Outstanding Writing in Animation (2009, 2012), Outstanding Music Direction and Composition (2009, 2013, 2014); Gemini Award and nomination (2007 and 2008, respectively) for Best Pre-School Program or Series; Gracie Allen Award for Outstanding Children/Adolescent Program (2008); Image Award nominations for Outstanding Children's Program (2007, 2010, 2011) and Outstanding Performance in a Youth/Children's Program (LaShawn Jefferies, 2010).

LYRICS AND MUSIC: Adam Peltzman and Evan Lurie, respectively.

SONGS: "Action Elves," "Magic Sack," "Snowball Fight," and "To Fill the Sack for Santa." The latter song is sung to the tune of "The Twelve Days of Christmas."

CHOREOGRAPHY: Beth Bogush

DANCERS: Hattie Mae Williams (Uniqua); Steven Konopelski (Pablo); Greg Sinacori (Tyrone); Amanda Ulibarri (Tasha); Kristen Frost (Austin).

PRODUCTION CREDITS—Writer: Adam Peltzman. Producer: Lynne Warner. Director: Dave Palmer. Production Companies: Nelvana and Nickelodeon Animation Studios. Rating: Not rated. Genres: Adventure, Children, Musical. Countries: Canada and USA. Run Time: 24 min.

REFERENCES: "The Action Elves Save Christmas Eve." Big Cartoon Database. http://www.bcdb.com/cartoon/114804-Action-Elves-Save-Christmas-Eve

"The Action Elves Save Christmas Eve." In *Christmas with The Backyardigans*. Hollywood, CA: Paramount Home Entertainment, 2010. DVD video.

"The Action Elves Save Christmas Eve." Internet Movie Database. http://www.imdb.com/title/tt1687145/

The Backyardigans. TV.com. http://www.tv.com/shows/the-backyardigans/

The Backyardigans. Wikipedia. https://en.wikipedia.org/wiki/The_Backyardigans

Wilson, Joanna. *Tis the Season TV: The Encyclopedia of Christmas-Themed Episodes, Specials and Made-for-TV Movies*. Akron, OH: 1701 Press, 2011.

The All Nighter Before Christmas —
(December 12, 2010)

Episode from the Animated Television Series *The Penguins of Madagascar*

THREAT TO CHRISTMAS: An argument between the animals at the Central Park Zoo over the theme for a Christmas Eve party degenerates into a snowball battle and general mayhem that may ruin "Kidsmas."

HOW CHRISTMAS IS SAVED: Santa provides sage advice that does the trick.

SYNOPSIS AND COMMENTARY: Elementary school children over preschoolers are more likely to appreciate the madcap comedy and shenanigans rampant in the entire *Madagascar* series of films from DreamWorks Animation, of which the present TV series and another TV short film discussed in this book, **Merry Madagascar**, are spinoffs. Premiering in 2008 on Nickelodeon in computer animation, *The Penguins of Madagascar* is set in the Central Park Zoo in New York City and follows the adventures of four penguin protagonists who are trained as spies: Skipper, the ringleader who is afraid of needles and views activities as military operations; Kowalski, an inventor who cannot read; Rico, a psychopathic weapons and explosives specialist who swallows tools and regurgitates them when needed; and Private, the rookie who speaks with a British accent. Other supporting characters include King Julien XIII, the ring-tailed, narcissistic monarch of the lemurs; Maurice, an aye-aye who disdains Julien; Mort, a dimwitted mouse lemur who is devoted to Julien; and Marlene, a female otter who serves as a buffer between the penguins and the lemurs.

In "All Nighter," it's Christmas Eve at the zoo, and the animals prepare to celebrate "Kidsmas," the penguins' term that describes

5   The All Nighter Before Christmas

The four protagonists from the TV series *The Penguins of Madagascar*. From left: Skipper, the ringleader, communicates via radio; Rico, the psychopathic weapons expert, is known for his excellent sushi; Private, the rookie, would like a nibble; and Kowalski, the technician, diddles with an abacus (Nickelodeon/Photofest).

Christmas for the animal children. Some of the animals vote for a contemporary party, whereas others desire a more traditional, 19th-century theme based on the Christmases of Charles Dickens, and an argument erupts. Although Marlene attempts to arbitrate, the scene degenerates into a snowball battle, which ruins many of the decorations. Meanwhile, Skipper and Private stalk bell-ringing street Santas in search of Santa's magic, and Julien wreaks havoc in search of the perfect Kidsmas tree when he, Maurice, and Mort steal the city's gigantic Christmas tree and attempt to haul it back to the zoo atop a stolen news van, which prompts a high-speed chase by the police. Just as Skipper and the animal children are sure that Kidsmas is ruined, the real Santa arrives and advises Skipper that he had Santa's magic all along, which is simply to make people happy. With that, Skipper conjures up colorful decorations and the Kidsmas party begins. The episode closes with the traditional greeting of "Merry Christmas" instead of the politically correct "Happy Holidays."

PRINCIPAL VOICES: Tom McGrath (*Shrek 3*) as Skipper, Jeff Bennett (*Johnny Bravo*) as Kowalski, John DiMaggio (*Futurama*) as Rico, James Patrick Stuart (*Pretty Woman*) as Private, Danny Jacobs (*Miles from Tomorrowland*) as King Julien, Kevin Michael Richardson (*Marvel's Guardians of the Galaxy*) as Maurice, Nicole Sullivan (*MADtv*) as Marlene, Andy Richter (*Late Night with Conan O'Brien*) as Mort, and Carl Reiner (*The Dick Van Dyke Show*) as Santa.

INTERESTING TIDBITS: Lemurs are prominent in the series, because they are endemic to the island of Madagascar, whereas penguins live almost exclusively in the Southern Hemisphere, especially Antarctica. Therefore, the irony of four penguins living up North in New York City contributes all the more to the comedy of the series. The animals' slapstick antics parallel those of the Warner Bros. cartoons of yesteryear in that animals may be "roughed up" a bit during all the excitement, but the animals suffer no long-term or fatal injuries such as being riddled with bullets or decapitation.

AWARDS: *The Penguins of Madagascar*—Among numerous awards and nominations, the series received 11 Emmy Awards for Outstanding Special Class Animated Program (2011); Outstanding Casting for an Animated Series/Special (2011); Outstanding Children's Animated Program (2011, 2012); Outstanding Music Direction and Composition (2011); Outstanding Performer in an Animated Program (Danny Jacobs, 2011); Outstanding Sound Editing (Live Action and Animation, 2011); Outstanding Writing in Animation (2011); Outstanding Original Song, Children's and Animation (2012); Outstanding Directing in an Animated Program (2012); and Outstanding Animated Program (2012).

PRODUCTION CREDITS—Writer: Brandon Sawyer. Producers: Dina Buteyn and Dean Hoff. Supervising Director: Nick Filippi. Production Company: DreamWorks Animation. Rating: Not rated. Genres: Animation, Action, Adventure, Comedy, Family. Country: USA. Run Time: 24 min.

REFERENCES: "The All Nighter Before Christmas." In *The Penguins of Madagascar: Operation Special Delivery*. Glendale, CA: DreamWorks Animation, 2014. DVD video.

"The All Nighter Before Christmas." Big Cartoon Database. http://www.bcdb.com/cartoon/130613-All-Nighter-Before-Christmas

"The All Nighter Before Christmas." Internet Movie Database. http://www.imdb.com/title/tt1780594/

Crump, William D. *The Christmas Encyclopedia*. Third Edition. Jefferson, NC: McFarland, 2013.

The Penguins of Madagascar. TV.com. http://www.tv.com/shows/the-penguins-of-madagascar/

The Penguins of Madagascar. Wikipedia. https://en.wikipedia.org/wiki/The_Penguins_of_Madagascar

The Amazing World of Gumball: Christmas Episode—December 4, 2013

Animated Television Short Film

THREAT TO CHRISTMAS: Richard runs down an old bum who turns out to be Santa suffering from amnesia.

HOW CHRISTMAS IS SAVED: Santa regains his memory when a present falls on his head.

SYNOPSIS AND COMMENTARY: Animated save-Christmas films often feature anthropomorphic animals as protagonists, but it's not every day that the protagonists consist of a biologically screwed-up "family," the supposedly related members of which are *different species* of animals. That's the case with *The Amazing World of Gumball*, a series of 11-minute animated episodes, created by Ben Bocquelet for Cartoon Network, ongoing since 2011. Set in the fictional town of Elmore, the series revolves around the shenanigans of the Watterson "family," the members of which are Gumball, a 12-year-old mischievous blue cat; his adopted brother Darwin, a ten-year-old air-breathing goldfish with legs; Anais, a pink rabbit and their precocious, four-year-old sister; Nicole, a blue cat and the workaholic mother; and Richard, a large pink rabbit and the witless, deadbeat father. The series is unusual in that it utilizes multiple animation formats, including traditional animation, puppetry, computer images, stop-motion figures, Flash animation, and live action.

While the Wattersons are driving around on Christmas Eve, Richard accidentally runs down a smelly old fly-infested, seemingly homeless bum, whom Richard believes to be Santa. Though the family rushes the bum to the hospital, Richard only worries about being on Santa's naughty list and seeks to make amends there and in his neighborhood by frantically performing "good deeds" that produce disastrous results. Since the bum only suffers from amnesia, he becomes the Wattersons' house guest over Nicole's objections, which prompts Richard to offer him everything, including the house, children, and wife. Attempting to jog the bum's memory, the kids kick out the mall's fake Santa and set up the bum instead, from whom Anais requests extravagant gifts, Darwin world peace, and Gumball to sit on his lap. When the bum rebuffs them, they vent their anger by destroying merchandise, then he joins their melee when he's denied a cookie. Back home, when the kids attempt to push the bum up the chimney, an exasperated Nicole deflates the kids' spirits by spilling the "truth" that Santa isn't real, because she had never received the gift she had wanted, despite having written Santa year after year. Elsewhere in the neighborhood, Richard stumbles across a one-reindeer sleigh while writing fence graffiti and then erasing it on pretense of being a good citizen. Believing he can save Christmas, Richard rockets away in the sleigh, zooming madly out of control such that a present falls from the sleigh, hits the bum on the head, and Santa regains his memory. Through a complicated mess, Gumball winds up in the sleigh with Richard, whereupon Santa unsuccessfully tries to talk them down with walkie-talkies; they successfully land only after Anais and Darwin fashion a runway by stringing flashing Christmas lights along the dark street. To wrap things up, Santa explains that Nicole had addressed those early letters to the *South* Pole, and though he's back on the nice list, Richard still wants $800 from Santa as reimbursement for the hospital bill.

PRINCIPAL VOICES: Logan Grove (*Christmas Do-Over*) as Gumball; Kwesi Boakye (*Flight*) as Darwin; Kyla Rae Kowalewski (*Adventure Time*) as Anais; Teresa Gallagher (*The Jacket*) as Nicole; Dan Russell (*Operation Flashpoint*) as Richard; Brian Blessed (*Alexander*) as Santa.

AWARDS: To date, the *Gumball* series has received numerous awards and nominations, including Annie Awards, British Academy Children's Awards, and Kids' Choice Awards, among others.

INTERESTING TIDBITS: Not that it really matters, but the film doesn't address how Santa originally suffers amnesia and becomes a homeless bum.

When Nicole informs the kids that Santa isn't real, the scene changes to black-and-white, in which the kids lament in song that Christmas is cancelled. The music for this scenario is an excerpt from the rather mournful Second Movement of Beethoven's Seventh Symphony, thus combining the classics with idiocy.

Other save-Christmas films in which Santa suffers amnesia include The **Boy Who Saved Christmas, Merry Madagascar, Miracle at the 34th Precinct, The Night Before the Night Before Christmas, Santa Who? The Search for Santa Paws,** and **Snow 2: Brain Freeze**.

REVIEWS: Brian Lowry of *Variety* reviewed the *Gumball* series (May 3, 2011): "…the show has an amusing look … but mostly a really clever spin on domestic chaos … qualifies as first-rate silliness."

Ken Tucker of *Entertainment Weekly* reviewed the series (August 15, 2012): "There are few examples of mainstream children's programming as wildly imaginative, as visually and narratively daring, as [this series] … a riot of animation looks and styles…. The visuals may hook very young viewers, but the sophisticated composition of the characters and the show's mastery of decades of pop fun … appeals to older viewers as well."

Emily Ashby of *Common Sense Media* reviewed the series: "…full of silly laughs and scrapes … absurdity is constant in this unpredictable cartoon … full of quirky characters … a lot of over-the-top humor…. Gumball's world is a place where kids' wildest imaginings will likely come to pass."

PRODUCTION CREDITS—Writers: Ben Bocquelet, Jon Foster, and James Lamont. Producer: Sarah Fell. Director: Mic Graves. Production Companies: Cartoon Network Development Studio Europe, Boulder Media Ltd., Studio SOI, and Dandelion Studios. Rating: TV-Y7. Genres: Animation, Comedy, Family, Fantasy. Countries: Ireland, United Kingdom, USA. Run Time: 11 min.

REFERENCES: *The Amazing World of Gumball: Christmas Episode*. In *Cartoon Network*

Holiday Collection. Burbank, CA: Warner Home Entertainment, 2014. DVD Video.

The Amazing World of Gumball: Christmas Episode. Internet Movie Database. http://www.imdb.com/title/tt1942683/

Ashby, Emily. *The Amazing World of Gumball*. Common Sense Media. https://www.commonsensemedia.org/tv-reviews/the-amazing-world-of-gumball

Lowry, Brian. "Cartoon Net Charms with Clever Import 'Gumball.'" *Variety*. http://variety.com/2011/voices/opinion/cartoon-net-charms-with-clever-import-gumball-3683/

Tucker, Ken. "'The Amazing World of Gumball' Season Premiere Review: Wildly Imaginative, with Tantrums and Giggles." *Entertainment Weekly*. http://www.ew.com/article/2012/08/15/the-amazing-world-of-gumball-season-2-review

An Angel for Christmas—1996

Direct-to-Video Animated Movie

THREAT TO CHRISTMAS: A town despot has cancelled Christmas for 25 years.

HOW CHRISTMAS IS SAVED: A little Christmas angel arrives to bring the spirit of Christmas back to the town.

SYNOPSIS AND COMMENTARY: Here's a story told in simple animation that focuses more on the true spirit of Christmas rather than on Santa, elves, and material gifts.

The year is 1901. In the town of Ironville, mean-spirited miser D.D. Kovet employs the vast majority of its citizens at his huge mill; without the mill, the town would not exist. Essentially holding the town hostage, Kovet has cancelled Christmas for the past 25 years for the sake of maintaining profits and keeps a Christmas Patrol to ensure that no one celebrates the holiday (Big Brother is watching you). All that changes when the little peasant girl Angela, accompanied by Wilfred, her talking pet wolf, arrives to bring the spirit of Christmas back into the town. When she unsuccessfully attempts to sell Christmas holly, the Christmas Patrol discovers a piece that had fallen in the square and launches a house-to-house search for the culprit. Although a brother and sister befriend Angela with kindness, another youth betrays her, whereupon the Christmas Patrol banishes her from town into the snowy weather. Initially dispirited, Angela would abandon her goal until, at Wilfred's request, she recalls the Christmas story from the Bible, which renews her faith. Determined to bring a Christmas tree into town, she receives aid from young friends and eventually from the Christmas Patrol itself, deeply moved when Angela's bravery saves a young friend from drowning. As the spirit of Christmas circulates among the town, its citizens congregate to decorate the tree erected in the town square, but an irate Kovet threatens to close the mill and move it to another town. Now Angela reveals herself as a Christmas angel, whereupon the Christmas spirit falls upon Kovet, whose reformation prompts behavior similar to that of a happy and benevolent Scrooge.

VOICES: Melissa Bathory, Don Francks, Edward Glen, Nonnie Griffin, Benji Plener, Paul Haddad, Jacelyn Holmes, James Rankin, Colette Stevenson.

INTERESTING TIDBITS: The villain's name, Kovet, is a play on "covet," because he covets cold hard cash.

Before Kovet's reformation, the narrator describes him as a man having a money chest the size of a truck and a heart the size of a pea. He's definitely a Scrooge-surrogate, for to him, Christmas is a "humbug."

REVIEWS: Tracy Moore of *Common Sense Media* (September 26, 2013): "…plots recycled from more popular Christmas tales about misers … kids who are in the Christmas mood may enjoy this tale of do-gooders in the name of the holiday spirit … it still imparts some decent lessons about compassion and the true meaning of the holiday."

PRODUCTION CREDITS—Writer: Mark Shekter and Sherman Snukal. Producer: Garry Blye. Director: Laura Shepherd. Production Companies: Blye Migicovsky Productions, Jaffa Road Management, and Phoenix Animation Studios. Rating: Not rated. Genre: Animation. Country: Canada. Run Time: 45 min.

REFERENCES: *An Angel for Christmas*. New York: GoodTimes Entertainment, 2003. DVD Video.

An Angel for Christmas. Internet Movie Database. http://www.imdb.com/title/tt1151447/

Moore, Tracy. *An Angel for Christmas.* Common Sense Media. https://www.commonsensemedia.org/movie-reviews/an-angel-for-christmas

Wilson, Joanna. *Tis the Season TV: The Encyclopedia of Christmas-Themed Episodes, Specials and Made-for-TV Movies.* Akron, OH: 1701 Press, 2011.

Angels Sing—March 10, 2013

Feature Film

THREAT TO CHRISTMAS: Painful memories of a childhood accident have caused Michael Walker to shun Christmas for 30 years.

HOW CHRISTMAS IS SAVED: Through the influence of old Nick, Michael finds "the courage to make peace with his past and find the hope, joy, and spirit that he lost."

SYNOPSIS AND COMMENTARY: Harry Connick, Jr. (*Dolphin Tale*), stars as college professor Michael Walker in this country-music adaptation of Turk Pipkin's novella, *When Angels Sing* (1999). The setting is Austin, TX. Thirty years ago, Michael's older brother David perished in an ice-skating accident on Christmas Day. Until that time, Michael had treasured Christmas, especially because he, David, and the rest of the family had always spent the holidays at their grandparents' home in the mountains. Filled with painful memories and blaming himself for David's death all those years, Michael has shunned Christmas ever since, to the disappointment of wife Susan (Connie Britton, *Nashville*) and young son David (Chandler Canterbury, *Repo Men*). Nick (Willie Nelson, *The Dukes of Hazzard*), a scruffy old stranger (perhaps Santa, perhaps an angel) who becomes most influential in turning Michael around, sells his spacious mansion to Michael at a fraction of its actual worth and stipulates that Michael must abide by all neighborhood standards. Nick fails to mention one of those standards, the "Trail of Lights," a garish house-decorating tradition that has gained worldwide fame with his house as the prime showpiece. Profoundly addicted to Christmas, all the neighbors (one played by Texas music icon Lyle Lovett) expect Michael likewise to adorn his new house with thousands of lights and decorations that they supply day after day. He refuses to participate and becomes the neighborhood Grinch, which parallels the sentiment in *Christmas with the Kranks* (but without nasty reprisals from the neighbors or the mandatory rooftop Frosty). The turning point for Michael is the death of his father "The Colonel" (Kris Kristofferson, *Miracle in the Wilderness*) a few days before Christmas, for which David blames himself and turns against Christmas just as Michael had done. Now Michael has only memories of his father and brother but, according to Nick, memories not only tie a family together for generations, they are the greatest gift a father can give to his son. Thenceforth, Michael chooses to focus on the good memories of father and brother, because both had adored Christmas. With his Christmas spirit restored, Michael imparts such wisdom to David.

Turk Pipkin's eclectic career includes work as an author, actor, comedian, and director. He is a co-founder of The Nobelity Project, a nonprofit organization that seeks solutions to global problems and is an advocate for children's rights worldwide. In addition to *When Angels Sing*, his notable works include *The Old Man and the Tee* and *Fast Greens*, among others.

INTERESTING TIDBITS: Ironically and contrary to the title, this production does not feature singing angels, but as expected, there are musical interludes, which include Willie Nelson's renditions of "Silent Night" and "Amazing Grace," a Lyle Lovett–Kat Edmonson duet on "Christmastime Is Here," and a Connick–Nelson duet on "When I'm Home" that accompanies the end credits. Because *Angels Sing* was filmed principally in Austin, a number of Texas musicians made cameo appearances, including The Trishas (Savannah Welch, Liz Foster, Kelley Mickwee, and Jamie Wilson), Dale Watson, Sara Hickman, Marcia Ball, Charlie Sexton, Miss Lavelle White, and Ray Benson.

REVIEWS: According to the Rotten Tomatoes film review site, 23 percent of critics gave this production a positive review. Metacritic gave it a score of 39/100 (generally unfavorable).

Ann Hornaday of *The Washington Post* (November 21, 2013): "Despite the story's tenuous rigging and too-obvious sentimentalism, the actors give it grounding and warm appeal…"

Annlee Ellingson of the *Los Angeles Times* (December 6, 2013): "Unfortunately, the juxtaposition of such country-music icons with the story's cringe-worthy treacle has one siding with Michael's bah-humbug attitude."

Neil Genzlinger of *The New York Times* (November 28, 2013): "*Angels Sing* is a music video disguised as a holiday movie, populated by musicians disguised as actors."

PRODUCTION CREDITS—Writer: Lou Berney. Producers: Elizabeth Avellán, Fred Miller, and Shannon McIntosh. Director: Tim McCanlies. Production Company: Angels Sing Productions. Rating: PG (mild thematic elements and brief language). Genres: Comedy, Drama, Family. Country: USA. Run Time: 87 min.

REFERENCES: *Angels Sing*. Internet Movie Database: http://www.imdb.com/title/tt1833888/

Angels Sing. Metacritic. http://www.metacritic.com/movie/angels-sing

Angels Sing. Official Web Site. http://www.angelssingmovie.com/

Angels Sing. Rotten Tomatoes. http://www.rottentomatoes.com/m/angels_sing/

Angels Sing. Santa Monica, CA: Lionsgate, 2013. DVD Video.

Crump, William D. *The Christmas Encyclopedia*. Third Edition. Jefferson, NC: McFarland, 2013.

Ellingson, Annlee. "Review: Even Willie Nelson and Harry Connick Jr. Can't Lift 'Angels Sing' Above Obviousness." *Los Angeles Times*. http://touch.latimes.com/#section/-1/article/p2p-78450294/

Genzlinger, Neil. "Holiday Movie or Music Video"? *The New York Times*. http://www.nytimes.com/2013/11/29/movies/holiday-movie-or-music-video.html

O'Sullivan, Michael, Ann Hornaday, and Stephanie Merry. "Watch Online: 'Sharknado,' 'Angels Sing,' 'Redlegs.'" *The Washington Post*. http://www.washingtonpost.com/news/going-out-guide/wp/2013/11/12/watch-online-sharknado-angels-sing-redlegs/

Pipkin, Turk. *When Angels Sing*. Chapel Hill, NC: Algonquin, 1999.

Anti-Claus Is Coming to Town—December 1, 2001

Episode from the Television Series *Big Wolf on Campus*

THREAT TO CHRISTMAS: Santa's jealous younger brother Roger swipes Santa's magical red coat and is determined to give the world a miserable Christmas.

HOW CHRISTMAS IS SAVED: Tommy-turned-werewolf and his friends put a stop to Roger.

SYNOPSIS AND COMMENTARY: According to the folklore in some countries, a child born during the 12 days of Christmas may become a werewolf (move over, Lon Chaney, Jr.). But that's not how teenage protagonist Tommy Dawkins (Brandon Quinn, *Kill Speed*) became a lycanthrope. Instead, he was mauled by one on a camping trip and thus followed in the footsteps of *I Was a Teenage Werewolf* (1957) and *Teen Wolf* (1985). Created by Peter Knight and Christopher Briggs, *Big Wolf on Campus* ran for 65 half-hour episodes from 1999 to 2002 (on YTV in Canada, Fox Family in the USA) and followed Tommy's adventures as he protected Pleasantville from a host of supernatural bogeys. The other principal characters included Merton Dingle (Danny Smith, *The Big Hit*), Tommy's effeminate goth friend and social outcast; and Lori Baxter (Aimée Castle, *Love and Human Remains*), a kickboxer and Tommy's sometime-sweetheart.

In "Anti-Claus," Santa's jealous younger brother Roger (David L. McCallum, *End of the Line*) swipes Santa's magical coat and, calling himself the "Anti-Claus," zooms about in Santa's no-reindeer jet sleigh to bring misery to the world, thus wrecking Christmas. A lousy pilot, Roger crashes the sleigh in Pleasantville and receives help from the three teens, who believe they have rescued Santa. Soon that moment shatters when the real Santa (Michel Perron, *Gothika*), sans red coat, proves himself by playing a segment from the sleigh's voice recorder (which smacks of police dash cams) that identifies Roger as the culprit. Santa and the teens find Roger sabotaging a house, but he escapes, Tommy wolfs out, and the foursome follows, but not until they pause to wax pseudo-philosophical about how wonderful Christmas can still be without presents—yeah, right! Meanwhile, Roger zooms about in the sleigh until werewolf-Tommy leaps aboard, retrieves Santa's coat, and tosses Roger out. With Tommy at the mercy of a runaway sleigh, Merton and Lori again wax sentimental about gifts, then turn the radio over to Santa, who talks Tommy down. Donning his coat, Santa's back in business, and he and Roger attend group therapy sessions at Sibling Rivalries Anonymous after Christmas.

INTERESTING TIDBITS: Danny Smith wrote, produced, and sang the show's theme song.

Sibling rivalry among the Clauses is also afoot in **Fred Claus**.

As of this writing, "Anti-Claus Is Coming to Town" was not available on DVD or VHS but could be seen on YouTube.com.

REVIEWS: *TV Tropes*: "[*Big Wolf on Campus* was] an incredibly lighthearted show that essentially existed to parody shows like *Buffy the Vampire Slayer* and *Charmed*, and replace their Wangsts with lighthearted slapstick and goofy wordplay."

PRODUCTION CREDITS—Writer: Rick Nyholm. Producer: Christian Gagné. Director: Erik Canuel. Production Companies: Ciné-Groupe, Fox Family Channel, Telescene Film Group Productions. Rating: TV-Y7. Genres: Action, Comedy, Horror. Country: Canada. Run Time: 30 min.

REFERENCES: "Anti-Claus Is Coming to Town." Internet Movie Database. http://www.imdb.com/title/tt0524436/

Big Wolf on Campus. Internet Movie Database. http://www.imdb.com/title/tt0189392/

"Series: Big Wolf on Campus." *TV Tropes*. http://tvtropes.org/pmwiki/pmwiki.php/Series/BigWolfOnCampus

Wilson, Joanna. *Tis the Season TV: The Encyclopedia of Christmas-Themed Episodes, Specials and Made-for-TV Movies*. Akron, OH: 1701 Press, 2011.

Arthur Christmas—November 23, 2011
Computer-Animated Feature Film

THREAT TO CHRISTMAS: Santa unwittingly overlooks one child. If her present isn't delivered by sunrise on Christmas Day, the North Pole will suffer a meltdown.

HOW CHRISTMAS IS SAVED: Arthur Christmas and Grandsanta deliver the gift amid wild and exciting adventures.

SYNOPSIS AND COMMENTARY: Despite an ultra-sophisticated, high-tech operation beneath the North Pole that delivers two billion presents in one night via a gigantic red spaceship/sleigh dubbed S-1, Santa, who is about to retire, manages to overlook one child. The mastermind behind the new technology is Santa's smug, older son Steve, who lacks the Christmas spirit and sees the holiday only from the viewpoint of statistics and production. On the other hand, Steve's clumsy but kind-hearted younger brother Arthur prefers to work in the mail room answering children's letters to Santa. Steve, next in line to be Santa, scoffs at Arthur's concern for Gwen, the little English girl who has been overlooked, and remarks, "Who cares about one single child?" Hardly possessing the child-friendly mindset necessary for a future Santa, Steve would dismiss the matter as a statistically acceptable error and convinces Santa to go along, which Arthur finds abominable. Taking the bull by the horns (or in this case the reindeer), Arthur and his mischievous grandfather, Grandsanta, head for England in "Evie," Grandsanta's old wooden sleigh pulled by descendants of the eight original reindeer (no Rudolph here). The elves prompt Steve and Santa to deliver a superior present to Gwen, but Santa's poor navigation in S-1 leads them to the wrong child. Meanwhile, after multiple twists and turns that include their being mistaken for aliens, temporarily stranded in Cuba, nearly eaten by lions in Africa, and losing reindeer, Arthur and Grandsanta arrive at Gwen's house just before sunrise, followed by Steve and Santa. When an argument erupts about who will place Gwen's gift, Arthur wins the honor after Santa realizes that his younger son has the true Christmas spirit and love for children, and it is Arthur who becomes the new Santa.

PRINCIPAL VOICES: James McAvoy (*Wanted*) as Arthur; Hugh Laurie (*House M.D.*) as Steve;

Younger son Arthur (center) awaits the arrival of his father, Santa, along with thousands of elves near Santa's gigantic spaceship/sleigh, S-1, in this scene from *Arthur Christmas* (2011) (Sony Pictures Releasing/Photofest).

Bill Nighy (*Hot Fuzz*) as Grandsanta; Jim Broadbent (*Cloud Atlas*) as Malcom Santa Claus; Imelda Staunton (*Maleficent*) as Margaret Claus; Ramona Marquez (*Outnumbered*) as Gwen; and Ashley Jensen (*Ugly Betty*) as Bryony, an elf obsessed with wrapping gifts.

Awards in 2011: Alliance of Women Film Journalists nomination for Best Animated Feature Film; Awards Circuit Community Award nomination for Best Animated Feature; Chicago Film Critics Association Award nomination for Best Animated Feature; Village Voice Film Poll nomination for Best Animated Feature Film; Village Voice Film Poll nomination for Best Animated Feature Film; Washington, D.C., Area Film Critics Association Award nomination for Best Animated Feature; Women Film Critics Circle Award nomination for Best Animated Female.

Awards in 2012: Annie Award for Voice Acting in a Feature Production (Bill Nighy); Central Ohio Film Critics Association Award for Best Animated Film ; San Diego Film Critics Society Award for Best Animated Film; Golden Globe nomination for Best Animated Feature Film; BAFTA Children's Award nomination for Best Feature Film; BAFTA Film Award nomination for Best Animated Film; Annie Award nominations for Best Animated Feature, Character Design, Storyboarding, Voice Acting (Ashley Jensen), and Writing in a Feature Production; Broadcast film Critics Association Award nomination for Best Animated Feature; Online Film and Television Association Award nominations for Best Animated Picture and Best Voice-Over Performance (Bill Nighy); Online Film Critics Society Award nomination for Best Animated Feature; Visual Effects Society Award nominations for Outstanding Virtual Cinematography and Outstanding Visual Effects in an Animated Feature Motion Picture; Young Artist Award nomination for Best Performance in a Voice-Over Role–Young Actress (Ramona Marquez).

Interesting Tidbit: With a budget of $100 million, the film earned over $46 million in domestic box office sales and over $147 million worldwide.

Reviews: According to the Rotten Tomatoes film review site, 92 percent of critics gave this production a positive review. Metacritic gave it a score of 69/100 (generally favorable).

Amy Biancolli of the *San Francisco Chronicle* (November 23, 2011): "It's as bright and twinkling as a Christmas tree, decked with warmth and humor."

Tom Russo of *The Boston Globe* (November 23, 2011): "…the film's indefatigable holiday spirit is infectious, and intimate as can be."

Michael O'Sullivan of the *Washington Post* (November 23, 2011): "A worthy addition to the Christmas movie canon."

Neil Genzlinger of *The New York Times* (November 22, 2011): "The plot may be a little too cluttered for the toddler crowd to follow, but the next age group up should be amused…"

PRODUCTION CREDITS—Writers: Peter Baynham and Sarah Smith. Producers: Peter Lord, David Sproxton, Carla Shelley, Steve Pegram. Director: Sarah Smith. Production Companies: Aardman Animations and Sony Pictures Animation. Rating: PG (mild crude humor). Genre: Animation, Comedy, Drama. Countries: United Kingdom and USA. Run Time: 97 min.

REFERENCES: *Arthur Christmas*. Big Cartoon Database. http://www.bcdb.com/cartoon/131013-Arthur-Christmas

Arthur Christmas. Box Office Mojo. http://www.boxofficemojo.com/movies/?id=arthurchristmas.htm

Arthur Christmas. Culver City, CA: Sony Pictures Home Entertainment, 2012. DVD Video.

Arthur Christmas. Internet Movie Database. http://www.imdb.com/title/tt1430607/

Arthur Christmas. Metacritic. http://www.metacritic.com/movie/arthur-christmas/critic-reviews

Arthur Christmas. Official Web Site: http://www.arthurchristmas.com

Arthur Christmas. Rotten Tomatoes. http://www.rottentomatoes.com/m/arthur_christmas

Arthur Christmas. Wikipedia. https://en.wikipedia.org/wiki/Arthur_Christmas

Biancolli, Amy. "'Arthur Christmas' Review: A Bright Holiday Film." *San Francisco Chronicle*. http://www.sfgate.com/movies/article/Arthur-Christmas-review-a-bright-holiday-film-2290414.php

Crump, William D. *The Christmas Encyclopedia*. Third Edition. Jefferson, NC: McFarland, 2013.

Fontes, Justine, and Ron Fontes. *Arthur Christmas: The Novel*. New York: Sterling Children's Books, 2011.

Genzlinger, Neil. "A Son of Santa Claus Takes the Reins." *The New York Times*. http://www.nytimes.com/2011/11/23/movies/arthur-christmas-voiced-by-james-mcavoy-and-hugh-laurie.html

O'Sullivan, Michael. "An Unexpected Holiday Gift." *The Washington Post*. http://www.washingtonpost.com/gog/movies/arthur-christmas,121022

Russo, Tom. "All Wrapped Up in Good Cheer." *The Boston Globe*. http://www.boston.com/ae/movies/articles/2011/11/23/santa_delivers_as_does_arthur_christmas/

Baby's First Christmas—November 12, 1983

Episode from the Animated Television Series *The Smurfs*

THREAT TO CHRISTMAS: Using a poisoned branch of mistletoe, the witch Chlorhydris plants the "kiss of hate" on Santa, and now the formerly jolly man despises Christmas.

HOW CHRISTMAS IS SAVED: A letter from a selfless boy to Santa and a kiss from Baby Smurf restore Santa's love of Christmas.

SYNOPSIS AND COMMENTARY: One of the most successful and longest-running Saturday morning cartoons in television history, *The Smurfs* aired on the NBC television network from 1981 to 1989. The creation of Belgian cartoonist Pierre "Peyo" Culliford, the Smurfs were blue, elfin characters "three apples high" who lived in mushroom-shaped houses and who first appeared as a comic strip in *Le Journal de Spirou* on October 23, 1958, where they were known as *Les Schtroumpfs*. A host of Smurf dolls and other merchandise followed, which inspired the television series after Fred Silverman, then-president of NBC, saw the pleasure that a Smurf doll brought to his daughter Melissa. Led by Papa Smurf, the more than 100 citizens of the sylvan Smurf Village bore names commensurate with personal characteristics: Brainy, Hefty, Handy, Grouchy, etc., with two female characters, Smurfette and tomboy Sassette. Serving as their principal nemeses were non–Smurf characters such as the evil wizard Gargamel, his young assistant Scruple, the diabolical cat Azrael, and the evil witch Chlorhydris, who strove to remove love from the world. The series featured 256 episodes (418 stories) and seven specials, one of the latter being **The Smurfs Christmas Special,** discussed in this volume. The Smurfs were also featured in several animated theatrical releases, for example, *The Smurfs and the Magic Flute* (1976), *The Baby Smurf* (1984), *The Smurfs* (2011), *The Smurfs 2* (2013), and *Get Smurfy* (2017).

In "Baby's First Christmas," Santa is known as Mr. Nicholas, his workshop has no elves, his four reindeer initially cannot fly, and there is no mention of the North Pole. Papa Smurf introduces the traditions of the holiday to Baby Smurf, such as making music, baking goodies, and gathering mistletoe to decorate Smurf Village. Gargamel's annual letter to Nicholas requesting no less than six Smurfs in his stockings always amuses the good toymaker, because he has no idea what Gargamel means. Determined to wipe out Christmas, Chlorhydris poses as Nicholas's neighbor bringing good cheer on Christmas Eve and bestows upon him the "kiss of hate" under poisoned mistletoe, which prompts Nicholas to loathe Christmas. When he abandons the unfinished toys, a small group of Smurfs, led by Papa Smurf, forgo their own holiday and volunteer to finish the job and deliver the gifts, yet the reindeer will not pull the sleigh without their master. Commencing with a kiss from Baby Smurf, the spell is broken after Nicholas reads a poor boy's selfless letter requesting that his mother's health be restored, but now Nicholas fears that it is too late to deliver all the presents in one night. With a wave of his hands, Baby Smurf miraculously enables the reindeer to fly, whereupon they, Nicholas, and the Smurfs take to the skies. On Christmas Morning, Gargamel and Chlorhydris curse their defeat, and the Smurfs, dancing around their Christmas tree, wish Baby Smurf a politically correct "Happy Holidays."

PRINCIPAL VOICES: Don Messick (*Tiny Toon Adventures*) as Papa Smurf, Frank Welker (*Aladdin*) as Hefty Smurf, Lucille Bliss (*Robots*) as Smurfette, Danny Goldman (*Young Frankenstein*) as Brainy Smurf, Michael Bell (*Rugrats*) as Grouchy Smurf, Hamilton Camp (*The Little Mermaid*) as Harmony Smurf, William Callaway (*Annie Hall*) as Clumsy Smurf, Alan Oppenheimer (*The NeverEnding Story*) as Vanity Smurf, Kip King (*Westworld*) as Tailor Smurf, Paul Winchell (*The AristoCats*) as Gargamel, and Amanda McBroom (*The Rose*) as Chlorhydris.

AWARDS: *The Smurfs*—Emmy Awards for Outstanding Children's Entertainment Series (1983, 1984); Emmy nominations for Outstanding Animated Program (1985–1989); Humanitas Prize for Children's Animation Category (1987); Blimp Award nominations for Favorite Cartoon (1988, 1989).

INTERESTING TIDBITS: Chlorhydris again threatens Christmas in a later *Smurfs* episode titled **The Magic Sack of Mr. Nicholas.** The *Smurfs* frequently utilized classical music in the background or for themes. Background music heard during this episode includes the haunting strains from the first movement of Franz Schubert's *Symphony No. 8* in B Minor ("Unfinished").

PRODUCTION CREDITS—Writers: Patsy Cameron and Tedd Anasti. Producer: Gerard Baldwin. Directors: Oscar Dufau, George Gordon, Carl Urbano, John Walker, Rudy Zamora, and Ray Patterson (Supervising Director). Production Companies: Hanna-Barbera Productions and SEPP International, S.A. Rating: Not rated. Genre: Animation, Family, Fantasy. Countries: Belgium and USA. Run Time: 23 min.

REFERENCES: "Baby's First Christmas." Big Cartoon Database. http://www.bcdb.com/cartoon/13604-Babys-First-Christmas

"Baby's First Christmas." In *The Smurfs: The Complete Third Season Volume One*. Amazon Instant Video.

"Baby's First Christmas" (*The Smurfs*). Wikia Christmas Specials. http://christmas-specials.wikia.com/wiki/Baby%27s_First_Christmas_(The_Smurfs)

Crump, William D. *The Christmas Encyclopedia*. Third Edition. Jefferson, NC: McFarland, 2013.

Lenburg, Jeff. *The Encyclopedia of Animated Cartoons*. Third Edition. New York: Facts on File, 2009.

Mallory, Michael. *Hanna-Barbera Cartoons*. Westport, CT: Hugh Lauter Levin Associates, 1998.

The Smurfs (TV Series). Wikipedia. http://en.wikipedia.org/wiki/The_Smurfs_(TV_series)

Wilson, Joanna. *Tis the Season TV: The Encyclopedia of Christmas-Themed Episodes, Specials and Made-for-TV Movies*. Akron, OH: 1701 Press, 2011.

A Barnyard Christmas Special—December 5, 2009

Also Known As "It's an Udderful Life"

Episode from the Computer-Animated Television Series *Back at the Barnyard*

THREAT TO CHRISTMAS: At the animals' Christmas Eve party, Santa catches ferret fever and cannot complete his rounds.

HOW CHRISTMAS IS SAVED: The animals take over for Santa.

SYNOPSIS AND COMMENTARY: Anthropomorphic barnyard animals horse around with bizarre and off-color humor in this series created by Steve Oedekerk. A spinoff of the computer-animated film *Barnyard: The Original Party Animals* (2006), it consisted of 52 half-hour episodes that ran on Nickelodeon from 2007 to 2011. The principal characters were the ringleader Otis, a gender-ambiguous male Holstein "cow" with inexplicable, pink udders; Pip, a barn mouse who spoke with a slight Mexican accent; Abby, a crazy, blonde, blue-eyed cow and Otis's love interest; Pig, a glutton; Freddy, a dimwitted ferret; Peck, an accident-prone rooster; Duke, an irresponsible sheepdog; Bessy, a sarcastic brown cow; Mrs. Beady, a woman who attempted to expose the talking animals; Farmer Buyer, the vegan owner of the barnyard.

In "Christmas Special," after some idiotic

Otis, the gender-ambiguous male Holstein "cow" and ringleader of the animals in the TV series *Back at the Barnyard*, shown here giving the mail carrier a real eyeful in a scene from *Barnyard: The Original Party Animals* (2006) (Paramount Pictures/Photofest).

preliminary scenes in which the animals dress up like humans to tour the town, Pig asks for a unicorn from a fake Santa, and Eugene "Snotty Boy" Beady (Mrs. Beady's bratty nephew) vows vengeance on Santa if he doesn't get a Red Ryder BB taser (a nod to *A Christmas Story* of 1983). Later, Otis and the gang throw a huge Christmas Eve party at which the guests of honor are Otis's old college chums, Donner and Blitzen, and Santa joins in to satisfy his raving fetish for cinnamon eggnog. During the evening, Santa unwittingly drinks from the cup belonging to Freddy (blame it on Otis), who is sick with ferret fever, and Santa also falls ill. If the remainder of Santa's gifts are not delivered by midnight, Christmas will end (the old Christmas-is-all-about-presents pitch). Fortunately, the animals' county is Santa's last stop, so they quickly make some new toys (Santa's bag will yield its toys only to Santa), decorate the tractor, and head out. The last house is Eugene's and, as expected, the kid lays a trap for Santa. With seconds to spare before midnight and before Christmas magic vanishes, Otis/Santa wrestles with Eugene and takes a flying leap to put the last gift under the tree. Finding his usual gift, a box of owl poop instead of the BB taser, Eugene attempts to pulverize Otis/Santa, whereupon the real Santa, having recovered, materializes and zaps the kid to the polar regions, where a hungry polar bear chases him into oblivion. For having saved Christmas, Santa makes all the gang honorary reindeer with fake antlers.

PRINCIPAL VOICES: Chris Hardwick (*Talking Dead*) as Otis/Blitzen/narrator; Leigh Allyn Baker (*Good Luck Charlie*) as Abby; Jeff Bennett (*Johnny Bravo*) as the mayor; Cam Clarke (*Teenage Mutant Ninja Turtles*) as Freddy; Jim Cummings (*Shrek*) as the polar bear; John DiMaggio (*Futurama*) as Donner; Jeffrey Garcia (*Happy Feet*) as Pip; Tino Insana (*Barnyard*) as Pig; Dom Irrera (*Barnyard*) as Duke; Steve Oedekerk (*Evan Almighty*) as Snotty Boy; Rob Paulsen (*The Mask*) as Peck; Kevin Michael Richardson (*Lilo and Stitch*) as Santa; Lloyd Sherr (*Turbo*) as Everett; Nick Simotas (*Back at the Barnyard*) as Goat; Wanda Sykes (*Evan Almighty*) as Bessy.

AWARDS: *Back at the Barnyard* received Annie nominations for Best Writing in an Animated Television Production (2008) and Best Music in an Animated Television Production or Short Form (2009); Artios nomination for Outstanding Achievement in Casting–Animation TV Programming (2008); Daytime Emmy nominations for Outstanding Special Class Animated Program and Outstanding Directing in an Animated Program (2008); won Daytime Emmy for Outstanding Special Class Animated Program and Daytime Emmy nomination for Outstanding Writing in Animation (2009); won Daytime Emmy for Outstanding Writing in Animation (2010); Daytime Emmy nominations for Outstanding Special Class Animated Program and Outstanding Writing in Animation (2011); Writers Guild of America Award (TV) nomination for Animation (2011).

INTERESTING TIDBITS: As a running gag through the show, a human narrator interrupts the story periodically to garner interest in a root canal, to file his toenails, and to ask about his huge, infected neck mole. Each time, the animals rush in, roll him up in a carpet, and toss him out the window. On the final run, they join the narrator in singing an armpit version of "Deck the Halls" (it should be obvious where the armpit sounds are inserted).

Is it necessary to add that "It's an Udderful Life" is a nod to *It's a Wonderful Life*?

REVIEW: While the humor rampant in *Back at the Barnyard* is clearly more suitable for adults, Emily Ashby of *Common Sense Media* is concerned about the series' potential impact on children: "Potty humor is popular … tamer than its big-screen predecessor … sends some iffy messages to kids. Otis often coerces his peers … to pull one over on the Farmer.... Perhaps most eyebrow-raising of all are the misconceptions kids might develop about barnyard animals.... Otis the *male* cow sports a protruding set of udders. A biology lesson this is not…"

PRODUCTION CREDITS—Writer: Gene Grillo. Producer: Paul Marshal. Director: T.J. Sullivan. Production Companies: Nickelodeon Animation Studios and O Entertainment. Rating: TV-Y7 (some rude humor). Genres: Animation, Comedy, Family. Country: USA. Run Time: 24 min.

REFERENCES: Ashby, Emily. *Back at the Barnyard. Common Sense Media*. https://www.commonsensemedia.org/tv-reviews/back-at-the-barnyard

Back at the Barnyard. Internet Movie Database. http://www.imdb.com/title/tt0857277/

"A Barnyard Christmas Special." Internet Movie Database. http://www.imdb.com/title/tt1581694/

"It's an Udderful Life." In *Back at the Barnyard Season 2*. Amazon Instant Video.

Wilson, Joanna. *Tis the Season TV: The Encyclopedia of Christmas-Themed Episodes, Specials and Made-for-TV Movies*. Akron, OH: 1701 Press, 2011.

The Bears Who Saved Christmas—
December 1994

Animated Television Short Film

THREAT TO CHRISTMAS: Two snowbound children fear that their Christmas will be ruined if Santa cannot find them.

HOW CHRISTMAS IS SAVED: Two teddy bear dolls come to life and provide the best Christmas the children ever had.

SYNOPSIS AND COMMENTARY: Snowbound en route to Grandma's house on Christmas Eve, a family of four finds shelter in a deserted cabin in the woods. When the two children, Tom and Suzie, lament that Santa will not find them and that Christmas will be ruined, their father reassures them that Santa will find a way, then mumbles to the mother, "with a miracle." That night while the children sleep, the Christmas Star shines upon their two teddy bear dolls, Christopher and Holly, and gives them life. The little bears trek through the forest to search for the perfect Christmas tree, together with friends Flashy, a flashlight; Charlie, a compass; and Bobby Bucktooth, a beaver whom the bears rescue from drowning in an icy pond. Bobby expresses his gratitude by gnawing down a gorgeous fir tree, but the commotion disturbs the hibernation of Black Bart, a huge, mean-tempered bear. Bart gives chase, and when he is about to strike, Holly warns him about a deadly bear trap in his path. Grateful, Bart repays the kindness by hauling the fir tree back to the cabin. The teddy bears decorate the cabin with garlands and holly and the tree with fruit, while numerous fireflies light the tree. When dawn breaks, the two little bears become dolls again, and the children are surprised to find them under the tree, along with many wrapped gifts. The implication is that Santa had visited the children after all. For the family, together, safe, and happy with love for one another, it is indeed their best Christmas.

PRINCIPAL VOICES: Charlie Adler (*Aladdin*) as Christopher and Bobby, Mary Kay Bergman (*South Park*) as Holly, Pam Dawber (*Mork and Mindy*) as Mom, Brad Garrett (*Everybody Loves Raymond*) as Black Bart, Henry Gibson (*Wedding Crashers*) as Flashy, Dan Gilvezan (*The Transformers*) as Dad, Haven Hartman (*Red Planet*) as Suzie, Adam Henderschott (*Celtic Pride*) as Tom, B.J. Ward (*The Return of Jafar*) as Mrs. Bucktooth, and Jonathan Winters (*Santa vs. the Snowman*) as Charlie.

INTERESTING TIDBITS: Appealing more to elementary school children, this squeaky-clean little program was presented on the *Toys "R" Us Family Theater*. The central focus is not on rescuing a harried Santa in trouble (indeed, Santa never makes an appearance on camera), but on two anthropomorphic teddy bears miraculously brought to life to become Santa-surrogates of a sort. The tone is overwhelmingly secular, save for a brief, spiritual moment when the Christmas Star shines upon the bear dolls.

PRODUCTION CREDITS—Writers: Rachel Koretsky and Steve Whitestone. Producer: Carol Corwin. Director: Allen Foster. Production Company: Film Roman Productions. Rating: Not rated. Genre: Adventure, Animation, Short. Country: USA. Run Time: 22 min.

REFERENCES: *The Bears Who Saved Christmas*. Big Cartoon Database. http://www.bcdb.com/cartoon/109092-Bears-Who-Saved-Christmas

The Bears Who Saved Christmas. In *Magical Christmas Collection*. Chatsworth, CA: Image Entertainment, 2009. DVD Video.

The Bears Who Saved Christmas. Internet Movie Database. http://www.imdb.com/title/tt0303725/

Crump, William D. *The Christmas Encyclopedia*. Third Edition. Jefferson, NC: McFarland, 2013.

Wilson, Joanna. *Tis the Season TV: The Encyclopedia of Christmas-Themed Episodes, Specials and Made-for-TV Movies*. Akron, OH: 1701 Press, 2011.

Beauty and the Beast: The Enchanted Christmas—November 11, 1997

Direct-to-Video Animated Musical

THREAT TO CHRISTMAS: Having been transformed into a hideous Beast ten years ago at Christmastime, the Beast despises Christmas and has forbidden its celebration in his castle.

HOW CHRISTMAS IS SAVED: Learning from Belle that there is always hope that his plight will someday end, Beast gives her the Christmas she's always wanted.

SYNOPSIS AND COMMENTARY: A European folktale holds that, in order to free her father, a young Beauty voluntarily becomes the prisoner of a Beast, then falls in love with him, which breaks the spell that an enchantress had put on him. Multiple variations of the tale exist, the most classic and well known of which is that by French author Jeanne-Marie LePrince

Belle teaches the Beast about the joy of the holidays in *Beauty and the Beast: The Enchanted Christmas* (1997). To the left of the Beast are Fife, Chip, and Mrs. Potts. To the right of Belle are Lumiere and Cogsworth. Walt Disney Enterprises/MMG Photo Archives (collection of William D. Crump).

de Beaumont, published in 1756 in *Magasin des enfants* (*Little Misses Magazine*) and titled *La Belle et la Bête* (*The Beauty and the Beast*).

Just as plentiful are adaptations of the tale to stage, screen, prose, and television. In the Disney animated motion picture *Beauty and the Beast* (1991), an enchantress's spell transforms a selfish prince into a hideous Beast and his servants into anthropomorphic household items. The Beast later imprisons the beautiful peasant girl Belle in his castle in exchange for her father's freedom, then falls in love with her, and the spell is eventually broken when Belle reciprocates the Beast's love. The Disney film spawned two direct-to-video sequels, *Belle's Magical World* (1998) and the present film under consideration.

A "midquel," the principal story line of which unfolds within the time frame of the original Disney film shortly after the fight with the wolves, *The Enchanted Christmas* opens a year later with a grand festival at the castle after the spell had been broken. As the now-human chief steward Cogsworth and his friend Lumiere argue over who really "saved" Christmas last year, Mrs. Potts the maid sets the record straight in flashback scenes:

It's Christmas Eve, and Belle plans a festive celebration to ease the Beast's melancholy spirits, yet the Beast has forbidden Christmas observances because his transformation had occurred ten years ago at that time. Unaware of this history, Belle enlists the help of enchanted servants Cogsworth the clock; Lumiere the candelabrum; Mrs. Potts the teapot; her son Chip the cup; and treetop angel Angelique, the former court decorator. Conspiring not only to uphold the Christmas prohibition but also to destroy the Beast and Belle and thus prevent the spell from being broken are the former court composer Forte, now a giant pipe organ whose dirges please the Beast because they help him to forget the past, and the piccolo Fife, Forte's reluctant henchman. Thanks to Belle's influence and persistence, however, the Beast receives hope that he will eventually overcome his plight, hope that inspires him to accept Christmas and to rout Forte before the organ destroys the castle with his thunderous music.

PRINCIPAL VOICES: Paige O'Hara (*Beauty and the Beast*) as Belle; Robby Benson (*Beauty and the Beast*) as the Beast; Jerry Orbach (*Law and Order*) as Lumiere; David Ogden Stiers (*M*A*S*H*) as Cogsworth; Bernadette Peters (*Anastasia*) as Angelique; Tim Curry (*Legend*) as Forte; Haley Joel Osment (*The Sixth Sense*) as Chip; Jeff Bennett (*Enchanted*) as Axe; Kath Soucie (*Rugrats*) as the enchantress; Paul Reubens (*Pee-wee's Playhouse*) as Fife; Angela Lansbury (*Mrs. Santa Claus*) as Mrs. Potts.

MUSIC: Rachel Portman

SONGS: Rachel Portman and Don Black: "Stories"; "As Long As There's Christmas"; "Don't Fall in Love"; "A Cut Above the Rest"; "Enchanted Christmas."

AWARDS (1998): World Animation Celebration Awards for Best Direct-to-Video Production and Best Director of Home Video (Andy Knight); Saturn Award nomination for Best Home Video Release; and Annie Award nominations for Outstanding Individual Achievements in an Animated Feature Production in the following categories: Directing (Knight), Music (Rachel Portman and Don Black for the song "As Long As There's Christmas"), Voice Acting by a Male Performer (Tim Curry and Jerry Orbach), and Writing (see below).

INTERESTING TIDBITS: As Belle ponders why Beast is so grumpy at Christmas, Chip asks, "What's Christmas?" In reply, Belle lists stockings in front of the fire, the tree, tinsel, and *presents*—in short, a typically secular, commercialized view of the holiday.

On her mission to find the perfect Christmas tree, Belle carries an axe, appropriately named Axe, the chief of the boiler room, who speaks with a Yiddish accent. Despite the fact that there are no obvious menorahs anywhere in the film (Lumiere is hardly one), Axe exclaims, "Merry Christmas and a Happy Hanukkah!" when Belle chooses her tree. This caught the ear of one reviewer (see below).

REVIEWS: There's a mixed bag here. Timothy Brayton of *Antagony and Ecstasy* (September 20, 2012): "…a vigorously non-denominational [Christmas celebration], in which even the name 'Santa Claus' is off-limits, for fear of depressing sales. Or offending the castle's woodman, now transformed into an axe ... who for a reason that beggars my understanding is being played as an enormously broad caricature of a Jewish shopkeeper, complete with the thing, and the oy gevalt, already."

David Nusair of *Reel Film Reviews* (November 30, 2010): "A typically low-rent direct-to-video Disney sequel."

At-A-Glance Film Reviews had a different take: "The interplay between Belle and the Beast was a bit overdone ... and the new character Angelique is tiresome, but thanks to Forte, his deluded minion Fife, and the antics of the old standbys Lumiere and Cogsworth, *An Enchanted Christmas* is quite enjoyable."

PRODUCTION CREDITS—Writers: Flip Kobler, Cindy Marcus, Bill Motz, and Bob Roth. Producer: Susan Kapigian (line producer). Director: Andy Knight. Production Companies: Walt Disney Animation Canada and Walt Disney Television Animation. Rating: G. Genre: Animation, Family, Fantasy. Countries: Canada and USA. Run Time: 72 min.

REFERENCES: *At-a-Glance Film Reviews*. http://www.rinkworks.com/movies/m/beauty.and.the.beast.the.enchanted.christmas.1997.shtml

Beauty and the Beast: The Enchanted Christmas. Big Cartoon Database. http://www.bcdb.com/cartoon/7272-Beauty-And-The-Beast-The-Enchanted-Christmas

Beauty and the Beast: The Enchanted Christmas. Burbank, CA: Buena Vista Home Entertainment, 2011. DVD Video.

Beauty and the Beast: The Enchanted Christmas. Internet Movie Database. http://www.imdb.com/title/tt0118692/

Brayton, Timothy. *Antagony and Ecstasy*. http://antagonie.blogspot.com/2012/09/disney-animation-looking-like-some-poor.html

Crump, William D. *The Christmas Encyclopedia*. Third Edition. Jefferson, NC: McFarland, 2013.

Haase, Donald. *The Greenwood Encyclopedia of Folktales and Fairy Tales*. Westport, CT: Greenwood Press, 2008.

LePrince de Beaumont, Jeanne-Marie. *Beauty and the Beast*. 1756. Reprint, Lexington, KY: Forgotten Books, 2008.

Nusair, David. *Film Reel Reviews*. http://reelfilm.com/beautytr.htm#2

Wilson, Joanna. *Tis the Season TV: The Encyclopedia of Christmas-Themed Episodes, Specials and Made-for-TV Movies*. Akron, OH: 1701 Press, 2011.

Beethoven's Christmas Adventure—
November 8, 2011

Direct-to-Video Movie

THREAT TO CHRISTMAS: When Henry the elf falls from Santa's sleigh and crashes in a small town, the magic sack of toys winds up in the hands of scam artists.

HOW CHRISTMAS IS SAVED: Beethoven is a key factor in finding the sack and routing the scammers.

SYNOPSIS AND COMMENTARY: What enables Henry (Kyle Massey, *Fish Hooks*), a stable elf at the North Pole, to communicate with animals? He licks a special, foul-tasting candy cane designed for the appropriate species, which in this case happens to be a dog; not just any dog but Beethoven, a big, sloppy St. Bernard (named after the composer Ludwig van Beethoven), who appears in this, his seventh movie in the *Beethoven* film series that was launched in 1992.

Having fallen into Santa's sleigh when his attempt at toymaking backfires, Henry takes an unscheduled joyride with the reindeer but topples out and crashes in snowy Woodhaven, MN. When last seen, the sleigh and reindeer continued on but probably headed back to the North Pole, though their fate is not specified. Santa's magic bag of toys, lost during the fall, ends up in the hands of greedy, bumbling scam artists Smirch (Robert Picardo, *Total Recall*) and Kenny (Curtis Armstrong, *Ray*), who use it to stock their toy store with an unlimited supply of merchandise at markedly inflated prices. Meanwhile, Henry solicits help from Mason (Munro Chambers, *Godsend*), a teenager looking after canine celebrity Beethoven and whose widowed, workaholic mom Christine (Kim Rhodes, *Another World*) is preoccupied with promotional ideas about the dog (which is a subplot all unto itself, complete with the neglectful mom scenario). With clues from a talking Beethoven, Mason and

Henry discover Santa's bag at the toy store and create a diversion there, during which Beethoven attempts to retrieve the bag. When the plan fails, Smirch kidnaps Henry and escapes on a motorcycle pulled from the bag, but instead plows into a crowd assembling for the town's Christmas parade, and the jig is up. The picture winds down with Beethoven as a surrogate reindeer who, having eaten Henry's magic berries for flying, pulls him in a sleigh back to the North Pole.

Dog Voices: Tom Arnold (*True Lies*) as Beethoven and John Kassir (*Pocahontas*) as Stray Dog.

Awards: ACTRA Award of Excellence nomination for Best Performance for a Male Artist (Manitoba, Ryan Miller, 2012) and Golden Reel Award nomination for Best Sound Editing–Direct to Video–Live Action (2012).

Interesting Tidbits: Aside from the commercialization in most save-Christmas movies, which stresses that without presents there can be no Christmas, this movie makes a pitch for the ASPCA. As grand marshal for the town's Christmas parade, Beethoven enters into a partnership with the ASPCA, which encourages everyone to free animals from shelters and give them good homes as Christmas pets. Riding with Beethoven on his float are all the animals from local shelters.

In an extended scene that will tickle children and the young-at-heart but probably not stodgy or dour adults, Beethoven and Stray Dog (a little pooch that takes up with Mason), experience much belching and flatulence amid vigorous tail-wagging after wolfing down Henry's candy. Similar scenes grace **Get Santa**, for those who are interested.

This is the only *Beethoven* movie that features talking dogs.

In a movie of this sort, expect much slapstick comedy with Beethoven running pell-mell, chase scenes, and general chaos in large crowds.

Review: Renee Schonfeld of *Common Sense Media* (November 8, 2011): "…bright, colorful, with a simply told story, engaging animal heroes, very silly comic villains, and plenty of slapstick action (including an extensive dog fart sequence that attempts to give the scientific facts about passing gas)."

Production Credits—Writers: Steven Altiere and Daniel Altiere. Producer: Jeff Freilich. Director: John Putch. Production Companies: Manitoba Film and Video Production Tax Credit, Original Pictures, and Universal International Pictures. Rating: PG (mild rude humor). Genre: Comedy, Fantasy. Countries: Canada and USA. Run Time: 90 min.

References: *Beethoven's Christmas Adventure*. Internet Movie Database. http://www.imdb.com/title/tt1855134/

Beethoven's Christmas Adventure. Universal City, CA: Universal Studios Home Entertainment, 2011. DVD Video.

Schonfeld, Renee. *Beethoven's Christmas Adventure. Common Sense Media*. https://www.commonsensemedia.org/movie-reviews/beethovens-christmas-adventure

Billy and Mandy Save Christmas—December 2, 2005

Episode from the Animated Television Series *The Grim Adventures of Billy and Mandy*

Threat to Christmas: Billy, Mandy, and Grim discover that Santa has become a vampire and is chained inside a coffin at the North Pole.

How Christmas Is Saved: Billy finds a stake-less antidote for Santa.

Synopsis and Commentary: Created by Maxwell Atoms (Adam Burton) for Cartoon Network, *The Grim Adventures of Billy and Mandy* first ran as one of two segments (the other being *Evil Con Carne*) in the children's animated television series *Grim and Evil* in 2001 and 2002, then ran as an independent spinoff series of 69 episodes (139 segments) from 2003 to 2007, plus three television movies, one special, and 19 shorts. The *Billy and Mandy* series followed the exploits of two neighborhood children: Billy, an energetic halfwit with a huge nose, and Mandy, a merciless, cynical girl thriving on hate. The other principal character was the Grim Reaper, whom the children finagled to be their companion after cheating him in a game of limbo. With a scythe as his source of power, Grim enabled the two children to venture into supernatural and macabre worlds.

"Billy and Mandy Save Christmas" is the answer to **Tim Burton's The Nightmare Before**

Christmas in that both combine the elements of Christmas and Halloween. Escaping from a burning shopping mall on Christmas Eve after Billy's visit with the fake Santa there spawns a riot, Mandy expresses skepticism about the existence of Santa. With his scythe, Grim rips a hole in the fabric of the universe (actually, Mother Earth's pants) and the three step through a portal to the North Pole, where they discover that Santa has become a vampire and is chained within his coffin. After a wild-goose chase that includes a failed attempt to eliminate Head Vampire Baron Von Ghoulish, the kids and Grim discover the cause of Santa's predicament: Nancy, his gap-toothed wife who, as the HEAD Head vampire, periodically turns Santa into one to appease her anger against him. As Mandy and Grim battle Nancy and her army of vampire elves, Billy whips up a vampire antidote of Christmas cookies and milk for Santa. Though Nancy will always remain a vampire, Santa has learned to have faith in her and believe in the goodness that is deep down inside her and all people. That's what Christmas is all about.

PRINCIPAL VOICES: Richard Horvitz (*The Angry Beavers*) as Billy; Grey DeLisle (*The Replacements*) as Mandy; Greg Eagles (*The Grim Adventures of Billy and Mandy*) as Grim; Malcom McDowell (*The Artist*) as Baron Von Ghoulish; Carol Kane (*Annie Hall*) as Nancy Claus; Gilbert Gottfried (*Aladdin*) as Santa; B.J. Ward (*The Return of Jafar*) as Mother Earth.

AWARDS: *The Grim Adventures of Billy and Mandy* series—Primetime Emmy Award for Outstanding Individual Achievement in Animation (2006); Annie Award for Directing in an Animated Television Production (2005); Annie nominations for Best Directing in an Animated Television Production (2005, 2007); Daytime Emmy nomination for Outstanding Broadband Children's Program (2007); Golden Reel nominations for Best Sound Editing in Television Animation (2002, 2005) and for Best Sound Editing in Television Animation Music (2003).

INTERESTING TIDBITS: At the North Pole, Billy is so excited to see Santa's motorized sleigh that when he kisses it, his tongue sticks to the icy vehicle. The scene is reminiscent of that in *A Christmas Story* (1983), when Flick, taking the "triple-dog-dare," sticks his tongue to an icy school flagpole and suffers the consequences.

With his fancy white coiffure, Head Vampire Baron Von Ghoulish is a caricature of Count Dracula from *Bram Stoker's Dracula* (1992).

Nancy Claus recalls when she witnessed vampire-Santa trying to drink the blood of "that poor elf who wanted to be a dentist," which alludes to Hermey the elf in the 1964 animated television special **Rudolph, the Red-Nosed Reindeer**.

As the end credits roll, Grim receives a new scythe for Christmas; Mandy, a lump of coal because she remains a skeptic; and Billy, leading the reindeer with his bulbous, red nose like Rudolph, flies away with Santa, who bids everyone a "Merry Christmas." Billy responds by hollering, "And Happy Hanukkah, too! That's what we have at our house and we get more presents!"

REVIEW: Joly Herman of *Common Sense Media* reviewed the series: "…this show isn't really appropriate for younger kids…. Some moments are truly scary and disgusting…. Lots of potty humor … those old enough to have a good sense of self might enjoy this program. It's clever, bizarre, and funny."

PRODUCTION CREDITS—Story: Maxwell Atoms. Writers: Nina Bargiel and Jeremy Bargiel. Producer: Louis J. Cuck. Directors: Russell Calabrese, Shaun Cashman, Robert Hughes, Sue Perrotto, and Juli Hashiguchi (supervising director). Production Companies: Cartoon Network Studios and Castle Creek Productions. Rating: TV-Y7. Genres: Animation, Comedy, Fantasy. Country: USA. Run Time: 30 min.

REFERENCES: "Billy and Mandy Save Christmas." Big Cartoon Database. http://www.bcdb.com/cartoon/108015-Billy-And-Mandy-Save-Christmas

"Billy and Mandy Save Christmas." In *Cartoon Network Christmas 3*. Burbank, CA: Warner Home Video, 2006. DVD Video.

"Billy and Mandy Save Christmas." Internet Movie Database. http://www.imdb.com/title/tt0592980/

The Grim Adventures of Billy & Mandy. Internet Movie Database. http://www.imdb.com/title/tt0292800/

The Grim Adventures of Billy & Mandy. Wikipedia. https://en.wikipedia.org/wiki/The_Grim_Adventures_of_Billy_%26_Mandy

Herman, Joly. *The Grim Adventures of Billy and Mandy. Common Sense Media.* https://www.commonsensemedia.org/tv-reviews/the-grim-adventures-of-billy-and-mandy

Lenburg, Jeff. *The Encyclopedia of Animated Cartoons*. Third Edition. New York: Facts on File, 2009.

Wilson, Joanna. *Tis the Season TV: The Encyclopedia of Christmas-Themed Episodes, Specials and Made-for-TV Movies.* Akron, OH: 1701 Press, 2011.

Booky and the Secret Santa—December 11, 2007

Television Movie

THREAT TO CHRISTMAS: Booky's family faces a bleak Christmas when her father loses his job just before the holidays in Depression-era Toronto.

HOW CHRISTMAS IS SAVED: Booky befriends the president of the T. Eaton Company, who becomes a secret Santa.

SYNOPSIS AND COMMENTARY: During the Great Depression, the T. Eaton Company Limited, founded by Timothy Eaton in Toronto in 1869, was one of the largest department stores in North America. Even then, it was conceivable that the company laid off employees from time to time because of budget cuts. When this happened at Christmastime, the holidays of families so affected promised to be quite bleak. This movie depicts such a fictional scenario, based on the *Booky* trilogy of novels by Canadian children's author Bernice Thurman Hunter, who set the stories in Toronto during the Depression era and incorporated many of her childhood experiences into the story lines.

Ten-year-old Beatrice "Booky" Thomson (Rachel Marcus, *Booky's Crush*) is determined to give her loving, working-class family a happy Christmas, despite the fact that her father Thomas (Stuart Hughes, *Cinderella Man*) has lost his job at Eaton's, where he had made harnesses. Now that Booky and her family are beneficiaries of Eaton's charity drive, she may also lose her best friend Laura Westover (Emilia McCarthy, *Zapped*), because the latter's social-climbing mother (Nahanni Johnstone, *The Doghouse*) desires a higher status of friends for her daughter. By chance, Booky manages to defuse a robbery attempt on company president Mr. Eaton (Kenneth Welsh, *The Aviator*), because she believes that the Santa she had seen in the Eaton Christmas Parade is Eaton himself. Though he initially denies the Santa claim, Eaton finally confesses and, in gratitude to Booky, grants her one "wish." In order to make Laura happy, Booky's selfless wish is for Eaton to be a secret Santa and invite Laura's parents to his grand Christmas party, but Eaton surprises the Thomsons with an invitation as well. Eaton promises Thomas a job when conditions improve, but it is Booky who ultimately aids her father and saves Christmas when she discovers a job opening at a chocolate factory while searching for chocolate scraps for her siblings' stockings.

AWARDS: In 2008, this picture received a Directors Guild of Canada Team Award for Family Television Movie; Gemini Award nominations for Best Supporting Actress (Johnstone), Best Actress in a Leading Role (Follows and Marcus), and Best Sound in a Dramatic Program; two Golden Reel Award nominations for Best Sound Editing.

INTERESTING TIDBITS: Megan Follows, who plays Francy Thomson, Booky's mother, is well known for having portrayed Anne Shirley in the television miniseries *Anne of Green Gables* (1985).

The movie depicts scenes of the Thomson family attending Eaton's Santa Claus Parade, which was an annual tradition in Toronto from 1905 until 1982, when it was cancelled for financial reasons. Stretching 1.5 miles with incredible floats originally drawn by horses and with costumed children marching, Eaton's was at one time the largest parade in North America. In the 1950s, it was televised over British and French networks and via CBS in the USA.

As hinted in the movie, the identity of each year's parade Santa was a well-guarded secret.

A native of Toronto, Bernice Thurman Hunter (1922–2002) was employed at Eaton's as an adult and did not publish her first book, *That Scatterbrain Booky*, until she was a grandmother. *Booky* sequels include *With Love from Booky* and *As Ever, Booky*. All of Hunter's novels depict scenes from the lives of children growing up in earlier days of Canadian history.

REVIEW: Donna Rolfe of The Dove Foundation: "…teaches many lessons about being kind, helping others and about pride … there is some minor language that may be offensive to some people. We award this film with the Dove 'Family-Approved' 12+ seal."

PRODUCTION CREDITS—Writer: Joe Wiesenfeld. Producer: Armand Leo, Laurie McLarty, and Phyllis Platt. Director: Peter Moss. Production Companies: Booky II, Platt Productions, and Shaftesbury Films. Rating: PG (mild thematic elements and brief language). Genre: Family. Country: Canada. Run Time: 90 min.

REFERENCES: *Booky and the Secret Santa*. Fort Mill, SC: Phase 4 Films, 2010. DVD Video.

Booky and the Secret Santa. Internet Movie Database. http://www.imdb.com/title/tt1129407/

Crump, William D. *The Christmas Encyclopedia*. Third Edition. Jefferson, NC: McFarland, 2013.

"Eaton's Santa Claus Parade." Ontario Archives. http://www.archives.gov.on.ca/en/explore/online/eatons/eatons_parade.aspx

Rolfe, Donna. *Booky and the Secret Santa*. The Dove Foundation. http://www.dove.org/review/8525-booky-and-the-secret-santa/

Sawyer, Deborah C. "The T. Eaton Company Limited." In *The Canadian Encyclopedia*. http://www.thecanadianencyclopedia.ca/en/article/t-eaton-company-limited/

Wilson, Joanna. *Tis the Season TV: The Encyclopedia of Christmas-Themed Episodes, Specials and Made-for-TV Movies*. Akron, OH: 1701 Press, 2011.

The Boy Who Saved Christmas—1998

Television Movie

THREAT TO CHRISTMAS: Santa's evil brother Atnas attempts to take over the North Pole and reverse Christmas, such that instead of Atnas giving gifts to everyone, they will give gifts to Atnas.

HOW CHRISTMAS IS SAVED: A young boy manages to supply Santa with his much-needed magic hat in order to defeat his brother.

SYNOPSIS AND COMMENTARY: In order to get into Santa's (Colin McLane, *Soul Survivor*) abode, Atnas (Douglas Robinson, *Big Bad Beetleborgs*)—"Santa" spelled backwards—and his minions pull a Trojan horse-like trick by boxing themselves up as a gift to Santa. Once inside, Atnas rockets Santa to the moon via a power chair, but he falls short, lands in the back yard of young Jeremy (Andre Bourque), and suffers brief amnesia. Just when Santa recovers, Atnas's two goofy minions kidnap him and deposit him in a cave. Soon arriving to investigate Santa's whereabouts is Pointer (Dana Woods, *Girl in Progress*), Santa's tech-savvy chief elf, who joins Jeremy in the search, and through the magic of an FOS (Friends of Santa) device, the two are transported to the cave, where the minions capture them as well. Having acquired the magic hat that Santa had left behind when he was kidnapped, Jeremy manages to toss the hat onto Santa's head. With his power restored, Santa reduces the minions to a flushing toilet. The three return to the North Pole via the FOS device, where Santa and Atnas do battle, and Jeremy ultimately rockets Atnas into oblivion via the same power chair he had attempted with Santa.

INTERESTING TIDBITS: To show more racial diversity, Santa's chief elf Pointer is black. Other films featuring a white Santa and a black chief elf include **Spike: The Elf That Saved Christmas** and **Santa Who?**

Two subplots involve the marital tension between Jeremy's parents and the constant bullying by his older brother.

Concerned that Santa may be gaining too much weight, Jeremy informs him via email to expect granola bars and mineral water instead of cookies and milk.

After Atnas ejects Santa from the North Pole, one of the elves expresses the typical relationship of Santa to Christmas: "No Santa, no Christmas!" Likewise, Mrs. Claus remarks, "If Santa doesn't return in time for Christmas, there will be no Christmas! It would be the end!"

Other films in which Santa is kidnapped include *The Elf and the Magic Key; The Glo Friends Save Christmas; The Great Santa Claus Switch; The Librarians and Santa's Midnight Run; Santa Claus Conquers the Martians; Sonic Christmas Blast; Spinach Greetings; Tim Burton's The Nightmare Before Christmas*; and *Who Stole Santa?*

Other save-Christmas films in which Santa suffers amnesia include *The Amazing World of Gumball: Christmas Episode; Merry Madagascar; Miracle at the 34th Precinct; The Night Before the Night Before Christmas; Santa Who? The Search for Santa Paws;* and *Snow 2: Brain Freeze.*

An Atnas character is also the villain in *A Freezerburnt Christmas.*

PRODUCTION CREDITS—Writer: Marc Vahanian. Producers: Ashok Amritraj and Andrew Stevens. Director: John Putch. Production Companies: Royal Oaks Entertainment and Cabin Fever Entertainment. Rating: Not rated. Genres: Family, Fantasy. Country: USA. Run Time: 94 min.

REFERENCES: *The Boy Who Saved Christmas.* In *Family Holiday Collection.* Universal City, CA: Vivendi Entertainment, 2012. DVD Video.

The Boy Who Saved Christmas. Internet Movie Database. http://www.imdb.com/title/tt0128083/

Wilson, Joanna. *Tis the Season TV: The Encyclopedia of Christmas-Themed Episodes, Specials and Made-for-TV Movies.* Akron, OH: 1701 Press, 2011.

Bratz Babyz Save Christmas: The Movie—2013

Direct-to-Video Computer-Animated Movie

THREAT TO CHRISTMAS: A crooked mall Santa and his minions threaten to ruin Christmas for a group of orphans.

HOW CHRISTMAS IS SAVED: By offering their help, the Bratz Babyz effect the capture of the crooked mall-Santa so the real Santa can delight the orphans with a special gift.

SYNOPSIS AND COMMENTARY: Bratz (a pun on "Brats") is a fashion doll line and assorted merchandise manufactured by Los Angeles-based Micro-Games America (MGA) Entertainment, a manufacturer of children's toys and entertainment products. Founded in 1979, the company released four original Bratz dolls in 2001—Cloe, Sasha, Jade, and Yasmin—featuring almond-shaped eyes, makeup, and clothing that followed pop-culture trends. These dolls generated multiple spinoff lines along with movies, TV series, interactive DVDs, music albums, and video games. One of these lines, Bratz Babyz, appeared in 2004 as much younger versions of the four original Bratz dolls with the same names and with a host of accessories.

Hardly crib babies, the four principals in *Bratz Babyz Save Christmas* are "mature" toddlers in trendy dress with makeup. Disappointed that their parents are snowed in elsewhere (doing who knows what) and will not be home for Christmas, the girls visit the mall on Christmas Eve with their elderly sitter, Gran, and overhear a mall-Santa remark that he will not be able to "deliver" that night. Believing that mall-Santa is the real deal and that Christmas will be a bust if he doesn't make his rounds, the girls decide to become Santa's extra elves and journey to the "North Pole" in their battery-powered toy sleigh-and-single-reindeer vehicle. Headed for the same destination are mall-Santa Max and his two adult but childlike minions, Ralphie and Reggie, three crooks who, in need of fast cash to repay a whopping gambling debt, plan to steal a kiddie car loaded with a million dollars in cash donations that real-Santa will deliver to a local orphanage. At the "North Pole," which is actually one of real-Santa's elf recruitment centers and a local tourist attraction, the crooks, together with their female boss, lock the girls and an elf attendant in the reindeer barn, only to be freed by a repentant Ralphie and Reggie, whose consciences will not allow them to rob orphans. Max and boss attempt to escape in the kiddie car, and the girls with Ralphie and Reggie pursue on flying reindeer in an extended, high-speed chase that terminates with the cops arresting the two malefactors. The elf attendant, vouching for Ralphie and Reggie, hires them as new reindeer trainers at the real North Pole, and the orphans receive their best Christmas ever. Considerably good work for toddlers.

PRINCIPAL VOICES: Britt Mckillip (*Mission to Mars*) as Cloe; Brittney Irvin (*Wasted*) as Jade; Dorla Bell (*Barbie and the Three Musketeers*) as Sasha; Maryke Hendrikse (*Johnny Test*) as Yasmin; Brian Drummond (*Dragon Ball Z*) as mall employee, real Santa, waiter, cop; Peter Kelamis (*Dragon Ball Z*) as Max and Dad; Betty Phillips (*The Crush*) as Gran; Dylan Lamoureux (*The Long Weekend*) as William; Jay Brazeau (*Watchmen*) as Ralphie; Laurie John Brunetti (*Rampage*) as Reggie; Qayam Devji (*Hulk Vs.*) as orphan Zachary; Andy Toth (*Mobile Suit Gundam Seed*) as male anchor and head elf; Marcy Goldberg (*Dreamcatcher*) as Milly.

INTERESTING TIDBITS: In the mall, when the girls conclude that Santa will not make his rounds, they express the ageless, materialistic sentiment of no-Santa-no-Christmas: "He can't deliver the presents? *No Christmas?*" then fall to pieces in a crying jag.

In a subplot, sweet old Gran, determined to give the girls the kind of Christmas they expect, dresses up as Santa with a bag of toys and expends much energy (and film footage, not to mention risking a broken neck) trying to climb a ladder onto her roof. She attempts to slide down the chimney but in the process becomes stuck at the top.

The film was originally released in 2008 as *Bratz Babyz Save Christmas* and was re-released in 2013 as *Bratz Babyz Save Christmas: The Movie*.

REVIEW: Tracy Moore of *Common Sense Media* (July 24, 2014): "The toddlers wear visible makeup, such as eye shadow, lipstick, and blush … [they] could not look less like actual toddlers in any shape or form … there are some positive messages here and a can-do spirit about problem solving. Overall, the adventure is a pretty convoluted one, but the themes are simple enough: We don't always get what we want, but sometimes we get something better if we can just keep a positive attitude."

PRODUCTION CREDITS—Writer: Karl Geurs. Producers: Mike Young and Bill Schultz. Director: Phil Weinstein. Production Companies: MGA Entertainment, Mike Young Productions, and Splash Entertainment. Rating: Not rated. Genres: Animation, Comedy, Family. Country: USA. Run Time: 70 min.

REFERENCES: Bratz. Official Site. http://www.bratz.com/

"Bratz." Wikipedia. https://en.wikipedia.org/wiki/Carter_Bryant

Bratz Babyz Save Christmas. Internet Movie Database. http://www.imdb.com/title/tt2297706

Bratz Babyz Save Christmas: The Movie. Santa Monica, CA: Lionsgate, 2013. DVD Video.

Moore, Tracy. *Bratz Babyz Save Christmas*. *Common Sense Media*. https://www.commonsensemedia.org/movie-reviews/bratz-babyz-save-christmas

Buster and Chauncey's Silent Night—October 13, 1998

Direct-to-Video Animated Musical

THREAT TO CHRISTMAS: Christmas sentiment is on the rocks when cat-and-mouse antics damage a church organ, and a little orphan is suspected of stealing the church's treasure.

HOW CHRISTMAS IS SAVED: Chauncey the mouse is instrumental in inspiring the music to "Silent Night"; he and his buddy Buster help to exonerate the orphan.

SYNOPSIS AND COMMENTARY: According to one of the myths surrounding the birth of the carol "Silent Night," in 1818 the organ in the Church of St. Nicholas in Oberndorf, Austria, was unplayable because mice had supposedly damaged the bellows. This quickly prompted the church organist, Franz Gruber, to set to music a poem that the priest, Father Josef Mohr, had written, and that Christmas Eve during Midnight Mass, the two men gave the first performance of "Silent Night" with guitar accompaniment.

In *Buster and Chauncey's Silent Night*, mice again play principal roles in the fictional origin of this beloved carol. Filled with dreams of fame and fortune, "mouse-icians" Buster and Chauncey arrive in Oberndorf to perform for the queen. Christmas sentiment quickly wanes when a vicious cat chases the two mice all through the sanctuary, demolishing the decorations and damaging the organ, for which the little orphan Christina receives the blame. She also becomes the prime suspect in the theft of the church's golden treasure of the three Wise Men. The real thieves, a Lady Gretchen and her "Uncle Otto," the Duke of Raoche, kidnap Christina when she discovers their deed, and the two mice set out to rescue her. As the thieves attempt to flee Oberndorf, a cat-and-mouse diversion uncovers the treasure with them, and Christina is exonerated. Meanwhile, the Christmas Eve service promises to be dismal because the organ is unplayable, but Franz Gruber receives inspiration from a little melody that Chauncey had composed and sets to music a poem that "Father Joseph" had written. Thus is born "Silent Night," which Father Joseph, Christina, and the queen sing at the service with guitar accompaniment from Gruber.

Buster (left), plump and egotistical, and Chauncey, skinny and selfless. Little did the world know that this Laurel-and-Hardy pair of mice composed the beloved Christmas carol "Silent Night"—that is, from the standpoint of the cartoon world in *Buster and Chauncey's Silent Night* (1998). Columbia TriStar International Television (collection of William D. Crump).

PRINCIPAL VOICES: Jim Cummings (*Star Wars Rebels*) as Buster; Phil Hartman (*Saturday Night Live*) as Chauncey; Marie Osmond (*Donnie and Marie*) as the queen; Tom Arnold (*Roseanne*) as the blue jay Fritz; Judy Blazer (*Anastasia*) as Lady Gretchen; Townsend Coleman (*Must See TV*) as Father Joseph; Gregg Edelman (*Spider-Man 2*) as Father Joseph's singing voice; Paul Kandel (*The Hunchback of Notre Dame*) as the Duke of Raoche; Harry Goz (*Sealab 2021*) as Mayor Huffenmeier; Lea Michele (*Glee*) as Christina; The Fitzerino Singers as the chorus.

SONGS: "Christmas in Oberndorf" and "Things That I've Collected," lyrics and music respectively by Lynn Ahrens and Stephen Flaherty. "Holiday for Thieves," lyrics and music respectively by Barry Harman and Keith Herrmann.

INTERESTING TIDBITS: This was Phil Hartman's final role (1948–1998). The film was released five months after his death.

This film was the first in-house, direct-to-video animated production from Columbia TriStar Home Video.

The characters Buster and Chauncey show parallels with the comedy team of Stan Laurel and Oliver Hardy. Like Hardy, Buster is obese and full of grandiose ideas, while Chauncey, like Laurel, is slender and childlike.

REVIEWS: Brian Webster of *Apollo Movie Guide*: "The Christmas theme of [this film] seems almost an afterthought, as the good-guys-versus-bad-guys story is what it's really all about. Religious themes make an appearance at several points, although they are relatively understated, despite the fact that it's about Christmas and much of the story takes place in a cathedral."

Lynne Heffley of the *Los Angeles Times* (November 26, 1998): "The animation is standard, but the message about the meaning of the season, based on the writing of the soulful Christmas carol, comes through. The most notable thing ... is the talent: The late Phil Hartman, Tom Arnold and Marie Osmond do expressive voice-overs."

PRODUCTION CREDITS—Writers: George Taweel and Rob Loos. Producer and Director: Buzz Potamkin. Production Company: Project X Productions. Rating: G. Genres: Animation, Comedy, Family, Musical. Countries: Canada and USA. Run Time: 48 min.

REFERENCES: *Buster and Chauncey's Silent Night*. Big Cartoon Database. http://www.bcdb.com/cartoon/77358-Buster-And-Chaunceys-Silent-Night

Buster and Chauncey's Silent Night. Culver City, CA: Columbia TriStar Home Video. DVD Video.

Buster and Chauncey's Silent Night. Internet Movie Database. http://www.imdb.com/title/tt0167064/

Crump, William D. *The Christmas Encyclopedia*. Third Edition. Jefferson, NC: McFarland, 2013.

Heffley, Lynne. *Buster and Chauncey's Silent Night*. Los Angeles Times. http://articles.latimes.com/1998/nov/26/entertainment/ca-47824

McCormick, Moira. "Musical Mice Enliven 'Silent Night.'" *Billboard* (July 25, 1998).

Webster, Brian. *Buster and Chauncey's Silent Night*. Apollo Movie Guide. Apollo Communications (February 9, 2006).

Wilson, Joanna. *Tis the Season TV: The Encyclopedia of Christmas-Themed Episodes, Specials and Made-for-TV Movies*. Akron, OH: 1701 Press, 2011.

Call Me Claus—December 2, 2001

Television Movie

THREAT TO CHRISTMAS: Santa has reigned for 200 years. Now he must choose a successor, lest the world face a watery Armageddon.

HOW CHRISTMAS IS SAVED: Santa makes history and chooses a black woman to bring the toys.

SYNOPSIS AND COMMENTARY: It's not uncommon for the movies to alter the gender and/or race of classic characters for the sake of variety or political correctness. Judging from the woodcuts in *A Christmas Carol*, Charles Dickens portrayed Ebeneezer Scrooge as an elderly white man. In film adaptations such as *Ebbie* and *Ms. Scrooge*, however, Scrooge is respectively depicted as a white woman and a black woman. And so it is with Santa Claus in *Call Me Claus*, in which a black woman becomes the new jolly ole elf.

With his 200-year-old contract soon to expire, Santa (Nigel Hawthorne, *Yes Minister*), calling himself "Nick," must find a suitable replacement by midnight on Christmas Eve, lest the "Or Else" clause be invoked—the entire polar ice cap will melt and flood planet Earth. According to Nick, such melting supposedly caused the Great Flood associated with Noah's Ark (according to history, however, St. Nicholas dates to the fourth century A.D.). Nick's choice is Lucy Cullins (Whoopi Goldberg, *The Color Purple*), the producer of a home shopping television network who has been cynical about Christmas since her childhood, because her soldier-father died at Christmastime in Vietnam. By accident, Lucy hires Nick to portray a merchandise-pitching Santa on her network all during December, and his authentic performance boosts sales to an all-time high by Christmas Eve. To prepare the world for the advent of a black, female Santa, Nick's frequently improvised dialogue includes a passage from "Can Santa Be Black?" a poem by B.J. Wrights, which implies that Santa becomes whatever race and form are suitable for the occasion or region of the world. As the polar ice slowly melts, if a magical trip to the North Pole doesn't convince Lucy of her destiny, her evil boss's comments do: if she would scheme with him, the two of them could *own* Christmas by next year. Unable to fathom Christmas as another item to be put on the block for sale, Lucy dons the magical stocking cap that Santa has left for her, an act that creates a snowfall in Los Angeles as well as at the North Pole. It is a sign that not only has the baton been passed, but that Christmas and the world are saved.

INTERESTING TIDBITS: Nigel Hawthorne (1929–2001) died at the age of 72 on December 26, just 24 days after the release of this film.

Country music artist Garth Brooks provided vocal music. In 2001, he released the album *Garth Brooks and the Magic of Christmas: Songs from Call Me Claus* on the Capitol label, which was a reissue of *Garth Brooks and the Magic of Christmas* (1999). The *Call Me Claus* album included the following that were exclusive to its release: "Call Me Claus" by Garth Brooks, Lisa Sanderson, and Jenny Yates; "Mary Had a Little Lamb" by Larry Bastian, Gordon Kennedy, and Wayne Kirkpatrick; "'Zat You, Santa Claus?" by Jack Fox. Other songs on the *Call Me Claus* release included "Baby Jesus Is Born" by Randy Handley and Cam King and "The Wise Man's Journey" (instrumental) by Bobby Wood," plus the following Christmas standards: "It's the Most Wonderful Time of the Year," "Have Yourself a Merry Little Christmas," "Let It Snow! Let It Snow! Let It Snow!" "Winter Wonderland," "The Christmas Song," "Sleigh Ride," "Silver Bells," "(There's No Place Like) Home for the Holidays," and "O Little Town of Bethlehem." The *Call Me Claus* album peaked at number 11 on the *Billboard* Top Christmas/Holiday Albums (November 17, 2001); number 8 on the *Billboard* Top Country Albums (November 24, 2001); number 99 on the *Billboard* 200 (December 1, 2001); and number 17 on the *Billboard* Top Country Albums (December 14, 2002).

Although the film is not rated, it should at least be rated as PG, because there is mild vulgarity and brief sexuality.

REVIEWS: Andrea Beach of *Common Sense Media* (July 3, 2014): "[This film] presents standard holiday fare along with a lot of mild profanity (especially 'crap') and some sexual innuendo … making it better suited for older kids…. The real strength of the movie is the way it presents a positive, multiracial society with African-Americans at the forefront…. But the contrived plot, flat acting … and dated, made-for-TV format keep it out of the pantheon of great holiday movies."

Andy Webb of *The Movie Scene*: "…90% of [this film] is child friendly…. But then it has some moments which jar with everything else from a scene where Lucy says the word 'crap' half a dozen times to a joke about how goblins are a misadventure on a beach between drunk gnomes and leprechauns. They are too in your face and seem out of place in a movie which for the most seems to be targeting a pre-thirteen year old market."

PRODUCTION CREDITS—Story: Paul Mooney, Sara Bernstein, and Gregory Bernstein. Teleplay: Sara Bernstein, Gregory Bernstein, and Brian Bird. Producers: Tom Leonardis and Jay Benson. Director: Peter Werner. Production Companies: Columbia TriStar Television Productions, Floresta Productions, Turner Network Television, One Ho Productions, and Red Strokes Entertainment. Rating: Not rated. Genres: Comedy, Family. Country: USA. Run Time: 90 min.

REFERENCES: Beach, Andrea. *Call Me Claus. Common Sense Media*. https://www.commonsensemedia.org/movie-reviews/call-me-claus

Brooks, Garth. *Garth Brooks and the Magic of Christmas: Songs from Call Me Claus*. Nashville: Capitol, 2001. Music CD Audio.

Call Me Claus. Culver City, CA: Columbia TriStar Home Entertainment, 2001. DVD Video.

Call Me Claus. Internet Movie Database. http://www.imdb.com/title/tt0272018/

Crump, William D. *The Christmas Encyclopedia*. Third Edition. Jefferson, NC: McFarland, 2013.

Webb, Andy. *Call Me Claus* (2001). *The Movie Scene*. http://www.themoviescene.co.uk/reviews/call-me-claus-2001/call-me-claus-2001.html

Whitburn, Joel. *Christmas in the Charts: 1920–2004*. Menomonee Falls, WI: Record Research, 2004.

Wilson, Joanna. *Tis the Season TV: The Encyclopedia of Christmas-Themed Episodes,*

Specials and Made-for-TV Movies. Akron, OH: 1701 Press, 2011.

Wrights, B.J. "Can Santa Be Black?" *Democratic Underground*. http://www.democraticunderground.com/10024189125

Cancel Christmas—November 13, 2011
Television Movie

THREAT TO CHRISTMAS: Santa must persuade two misfit boys to help a less fortunate boy, lest Christmas be cancelled.

HOW CHRISTMAS IS SAVED: Santa temporarily becomes a school janitor and uses his influence on his charges.

SYNOPSIS AND COMMENTARY: Displeased because so many children are selfish and lack the Christmas spirit, the Christmas Board of Directors gives Santa (Judd Nelson, *The Breakfast Club*) 30 days to inspire two privileged boys to help a less fortunate boy by midnight on Christmas Eve. If he fails, the board will fire Santa and cancel Christmas. Santa's assignments are Farley (Sante Scaletta, *My Family's Secret*) and Steve (Connor Price, *Cinderella Man*), two incorrigible students at a private school, and Adam (John Fleming, *The Barrens*), a paraplegic whose widowed mother teaches at the same school. Traveling in disguise under the respective aliases of Kris Frost and Randy Elfman, Santa and his chief elf Randal (Justin Landry, *Periods of Rain*) take jobs as a custodian and his assistant at the private school. Kris first persuades Farley and Steve to help him build a wheelchair access ramp at Adam's house, then poses as a mall Santa who encourages children to give gifts (even if it's just a hug) instead of asking for them. This innovation attracts a television news reporter who believes that he may have found the real Santa. Meanwhile, Steve launches a school fundraising drive to buy Adam a robotic wheelchair, but when the funds fall short, Steve sells his prize drum kit to make up the difference. On Christmas Eve, Kris, Randy, Steve, and many other school friends surprise Adam with the new wheelchair. Farley, having been reconciled to his workaholic father, arrives at the last moment and gives Kip, his beloved golden retriever, to Adam, who had never owned a dog. The boys' selfless acts enable Santa to retain his job in perpetuity.

AWARDS: In 2011, this picture received a Young Artist Award nomination for Best Performance in a TV Movie, Miniseries or Special–Leading Young Actor (John Fleming).

INTERESTING TIDBITS: Note the opposite parallels in this film and a film like *Casper's Haunted Christmas*. In both, a higher authority of sorts orders the two protagonists to fulfill a goal by Christmas, lest dire consequences befall them. Whereas Casper must scare at least one person or face eternal banishment to "The Dark," Santa must reform a couple of misfits or Christmas is "cancelled" forever. Then compare those scenarios with films like *Call Me Claus* and *The Santa Clause*. In the former, Lucy must become the new Santa, lest the polar ice cap melt and flood the earth; in the latter, whoever dons dead Santa's suit is drafted into the role of Santa forever. In those two scenarios, there's no specific higher authority as such (it's hard to imagine God behind such silliness), only the natural forces that have been set in motion for eons of time. In all such films, whatever the mechanism involved, the end result is the same: if the goal is not fulfilled, Christmas will be cancelled, ended, over, finished, *fin*, *kaput*. It's nonsensical, of course, but it's funny and entertaining nonetheless.

PRODUCTION CREDITS—Writer: David Alexander. Producer: Marek Posival. Director: John Bradshaw. Production Company: Chesler/Perlmutter Productions. Rating: G. Genres: Comedy, Family, Fantasy. Country: Canada. Run Time: 88 min.

REFERENCES: *Cancel Christmas*. Hallmark Channel, 2013. DVD Video.

Cancel Christmas. Internet Movie Database. http://www.imdb.com/title/tt1733111/

Crump, William D. *The Christmas Encyclopedia*. Third Edition. Jefferson, NC: McFarland, 2013.

The Case for Christmas—November 19, 2011
Television Movie

THREAT TO CHRISTMAS: Santa's popularity wanes when he is sued for ruining Christmas.

How Christmas Is Saved: Santa hires an attorney and has another day in court.

Synopsis and Commentary: As if the majority of the population's losing the Christmas spirit weren't bad enough, Santa, alias Kris Kringle (George Buza, *X-Men*), is in court … again. This time, instead of having to prove that he is the real deal, as in *Miracle on 34th Street*, he faces a class-action lawsuit by people claiming irreparable emotional distress over Christmas gifts they desired but never received as children. Never mind that Santa always gives children the most appropriate gifts, not necessarily what they always want. Instigating the suit is Braxton Bennett (Barry Flatman, *The Dead Zone*), a sporting-goods mogul whose secret motive is to replace Santa with "Santana Snow," a female figure who brings sporting goods to children at Christmas. Kris chooses widowed attorney Michael Sherman (Dean Cain, *Lois and Clark: The New Adventures of Superman*) in New York City to defend him, and Michael, in need of clients, takes the case. The media make a laughing stock of Michael, which shakes his reputation as public opinion of Kris drops, coupled with the fact that Kris had been a patient in a psychiatric hospital years ago. Michael then resigns but reconsiders after discovering that Kris had himself admitted to the hospital in order to give Christmas joy to a group of lonely children there. The proceedings at the trial look dismal for Kris, until Christmas Eve, when by chance Bennett tells a little girl all about Santana Snow, not knowing that the girl is Michael's daughter Lily (Helen Colliander, *Heartland*). When this information is revealed at the trial, Bennett is caught and drops the suit.

Interesting Tidbit: A subplot focuses on Lauren (Rachel Blanchard, *Fargo*), Michael's mechanic-friend who restores (with help from Kris's magic) the classic car Michael inherited from his parents and who falls in love with him. Since this movie premiered on the Hallmark Channel, we would expect nothing less.

Reviews: **Andy Webb** of *The Movie Scene*: "[This film] can be lumped in with the bulk of Christmas movies which are an enjoyable distraction … but don't demand you going out of your way to watch again, that is unless you are a fan of Dean Cain who still has that winning smile and charm."

Edwin L. Carpenter of The Dove Foundation: "The likeable cast is a joy to watch. We are pleased … to award it our Dove Seal for all ages. As Santa tells Michael Sherman when the heat is on during the trial, his reindeer fly because they believe in the impossible. [This film] makes its own case as a wonderful and warm film which will delight your family."

Production Credits—Screenplay: Tom Amundsen and Rickie Castaneda. Producer: Marek Posival. Director: Timothy Bond. Production Company: Chesler/Perlmutter Productions. Rating: G. Genres: Comedy, Drama, Family, Fantasy. Countries: Canada and USA. Run Time: 87 min.

References: *The Case for Christmas*. Hallmark Channel, 2012. DVD Video.

The Case for Christmas. Internet Movie Database. http://www.imdb.com/title/tt2039389/

Carpenter, Edwin L. *The Case for Christmas.* The Dove Foundation. http://www.dove.org/review/10619-the-case-for-christmas/

Crump, William D. *The Christmas Encyclopedia*. Third Edition. Jefferson, NC: McFarland, 2013.

Webb, Andy. *The Case for Christmas* (2011). *The Movie Scene.* http://www.themoviescene.co.uk/reviews/the-case-for-christmas/the-case-for-christmas.html

Casper's Haunted Christmas—October 31, 2000

Direct-to-Video, Computer-Animated Movie

Threat to Christmas: Failing to induce Casper to scare someone by Christmas Day, his three uncles decide to ruin Christmas by stealing all the presents in town.

How Christmas Is Saved: Casper and cousin Spooky thwart their three uncles by putting a scare into them, which fulfills Ghost Law.

Synopsis and Commentary: Casper the Friendly Ghost, the protagonist here as well as in comic books and a host of theatrical animated cartoon shorts, feature films, and television series, was created in 1940 by Seymour

Reit (author) and Joe Oriolo (illustrator) for either a short story or for an illustrated children's book that never sold (accounts are not in agreement). All rights to the Casper character were soon sold to Paramount Pictures' Famous Studios animation department, which developed Casper into one of its most famous properties during the 1940s and 1950s. *Casper* comic books first appeared in 1949 from St. John Publishing and from Harvey Comics in 1952, the latter also creating Casper's three pointy-headed uncles—Stinkie, Fatso, and Stretch—the "Ghostly Trio," who appear in *Casper's Haunted Christmas*. In 1959, Harvey Comics purchased the entire Famous line and distributed it to television as Harveytoons with Casper as the top draw. After several transfers of ownership, DreamWorks Classics currently owns Harvey Films, the animation department of Harvey Comics.

Since the first Casper Noveltoon, *The Friendly Ghost* (1946), Casper was always portrayed as a personable little ghost-child who sought friendship with all whom he met, unlike his spirit counterparts who enjoyed scaring the pants off the living. Casper managed to acquire a few friends, primarily in children and animals, despite the fact that, upon first seeing him, adults fled in terror, screaming, "A g-g-*ghost!*" In response to those wondering how Casper died, Harvey Comics remarked that he was a ghost because his parents were already ghosts when they married, which suggested supernatural beings. On the other hand, the feature film *Casper* (1995) portrayed him as a deceased human and provided an account of his death.

Finding that Casper has deliberately failed to scare at least one person per year according to Ghost Law, spectral authority Kibosh, a not-so-jolly green giant, banishes Casper and his three uncles (the Ghostly Trio) to Kriss, Massachusetts, "the most Christmasy town in the world," where they meet the syrupy Jollimore family, whose young daughter Holly regards Casper as a talking snowman. There in Kriss, the uncles must persuade Casper to scare someone by Christmas Day, lest all four be cast into "The Dark," the ghost equivalent of hell. Yet the uncles are not permitted to scare anyone themselves, because their "haunting licenses" have been revoked. Failing in the task, the uncles solicit help from Spooky, Casper's tough, look-alike cousin, but when he also fails, the uncles reject him as their equal and decide to ruin Christmas by stealing all the presents in town and framing the Jollimores, at which point Christmas must be saved. Humiliated, Spooky turns against his uncles and warns Casper of their imminent plan. Together with Pearl ("Poil"), Spooky's girlfriend,

Casper the Friendly Ghost experiences a brief period of The Dark, the ghost equivalent of hell. It will be his eternal fate if he fails to scare at least one person by Christmas in *Casper's Haunted Christmas* (2000) (Universal Studios Home Video/Photofest).

Casper and Spooky create a successful stunt that not only scares the uncles, thwarts their actions, and saves Christmas in Kriss, but it also fulfills Ghost Law and avoids an unpleasant final destiny.

PRINCIPAL VOICES: Theme song sung by Randy Travis (*Annabelle's Wish*). Brendon Ryan Barrett (*Soul Man*) as Casper; Kathleen Barr (*Re-Boot*) as Carol Jollimore; David Kaye (*Dragon Ball Z*) as the narrator; Graeme Kingston (*Mummies Alive!*) as Fatso; Terry Klassen (*The Cramp Twins*) as Stinkie; Scott McNeil (*Dragon Ball Z*) as Stretch and Noel Jollimore; Tegan Moss (*Little Women*) as Holly Jollimore; Colin Murdock (*Altitude*) as Kibosh; Tabitha St. Germain (*Captain Flamingo*) as Poil; Lee Tockar (*Johnny Test*) as Snivel, Kibosh's informant; and Sam Vincent (*Martin Mystery*) as Spooky.

AWARDS: In 2001, this video won the Santa Clarita International Film Festival Award for Best Foreign Animation and also won First Prize at the Vancouver Effects and Animation Festival for Animated Feature Film. It received a Leo Award nomination for Best Overall Sound in an Animation Program or Series.

INTERESTING TIDBIT: It's probably not a coincidence that *Casper's Haunted Christmas* was released on Halloween, since it combines the traditional elements of that holiday with those of Christmas, as is also evident in **Tim Burton's The Nightmare Before Christmas**.

REVIEWS: Critic reviews were mixed. Paul Trandahl of *Common Sense Media* (May 3, 2005): "A sweet and somewhat sophisticated holiday tale."

Morgan R. Lewis of *Morgan on Media* (December 19, 2013): "…one has to set the bar pretty low to give *Casper's Haunted Christmas* any praise at all."

PRODUCTION CREDITS—Writers: Ian Boothby and Roger Fredericks. Producer: Byron Vaughns. Director: Owen Hurley. Production Companies: The Harvey Entertainment Company and Mainframe Entertainment. Rating: G. Genres: Animation, Family, Fantasy. Countries: Canada and USA. Run Time: 84 min.

REFERENCES: *Casper's Haunted Christmas*. Big Cartoon Database. http://www.bcdb.com/cartoon/40992-Caspers-Haunted-Christmas

Casper's Haunted Christmas. Internet Movie Database. http://www.imdb.com/title/tt0284946/

Casper's Haunted Christmas. Universal City, CA: Universal Home Entertainment, 2012. DVD video.

Casper's Haunted Christmas. Wikipedia. https://en.wikipedia.org/wiki/Casper_the_Friendly_Ghost

Crump, William D. *The Christmas Encyclopedia*. Third Edition. Jefferson, NC: McFarland, 2013.

Holland, Steve. "Seymour Reit: The Man Behind the Genius of Casper the Friendly Ghost." *The Guardian* (December 23, 2001). http://www.theguardian.com/news/2001/dec/24/guardianobituaries.books

Lenburg, Jeff. *The Encyclopedia of Animated Cartoons*. Third Edition. New York: Facts on File, 2009.

Lewis, Morgan R. *Casper's Haunted Christmas*. Morgan on Media. https://morganrlewis.wordpress.com/2013/12/19/caspers-haunted-christmas/

Nash, Eric P. "Seymour V. Reit, 83, a Creator of Casper the Friendly Ghost." *The New York Times* (December 17, 2001). http://www.nytimes.com/2001/12/17/arts/seymour-v-reit-83-a-creator-of-casper-the-friendly-ghost.html

Trandahl, Paul. *Casper's Haunted Christmas*. Common Sense Media. https://www.commonsensemedia.org/movie-reviews/caspers-haunted-christmas

Wilson, Joanna. *Tis the Season TV: The Encyclopedia of Christmas-Themed Episodes, Specials and Made-for-TV Movies*. Akron, OH: 1701 Press, 2011.

A Christmas Adventure from a Book Called Wisely's Tales—October 2, 2001

Computer-Animated Direct-to-Video Movie

THREAT TO CHRISTMAS: A blizzard forces Santa's team down in the forest, and the reindeer scatter when they see a lion from a circus train.

HOW CHRISTMAS IS SAVED: Circus animals and woodland creatures join forces to help Santa find his missing reindeer.

SYNOPSIS AND COMMENTARY: On Christmas Eve, Wisely the owl reads a story to four human children about the introduction to Christmas that his forest friends experienced several years ago. The setting is also Christmas Eve when a blizzard forces Santa's team down in the forest. Upon meeting locals Rockin' Raccoon and Honey Bunny, who know nothing of Christmas, Santa and the reindeer gladly explain the meaning of the holiday. Although the audience is not party to the actual explanation, the animals' comments later on imply that Christmas involves being with family, sharing, and giving; the birth of Christ is not mentioned. Meanwhile, a rock avalanche jolts a nearby circus train and bounces three animals off—Kingly the lion, Kimberoo the kangaroo, and Mousel the mouse. Their wanderings lead them to Santa, a familiar person, because their contact with humans has taught them about Christmas. Yet when the reindeer spot Kingly, they bolt and scatter, requiring the others to split into teams to search for them. They find six of the eight reindeer (Rudolph sits this one out), but Donner and Vixen are still missing, whereupon the plot thickens as those two are victorious against vicious wolves, and Kingly saves Mousel from plunging over a raging waterfall after falling through the ice. At the close, Santa shames the wolf pack leader for being a "bad wolf" and teaches him to be a better representative of his pack.

PRINCIPAL VOICES: Joey Lawrence (*Blossom*) as the wolf pack leader; Tiffani-Amber Thiessen (*Saved by the Bell*) as Vixen; Dean Cain (*Bloopers*) as Donner; Richard Newman (*Escaflowne*) as Wisely; Fran Dowie (*Timothy Tweedle the First Christmas Elf*) as Santa; Saffron Henderson (*Dragon Ball Z*) as Rachael and Cupid; Cathy Weseluck (*Dragon Ball Z*) as Darryl and Kimberoo; Andrew Francis (*Max Steel*) as Nick; Andrea Libman (*Dragon Ball Z*) as Natalie; Paul Dobson (*Dragon Ball Z*) as Rockin' Raccoon; Kathleen Barr (*ReBoot*) as Honey Bunny; Gerald Plunlett (*Sucker Punch*) as Kingly; Lee Tockar (*Johnny Test*) as Mousel; Terry Klassen (*Dragon Ball Z*) as Bear; P.J. Barbera (*A Christmas Adventure*) as Dasher; Venus Terzo (*It*) as Dancer; Linda Boyd (*Republic of Doyle*) as Prancer; Michael Dobson (*Dragon Ball Z*) as Comet.

INTERESTING TIDBITS: Before Wisely begins his story, the children banter about Christmas presents. When one girl remarks that her best Christmas gifts are being with family and sharing love, one of the boys scoffs, "You don't know nothin' about Christmas! Christmas is about getting *real* presents!" Of course, as expected, by the end of the story, the boy has a different attitude about Christmas.

The story teaches the moral that it is not wise to make judgments about people and animals based entirely on their appearances. For example, the reindeer scatter, because they see Kingly as a threat, when he is anything but that. Rockin' Raccoon and Honey Bunny initially perceive Santa as "bad," because he is a human; from their experiences, humans invade the forest to chop down trees (home to some animals) and disturb the tranquility with their noisy "snow beasts" (snowmobiles).

PRODUCTION CREDITS—Creators: Anthony Asfur and Dale Sexton. Original Story: Anthony Asfur, Dale Sexton, and Jack Olesker. Screenplay: Jack Olesker. Producer and Director: Dale Sexton. Production Companies: Aston Entertainment and Columbia Pictures. Rating: G. Genres: Animation, Family. Countries: Canada and USA. Run Time: 50 min.

REFERENCES: *A Christmas Adventure from a Book Called Wisely's Tales*. Big Cartoon Database. http://www.bcdb.com/cartoon/55357-Christmas-Adventure-From-A-Book-Called-Wiselys-Tales

A Christmas Adventure from a Book Called Wisely's Tales. Culver City, CA: Columbia TriStar Home Entertainment, 2001. VHS Video.

A Christmas Adventure from a Book Called Wisely's Tales. Internet Movie Database. http://www.imdb.com/title/tt0293783/

Wilson, Joanna. *Tis the Season TV: The Encyclopedia of Christmas-Themed Episodes, Specials and Made-for-TV Movies*. Akron, OH: 1701 Press, 2011.

The Christmas Angel (Détresse et Charité)—1904

Silent Black-and-White Short Film

THREAT TO CHRISTMAS: A poverty-stricken family faces a bleak Christmas.

HOW CHRISTMAS IS SAVED: Depending on the ending, either the family's daughter perishes in the snow and the Christmas angel takes her to heaven, or a kind-hearted couple rescue her and give her family a really wonderful Christmas.

SYNOPSIS AND COMMENTARY: Given the date of this French film, it would be presumptuous to state that it is *the* first save-Christmas film, but it is certainly one of the earliest. It was originally released in France as *Détresse et Charité* (*Distress and Charity*), in the USA as *The Christmas Angel*, and in the United Kingdom as *The Beggar Maiden*. The film is somewhat similar to another silent French production, **The Christmas Miracle** (1912).

Christmas promises to be bleak for one poverty-stricken family: the mother lies ill in bed, there's no fuel for a fire, a hole in the roof allows snow to fall through, and the landlord or tax collector is about to evict the family. Showing his despair through melodramatic acting, the worried father sends his young daughter Marie (Rachel Gillet) in rags out into the snowy streets to beg. Wealthy worshipers exiting a church spare a few coins for a group of "professional" beggars crowded about, but they all rebuff Marie. Likewise, a butcher's shop casts her out, and a couple of gendarmes move her along. A poor ragman (director Georges Méliès) collecting litter in the street does more for Marie than the others so far by providing a crust of bread and an old shawl. After wandering penniless all day, Marie collapses in the snow.

Here, the film provides two endings. In the version shown to French audiences, Marie perishes there in the snow and the Christmas angel takes her away to heaven. For American and British audiences, who seemed to prefer happier endings, a Good Samaritan couple approaching in a car rescue Marie and bring her home. Prior to that, her mother recovers, whereupon the Christmas angel momentarily appears to the parents as if to reassure them. Soon Marie returns with the Good Samaritans along with a host of merchants bearing an abundance of food and supplies, courtesy of the philanthropists, who also satisfy the landlord or tax collector, and there's the happy ending.

INTERESTING TIDBITS: Even at this early stage of film-making, director Georges Méliès, known more for his fantasy films, was also known for his special effects, which in this film include artificial snow, superimposing the image of the Christmas angel into the scene before Marie returns, and scenes that "dissolve" gradually into other scenes. One particular special effect is the cross-section set at the butcher's shop, which allows viewers to see both inside and outside the shop. When the ragman "shines" his lantern to see Marie lying in the snow, the effect of a light beam is created with a "substitution splice" that involves film editing instead of stopping and restarting the camera.

The French ending is similar to that in Hans Christian Andersen's story "The Little Match Girl." Though the setting there is New Year's Eve rather than Christmas, a little girl perishes in the snow after her unsuccessful attempts to sell matches, after which an angel in the form of her late grandmother appears and takes her away to heaven.

REVIEW: Dave Sindelar of *Fantastic Movie Musings and Ramblings* (September 7, 2014): "…dramas are not Melies's forte, and this one has its fair share of flaws, such as some over-theatrical acting and a story that tries to push the pity buttons a little too insistently. Nevertheless, this is perhaps one of Melies's more successful forays into drama; the story is efficiently told and easy to follow … the sets are wonderful, and it maintains the right mood.… It's one of Melies's better departures from his usual style."

PRODUCTION CREDITS—Writer and Producer: Unknown. Director: Georges Méliès. Production Company: Star-Film. Rating: Not rated. Genre: Drama. Country: France. Run Time: 10 min.

REFERENCES: *The Christmas Angel*. In *Georges Méliès Encore: New Discoveries: 26 films (1896–1911)*. Los Angeles: Flicker Alley, 2010. DVD Video.

The Christmas Angel. Internet Movie Database. http://www.imdb.com/title/tt0228014/

The Christmas Angel. Wikipedia. https://en.wikipedia.org/wiki/The_Christmas_Angel

Sindelar, Dave. *The Christmas Angel* (1904). *Fantastic Movie Musings and Ramblings.* http://www.scifilm.org/musing4624.html

The Christmas Angel: A Story on Ice—
December 23, 1998

Television Movie

THREAT TO CHRISTMAS: An evil gargon prevents the coming of Christmas when he steals an angel atop a village's Christmas tree.

HOW CHRISTMAS IS SAVED: A young mother and come-to-life Christmas presents rescue the angel and turn the gargon to good.

SYNOPSIS AND COMMENTARY: Similar to ice performances of *The Nutcracker* ballet, world-champion ice skaters perform this fantasy story amid breathtaking special effects, with Mannheim Steamroller providing contemporary arrangements of traditional Christmas carols. As if reading from a storybook to a small group of children, hosts Olivia Newton-John (*Grease*) and Mannheim Steamroller's founder Chip Davis provide intermittent narration, which is the only dialogue. Because the story is quite simple, most of the footage is devoted to showcasing the artistic merits of the skaters.

Each year on Christmas Eve, a small village crowns its Christmas tree in the public square with an ornate angel tree topper. This year, however, a horned male demon dressed in black, known as the "gargon" (as opposed to the female Gorgon of Greek mythology), steals the angel at midnight and takes her to his realm of lost souls in the "nether world" (which sounds a lot like hell). Without the angel, Christmas will not arrive, because the various toys under that three cannot become presents for the village children (no presents, no Christmas). A young mother first discovers the tragedy, whereupon the toys come to life and accompany her through a spooky forest to the gargon's lair to rescue the angel. There, the troupe encounters other demons, the lost souls, and after a series of skating routines, the mother's magic weakens the gargon such that she unmasks him (not exactly like *The Phantom of the Opera*), and he is transformed into the Christmas angel that he once was. In so doing, all the other demons shed their facades and become the Christmas angels that they had been as well. The return of the village's Christmas angel opens Christmas, and the other angels return to their respective villages whence they had come.

PRINCIPAL CAST: Dorothy Hamill (*Blades of Glory*) as the mother; Elvis Stojko (*Ice Angel*) as the gargon; Rudy Galindo (*Nutcracker on Ice*) as the gargon's sidekick; Tonia Kwaitkowski (*Cook's Champagne on Ice*) as the stolen Christmas angel; Tiffany Chin (*Gershwin on Ice*) as the marionette; Liz Punsalan (*Halloween on Ice*) and Jerod Swallow (*Halloween on Ice*) as the pair of dolls; Rocky Marval (*Nutcracker on Ice*) as the woodcutter; Calla Urbanski (*Nutcracker on Ice*) as the cat; Lisa Cricks (*The Christmas Angel: A Story on Ice*) as the teddy bear; Ryan Hunka (*The Christmas Angel: A Story on Ice*) as the snowman.

INTERESTING TIDBITS: In 1998, Mannheim Steamroller produced a platinum album on the American Gramaphone label titled *The Christmas Angel: A Family Story* about the gargon stealing a Christmas angel. Olivia Newton-John and Chip Davis also narrated that story which was subsequently made into the ice-skating production as described above. The album peaked at number 25 on the *Billboard* 200 chart and number 2 on the Top Christmas/Holiday Albums chart (1998); numbers 10 and 11 respectively on the Top Christmas/Holiday Albums chart and the *Billboard* 200 chart (1999); and numbers 39 and 41 respectively on the *Billboard* 200 chart and the Top Christmas/Holiday Albums chart (2002).

PRODUCTION CREDITS—Story: Chip Davis. Writer: Noah Zachary. Producer: Chip Davis. Director: Andy Picheta. Production Company: American Gramaphone. Rating: Not rated. Genre: Family. Country: USA. Run Time: 45 min.

REFERENCES: *The Christmas Angel: A Family Story.* Omaha, NE: American Gramaphone, 1998. Music CD.

The Christmas Angel: A Story on Ice. Internet Movie Database. http://www.imdb.com/title/tt0245836/

The Christmas Angel: A Story on Ice. Omaha, NE: American Gramaphone, 1998. DVD Video.

Whitburn, Joel. *Christmas in the Charts: 1920-2004*. Menomonee Falls, WI: Record Research, 2004.

Wilson, Joanna. *Tis the Season TV: The Encyclopedia of Christmas-Themed Episodes, Specials and Made-for-TV Movies*. Akron, OH: 1701 Press, 2011.

The Christmas Candle—November 22, 2013

Feature Film

THREAT TO CHRISTMAS: A progressive young minister struggling with his own faith threatens to end a beloved, long-standing Christmas tradition that has otherwise brought hope and joy to a quaint English village.

HOW CHRISTMAS IS SAVED: The Christmas Candle is the instrument of a Christmas "miracle."

SYNOPSIS AND COMMENTARY: No Santa Claus, no sleigh, and no reindeer. Can Christmas be "saved" if those three elements are not part of the equation? There is a special gift, however, the gift of the Christmas Candle in this adaptation of Max Lucado's Christian-based novel of the same title.

Every 25 years since 1664, an angel has visited the chandler's shop in the little village of Gladbury, England (Gladstone in the novel), and touched one candle on the eve of the last Sunday in Advent. Whoever received that candle and said a prayer over it always had his prayer answered.

The year is now 1864, the 25th year, and Gladbury receives a new, young rector, the Rev. David Richmond (Hans Matheson, *Sherlock Holmes*), who dismisses the story of the Christmas Candle as superstitious nonsense and refuses to preach about it on Advent Sundays. Nonetheless, each needy villager hopes to be the recipient and makes his request known to Edward Haddington (Sylvester McCoy, *Doctor Who*), the aging chandler, and his wife Bea (Lesley Manville, *Maleficent*). The Haddingtons find themselves in a quandary when, following the angel's latest visit, the Christmas Candle is lost among 30 identical candles during an accident. Rather than confess the mistake, the Haddingtons give the 30 candles to those needy villagers and pledge them to secrecy about being recipients. Whereas in the novel the Haddingtons use the last candle to pray for their wayward granddaughter, that candle instead goes to Richmond, who needs a miracle to restore his waning faith. At the Christmas Eve service, Richmond is certain that he will expose the Candle story as a myth, which would ruin Gladbury's greatest Christmas tradition. Instead of one recipient as expected, multiple candle recipients present their testimony of prayers answered, for God had redirected their faith in candles to Him alone. Richmond remains skeptical, however, until the candle he had received is instrumental in rescuing a storm victim, for it proves to be the Christmas Candle.

Whereas the novel ends with the angel touching another candle in present-day Ed Haddington's store, the film closes with happy church members singing "Miracles All Around" (by Luke Atencio and Candace Lee) at Christmas services the following year.

INTERESTING TIDBITS: This production focuses on the Advent season in which the minister frequently quotes Jesus from the New Testament Gospels and incorporates a mix of Protestant and Roman Catholic theology. The film also features famed Scottish singer Susan Boyle in her feature film debut as Eleanor Hopewell, the inn-keeper's wife.

Domestic box office sales barely exceeded two million dollars.

Max Lucado is a minister and host of the teaching ministry *UpWords*. He is the author of multiple best-sellers and is said to be America's leading inspirational author.

REVIEWS: According to the Rotten Tomatoes film review site, 18 percent of critics gave this production a positive review. Metacritic gave it a score of 33/100 (generally unfavorable).

Joe Neumaier of the *New York Daily News*

(November 21, 2013): "This odd Dickens-meets-Sunday-school movie is as artless as the setup is muddled."

Martin Tsai of the *Los Angeles Times* (November 21, 2013), "…in spite of the hammy histrionics requisite for the genre, it is not at all a turkey."

Frank Scheck of *The Hollywood Reporter* (November 21, 2013): "…its hopelessly stodgy execution will test the patience of even the most enthusiastic audiences for faith-based films."

PRODUCTION CREDITS—Writers: Candace Lee and Eric Newman. Producers: Hannah Leader and Tom Newman. Director: John Stephenson. Production Companies: Pinewood Studios, Big Book Media, and Impact Productions LLC. Rating: PG (mild thematic elements). Genres: Drama, Family. Countries: United Kingdom and USA. Run Time: 100 min.

REFERENCES: *The Christmas Candle*. Box Office Mojo. http://www.boxofficemojo.com/movies/?id=christmascandle.htm

The Christmas Candle. Christian Film Database. http://www.christianfilmdatabase.com/review/christmas-candle/

The Christmas Candle. EchoLight Studios, 2014. DVD Video.

The Christmas Candle. Metacritic. http://www.metacritic.com/movie/the-christmas-candle

The Christmas Candle. Official Web Site: http://www.thechristmascandlemovie.com

The Christmas Candle. Rotten Tomatoes. http://www.rottentomatoes.com/m/the_christmas_candle_2013

Crump, William D. *The Christmas Encyclopedia*. Third Edition. Jefferson, NC: McFarland, 2013.

Lucado, Max. *The Christmas Candle*. Nashville: WestBow Press, 2006

Max Lucado. Official Web Site: http://maxlucado.com

Neumaier, Joe. *The Christmas Candle*. *New York Daily News*. http://www.nydailynews.com/entertainment/tv-movies/christmas-candle-everyday-movie-reviews-article-1.1525043

Scheck, Frank. *The Christmas Candle*. *The Hollywood Reporter*. http://www.hollywoodreporter.com/review/christmas-candle-film-review-658549

Tsai, Martin. "Review: 'Christmas Candle' Beams with Holiday Spirit." *Los Angeles Times*. http://touch.latimes.com/#section/-1/article/p2p-78270858/

Christmas Comes but Once a Year—
December 4, 1936
    Remade as *True Boo*
    October 24, 1952
    Animated Theatrical Cartoon Shorts

THREAT TO CHRISTMAS: Innocent children despair over having received either useless toys or no toys at all for Christmas.

HOW CHRISTMAS IS SAVED: Professor Grampy and Casper the Friendly Ghost create new toys from household items.

SYNOPSIS AND COMMENTARY: *Christmas Comes* was numbered among the *Color Classics* series of theatrical cartoons that Fleischer Studios produced for Paramount Pictures from 1934 to 1941. A collection of musical cartoons that showcased creator Max Fleischer's patented "stereo-optical process," the *Color Classics* created the illusion of depth by animating the characters over three-dimensional, live-action backgrounds.

Christmas Comes opens to survey the wretched conditions at a dilapidated orphanage as a tenor in the background delivers a mournful rendition of "The First Nowell." It is Christmas morning, and the children in the dormitory are heartbroken when they discover that the toys in their stockings are old and quickly fall to pieces. Whether they are "gifts" from a heartless Santa or from the orphanage is not revealed. The children's pitiful crying catches the attention of Professor Grampy, a bald, bearded, brilliant old inventor who is passing by the orphanage in his self-propelled sleigh. Moved with compassion, the professor sneaks into the kitchen and, in the role of a Santa-surrogate, creates a series of simple toys from ordinary kitchen utensils. Then dressed as Santa, the professor decorates the living room with strings of popcorn, creates an indoor path for sleds with a shredded bar of soap, and fashions a Christmas tree from several umbrellas stacked on a phonograph turntable. Ringing a bell, the professor/Santa then bids the children to enjoy their "new" toys.

True Boo features Casper the Friendly Ghost of Harvey Cartoons (see **Casper's Haunted Christmas** for a brief history of Casper) in a similar role as a surrogate-Santa. Upon wandering the streets in search of a Christmas friend after his three uncles (the Ghostly Trio) destroy his letter to Santa, the sobbing of little Billy, a poor child whom Santa has overlooked, induces Casper to dress as the jolly man and fashion toys from simple items in the boy's house. Even the Christmas tree and some of the toys are created in virtually the same manner as in the 1936 cartoon.

PRINCIPAL VOICES: *Christmas*—Jack Mercer (*Felix the Cat*) as Grampy; Mae Questel (*Funny Girl*) as the orphans. *True Boo*—Alan Shay (*Ghost of the Town*) as Casper; Mae Questel as Billy and Billy's mother; Jack Mercer as other voices.

INTERESTING TIDBITS: According to Jennie Rothenberg Gritz, a senior editor for *The Atlantic*, the spirit of Professor Grampy's ingenuity evident in *Christmas Comes* parallels that of the founders of not only Paramount Pictures, but also Universal, MGM, Twentieth-Century Fox, and Warner Bros. studios, as well as Max Fleischer, all of whom were European Jewish immigrants. More than that, she notes, with *Christmas Comes*, "there's a note of real pathos, too. For the men listed on the credits, a house full of crying orphans wasn't an abstract idea. All of them had family living in Nazi-occupied territories … these filmmakers also knew about ingenuity, and that's what their Christmas fable was all about."

Professor Grampy regularly appeared in Max Fleischer's *Betty Boop* series of cartoon shorts released by Paramount Pictures during the 1930s. *Christmas Comes* is the only color cartoon in which Professor Grampy appeared without Betty Boop, and *True Boo* was the first Christmas cartoon in the *Casper* series of shorts.

PRODUCTION CREDITS—Writers: None listed for *Christmas*; Larz Bourne for *True Boo*. Producers: Max Fleischer (*Christmas*); Seymour Kneitel and Isadore Sparber (*True Boo*). Directors: Dave Fleischer (*Christmas*); Isadore Sparber (*True Boo*). Production Companies: Fleischer Studios (*Christmas*); Famous Studios (*True Boo*). Rating: Not rated. Genres: Animation, Short. Country: USA. Run Time: 8 min. (*Christmas*); 6 min. (*True Boo*).

REFERENCES: *Christmas Comes but Once a Year*. Big Cartoon Database. http://www.bcdb.com/cartoon/1716-Christmas-Comes-But-Once-A-Year

Christmas Comes but Once a Year. In *Max Fleischer's Color Classics: Somewhere in Dreamland*. Tulsa, OK: VCI Entertainment, 2002. DVD Video

Christmas Comes but Once a Year. Internet Movie Database. http://www.imdb.com/title/tt0027446/

Crump, William D. *The Christmas Encyclopedia*. Third Edition. Jefferson, NC: McFarland, 2013.

Gritz, Jennie Rothenberg. "The Jewish Cartoonists Who Reinvented Christmas." *The Atlantic* (December 23, 2014). http://www.theatlantic.com/entertainment/archive/2014/12/the-jewish-cartoonists-who-tried-to-reinvent-christmas/384007/

Lenburg, Jeff. *The Encyclopedia of Animated Cartoons*. Third Edition. New York: Facts on File, 2009.

True Boo. Big Cartoon Database. http://www.bcdb.com/cartoon/16010-True-Boo

True Boo. In *Harvey Toons: The Complete Collection*. New York: Sony Wonder, 2006. DVD Video

True Boo. Internet Movie Database: http://www.imdb.com/title/tt0149297/

Wilson, Joanna. *Tis the Season TV: The Encyclopedia of Christmas-Themed Episodes, Specials and Made-for-TV Movies*. Akron, OH: 1701 Press, 2011.

Christmas Comes to Pac-Land—December 16, 1982

Animated Television Short Film

THREAT TO CHRISTMAS: Santa crashes his sleigh in Pac-Land and loses his bag of toys.

HOW CHRISTMAS IS SAVED: The Pac-

Christmas Comes to Pac-Land

Landers pitch in to fend off the menacing ghosts and help return Santa to his route.

SYNOPSIS AND COMMENTARY: *Pac-Man* was a cartoon series of 42 episodes that aired on the ABC Network from 1982 to 1983 with a Halloween and a Christmas special. The series was based on a popular video game of the same title at the time from Bally Midway Manufacturing Company/Namco, Ltd., the principal characters of which were round, colored balls named Pac-Man, wife Pepper, Pac-Baby, pet dog Chomp-Chomp, and pet cat Sour Puss, all of whom lived in Pac-Land. Their only nemeses were "ghost" monsters named Inky, Blinky, Pinky, Clyde, and Sue, who worked for Mezmaron, a Darth Vader–like figure whose mission was to control the supply of power pellets that served as the food and energy source for Pac-Land. The ghosts had a never-ending desire to chomp Pac-Man and his family.

In the series' only Christmas special, imagine a scenario in which Santa flies all over the world yet knows nothing of Pac-Land, until he accidentally crashes the reindeer sleigh in that cyberworld on Christmas Eve and loses his bag of toys. Perhaps his ignorance is based on the fact that Christmas doesn't exist in Pac-Land. Pac-Man and his peers find Santa a most intriguing stranger who explains his mission as gift-giver and that all of his toys must be retrieved, lest there be no Christmas for all the world's children. While Pepper nurses a shaken Santa and the reindeer, the Pac-Landers agree to repair Santa's sleigh as Pac-Man battles the ever-present ghosts and a howling blizzard to round up the gifts. Despite all the misery that

After crashing his sleigh in Pac-Land, Santa recuperates under the care of Pac-Man (left), Pac-Baby, pet dog Chomp-Chomp, and wife Pepper. Pet cat Sour Puss gives Santa the evil eye from her perch on the mantel, while ghosts Inky, Blinky, Pinky, Clyde, and Sue peer in the window outside in *Christmas Comes to Pac-Land* (1982). ABC Television (collection of William D. Crump).

Pac-Man suffers to retrieve those toys, Santa nevertheless decides to cancel Christmas because of reindeer fatigue and the late hour. But Pac-Man isn't about to be defeated, for he leads the troupe into the fabled Power Pellet Forest (after persuading the ghosts to let them pass "in the spirit of the holidays"), where the reindeer gain super energy by consuming power pellets. Thus revived, Santa and his reindeer zoom away, but not before stopping at Pac-Man's house to deliver special gifts for them and the ghosts as well.

PRINCIPAL VOICES: Marty Ingels (*I'm Dickens, He's Fenster*) as Pac-Man; Barbara Minkus (*Lady Sings the Blues*) as Pepper; Russi Taylor (*The Simpsons*) as Pac-Baby; Frank Welker (*Aladdin*) as Chomp-Chomp; Peter Cullen (*Ghostbusters*) as Sour Puss and Santa; Barry Gordon (*Teenage Mutant Ninja Turtles*) as Inky; Chuck McCann (*Little Orphan Annie*) as Blinky and Pinky; Neilson Ross (*Rambo*) as Clyde; Susan Silo (*Once upon a Forest*) as Sue.

INTERESTING TIDBITS: *Christmas Comes to Pac-Land* is broadcast annually on the Boomerang cable channel. Often retitled as *Pac-Man's Christmas*, it has aired on Cartoon Network and TNT.

Pepper finds reindeer Rudolph's blinking red nose perplexing and interprets it as a warning light that he has not fully recovered.

Mezmaron is the only character from the *Pac-Man* series that is not present in this Christmas special.

As Santa flies away, he modifies his usual farewell to "Merry Christmas to all, and to all a good chomp!" This is an allusion to the last line of the poem "A Visit from St. Nicholas" (AKA "'Twas the Night Before Christmas"), which reads, "Happy Christmas to all, and to all a good night."

Pac-Man was the first animated series to be based on a video game.

REVIEW: J.P. Roscoe of *Basement Rejects* (December 25, 2012): "[This film] would be fun for kids from the '80s and the story is basic enough that younger kids might like it without knowing the characters. I just wish Santa Claus had eaten a power pellet and went after the ghosts."

PRODUCTION CREDITS—Writer: Jeffrey Scott. Producer: Kay Wright. Director: Ray Patterson. Production Company: Hanna-Barbera Productions. Rating: G. Genres: Animation, Family. Country: USA. Run Time: 30 min.

REFERENCES: *Christmas Comes to Pac-Land*. Big Cartoon Database. http://www.bcdb.com/cartoon/54916-Christmas-Comes-To-PacLand

Christmas Comes to Pac-Land. In *Pac-Man: The Complete Second Season*. Burbank, CA: Warner Home Video, 2012. DVD Video.

Christmas Comes to Pac-Land. Internet Movie Database. http://www.imdb.com/title/tt0499003/

Crump, William D. *The Christmas Encyclopedia*. Third Edition. Jefferson, NC: McFarland, 2013.

Lenburg, Jeff. *The Encyclopedia of Animated Cartoons*. Third Edition. New York: Facts on File, 2009.

Roscoe, J.P. "Christmas Comes to Pac-Land (1982)." *Basement Rejects*. http://basementrejects.com/review/christmas-comes-to-pac-land-1982/

Wilson, Joanna. "Christmas Comes to PacLand—The Weirdest Holiday Special Starring Pac-Man." About.com. http://classicgames.about.com/od/popculture/p/Christmas-Comes-To-Pac-Land.htm

_____. *Tis the Season TV: The Encyclopedia of Christmas-Themed Episodes, Specials and Made-for-TV Movies*. Akron, OH: 1701 Press, 2011.

Christmas Con Carne—October 11, 2002

Episode Short from the Animated Television Series *Evil Con Carne*

THREAT TO CHRISTMAS: In his quest for world domination, Hector Con Carne attempts to take over the North Pole with mind-control devices.

HOW CHRISTMAS IS SAVED: Rupert, the green-nosed reindeer, foils Hector.

SYNOPSIS AND COMMENTARY: This series would have been Dr. Frankenstein's dream come true. Created by Maxwell Atoms (Adam Burton), this series of only 14 half-hour episodes (with several cartoon shorts per episode) ran on Cartoon Network as one of two segments of the show *Grim and Evil* (2001–2002), the other segment being *The Grim Adventures of Billy and Mandy*; both segments became independent in 2003. The protagonist, Hector Con Carne, was a rich crime lord bent on conquering the world, but an explosion reduced him to an anthropomorphic brain and stomach, which the scientist, Major Dr. Ghastly, using containment units, implanted into Boskov, a purple Russian circus bear. Mustering an army commanded by General Skarr, Hector resumed his quest for world domination.

In "Christmas Con Carne," Hector, attached to Boskov's head, and his troops attack Santa at the North Pole with bazookas that shoot snowballs as Santa yells, "Protect the presents!" (that all-important part of Christmas). Once Santa is overcome, his head receives Hector, whose troops install mind-control devices in all the presents. A snowman watching from a distance rushes to summon Rupert, the green-nosed reindeer and superhero-bodybuilder, who lives in isolation after the other reindeer ostracized him from the reindeer games (a parody of Rudolph). Entering Santa's abode disguised as a Christmas tree, Rupert battles Skarr's troops and persuades Santa to dislodge Hector, who returns to Boskov, then flees in his rocket ship with the tainted presents. Flying in pursuit in typical superhero fashion, Rupert fires a beam from his nose that cuts a hole in the ship, then battles more troops and retrieves the sleigh with the tainted gifts as the ship crashes in the distance. Rupert's reward from Santa: "Rupert, with your muscles and might, won't you guide my sleigh tonight?" Hector, Ghastly, and Skarr all receive coal for Christmas.

VOICES: Phil LaMarr (*Pulp Fiction*) as Hector; Armin Shimerman (*The Hitcher*) as General Skarr; Grey DeLisle (*The Replacements*) as Major Dr. Ghastly; Charlie Adler (*Aladdin*) as the snowman; Frank Welker (*Aladdin*) as Santa; Michael Dorn (*Star Trek: The Next Generation*) as Rupert.

AWARDS: In 2005, *Evil Con Carne* received a Golden Reel nomination for Best Sound Editing in Television Animation.

INTERESTING TIDBIT: Meaning "with meat" in Spanish, "Con Carne" is a play on "evil incarnate" and "chili con carne."

NOTE: At the time of this writing, "Christmas Con Carne" was not available on DVD or VHS but could be seen on YouTube.

PRODUCTION CREDITS—Writer: Gord Zajac. Producer: Louis J. Cuck. Directors: John McIntyre and Robert Alvarez. Production Company: Cartoon Network Studios. Rating: Not rated. Genres: Animation, Comedy, Family. Country: USA. Run Time: 6 min.

REFERENCES: "Christmas Con Carne." Big Cartoon Database. http://www.bcdb.com/cartoon/72463-Christmas-Con-Carne

Evil Con Carne. Internet Movie Database. http://www.imdb.com/title/tt0419322/

Wilson, Joanna. *Tis the Season TV: The Encyclopedia of Christmas-Themed Episodes, Specials and Made-for-TV Movies.* Akron, OH: 1701 Press, 2011.

The Christmas Conspiracy—December 7, 2008

Animated Short Film

THREAT TO CHRISTMAS: A community conspiracy to make skeptical children believe in Santa goes up in flames.

HOW CHRISTMAS IS SAVED: Santa proves that he is perfectly capable of making believers of children despite the bumbling efforts of well-meaning people.

SYNOPSIS AND COMMENTARY: At first, the title of this production that features stop-motion clay humanoid puppets might suggest a plot involving international intrigue, but it's nothing nearly as exciting as that. Instead, the setting is the little town of Bedsbottom, where the recently widowed Mrs. Duckett calls an emergency meeting of the Community Board on Christmas Eve when she discovers that the town's youth no longer believe in Santa. Convinced that the children will believe if they make Santa real, Doug outlines a Christmas Conspiracy such that the Board members round up all the parents' presents in town and deposit them in a local warehouse, then Doug dressed as Santa would deliver the presents to the homes at midnight. As planned, Doug arrives at the warehouse in costume puffing a cigarette, but during a coughing fit, he drops the cigarette and the warehouse explodes like a bomb. With the presents reduced to ashes and no solution in sight, Christmas is ruined—or is it? Either way, it sends the common message that Christmas exists only if Santa delivers the presents, which he does here. Yes, on Christmas morning, the Bedsbottomites awaken to presents under their Christmas trees, courtesy of the big guy, who leaves a special message for Doug: "Ho, Ho, Ho! It's not so easy being me, is it?—Santa." Though the Christmas Conspiracy fails, Santa proves that "hope makes all things possible."

PRINCIPAL VOICES: Dick Van Patten (*Eight Is Enough*) as the narrator; Josh Blanford (*The Christmas Conspiracy*) as Jim Duckett; Sarah Blanford (*The Christmas Conspiracy*) as Jane Duckett; Jennifer Clary (*The Potters*) as Mrs. Duckett; Kevin Haberer (*Discover Me*) as Mr. Halbert and Mr. Shingle; Christian Kane (*Leverage*) as Doug.

AWARD: In 2009, this film received a Silver Award for Short Film at WorldFest Houston.

INTERESTING TIDBIT: The background music consists of excerpts from Tchaikovsky's *The Nutcracker Suite* with background art by Vincent Van Gogh.

NOTE: At the time of this writing, this film was not available on DVD or VHS but could be seen on YouTube.

PRODUCTION CREDITS—Story: Kevin Haberer. Writers and Producers: Jennifer Clary and Kevin Haberer. Director: Jennifer Clary. Production Company: Jenkev Productions. Rating: Not rated. Genres: Animation, Family, Short. Country: USA. Run Time: 10 min.

REFERENCE: *The Christmas Conspiracy*. Internet Movie Database. http://imdb.com/title/tt1326751/

The Christmas Dragon—November 7, 2014

Direct-to-Video Movie

THREAT TO CHRISTMAS: Father Christmas is dying because his magic orb has been stolen.

HOW CHRISTMAS IS SAVED: With the help of a dragon, a group of orphans find and return the orb.

SYNOPSIS AND COMMENTARY: The setting is medieval Europe in a fantasy land of magic, spells, dragons, ogres, goblins, as well as elves. Now imagine that Santa, or in this case Father Christmas (Adam Johnson, *Frozen*), lives not at the North Pole as such but in the North country without snow. His magic, in fact his very existence, depends on the Orb of Borealis, a sphere that his now-estranged, adult son Airk (Jake Stormoen, *Mythica: A Quest for Heroes*) had stolen five years earlier in an unsuccessful attempt to save his dying mother. Without his magic, Father Christmas and his elves are now dying. An ancient elf conveys this information to Ayden (Bailee Johnson, *Abide with Me*), a young orphan girl, together with a magic crystal that will lead her and her orphan friends on a trek to find and return the stolen Orb to the North. Their paths link with Airk and the elf Saerwen (Melanie Stone, *Mythica: A Quest for Heroes*), Airk's love-interest, who join the orphans. Along the way, Ayden nurses an injured young dragon that later saves the troupe from certain death during the many perils they face, including two bounty hunters in pursuit who would sell the orphans into slavery as workers in the mines. Finally replacing the Orb on the staff of the comatose Father Christmas and loading his sleigh with his toys, the troupe hitches the dragon to the sleigh (no reindeer in this story) and flies to the orphans' village to deliver the presents on Christmas Eve. The resulting merriment triggers Father Christmas's magic, and the 1,000-year-old man recovers not only to forgive his son and banish the two party-crashing bounty hunters from the land but also to unite Airk and Saerwen in marriage.

OTHER CAST: Jacob Buster (*Christmas for a Dollar*) as orphan Rand; David DeVilliers (*The Aquabats! Super Show!*) as orphan Fin; Ruby Jones (*Christmas for a Dollar*) as orphan Hoyt; Paris Warner (*Once I Was a Beehive*) as orphan Rosalynne; Renny Grames (*Blue Door*) as bounty hunter Gazared; Danny James (*Mercer*) as bounty hunter Borntall; Heather Beers (*Christmas for a Dollar*) as Sister Lenora; Michael Flynn (*Stripes*) as Father Mendel.

AWARDS: In 2015, this production won a Filmed in Utah Award for Best Makeup and received a Golden Reel Award nomination for Best Sound Editing, Direct-to-Video, Live Action.

INTERESTING TIDBITS: Ironically, though the subject is Christmas, it's an alien concept to most of the orphans. Ayden seems to know more about the holiday only to the point that Father Christmas is the chief figure, but all the orphans appear to be ignorant of any religious connection of Christmas with the birth of Christ. Indeed, Father Christmas is the godlike gift-giver here. To that end, at the beginning of the film, when Ayden's parents give her a kite for Christmas, they bid her to thank Father Christmas, whereupon she looks above and gives thanks, as if she were praying. Father Christmas hears her "prayer" and is pleased.

PRODUCTION CREDITS—Story: John Lyde. Screenplay: David Addante and Shylah Addante. Producers: Jennifer Griffin and John Lyde. Director: John Lyde. Production Companies: Arrowstorm Entertainment and Mainstay Productions. Rating: Not rated. Genres: Adventure, Drama, Fantasy. Country: USA. Run Time: 106 min.

REFERENCES: *The Christmas Dragon*. Internet Movie Database. http://www.imdb.com/title/tt3918686

The Christmas Dragon. Salt Lake City: Excel Entertainment Group, 2014. DVD Video.

Christmas Evil—2005

Episode from the Animated Television Series *Robotboy*

THREAT TO CHRISTMAS: Dr. Kamikazi creates a ruse to conquer the North Pole in order to capture Robotboy.

HOW CHRISTMAS IS SAVED: Tommy "rescues" Santa, who rescues Robotboy.

SYNOPSIS AND COMMENTARY: Created by Belgian designer and producer Jan Van Rijsselberge, *Robotboy* consisted of 104 segments in 52 half-hour episodes that premiered in the United Kingdom and the USA in 2005 on Cartoon Network. While the series is ongoing in the UK and other portions of Europe, airing ceased in the USA in 2008. A small but powerful fighting machine with superhuman abilities, Robotboy was the creation of Professor Moshimo, whose enemies, Dr. Kamikazi (a play on the Japanese "kamikaze") and his hulking henchman Constantine, consistently sought to capture the robot for world domination. Therefore, Moshimo entrusted his creation to ten-year-old Tommy Turnbull, who protected him together with his friends Lola and Gus.

Appearing in disguise on a TV talent show, Kamikazi and Constantine send a message to the world that Christmas will not come that year because Santa will be in chains. Of course, it's just a ruse to get Robotboy, and Tommy falls for it. Riding on Robotboy, Tommy rockets to the North Pole, where Kamikazi and Constantine have already subdued Santa. They freeze Robotboy's batteries, rendering him powerless, and escape with him. Shedding his suit, Santa displays his massive physique, despite all those cookies and milk, while sporting a pair of automatic weapons, then he zooms off in pursuit of the villains with Tommy in a reindeer jet. After they evade Kamikazi's laser defenses and blast their way into his lair, Santa smashes a herd of cloned blue bulls that serve as guards, then leaves for Christmas rounds. On his own, Tommy enters the lair via the chimney to replace Robotboy's batteries, and a battle commences between Robotboy and the guards, but when Robotboy is caught in a laser crossfire, Santa returns to save the day. Cut to Christmas morning. Since Santa really doesn't like Gus, he just can't resist leaving an obnoxious present that befits the obnoxious boy: a box filled with one of Santa's own copious *farts*. Repulsive, oh yes; hilarious, you bet!

PRINCIPAL VOICES: Laurence Bouvard (*Planet 51*) as Robotboy and Lola; Lorraine Pilkington (*Human Traffic*) as Tommy; Rupert Degas (*Planet 51*) as Gus and Constantine; Togo Igawa (*The Last Samurai*) as Moshimo; Eiji Kusuhara (*Eyes Wide Shut*) as Kamikazi; Lewis Macleod (*Planet 51*) as Santa.

NOTE: At the time of this writing, this episode was not available on DVD or VHS but could be seen on YouTube.

REVIEW: Emily Ashby of *Common Sense Media* reviewed the series: "Robotboy's arms transform into guns, and he shoots robotic enemies in defense of his friends. The Japanese villain and his servant are portrayed as bumbling fools with exaggerated accents. While teamwork and friendship are embedded in the moral of each episode, the lessons are overshadowed by the show's action…. The show also offers some gross-out moments, which are always hits with kids…"

PRODUCTION CREDITS—Writers: Robert Mittenthal and Mike Rubiner. Executive Producers: Christian Davin, Clément Calvet, Daniel Lennaro, and Finn Arnesen. Director: Charlie Bean. Production Companies: Alphanim, Cartoon Network, France 3, LuxAnimation, and Cofinova 1. Rating: Not rated. Genres: Animation, Comedy, Action-Adventure, Sci-Fi. Countries: France, United Kingdom, Luxembourg, and USA. Run Time: 11.5 min.

REFERENCES: Ashby, Emily. *Robotboy*. Common Sense Media. https://www.commonsensemedia.org/tv-reviews/robotboy

Robotboy. Internet Movie Database. http://www.imdb.com/title/tt0482870/

Wilson, Joanna. *Tis the Season TV: The Encyclopedia of Christmas-Themed Episodes, Specials and Made-for-TV Movies*. Akron, OH: 1701 Press, 2011.

Christmas Flintstone—December 25, 1964

Episode from the Animated Television Series *The Flintstones*

THREAT TO CHRISTMAS: Santa is sick in bed with a cold and cannot deliver his presents.

HOW CHRISTMAS IS SAVED: Santa drafts Fred Flintstone to make the deliveries.

SYNOPSIS AND COMMENTARY: Stone-Age people celebrating Christmas? Isn't that a bit far-fetched? In the real world, thousands of years would pass from the time of the Stone Age until Christmas would become a reality. In the world of animation, however, anachronistic settings are not uncommon and link the present with the distant past. Such is the case with *The Flintstones*, the first primetime, made-for-television animated situation comedy series, created by the animation giant Hanna-Barbera Studios. Inspired by the 1950s television series *The Honeymooners* and set during the Stone Age, *The Flintstones* aired on the ABC network from 1960 to 1966 with 166 half-hour episodes. The principal characters included Fred and Wilma Flintstone with daughter Pebbles; Dino, the Flintstones' little pet dinosaur who barked and behaved like a dog; neighbors Barney and Betty Rubble with adopted son Bamm-Bamm; Hoppy, the Rubbles' pet hopparoo (a combination of kangaroo and dinosaur); and Mr. Slate, Fred's boss at the rock quarry. *The Flintstones* revolved around Fred's and Barney's shenanigans in the town of Bedrock, where every name was derived from some form of stone or prehistoric creature. The principal characters also appeared in a host of other incarnations.

In "Christmas Flintstone," Fred needs some extra Christmas cash and takes a part-time job in the Macyrock Department Store during the week before Christmas. Inept as a gift wrapper and stock boy, Fred would have been terminated, until his boss, needing a last-minute replacement for the store's ailing Santa Claus, gives Fred one last chance, whereupon in costume, he uncharacteristically bursts into song with "Merry Christmas Is My Favorite Time of Year" and "Dino the Dinosaur." His portrayal of the jolly man and his warm interaction with children greatly impresses the real Santa, who sends elves Winkie and Blinkie on Christmas Eve to offer Fred the opportunity to take over Christmas rounds, because Santa is sick with a cold. Fred speeds around the world with the two elves in a sleigh drawn by three little barking dinosaurs with antlers (who otherwise resemble Dino) and shouts "Merry Christmas" in the languages of the respective countries as he flies by, hamming it up all the way with a reprise of "Merry Christmas Is My Favorite Time of Year." As he drops presents from the sleigh, they parachute into the chimneys of homes. After the elves depart, Fred realizes that he has nothing for his own family, because their gifts were aboard the sleigh. On returning home, he is relieved to find that Santa had rallied and had made a special delivery to everyone there, sneezing all the way.

PRINCIPAL VOICES: Alan Reed as Fred; Jean Vander Pyl as Wilma and Pebbles; Mel Blanc as

Barney, Mr. Macyrock, and Dino; Gerry Johnson as Betty; Don Messick as Bamm-Bamm and Hoppy; and Hal Smith as Santa. All these voice actors worked on *The Flintstones* TV series.

ORIGINAL SONGS: John McCarthy

AWARDS: *The Flintstones*—Primetime Emmy nomination for Outstanding Program Achievement in the Field of Humor (1961); Online Film and Television Association TV Hall of Fame Award for Television Programs (2006); TV Land Award nomination for Greatest TV Dance Craze ("The Twitch," 2006).

INTERESTING TIDBITS: A somewhat similar story line is found in the television special *A Flintstone Christmas*, in which Fred and Barney save Christmas when Santa once again becomes incapacitated. There, instead of utilizing parachutes, the presents are dropped from the sleigh like bombs into chimneys. Other films in which presents are delivered via parachutes include *The Christmas Orange, Christmas Present Time, A Monster Christmas,* and *The Super Special Gift.*

A cold also prevents Santa from delivering gifts in *The Year without a Santa Claus*. Santa-surrogate Granny Rose suffers a cold in *How the Toys Saved Christmas*.

PRODUCTION CREDITS—Writer: Warren Foster. Producers and Directors: William Hanna and Joseph Barbera. Production Company: Hanna-Barbera Productions. Rating: G. Genres: Animation, Comedy, Family. Country: USA. Run Time: 27 min.

REFERENCES: "Christmas Flintstone." In *The Flintstones: The Complete Fifth Season.* Burbank, CA: Warner Home Video, 2006. DVD Video.

"Christmas Flintstone." Big Cartoon Database. http://www.bcdb.com/cartoon/3292-Christmas-Flintstone

"Christmas Flintstone." Internet Movie Database. http://www.imdb.com/title/tt0580153/

Crump, William D. *The Christmas Encyclopedia*. Third Edition. Jefferson, NC: McFarland, 2013.

Lenburg, Jeff. *The Encyclopedia of Animated Cartoons*. Third Edition. New York: Facts on File, 2009.

Mallory, Michael. *Hanna-Barbera Cartoons*. Westport, CT: Hugh Lauter Levin Associates, 1998.

Wilson, Joanna. *Tis the Season TV: The Encyclopedia of Christmas-Themed Episodes, Specials and Made-for-TV Movies*. Akron, OH: 1701 Press, 2011.

Christmas in Cartoontown—1996

Direct-to-Video Animated Musical

THREAT TO CHRISTMAS: A witch and an evil toymaker try to shut down Santa's operation.

HOW CHRISTMAS IS SAVED: Two children and an elf foil the malefactors.

SYNOPSIS AND COMMENTARY: Bent on sabotaging Santa's operation, a mysterious stranger at the North Pole traps Irv the elf in a snow globe so that he cannot assist the reindeer to fly. The snow globe winds up in a toy shop, where young Alex buys it as a present for his sister Heidi. On Christmas Eve, the two children discover Irv and free him, and the three begin a journey back to the North Pole through a mirror into a fantasy land of storybook characters: Pinocchio, a huckster selling a magic bean that sprouts the beanstalk with Jack and the giant, the witch from Hansel and Gretel, Snow White, and Cinderella. These characters, included to hold the interest of young viewers, are simply filler material and are not germane to the story except for the witch who, as expected, is the real bugaboo. She threatens the children's lives and is in cahoots with Mr. Trench, the stranger and head of a toy company who wants to put Santa out of business. At the North Pole, although the witch initially destroys Santa's presents, she and Trench have a falling out such that she sides with the children, restores the gifts, and Trench ends up imprisoned in a snow globe as Irv had been. Now with Irv back, the reindeer can fly again, and Santa returns the children back home during his rounds.

SONGS: (Music by Megan Cavallari; Lyrics by David Goldsmith). "An Elf's Work Is Never Done"; "Wicked Little Me"; "Good Things Come in Small Packages"; "What Makes Christmas Merry."

VOICES: Alex Hugh (*Lost Stallions: The Journey Home*) as Alex; Oliver Clark (*Ernest Saves Christmas*) as Santa; Brad Kane (*Aladdin*) as Jack and Pinocchio. Other voices: John Beach, Kimberly Brown, Spencer Treat Clark, Laura Dean, Peter Fernandez, Donna Coney Island, Bob Kaliban, Barbara Jean Kearney, Liz Moses, Dennis Predovic.

INTERESTING TIDBITS: Irv's magic snowflake allows him to transport the children and himself through the mirror, but they may return only as long as the snowflake does not completely melt. As expected, the snowflake melts, whereupon it's up to Santa to deliver the kids back home on his sleigh.

When the witch initially destroys Santa's presents, she declares the typical sentiment about Christmas: "Christmas is cancelled! No presents, so no Christmas!"

PRODUCTION CREDITS—Original Story: Jerry Pettus, Jr., and Bill Schwartz. Writer: James Iver Mattson. Producers: Bill Schwartz and Winnie Chaffee. Director: Lon Moore. Production Company: Schwartz and Company. Rating: Not rated. Genres: Animation, Musical. Country: USA. Run Time: 60 min.

REFERENCES: *Christmas in Cartoontown*. Fort Mill, SC: Sterling, 2002. DVD Video.

Christmas in Cartoontown. Internet Movie Database. http://www.imdb.com/title/tt0122019/

Wilson, Joanna. *Tis the Season TV: The Encyclopedia of Christmas-Themed Episodes, Specials and Made-for-TV Movies*. Akron, OH: 1701 Press, 2011.

The Christmas Invasion—December 25, 2005

David Tennant as the Tenth Doctor with one of his hottie companions, Billie Piper as Rose Tyler, from the British TV series *Doctor Who*. Both starred in the episode "The Christmas Invasion." By the way, both are gesturing for silence with their *index* fingers, not their "bird" fingers. BBC Television (collection of William D. Crump).

Christmas Special from the Television Series *Doctor Who*

THREAT TO CHRISTMAS: An alien invasion attempts to enslave Earth at Christmastime.

HOW CHRISTMAS IS SAVED: The Doctor fights a duel with the alien leader and sends the creatures packing in time for Christmas dinner.

SYNOPSIS AND COMMENTARY: A significant part of British pop culture and created by Sydney Newman, C.E. Webber, and Donald Wilson, *Doctor Who* is a science-fiction series that initially ran on the BBC from 1963 to 1989; revived in 2005, the series has been ongoing since that time. The series protagonist is a time-traveling alien in humanoid form known simply as "the Doctor," originally from the planet Gallifrey, who travels through time and space in a Time and Relative Dimension in Space (TARDIS), a spacecraft with the deceptive, exterior appearance of a blue British police call box. Traveling with one or more human companions from Earth (usually female), the Doctor battles evil forces in the universe with just a few resources such as his sonic screwdriver. When mortally wounded, the Doctor can regenerate himself by taking on a new appearance and personality; thus, a slew of different actors have portrayed the Doctor over the years, the First Doctor being William Hartnell from 1963 to 1966. The series boasts a number of spinoffs.

Warning: Santa Claus does *not* appear in this film, only imposters. Now in the throes of his most recent regeneration, the Tenth Doctor (David Tennant, *Fright Night*) and his young, hottie blonde companion Rose Tyler (Billie Piper, *Spirit Trap*) crash the TARDIS on Christmas Eve in London. Although the Doctor spends most of the episode in a coma at the home of Rose's mom, Jackie Tyler (Camille Coduri, *Nuns on the Run*), together with Rose's black boyfriend Mickey Smith (Noel Clarke, *Storage 24*), there's plenty of action for the Doctor later on. Following an incident in which three masked, robot Santas attack the young couple in public with flame-throwing trumpets, there's more mayhem when a mysterious Christmas tree found at Jackie's home spins like a buzz saw to create a shambles. Miraculously, the Doctor awakens long enough to destroy the tree with his sonic screwdriver, and upon informing his friends that the strong energy from his regeneration is luring a deadly foe to him, he relapses. Meanwhile, the Sycorax, invading aliens bound for Earth, intercept a British space probe en route to Mars and deliver an ultimatum to Prime Minister Harriet Jones (Penelope Wilton, *Match Point*) on Christmas Day: Earth will surrender and half its population will become slaves. To seal their threat, the Sycorax, through blood control, force a third of the world's population (including the Royal Family), all of whom have the same blood type, to the roofs of tall buildings, where they will fall to their deaths if Earth fails to surrender. As the alien ship looms over London (which smacks of *Independence Day*), Rose and Mickey haul the Doctor to the TARDIS, which the Sycorax teleport aboard, along with Harriet Jones and her staff. Through idiotic babblings, Rose stalls the Sycorax long enough for the Doctor to recover upon inhaling the aroma of spilled tea (definitely a British cure-all). After disabling the blood control device which frees the people below, the Doctor then challenges the alien leader (Sean Gilder, *King Arthur*) to a one-on-one swordfight for Earth. Though the Doctor loses a hand in the battle (no blood anywhere), it regenerates; though the leader initially submits, he attacks the Doctor again, who dispatches him and orders the Sycorax to leave, never to return. Nevertheless, back on Earth, Jones orders the secret organization Torchwood to destroy the departing ship with lasers to deter other potential invaders. Her act of "murder" spawns repercussions, including false rumors of her ill health and a pending vote of no confidence. The good Doctor, having soundly denounced Jones, enjoys Christmas dinner with Rose, Jackie, and Mickey, along with the traditional trinket-laden British noisemakers, "Christmas crackers," then he and Rose prepare to head out again in the TARDIS.

AWARDS: *Doctor Who* has won nearly 130 awards and received over 230 nominations, primarily during the revival period. Some of the wins include 27 BAFTA Cymru Awards, 12 BBC's "Drama Best of" Awards, 11 Constellation Awards, 14 National Television Awards, 19 SFX Awards, and many others.

INTERESTING TIDBITS: The Doctor dispatches the Sycorax leader by triggering a sensor on the ship's exterior with an orange from his bathrobe. A portion of the wing drops and the leader plummets to his death. The orange is significant in that it is linked with the tradition of placing one or more oranges in the toes of Christmas stockings. The tradition in turn stems from legends about the benevolence of Bishop Nicholas (later St. Nicholas), who paid the dowries of three penniless maidens by tossing three bags of gold through their windows (or down their chimneys according to other versions of the story) and thence into their stockings that hung by the fireplace. Over time, the bags of gold were represented by three gold balls, which ultimately became the symbols of pawnbrokers, since St. Nicholas is their patron saint, and the oranges came to represent the gold balls as delicious, Christmas treats.

"The Christmas Invasion" is the first full episode starring David Tennant as the Tenth Doctor. In 2014, readers of *Radio Times* voted "The Christmas Invasion" as the best *Doctor Who* Christmas special. There has been an annual Christmas special since the series' revival in 2005.

"Sycorax" is the name of the unseen witch in Shakespeare's play *The Tempest* as well as a moon of Uranus, named after the fictional character.

In a running gag, whenever the Prime Minister greets anyone, including the aliens, she whips out her badge and says, "Harriet Jones, Prime Minister." Those addressed respond with, "Yes, we know who you are."

The aliens control all people with blood type A positive, which supposedly includes the Royal Family. In reality, none of the Royals has that blood type.

REVIEWS: Metacritic gave the revival series of *Doctor Who* a score of 70/100 (generally favorable reviews).

The New York Times reviewed the revived series (March 17, 2006): "Like so much British science fiction, especially Douglas Adams's 'Hitchhiker's Guide to the Galaxy' series, this 'Doctor Who' has a goofy, homemade quality; it's less interested in gizmos than in characters."

Sharon Eberson of the *Pittsburgh Post-Gazette* reviewed the revived series (March 16, 2006): "BBC execs thought they could update the series, take a giant leap in production values and regenerate ratings, and they were right…. Some of the pop-culture humor and creatures owe a nod to 'Farscape,' but the camp level is high and can be mighty funny…"

Will Wade of *Common Sense Media* reviewed the series: "As sort of an anti-action-hero, the Doctor uses charm and quick thinking to disarm his foes rather than guns or fists. Among other likable traits, this gives his character strong appeal and broadens the show's potential fan base. There's still a fair amount of violence and plenty of tense moments, but they're offset by a real joviality that all ages will enjoy."

PRODUCTION CREDITS—Writer: Russell T. Davies. Producer: Phil Collision. Director: James Hawes. Production Companies: BBC Wales and the Canadian Broadcasting Corporation. Rating: PG. Genres: Adventure, Drama, Family, Mystery, Sci-Fi. Country: United Kingdom. Run Time: 60 min.

REFERENCES: "The Christmas Invasion." In *Doctor Who: The Complete Second Series*. United Kingdom: BBC Video and 2 Entertain, 2007. DVD Video.

"The Christmas Invasion." Internet Movie Database. http://www.imdb.com/title/tt0562994/

Doctor Who. Metacritic. http://www.metacritic.com/tv/doctor-who

Eberson, Sharon. "'Doctor Who' Pays Return Visit to the U.S." *Pittsburgh Post-Gazette*. http://old.post-gazette.com/pg/06075/670867.stm

Fullerton, Huw. "David Tennant's Debut Voted Best Doctor Who Christmas Special." *Radio Times*. http://www.radiotimes.com/news/2014-12-28/david-tennants-debut-voted-best-doctor-who-christmas-special

"The Return of the Regenerated: A New 'Doctor Who.'" *The New York Times*. http://www.nytimes.com/2006/03/17/arts/television/17who.html?_r=2&oref=slogin&

Wade, Will. *Doctor Who. Common Sense*

Media. https://www.commonsensemedia.org/tv-reviews/doctor-who

Wilson, Joanna. *Tis the Season TV: The Encyclopedia of Christmas-Themed Episodes, Specials and Made-for-TV Movies.* Akron, OH: 1701 Press, 2011.

Christmas Is Here Again—October 19, 2007

Direct-to-Video Animated Musical

THREAT TO CHRISTMAS: Because Santa's magic sack was stolen years ago, there's been no Christmas since that time.

HOW CHRISTMAS IS SAVED: A little orphan girl and her friends brave perils to retrieve the sack.

SYNOPSIS AND COMMENTARY: Thirty years ago, the evil Krad had stolen Santa's magic sack that had been made from the swaddling clothes of the Baby Jesus. Krad, residing in the bowels of the earth, had formerly supplied Santa with coal for naughty children, but when Santa decided to forgo that practice, Krad retaliated and stole the sack. Now a whole generation of children such as the little handicapped orphan Sophiana has grown up without knowing about Santa and Christmas. While wandering in the forest, Sophiana liberates Paul Rocco, an elf who had been trapped in ice all this time and who shares the story about Krad. Determined to find Santa's sack, Sophiana sets out with Mr. Caterpillar (her pet insect), Paul, the young reindeer Dart (Prancer's grandson), the wily fox Buster, and the dimwitted polar bear Charlee. After an arduous journey climbing a mountain, the group accidentally falls into Krad's lair, where Buster turns traitor and betrays the others to Krad for pieces of gold, but eventually Buster's good conscience forces him to liberate his friends from Krad's dungeon. After a number of twists and turns, during which time Dart learns to fly and saves the group from certain death, Sophiana buries Krad and his minions in coal that was stored in Santa's sack and returns it to the North Pole. With Christmas restored, Sophiana receives her fondest wish to be part of a family when Santa and Mrs. Claus adopt her.

PRINCIPAL VOICES: The film sports an all-star cast: Jay Leno (*The Tonight Show*) as the narrator; Ed Asner (*The Mary Tyler Moore Show*) as Krad; Kathy Bates (*Fried Green Toma-*

Sophiana and Paul Rocco the elf ride Dart the young reindeer in search of Santa's stolen sack in *Christmas Is Here Again* (2007). This is one of few save–Christmas films that mentions the birth of Christ (screen Media Films/Photofest).

toes) as Miss Dowdy; Madison Davenport (*While the Children Sleep*) as Sophiana; Colin Ford (*Sweet Home Alabama*) as Dart; Brad Garrett (*Everybody Loves Raymond*) as Charlee; Shirley Jones (*The Partridge Family*) as Mrs. Claus; Norm MacDonald (*Screwed*) as Buster; Daniel Roebuck (*Grumpy Cat's Worst Christmas Ever*) as Paul; Andy Griffith (*The Andy Griffith Show*) as Santa.

SONGS: The musical numbers are far from memorable, but young children probably couldn't care less: "Who Stole Santa's Sack?" by Marco Zappia; "I Stole Santa's Sack" by Marco Zappia; "Will I Ever See?" by Marco Zappia and Sherry Hackney Cade; "The Un-Christmas Song" by Robert Zappia; "Easy to Dream" by Rocco Zappia; "I'm Evil" by Robert Zappia; "Storytelling Song" by Marco Zappia; "Christmas Is Here Again" by Marco Zappia; "All Because of Me" by Robert Zappia; "You've Got Me, Honey" by Rocco Zappia.

AWARDS: Annie Award nominations for Best Voice Acting in an Animated Television Production (Madison Davenport, 2008); Best Animated Home Entertainment Production (2009); Best Performance in a Voice-Over Role, Young Actor (Colin Ford, 2009).

INTERESTING TIDBITS: Although the film centers around Santa, it is one of few save-Christmas productions to mention the birth of Christ. Paul provides a brief recap of the birth to Sophiana, and the inscription on a plaque where the sack had once stood in Santa's domain is taken from Luke 2:7 in the Bible: "…and Mary brought forth her first born son, Jesus, wrapped him in swaddling clothes, and laid him in a manger."

Sophiana walks with a cane, but the reason for her infirmity is not revealed.

Given the very simple animation, Krad resembles either a red-hooded Grim Reaper or the Ghost of Christmas Yet to Come from Dickens's *A Christmas Carol*.

Buster's betraying his friends to Krad for gold smacks of Judas Iscariot, who betrayed Jesus for 30 pieces of silver. But rather than hang himself as Judas did, Buster confesses his fault and liberates his friends.

Other save-Christmas films that involve Santa's missing sack include **Beethoven's Christmas Adventure, The Magic Sack of Mr. Nicholas,** and **My Friends Tigger and Pooh: Super Sleuth Christmas Movie**.

This film was the first feature production from Renegade Animation Studio and premiered at the Heartland Film Festival in 2007.

REVIEWS: Deb Berkenpas of The Dove Foundation: "…the birth of Jesus … and its significance to Santa's magic sack and the reminder of why gifts are given on Christmas [are] told … we see that children hold the hopes and dreams of tomorrow … dreams really do come true and, sometimes, in amazing ways … teaches some good life lessons. We approve it for all ages and we award it five doves."

Lauren Perry of *Parents Television Council*: "Because of its portrayal of positive, family-friendly values, its relevance to children, and its delightful holiday spirit, the Parents Television Council is proud to award [this film] with the *PTC Seal of Approval*™. The PTC recommends this film for children over the age of six."

Will Brownridge of *The Film Reel* (December 16, 2013): "This is a great holiday film, but the songs are really a chore to sit through … plenty of slow[-]paced songs. It's worth a look, but if the first song doesn't appeal to you, you may be better off stopping the film there, because it's not going to get better."

PRODUCTION CREDITS—Story: Marco Zappia. Writer and Director: Robert Zappia. Producers: Jim Praytor and Robert Zappia. Production Companies: Easy to Dream Entertainment, Asylum Hill Productions LLC, Renegade Animation. Rating: G. Genres: Animation, Adventure, Comedy, Family, Musical. Country: USA. Run Time: 74 min.

REFERENCES: Berkenpas, Deb. *Christmas is Here Again*. The Dove Foundation. http://www.dove.org/review/6517-christmas-is-here-again/

Brownridge, Will. *Christmas Is Here Again. The Film Reel*. http://www.the-filmreel.com/2013/12/16/review-christmas-2007-please-stop-singing/

Christmas Is Here Again. Big Cartoon Database. http://www.bcdb.com/cartoon/97786-Christmas-Is-Here-Again

Christmas Is Here Again. Internet Movie Database. http://www.imdb.com/title/tt0762148/

Christmas Is Here Again. New York: Screen Media Films, 2008. DVD Video.

Crump, William D. *The Christmas Encyclopedia.* Third Edition. Jefferson, NC: McFarland, 2013.

Perry, Lauren. *Christmas Is Here Again. Parents Television Council.* http://www.parentstv.org/ptc/publications/moviereviews/PTC/2008/christmashereagain.asp

Wilson, Joanna. *Tis the Season TV: The Encyclopedia of Christmas-Themed Episodes, Specials and Made-for-TV Movies.* Akron, OH: 1701 Press, 2011.

The Christmas Miracle—1912

Silent Black-and-White Short Film

THREAT TO CHRISTMAS: The holiday looks bleak for a poor mother and her three little girls.

HOW CHRISTMAS IS SAVED: The kind mother befriends an old beggar and takes in an infant orphan, whereupon Jesus saves her Christmas with a miracle of bounty.

SYNOPSIS AND COMMENTARY: Hardly anything is known about this little French film, including the original French title (perhaps it was *Le miracle de Noël*), though the title on the film is given in English as are the intertitles within the film. It is somewhat similar to another silent French production, ***The Christmas Angel*** (1904).

On a snowy Christmas Eve, a poor, single or widowed mother prepares her three little girls for bed in their miserable shack. There are no decorations, no Christmas tree, little food, and no warmth. Though the girls remove their shoes and place them by the fireless hearth in anticipation of a visit from *Père Noël* (Father Christmas, whom they imagine in a special-effects vision as placing little gifts on a Christmas tree), their mother despairs through melodramatic sighing and shaking her head that there will be nothing for them. The kind mother admits a bearded old beggar who seeks shelter, and after receiving a bit of bread and a cloak, he departs. For some inexplicable reason, the mother follows the beggar, who deposits a bundle by the church door and leaves as people file in for Midnight Mass. The curious mother discovers a tiny infant, likely an orphan, within the bundle, whereupon she carries it back home and makes a crib for it from a basket filled with straw. After introducing her girls to their new sibling, suddenly a light radiates from the baby, the door opens, and there stands the old beggar, who morphs into Jesus in white robes. The mother and girls kneel in worship, and Jesus quotes from Matthew 25:40 in an intertitle: "For as much as ye have done it unto the least of these, ye have done it unto me." Jesus rewards them with a Christmas miracle as their rags morph into new clothes with good food on the table, a full larder, toys for the kids, and even a little purse with coins. Their Christmas "cup runneth over."

INTERESTING TIDBITS: The identities of the cast members are unknown.

Today, an old male beggar toting around and abandoning an infant would raise serious questions.

NOTE: At the time of this writing, this film was not available on DVD or VHS but could be seen on YouTube.

REVIEW: Dave Sindelar of *Fantastic Movie Musings and Ramblings* (November 28, 2014): "…if you [saw] the title of this one and … the plot description [confined to the mother, children, and beggar], you could write the ending yourself and not be far off. You might get specific details wrong … but [you'd] probably get the fate of the mother and the three children right … those specific details are the most interesting bits of this otherwise unremarkable short."

PRODUCTION CREDITS—Writer, Producer, and Director: Unknown. Production Company: Compagnie Genérale des Établissements Pathé Frères Phonographes & Cinématographes. Rating: Not rated. Genre: Drama. Country: France. Run Time: 12 min.

REFERENCES: *The Christmas Miracle.* Internet Movie Database. http://ww.imdb.com/title/tt1269539/

Sindelar, Dave. *The Christmas Miracle.*

Fantastic Movie Musings and Ramblings. http://www.scifilm.org/musing4695.html

The Christmas Orange—December 9, 2002

Animated Television Movie

THREAT TO CHRISTMAS: When a greedy kid gets one orange for Christmas and hauls Santa into court for breach of promise, Santa quits.

HOW CHRISTMAS IS SAVED: Repenting, the kid performs a selfless act that changes Santa's mind.

SYNOPSIS AND COMMENTARY: Oh no! Santa's in court ... again? This time, he's actually being *sued* by a greedy, six-year-old kid in this adaptation of the children's book of the same title by Canadian author Don Gillmor, published in 1998. Born on Christmas Day, young Anton Stingley is unhappy because he gets presents only one day a year, whereas most other kids get them on their birthdays *and* at Christmas. Throughout the year, he compiles a 92-page wish-list of 600 gifts and presents it to Santa at the mall. But on Christmas morning, all he receives is one perfect orange. Outraged, Anton hires vicious attorney Wiley Studpustle and sues Santa for 11 million bucks for breach of promise. In court a year later, Studpustle attempts to make Santa look like a cruel, heartless villain who, if he were innocent, wouldn't need to hide behind such aliases as Kris Kringle, Father Christmas, and others. Santa argues that since Anton owns more than 2,700 toys, over 1,800 of which have never been used, he didn't need 600 more toys. Yet public opinion sides with Anton, whereupon Santa decides to quit, not wishing that people remain unhappy because they don't always get what they request, and Anton becomes the town pariah. Initially failing to persuade Santa to return and not willing that everyone go empty-handed, Anton dispenses all his unused toys around town as gifts. That one orange remains (miraculously it never rotted or became moldy in a year's time), which he gives to an old man, who morphs into Santa. Now Anton understands why he received that orange in the first place: it wasn't a punishment but a tool for teaching about generosity. As Santa makes his rounds, he and Anton drop oranges via parachutes over the town.

VOICES: Danny McKinnon (*Dragon Tales*) as Anton; Don Brown (*G.I. Joe*) as Studpustle; French Tickner (*Double Jeopardy*) as Santa; Scott McNeil (*Dragon Ball Z*) as Lenny the elf foreman; Ellen Kennedy (*Dragon Ball Z*) as Judge Marion Oldengray (a play on "old and gray").

AWARDS: In 2003, this film won a Leo Award for Best Music in an Animation Program or Series and received a Gemini nomination for Best Original Music Score for a Program or Miniseries.

INTERESTING TIDBITS: This story stems from the tradition of placing one or more oranges in the toes of Christmas stockings. The tradition in turn stems from legends about the benevolence of Bishop Nicholas (later St. Nicholas), who paid the dowries of three penniless maidens by tossing three bags of gold through their windows (or down their chimneys according to other versions of the story) and thence into their stockings that hung by the fireplace. Over time, the bags of gold were represented by three gold balls, which ultimately became the symbols of pawnbrokers, since St. Nicholas is their patron saint, and the oranges came to represent the gold balls as delicious, Christmas treats.

When Santa vows to quit, Judge Oldengray declares the popular sentiment about the relationship between Santa and Christmas: "Without Santa Claus, I might as well cancel Christmas!"

The roof of Anton's house sports a snowman figure, complete with black top hat. It's probably just a coincidence, but it smacks of the rooftop Frosty scenario in John Grisham's novel *Skipping Christmas* (2001).

An image of a shark befittingly graces the office door of attorney Wiley Studpustle.

Other save-Christmas films in which presents parachute down include ***Christmas Flintstone, Christmas Present Time, A Monster Christmas,*** and ***The Super Special Gift.***

Don Gillmor is an award-winning journalist and travel writer from Toronto. His other books include *The Trouble with Justin, When*

Vegetables Go Bad, and *The Fabulous Song*. The latter book won the Mr. Christie's Book Award.

PRODUCTION CREDITS—Screenplay: Cindy Filipenko and Geoff Berner. Producer: Cathy Schoch. Director: Ian Freedman. Production Company: Bardel Entertainment. Rating: Not rated. Genres: Animation, Comedy, Family. Country: Canada. Run Time: 22 min.

REFERENCES: *The Christmas Orange*. Big Cartoon Database. http://www.bcdb.com/cartoon/58547-Christmas-Orange

The Christmas Orange. British, Columbia, Canada: StudioWorks Entertainment, 2002. DVD Video.

The Christmas Orange. Internet Movie Database. http://www.imdb.com/title/tt0366307/

Crump, William D. *The Christmas Encyclopedia*. Third Edition. Jefferson, NC: McFarland, 2013.

Gillmor, Don. *The Christmas Orange*. Illustrated by Marie-Louise Gay. Toronto: Stoddart Kids, 1998.

Wilson, Joanna. *Tis the Season TV: The Encyclopedia of Christmas-Themed Episodes, Specials and Made-for-TV Movies*. Akron, OH: 1701 Press, 2011.

The Christmas Path—1998

Television Movie

THREAT TO CHRISTMAS: A young boy's cynicism creates a gap in the Christmas Path, thus preventing Santa from reaching Earth.

HOW CHRISTMAS IS SAVED: The Christmas angel persuades the boy to believe in Santa.

SYNOPSIS AND COMMENTARY: Rebellious and cynical since his father's death, young Cal Banks (Shia LaBeouf, *Transformers*) unwittingly creates a gap in the mystical path by which Santa (Bill Lucking, *Contraband*) gains access to all people of Earth. To save Cal and ultimately Christmas itself, Santa hands this assignment to Balthazar (Vincent Spano, *City of Hope*), the problematic Christmas angel. His task becomes more difficult after he defies Santa and swipes a bag of magic angel dust, for which his powers are revoked until a time when he is deemed worthy to receive them again. Back on Earth, Cal's adorable little sister Dora (Madylin Sweeten, *Everybody Loves Raymond*) is the epitome of the Christmas spirit, while their mother Jenny (Dee Wallace Stone, *Cujo*) struggles to make ends meet. At first, Balthazar's interactions with Jenny and her children are casual, until she receives an eviction notice, and Cal overreacts by breaking into a plush home. Yet it is Balthazar whom the police arrest, for he had followed Cal to protect him. His powers now restored because of this selfless act, the angel makes a believer of Cal when Balthazar's vision of Dora's imminent danger allows the youth to save his sister from being struck by a car. The final moments of the picture recall scenes from *Miracle on 34th Street*, for Balthazar must prove that he is a Christmas angel and answer the charges of attempted burglary in a court of law. Now it's Cal's turn to reciprocate, for he confesses his guilt. But when the homeowner (Diane McBain, *General Hospital*) realizes that Cal's father had died while saving her grandson from a car crash, she drops all charges, and the gap in the Christmas path is closed.

INTERESTING TIDBITS: This picture casts Santa in the unorthodox role of a heavenly being (perhaps a god) with power over angels. Other films in which the North Pole is depicted as a heavenly abode include **Must Be Santa** and **One Magic Christmas**.

PRODUCTION CREDITS—Writer and Director: Bernard Salzman. Producers: Ami Artzi and Bernard Salzman. Production Companies: Amco Entertainment in association with Dream Vision Entertainment III. Rating: Not rated. Genres: Drama, Fantasy. Country: USA. Run Time: 95 min.

REFERENCES: *The Christmas Path*. Internet Movie Database. http://www.imdb.com/title/tt0264483/

The Christmas Path. New York: GoodTimes Home Video, 2002. DVD Video.

Crump, William D. *The Christmas Encyclopedia*. Third Edition. Jefferson, NC: McFarland, 2013.

Wilson, Joanna. *Tis the Season TV: The Encyclopedia of Christmas-Themed Episodes, Specials and Made-for-TV Movies*. Akron, OH: 1701 Press, 2011.

Christmas Present Time—December 14, 2013

    Episode from the Computer-Animated Television Series *Tickety Toc*

    THREAT TO CHRISTMAS: Santa crash-lands his sleigh in Tickety Town.

    HOW CHRISTMAS IS SAVED: Twin siblings and their friends help Santa gather the presents, repair the sleigh, and deliver the presents.

    SYNOPSIS AND COMMENTARY: Imagine a fantasy world that exists behind a shop's cuckoo clock. That's the situation with *Tickety Toc*, an ongoing series of 30-minute episodes for preschoolers from the United Kingdom and South Korea that premiered in 2012. In the USA, the series first aired on Nickelodeon and then on Nick Jr. Dominated by a giant hourglass that marks the passage of time, the setting is Tickety Town, where eight-year-old twin protagonists Tommy and Tallulah experience their adventures. Regardless of the SNAFUs that frequently arise, the twins must set things right in time for them to return to the clock face for their hourly Chime Time duties. Other principal characters include Pufferty, a talking dog-train who delivers the twins to the clock on time; McCoggins, the town's maintenance creature (perhaps a cow?); Hopparoo, an accident-prone bunny who occasionally assists McCoggins.

    In "Christmas Present Time," the reindeer catch a cold while out on rounds and their sneezing causes Santa to crash-land in Tickety Town. Tommy and Tallulah gladly round up the presents that are scattered about, while McCoggins and Hopparoo find that repairing the damaged sleigh will take more time than Santa had planned. Loading up McCoggins's hot-air balloon, Santa and the twins commence delivering presents by dropping them via parachutes on the townspeople, but the balloon hits the star atop the community Christmas tree and bursts. With seemingly no time to deliver the remaining presents around Tickety Town *and* be punctual for Chime Time, Santa tosses a bit of Christmas dust on Pufferty, who flies the three to complete their mission around town. Meanwhile, Madame Au Lait, a huge, anthropomorphic cow, has purged the reindeer of their sniffles with her hot-as-blazes Christmas chili cheese bites, just as Santa and the twins return. With the sleigh repaired, Santa and his team of *six* reindeer head out to the rest of the world, and Pufferty delivers the twins on time for Chime Time.

    PRINCIPAL VOICES: Ruby Love (*Tickety Toc*) as Tallulah; Toby Ralph (*Tickety Toc*) as Tommy; Lewis Macleod (*Minions*) as McCoggins; David Holt (*Tickety Toc*) as Hopparoo; Katy Wix (*Magicians*) as Chickidee; Felicity Duncan (*Tickety Toc*) as Madame Au Lait; Elly Fairman (*Tickety Toc*) as Pufferty.

    INTERESTING TIDBIT: Other films in which the presents are delivered via parachutes include **Christmas Flintstone, The Christmas Orange, A Monster Christmas**, and **The Super Special Gift**.

    REVIEW: Emily Ashby of *Common Sense Media* reviewed the *Tickety Toc* series: "…[introduces] tots to the concept of time … delightful animation and colorful, comical community of characters … [carries] the clock theme through every scene, incorporating gears and pendulums into background scenery…"

    PRODUCTION CREDITS—Writer: Dave Ingham. Producers: Jung Jin Hong and Do Uk Kim. Animation Director: Jin Yong Kim. Production Companies: The Foundation, Zodiak Media Group, FunnyFlux [*sic*] Entertainment, High 1 Entertainment. Rating: Not rated. Genre: Animation. Countries: United Kingdom and South Korea. Run Time: 24 min.

    REFERENCES: Ashby, Emily. *Tickety Toc. Common Sense Media*. https://www.commonsensemedia.org/tv-reviews/tickety-toc

    "Christmas Present Time." In *Tickety Toc. Christmas Present Time*. Beverly Hills, CA: Anchor Bay Entertainment, 2014. DVD Video.

    Tickety Toc. Internet Movie Database. http://www.imdb.com/title/tt2369946/

Christmas Rescue—December 1991

    Also Known as *Mr. Men, Little Misses*

    Animated Television Short Film

    THREAT TO CHRISTMAS: Hating Christmas, the queen of MiseryLand sends her knights to seize Father Christmas's presents.

How Christmas Is Saved: Little Miss Magic speeds up production of new toys at the North Pole, but the confused knights end up returning the stolen presents anyway.

Synopsis and Commentary: Commencing in 1971, British author Roger Hargreaves wrote two series of children's books, the *Mr. Men* series, followed by the *Little Miss* series. Presenting a simple moral lesson with simple illustrations, each book featured a respective male or female title character whose name reflected his or her dominant personality, such as Mr. Happy, Mr. Silly, Little Miss Bossy, Little Miss Splendid, etc. Following Hargreaves's death in 1988, his son Adam took over the franchise. The books included some 85 characters that were adapted into several animated television series, one being *Mr. Men and Little Miss* that first aired in the United Kingdom (1994–1997) and then in the USA as *The Mr. Men Show* (1997–1999). Although *Christmas Rescue* predated the aforementioned series by several years, it is considered to be a special episode of that series.

The setting is Misterland, where Mr. Clever and Little Miss Star are the hosts of a TV show titled *The Misterland Breakfast Chat*. After some rapid, idiotic blather from Mr. Chatterbox about the Christmas goings-on in town, followed by a brief interview between Mr. Snow the snowman and Father Christmas, the hosts receive an urgent broadcast from Mr. Nosey, reporting live on location in Miseryland. The court jester having failed to entertain the queen there, she drops a load of glop on him (and accidentally on herself as well), then decides to ruin Christmas by sending three knights (Dark Knight, Starry Knight, and Stormy Knight) to the North Pole to seize all the presents from Father Christmas's workshop and tie up the old gent, his elves, and Mr. Snow. The hosts dispatch a helicopter to the North Pole with Mr. Impossible, Little Miss Magic, Mr. Rush, Mr. Busy, and Mr. Strong on board, who note that the knights below are escaping with the presents in a truck. When the helicopter arrives at Father Christmas's workshop, Mr. Strong having crashed through the barricaded door, Father Christmas needs to replace the stolen presents, so Little Miss Magic waves her wand, which doubles the speed of production. Soon the three bumbling knights arrive back at the workshop, because they had been driving around in circles in a snowstorm, but Father Christmas believes they decided to return the presents after all, and the knights offer no arguments.

Voices: David Shaw Parker (*The Muppet Christmas Carol*) and Jill Shilling (*Pets*).

Interesting Tidbit: Mr. Impossible's voice is a parody of actor John Wayne.

Note: At the time of this writing, this film was not available on DVD or VHS but could be seen on YouTube.

Production Credits—Writer: Bernie Kay. Director: Terry Ward. Production Companies: Flick Films Ltd, TV-AM Enterprises Ltd, and Mr. Films Ltd. Rating: Not rated. Genres: Animation, Family. Country: United Kingdom. Run Time: 13 min.

References: *Mr. Men and Little Miss*. Web Site. http://www.mrmen.com/index.html

"Mr. Men and Little Miss Christmas Special." Mr. Men Wiki. http://mrmen.wikia.com/wiki/Mr._Men_And_Little_Miss_Christmas_Special

Wilson, Joanna. *Tis the Season TV: The Encyclopedia of Christmas-Themed Episodes, Specials and Made-for-TV Movies*. Akron, OH: 1701 Press, 2011.

A Christmas Snow—October 1, 2010
Direct-to-Video Movie

Threat to Christmas: Because her father had abandoned her and her mother 30 years ago on Christmas Eve, a woman has rejected the holiday ever since.

How Christmas Is Saved: Snowbound in her home at Christmastime with her future stepdaughter and an elderly stranger, the woman rediscovers the essence of family and the spirit of Christmas.

Synopsis and Commentary: While the majority of save-Christmas films focus on saving Santa and the North Pole from various bogeys, some films like the inspirational *A Christmas Snow* focus on restoring the Christmas spirit to individuals who have lost it because of tragedies or other unfortunate circumstances. The film, which bears the tagline, "The storm of the century brings the gift of a lifetime," was subsequently novelized by American author Jim Stovall in 2010 under the same title.

For 30 years, successful restaurateur Kathleen Mitchell (Catherine Mary Stewart, *Night of the Comet*) has borne the wound left after her father walked out on her family on Christmas Eve when she was ten years old. Not only did Kathleen spurn Christmas from that point, she locked away all her emotions and never forgave her mother whom she blamed. A few days before Christmas, a freak blizzard leaves Kathleen snowbound in her home with two unlikely guests: Lucy Wright (Cameron Ten Napel, *Cool Dog*), the young daughter of her widower-boyfriend Andrew (Anthony Tyler Quinn, *Boy Meets World*), who is away on business; and Sam (Muse Watson, *Assassins*), an older, seemingly homeless man to whom Kathleen has offered shelter. A power failure forces the three to entertain themselves in simple family ways through board games, making snow angels, snowball fights, homemade decorations and confections, a holiday wish list, and even staging their own Christmas pageant. Their togetherness and Sam's special influence help Kathleen to rediscover her emotions of family and to dispel Lucy's fear that Kathleen will displace her as an important part in her father's life. Having confessed that he had left his own family years ago, had become an alcoholic, and had found a way back through faith in God, Sam urges Kathleen to be reconciled with her mother and to find her father. On Christmas Eve, Sam mysteriously disappears. In a box that had been delivered to her five days ago but was overlooked, Kathleen discovers her recently deceased father's personal effects: the same Bible and hand-crafted pocket watch that Sam had utilized during his stay. Within the Bible, her father had written his final gifts for "Katie": Faith in God, Friendship, Peace, Family, and Forgiveness, all of which comprise the Christmas spirit. The spirit of Kathleen's father had returned to her at a time when she most needed him, and on Christmas Day, as Lucy and her father enjoy a Christmas reunion, a new Kathleen takes a flight to be reconciled with her mother and stepfather.

AWARDS: In 2011, this film won Best Actor in a Feature Film (Muse Watson) at the Trail Dance Film Festival.

INTERESTING TIDBIT: Jim Stovall is the founder and president of the Emmy Award-winning Narrative Television Network, which makes movies and television accessible to blind audiences. His best-known novel is *The Ultimate Gift* (2001), which also became a major motion picture.

REVIEW: From *Movie Guide*: "Very strong evangelistic Christian, biblical movie with repeated readings of the Nativity Story about the virgin birth of Jesus Christ, explicit testimony of being saved ... with a character that may be a ghost a la *The Sixth Sense* but it's more ambiguous..."

PRODUCTION CREDITS—Screenplay: Candace Lee and Tracy Trost. Producer: Chad Gundersen. Director: Tracy Trost. Production Company: Trost Moving Pictures. Rating: G. Genre: Drama, Family. Country: USA. Run Time: 110 min.

REFERENCES: *A Christmas Snow*. Internet Movie Database. http://www.imdb.com/title/tt1606191/

A Christmas Snow. *Movie Guide*. https://www.movieguide.org/reviews/a-christmas-snow.html

A Christmas Snow. Shippensburg, PA: Destiny Image Films, 2010. DVD Video.

Crump, William D. *The Christmas Encyclopedia*. Third Edition. Jefferson, NC: McFarland, 2013.

Stovall, Jim. *A Christmas Snow*. Shippensburg, PA: Destiny Image Publications, 2010.

A Christmas Story—December 9, 1972

Animated Television Short Musical

THREAT TO CHRISTMAS: A little boy forgets to mail his letter to Santa.

HOW CHRISTMAS IS SAVED: Santa finds the letter anyway, despite the failed efforts of a mouse and a dog to deliver the letter.

SYNOPSIS AND COMMENTARY: Note: Ralphie Parker and his BB gun are not in this one. Here's a film that focuses on the heroic efforts of two animals to save one little boy's Christmas. When Timmy forgets to mail his letter to Santa, Gumdrop, the mouse-in-residence, discovers it under a table on Christmas Eve after Timmy goes to bed and sets out with Goober the family dog to intercept Santa and deliver the letter. They ramble around the neighborhood all evening chasing after Santa, who always stays one step ahead. At one point, Goober rescues Gumdrop from a bunch of alley cats bent on making him their Christmas feast, and on another occasion, the two make it onto a rooftop ahead of Santa, but a gust of wind whips the letter away, requiring Goober to chase it down; upon his return, Santa has departed again. When a neighborhood animal relay (consisting of dogs, cats, and squirrels) also fails to locate Santa, all that remains is for the two dejected searchers to return home with hope that Santa will visit there anyway and see Timmy's letter. As they sleep by the Christmas tree, Santa does indeed find the letter and fills Timmy's wish list.

PRINCIPAL VOICES: Daws Butler (*The Cat in the Hat*) as Gumdrop; Paul Winchell (*The Smurfs*) as Goober; Walter Tetley (*The Bullwinkle Show*) as Timmy; Don Messick (*The Smurfs*) as the father; Janet Waldo (*The Jetsons*) as the mother; Hal Smith (*The Andy Griffith Show*) as Santa. Other voices: John Stephenson (*The Flintstones*). Singers: Paul DeKorte, Randy Kemner, Stephen McAndrew, Ida Sue McCune, and Judi Richards.

ORIGINAL SONGS: "Sounds of Christmas Day," "Hope," "Which One Is the Real Santa Claus?" and "Where Do You Look for Santa?" The composers are not credited. The first three songs were reused in *A Flintstone Christmas* (1977), and "Hope" was reused in *Yogi's First Christmas* (1980).

INTERESTING TIDBITS: In the opening segment, Timmy's father reads the poem "A Visit from St. Nicholas" ("'Twas the Night Before Christmas"). He quotes the last line as "Merry Christmas to all, and to all a good night." Actually, the last line is "*Happy* Christmas to all,…" etc. We're far more used to saying "Merry Christmas" than "Happy Christmas" (unless we're bent on being politically correct and saying "Happy Holidays"). Other save-Christmas films with the same error are **Mary Engelbreit's The Night Before Christmas and 'Twas the Night**.

The appearance of the mother's and father's period dress and the antique mail truck suggest a setting in the early 1900s.

PRODUCTION CREDITS—Story: Ken Spears and Joe Ruby. Producers and Directors: William Hanna and Joseph Barbera. Production Company: Hanna-Barbera Productions. Rating: Not rated. Genres: Animation, Family. Country: USA. Run Time: 30 min.

REFERENCES: *A Christmas Story (Hanna-Barbera)*. Christmas Specials Wiki. http://christmas-specials.wikia.com/wiki/A_Christmas-Story_(Hanna-Barbera)

A Christmas Story. In *Hanna-Barbera Christmas Classics Collection*. Burbank, CA: Warner Home Video, 2012. DVD Video.

Crump, William D. *The Christmas Encyclopedia*. Third Edition. Jefferson, NC: McFarland, 2013.

Wilson, Joanna. *Tis the Season TV: The Encyclopedia of Christmas-Themed Episodes, Specials and Made-for-TV Movies*. Akron, OH: 1701 Press, 2011.

The Christmas That Almost Wasn't—
November 23, 1966

Feature Film

THREAT TO CHRISTMAS: When Phineas T. Prune buys the North Pole and Santa can't pay the rent, Prune offers to waive the rent if Santa will no longer deliver toys to children.

HOW CHRISTMAS IS SAVED: Thousands of children surrender their piggy banks to pay the rent.

SYNOPSIS AND COMMENTARY: It's ridiculous to imagine that one Christmas wish not granted in childhood would spawn lifelong, bitter feelings toward Christmas and children, but that's the case with wealthy villain Phineas T. Prune (Rossano Brazzi, *South Pacific*). His postcard to Santa requesting a toy sailboat was lost years ago, and Prune has been at war with Christmas ever since. When Prune purchases the North Pole a few weeks before Christmas, Santa (Alberto Rabagliati, *The Barefoot Con-*

A very worried Santa (Alberto Rabagliati, left) in street dress and more upbeat attorney Sam Whipple (Paul Tripp) confer with Mr. Prim (Sonny Fox, seated) about Santa's job in Prim's department store in *The Christmas That Almost Wasn't* (1966). Metro-Goldwyn-Mayer (collection of William D. Crump).

tessa) becomes his tenant. Santa must either pay the rent by midnight on Christmas Eve or surrender all the toys in his workshop to Prune, who offers to waive the rent if Santa will promise never again to deliver presents to children. Strapped for cash, a sad-sack Santa elects to scrape up the rent and takes a job portraying himself in a department store with assistance from an old friend, attorney Sam Whipple (Paul Tripp, *Maybe Baby*). Prune, determined to foil Santa at every turn, buys the store on Christmas Eve and fires him, which again leaves Santa short on the rent. The outlook is grim until thousands of children come to the rescue after learning about Santa's plight and donate their piggy banks to save Christmas. Kind-hearted Santa has one present for Prune, the long-belated sailboat, which melts Prune's heart.

LYRICS AND MUSIC: Paul Tripp and Bruno Nicolai, respectively.

INTERESTING TIDBITS: Prune's mean-spiritedness parallels that of Scrooge in *A Christmas Carol*, and the children's cash-for-Santa scenario parallels that in *It's a Wonderful Life*, when the citizens of Bedford Falls rally to pay George Bailey's debt.

REVIEWS: Critic reviews were mixed. Bosley Crowther of *The New York Times* (November 24, 1966): "…a pleasant but highly derivative fable … appears to be a direct descendant of Dickens' *A Christmas Carol* and *Miracle on 34th Street*."

Tracy Moore of *Common Sense Media* (October 24, 2013): "Maudlin tone and overly long, but some lessons in kindness."

PRODUCTION CREDITS—Writer: Paul Tripp. Producer: Barry B. Yellen. Director: Rossano

Brazzi. Production Companies: Bambi Productions and Childhood Productions. Rating: G. Genres: Family, Fantasy. Countries: Italy and USA. Run Time: 89 min.

REFERENCES: *The Christmas That Almost Wasn't.* Bellingham, WA: Hen's Tooth Video, 2003. DVD Video.

The Christmas That Almost Wasn't. Internet Movie Database. http://www.imdb.com/title/tt0059032/

Crowther, Bosley. *The Christmas That Almost Wasn't. The New York Times.* http://www.nytimes.com/movie/review?res=9506E3D91030E43BBC4C51DFB767838D679EDE

Crump, William D. *The Christmas Encyclopedia.* Third Edition. Jefferson, NC: McFarland, 2013.

Duralde, Alonso. *Have Yourself a Movie Little Christmas.* New York: Limelight Editions, 2010.

Moore, Tracy. *The Christmas That Almost Wasn't. Common Sense Media.* https://www.commonsensemedia.org/movie-reviews/the-christmas-that-almost-wasn't

Thompson, Frank T. *American Movie Classics Great Christmas Movies.* Dallas, TX: Taylor Publishing, 1998.

A Christmas Visitor—December 21, 2002

Television Movie

THREAT TO CHRISTMAS: A family grieving over the loss of a loved one has shunned Christmas for more than a decade.

HOW CHRISTMAS IS SAVED: A mysterious war veteran restores the family's faith and Christmas spirit.

SYNOPSIS AND COMMENTARY: On Christmas Eve twelve years ago, George and Carol Boyajian (William Devane, *Interstellar*, and Meredith Baxter, *Family Ties*) and daughter Jean (Reagan Pasternak, *Being Erica*) received the news that their son and brother John (Aaron Ashmore, *Smallville*) had been killed in action during the Persian Gulf War. Since that time, the family, living under a cloud of profound grief, has completely boycotted Christmas. Through a series of flashback scenes, the family relives poignant moments in John's life and death: his departure from town for basic training, the fateful Christmas Eve that brought the tragic news, his funeral with full military honors, and other memories. This year, the holidays are an especially tense time for Jean, who is worried that she may have breast cancer. Determined to lift everyone's spirits, George sets out to restore Christmas to his family, although Carol and Jean are strongly opposed initially. On Christmas Eve, George surprises his family by inviting Matthew (Dean McDermott, *Open Range*), a hitchhiker and veteran of the Gulf War, to share their first Christmas in more than a decade. Little do the Boyajians know that this gentle stranger will bring unimaginable peace as well as emotional, spiritual, and physical healing, leaving them to wonder if perhaps their Christmas visitor had been a supernatural entity or even the ghost of John himself.

INTERESTING TIDBITS: David Saperstein and George Samerjan published the story as a novel in 2004 under the same title.

REVIEW: Edwin L. Carpenter of The Dove Foundation: "The viewer will feel the turmoil the parents go through and the release when their faith is restored. The ending might also have some viewers scratching their heads regarding the visitor, but the love of the son and brother is definitely burned into the family's hearts. We award [this film] five Doves. It is a film that just might renew your faith in any area where it is lacking. Yes, it is that good!"

PRODUCTION CREDITS—Writers: David Saperstein and George Samerjan. Producers: Paul D. Goldman and Frank Siracusa. Director: Christopher Leitch. Production Company: Cypress Point Productions. Rating: Not rated. Genre: Drama. Country: USA. Run Time: 87 min.

REFERENCES: Carpenter, Edwin L. *A Christmas Visitor.* The Dove Foundation. http://www.dove.org/review/6905-a-christmas-visitor/

A Christmas Visitor. Internet Movie Database. http://www.imdb.com/title/tt0343531/

A Christmas Visitor. Santa Monica, CA: Platinum Disc, 2005. DVD Video.

Crump, William D. *The Christmas Encyclopedia.* Third Edition. Jefferson, NC: McFarland, 2013.

Saperstein, David, and George Samerjan. *A Christmas Visitor*. New York: Kensington Books, 2004.

Wilson, Joanna. *Tis the Season TV: The Encyclopedia of Christmas-Themed Episodes, Specials and Made-for-TV Movies*. Akron, OH: 1701 Press, 2011.

Christmas with a Capital C—December 24, 2011

Direct-to-Video Movie

THREAT TO CHRISTMAS: An atheist is bent on destroying Christmas in a small town.

HOW CHRISTMAS IS SAVED: Compassion and understanding allow all parties involved to compromise without undermining their beliefs.

SYNOPSIS AND COMMENTARY: Just about the time Thanksgiving is over, people really get into the Christmas spirit (except that department stores often have Christmas paraphernalia on display before Halloween). Then the annual "Christmas wars" begin: "It's 'Merry Christmas,' not 'Happy Holidays'"; "It's a 'Christmas tree,' not a 'holiday tree'"; "It's 'Christmas break,' not 'Winter break'"; "Jesus is the reason for the season"; "Christmas has pagan origins, and 'Santa' is just an anagram for 'Satan'"; "This Christmas symbol offends me"; "That Nativity scene is illegal on public property"; "Our school system prohibits wearing the traditional Christmas colors of red and green," and so forth. It's all over Facebook, the Internet, and religious message boards. Now imagine one atheist who wages his own personal war against Christmas in a small town.

For years, the citizens of Trapper Falls, Alaska, have celebrated Christ-centered Christmases that are currently led by Mayor Dan Reed (Ted McGinley, *Married … with Children*) and his brother Greg (Brad Stine, *Run On*). The town is fully draped in Christmas cheer, all public signs include the word "Christmas," and City Hall features a Nativity scene out front. After a 20-year absence, the sudden return of big-city attorney Mitch Bright (Daniel Baldwin, *Born on the Fourth of July*) to his hometown jeopardizes Christmas in Trapper Falls. An atheist and Dan's old high school rival, Mitch launches a campaign to attack all religious beliefs, beginning with Christmas. Mitch successfully removes the public Nativity scene, demands that all public signs sport "Happy Holidays" or "Season's Greetings" instead of "Merry Christmas," then decides to run against Dan for mayor. Outraged, Greg counters by persuading his niece Makayla (Francesca DeRosa, *Are You Smarter Than a 5th Grader?*) to dress as an angel and sing sacred carols where the Nativity scene had been, but Mitch has the police to remove her. With the goodwill of the town dissolving, Dan's wife Kristen (Nancy Stafford, *Matlock*) and her daughter Makayla launch their own "Christmas with a Capital C" campaign to remind everyone that the love of Christ and giving to others is for all mankind, "even those whose hearts seem closed to Him." Their example helps to reveal the ulterior motive that prompted Mitch's return.

AWARDS: In 2011, this film received Grace Award nominations for Most Inspiring Television Acting (Brad Stine and Nancy Stafford).

INTERESTING TIDBITS: This film is based on the song "Christmas with a Capital C," written by the American contemporary Christian band Go Fish (Jamie Statema, Jason Folkmann, and Andy Selness). It first appeared on the band's Christmas album *Snow* (2006, Go Fish Kids label), which was remastered as *Christmas with a Capital C—Snow: The Deluxe Edition* (2010, same label). The song gained considerable popularity after a fan-created video appeared on the Internet's YouTube.com that has been viewed over 18 million times. Taking a stand against efforts to remove God from American culture, the song features an opening monologue from comedian Brad Stine's album *Put a Helmet On* with lyrics that remind everyone that the birth of Christ is the prime focus of Christmas. According to Statema, "'Christmas with a Capital C' has become an anthem for Christians all over the United States."

REVIEWS: Tracy Moore of *Common Sense Media* (January 19, 2015): "There's nothing inappropriate here for kids, but much of the film's plot and discussion involves debating how to get around the legal loophole and still celebrate Christmas just as they always have, and it heavily promotes the idea that saying 'happy holidays' is not something you do for religious tolerance but rather it's an idea 'God haters' have promoted to get rid of religion altogether."

Christopher Gildemeister of the *Parents Television Council*: "[This film] is unapologetic in its position on the importance of Christian customs and traditions in the public square, at Christmas and year-round; but it also demonstrates the importance of Christian compassion for others, and of making a genuine effort to understand them … the Parents Television Council is proud to award [this film] with the *PTC Seal of Approval*™."

Edwin L. Carpenter of The Dove Foundation: "This is a nicely made film with some good themes including forgiveness, loyalty, and standing up for one's beliefs. We are more than pleased to award our Dove 'Family-Approved' Seal to this movie. It is an inspiring film."

Angela Walker of *Christian Cinema*: "What if, instead of trying to fight back and demand 'rights' as believers, we showed what the true spirit of Christmas really is? That's the best part of this story. Don't look for a legal way to keep Christ in Christmas[;] do it through your own attitude and choices for celebrations."

PRODUCTION CREDITS—Writer: Andrea Gyertson Nasfell. Producers: James Chankin and Michael Scott. Director: Helmut Schleppi. Production Company: Ranch Studios. Rating: Not rated. Genres: Drama, Family. Country: USA. Run Time: 81 min.

REFERENCES: Carpenter, Edwin L. *Christmas with a Capital C*. The Dove Foundation. http://www.dove.org/review/8463-christmas-with-a-capital-c/

Christmas with a Capital C. Internet Movie Database. http://www.imdb.com/title/tt1640116/

Christmas with a Capital C (album). Medford, MN: GFK Records, 2010. Audio CD Recording.

"Christmas with a Capital C" (song). YouTube. https://www.youtube.com/watch?v=IAckfn8yiAQ

Christmas with a Capital C. Scottsdale, AZ: Pure Flix Entertainment, 2011. DVD Video.

Crump, William D. *The Christmas Encyclopedia*. Third Edition. Jefferson, NC: McFarland, 2013.

Gildemeister, Christopher. *Christmas with a Capital C. Parents Television Council*. http://www.parentstv.org/PTC/publications/reviews/ChristmaswithaCapitalC.asp

Moore, Tracy. *Christmas with a Capital C. Common Sense Media*. https://www.commonsensemedia.org/movie-reviews/christmas-with-a-capital-c

Walker, Angela. "Christmas with a Capital C Spells a Charming Film." *Christian Cinema*. http://www.christiancinema.com/catalog/article_info.php?articles_id=7622#

A Christmoose Story (Midden in De Winternacht)—November 27, 2013

Feature Film

THREAT TO CHRISTMAS: Santa's test-pilot Moose crashes the sleigh, Santa is incarcerated, and a hunter steals Moose's medallion that enables him to fly.

HOW CHRISTMAS IS SAVED: Young Max and Moose rescue Santa and retrieve the medallion.

SYNOPSIS AND COMMENTARY: Whenever Santa is out on a test-run with his sleigh, most Christmas movies depict him in exercises with the full reindeer team. In this Dutch/Swedish/Belgian production dubbed in English, however, Santa (Derek de Lint, *Black Book*) utilizes a large talking, belching moose named—for lack of originality—"Moose" (an animatronic creation voiced by Jeroen van Koningsbrugge, *Smeris*), because the reindeer are much too fragile to risk in such matters. Titled *Midden in De Winternacht* (*Middle of the Winter Night*) in Dutch, the film is an adaptation of *Es ist ein Elch entsprungen* (*A Moose Dropped In*), a children's novel by German author Andreas Steinhöfel, published in 2002.

Ten-year-old Max (Dennis Reinsma, *The Little Gangster*) expects this first Christmas since his parents' recent divorce to be a real drag; that is, until Moose loses control in mid-flight, crashes into Max's barn, and injures his leg. Santa and the sleigh crash elsewhere, and while he's out searching for Moose, the latter, fearing that Santa will fire him because he feels responsible for the mishap, recuperates with

Max as his nurse. Max's mother Kirsten (Jelka van Houten, *Summer Heat*) tolerates Moose for the boy's sake, but her know-it-all younger sister Kiki (Dana Goldberg, *Vrolijke Kerst*) rejects the idea that Moose belongs to Santa, let alone that Santa even exists. By coincidence, Max's Grandma (Carla Hardy, *The Ninth Hour*), never once doubting his identity, arrives with Santa in tow, having given him a lift on the highway. When Santa learns that Moose has lost the medallion containing the stardust that empowers them with flight, he first attempts to strangle Moose, then falls into a funk and cancels Christmas, but flirtatious Grandma counters with a pep-talk laced with booze that pumps up Santa in more ways than one (*wink!*). Thinking back, Max recalls that grumpy neighbor Panneman (Arjan Ederveen, *Still Smokin*), an avid hunter who desires Moose's head on his wall, had pocketed the medallion earlier, whereupon Santa's drunken, nocturnal confrontation with Panneman lands him in a mental asylum for claiming to be the jolly gent. If there's going be a Christmas, Moose must have that medallion, so he and Max create a diversion at Panneman's house while Max slips in to retrieve the medallion, then Max sprinkles Panneman with the stardust when he's about to shoot Moose. As Panneman rockets away into the wild blue yonder, Max and Moose fly to the asylum to free Santa, who escapes by shinnying up the chimney, after which they return home where, upon bidding farewell to all, Santa and Moose head into the skies.

AWARDS: In 2013, this film won a Golden Film Award at the Golden and Platin Film, Netherlands. In 2014, it received a Crystal Bear nomination for Generation K Plus, Best Film, at the Berlin International Film Festival; an Audience Award nomination for Best Film at the Nederlands Film Festival; a Rembrandt Award nomination for Best Dutch Youth Film; a Just Film Award nomination for Best Children's Film at the Tallinn Black Nights Film Festival; and nominations for the Children's Jury Main Prize and Golden Slipper for Best Feature Film for Children at the Zlín International Film Festival for Children and Youth.

INTERESTING TIDBITS: This film is a remake of *A Christmoose Carol*, the English-language title of a German film adaptation of Andreas Steinhöfel's book, released in 2005. Directed by Ben Verbong with a screenplay co-written by Steinhöfel, the earlier version bears no relationship to Dickens's tale. Both titles reflect obvious puns, and their plots are quite similar with a few changes in characters' names. For example, it's Moose here and Mr. Moose there; Max here and Bertil (Raban Bieling) there; Panneman vs. Pannecke (Jürgen Tarrach); Santa vs. *Weihnachtsmann* (Mario Adorf). The characters of Kirsten (Anja Kling there) and Kiki (Sarah Beck there) remain the same. The DVD for the earlier version is in non–USA format, PAL/Region 2.

Embarrassed that his name is nothing more spectacular than "Moose," Moose initially informs Max that his name is "Apollo" and that the American lunar missions were named after him.

The picture was filmed in Sweden and Swedish Lapland, which provided for some stunning landscape scenes.

REVIEWS: Bernardo Villela of *The Movie Rat* (December 7, 2014): "The bones of this version and the prior [one] are essentially the same. Much of the humor being intended to stem from the situations the characters find themselves in this well-crafted world. However, through more sure-handed filmmaking, better implementation of practical and digital effects work as well as a more prominent, comedic presence from supporting actors makes this film work even better."

Monica Meijer of the Dutch *Cinemagazine* (November 26, 2013) implied that because the earlier version, which appeared in Dutch theaters in 2006 under the title *Prettige kerst, Mr. Moose* (*Merry Christmas, Mr. Moose*), was not spectacularly successful at the box office, it was time for a remake. "*Middle of the Winter Night* is a smooth, touching family film. The jokes range from bland to hilarious, but you can speak of a successful remake across the board." [Quotes translated by Google Translate.]

PRODUCTION CREDITS—Scenario: Daan Bakker and Marco van Geffen. Producers: Eva

Eisenloeffel, Leontine Petit and Joost de Vries. Director: Lourens Blok. Production Companies: Lemming Film, Svensk Filmindustri, Davaj Film, Anchorage Entertainment, and Filmpool Nord. Rating: Not rated. Genres: Adventure, Comedy, Family. Countries: Netherlands, Sweden, Belgium. Run Time: 85 min.

References: *A Christmoose Story*. Burbank, CA: Warner Home Video, 2015. DVD Video.

Meijer, Monica. "Midden in De Winternacht (2013)." *Cinemagazine* (Dutch language). http://cinemagazine.nl/midden-in-de-winternacht-2013-recensie/

Midden in De Winternacht. Internet Movie Database. http://www.imdb.com/title/tt2389456/

Steinhöfel, Andreas. *Es ist ein Elch entsprungen*. Illustrated by Kerstin Meyer. Hamburg: Carlsen, 2002 (German language).

Villela, Bernardo. "Review: A Christmoose Story (2013)." *The Movie Rat*. https://themovierat.com/2014/12/07/review-a-christmoose-story-2013/

The ChubbChubbs Save Xmas—August 8, 2007

Computer-Animated Short Comedy Film

Threat to Christmas: Meeper the alien and his ChubbChubbs crash into Santa and put him in traction.

How Christmas Is Saved: The gang dissuades a troublesome kid from being a pest to Santa.

Synopsis and Commentary: Meeper, the bulbous-nosed alien, and the ChubbChubbs first appear in the computer-animated short comedy film *The ChubbChubbs!* (2002). There Meeper, who aspires to be a karaoke performer, loses his job as a janitor at the Ale-E-Inn pub (a play on "Alien") after accidentally electrocuting a performer. Following an attack by alien monsters, Meeper becomes a surrogate "mother" to four ChubbChubbs that look like innocent little yellow chicks but are really fearsome creatures with spinning, razor-sharp teeth that can quickly rip anything to shreds.

In the sequel *The ChubbChubbs Save Xmas*, which is just as fast-paced as *The ChubbChubbs!* Meeper and the ChubbChubbs have been traveling the universe looking for a home, but every planet they've visited has tossed them out. They try Earth but crash-land on top of Santa, who fractures his beard and just about everything else. With Santa in traction, Meeper volunteers to deliver the gifts, whereupon he and the ChubbChubbs don Santa suits and go to it in a rocket-powered sleigh (no reindeer here). Meanwhile, the little hellion Brad Spoylt, who has irked Santa from his infancy, hacks into Santa's www.I'veBeenGood.com Web Site, puts himself back on the nice list, and receives a visit from Meeper/Santa. Inside, the ChubbChubbs reduce the milk-and-cookies table and Christmas tree to sawdust. When Brad grabs a ChubbChubb and, thinking it's a toy, tries to cram a battery up its tail, a TV news flash soon reports that a "killer chicken" attacked a young boy who vowed never to be naughty again. Back at the North Pole, though Meeper botched delivering the presents, Santa is so happy to have Brad out of his hair during future Christmases that he rewards Meeper and the gang with a new trailer-home, which the ChubbChubbs promptly demolish.

Voices: Jeffrey Tambor (*Transparent*) as Santa; Brad Simonsen (*Big Fish*) as Meeper; Jeff Wolverton (*Ghost Rider*) as the ChubbChubbs; Zachary Gordon (*Diary of a Wimpy Kid*) as Brad; Mandy Freund (*The Little Death*) as nurse and reporter; Cody Cameron (*Shrek*) as elf and aliens; Matthew W. Taylor (*Open Season*) as elf, snowman, fly, and witness.

Awards: In 2003, the five-minute *The ChubbChubbs!* won an Academy Award for Best Short Film, Animated, and received nominations for a BAFTA Film Award and a Golden Berlin Bear, respectively, for Best Short Animation and Best Short Film.

Interesting Tidbits: As Meeper is about to board the rocket-sleigh, he tosses a top hat onto a nearby snowman who, in a parody of Frosty, yells, "I'm alive!" but is immediately vaporized by the rocket blast.

Meeper is preoccupied with singing Hoyt Axton's "Joy to the World."

The ChubbChubbs' spinning teeth recall those of the flying creatures in the TV mini-

Always desiring to be a karaoke performer, here's Meeper the alien on stage with his four little ChubbChubbs in *The ChubbChubbs!* (2002); they also star in *The ChubbChubbs Save Xmas* (2007). Though they appear as cute chicks, the ChubbChubbs won't hesitate to rip anything to shreds with their razor-sharp teeth (Columbia Pictures/Photofest).

series *The Langoliers* (1995), which devoured everything in their path.

PRODUCTION CREDITS—Story: Dave Feiss, Jurgen Gross, and Cody Cameron. Producer: Kirk Bodyfelt. Director: Cody Cameron. Production Companies: Prana Studios and Sony Pictures Imageworks. Rating: PG (mild rude humor). Genres: Animation, Comedy, Short. Country: USA. Run Time: 5 min.

REFERENCES: *The ChubbChubbs Save Xmas*. Big Cartoon Database. http://www.bcdb.com/cartoon/

The ChubbChubbs Save Xmas. In *Surf's Up*. Culver City, CA: Sony Pictures Home Entertainment, 2007. DVD Video.

The ChubbChubbs Save Xmas. Internet Movie Database. http://www.imdb.com/title/tt1103971/

The City That Forgot About Christmas—1974

Animated Television Short Film

THREAT TO CHRISTMAS: After years of godless living, the citizens of a small city lose all knowledge of God and Christmas.

HOW CHRISTMAS IS SAVED: The old carpenter Matthew steers the town toward God and Christmas.

SYNOPSIS AND COMMENTARY: Emerging from a flood of movies about Santa and presents, it's rather refreshing to find a film that deals with the true meaning of Christmas. When the boy Benji becomes frustrated with the hubbub of Christmas preparations, he wishes that there were no Christmas, whereupon his grandfather relates the following tale that improves the boy's attitude:

Anger and hostility reign in a small city in which the citizens have forgotten about God and Christmas. There is no love, children steal food, and the sick are neglected. Then an old carpenter named Matthew arrives and, through deeds of kindness, melts the stony hearts of the townspeople, except for the mayor and his minions. As the others become interested in a set of life-size figures that Matthew carves late in the year, he tells them all about the Biblical account of the birth of Christ and God's love, whereupon the town decides to celebrate the holiday. As the people bustle about in their preparations, Matthew enlists their help to paint and finish the figures, which form a beautiful Nativity scene in a stable. Everything is ready for Christmas Eve, except that the manger is missing the figure of Baby Jesus (the mayor secretly stole it to ruin the celebration). More mysterious is the fact that Matthew disappears early on Christmas Eve without a word. When the hour arrives for the people to gather at the stable for prayer, a mother places her baby in the manger in recognition of the message that Matthew had brought: "On the first Christmas, God came to earth as a *real live baby*." Believing that God has visited their city, the people also surmise that the Christmas angel had come in the guise of Matthew.

VOICES: Sebastian Cabot (*Family Affair*) as the narrator; Charles Nelson Reilly (*All Dogs Go to Heaven*) as the mayor. Other voices: Joan Gardner, Casey Kasem, David Kelley, Robie Lester, Dina Lynn, Sonny Melendrez, Don Messick, Philip Morris, Louis Nye, and Gary Shapiro.

INTERESTING TIDBITS: This film is a faithful adaptation of a children's Christian picture book of the same title, published in 1968 by Mary Warren. In 2006, Susan K. Leigh again adapted the story into a more contemporary setting in a book titled *The Town That Forgot About Christmas*.

The grandfather and old Matthew closely resemble each other, which leaves the viewer wondering.

The characters of Benji and his dog Waldo also appear in the animated television special *Christmas Is* (1970).

PRODUCTION CREDITS—Writer: Don Hinchey. Executive Producer: Martin J. Neeb, Jr. Director: Not credited. Production Companies: Lutheran Television; Screen Images; Lutheran Church, Missouri Synod; International Lutheran Laymen's League. Rating: Not rated. Genres: Animation, Family, Short. Country: USA. Run Time: 22 min.

REFERENCES: *The City That Forgot About Christmas*. Big Cartoon Database. http://www.bcdb.com/cartoon/54930-City-That-Forgot-About-Christmas

The City That Forgot About Christmas. In *Three Christmas Classics*. Worcester, PA: Vision Video, 2002. DVD Video.

The City That Forgot About Christmas. Internet Movie Database. http://www.imdb.com/title/tt0441610/

Crump, William D. *The Christmas Encyclopedia*. Third Edition. Jefferson, NC: McFarland, 2013.

Leigh, Susan K. *The Town That Forgot About Christmas*. Illustrated by David Gordon. St. Louis: Concordia, 2006.

Lenburg, Jeff. *The Encyclopedia of Animated Cartoons*. Third Edition. New York: Facts on File, 2009.

Warren, Mary. *The City That Forgot About Christmas*. Illustrated by Rudolph Wendelin. St. Louis: Concordia, 1968.

Wilson, Joanna. *Tis the Season TV: The Encyclopedia of Christmas-Themed Episodes, Specials and Made-for-TV Movies*. Akron, OH: 1701 Press, 2011.

A Country Christmas—October 27, 2013

Also Known As *The Great Santa Rescue*
Direct-to-Video Movie

THREAT TO CHRISTMAS: A disgruntled senator passes a law that causes Santa to loses his powers.

HOW CHRISTMAS IS SAVED: Two children and Santa convince the senator to drop his grudge against Santa.

SYNOPSIS AND COMMENTARY: Banning Bible reading and prayer in schools is now the law, but Senator Max Schmucker (Kevin Pollak, *A Few Good Men*) takes this a bit further by passing a law that bans the belief in and all references to Santa Claus (Abraham Benrubi, *ER*). The movement takes the world by storm, and as people lose faith in Santa, his magic powers dissipate. While out performing pre–Christmas duties, Santa and his dwarf-elf Elliot (Mikey Post, *Black Knight*) crash-land and become stranded in the Logan family's barn in Arizona and are discovered by the two Logan children, Miley (Caitlin Carmichael, *Lizzie*) and Zach (Benjamin Stockham, *About a Boy*). In order to persuade people to believe in Santa again, Miley makes a video challenging Schmucker to a public debate and manages to get this aired at the local TV station with help from Santa and Elliot, which generates a flood of media interest. Yielding to advice from his publicist, Schmucker accepts the challenge on Miley's turf, but just prior to the debate, Miley learns that her mother has terminal cancer, yet Santa can do nothing, for a cardinal rule forbids him to interfere in the affairs of mortals. The debate is a bust, because Miley cannot provide incontrovertible proof that Santa exists. Confronting a dying Santa in the barn, Schmucker faces the truth regarding his vendetta against Santa: as a boy, Schmucker had received a lump of coal because he had everything in life except the most important thing—love. Such truth changes Schmucker, who now encourages everyone to believe in Santa, the very epitome of love, and Santa regains his powers. On Christmas Eve, Santa sheds his immortality in order to heal Miley's mom, and thus he becomes Nick the mortal, which leaves Elliot as the new Santa.

INTERESTING TIDBITS: To Miley's query about how to handle the predicament, Santa, referring to God, points to heaven and says, "The Man upstairs has a plan; He always does."

With the exception of the farm setting in Arizona, the only "country" aspects of this film are cameo appearances by country artists Jay DeMarcus and Trace Adkins and the opening song, "Who Says There Ain't No Santa?" written by Larry Boone, Kix Brooks, and Paul Nelson, performed by Brooks and Dunn.

REVIEWS: David Brook of *Blueprint Review* (December 8, 2013): "…this is far too dull for a children's film. The stakes are clearer and stronger here and the writers throw in a dying mother subplot to tug at the heartstrings, but there are no fun or exciting scenes or set-pieces to keep you interested. Children in particular will struggle to sit through a film whose finale sees the heroine taking part in a political debate."

Andrea Beach from *Common Sense Media* (July 23, 2014): "Big-hearted, kid-friendly holiday film with shallow plot…. The story's formulaic, broad strokes feel emotionally manipulative, as when Miley makes no effort to prepare for her big debate with a U.S. senator and … makes no actual arguments to prove her point, appealing to emotion to win the day. The cast's flat performances don't add any depth, either. The warm holiday messages of love and family shine through…"

Edwin L. Carpenter of The Dove Foundation: "The acting is excellent … making the plot that could have come off as unintentionally funny instead work great…. The kids do tell a few lies … to protect and cover up for Santa but the truth eventually comes out…. The theme of believing when things are the worst is to be commended. We are very pleased to award this movie our Dove "Family-Approved" Seal for all ages."

PRODUCTION CREDITS—Writers and Producers: William Shockley, Dustin Rikert, and Eric Brooks. Director: Dustin Rikert. Production Company: Team 2 Entertainment. Rating: PG (mild thematic elements). Genre: Family. Country: USA. Run Time: 91 min.

REFERENCES: Beach, Andrea. *A Country Christmas. Common Sense Media.* https://www.commonsensemedia.org/movie-reviews/a-country-christmas

Brook, David. *The Great Santa Rescue. Blueprint Review.* http://blueprintreview.co.uk/2013/12/3-christmas-films-from-metrodome-releasing/

Carpenter, Edwin L. *A Country Christmas.* The Dove Foundation. http://www.dove.org/review/10063-a-country-christmas/

A Country Christmas. Fort Mill, SC: Phase 4 Films, 2013. DVD Video.

A Country Christmas. Internet Movie Database. http://www.imdb.com/title/tt2098799/

Diego Saves Christmas!—December 8, 2006

Episode from the Animated Television Series *Go, Diego, Go!*

THREAT TO CHRISTMAS: Santa's sleigh is stuck in a snowbank, and the reindeer are not strong enough to pull it out.

HOW CHRISTMAS IS SAVED: Diego rounds up Linda the Llama to help the reindeer.

SYNOPSIS AND COMMENTARY: Created by Chris Gifford and Valerie Walsh with a target audience of young children, this educational series of 75 episodes ran initially on the Nickelodeon network and later on CBS from 2005 to 2011. A spinoff of the *Dora the Explorer* series, the program focused on the adventures of Dora's eight-year-old cousin, Diego Marquez, a bilingual, Latino boy whose family ran an animal rescue center in a tropical forest. Diego's prime objective was to rescue animals around the world, assisted by his eleven-year-old sister and computer whiz Alicia, a young jaguar named Baby Jaguar, a self-operating camera named Click, and a backpack named Rescue Pack. Other principal characters included Linda the Llama and mischievous spider monkeys, the Bobo Brothers. Along with musical interludes, the interactive episodes presented pictorial information about the characteristics and habitats of different animals and elicited responses from the audience by asking simple questions with two possible answers; after a brief pause, the correct answer was revealed and repeated to boost the learning process. Upon hearing the cry of animals in trouble, Click zoomed in on their location, and Diego was off to the rescue.

In *Diego Saves Christmas!* it's Christmas Eve, and because all the animals at the rescue center are expecting presents, Diego places pictures of Santa at their respective locales, so that Santa can easily find them. Suddenly, when animals cry for help (which sounds more like cats meowing), with the help of Click, the audience matches the cry to a picture of the animals in question which, in this case, are six reindeer that cannot pull Santa's sleigh, because it's stuck in a snowbank on a mountain. The audience also interacts with Click to help Diego locate Linda the Llama, a strong, mountain-climbing animal that only speaks Spanish. After reassuring the naughty but repentant Bobo Brothers that Santa will not forget them, Diego and Linda navigate a large span of hazardous ice to reach the reindeer. Hitched together, Linda and the team free the sleigh, thus saving Christmas, after which Santa enables Linda to fly with magic Christmas sparkles, and the animals at the rescue center receive their presents on schedule.

PRINCIPAL VOICES: Jake T. Austin (*Rio*) as Diego, Constanza Sperakis (*Go, Diego! Go!*) as Alicia, Rosie Perez (*Pineapple Express*) as Click, Jose Zelaya (*Dora the Explorer*) as Bobo Brothers, Thomas Sharkey (*The Backyardigans*) as Baby Jaguar, Laura Abreu (*Go, Diego! Go!*) as Linda the Llama, Sebastian Arcelus (*House of Cards*) as Mr. Marquez, Karen June Sanchez (*Dora the Explorer*) as Mrs. Marquez, and Harry Chase (*Hello Lonesome*) as Santa.

AWARDS: *Go, Diego, Go!*—The series received nominations in the following categories: Young Artist Award for Best Performance in a Voice-Over Role—Young Actor (Jake T. Austin, 2006); Imagen Award for Best Actor—Television (Jake T. Austin, 2007); Image Award for Outstanding Children's Program (2008, 2009, 2010, 2012); and an Artios Award for Outstanding Achievement in Casting—Television Animation.

INTERESTING TIDBIT: Since Christmas receives secular treatment, upbeat Latin American music permeates the episode instead of traditional carols, along with frequent usage of the Spanish holiday greeting, "Feliz Navidad." Ironically, the episode does not mention *Las Posadas* ("The Lodgings"), a highly traditional Latin American Christmas custom.

PRODUCTION CREDITS—Writer: Chris Gifford. Producers: Cathy Galeota and Miken Wong. Director: George Chialtas. Production Company: Nickelodeon Studios. Rating: G. Genres: Animation, Family. Country: USA. Run Time: 25 min.

REFERENCES: "Diego Saves Christmas!" Big Cartoon Database. http://www.bcdb.com/cartoon/114825-Diego-Saves-Christmas

"Diego Saves Christmas!" Internet Movie Database. http://www.imdb.com/title/tt0904491/

"Diego Saves Christmas!" Hollywood, CA: Paramount, 2007. DVD Video.

Go, Diego, Go! Wikipedia. https://en.wikipedia.org/wiki/Go,_Diego,_Go!

Lenburg, Jeff. *The Encyclopedia of Animated Cartoons*. Third Edition. New York: Facts on File, 2009.

Wilson, Joanna. *Tis the Season TV: The Encyclopedia of Christmas-Themed Episodes, Specials and Made-for-TV Movies*. Akron, OH: 1701 Press, 2011.

Dr. Seuss' How the Grinch Stole Christmas!—December 18, 1966

Animated Television Special

THREAT TO CHRISTMAS: Desiring to keep Christmas from coming, the grouchy Grinch steals all the holiday paraphernalia in Who-ville.

HOW CHRISTMAS IS SAVED: The Whos' example of expressing Christmas joy despite a lack of presents teaches the Grinch that Christmas "means a little bit more."

SYNOPSIS AND COMMENTARY: If one were to name the top three most enduring animated television Christmas specials of all time, the list would likely include, in no particular order, *A Charlie Brown Christmas*, **Rudolph, the Red-Nosed Reindeer**, and ***Dr. Seuss' How the Grinch Stole Christmas!*** All three are classic productions from the 1960s that are still telecast annually. The latter is an adaptation of *How the Grinch Stole Christmas!* a children's rhyming picture book published in 1957 by American author Theodor Seuss Geisel, who wrote under the pseudonym of "Dr. Seuss."

A nasty, cave-dwelling creature who lives on Mt. Crumpit, the Grinch hates Christmas for three possible reasons: his shoes are too tight, his head is not screwed on right, or his heart is two sizes too small. Hearing the little Whos gaily preparing for Christmas in the nearby town of Who-ville only irritates him that much more. Determined to keep Christmas from coming, the Grinch, disguised as Santa, steals into Who-ville on Christmas Eve with his dog Max disguised as a reindeer and, while the Whos sleep, strips the town of every Christmas item, including the Who-pudding, the roast beast, and the last can of Who-hash. When tiny Cindy Lou Who discovers him stealing her Christmas tree, the lying Grinch claims that he's merely taking the tree away to replace a broken light bulb and will return it shortly. On Christmas morning, instead of witnessing a scene of despair, the Grinch hears joyful singing as the Whos welcome Christmas despite the absence of gifts and decorations. Learning that the true meaning of Christmas doesn't come from a store, his heart grows three sizes larger, whereupon he restores the Whos' possessions and joins in the festivities

Dressed as a phony Santa, the Christmas-hating Grinch steals a Christmas tree in the animated TV special *Dr. Seuss' How the Grinch Stole Christmas* (1966). CBS Television (collection of William D. Crump).

as the guest of honor who carves the roast beast.

SONGS: Lyrics by Dr. Seuss; music by Albert Hague. "Opening Song"; "Trim Up the Tree"; "Welcome, Christmas"; and "You're a Mean One, Mr. Grinch."

VOICES: The only voice-actor credited is Boris Karloff (well known for his portrayal of the Frankenstein monster) who serves as narrator and voices the Grinch. Other voices include June Foray (*The Smurfs*) as Cindy Lou Who, Dal McKennon (*Daniel Boone*) as Max, and Thurl Ravenscroft (who sang "You're a Mean One, Mr. Grinch").

AWARDS: In 1968, *Grinch* won a Grammy for Best Recording for Children.

INTERESTING TIDBITS: *Grinch* originally aired on CBS but has since aired on other networks and cable channels.

Unlike many save-Christmas movies, which emphasize the importance of Santa's delivering presents lest Christmas be "cancelled," *Grinch* criticizes the commercialization of Christmas, as does *A Charlie Brown Christmas*, but without the obviously religious overtones that permeate the latter. In fact, Geisel had originally thought of ending *Grinch* on a religious note but, not wishing to sound "preachy," opted instead for a neutral ending at the Christmas table.

The Grinch character was the first adult and the first villain to be a protagonist in a Dr. Seuss book.

The Grinch remarks that he's been hating Christmas for 53 years. That's no coincidence, because Geisel was 53 when *Grinch* was published.

Grinch was remade as a live-action feature film in 2000.

Theodor Geisel (1904–1991) wrote over 60 children's books, including *The Cat in the Hat* (his most famous book, consisting of 223 words), *Green Eggs and Ham* (his second-most successful book of just 50 words), *Horton Hatches the Egg*, and others. According to the *Encyclopedia of World Biography*, "As Dr. Seuss, Geisel brought a whimsical touch and a colorful imagination to the world of children's books…. All of Geisel's books … feature crazy-looking creatures that are sometimes based on real animals, but which usually consist of such bizarre combinations of objects as a centipede and a horse and a camel with a feather duster on its head."

REVIEWS: According to the Rotten Tomatoes film review site, 100 percent of critics gave this production positive reviews.

James Poniewozik of *Time Magazine* (November 29, 2007): "This lusty, garishly colored, good-hearted cartoon was a wonderful, awful idea."

Heather Boerner of *Common Sense Media* (November 15, 2006): Heartwarming TV special true to Seuss' classic."

PRODUCTION CREDITS—Writer: Dr. Seuss. Additional Story: Irv Spector and Bob Ogle. Producers: Chuck Jones and Ted Geisel. Director: Chuck Jones. Production Companies: Chuck Jones Enterprises, The Cat in the Hat Productions, and Metro-Goldwyn-Mayer Television. Rating: Not rated. Genres: Animation, Comedy, Family. Country: USA. Run Time: 26 min.

REFERENCES: Boerner, Heather. *Dr. Seuss' How the Grinch Stole Christmas! Common Sense Media.* https://www.commonsensemedia.org/movie-reviews/dr-seuss-how-the-grinch-stole-christmas

Crump, William D. *The Christmas Encyclopedia*. Third Edition. Jefferson, NC: McFarland, 2013.

Dr. Seuss' How the Grinch Stole Christmas! Big Cartoon Database. http://www.bcdb.com/bcdb/cartoon.cgi?film=15585

Dr. Seuss' How the Grinch Stole Christmas! Burbank, CA: Warner Home Video, 2008. DVD Video.

Dr. Seuss' How the Grinch Stole Christmas! Internet Movie Database. http://www.imdb.com/title/tt0060345/

Dr. Seuss. *How the Grinch Stole Christmas.* New York: Random House, 1957.

Dr. Seuss' How the Grinch Stole Christmas! Rotten Tomatoes. http://www.rottentomatoes.com/m/1006223-how-the-grinch-stole-christmas/

Fensch, Thomas. *The Man Who Was Dr. Seuss: The Life and Work of Theodor Geisel.* Woodlands, TX: New Century Books, 2000.

Lenburg, Jeff. *The Encyclopedia of Animated Cartoons.* Third Edition. New York: Facts on File, 2009.

Morgan, Judith, and Neil Morgan. *Dr. Seuss and Mr. Geisel: A Biography.* New York: Random House, 1995.

Poniewozik, James. *Dr. Seuss' How the Grinch Stole Christmas! Time Magazine.* http://content.time.com/time/specials/2007/article/0,28804,1689075_1689089_1689105,00.html

"Theodor Geisel Biography." In *Encyclopedia of World Biography.* http://www.notablebiographies.com/Fi-Gi/Geisel-Theodor.html

Werts, Diane. *Christmas on Television.* Westport, CT: Praeger, 2006.

Wilson, Joanna. *Tis the Season TV: The Encyclopedia of Christmas-Themed Episodes, Specials and Made-for-TV Movies.* Akron, OH: 1701 Press, 2011.

Dr. Seuss' How the Grinch Stole Christmas—November 17, 2000

Also Known As *The Grinch*
Feature Film

THREAT TO CHRISTMAS: As in the Dr. Seuss book and the 1966 animated television special, the Grinch attempts to keep Christmas from coming.

HOW CHRISTMAS IS SAVED: The kindness of little Cindy-Lou Who has much to do with countering the Grinch as a big bugaboo.

SYNOPSIS AND COMMENTARY: Imagine an entire village of Whos celebrating Christmas within the confines of one single snowflake. Even in such a microscopic world, the green Grinch (Jim Carrey, *Dumb and Dumber*) hates Christmas, as narrator Anthony Hopkins (*The Silence of the Lambs*) explains through rhymes, many of which remain faithful to Dr. Seuss, while others are altered and new rhymes are added to accompany a feature-length story line. While the Grinch remains the star villain, little Cindy Lou Who (Taylor Momsen, *Gossip Girl*) shines as the featured protagonist, who struggles to understand the true meaning of Christmas amid Who-ville's rampant commercialism. Moreover, contrary to her peers, she forms a different opinion about the Grinch when, after sneaking into town to pull a few practical jokes, he rescues her from certain injury. Maybe the Grinch isn't so bad after all. But what made him so mean? After interviewing several Whos, Cindy Lou discovers the Grinch's tragic past. Adopted by two elderly sisters, he was bullied in school because of his odd appearance, and following an exceptionally humiliating experience at Christmastime, he eventually fled to Mt. Crumpit, the local garbage dump, where he had lived in a cave ever since, hating the Whos and Christ-

This poster for the live-action film *Dr. Seuss' How the Grinch Stole Christmas* (2000) depicts Jim Carrey as a most frightful-appearing Grinch looming over the town of Who-Ville below. MCA/Universal Pictures (collection of William D. Crump).

mas. Upon Cindy Lou's nomination, the Grinch becomes Who-ville's "Cheermeister" at their annual "Who-bilation" on Christmas Eve, but an event there reminds him of his childhood humiliation, whereupon the Grinch flies into a rage, berates the Whos' lust for presents, and burns the community Christmas tree. Then follows the scenario of his dressing as Santa and stealing the town's presents, which is probably the most poignant moment of the movie, when Cindy Lou catches the Santa-Grinch in the act. She asks, "What's Christmas really about?" and the Grinch at first barks, "*Vengeance!*" then mellows with, "Presents, I suppose." Dejected, Cindy Lou asks "Santa" to remember the Grinch, because he's "sorta sweet." That someone cares about him is the turning point for the Grinch. On Christmas morning, Mayor Augustus May Who (Jeffrey Tambor, *Transparent*) denounces Cindy Lou as the root of the Grinch's devilment, whereupon her father, in her defense, assures everyone that presents do not define Christmas, the true meaning of which is spending time with family and friends. Then follows the scenario atop Mt. Crumpit as the Grinch, hearing the Whos singing instead of crying, receives his epiphany about Christmas and hosts the feast for Who-ville in his decorated cave.

Songs: "Where Are You Christmas?" (by James Horner, Will Jennings, and Mariah Carey); "Happy Who-lidays," "How I Love Who-liday Shopping," "Who-bilation," and "Come, Come All Ye Whos" (latter four by James Horner and Cynthia Weil); "Christmas, Why Can't I Find You?" (by James Horner and Will Jennings).

Awards: With more than 50 nominations, the film won an Oscar for Best Makeup and Academy nominations for Best Costume Design and Best Art Decoration/Set Decoration. Other wins included a BAFTA Film Award for Best Makeup/Hair, ASCAP Award for Top Box Office Films, Saturn Awards for Best Music and Best Makeup, Awards Circuit Community Award for Best Makeup, Blockbuster Entertainment Award for Favorite Comedy Actor (Carrey), Costume Designers Guild Award for Excellence in Period/Fantasy Film, Hollywood Makeup Artist and Hair Stylist Guild Awards for Best Special Makeup Effects–Feature and Best Innovative Hair Styling–Feature, Blimp Awards for Favorite Movie and Favorite Movie Actor (Carrey), MTV Movie Award for Best Villain (Carrey), Phoenix Film Critics Society Awards for Best Costume Design and Best Makeup, Golden Satellite Award for Best Costume Design, Teen Choice Award for Choice Hissy Fit (Carrey), and a Young Artist Award for Best Family Feature Film–Comedy. The film also received Razzie Award nominations for Worst Remake or Sequel and Worst Screenplay. For her role as Cindy Lou Who, Taylor Momsen received a Blockbuster Entertainment Award nomination for Favorite Female Newcomer, a Saturn Award nomination for Best Performance by a Young Actor, and a Young Artist Award nomination for Best Performance in a Feature Film–Young Actress Age Ten or Under.

Interesting Tidbits: The film inserts a love-triangle subplot involving Mayor May Who (age eight, Ben Bookbinder) and the Grinch (age eight, Josh Ryan Evans), rivals who, since their school days, had vied for the affection of Martha May Whovier (age eight, Landry Albright; adult, Christine Baranski). Though May Who and his cronies had bullied the Grinch because he was different, Martha did not, which smacks of similar sentiment in the 1998 **Rudolph** movie with his doe friend Zoey. Like misfit Rudolph, the Grinch ran away from society.

With a budget of $123 million, *Grinch* grossed over $260 million at domestic box offices and over $345 million worldwide, making it the highest grossing holiday film of all time.

Newcomer Taylor Momsen was six years old when she portrayed Cindy Lou Who, compared with her character in the Dr. Seuss book and the television special, who was two years old. She is known for her role in the television series *Gossip Girl* and fronts the rock band The Pretty Reckless.

Reviews: According to the Rotten Tomatoes film review site, 53 percent of critics gave this film a positive review. Metacritic gave it a score of 46/100 (mixed/average).

Nell Minow of *Common Sense Media* (May 18, 2003): "Live-action version of classic has crude, scary moments."

Steve Simels of TV Guide: "Parents can relax: Ron Howard's version of the Christmas-napping Grinch is a smartly stylized hoot. It features a virtuoso performance by Jim Carrey, great-looking Seussian sets, and enough sophisticated in-jokes to keep adults interested when the whimsy level threatens to get out of hand."

Todd McCarthy of *Variety* (November 16, 2000): "Shrill, strenuous and entirely without charm … in the long run, the 1966 animated version will certainly prevail in viewers' hearts, if not on the bottom line."

Peter Stack of the San Francisco Chronicle (November 17, 2000): "Overall, the film sparkles. But it's a curiously unaffecting sparkle, an example, almost, of how the special effects stole Christmas."

PRODUCTION CREDITS—Screenplay: Jeffrey Price and Peter S. Seaman. Producers: Brian Grazer and Ron Howard. Director: Ron Howard. Production Companies: Universal Pictures, Imagine Entertainment, LUNI Productions GmbH and Company KG. Rating: PG (some crude humor). Genres: Comedy, Family, Fantasy. Countries: Germany and USA. Run Time: 104 min.

REFERENCES: Crump, William D. *The Christmas Encyclopedia*. Third Edition. Jefferson, NC: McFarland, 2013.

Dr. Seuss. *How the Grinch Stole Christmas*. New York: Random House, 1957.

Dr. Seuss' How the Grinch Stole Christmas. Internet Movie Database. http://www.imdb.com/title/tt0170016/

Dr. Seuss' How the Grinch Stole Christmas. Metacritic. http://www.metacritic.com/movie/how-the-grinch-stole-christmas

Dr. Seuss' How the Grinch Stole Christmas. Rotten Tomatoes. http://www.rottentomatoes.com/m/how_the_grinch_stole_christmas/

Dr. Seuss' How the Grinch Stole Christmas. Universal City, CA: Universal Studios, 2003. DVD Video.

How the Grinch Stole Christmas. Box Office Mojo. http://www.boxofficemojo.com/movies/?id=grinch.htm

McCarthy, Todd. *Dr. Seuss' How the Grinch Stole Christmas*. Variety. http://variety.com/2000/film/reviews/dr-seuss-how-the-grinch-stole-christmas-1200465392/#

Minow, Nell. *How the Grinch Stole Christmas*. Common Sense Media. https://www.commonsensemedia.org/movie-reviews/how-the-grinch-stole-christmas

Simels, Steve. *Dr. Seuss' How the Grinch Stole Christmas*. TV Guide. http://www.tvguide.com/movies/dr-seuss-grinch/review/134709

Stack, Peter. "How Effects Stole 'Christmas' / Supercharged 'Grinch' Stays True to Seuss but Amps Up Carrey's Character." *San Francisco Chronicle*. http://www.sfgate.com/movies/article/How-Effects-Stole-Christmas-Supercharged-3302567.php

Wilson, Joanna. *Tis the Season TV: The Encyclopedia of Christmas-Themed Episodes, Specials and Made-for-TV Movies*. Akron, OH: 1701 Press, 2011.

The Dog Who Saved Christmas—November 29, 2009

Television Movie

THREAT TO CHRISTMAS: Two thieves break into a house on Christmas Eve.

HOW CHRISTMAS IS SAVED: The guard dog on duty inside foils the burglars.

SYNOPSIS AND COMMENTARY: If you're a big fan of the *Home Alone* series of films, substitute a dog for the protagonist, and you have this film. If you're not a fan of that series, substitute a dog anyway, because that's the hero here.

When the Bannister family learns about a rash of robberies in their neighborhood, husband George (Gary Valentine, *The King of Queens*) sets out to find the perfect guard dog. He adopts Zeus (voiced by Mario Lopez, *Saved by the Bell*), a yellow Labrador retriever and former award-winning police dog, from the pound as an early Christmas present for his family. Yet wife Belinda (Elisa Donovan, *Eve's Christmas*), who never wanted a dog, is doubtful that Zeus will be useful as a guard dog, because he never barks and seems too playful. With plans to return Zeus to the pound after the holidays, the Bannisters leave for Grandma Bannister's (Mindy Sterling, *Austin Powers: The*

Spy who Shagged Me) house on Christmas Eve, while Zeus remains at home alone. Ted Stein (Dean Cain, *Lois and Clark*) and Stewey McMann (Joey Diaz, *The Longest Yard*), the two neighborhood robbers who have been watching the Bannisters' home, now seize the opportunity to break in, whereupon Zeus proves his worth by foiling the robbers' bumbling efforts with a series of canine maneuvers. These include, for example, dropping flour and Christmas ornaments on the intruders from above, pushing bowling balls down the stairs, and dropping an entire chandelier on them.

AWARDS: In 2009, this film won a couple of "Yulies," spoof awards from *Entertainment Weekly*: MVP (Most Valuable Pooch) and Best Use of Dean Cain.

INTERESTING TIDBITS: Two of the film's writers, Michael Ciminera and Richard Gnolfo, appear as police officers, while producer/director Michael Feifer appears as Officer Billing. Executive producer Barry Barnholtz appears as incidental character Jack.

Sequels include **The Dog Who Saved Christmas Vacation** (2010), *The Dog Who Saved Halloween* (2011), **The Dog Who Saved the Holidays** (2012), *The Dog Who Saved Easter* (2014), and *The Dog Who Saved Summer* (2015).

REVIEWS: Emily Ashby of *Common Sense Media* (November 22, 2009): "There's no reason to sweat the content in this family-friendly comedy (a gun with suction-cup ammo and one noisy farting scene are about as iffy as things get)… Fiction or not, it's hard not to be moved by Zeus' desperate quest for a forever home."

Will Brownridge of *The Film Reel* (December 31, 2014): "Essentially, this is really just *Home Alone* but with a dog. [There are] two bumbling crooks, and Zeus actually sets up a few traps that will remind you of Kevin in the *Home Alone* films. Of course, the movie can't come close to the hilarity of *Home Alone*, but … it helps that Zeus is such a cute dog to headline the movie."

Donna Rolfe of The Dove Foundation: "Like many movies in the past, you have animals that can talk to each other which adds humor to many situations as you learn what these animals are thinking. [This film] is entertaining and will be a family favorite. We award this film the Dove 'Family-Approved' Seal for all ages."

PRODUCTION CREDITS—Story: Michael Ciminera, Richard Gnolfo, and Jeffrey Schenck. Screenplay: Michael Ciminera and Richard Gnolfo. Producer and Director: Michael Feifer. Production Companies: ARO Entertainment, Barnholtz Entertainment, Feifer Worldwide, and Hybrid. Rating: PG (mild language and rude humor). Genres: Comedy, Family. Country: USA. Run Time: 89 min.

REFERENCES: Ashby, Emily. *The Dog Who Saved Christmas. Common Sense Media.* https://www.commonsensemedia.org/movie-reviews/the-dog-who-saved-christmas

Brownridge, Will. "Review: The Dog Who Saved Christmas (2009)—or—Home Alone with Dogs." *The Film Reel.* http://www.thefilmreel.com/2014/12/31/review-the-dog-who-saved-christmas-2009/

Crump, William D. *The Christmas Encyclopedia.* Third Edition. Jefferson, NC: McFarland, 2013.

The Dog Who Saved Christmas. Beverly Hills, CA: Anchor Bay Entertainment, 2009. DVD Video.

The Dog Who Saved Christmas. Internet Movie Database. http://www.imdb.com/title/tt1356395/

Rolfe, Donna. *The Dog Who Saved Christmas.* The Dove Foundation. http://www.dove.org/review/8057-the-dog-who-saved-christmas/

Snierson, Dan. "The 2nd Annual Yulies: An Absurd Celebration of the Holiday TV-Movie Genre." *Entertainment Weekly.* http://www.ew.com/article/2009/11/29/the-2nd-annual-yulies-an-absurd-celebration-of-the-holiday-TV-movie-genre

Wilson, Joanna. *Tis the Season TV: The Encyclopedia of Christmas-Themed Episodes, Specials and Made-for-TV Movies.* Akron, OH: 1701 Press, 2011.

The Dog Who Saved Christmas Vacation—November 28, 2010
Television Movie

THREAT TO CHRISTMAS: Two thieves threaten to ruin the Bannisters' Christmas vacation.

How CHRISTMAS IS SAVED: Zeus the dog must once again foil the thieves.

SYNOPSIS AND COMMENTARY: In this dog-gone-it sequel to *The Dog Who Saved Christmas*, Gary Valentine and Elisa Donovan reprise their roles as George and Belinda Bannister who, along with their dog Zeus, are spending Christmas at a mountain ski resort. Crashing the tranquility is Belinda's obnoxious brother Randy (Casper Van Dien, *Starship Troopers*) and his haughty French poodle Bella. Although Zeus attempts a relationship with Bella, she is not impressed, and the macho avalanche dog Trooper provides stiff competition. Meanwhile, talk about lucky coincidences, Ted and Stewey (Dean Cain and Joey Diaz), the same two housebreakers whom Zeus foiled a year ago, have been released from prison and have followed London James (Carlson Young, *Key and Peele*), a young celebrity, to the resort to steal her diamond necklace. After a bungled heist, the crooks stash the necklace in the gift shop, where the Bannisters mistake it for a cheap dog collar and purchase it as a gift from Zeus to Bella. The desperate crooks now stalk Bella, Zeus, and the Bannisters to retrieve the necklace, and Zeus must once again use his woofy ingenuity to outwit the thieves.

DOG VOICES: Mario Lopez (*Saved by the Bell*) as Zeus; Paris Hilton (*House of Wax*) as Bella; Michael Healey (*The Dog Who Saved Christmas*) as Trooper.

AWARDS: In 2011, this picture won a Young Artist Award for Best Performance in a TV Movie, Miniseries or Special–Leading Young Actor (Brennan Bailey) and a Young Artist Award nomination for the same category (Michael William Arnold).

INTERESTING TIDBITS: Executive producers Barry Barnholtz and Jeffrey Schenck appear respectively as incidental characters Russell and Clark.

This was Paris Hilton's first voice-acting role.

Other sequels include *The Dog Who Saved Halloween* (2011), **The Dog Who Saved the Holidays** (2012), *The Dog Who Saved Easter* (2014), and *The Dog Who Saved Summer* (2015).

REVIEWS: Emily Ashby of *Common Sense Media* (November 28, 2010): "…the chronic misfortunes of the 'villains' are good for some laughs, and George and Randy's infighting will ring true with viewers who have experience spending the holidays with obnoxious relatives, but overall, this movie lacks both sugar and spice."

Will Brownridge of *The Film Reel* (December 31, 2014): "This one is a bit more *Christmas Vacation* instead of *Home Alone*, as George Bannister seems to find himself in the same types of problems that the Griswold family would…. Valentine makes the character work, though, so it's never annoying…. Zeus and Bella aren't quite as featured here as Zeus was in the first film, so most of the ridiculous comedy comes from Ted and Stewey…"

Donna Rolfe of The Dove Foundation: "…this film is a treat for the entire family. We award this DVD the Dove 'Family-Approved' 12+ Seal due to the use of the D-word by a bad guy."

PRODUCTION CREDITS—Story: Michael Ciminera, Richard Gnolfo, Jeffrey Schenck, and Peter Sullivan. Screenplay: Michael Ciminera, Richard Gnolfo, and Peter Sullivan. Producer and Director: Michael Feifer. Production Companies: Barnholtz Entertainment, ARO Entertainment, and Hybrid. Rating: PG (brief language and rude humor). Genres: Comedy, Family. Country: USA. Run Time: 89 min.

REFERENCES: Ashby, Emily. *The Dog Who Saved Christmas Vacation. Common Sense Media.* https://www.commonsensemedia.org/movie-reviews/the-dog-who-saved-christmas-vacation

Brownridge, Will. *The Dog Who Saved Christmas Vacation. The Film Reel.* http://www.the-filmreel.com/2014/12/31/review-the-dog-who-saved-christmas-vacation-2010/

Crump, William D. *The Christmas Encyclopedia*. Third Edition. Jefferson, NC: McFarland, 2013.

The Dog Who Saved Christmas Vacation. Beverly Hills, CA: Anchor Bay Entertainment, 2010. DVD Video.

The Dog Who Saved Christmas Vacation. Internet Movie Database. http://www.imdb.com/title/tt1691012/

Rolfe, Donna. *The Dog Who Saved Christmas Vacation.* The Dove Foundation. http://www.dove.org/review/8564-the-dog-who-savved-christmas-vacation/

The Dog Who Saved the Holidays—
December 4, 2012

Direct-to-Video Movie

THREAT TO CHRISTMAS: Two housebreakers are after Aunt Barbara's diamond-studded tree topper.

HOW CHRISTMAS IS SAVED: Zeus and his new puppy "sister" Eve rout the villains.

SYNOPSIS AND COMMENTARY: George and Belinda Bannister (Gary Valentine and Elisa Donovan) just can't seem to shake off housebreakers Ted and Stewey (Dean Cain and Joey Diaz) in this yet another sequel to ***The Dog Who Saved Christmas***. The Bannisters are on the road again for Christmas, this time to Southern California to visit their Aunt Barbara (Shelley Long, *Cheers*), who surprises them with the gift of a new puppy named Eve (voiced by Peyton List, *Jessie*). Seemingly cute and adorable, Eve captures the humans' hearts, yet the Bannisters' dog Zeus (voiced by Joey Lawrence, *Blossom*) isn't fooled, for he observes how utterly mischievous the little pooch can be when no humans are watching. Zeus wants nothing to do with Eve, until he notices that the familiar housebreakers Ted and Stewey, in debt to a hostile loan shark, are up to their old tricks while the Bannisters are at church. The crooks' goal is Barbara's diamond-studded tree topper. Now Zeus must join forces with his "little sister" and use similar doggy techniques as before to foil the villains and save Christmas.

INTERESTING TIDBITS: Executive producers Barry Barnholtz and Jeffrey Schenck appear respectively as incidental characters Cousin Randy and Cousin Jamie.

Elisa Donovan's actual pregnancy during this film is incorporated into her role.

Other sequels include ***The Dog Who Saved Christmas Vacation*** (2010), *The Dog Who Saved Halloween* (2011), *The Dog Who Saved Easter* (2014), and *The Dog Who Saved Summer* (2015).

REVIEWS: Tracy Moore of *Common Sense Media* (November 21, 2013): "Nothing wrong with a little bawdy action, but [this film] is a poor man's *Home Alone* that relies too heavily on tired tropes (the nagging pregnant wife, the insensitive husband) and fart jokes to really pull off what could be a cute, if sentimental, holiday movie that owes its best scenes to Shelley Long."

Edwin L. Carpenter of The Dove Foundation: "…a warm and inspiring film which contains a lot of cute moments … features a theme of growing up and evolving into people (or dogs) of character…. We are pleased to award it our Dove 'Family-Approved' Seal for all ages."

Will Brownridge of *The Film Reel* (December 31, 2014): "It's still fun to watch Ted and Stewey be complete fools, and it's hard to get tired of a little puppy, but the fun that everybody seemed to have in the previous films looks to be wearing thin." In other words, it's about time to close out this particular dog-saves-Christmas series.

PRODUCTION CREDITS—Story: Michael Ciminera, Richard Gnolfo, Jeffrey Schenck, and Peter Sullivan. Screenplay: Michael Ciminera and Richard Gnolfo. Producer and Director: Michael Feifer. Production Companies: ARO Entertainment and Lancom Entertainment. Rating: PG (rude humor and some language). Genres: Comedy, Family. Country: USA. Run Time: 83 min.

REFERENCES: Brownridge, Will. *The Dog Who Saved the Holidays.* The Film Reel. http://www.the-filmreel.com/2014/12/31/review-the-dog-who-saved-the-holidays-2012/

Carpenter, Edwin L. *The Dog Who Saved the Holidays.* The Dove Foundation. http://www.dove.org/review/9432-the-dog-who-saved-the-holidays/

Crump, William D. *The Christmas Encyclopedia.* Third Edition. Jefferson, NC: McFarland, 2013.

The Dog Who Saved the Holidays. Beverly Hills, CA: Anchor Bay Entertainment, 2012. DVD Video.

The Dog Who Saved the Holidays. Internet Movie Database. http://www.imdb.com/title/tt2294853/

Moore, Tracy. *The Dog Who Saved the Holidays. Common Sense Media.* https://www.commonsensemedia.org/movie-reviews/the-dog-who-saved-the-holidays

A Doomed Christmas—December 10, 2011

Episode from the Animated Television Series *T.U.F.F. Puppy*.

THREAT TO CHRISTMAS: Villains from Petropolis take over the North Pole.

HOW CHRISTMAS IS SAVED: The gang from T.U.F.F. stop the villains.

SYNOPSIS AND COMMENTARY: It could have been a dog-and-pony show, but in this case, *T.U.F.F. Puppy*, created by Butch Hartman, was a dog-and-cat series with a penchant for acronyms that ran for 60 half-hour episodes on Nickelodeon and then on Nicktoons from 2010 to 2015. Set in fictional Petropolis, a town appropriately populated by anthropomorphic animals, the series revolved around the adventures of Dudley Puppy, an idiotic, hyperactive mutt, who worked as a spy for the Turbo Undercover Fighting Force (T.U.F.F.), and his feline partner, Kitty Katswell (such overwhelming originality). Other principal characters included The Chief, a flea who ran T.U.F.F., and Keswick, a T.U.F.F. inventor and stuttering creature of ambiguous species, whose function mirrored that of "Q" in the *James Bond* films, albeit with less reliable results. Serving as the principal villains: Verminious Snaptrap, a stupid rat who led the Diabolical Order of Mayhem (D.O.O.M.); Chameleon, a shape-shifting chameleon who spoke like actor Peter Lorre; and Bird Brain, a flightless, blue-footed booby.

Finding themselves together in the Petropolis prison on Christmas Eve, the villainous trio have grown weary of being on Santa's naughty list and decide to take their revenge. After they escape (Bird Brain lays an egg containing the key to their cell), Chameleon masquerading as Santa with his two companions stuffed in a sack travels to the North Pole via the T.U.F.F. transport tubes. Bird Brain throws a force field around Santa's workshop, and the villains lock Santa, the elves, and reindeer away. While Snaptrap destroys the presents and Bird Brain interrogates the reindeer about their flying, Santa alerts T.U.F.F. at their holiday party, whereupon Keswick supplies Dudley and Kitty with a series of holiday-themed weapons: ornament grenades, candy cane lasers, and Mama Keswick's hard fruitcake for smashing. The latter enables Dudley and Kitty to free themselves from Santa's machine that crushes defective toys after the villains capture them (Dudley having eaten the candy cane lasers). When Snaptrap and Bird Brain attempt to escape in a Chameleon-turned-rocket sleigh, Dudley lassos them with Christmas lights, but it's too late—as midnight strikes, Santa's reindeer lose their flying ability, Santa having failed to get under way by that hour. Oh boo, no Christmas! Yet all is not lost. Keswick arrives in a flash with the T.U.F.F. jet, the elves make new toys in a flash (only in a cartoon), the gang deliver the presents with Santa, and the three villains are thrown back into prison. Santa's last stop is the home of a little bunny who wants a coveted race-car bed, just as Dudley does (he's been wildly raving about that bed all through the story), but the bunny's present is missing. Rather than disappoint the bunny, Dudley surrenders the race-car bed that would have been his present, after which Santa greatly rewards Dudley's kindness.

PRINCIPAL VOICES: Jerry Trainor as Dudley; Grey DeLisle as Kitty; Daran Norris as The Chief and Chameleon; Rob Paulsen as Bird Brain. All these voice actors are known for their work on the *T.U.F.F. Puppy* series.

AWARDS: *T.U.F.F. Puppy* won Annies for Best Character Design and Best Storyboarding in an Animated Television Production (2011), and Daytime Emmys for Outstanding Individual Achievement in Animation (2011, 2012, 2014). The series also received Annie nominations for Outstanding Achievement in Music (2013, 2014), Best Character Design (2011, 2012, 2013), Voice Acting (Jeff Bennett, 2013), Directing (2012), Storyboarding (2012), and Writing (2012); Daytime Emmy nominations for Outstanding Performer (Jerry Trainor, 2013), Outstanding Music (2012, 2013); and a

Golden Reel nomination for Best Sound Editing (2014).

INTERESTING TIDBITS: Upon capturing Dudley and Kitty, the three villains engage in a series of rapidly executed word plays involving homonyms. An example from Snaptrap: "Your presence is unwanted, unlike these presents that I wanted in the past, but never got, until presently—let me start again!"

In a running gag, Chameleon attempts to serve poisoned eggnog on several occasions.

REVIEW: Emily Ashby of *Common Sense Media* reviewed *T.U.F.F. Puppy*: "While tweens might be able to see the ironic humor in a partnership as lopsided as Kitty and Dudley's, younger kids won't, and the messages *they'll* pick up from the characters' interactions will reflect the fact that Dudley's accidental heroism always outshines Kitty's careful training and rule following. In other words, the show tells kids that it's better to be lucky than to be prepared."

PRODUCTION CREDITS—Writers: Ray DeLaurentis, Will Schifrin, and Kevin Sullivan. Producers: George Goodchild and Dave Thomas. Directors: Ken Bruce and Michelle Bryan. Production Companies: Billionfold and Nicktoons Productions. Rating: TV-Y7. Genres: Animation, Action, Adventure, Comedy. Country: USA. Run Time: 24 min.

REFERENCES: Ashby, Emily. *T.U.F.F. Puppy*. *Common Sense Media*. https://www.commonsensemedia.org/tv-reviews/tuff-puppy

"A Doomed Christmas." In *T.U.F.F. Puppy*. Season One. New York: Viacom International, 2014. DVD Video.

T.U.F.F. Puppy. Internet Movie Database. http://www.imdb.com/title/tt1710310/

Dot and Spot's Magical Christmas Adventure—1996

Direct-to-Video Animated Short Film

THREAT TO CHRISTMAS: When the reindeer harness snaps, Santa's sleigh crashes in the snow and is damaged.

HOW CHRISTMAS IS SAVED: Children and their pups work together as a team with Santa and the reindeer to repair the sleigh.

SYNOPSIS AND COMMENTARY: While tracking Santa's flight with the family's new telescope, Dalmatian puppies Dot and Spot, trained for rescue, witness Santa's sleigh crash in the snow and hit a boulder. Although the puppies cannot speak at the moment, their frantic barking alerts young Ryan and his older sister Robin (but somehow not their parents), and the four trek through the snow to find Santa. On the way, they must overcome several obstacles, such as a navigating a large snowbank, crossing thin ice, and scaling a cliff. Because it's Christmas Eve and because of the crisis at hand, the puppies are now gifted with speech (which they will lose at midnight), which enables them to work together with the children, Santa, and the reindeer to remove the boulder and repair his damaged sleigh. The kids are incredulous over the puppies' speech, but Santa teaches that all living things can communicate; we just have to listen with an open heart.

SONGS: "In the Woods" and "If We All Pull Together." Music by Thomas Chase and Steve Rucker; lyrics by Pamela Phillips-Oland.

VOICES: Debi Derryberry as Dot (*Toy Story*); Cam Clarke as Spot (*Teenage Mutant Ninja Turtles*); Anndi McAfee as Robin (*Tom and Jerry: The Movie*); Adam Wylie as Ryan (*Picket Fences*); Jeff Glen Bennett as Steve (*Johnny Bravo*); Ellen Gerstell as Maggie (*Little Nemo: Adventures in Slumberland*); Earl Boen as Santa (*Terminator 2: Judgment Day*).

INTERESTING TIDBITS: According to an ancient legend, at midnight on Christmas Eve, the traditional hour of Christ's birth, animals are empowered with speech, cattle kneel facing east, and bees hum Psalm 100. This cartoon modifies the legend such that the puppies' ability to speak on Christmas Eve *terminates* at midnight. There is no indication that Santa's *six* reindeer speak, however.

Dot and Spot's Magical Christmas Adventure should not be confused with another children's animated production, **Spot's Magical Christmas**, the principal character of which is also a dog, but of a different breed.

PRODUCTION CREDITS—Writer: Brynne Chandler Reaves. Producer: Charles Zembillas. Director: David Schwartz. Production Companies: Geoffrey, Inc., and Epoch Ink Animation. Rating: G. Genres: Animation, Family, Short. Country: USA. Run Time: 25 min.

REFERENCES: Crump, William D. *The Christmas Encyclopedia*. Third Edition. Jefferson, NC: McFarland, 2013.

Dot and Spot's Magical Christmas Adventure. Big Cartoon Database. http://www.bcdb.com/cartoon/77744-Dot-And-Spots-Magical-Christmas-Adventure

Dot and Spot's Magical Christmas Adventure. In *Magical Winter Tales*. Genius Entertainment, 2007. DVD Video.

Dot and Spot's Magical Christmas Adventure. Internet Movie Database. http://www.imdb.com/title/tt1353092/

Wilson, Joanna. *Tis the Season TV: The Encyclopedia of Christmas-Themed Episodes, Specials and Made-for-TV Movies*. Akron, OH: 1701 Press, 2011.

The Elf and the Magic Key—1993

Television Movie

THREAT TO CHRISTMAS: Two misfits kidnap Santa on Christmas Eve.

HOW CHRISTMAS IS SAVED: Toby the elf solves the riddle of a magic key to rescue Santa.

SYNOPSIS AND COMMENTARY: In this sequel to *The Elf Who Saved Christmas*, the principals there reprise their roles. On Christmas Eve, two misfits (Dink O'Neal, *Caged Hearts*, and Lara Teeter, *The Pirates of Penzance*) kidnap Santa (Harry Frazier, *The Elf Who Saved Christmas*) and demand all his toys for the ransom. Any other crooks would have demanded cash, but with misfits, what else can you expect? Gaining access to Mrs. Buzzard the witch (Jo Anne Worley, *Rowan and Martin's Laugh-In*) through Santa's mailbox, Toby the mailroom elf (Wendy Cooke, *The Elf Who Saved Christmas*) solicits her help, but a wizard has imprisoned her in her den with a magic key that can only be used by solving its riddle. Armed with the key and a compass, Toby discovers Santa bound in an old house, and the misfits capture her as well while boasting that they will have more toys than all people in the world, which provides Santa with an opportunity to wax philosophical that "things" are not the most important part of life. While the misfits are out, Santa and Toby easily cast off their bonds. When Toby wishes that she were back at the workshop, a magic door appears that the key unlocks when Toby solves the riddle, and the two return home through the portal. Soon the misfits arrive for the toys, and the ensuing commotion reveals that they are the Buzzard Brothers, Mrs. Buzzard's sons. The magic key reunites them with the mother they haven't seen in ages; after all, she is an infinitely better gift than all the toys in the world.

OTHER CAST: Roger Perry (*Arrest and Trial*) as the head elf; Barry Livingston (*My Three Sons*) as elf Hoot; F. Thom Spadaro (*The Elf Who Saved Christmas*) as elf Smitty; Lee Wilson (*The Elf Who Saved Christmas*) as Trixie.

INTERESTING TIDBIT: Other save-Christmas movies in which Santa is kidnapped include ***The Boy Who Saved Christmas; The Glo Friends Save Christmas; The Great Santa Claus Switch; The Librarians and Santa's Midnight Run; Santa Claus Conquers the Martians; Sonic Christmas Blast; Spinach Greetings; Tim Burton's The Nightmare Before Christmas***; and ***Who Stole Santa?***

PRODUCTION CREDITS—Writer: Lee Wilson. Producer: Robert Woods and Lee Wilson. Director: Bob Sykes. Production Company: Rim of the World Productions. Rating: Not rated. Genre: Fantasy. Country: USA. Run Time: 30 min.

REFERENCES: *The Elf and the Magic Key*. Internet Movie Database. http://www.imdb.com/title/tt0298315/

The Elf and the Magic Key. New York: GoodTimes Home Video, 1994. VHS Video.

Wilson, Joanna. *Tis the Season TV: The Encyclopedia of Christmas-Themed Episodes, Specials and Made-for-TV Movies*. Akron, OH: 1701 Press, 2011.

The Elf Who Didn't Believe—1997

Television Movie

THREAT TO CHRISTMAS: Elmer the young elf wants to be a boy in the outside world and departs from the North Pole in Santa's sleigh.

HOW CHRISTMAS IS SAVED: Santa journeys into the world to rescue Elmer and retrieve his sleigh before Christmas.

SYNOPSIS AND COMMENTARY: Weary of being one of Santa's elves and desiring instead to be a regular boy who receives Christmas presents, young Elmer (Sean Donnelly) diddles with Santa's super-tech sleigh a couple of days before Christmas and is transported to Plantville, Ohio, where he meets Jolie (Margo Harshman, *Even Stevens*), a young girl in need of a heart transplant. Jolie introduces Elmer to life in the outside world, but there is intrigue afoot, for the townspeople, having seen the sleigh streaking across the night sky, suspect that Elmer is a space alien. Moreover, the unscrupulous businessman Slick (Burke Morgan, *Lap Dancing*), having found the sleigh and captured Elmer, plans to steal Christmas by turning his defunct plastics plant into a lucrative tourist attraction by putting the sleigh and Elmer on display. With time running out on Christmas Eve, Santa (Rich Mann) journeys by plane and bus to Plantville incognito (although his abundant white hair and beard are hard to hide) to rescue Elmer, retrieve his sleigh, and give Slick his comeuppance. With all that Elmer has been through, he's happy to remain an elf and receives his first Christmas present from Jolie.

INTERESTING TIDBIT: According to the DVD promotional description: "Elmer is one of Santa's elves but he doesn't believe in Christmas anymore. He flees from the North Pole and is taken in by an orphanage. There he tries to get adopted by a nice couple." The film title is a bit misleading, and that description is not quite accurate. While Elmer is an elf who leaves the North Pole, he still believes in Christmas but wants to enjoy it as a real boy would and not as a working elf. In other words, the grass is always greener, etc. Neither is there an orphanage involved nor does Elmer seek adoption. Instead, most of his time is spent evading those who would make something of a circus freak of him.

PRODUCTION CREDITS—Writer: Karen Kelly. Producers: Ashok Amritraj and Andrew Stevens. Director: Rodney McDonald. Production Companies: Cabin Fever Entertainment, Eagle Pictures SRL, Green Communications LTD, and Royal Oaks Entertainment. Rating: G. Genres: Comedy, Family. Country: USA. Run Time: 91 min.

REFERENCES: *The Elf Who Didn't Believe.* In *Family Holiday Collection.* Universal City, CA: Vivendi Entertainment, 2012. DVD Video.

The Elf Who Didn't Believe. Internet Movie Database. http://www.imdb.com/title/tt0123055/

Wilson, Joanna. *Tis the Season TV: The Encyclopedia of Christmas-Themed Episodes, Specials and Made-for-TV Movies.* Akron, OH: 1701 Press, 2011.

The Elf Who Saved Christmas—1991
Television Special

THREAT TO CHRISTMAS: Santa decides to retire when he doesn't receive any Christmas letters.

HOW CHRISTMAS IS SAVED: Toby the elf discovers the source of the problem and how to get the missing letters back.

SYNOPSIS AND COMMENTARY: When Santa (Harry Frazier, *The Elf and the Magic Key*) receives no letters all year, he's convinced that no one believes in the spirit of Christmas anymore and decides to retire on Christmas Eve. Rechecking Santa's mailbox, Toby the mailroom elf (Wendy Cooke, *The Elf and the Magic Key*) is sucked down into the den of the evil witch Mrs. Buzzard (Jo Anne Worley, *Rowan and Martin's Laugh-In*), who, in an effort to ruin Christmas, placed a spell on the mailbox and now possesses all of Santa's letters. Toby's efforts to leave are futile until she thrice chants, "I'll always believe in Christmas," which shoots her back outside. She returns to the mailbox with Santa and others, who chant the same words, but no letters appear. Because children wrote those letters, the children must chant the words, whereupon Toby turns to the audience and exhorts them to repeat, "I'll always believe in Christmas," which does the trick. As millions of letters pour from the mailbox, Santa regains his Christmas spirit, and the holiday is saved, thanks to Toby, who sends Mrs. Buzzard a special gift in the spirit of goodwill.

OTHER CAST: Roger Perry (*Arrest and Trial*) as the head elf; Barry Livingston (*My Three Sons*) as elf Hoot; F. Thom Spadaro (*The

Elf and the Magic Key) as elf Smitty; Lee Wilson (*The Elf and the Magic Key*) as Trixie; Linda Martin (*Shelter in the Storm*) as elf Robin.

INTERESTING TIDBITS: Toby's plea to the audience parallels that in J.M. Barrie's play *Peter Pan* (1904), when at Peter's behest, the audience applauds to indicate their belief in fairies, which saves the poisoned fairy Tinker Bell. A similar scenario is found in **Elmo's Christmas Countdown, It Nearly Wasn't Christmas,** and **Raggedy Ann and Andy in the Great Santa Claus Caper**.

All the elves are of normal size; no dwarfs portray elves here.

Although the setting is the North Pole, the production was filmed entirely on location in California at Santa's Village in Skyforest and at Antlers Inn in Twin Peaks. Therefore, a snow-covered forest surrounds Santa's residence, which is rather incongruous for the polar region.

This film should not be confused with the animated production, **Snuffy, the Elf Who Saved Christmas** (1991).

Check out the sequel: **The Elf and the Magic Key**.

PRODUCTION CREDITS—Writer: Lee Wilson. Producer: Robert Woods. Director: Bob Sykes. Production Company: Rim of the World Productions. Rating: Not rated. Genre: Fantasy. Country: USA. Run Time: 30 min.

REFERENCES: *The Elf Who Saved Christmas*. Internet Movie Database. http://www.imdb.com/title/tt0289700/

The Elf Who Saved Christmas. Los Angeles: J2 Communications, 1991. VHS Video.

Wilson, Joanna. *Tis the Season TV: The Encyclopedia of Christmas-Themed Episodes, Specials and Made-for-TV Movies*. Akron, OH: 1701 Press, 2011.

Elmo Saves Christmas—1996

Television Special and Musical

THREAT TO CHRISTMAS: Santa becomes stuck in Elmo's chimney, and Elmo's wish for Christmas 365 days of the year turns sour.

HOW CHRISTMAS IS SAVED: Elmo pulls Santa from the chimney and travels back in time to undo his wish.

SYNOPSIS AND COMMENTARY: Jim Henson's Muppets of PBS's *Sesame Street* glow with Christmas cheer in this musical parody of "Christmas Every Day" (a classic short story by American author William Dean Howells, first published in 1892) that smacks of *Back to the Future*.

Surrounded by a group of young Muppets, poet Maya Angelou (*I Know Why the Caged Bird Sings*) narrates how the little red Muppet monster Elmo saved Christmas. Stuck in Elmo's fireplace because of an oversized bag of toys, Santa (Charles Durning, *The Sting*) receives some much-needed assistance from Elmo (Kevin Clash, *Sesame Street*), who pulls him out. (That's really how Elmo saves Christmas, but the story continues to make things a bit more complicated.) Santa's bag is so large because Lightning (Joey Mazzarino, *Sesame Street*), a curious little reindeer in training, stowed away there. A grateful Santa offers Elmo a special gift, the choice between a pink bear doll or a magical snow globe that grants three wishes. Choosing the globe, Elmo wastes his first wish on a glass of water. His second wish is worse, for he wishes that every day of the year could be Christmas. At Santa's command, Lightning escorts Elmo forward in time to glimpse the future impact of his folly: work piles up because people are on Christmas break, daily carol singing produces hoarse voices, other holidays overlap with Christmas, and endless shopping for gifts breeds poverty and contempt for the season. Repenting, Elmo accidentally breaks his globe while casting his final wish for all to be restored as it was. The only hope is for Lightning and Elmo to reverse their path and return to that part of time before Elmo received the globe. This time he chooses a bizarre but innocuous moo-bunny doll (combination of a cow and a rabbit) over the pink bear doll.

OTHER CAST: Harvey Fierstein (*Independence Day*) as the Easter Bunny; Caroll Spinney (*Sesame Street*) as Big Bird and Oscar the Grouch; Jerry Nelson (*Sesame Street*) as Count von Count; Martin P. Robinson (*Sesame Street*) and Bryant Young (*Sesame Street*) as Mr. Snuffleupagus; Steve Whitmire (*The Muppets*) as

Muppets Elmo (left) and Kermit the Frog in a scene from *Sesame Street*. Elmo is the featured Muppet in *Elmo Saves Christmas* (1996) and *Elmo's Christmas Countdown* (2007), while Kermit appears with the Muppet gang in *A Muppets Christmas: Letters to Santa* (2008) (PBS/Photofest).

Kermit the Frog; Frank Oz (*Star Wars*) as Cookie Monster; Sonia Manzano (*The Adventures of Elmo in Grouchland*) as Maria; Emilio Delgado (*Sesame Street*) as Luis; Roscoe Orman (*Sesame Street*) as Gordon; David Smyrl (*The Preacher's Wife*) as Mr. Handford; Carlo Alban (*21 Grams*) as Carlo; 14 Karat Soul as themselves.

CHILD TALENT: Desiree Casado, Mara Feinstein, Noemi Hernandez, Andrew Mackasek, and Theresa Sophia Rivera.

SONGS: Music and lyrics by Tony Geiss: "It's Christmas Again," "Every Day Can't Be Christmas," "Give Your Friends an Easter Egg for Christmas," "All I Want for Christmas Is You." "Keep Christmas with You" (music and lyrics respectively by Sam Pottle and David Axlerod).

AWARDS: In 1997, the production received Daytime Emmy Awards for Outstanding Achievement in Costume Design/Styling and Outstanding Children's Special. It received Daytime Emmy nominations for Outstanding Directing and Writing in a Children's Special and Outstanding Achievement in Multiple Camera Editing.

INTERESTING TIDBITS: While rebuking Lightning, Santa voices the timeless, materialistic view of Christmas: "Sonny boy, I could have been stuck in this chimney all night. Then what would have happened? There would have been no Christmas because of you!"

Elmo settles down to wait for Santa by watching *It's a Wonderful Life* on television. After Elmo wishes for 365 days of Christmas, all television stations broadcast nothing but IAWL.

Dubbed the "black woman's poet laureate," Maya Angelou (born Marguerite Annie Johnson, 1928–2014) was an American author, actress, civil rights activist, and raconteur, who appeared in several *Sesame Street* insert segments during the 1990s. Her many works included essays, poetry, television scripts, documentaries, short stories, movie scores and directing, and plays. At the inauguration of President Bill Clinton in 1993, she read her poem, "On the Pulse of Morning"; no poet had made such an inaugural recitation since Robert Frost at the inauguration of President John F. Kennedy in 1961. The first of her seven autobiographies, *I Know Why the Caged Bird Sings* (1969) brought her international recognition and acclaim.

Premiering on PBS in 1969, *Sesame Street* is the longest-running children's show in history, reaching some eight million preschoolers on 350 PBS stations in 120 countries. It has taught not only basic letters and numbers but also cooperation with others, fair play, tolerance, self-respect, conflict resolution, and the importance of listening.

William Dean Howells (1837–1920) served as editor for the *Atlantic Monthly* from 1871 to 1881. His works include literary criticisms and some thirty novels. *The Rise of Silas Lapham* (1885) is perhaps his most famous book.

PRODUCTION CREDITS—Writers: Christine Ferraro and Tony Geiss. Producer: Karin Young Shiel. Director: Emily Squires. Production Companies: Children's Television Workshop and the Jim Henson Company. Rating: Not rated. Genre: Family. Country: USA. Run Time: 60 min.

REFERENCES: Angelou, Maya. *The Collected Autobiographies of Maya Angelou*. New York: Modern Library, 2004.

Crump, William D. *The Christmas Encyclopedia*. Third Edition. Jefferson, NC: McFarland, 2013.

Davis, Michael. *Street Gang: The Complete History of Sesame Street*. New York: Viking, 2008.

Elmo Saves Christmas. Internet Movie Database. http://www.imdb.com/title/tt0116189/

Elmo Saves Christmas. Sesame Street, 2010. DVD Video.

Jones, Brian Jay. *Jim Henson: The Biography*. New York: Ballantine, 2013.

Wilson, Joanna. *Tis the Season TV: The Encyclopedia of Christmas-Themed Episodes, Specials and Made-for-TV Movies*. Akron, OH: 1701 Press, 2011.

Elmo's Christmas Countdown—
December 23, 2007
Television Special

THREAT TO CHRISTMAS: A disrupted Christmas Countdown jeopardizes the holiday.

HOW CHRISTMAS IS SAVED: The Muppets help to locate the missing counting blocks in the "Christmas Counterdowner."

SYNOPSIS AND COMMENTARY: Featuring Jim Henson's Muppets from *Sesame Street* with a gang of celebrity guests and hosted by Stiller the Elf (voice of Ben Stiller, *Tropic Thunder*) and Stan the Snowball (voice of Joey Mazzarino, *Ghost Town*), this special offers a small lesson in counting for preschoolers apart from all the Christmas pizzazz. On Christmas Eve, the traditional Christmas Countdown begins when a selected person opens a little door in each of ten numbered counting blocks on the magical "Christmas Counterdowner," which is basically a modified, fast-track Advent calendar but without religious implications, of course. Behind each door is a surprise, and completion of the Countdown then allows Santa and Christmas to arrive. On the other hand, since no Countdown means no Santa and no Christmas, it's quite obvious what's about to happen as Stiller recalls the year when Christmas almost didn't come, because of a bungled Countdown.

"Research" having revealed that Oscar the Grouch has the best Christmas spirit that year, Stiller selects him to start the Countdown, but since he cares nothing for Christmas, he sings "I Hate Christmas" and tosses the blocks into the air, whereupon they disappear. Now with Christmas in jeopardy, various Muppets help to find the missing blocks with their surprises as follows:

Abby Cadabby (a play on "Abracadabra"), a fairy in training, finds block number 10. The surprise: Jennifer Hudson (*American Idol*) sings "Carol of the Bells" with forest animals.

Bert finds block number nine in his oatmeal. The surprise: reindeer newscaster Charles Blitzen (a parody of and voiced by newsman Charles Gibson) blames Stiller for failing to prevent Oscar's mishap.

Super Grover finds block number eight in his cape. The surprise: Anne Hathaway (*The Devil Wears Prada*) sings "I Want a Snuffleupagus for Christmas" (a parody of the 1953 novelty song "I Want a Hippopotamus for Christmas") with Big Bird and Snuffy.

Big Bird finds block number seven. The surprise: Tony Sirico and Steve Schirripa of *The Sopranos* portray Bert and Ernie in *The Bert and Ernie Christmas Special* spoof with Muppets Bert, Ernie, and Prairie Dawn.

Ernie finds block number five out of order; hence, nothing happens.

Alicia Keys (*The Great Gatsby*) consoles a depressed Elmo by singing "Do You Hear What I Hear?" with him, after which she produces block number six. The surprise: Charles Blitzen reports that Stiller's goof is producing mass hysteria.

Block number five then opens with the surprise: Jamie Foxx (*Collateral*) sings a hip-hop version of *The Nutcracker Suite* with Nutcracker Elmo and choreographer Tiffany Curl.

Papa Bear finds block number four. The surprise: Charles Blitzen gives Stiller the Bronx Cheer (AKA the raspberries).

Mama Bear finds block number three. The surprise: Count von Count sings "I Saw Three Ships" with Ty Pennington in a spoof of the latter's show *Extreme Makeover: Home Edition*. Here, it's the *Christmas Carol Edition* in which they add more ships to the song.

Baby Bear finds block number two. The surprise: country star Brad Paisley on guitar sings "Jingle Bells" with Grover and penguins (out of place in the Northern Hemisphere) in a sleigh.

Stiller himself finds block number one. The surprise: a Christmas cookie, which Cookie Monster promptly devours, along with the Counterdowner. Yet Elmo and Abby, who believe in Christmas miracles, persuade Stiller to believe, and he encourages the audience to believe, all of which brings on Santa (Kevin James, *The King of Queens*), who sings "You Gotta Believe" with the Sesame Street gang and guests.

PRINCIPAL MUPPET PERFORMERS: Kevin Clash as Elmo and Mouse King; Jennifer Barnhart as Mama Bear; Fran Brill as Prairie Dawn; Leslie Carrara-Rudolph as Abby; Eric Jacobson as Bert and Ernie; Joey Mazzarino as Stan and Papa Bear; Jerry Nelson as the Count; Martin P. Robinson and Bryant Young as Snuffy; David Rudman as Cookie Monster and Baby Bear; Carrol Spinney as Big Bird and Oscar; Matt Vogel as Stiller; Steve Whitmire as Ernie.

OTHER CREDITS: Music composed by Mark Radice and John Califra. Lyrics by Mark Radice, Joey Mazzarino, Byron Breeze, Daniel Butler, Kivel Jones, and William Turner. Choreographed by Tiffany Curl and Brian Thomas. With the Brooklyn Youth Chorus.

AWARD: In 2009, this production won a Kids First! Best Award for Feature Film, Ages 2–5.

INTERESTING TIDBITS: For an opening number, Sheryl Crow sings "Almost Christmas Day" with Elmo.

Although *Sesame Street* has had a long run on PBS, this special premiered on ABC.

Stiller's plea to the audience to believe in Christmas miracles parallels that in J.M. Barrie's play *Peter Pan* (1904), when at Peter's behest, the audience applauds to indicate their belief in fairies, which saves the poisoned fairy Tinker Bell. A similar scenario is found in **The Elf Who Saved Christmas, It Nearly Wasn't Christmas,** and **Raggedy Ann and Andy in the Great Santa Claus Caper**.

REVIEW: Emily Ashby of *Common Sense Media* (December 20, 2007): "…young *Sesame Street* fans will no doubt love this holiday special's story and age-appropriate pacing, while parents will appreciate the collective talent of the musical guests. Though there are few overt learning opportunities here, it's a worry-free way to enjoy some family-friendly holiday TV time with your kids."

PRODUCTION CREDITS—Writer: Joey Mazzarino. Senior Producer: Tim Carter. Director: Gary Halvorson. Production Companies: Gotham Group and Sesame Workshop. Rating: Not rated. Genres: Family, Music. Country: USA. Run Time: 44 min.

REFERENCES: Ashby, Emily. *Elmo's Christmas Countdown*. Common Sense Media. https://www.commonsensemedia.org/movie-reviews/elmos-christmas-countdown

Elmo's Christmas Countdown. Internet Movie Database. http://www.imdb.com/title/tt1077081/

Sesame Street: Elmo's Christmas Countdown. Santa Monica, CA: Genius Entertainment, 2008. DVD Video.

Wilson, Joanna. *Tis the Season TV: The Encyclopedia of Christmas-Themed Episodes, Specials and Made-for-TV Movies.* Akron, OH: 1701 Press, 2011.

Ernest Saves Christmas—November 11, 1988

Feature Film

THREAT TO CHRISTMAS: After serving for 151 years, Santa must find a replacement, lest the magic of Christmas be lost forever.

HOW CHRISTMAS IS SAVED: Ernest bails Santa out of trouble and assists him in finding the ideal replacement.

SYNOPSIS AND COMMENTARY: If you're looking to have a Christmas filled with slapstick comedy, accidents, madcap adventure, and general chaos served up with a heaping dose of Christmas spirit, then Ernest P. Worrell is the man to call. Preceded by *Dr. Otto and the Riddle of the Gloom Beam* (1986) and *Ernest Goes to Camp* (1987), *Ernest Saves Christmas* is the third feature film in which Jim Varney stars as the wacky, drawling, accident-prone know-it-all hick, Ernest P. Worrell.

For centuries, the role of Santa Claus has been passed from one deserving man to the next, each endowed with that special spirit, a love for children, that makes him worthy of receiving the role. The time has arrived when the present Santa (Douglas Seale, *Aladdin*), now 151 years old, must name his successor by 7 PM on Christmas Eve, lest the magic of Christmas die forever. Two days remain. Having chosen Joe Carruthers (Oliver Clark, *Lost Souls*), a gentle, highly moral man and host of a recently cancelled children's television show in Orlando, Florida, Santa arrives by commercial aircraft in street dress with his sleigh and reindeer crated on board. Now all he has to do is find Joe and transfer the magic. As Ernest, a cabby oozing Christmas spirit from every pore, chauffeurs Santa around town, the two experience plenty

The future of Christmas may never be the same after everybody's favorite buttinski Ernest P. Worrell (Jim Varney, right) takes the reins of Santa's sleigh to help his elves (Buddy Douglas, left, and Patty Maloney) in *Ernest Saves Christmas* (1988) (Buena Vista Pictures Distribution/MMG Photo Archives. Collection of William D. Crump).

of complications. For one, Santa freely uses his moniker, "Santa Claus," for which he is branded as a lunatic and thrown in jail for vagrancy. For another, the powers at hand evidently thought that a cute, cynical, runaway teenager would spice up the plot. Thus enters one Harmony Starr, AKA Pamela Trent (Noelle Parker, *At Close Range*), who falls in with Ernest and Santa and crashes at Ernest's house (which should raise a few eyebrows). Adept at trickery, disguises, and deception, Ernest serves Santa well by bailing him out of jail, discovering Joe's whereabouts from a talent agency and, posing as a filthy "snake man," sneaking Santa onto the studio lot where Joe contemplates starring in a movie filled with violence and profanity. Meanwhile, the reindeer at the airport baggage hangar have kicked themselves out of their crates and have attached themselves upside down to the ceiling (they have a natural affinity for roofs), and Harmony, believing that wealth is to be had, has absconded with Santa's sack. As expected, there's an extended scene with Ernest and two screaming, terrified elves rocketing wildly through the skies and briefly into outer space after they claim the sleigh and reindeer, as Ernest, fighting for control, manages to keep them all from being shot down as a UFO. With minutes to spare on Christmas Eve, Harmony returns along with Joe, who has declined the smut movie, and Santa confers the Christmas magic through a simple handshake.

INTERESTING TIDBITS: Whereas the sack in most Santa films contains an endless supply of toys, here, Santa's sack is filled with balls of light that, when withdrawn, produce toys that children desire, but only when Santa is in control. When Ernest attempts the same, the balls only produce worthless junk.

At the police station, the officers are shocked to see that patterns of snowflakes adorn Santa's fingerprints.

Jim Varney (1949–2000) was initially known for portraying Ernest in a long series of television commercials, in which he talked to an unseen friend named Vern and whose catch phrase was "Know what I mean?" As Frank Thompson noted in *AMC Great Christmas Movies*, Ernest was "a dim-bulb hick with a highly inflated opinion of his own intellect and a penchant for long and rambling flights of fancy that [made] sense only to himself ... the situations he found himself in were designed for maximum mayhem."

Ernest feature films following *Ernest Saves Christmas*: *Ernest Goes to Jail* (1990), *Ernest Scared Stupid* (1991), and *Ernest Rides Again* (1993). The remaining *Ernest* films were all direct-to-video: *Ernest Goes to School* (1994), *Slam Dunk Ernest* (1995), *Ernest Goes to Africa* (1997), and *Ernest in the Army* (1998). With the exception of *Ernest Saves Christmas*, Ernest battled some kind of villain in all of the *Ernest* films.

Budgeted at approximately six million dollars, this film's domestic gross earnings at the box office were over $28 million.

REVIEWS: According to the Rotten Tomatoes film review site, 38 percent of critics gave this film a positive review.

Rita Kempley of *The Washington Post* (November 11, 1988): "Varney's cretinous character—part Francis the Talking Mule, part Minnie Pearl, part auto parts aficionado—will not disappoint fans with this antic combo of candy canes and slapstick."

Emily Ashby of *Common Sense Media* (December 19, 2011): "Goofy holiday movie is OK fun for families, knowhatImean?"

Caryn James of *The New York Times* (November 11, 1988): "The best thing that can be said for the film is that it leaves Ernest behind now and then to focus on Santa, who is played by Douglas Seale with sweetness, sincerity and an amazing amount of dignity, considering his surroundings."

Ryan Cracknell of *Movie Views* (December 14, 2003): "*Ernest Saves Christmas* is an innocent enough film that will likely appeal more to the children than their parents."

PRODUCTION CREDITS—Story: Ed Turner. Screenplay: B. Kline and Ed Turner. Producers: Doug Claybourne and Stacy Williams. Director: John Cherry. Production Companies: Touchstone Pictures, Silver Screen Partners III, and Emshell Producers. Rating: PG (some crude humor). Genres: Comedy, Family, Fantasy. Country: USA. Run Time: 95 min.

REFERENCES: Ashby, Emily. *Ernest Saves*

Christmas. Common Sense Media. https://www.commonsensemedia.org/movie-reviews/ernest-saves-christmas

Cracknell, Ryan. *Ernest Saves Christmas. Movie Views.* http://movieviews.ca/ernest-saves-christmas

Crump, William D. *The Christmas Encyclopedia.* Third Edition. Jefferson, NC: McFarland, 2013.

Duralde, Alonso. *Have Yourself a Movie Little Christmas.* New York: Limelight Editions, 2010.

Ernest Saves Christmas. Box Office Mojo. http://www.boxofficemojo.com/search/?q=ernest%20saves%20christmas

Ernest Saves Christmas. Burbank, CA: Touchstone Home Video, 2002. DVD Video.

Ernest Saves Christmas. Internet Movie Database. http://www.imdb.com/title/tt0095107

Ernest Saves Christmas. Rotten Tomatoes. http://www.rottentomatoes.com/m/ernest_saves_christmas/

James, Caryn. *Ernest Saves Christmas. The New York Times.* http://www.nytimes.com/movie/review?res=940DEED91339F932A25752C1A96E948260&partner=Rotten%2520Tomatoes

Kempley, Rita. *Ernest Saves Christmas. The Washington Post.* http://www.washingtonpost.com/wp-srv/style/longterm/movies/videos/ernestsaveschristmas.htm

Thompson, Frank T. *American Movie Classics Great Christmas Movies.* Dallas, TX: Taylor Publishing, 1998.

Wilson, Joanna. *Tis the Season TV: The Encyclopedia of Christmas-Themed Episodes, Specials and Made-for-TV Movies.* Akron, OH: 1701 Press, 2011.

A Fairly Odd Christmas—November 29, 2012

Television Movie

THREAT TO CHRISTMAS: When Timmy Turner's bungling causes Santa to lose his mind, the North Pole shuts down.

HOW CHRISTMAS IS SAVED: Timmy overcomes being on the naughty list to save Santa.

SYNOPSIS AND COMMENTARY: A sequel to the television movie *A Fairly Odd Movie: Grow Up, Timmy Turner!* (2011), *A Fairly Odd Christmas*, like its predecessor, combines live-action adventure with computer-animated characters. Both films are based on *The Fairly OddParents*, an ongoing, animated television series created by Butch Hartman in 2001 for Nickelodeon that revolves around the misadventures of Timmy Turner, a boy living in the city of Dimmsdale, who acquires oddball fairy godparents Cosmo and Wanda with their baby Poof. The latter three in turn grant Timmy's every wish to improve his life, often with comically disastrous consequences. Note that the title *Fairly OddParents* is a play on "fairy godparents."

In *Odd Christmas*, Timmy Turner (Drake Bell, *A Fairly Odd Movie: Grow Up, Timmy Turner!*) is now a 23-year-old man who acts like a child and is in the fifth grade. He may keep his animated fairies as long as he wishes nothing for himself. Together with the fairies and his girlfriend Tootie (Daniella Monet, *A Fairly Odd Movie: Grow Up, Timmy Turner!*), Timmy has been zipping around the world in his flying "Wishful Thinking" van, indiscriminately granting thousands of wishes, which attracts Santa's (Donavon Stinson, *Fantastic Four*) attention, because the names of those wish recipients are disappearing from his nice list, and Santa fears for his job. Timmy and the gang, along with Timmy's nerdy principal Mr. Crocker (David Lewis, *Man of Steel*), who stowed away to get his name removed from the naughty list, are summoned to the North Pole, where Santa pleads for Timmy to stop his wish-granting spree. When a gift-wrapping machine malfunctions and Santa wishes that it were fixed, Timmy grants the wish, but since an elf environment snafus fairy magic, Santa instead falls into the machine and becomes an idiot who believes he's the Easter Bunny, Superman, and other iconic figures. With Santa incapacitated, the North Pole shuts down, Christmas gloom plagues the world, and Timmy winds up on the naughty list. Now protocol dictates that Timmy assume Santa's role, yet being on the naughty list, he cannot, and his friends are powerless to help. Only Elmer the Elder Elf (Tony Cox, *Bad Santa*), the black dwarf-keeper of the naughty list, can remove Timmy's name. The journey to Elmer's domain is treacherous, yet Timmy and the gang, along with Crocker and two other elves, endure the perils involved, such as an avalanche, being chased by angry gingerbread men when hungry Crocker takes a bite of one, and crossing a dangerous bridge over boiling eggnog. Hardly civil, Elmer refuses to accommodate Timmy until he discovers how much Timmy risked his life for Christmas. Even with Timmy back as the new temporary Santa, there's another hurdle: the reindeer have escaped from their barn, thanks to Crocker's carelessness, whereupon the fairies arrive with Timmy's flying van that pulls the sleigh through the gap to the North Pole before Christmas gloom closes it, and Christmas is saved. Yes, the real Santa recovers. No, Elmer does not remove Crocker's name from the naughty list.

OTHER CAST: Devyn Dalton (*Godzilla*) as elf Christmas Carol; Travis Turner (*Some Assembly Required*) as elf Dingle Dave; Dalila Bela (*Odd Squad*) as elf Jingle Jill; Mark Gibbon (*Man of Steel*) as fairy king Jorgen von Strangle.

FAIRY VOICES: Daran Norris as Cosmo; Susanne Blakeslee as Wanda; Tara Strong as Poof. All three provided voices for *The Fairly OddParents*.

AWARDS: Young Artist Award nominations for Best Performance in a TV Movie, Miniseries, Special or Pilot–Supporting Young Actress (Dalila Bella and Olivia Steele-Falconer).

INTERESTING TIDBITS: The elves at the North Pole are primarily children.

In a running gag, Mr. Crocker often exhales a green vapor, which represents halitosis. Those close by make disgusting faces, hold their noses, and walk away. When elf Jingle Jill experiences this, she blurts out, "Your breath smells like a reindeer's butt!"

Note the ongoing feud between Santa's elves and Timmy's fairies.

The Fairly OddParents series is the second longest-running Nicktoon, the longest being *SpongeBob SquarePants*.

Check out **Merry Wishmas**, an episode from *The Fairly OddParents*.

REVIEW: Emily Ashby of *Common Sense Media* (November 28, 2012): "Bell and Monet are the story's shining stars, followed closely by Lewis, who so masters the ludicrous villain's character that he accounts for a lot of the laughs. The story itself is neither noteworthy nor unique, but the cast's talents and the characters' wacky predicaments are enough to carry kids' attention to the end."

PRODUCTION CREDITS—Story: Butch Hartman, Ray DeLaurentis, and Will Schifrin. Teleplay: Butch Hartman and Savage Steve Holland. Executive Producers: Marjorie Cohn, Butch Hartman, and Lauren Levine. Director: Savage Steve Holland. Production Companies: Billionfold Inc., Frederator Studios, and Pacific Bay Entertainment. Rating: G. Genres: Comedy, Family, Fantasy. Country: USA. Run Time: 68 min.

REFERENCES: Ashby, Emily. *A Fairly Odd Christmas. Common Sense Media.* https://www.commonsensemedia.org/movie-reviews/a-fairly-odd-christmas

A Fairly Odd Christmas. Internet Movie Database. http://www.imdb.com/title/tt2299368/

A Fairly Odd Christmas. Viacom International, 2013. DVD Video.

Lenburg, Jeff. *The Encyclopedia of Animated Cartoons.* Third Edition. New York: Facts on File, 2009.

Felix the Cat Saves Christmas—October 12, 2004

Direct-to-Video Animated Musical

THREAT TO CHRISTMAS: The Professor wants to shut down Christmas by trapping Santa in a horrendous blizzard.

HOW CHRISTMAS IS SAVED: Felix the Cat and his friend Poindexter put a cork in the Professor's operation.

SYNOPSIS AND COMMENTARY: Dubbed as animation's first superstar, Felix the Cat was born during the silent era of theatrical animated cartoon shorts. This anthropomorphic black cat was initially known as "Master Tom" in his first two cartoons, *Feline Follies* and *Musical Mews*, which were products of the Pat Sullivan Studio in 1919, then with *The Adven-*

tures of Felix, also from Sullivan that same year, he acquired his now-famous name. The creation of Sullivan animator Otto Messmer, Felix enjoyed much success during the 1920s, but the advent of Disney's Mickey Mouse character and sound cartoons eclipsed Felix, and the series ended in 1932, followed by a brief, three-cartoon resurrection by the Van Beuren Studios in 1936. Although the Sullivan-Messmer shorts with added soundtracks had been airing on television since the early 1950s, Messmer's assistant, Joe Oriolo (also known for *Casper the Friendly Ghost*), redesigned Felix for a new television series launched in 1958 that introduced new characters and features: Felix's magic bag of tricks that helped in dangerous situations; the Professor, a mad scientist and Felix's archenemy; Poindexter, the Professor's nerdy scientist-nephew who sports thick glasses and a mortarboard; Rock Bottom, the Professor's cigar-chewing, bulldog-faced henchman; Master Cylinder, an evil robot; Martin the Martian; General Clang, an evil general in space; and Vavoom, a small Inuit. Felix's career has led him into other television series, two feature films, comic strips, comic books, and he has graced a host of merchandise.

A poster for a cartoon short during the silent film era, *Felix the Cat Shatters the Sheik* (1926), starring the iconic feline and animation's first superstar. Felix is seen here prior to the advent of his magic bag of tricks, his archenemy the Professor, and Poindexter. The latter three are featured in *Felix the Cat Saves Christmas* (2004) (Educational Film Exchanges/Photofest).

In *Felix the Cat Saves Christmas*, the Professor attempts to stop Santa from delivering Christmas toys by creating a worldwide blizzard with his "hyper-horrible snowmaking machine." His loathing of Christmas stems from his childhood because, being a misfit like Rudolph, children ostracized him from Christmas games in the snow and because Santa only brought him lumps of coal. En route to the North Pole to assess Santa's situation, Felix and Poindexter experience several adventures, such as bailing out of the latter's rocket funmobile when it malfunctions over the Arctic (Felix turns his bag into a hang glider), meeting a village of "snowkids" who consume much footage in snowboarding, and battling the haunted ice forest's snow monster. Following a tour of Santa's operation, Poindexter equips the reindeer with bifocals for night vision, Felix's bag becomes a giant hair dryer that clears a runway for the sleigh, and Santa is off. Felix finally foils the Professor's setup by using his bag as a giant cork on the snow machine, which explodes.

VOICES: Dave Coulier (*Full House*) as Felix and Tom Bosley (*Happy Days*) as Santa. Other voices: Don Oriolo, Jason Marsden, Catie Gresham, and Erika Hays.

SONGS: "It's Not Easy Being Mean" (by Don Oriolo and Jay Thompson, performed by Mongo Joey, Ed Stassium, and Amy Hartman); "It's Christmas" (by Don Oriolo and Paul Christianson, performed by The FTC Singers); "It's Christmas Time of Year" (by Don Oriolo, performed by Mongo Joey); "Happy Day" (by Don Oriolo, performed by Amy Hartman); "Snowkids Rock" (by Don Oriolo, performed by Mongo Joey, Ed Stassium, and Amy Hartman); "Felix the Cat Theme" (by Winston Sharples, performed by Nancy Calo); "Hallelujah" (by Don Oriolo, performed by Gloria Gaynor during end credits).

INTERESTING TIDBITS: In running gags throughout the movie, Rock Bottom is obsessed with food, Rock repeatedly hauls the Professor from icy waters encased in a block of ice, and Felix and Poindexter banter back and forth with corny jokes. For example, when Felix presents him with a new pair of glasses, he says, "I hope I don't make a spectacle out of myself wearing them!"

Consuming more footage than necessary, the Professor uses all manner of tools and a jackhammer to dislodge Rock, when his tongue sticks to an icy window. The scenario recalls *A Christmas Story* (1983), in which Flick, taking the "triple-dog-dare," sticks his tongue to an icy flag pole and suffers the consequences. A similar scenario is found in **Billy and Mandy Save Christmas**.

Background music includes snippets of Tchaikovsky's *Nutcracker Suite*, and there is a brief nod to the Radio City Music Hall Rockettes in caricatures.

REVIEW: Donna Rolfe of The Dove Foundation: "This is one of those classic little cartoons from the past, filled with funny comic-strip tricks, dialogue and one-dimension animation, plus fun, toe-tapping music…. We award [this film] with the Dove Family Approved Seal for all ages."

PRODUCTION CREDITS—Writer, Producer, and Director: Don Oriolo. Production Companies: Felix the Cat Creations. Rating: Not rated. Genres: Animation, Family, Musical. Countries: China and USA. Run Time: 72 min.

REFERENCES: Canemaker, John. *Felix: The Twisted Tale of the World's Most Famous Cat*. New York: Pantheon, 1991.

Felix the Cat Saves Christmas. Big Cartoon Database. http://www.bcdb.com/cartoon/127608-Felix-the-Cat-Saves-Christmas

Felix the Cat Saves Christmas. The Dove Foundation. http://www.dove.org/review/10659-felix-the-cat-saves-christmas/

Felix the Cat Saves Christmas. Internet Movie Database. http://www.imdb.com/title/tt0439567/

Felix the Cat Saves Christmas. New York: GoodTimes Entertainment, 2004. DVD Video.

Lenburg, Jeff. *The Encyclopedia of Animated Cartoons*. Third Edition. New York: Facts on File, 2009.

Markstein, Don. "Felix the Cat." Toonopedia. http://www.toonopedia.com/felix.htm

Rolfe, Donna. *Felix the Cat Saves Christmas*. The Dove Foundation. http://www.dove.org/review/10659-felix-the-cat-saves-christmas/

Wilson, Joanna. *Tis the Season TV: The Encyclopedia of Christmas-Themed Episodes, Specials and Made-for-TV Movies*. Akron, OH: 1701 Press, 2011.

Flicker Saves Christmas—November 29, 2010

Episode from the Computer-Animated Television Series *Handy Manny*

THREAT TO CHRISTMAS: When a snowstorm forces Santa to make an emergency landing, he damages his sleigh.

HOW CHRISTMAS IS SAVED: Handy Manny and his talking tools put Santa back in the skies.

Flicker Saves Christmas

SYNOPSIS AND COMMENTARY: Created by Roger Bollen, Marilyn Sadler, and Rick Gitelson, the preschool series *Handy Manny* ran on the Disney Channel and then on Disney Jr., for 113 half-hour episodes from 2006 to 2013. Manny was a Latino handyman who ran a fix-it shop in the fictional town of Sheetrock Hills and worked with a group of talking, anthropomorphic tools named Felipe, a Phillips-head screwdriver; Turner, a flat-head screwdriver; Pat, a hammer; Dusty, a hand saw; Squeeze, a pair of pliers; Stretch, a tape measure; Rusty, a monkey wrench; and Flicker, a predominantly Spanish-speaking flashlight. Though the story lines were conducted mainly in English, the show featured an abundance of basic Spanish words and phrases as a means of introducing young English-speaking children to Spanish.

By the time kids finish watching "Flicker Saves Christmas," they should know that "Feliz Navidad" and "árbol de Navidad" are the respective Spanish phrases for "Merry Christmas" and "Christmas tree"; if they don't, they haven't been paying attention, because those phrases are repeated multiple times. Not long after Santa begins his rounds on Christmas Eve, a snowstorm precludes navigation, whereupon he makes an emergency landing in Sheetrock Hills and damages the sleigh in the process (at least he doesn't crash like he does in so many other films). When Santa walks into Manny's shop to solicit repairs, the excited tools all but fall down and worship the old gent as if he were a god. The sleigh needs a new runner, and the local hardware store just happens to have one remaining in stock (as if people had been storming the store to buy runners), so Manny and his tools get to work. Now because Santa has much trouble climbing into his sleigh (either it's too high or he's just too fat), Manny surprises him with a little handmade step-stool as a gift, and because he's running behind, Santa invites Manny and tools to help him deliver the presents. There's one last problem: the reindeer still cannot navigate in the blinding snow. Since there's no indication that Rudolph with his red beacon is a member of this team, Flicker the flashlight has the honors and thus saves Christmas.

PRINCIPAL VOICES: Wilmer Valderrama (*Unaccompanied Minors*) as Manny; Carlos Alazraqui (*Inside Out*) as Felipe; Dee Bradley Baker (*American Dad!*) as Turner; Nika Futterman (*The Boxtrolls*) as Stretch and Squeeze; Grey DeLisle (*The Replacements*) as Flicker; Kath Soucie (*Rugrats*) as Dusty; Fred Stoller (*Littleman*) as Rusty; Daniel Hagen (*The Informant!*) as Santa.

SONGS: "Hop Up, Jump In" and "We Work Together" by Randy Miller and Rick Gitelson; "You Can Always Count on Santa" by Andy Paley and Tom Kenny.

AWARDS: In 2008, *Handy Manny* won a Vision Award for Animation, won two Genesis Awards for Animated Television Children's Programming, and won an Environmental Media Award USA for Children's Live-Action/Animated Program. In 2009, it won a Vision Award for Animation, won a Genesis Award for Children's Programming, and received a Primetime Emmy nomination for Outstanding Special Class Animated Program. In 2013, it won an Imagen Award for Best Children's Programming.

INTERESTING TIDBITS: In films that focus on Santa and receiving presents, it's common to hear sentiments about Santa's presence being absolutely necessary for Christmas. To that end, when it appears that the snowstorm may hinder or prevent Santa from arriving, Manny's tools exclaim, "You can't have Christmas without Santa!" Manny somewhat counters with the observation that Christmas isn't just about presents. Pat the hammer replies with, "It isn't?" whereupon Manny then provides the usual, politically correct pitch that Christmas is all about helping friends and neighbors and giving. Religious sentiments are neither suggested nor implied.

NOTE: At the time of this writing, this film was not available on DVD or VHS but could be seen on Hulu.

REVIEW: Emily Ashby of *Common Sense Media* reviewed the series: "…brimming with positive content … themes of teamwork, preparedness, and mutual respect … exposes preschoolers to aspects of Latino culture … when he introduces less-familiar Spanish terms, Manny includes their English translations ... colorful animation, engaging storylines, and rich characters..."

PRODUCTION CREDITS—Writer: Mike Rabb. Producers: Roger Bollen, Rick Gitelson, and Marilyn Sadler. Director: Charles E. Bastien. Production Company: Nelvana. Rating: TV-Y. Genres: Animation, Family. Countries: Canada and USA. Run Time: 24 min.

REFERENCES: Ashby, Emily. *Handy Manny*. Common Sense Media. https://www.commonsensemedia.org/tv-reviews/handy-manny

"Flicker Saves Christmas." Big Cartoon Database. https://www.bcdb.com/cartoon/166590-Flicker-Saves-Christmas

"Flicker Saves Christmas." Internet Movie Database. http://www.imdb.com/title/tt1777170/

Handy Manny. Internet Movie Database. http://www.imdb.com/title/tt0451460/

Handy Manny Web Site: http://disneyjunior.disney.com/handy-manny

The Flight Before Christmas—October 10, 2008

Computer-Animated Feature Film

THREAT TO CHRISTMAS: A pack of wolves plans to eat Santa, his Flying Forces, and the children to whom he gives presents.

HOW CHRISTMAS IS SAVED: Little Niko and Santa's Flying Forces stave off the wolves.

SYNOPSIS AND COMMENTARY: *The Flight Before Christmas* is the English-language title for *Niko—Lentäjän poika*, a film made predominantly in Finland with contributions from Danish, German, and Irish studios. It's also known in English as *Niko—The Way to the Stars*. The story centers around Niko, a little reindeer buck who believes that his father, whom he has never met, is a member of Santa's reindeer team known as the Flying Forces. Desiring to join his father as well as to fly, Niko receives flying lessons from his friend Julius, a flying squirrel who has become a mentor and father figure, but Niko repeatedly fails and the adult reindeer mock him. When Niko sneaks away from his community of Home Valley to practice alone, a pack of hungry wolves led by Black Wolf catches Niko's scent, follows him back home, attacks the herd, and Niko is blamed for the melee. Feeling ostracized, Niko leaves the community with Julius and Wilma, a singing weasel, and sets out to find Santa's Fell and his father. The mission is fraught with hazards, the most significant of which is the wolf pack, which hatches a diabolical plan to raid Santa's Fell and devour not only Santa and his Flying Forces but also the children of the world who receive Santa's gifts. Following Niko into the Fell, the wolves put such fear into the Flying Forces that they lose faith and cannot fly, whereupon Julius shames them into flying to save Niko from Black Wolf; in turn, Niko gains the faith to fly to save Julius from the wolf. With renewed faith in themselves, Niko and the Flying Forces chase the wolves out, after which Niko learns that Prancer is his father and flies with Santa's team. But rather than remain with Santa's team, Niko returns to his mother, the herd, and Julius, who had been his "father" all along.

PRINCIPAL VOICES (ENGLISH VERSION): Andrew McMahon (*The Flight Before Christmas*) as Niko; Norm MacDonald (*Dirty Work*) as Julius; Emma Roberts (*Wild Child*) as Wilma; Alan Stanford (*Animal Farm*) as Black Wolf; Gavin Morgan (*Zombie Hotel*) as Smiley; Paul Tylak (*Skunk Fu!*) as Specs and Prancer; Carly Baker (*I Went Down*) as Saga; Morgan Jones (*Creep*) as Dasher; Susan Zelouf (*Zombie Hotel*) as Essie; Susan Slott (*Zombie Hotel*) as Oona; Patrick Fitzsymons (*Zombie Hotel*) as Grandpa.

AWARDS: In 2008, this picture received the Cinekid Audience Award, the Cinekid Film Award, and the *Centre International du Film pour l'Enfance et la Jeunesse* Award—Special Mention from the Oulu International Children's Film Festival. In 2009, it received Jussi Awards for Best Film and Best Script; a Jussi nomination for Best Direction; and Irish Film and Television Award nominations for Best Animation, Best Original Score, and Best Sound.

INTERESTING TIDBITS: With an estimated budget of 6,100,000 Euros, this production is reported to be the most expensive Finnish animated film.

In the original Finnish version, Niko journeys to Mount Korvatunturi, Santa's abode in Finnish folklore.

REVIEWS: Nancy Davis Kho of *Common Sense Media* (November 21, 2008): "…beautifully animated and imagined … the wolves are truly scary, and the fact that they are chasing Niko and the herd is bad enough; then they decide to eat Santa. The subplot about Niko determining which of the Flying Force reindeer is his father borders on creepy, especially as his mother relays the tale of one night with Daddy Reindeer … not a movie that embodies the Christmas spirit…"

Jen Johans of *Film Intuition* (October 22, 2008): "…macabre … sinister plot … upsetting to young children who may develop nightmares about wolves aspiring to eat Santa and babies … doesn't fit the holiday film paradigm…. Santa's reindeer who act like a bunch of hard-drinking, horny frat-boys, and a teenage runaway … excellent message of being true to yourself … gorgeous quality of the animation…"

PRODUCTION CREDITS—Writers: Marteinn Thorisson and Hannu Tuomainen. Additional Dialogue: Mark Hodkinson. Producers: Petteri Pasanen and Hannu Tuomainen. Directors: Michael Hegner and Kari Juusonen. Production Companies: Cinemaker Oy, Anima Vitae, A. Film, Animaker, Europool, Magma Films Ltd., TV2 Danmark [sic], Ulysses Filmproduktion, Universum Film, The Weinstein Company, Yleisradio, and ZDF Tivi. Rating: G. Genres: Animation, Adventure, Family, Fantasy. Countries: Finland, Denmark, Germany, Ireland. Run Time: 81 min.

REFERENCES: Crump, William D. *The Christmas Encyclopedia*. Third Edition. Jefferson, NC: McFarland, 2013.

The Flight Before Christmas. Internet Movie Database. http://www.imdb.com/title/tt0885415/

The Flight Before Christmas. Santa Monica, CA: Genius Products, 2008. DVD Video.

Johans, Jen. *The Flight Before Christmas. Film Intuition*. http://reviews.filmintuition.com/2008/10/flight-before-christmas-2008.html

Kho, Nancy Davis. *The Flight Before Christmas. Common Sense Media*. https://www.commonsensemedia.org/movie-reviews/the-flight-before-christmas

Wilson, Joanna. *Tis the Season TV: The Encyclopedia of Christmas-Themed Episodes, Specials and Made-for-TV Movies*. Akron, OH: 1701 Press, 2011.

A Flintstone Christmas—December 7, 1977

Animated Television Musical Special

THREAT TO CHRISTMAS: When Santa slips on Fred Flintstone's roof, sprains his ankle, and takes a cold, he cannot finish delivering his presents.

HOW CHRISTMAS IS SAVED: Fred and friend Barney Rubble take over Santa's route.

SYNOPSIS AND COMMENTARY: Stone-Age people celebrating Christmas? Isn't that a bit far-fetched? In the real world, thousands of years would pass from the time of the Stone Age until Christmas would become a reality. In the world of animation, however, anachronistic settings are not uncommon and link the present with the distant past. Such is the case with *The Flintstones*, the first primetime, made-for-television animated situation comedy series, created by the animation giant Hanna-Barbera Studios. Inspired by the 1950s television series *The Honeymooners* and set during the Stone Age, *The Flintstones* aired on the ABC network from 1960 to 1966 with 166 half-hour episodes. The principal characters included Fred and Wilma Flintstone with daughter Pebbles; Dino, the Flintstones' little pet dinosaur who barked and behaved like a dog; neighbors Barney and Betty Rubble with adopted son Bamm-Bamm; Hoppy, the Rubbles' pet hopparoo (a combination of kangaroo and dinosaur); and Mr. Slate, Fred's boss at the rock quarry. *The Flintstones* revolved around Fred's and Barney's shenanigans in the town of Bedrock, where every name was derived from some form of stone or prehistoric creature. The principal characters also appeared in a host of other incarnations.

To keep his job at the rock quarry, Fred agrees to play Santa at a benefit for the Bedrock Orphanage, as requested by Mr. Slate. But when the real Santa falls off Fred's roof, sprains

The four principals of the animated TV series *The Flintstones* making merry at holiday time. Shown from left are Fred and Wilma Flintstone and neighbors Barney and Betty Rubble. Fred bails Santa out of a jam in the episode "Christmas Flintstone" (1964), and Fred and Barney come to Santa's rescue in the TV special *A Flintstone Christmas* (1977) (ABC/Photofest).

his ankle, and catches a cold, Fred and Barney take over Santa's Christmas Eve rounds. With Fred in Santa's own suit and Barney dressed as an elf, the two bumble their way around the world in a sleigh pulled by the eight reindeer and lose half of the presents in a snow storm. Forced to return to the North Pole for another load and with time drawing nigh for the benefit, Fred kicks the sleigh into high gear and drops presents like bombs into chimneys. The two arrive back at the orphanage just in the (St.) Nick of time as Mr. Slate is about to fire Fred. Arriving with an empty sack, Fred quickly takes advantage of Santa's magical suit and conjures up abundant gifts for the children.

PRINCIPAL VOICES: Henry Corden (*A Flintstone Family Christmas*) as Fred; Jean Vander Pyl (*The Flintstones*) as Wilma and Pebbles; Mel Blanc (*The Flintstones*) as Barney, Gay Hartwig (*The Flintstones' New Neighbors*) as Betty; Lucille Bliss (*The Smurfs*) as Bamm-Bamm; John Stephenson (*The Flintstones*) as Mr. Slate; and Hal Smith (*The Andy Griffith Show*) as Santa.

ORIGINAL SONGS: "Sounds of Christmas Day," "Hope," "Which One Is the Real Santa Claus?" "Brand New Kind of Christmas Song," and "It's Our Favorite Time of the Year." The composers are not credited. The first three songs had been featured in ***A Christmas Story*** (1972), and the fifth was reused in *Yogi's First Christmas* (1980).

AWARDS: *The Flintstones*—Primetime Emmy nomination for Outstanding Program Achievement in the Field of Humor (1961); Online Film and Television Association TV Hall of Fame Award for Television Programs (2006); TV Land Award nomination for Greatest TV Dance Craze ("The Twitch," 2006).

INTERESTING TIDBITS: *A Flintstone Christmas* was the first *Flintstones* special to premiere on the NBC network.

Fred alone bailed out an ailing Santa in an earlier episode from the original *Flintstones* series titled **Christmas Flintstone** (1964). There, the presents fell into the chimneys via little parachutes.

Other films in which Santa or his surrogate suffers a cold and cannot deliver his presents include: **How the Toys Saved Christmas** and **The Year Without a Santa Claus**.

PRODUCTION CREDITS—Writers: Duane Poole and Dick Robbins. Executive Producers: William Hanna and Joseph Barbera. Director: Charles A. Nichols. Production Company: Hanna-Barbera Productions. Rating: Not rated. Genres: Animation, Family. Country: USA. Run Time: 48 min.

REFERENCES: Crump, William D. *The Christmas Encyclopedia*. Third Edition. Jefferson, NC: McFarland, 2013.

A Flintstone Christmas. Big Cartoon Database. http://www.bcdb.com/bcdb/cartoon.cgi?film=28593

A Flintstone Christmas. Christmas Specials Wiki. http://christmas-specials.wikia.com/wiki/A_Flintstone_Christmas

A Flintstone Christmas. In *A Flintstone Christmas Collection: A Flintstone Christmas and A Flintstone Family Christmas*. Burbank, CA: Warner Home Video, 2011. DVD Video.

A Flintstone Christmas. Internet Movie Database. http://www.imdb.com/title/tt0193163/

Lenburg, Jeff. *The Encyclopedia of Animated Cartoons*. Third Edition. New York: Facts on File, 2009.

Mallory, Michael. *Hanna-Barbera Cartoons*. Westport, CT: Hugh Lauter Levin Associates, 1998.

Wilson, Joanna. *Tis the Season TV: The Encyclopedia of Christmas-Themed Episodes, Specials and Made-for-TV Movies*. Akron, OH: 1701 Press, 2011.

For Whom the Sleigh Bell Tolls—
December 12, 2010

Episode from the Animated Television Series *American Dad!*

THREAT TO CHRISTMAS: A boy accidentally kills a mall Santa who turns out to be the real Santa.

HOW CHRISTMAS IS SAVED: The elves revive Santa at the North Pole, but Santa turns homicidal against the boy and his family.

SYNOPSIS AND COMMENTARY: In **Road to the North Pole**, an episode from Seth MacFarlane's adult animated sitcom *Family Guy*, a kid seeks revenge against Santa for snubbing him at the mall. Since *American Dad!* is also MacFarlane's brainchild, then it's not surprising to find a reverse situation in **For Whom the Sleigh Bell Tolls**: Santa seeks revenge against a kid and his family for shooting him. MacFarlane, together with Mike Barker and Matt Weitzman, created *American Dad!* for the Fox Network, and the series has been ongoing since 2005; currently it airs on TBS. Relying more on observational comedy and farce with often absurd plots, *American Dad!* sports fewer cutaway gags and allusions to pop culture that are more prevalent in *Family Guy*. Set in the fictional town of Langley Falls, VA, *American Dad!* revolves around the adventures of Stan Smith, an ultraconservative, insensitive CIA agent; nagging wife Francine; hippie, liberal daughter Hayley; nerdy teenage son Steve; Jeff Fischer, Hayley's emasculated, deadbeat husband who lives with the Smiths; Klaus Heissler, the family's pet goldfish, whose mind formerly resided in the body of an East German athlete; and Roger, a gray, brazen alien who lives in the Smith family attic.

Desiring to bond more with son Steve, Stan gives him an assault rifle, his first gun, a few days before Christmas, over Francine's objections. Stan's instructions: "Shooting a gun is like being intimate with a woman. First you inspect it to make sure it's clean. Then you grab it on the butt and jam the magazine in; if it doesn't fit, make it!" During practice, Steve nearly shoots his eye out (a nod to Ralphie Parker in *A Christmas Story*). Outside the mall at Stan's urging, Steve targets what appears to be a snowman and blasts away, then realizes he's just killed a mall Santa. Since the latter's prints are not on file with the CIA, the family sans Jeff and Roger covertly bury the body in the woods but prevent Francine from cutting off his hands and smashing his teeth to conceal his identity. After receiving anonymous notes claiming to know about their foul deed, the Smiths return to the now-empty grave on

Life's initially a dull roar for the Stan Smith family, the protagonists in the animated TV series *American Dad!* until the son Steve accidentally shoots Santa, who turns homicidal and stalks the family in the episode "For Whom the Sleigh Bell Tolls" (2010). From left: Hayley, Stan, Steve, Francine holding Klaus, and Roger the alien (Fox/Photofest).

Christmas Eve, where an angry elf appears with news that, although Steve had killed the real Santa, he's been revived back at the North Pole. Therefore, Santa will return to annihilate the Smiths before sunrise on Christmas Day (so much for believing that Santa merely punishes the naughty with coal). Although the Smiths attempt to hide with Roger in aircraft wreckage serving as the mountain "home" of Bob Todd the moonshiner, Haley summons clueless hubby Jeff, who arrives after having written Santa about their new location for receiving presents. Leading a vast army of reindeer-riding elves toting bows and arrows, a homicidal Santa soon plunges into a bloody slaughter against the Smiths with their automatic weapons, courtesy of Bob's arsenal (moral: never bring bows and arrows to a gunfight). Santa fails to lure innocent Jeff to his side with a coveted polar bear helmet from the film *The Golden Compass*, Jeff instead pulling an injured Stan to safety. Though the elves fall by the hundreds, they almost overrun the Smiths, until dawn puts a halt to the battle as Santa retreats, but he promises to return next year to finish the job.

PRINCIPAL VOICES: Seth MacFarlane as Stan and Roger; Wendy Schaal as Francine; Scott Grimes as Steve; Rachael MacFarlane as Haley; Dee Bradley Baker as Klaus; Jeff Fischer as Jeff Fischer; Erik Durbin as Bob Todd; Matt McKenna as Santa. All these voice actors are known for their work on *American Dad!* Guest actor: Clancy Brown (*The Shawshank Redemption*) as the liquor store manager.

AWARDS: In 2013, *American Dad!* won the ASCAP Film and Television Music Award for Top Television Series. The series has been nominated for Primetime Emmys, Annies, People's Choice Awards, and Teen Choice Awards, among others.

INTERESTING TIDBITS: The title is an obvious parody of Hemingway's novel *For Whom the Bell Tolls*.

Seeking to make the story line as bloody as possible, the writer modeled the cartoon after the film *300* (2006).

During the battle scenes, the background music consists of a rendition of "Carol of the Bells" by the American metalcore band August Burns Red.

The Golden Compass (2007) is a British-American fantasy adventure film based on Philip Pullman's novel *Northern Lights*, the first in his trilogy titled *His Dark Materials*.

REVIEWS: Scott D. Pierce of *The Salt Lake Tribune* (December 6, 2010): "…If a TV show is funny, that makes up for a lot. Like being crude, stupid, offensive and disturbing. If the show isn't funny—and the Christmas episode of *American Dad* … is not—all you're left with is crude, stupid, offensive and disturbing … includes gay slurs, profanity and jokes about vibrators … somehow mistakes crude for funny."

Tony Nigro of *Common Sense Media* reviewed *American Dad!*: "Like its sister series *Family Guy*, *American Dad* combines edgy humor and fantasy to poke fun at today's contemporary family and, by association, the state of American society.… This is one of those instances in which the show's animated style gives a false impression of its appropriateness for kids. Sexual content, violence, and language push the envelope on acceptability, making it a less-than-ideal choice for tweens and young teens."

PRODUCTION CREDITS—Writer: Erik Durbin. Producers: Erik Sommers and Kara Vallow. Director: Bob Bowen. Production Companies: Fuzzy Door Productions, 20th Century Fox Television, Atlantic Creative, and Underdog Productions. Rating: TV-14. Genres: Animation, Comedy. Country: USA. Run Time: 22 min.

REFERENCES: *American Dad!* Internet Movie Database. http://www.imdb.com/title/tt0397306/

"For Whom the Sleigh Bell Tolls." In *American Dad! Volume 7*. 20th Century Fox Home Entertainment, 2012. DVD Video.

"For Whom the Sleigh Bell Tolls." Internet Movie Database. http://www.imdb.com/title/tt1640758/

Nigro, Tony. *American Dad. Common Sense Media*. https://www.commonsensemedia.org/tv-reviews/american-dad

Pierce, Scott D. "'American Dad' Gives Us a Crude Christmas." *The Salt Lake Tribune*.

http://archive.sltrib.com/story.php?ref=/sltrib/entertainment/50786704-81/santa-american-dad-christmas.html.csp

Fred Claus—November 9, 2007
Feature Film

THREAT TO CHRISTMAS: An efficiency expert wants to shut down Santa's operation.

HOW CHRISTMAS IS SAVED: Santa and his brother Fred overcome sibling rivalry and work together to keep the North Pole afloat.

SYNOPSIS AND COMMENTARY: Even the Claus Brothers can demonstrate sibling rivalry. All his life, a jealous Fred Claus (Vince Vaughn, *The Internship*) has lived in the shadow of his saintly younger brother Nick (Paul Giamatti, *Cinderella Man*), better known as Santa Claus. In spite of the rift between the two brothers, when Fred needs $50,000 to open a gambling facility, he turns to Santa, who offers him a job at the North Pole. There, Fred is assigned the task of examining children's files to determine if they are naughty or nice. Being unconventional, Fred manages to disrupt the elves' work routine and decides that all children should be marked as nice. The chaos that ensues pleases Clyde Northcutt (Kevin Spacey, *The Usual Suspects*), a newly arrived, hard-nosed efficiency expert bent on shutting down Santa and creating a new, more efficient operation at the South Pole that focuses on giving fewer gifts. With Christmas in jeopardy, the Claus brothers must work together to sweeten Clyde's bitter disposition. During a physical altercation between the two brothers, Santa throws his back out and cannot make the Christmas rounds, but Fred, being a Claus, is entitled to fill in, so he dons the red suit (sans beard) and zips away with chief elf Willie (John Michael Higgins, *Yes Man*) and the reindeer. Meanwhile, Santa discovers the reason for Clyde's aversion to Santa and rectifies it with the Superman cape that he had always wanted as a kid. In films like this, the villain's problem almost always dates from a childhood disappointment at Christmastime.

OTHER CAST: Miranda Richardson (*Sleepy Hollow*) as Mrs. Claus; Rachel Weisz (*The Mummy*) as Wanda, Fred's meter-maid girlfriend; Kathy Bates (*Fried Green Tomatoes*) as Mother Claus; Trevor Peacock (*Quartet*) as Papa Claus; Chris "Ludacris" Bridges (*Fast Five*) as elf D.J. Donnie; Elizabeth Banks (*The Hunger Games*) as Charlene, elf Willie's love interest.

INTERESTING TIDBITS: Moments after his birth, baby Nick utters, "Ho Ho!" The third "Ho" would come later.

Santa's domain at the North Pole is a sprawling city with a gigantic workshop that sports an ornate dome like a basilica. The toys are made in factory assembly-line fashion, primarily by elves who are ethnically diverse. Computer technology shortened the heights of the elf-actors, particularly John Michael Higgins and Chris "Ludacris" Bridges .

Three elves parody members of the U.S. government's Secret Service. Wearing dark suits, sunglasses, and wireless headset microphones, they keep constant vigil over Santa and are quick to jump Fred if they perceive his movements as "threatening" to Santa.

Making cameo appearances as themselves during a group session of Siblings Anonymous with Fred are Frank Stallone, younger brother of Sylvester Stallone; Roger Clinton, Jr., younger half-brother of former U.S. President Bill Clinton; and Stephen Baldwin, the youngest brother of actors Alec, Daniel, and William Baldwin.

The film earned about $72 million in lifetime domestic box office sales and nearly $26 million in foreign sales for a total of nearly $98 million worldwide.

REVIEWS: According to the Rotten Tomatoes film review site, 21 percent of critics gave this film a positive review. Metacritic gave it a score of 42/100 (mixed/average reviews).

Tom Keogh of *The Seattle Times* (November 9, 2007): "Vaughn gets plenty of mileage exploring both the painful and fun sides of Fred…. The sight of him leading a few hundred elves in a groovy dance is reason enough to see the movie…"

Wesley Morris of *The Boston Globe* (November 9, 2007): "Vaughn's crude stylings are mercifully intact. More than ever, he resembles a giant, hungover, vaguely bloated Tony Curtis, and he still talks with an auctioneer's velocity. But his naughtiness has never seemed so approachably nice."

Sandie Angulo Chen of *Common Sense Media* (November 23, 2008): [This film] features a top-notch cast, slapstick gags, and plenty of North Pole Mayhem. Most of the film's humor comes from Vaughn in improv mode. His lightning-paced delivery is always a treat ... by the time 'Silent Night' starts playing, even the Grinchiest viewer will feel a slight tug on the heartstrings."

Jack Mathews of the *New York Daily News* (November 9, 2007): "The story's fantasy hook is so illogical, no amount of suspended disbelief can accommodate it. Even true believers in Santa—i.e., toddlers—will find it a stretch that Santa is on somebody's payroll and is subject to disciplinary action."

PRODUCTION CREDITS—Story: Dan Fogelman and Jessie Nelson. Screenplay: Dan Fogelman. Producers: David Dobkin, Joel Silver, and Jessie Nelson. Director: David Dobkin. Production Companies: Warner Bros. Pictures, Silver Pictures, David Dobkin Productions, and Jessie Nelson Productions. Rating: PG (mild language and some rude humor). Genres: Comedy, Family, Fantasy. Country: USA. Run Time: 116 min.

REFERENCES: Chen, Sandie Angulo. *Fred Claus. Common Sense Media.* https://www.commonsensemedia.org/movie-reviews/fred-claus

Crump, William D. *The Christmas Encyclopedia.* Third Edition. Jefferson, NC: McFarland, 2013.

Fred Claus. Box Office Mojo. http://www.boxofficemojo.com/movies/?id=fredclaus.htm

Fred Claus. Burbank, CA: Warner Home Video, 2008. DVD Video.

Fred Claus. Internet Movie Database. http://www.imdb.com/title/tt0486583/

Fred Claus. Metacritic. http://www.metacritic.com/movie/fred-claus

Fred Claus. Rotten Tomatoes. http://www.rottentomatoes.com/m/1175076-fred_claus/

Keogh, Tom. "Vaughn Takes 'Claus' for a Slay Ride." *The Seattle Times.* http://www.

Despite their sibling rivalry, Santa Claus (Paul Giamatti, left) and his older brother Fred (Vince Vaughn) manage to sit down together for a holiday meal in *Fred Claus* (2007) (Warner Bros./Photofest).

seattletimes.com/entertainment/vaughn-takes-claus-for-a-slay-ride/

Mathews, Jack. "No Ho-Ho-Ho at This North Pole." New York Daily News. http://www.nydailynews.com/entertainment/tv-movies/no-ho-ho-ho-north-pole-article-1.257573

Morris, Wesley. "Sweet and Seasonal, 'Fred' Makes Naughty and Nice." *The Boston Globe*. http://www.boston.com/ae/movies/articles/2007/11/09/sweet_and_seasonal_fred_makes_naughty_and_nice/

A Freezerburnt Christmas—1997

Animated Television Short Film

THREAT TO CHRISTMAS: An evil toy tycoon grounds Santa's reindeer on Christmas Eve.

HOW CHRISTMAS IS SAVED: Santa delivers his presents in an ice cream truck pulled by arctic animals.

SYNOPSIS AND COMMENTARY: This film using clay puppets in stop-motion animation should have been subtitled *The Fudgesicle That Saved Christmas*. Weary of Santa's giving away free toys every Christmas, his nemesis, the evil toy tycoon Sualc Atnas ("Santa Claus" spelled backwards) launches a plot to put Santa out of business. Ransacking the home of Professor Crenshaw, Atnas's goons steal a heavy gravity formula that will neutralize Santa's magic flying dust and keep Santa's reindeer grounded. When Freezerburn, a hapless ice cream vendor, learns of the plot, he drives to the North Pole in his ice cream truck, along with pet penguin Chill and Anna, Crenshaw's niece, with whom Freezerburn is smitten (his eyes bug out, tongue lolls, the usual signs). Although they warn Santa, Atnas and company have already put their moves on the reindeer and have trashed Santa's sleigh. Anointed with some magic flying dust, Chill flies to summon other arctic animals who hitch themselves to Freezerburn's truck, and Santa and the gang take off with Atnas and company in pursuit, the latter having swiped some magic dust. An aerial "battle" of sorts commences, with Anna and Freezerburn raining fudgesicles on Atnas and goons while Santa's toy planes buzz them. Just as Atnas shoots a cloud of heavy gravity mist, a member pulling the truck sneezes, the cloud bounces back, Atnas and goons drop like a rock, and Santa continues his rounds, exclaiming, "Let's kick some Christmas butt!"

PRINCIPAL VOICES: Chris Parnell (*21 Jump Street*) as Freezerburn; Horatio Sanz (*The Dictator*) as Gus the narrator; Darrell Hammond (*Epic Movie*) as Atnas.

INTERESTING TIDBITS: Atnas remarkably resembles the late Soviet dictator Joseph Stalin.

The principal voice actors are all members of *Saturday Night Live*.

An Atnas character is also the villain in ***The Boy Who Saved Christmas***.

PRODUCTION CREDITS—Writer and Director: Michael Bannon. Producers: Mark Bannon and Michael Bosze. Production Company: Wreckless Abandon Studios. Rating: Not rated. Genres: Animation, Family. Country: USA. Run Time: 22 min.

REFERENCES: *A Freezerburnt Christmas*. Internet Movie Database. http://www.imdb.com/title/tt2393697/

A Freezerburnt Christmas. Santa Monica, CA: MGM Home Entertainment, 2001. DVD Video.

Wilson, Joanna. *Tis the Season TV: The Encyclopedia of Christmas-Themed Episodes, Specials and Made-for-TV Movies*. Akron, OH: 1701 Press, 2011.

Gekko Saves Christmas—December 4, 2015

Episode Segment from the Computer-Animated Television Series

PJ Masks

THREAT TO CHRISTMAS: Luna Girl covertly steals people's presents all over town.

HOW CHRISTMAS IS SAVED: It's up to Gekko and the other PJ Masks to stop Luna Girl.

SYNOPSIS AND COMMENTARY: By day, Greg, Connor, and bespectacled Amaya are just three ordinary elementary school kids learning their three Rs, but by night when crises arise, they don their PJs (pajamas), activate their amulets, and respectively become Gekko, Catboy, and Owlette, masked, crime-fighting superheroes known as the "PJ Masks." Though endowed with various superpowers not unlike those of Superman and Batman, ironically they're still too young to drink and vote. Gekko's green costume resembles a gecko; Catboy's blue costume sports cat's ears; and Owlette's red costume sans glasses comes equipped with a cape that can morph into wings. Their nocturnal nemeses are the mad scientist Romeo; Luna Girl, who flies on a luna board; and Night Ninja, whose minions are the Ninjalinos.

An ongoing preschool series of 24-minute episodes (two segments per episode) that premiered on Disney Junior in 2015, *PJ Masks* is the English-language version of *Les Pyjamasques*, the French TV version of the series, which in turn is based on a children's picturebook series of the same title by French author Romuald Racioppo.

It's Christmas Eve. Though Greg is a bit embarrassed because he's never learned to ice-skate like Amaya and Connor, it's moot when the three realize that all the town's decorations are missing. Most superheroes would launch an immediate search for the culprit, but the three must wait until nightfall when, as the PJ Masks, they zip to their headquarters (which resembles a totem pole) and search the city in their owl glider. Using her special night vision, Owlette discovers Luna Girl on her luna board pulling a reverse-Santa routine as she uses her telekinetic luna magnet to steal presents from homes through chimneys and deposit them in a sack carried by two swarms of moths. The bulk of the story consists of a battle between good and corrupt superpowers as the PJ Masks chase Luna Girl all over the city while attempting to capture her luna board. As with ice-skating, Gekko has no experience with a luna board, but time and again, though he doubts himself, he's forced to *try* in order to keep his pals from harm. As expected, the Masks finally restrain Luna Girl, who relates a sob-story that she's all alone, whereupon the do-gooder Masks invite her to spend Christmas with them as they all return the presents down the chimneys and restore the town's decorations.

PRINCIPAL VOICES: Jacob Ewaniuk (*Chirp*) as Connor; Kyle Harrison Breitkopf (*Parental Guidance*) as Greg; Addison Holley (*Annedroids*) as Amaya; Brianna Daguanno (*Chirp*) as Luna Girl.

AWARDS: In 2015, the *PJ Masks* series won a Joey Award, Vancouver, for Best Male Voiceover Performance Age 11–13 years (Alex Thorne); it received a Joey Award, Vancouver, nomination for Best Young Ensemble In a Voiceover Performance.

INTERESTING TIDBIT: This episode segment imparts the following "Hero Revelation" to preschool viewers: You won't know if you're able to do something unless you *try*. Keep trying.

NOTE: At the time of this writing, this episode segment was not available on DVD or VHS but could be seen on YouTube.

REVIEW: Emily Ashby of *Common Sense Media* reviewed the TV series: "…these three cuties are the first to fight bad guys in their jammies and at the tender age of 5 … [the series] has generally empowering messages for preschoolers and never misses an opportunity to teach a lesson about friendship and cooperation that's easily applicable to kids' experiences."

PRODUCTION CREDITS—Writer: Justine Cheynet. Producers: Guillaume Hellouin and Corrine Kouper. Director: Christian De Vita. Production Companies: Entertainment One, Frog Box, and Team TO. Rating: Not rated. Genre: Animation. Country: France. Run Time: 12 min.

REFERENCES: Ashby, Emily. *PJ Masks. Common Sense Media*. https://www.commonsensemedia.org/tv-reviews/pj-masks

PJ Masks. Internet Movie Database. http://www.imdb.com/title/tt4148744/

Get Santa—December 12, 2014

Feature Film

THREAT TO CHRISTMAS: Santa crashes his sleigh, loses his reindeer, and lands in prison.

HOW CHRISTMAS IS SAVED: Santa solicits help from a parolee and his young son.

SYNOPSIS AND COMMENTARY: While test-driving his new sleigh, Santa (Jim Broadbent, *Cloud Atlas*), more formally known as Father Christmas in the United Kingdom, crashes in London and is thrown in prison for attempting to rescue his impounded reindeer. There, his penchant for making toys for the inmates' children and his mistaking "Sally" (Warwick Davis,

Harry Potter), a dwarf inmate, for an elf prompt the authorities to dismiss him as a delusional old crock, much like *Miracle on 34th Street*. Santa's only hope for escape lies with Steve (Rafe Spall, *Prometheus*), a recent parolee and Santa skeptic, who just wants to reconnect with his estranged young son Tom (Kit Connor, *Mr. Holmes*). Led by reindeer Dasher, who "communicates" through flatulence, father and son find the wrecked sleigh and from there proceed to a rural tower that serves as a magic, emergency portal back to Santa's abode in Lapland, an area with reindeer aplenty in the Arctic Circle that spreads across Finland, Sweden, Norway, and Russia. There in glorious Elf Village, wizened elves provide Steve and Tom with everything necessary to liberate Santa: his original sleigh with one decrepit reindeer and magic dust to fly to the prison; a squirrel that will round up the other *six* reindeer aside from Dasher; keys to unlock all doors; and, instead of assault weapons, a device for shooting reindeer poop pellets at police cars during extended chase scenes.

INTERESTING TIDBITS: Note that after Tom writes a letter to Santa, instead of mailing it, he places it in the fireplace where, in this instance, it is whisked up the chimney and out to Santa. According to strict British tradition, children throw their letters into the fire, for it is believed that Father Christmas will favor those letters that burn quickly; otherwise they must be rewritten. That Father Christmas resides in Lapland is more of a Finnish tradition, yet of the more than 500,000 letters received annually by the Santa Claus Post Office near the city of Rovaniemi in Finnish Lapland, about one-fifth are from British children.

While expounding upon his personal history to the prison barber (Stephen Graham), Santa mentions that he was born in the Laughing Valley of Ho Ha Ho and was inspired to make toys for children at Christmastime when an old wood-cutter showed him all the poverty in the world. These statements are allusions to events found in *The Life and Adventures of Santa Claus* (1902), a children's novel by L. Frank Baum, who also wrote *The Wonderful Wizard of Oz*.

Santa's escape through a tunnel in the prison wall that "Sally" had dug over time and had covered with a nude picture is a nod to *The Shawshank Redemption* (1994).

Similar scenes with dog flatulence grace **Beethoven's Christmas Adventure**, for those who are interested.

REVIEWS: According to the Rotten Tomatoes film review site, 76 percent of critics gave this production a positive review. Metacritic gave it a score of 52/100 (mixed/average).

Charles Gant of *Variety* (December 17, 2014): "Overall, there's as much for adults to enjoy as kids, although the latter will probably be the only ones to appreciate the farting reindeer and the poop pellets fired at cop cars in pursuit."

Trevor Johnston of *Time Out London* (December 1, 2014): "…there's enough sly wit in the margins to engage the grown-ups and the whole thing conveys Christmas cheer without being overly cynical."

Tim Robey of *The Telegraph* (December 5, 2014): "Jim Broadbent gets the balance of jollity and melancholy just right as Santa."

Mark Kermode of *The Guardian* (December 6, 2014): "Former horror maestro Christopher Smith, who made his name with *Severance*, *Triangle* and *Black Death*, goes in search of his inner child with this moderately likable Christmas romp."

PRODUCTION CREDITS—Writer and Director: Christopher Smith. Producer: Liza Marshall. Production Companies: Scott Free Productions, British Film Institute, Screen Yorkshire, and Ingenious Media. Rating: PG (mild rude humor and language). Genres: Comedy, Family. Countries: United Kingdom and USA. Run Time: 102 min.

REFERENCES: Blackhurst, Rob. "Who Answers All the Letters Sent to Father Christmas?" *The Telegraph* (December 5, 2013). http://www.telegraph.co.uk/topics/christmas/10494193/Who-answers-all-the-letters-sent-to-Father-Christmas.html

Gant, Charles. Get Santa. *Variety*. http://variety.com/2014/film/reviews/film-review-get-santa-1201375759/#

Get Santa. Internet Movie Database Web Site. http://www.imdb.com/title/tt1935940/

Get Santa. Metacritic Web Site. http://www.metacritic.com/movie/get-santa

Get Santa. Rotten Tomatoes Web Site. http://www.rottentomtoes.com/m/Get_Santa/

Get Santa. Santa Monica, CA: Lionsgate, 2015. DVD Video.

Johnston, Trevor. *Get Santa. Time Out London.* http://www.timeout.com/london/film/get-santa

Kermode, Mark. "*Get Santa* Review—Sweet-Natured Seasonal Fare." http://www.theguardian.com/film/2014/dec/07/get-santa-review-jim-broadbent-rafe-spall

Robey, Jim. "*Get Santa*, Review: 'Surprisingly Characterful.'" *The Telegraph.* http://www.telegraph.co.uk/culture/film/filmreviews/11272443/Get-Santa-review-surprisingly-characterful.html

The Gift—2002

Direct-to-Video Musical from the Computer-Animated Series
Kingdom Under the Sea

THREAT TO CHRISTMAS: The kingdom residents forget what Christmas really means, and Professor Pinch ruins the kingdom's tree-lighting ceremony.

HOW CHRISTMAS IS SAVED: Realizing that Christmas is not all about presents and decorations, Mayor Finley restores the true meaning of Christmas to the kingdom with the biblical account of the birth of Jesus.

SYNOPSIS AND COMMENTARY: *Kingdom* is a series of videos that helps children learn basic Christian concepts such as faith, salvation, trust, and forgiveness. With the exception of narrator Wally Walrus, the characters consist primarily of talking fish and crustaceans who live in a kingdom on the ocean floor. The protagonists are the Finleys, a family of fish: Mayor Finley and his wife; their two children Splash and Coral; Grandpa; and their pet Slugger, a slug that acts and barks like a dog. Then there's Sharky, the small business shark with a lust for cash; Splash's best friend Tommy; and the Plankton, who serve the kingdom in various ways. The chief villains are Professor Pinch, a lobster with a German accent bent on delivering misery to the kingdom because he despises its clean-living residents; and the small crustacean Clawed (a play on "Claude"), Pinch's sidekick and spy.

It's Christmas Eve in the kingdom as all the residents are caught up in a frenzy of holiday commercialism. Splash and Coral sing a lengthy number about all the "stuff" they hope to get, Sharky declares that Christmas is all about sales, while Mayor Finley expounds on the virtues of shopping and decorating. In a parody of the Nativity, Toby and Gracie are newly arrived turtles who seek shelter at the local inn, because Gracie's egg is about to hatch. Yet when there is no vacancy, Gracie expresses her faith in God through song, after which Splash finds them and brings them to his family's house for Christmas. Meanwhile, as the Plankton haul a Christmas tree to the town square, Pinch and Clawed carry out their plan to ruin the upcoming tree-lighting ceremony at high-tide by boring through the earth to the decorated tree and cutting it down. So what does Christmas mean without a tree, presents, and decorations? No one seems to know, until the mayor reminds everyone that he and they had forgotten what Christmas is really about, then he relates the biblical story of the birth of Jesus and states that Jesus was God's first Christmas gift to mankind. Therefore, Christmas is about giving, not getting. And speaking of giving, after the little turtle hatches, the kingdom provides a home for him and his parents.

PRINCIPAL VOICES: Jonathan Abel (*Geronimo*) as Wally; Eric Shawkey (*Greener Mountains*) as Splash; Dick Baniszewski (*Spies, Lies and the Superbomb*) as Sharky, Mayor Finley, Pinch, and Tommy; Maggie Hunts (*Ark*) as Mom Finley and Mrs. Fishburn; Stephanie Likes (*Jolene*) as Coral; Chris Daly (*Icarus Descending*) as Grandpa, Toby, and Mr. Fishburn; Curt Anthon (*Anastasia*) as Plankton leader and starfish; Ali Stelzer (*The Gift*) as Clawed and Gracie.

SONGS: Music by Scott B. Seymann. "Stuff!" lyrics by Scott B. Seymann, Michelle Bizzarro, Martha Gold, and Marc Reilly, performed by Stephanie Likes and Teddy Overton; "Shop, Shop, Shop" lyrics by Scott B. Seymann, performed by Dick Baniszewski; "Faith (Gracie's Song)" lyrics by Tim Owens, performed by Stephanie Bianchi and Dunamis; "Faith" and "It's All About" lyrics by Tim Owens, performed by Dunamis.

INTERESTING TIDBITS: Clawed is an Igor-like character whose appearance and "Yes, master!" vocalizations are a parody of actor Peter Lorre.

As the exhausted Plankton pull the tree, one of their number with a Scottish accent informs the leader, "But Captain, I cannah go another step!" This is a nod to the original *Star Trek* series with engineering officer Scotty and Captain Kirk. Another save-Christmas film with a similar scenario is ***Gotta Catch Santa Claus***.

REVIEW: Donna Rolfe of The Dove Foundation: "This colorful animated story will remind everyone, young and old alike, about the true reason we celebrate Christmas. It is a fun entertaining movie for the entire family. Dove proudly awards the Dove "Family-Approved" Seal to this DVD."

PRODUCTION CREDITS—Story: Stacie Ghali, Martha Gold, and Marc Reilly. Producers and Directors: Michelle Bizzarro and Stephen Reid. Production Company: Alpha Omega Publications. Rating: Not rated. Genres: Adventure, Animation, Children, Short Films. Country: USA. Run Time: 25 min.

REFERENCES: *Kingdom Under the Sea: The Gift*. Chandler, AZ: Alpha Omega Publications, 2002. DVD Video.

Kingdom Under the Sea: The Series. Christian Film Database. http://www.christianfilmdatabase.com/review/kingdom-under-the-sea-the-series/#

Kingdom Under the Sea. Web Site. http://www.kingdomunderthesea.com/index/php

Rolfe, Donna. *Kingdom Under the Sea: The Gift*. The Dove Foundation. http://www.dove.org/review/7718-kingdom-under-the-sea-the-gift/

The Glo Friends Save Christmas—December 1985

Animated Television Musical

THREAT TO CHRISTMAS: A jealous witch kidnaps and imprisons Santa and his reindeer in an ice cage.

HOW CHRISTMAS IS SAVED: It's up to the Glo Friends to join together to foil the witch and melt the cage.

SYNOPSIS AND COMMENTARY: In 1982, Hasbro Toys introduced "Glo Friends," a line of small, glow-in-the-dark toys in the shapes of insects and other small creatures, including the Glo Worm. That toy line spawned a television Christmas special, followed by a short-lived, animated television series of 26 segments titled *The Glo Friends* that aired for one season, commencing in 1986 as part of the *My Little Pony and Friends* series.

In *Christmas*, Blanche, the wicked witch of the North Pole, is jealous of Santa's worldwide fame and decides to create her own fame by being "the witch who stopped Christmas." As Santa begins his rounds with the reindeer team on Christmas Eve, Blanche zaps them into an ice cage in a raging river and initially prevents the Glo Friends from taking action by whisking them far away into a scary forest. There, a cluster of Blanche's magic flowers trap some of them, but their cohorts soon arrive along with Moose, Blanche's former steed, and release them (by the way, Moose, who wants no part of Blanche's misdeeds, is just that ... a lumbering moose, not a horse). Moose leads the Glo Friends to Santa's location and, after braving the turbulent river, deposits them onto the ice, where they join hands in a circle around the ice cage to melt it with their glowing bodies. Blanche attempts one last-ditch effort to crash the scene, but she falls into the river and is swept downstream. Now free, a grateful Santa invites Moose (who had always wanted to be a reindeer) to lead his team as the Glo Friends light the way in the spirit of Rudolph.

PRINCIPAL VOICES: Carroll O'Connor (*All in the Family*) as Santa; Sally Struthers (*All in the Family*) as Blanche; Charlie Adler (*Aladdin*) as Blanche's fox-scarf; Lorenzo Music (*Garfield and Friends*) as Moose.

SONGS: "Say Goodbye to Christmas"; "I've Got the Blues"; "It's Time to Be Brave"; "Everybody Glo." Music and lyrics respectively by Tommy Goodman and Barry Harman.

INTERESTING TIDBITS: When Blanche expresses a desire to take revenge on Santa for being famous, Moose voices a typically secular sentiment about Christmas: "Santa brings joy to the whole world every year. Without Santa, there wouldn't even *be* a Christmas!" The Glo Friends voice a similar opinion when, after Santa's rescue, they exclaim, "We almost lost you, Santa, and we almost lost Christmas." Santa, though, has a more realistic take on the matter: "Oh, no. As long as the spirit of Christmas glows within our hearts, it can never be stopped." Of course, no religious sentiment is intended.

Other save-Christmas films in which Santa is kidnapped include *The Boy Who Saved Christmas; The Elf and the Magic Key; The Great Santa Claus Switch; The Librarians and Santa's Midnight Run; Santa Claus Conquers the Martians; Sonic Christmas Blast; Spinach Greetings; Tim Burton's The Nightmare Before Christmas*; and *Who Stole Santa?*

PRODUCTION CREDITS—Writer: George Arthur Bloom. Producer: Mike Joens. Supervising Director: Terry Lennon. Production Companies: Sunbow Productions, Marvel Productions, and Hasbro. Rating: Not rated. Genres: Animation, Family. Country: USA. Run Time: 23 min.

REFERENCES: *The Glo Friends Save Christmas*. Big Cartoon Database. http://www,bcdb.com/cartoon/55076-Glo-Friends-Save-Christmas

The Glo Friends Save Christmas. Internet Movie Database. http://www.imdb.com/title/tt0225829/

The Glo Friends Save Christmas. Stamford, CT: Children's Video Library, 1986. VHS Video.

Lenburg, Jeff. *The Encyclopedia of Animated Cartoons*. Third Edition. New York: Facts on File, 2009.

Wilson, Joanna. *Tis the Season TV: The Encyclopedia of Christmas-Themed Episodes, Specials and Made-for-TV Movies*. Akron, OH: 1701 Press, 2011.

Gotta Catch Santa Claus—December 11, 2008

Computer-Animated Television Movie

THREAT TO CHRISTMAS: An ice monster from space with a grudge against Santa is bent on capturing him.

HOW CHRISTMAS IS SAVED: Santa gives the monster the gift he's always wanted, which settles the matter.

SYNOPSIS AND COMMENTARY: When tween Trevor learns on Christmas Eve that his friend Veronica is a Santa skeptic, Trevor sets out to catch the old gent to prove that he's the real deal. Together with his two nerdy black friends, twins Errol and Gabriel, Trevor rigs a laser to his parents' telescope in their observatory and shoots Santa out of his sleigh during his rounds. Santa parachutes down and lands in Trevor's basement, where he's trapped in a cage but manages to free himself with a chainsaw from his sack. Meanwhile, a longstanding grudge against Santa compels the ice monster LeFreeze and his trio of snowmen goons to leave their comet in space and zoom to Earth to capture Santa. After freezing most of Trevor's town, LeFreeze and minions engage in a snowball "battle" with Santa, backed by Trevor and friends, but when nothing comes of that, LeFreeze captures Veronica as a hostage. Santa settles the feud by giving LeFreeze what he's always wanted but never got: a little teddy bear, which does the trick, and LeFreeze becomes as docile as a lamb. And to mollify the snowmen goons, Santa has carrot noses for them.

PRINCIPAL VOICES: Cory Doran (*Jimmy Two-Shoes*) as Trevor; Lisa Lennox (*The Doodlebops*) as Veronica; William Shatner (*Star Trek*) as Santa; Nathan Stephenson (*Skyrunners*) as Errol and Gabriel; Sweeney MacArthur (*The Tracker*) as Barky Elf; Kristina Nicoll (*Pompeii*) as Mrs. Claus; Cathal J. Dodd (*X-Men*) as LeFreeze.

INTERESTING TIDBITS: The film gives a nod to the original *Star Trek* series that starred William Shatner as Captain James Kirk: Barky, Santa's chief elf, speaks with a Scottish accent (similar to that of engineering officer Mr. Scott, "Scotty," played by James Doohan in the series) and refers to Santa as "Captain." Another save-Christmas film with a similar scenario is *The Gift*.

Whereas most Santa films depict Mrs.

Claus as equally rotund as her husband, in this film, she is skinny and quite sexy.

Several famous, fictitious places also receive mention as nods to their respective films or TV series: Bedford Falls (*It's a Wonderful Life*), Walton's Mountain (*The Waltons*), Avonlea (*Anne of Green Gables*), and Meisterburger Village (*Santa Claus Is Comin' to Town*).

REVIEWS: Sierra Filucci of *Common Sense Media* (October 12, 2009): "A mix of messages. The primary one is that science isn't always right and magic has an important place in childhood … less positive are the confusing messages about junk food (Santa eats tons of donuts…), women (Mrs. Claus … wears skin-tight clothes while cavorting provocatively), and friendship (Trevor locks [Veronica] in a shed when she tries to get in his way)."

Erich Asperschlager of *DVD Verdict* (October 13, 2009): "…the first [special] I've seen to tackle the philosophical and theological questions Santa's yearly journey raises. Is it better to believe in something you've never seen than to have undeniable proof? Does cold calculation trump the certainty of the heart? … the whole thing gets hijacked by the unnecessary inclusion of an ice beast from space … by the time [the film] reaches its climactic conclusion, all of the interesting questions raised in the first half are long since forgotten … harmless holiday fun."

PRODUCTION CREDITS—Writer: Steven E. de Souza. Producer: Jamie Waese. Directors: Jin Choi, Peter Lepeniotis, and Jamie Waese. Production Companies: Enemes, Cookie Jar Entertainment, and Gotta Catch Santa Productions. Rating: Not rated. Genres: Animation, Fantasy. Countries: Canada and USA. Run Time: 66 min.

REFERENCES: Asperschlager, Erich. *Gotta Catch Santa Claus. DVD Verdict.* http://www.dvdverdict.com/reviews/gottacatchsanta.php

Filucci, Sierra. *Gotta Catch Santa Claus. Common Sense Media.* https://www.commonsensemedia.org/movie-reviews/gotta-catch-santa-claus

Gotta Catch Santa Claus. Internet Movie Database. http://www.imdb.com/title/tt1312972/

Gotta Catch Santa Claus. Santa Monica, CA: Lionsgate, 2007. DVD Video.

Poster art for *Gotta Catch Santa Claus* (2008), showing Santa fleeing from (top to bottom) LeFreeze the ice monster and Veronica with a net on the shoulders of Trevor (ABC Family/Photofest).

Wilson, Joanna. *Tis the Season TV: The Encyclopedia of Christmas-Themed Episodes, Specials and Made-for-TV Movies*. Akron, OH: 1701 Press, 2011.

Grandma Got Run Over by a Reindeer—October 31, 2000

Television/Video Animated Musical

THREAT TO CHRISTMAS: Santa stands trial for hit-and-run and kidnapping Grandma.

HOW CHRISTMAS IS SAVED: Young grandson Jake exposes his Cousin Mel as the culprit who framed Santa.

SYNOPSIS AND COMMENTARY: Spiked with the right ingredients, the proverbial and dreaded Christmas fruitcake can become "reindeernip," similar to catnip, with untoward consequences. When Grandma Spankenheimer refuses to sell her shop to wealthy land developer Austin Bucks, her greedy granddaughter, Cousin Mel, plots to take over the shop and spikes Grandma's famous fruitcakes with a disgusting brew. Her rationale: the awful fruitcakes will drive Grandma's customers away and she'll be forced to sell. But as Grandma heads out on Christmas Eve to deliver her goodies, the heavy fruitcake aroma overpowers Santa's team flying overhead, and they run her down. Grandma only suffers amnesia, whereupon Santa, after leaving a note at the scene (which Cousin Mel swipes), carries her back to the North Pole to recuperate, and her family soon reports her as missing. With Grandma out of her way, Cousin Mel puts pressure on befuddled Grandpa to become his power of attorney. The deal with Bucks is nearly set, until young Jake learns of his Grandma's whereabouts; following a trip to the North Pole, courtesy of elf Quincy, Jake returns with Grandma and Santa to the city. When Grandma disappears again, courtesy of Cousin Mel, Santa is charged with kidnapping as well as hit-and-run and is placed on trial, which smacks of *Miracle on 34th Street*. Jake and Quincy track down Grandma, who returns to her store and regains her memory when she eats her untainted fruitcake, then it's a rush to the court to exonerate Santa, at which time Cousin Mel confesses to her crimes. As Santa heads back to the North Pole, Grandma accidentally diddles with the tainted fruitcake, whereupon the reindeer, overpowered again, swoop down for a second hit.

PRINCIPAL VOICES: Elmo Shropshire (*One Hit Wonderland*) as the narrator/Grandpa; Sue Blu (*Finding Nemo*) as Grandma; Alex Doduk (*Brain Powered*) as Jake; Michele Lee (*Knots Landing*) as Cousin Mel; Jim Staahl (*Bobby's World*) as Santa; Cam Clarke (*Hotel Transylvania*) as Austin Bucks.

SONGS: "Grandma Got Run Over by a Reindeer" by Randy Brooks, performed by Gary Chase; "Feels Like Christmas" by Pam Wendell and Elmo Shropshire, performed by Gary Chase; "Grandpa's Gonna Sue the Pants Off Santa" by Rita Abrams, Elmo Shropshire, and Jon Gauger, performed by Michelle Lee; "Grandma's Spending Christmas with the Superstars" by Rita Abrams and Elmo Shropshire, performed by Gary Chase; "Grandma's Killer Fruitcake" by Rita Abrams and Elmo Shropshire, performed by Gary Chase.

INTERESTING TIDBITS: This film is loosely based on Randy Brooks's novelty song of the same title that became a holiday favorite with the recording by the former husband-and-wife singing group Elmo & Patsy (Dr. Elmo Shropshire, a former veterinarian, and Patsy Trigg). The song was first released in 1979 on their label, Oink Records.

Crazy end-credits include the following: "No reindeer were harmed during the production of this motion picture"; "Santa Claus performed all of his own stunts"; and "The portrayal of fruitcake represented in this story is not necessarily the opinion of the producers."

REVIEWS: Jerry Beck of *Animation World Network* (November 23, 2001): "There are echoes of *It's a Wonderful Life* and *Miracle on 34th Street* ... and lots of good old-fashioned American values intertwined into the plot. None of this is very original.... But small kids, the ones who know Santa is real, should enjoy all the goings on just fine."

Erick Harper of *DVD Verdict* (December 12, 2001): "It takes a lot of padding to turn a three-minute song into an hour-long cartoon, and it shows ... a storyline that is unbelievable and unoriginal ... the additional songs ... lack any sort of punch or humor ... the apparent need to shoehorn every last detail from the song into odd places in the movie ... the quality of the animation ... is all fairly crudely done ... flat and unimaginative..."

PRODUCTION CREDITS—Story: Fred A. Rappoport, Elmo Shropshire, Jim Fisher, and Jim Staahl. Screenplay: Jim Fisher and Jim Staahl. Producers: Noel Roman, Jim Fisher, and Jim Staahl. Director: Phil Roman. Production Companies: The Fred Rappoport Company and Phil Roman Entertainment. Rating: G. Genres: Animation, Comedy, Family. Countries: Canada and USA. Run Time: 51 min.

REFERENCES: Beck, Jerry. *Grandma Got Run Over by a Reindeer*. Animation World Network. http://www.awn.com/animationworld/dvd-review-robbie-reindeer-and-grandma-got-run-over-reindeer

Crump, William D. *The Christmas Encyclopedia*. Third Edition. Jefferson, NC: McFarland, 2013.

Grandma Got Run Over by a Reindeer. Big Cartoon Database. http://www.bcdb.com/cartoon/55348-Grandma-Got-Run-Over-By-A-Reindeer

Grandma Got Run Over by a Reindeer. Burbank, CA: Warner Home Video, 2001. DVD Video.

Grandma Got Run Over by a Reindeer. Internet Movie Database. http://www.imdb.com/title/tt0267536/

Harper, Erick. *Grandma Got Run Over by a Reindeer*. DVD Verdict. http://www.dvdverdict.com/reviews/grandmareindeer.php

Lenburg, Jeff. *The Encyclopedia of Animated Cartoons*. Third Edition. New York: Facts on File, 2009.

Wilson, Joanna. *Tis the Season TV: The Encyclopedia of Christmas-Themed Episodes, Specials and Made-for-TV Movies*. Akron, OH: 1701 Press, 2011.

The Great Santa Claus Switch—
December 20, 1970

Television Special Musical Episode from *The Ed Sullivan Show*

THREAT TO CHRISTMAS: Cosmo Scam impersonates Santa and kidnaps him in order to burglarize homes.

HOW CHRISTMAS IS SAVED: Fred the elf is instrumental in foiling Scam's scam.

SYNOPSIS AND COMMENTARY: Originally known as *Toast of the Town* and hosted by New York entertainment columnist Ed Sullivan, the highly popular, hour-long television variety show that later bore his name ran for 1,068 episodes on CBS from 1948 to 1971. In appreciation for the Muppets' nearly two-dozen appearances on his show, Sullivan granted their creator Jim Henson a full time-slot for a Christmas musical.

Reading to a group of children, Ed Sullivan narrates this story that stars Art Carney (*The Honeymooners*) in dual roles as Santa and as his nemesis, Cosmo Scam, an evil, cigar-smoking magician who lives in a secret cave beneath the North Pole with assorted monsters known as Frackles (portrayed by the Muppets). Impersonating Santa with intent on using his benign physiognomy as a free ticket to burglarize homes, Scam kidnaps Santa, tosses him into a dungeon, then takes his place in his workshop. As each of the elves (more Muppets) discover the ruse, Scam kidnaps them one by one to his dungeon and replaces them with Frackles in elf costumes. In a separate cell, Santa is most kind to his two huge, lumbering guards and gives them desirable Christmas presents, then wins them over by waxing philosophical in song about the goodness and magic of Christmas. Meanwhile in another cell, the elves, disguised as rocks, escape past their guards, but Scam recaptures them. Only Fred, the youngest elf, evades capture and, finding the key to Santa's cell, releases his boss. Then it's a race to prevent Scam from heading out in the sleigh at midnight on Christmas Eve, which Fred accomplishes by disconnecting the reindeer harness. As Christmas arrives at midnight, Santa spreads Christmas spirit to all the Frackles and Scam becomes powerless, yet the ever-benevolent Santa still has special gifts for them all.

SONGS: Lyrics and music respectively by Jerry Juhl and Joe Raposo. "We're Happy Little Christmas Elves"; "I Want to Help"; "It's Christmas Time"; "Rock Music."

The Great Santa Claus Switch

In a special presentation of *The Ed Sullivan Show*, Art Carney portrays Santa in *The Great Santa Claus Switch* (1970) and also portrays Santa's nemesis, the cigar-smoking Cosmo Scam, as shown here. Cosmo kidnaps Santa and switches places with him in order to burglarize homes. The Muppets are also featured. CBS/MMG Photo Archives (collection of William D. Crump).

1963, this production was initially titled *The Witch Who Stole Santa Claus* and later *The Sinister Santa Claus Switch*. To aid his pitch to TV executives, Henson created a series of watercolor sketches of Frackles that accompanied his written proposal. Nevertheless, several more years elapsed before the project got the attention of Ed Sullivan.

The Muppet that later would become Gonzo on *The Muppet Show* made his first appearance in this production. Here, he is known as Snarl.

Other save-Christmas films in which Santa is kidnapped include ***The Boy Who Saved Christmas; The Elf and the Magic Key; The Glo Friends Save Christmas; The Librarians and Santa's Midnight Run; Santa Claus Conquers the Martians; Sonic Christmas Blast; Spinach Greetings; Tim Burton's The Nightmare Before Christmas***; and ***Who Stole Santa?***

This production aired only once; as of this writing, it was not available on DVD or VHS but could be seen on YouTube.com.

PRODUCTION CREDITS— Writer: Jerry Juhl. Producer: Bob Precht. Director: John Moffitt. Production Companies: Sullivan Productions and CBS Television. Rating: Not rated. Genres: Comedy, Family. Country: USA. Run Time: 60 min.

PRINCIPAL MUPPET PERFORMERS: Cary Antebi (*The Magic Garden*) as Fred; Fran Brill (*What About Bob?*) as Snerf; Jim Henson (*The Muppets*) as Fred and Lothar; Richard Hunt (*The Muppet Show*) as Bing and Match Frackle; John Lovelady (*The Muppet Show*) as Bong, Snake Frackle, Scoff, Snerf, Alarm Frackle; Jerry Nelson (*The Muppet Show*) as Thog, Zippity, Snivelly; Frank Oz (*Star Wars*) as Thig, Skippity, Hoppity, Boppity, Snerf; Danny Seagren (*The Electric Company*) as Gloat, Snarl, Snerf.

INTERESTING TIDBITS: In the works since

REFERENCES: *The Great Santa Claus Switch*. Internet Movie Database. http://www.imdb.com/title/tt0445979/

The Great Santa Claus Switch. Muppet Wiki. http://muppet.wikia.com/wiki/The_Great_Santa_Claus_Switch

Wilson, Joanna. *Tis the Season TV: The Encyclopedia of Christmas-Themed Episodes, Specials and Made-for-TV Movies.* Akron, OH: 1701 Press, 2011.

The Great Toy Robbery—1963

Animated Short Film

THREAT TO CHRISTMAS: Crooks hold up Santa in the Old West.

HOW CHRISTMAS IS SAVED: A cowboy unwittingly incapacitates the crooks.

SYNOPSIS AND COMMENTARY: In most cases, whenever a cartoon title includes the words "The Great This" or "The Great That," it's usually hyperbole. And so it is in this spoof of the Old West using very simple animation. Three crooks hold up Santa and his one-reindeer sleigh in the desert, then ride into town with the sack of toys and head for the saloon where, after running everybody out, they enjoy a round of guzzling and playing with the toys like children. A stereotypically yodeling cowboy all dressed in white with a guitar moseys into town astride a horse he can't control and would join in the festivities but quickly changes his mind (no brave good-guy there). The plot thickens when Santa arrives with the sheriff in tow as the two engage in a shootout with the crooks inside. Though bullets fly like rain, no one is killed, and as the crooks back into the street, the cowboy, bashing his stubborn horse in the head with his guitar, unwittingly bashes the crooks on the backstroke as well. They're arrested, the cowboy chooses a present from Santa's bag and plays with it, Santa heads out, and the show's done.

VOICES: Richard Gilbert.

NOTE: At the time of this writing, this cartoon could be seen on YouTube.

PRODUCTION CREDITS—Writer: Not credited. Producers: Robert Verrall and Wolf Koenig. Director: Jeffrey Hale. Production Company: The National Film Board of Canada. Rating: Not rated. Genres: Animation, Short. Country: Canada. Run Time: 7 min.

REFERENCES: *The Great Toy Robbery.* Big Cartoon Database. http://www.bcdb.com/cartoon/65000-Great-Toy-Robbery

The Great Toy Robbery. Montreal: The National Film Board of Canada, 1963. eVideo.

Wilson, Joanna. *Tis the Season TV: The Encyclopedia of Christmas-Themed Episodes, Specials and Made-for-TV Movies.* Akron, OH: 1701 Press, 2011.

The Guild of Thespian Puppets Save Christmas—2014

Short Film

THREAT TO CHRISTMAS: Nancy the Shark eats Santa.

HOW CHRISTMAS IS SAVED: Krampus induces Nancy to puke up Santa with a sneeze.

SYNOPSIS AND COMMENTARY: Based in Central New York State and founded by Michael Patrei, The Guild of Thespian Puppets is a puppet acting troupe that showcases original, handmade hand puppets through its "quirky and at times educational videos along with live puppet shows for both children and adults." Among the many varieties of puppets within the Guild, its featured puppets include Hamlet the Monkey; Clemens the Alligator; Scrooge-surrogate Dickens the Cat; Biggles the Cardinal; Darwin the Squirrel; Barry Plumpit, a whiz about bargains; Scout, a little white female of unspecified species; and Flappy, a bag puppet. They're not the Muppets, of course, but they are similar, nonetheless.

Following several verses of "Here We Come A-Caroling" to open the show, the members of the Guild have agreed to assist Dakota (Catherine Hood, *Brackish*) at a party for orphans on Christmas Eve. Dickens, on the other hand, would rather the orphans be put to work in factories. When Santa foolishly offers a candy cane to Nancy the Shark (who ironically speaks with a male voice), she devours it—and Santa too. In fact, she eats Hamlet and Dickens when they find candy canes. Meeting them in Nancy's stomach are Livingstone the Elephant (who's searching for his Snickers bar); Bing the Bigfoot; composer Roger Smith on guitar, who encourages them to sing a round of "Jingle Bells"; and Lenny (Gary Hood, *Falling Frames*), a young man who's been trapped within Nancy for the past 20 years. Being an orphan, Lenny along with Santa commiserates with Dickens, also an orphan, through brief black-and-white flashback scenes in England. For a diversion topside, Shackleton the nervous Yeti embarrasses a large man (Mike Cecconi, *Clerks* II) by insisting that the man is Santa, then claims that Dakota is Mrs. Claus; the latter regards such an assertion as an insult, especially when the man takes a fancy to her. Meanwhile, furry Krampus induces Nancy to sneeze with reindeer salt-and-pepper shakers. With her first sneeze, out pops Hamlet, followed shortly thereafter by Dickens, Santa, and Bing after presumably more sneezes (or perhaps Krampus added a wee bit of syrup of ipecac to induce some really good sneeze-pukes). However, it is presumed that Roger, Lenny, and Livingstone remain as Nancy's internal "guests." Whatever, the remaining members of the Guild close by singing verses of "Up on the Housetop."

VOICES/PUPPETEERS: Anthony Angiulli as Livingstone; Alexandria Compo as Scout; Garrett Ingraham as Shackleton and Clemens; Douglas Keyes as Dickens; Gregory Scott Mirell as Bing; Justin Parker as Nancy; Michael Patrei as Hamlet; Nicholas Patrei as Krampus. All these puppeteers have worked with The Guild of Thespian Puppets.

INTERESTING TIDBIT: Check out the film *Krampus* for more insight into this figure of German folklore.

PRODUCTION CREDITS—Writer, Producer, and Director: Michael Patrei. Production Company: Ilion Film Company. Rating: Not rated. Genre: Family. Country: USA. Run Time: 20 min.

REFERENCES: *The Guild of Thespian Puppets Save Christmas*. The Guild of Thespian Puppets Web Site. http://www.guildofthespianpuppets.com. Instant Video.

The Guild of Thespian Puppets Save Christmas. Internet Movie Database. http://www.imdb.com/title/tt4333722/

The Hebrew Hammer—December 19, 2003

Feature Film

Threat to Hanukkah and Kwanzaa: Santa's evil son Damien murders him and sets out to exterminate Hanukkah and Kwanzaa.

How Hanukkah and Kwanzaa Are Saved: A Jewish private-eye teams up with the leader of the Kwanzaa Liberation Front to stop Damien.

SYNOPSIS AND COMMENTARY: Since several films in this book mention Hanukkah along with saving Christmas, it's only fitting that the book include a film (which seems to be the only one) that focuses entirely on saving Hanukkah; in this case, from an anti–Semitic, anti-black Santa who would destroy Hanukkah as well as Kwanzaa and keep December for Christmas alone. The film is an adult comedy that parodies many common Jewish stereotypes.

After Damien Claus (Andy Dick, *Road Trip*), the nerdy yet evil son of Santa (Richard Riehle, *Office Space*), murders and replaces his father for having advocated too much tolerance between Jews, blacks, and white Christians, Damien launches his campaign against Hanukkah and Kwanzaa. To stop Damien, the Jewish Justice League (JJL, a parody of the Jewish Anti-Defamation League) reluctantly recruits protagonist Mordechai Jefferson Carver (Adam Goldberg, *Saving Private Ryan*), a hero known as the "Hebrew Hammer" in New York City's Jewish community. A private investigator fighting Jewish injustice whose appearance is a cross between that of a pimp and a Hasidic Jew, Hammer receives assistance from the JJL chief's daughter, lovely Esther Bloomenbergensteinenthal (Judy Greer, *Jurassic World*), as well as from the Kwanzaa Liberation Front (KLF), led by Mohammed Ali Paula Abdul Rahim (Mario Van Peebles, *Ali*). Damien's tactics include an attempt to weaken Jewish pride by flooding Jewish communities nationwide with free, bootleg copies of *It's a Wonderful Life*, while Hammer counters with copies of positive Jewish movies like *Yentl* and *Fiddler on the Roof*; and indoctrinating kids against Jews (they worship Satan and sacrifice gentile children). This precipitates an attack on Hammer and Esther when the latter two would apprehend Damien at a department store booking, though they're rescued by Harriet "Moses" Tubbleman (Anna Berger, *Ghost World*) of the Underground Jewish Railroad. Damien's plan to sabotage the atomic clock in Jerusalem, thus ending the Jewish calendar and Hanukkah, sends Hammer and Esther to Israel where a shootout erupts between them and Damien's forces. Though Damien overpowers them and kidnaps Esther back to the North Pole, Rahim and his KLF team arrive on the scene in Israel to rescue Hammer. In the final confrontation at the North Pole, Hammer and Rahim infiltrate the compound, put the drop on Damien, and free Esther as well as former New York City Mayor Ed Koch in a cameo role. Rahim leads Damien away to spend the rest of his days in a home for the "religiously [sic] insane," after which Hammer proposes to Esther. Cut to Hanukkah a year later. A working relationship between the JJL and the KLF introduces as the new Santa-elect the foul-talking black dwarf elf Jamal (Tony Cox, *Bad Santa*), who flies in a sleigh with two hottie black women. Seeing Hammer and Esther below, though they're not black, he shouts, "Merry Christmas, [N-words], and a Happy *Jew* Year!"

INTERESTING TIDBITS: An early flashback shows the young Mordechai (Grant Rosenmeyer, *Temps*) ostracized as a Jew at the Saint Peter, Paul, and Mary Elementary School which, if not a nod to three biblical characters, is certainly a nod to the 1960s folk-singing trio of Peter Yarrow, Paul Stookey, and Mary Travers.

A sign on Hammer's office door reads "Certified Circumcised Dick," a colloquial expression ordinarily meaning that he's a certified Jewish private investigator, but viewers will note the not-so-subtle pun.

The name "Damien" is a nod to the anti-Christ of the same name in *The Omen* (1976).

Damien's too-tolerant father takes credit for pushing the trans-religious phrase "Happy Holidays" over "Merry Christmas," after which two reindeer with knives strapped to their antlers (shown in silhouette) betray Santa by cutting him down. His dying words are, "Et tu, Blitzen?" which is a nod to Caesar's murder in William Shakespeare's play *Julius Caesar*.

"Harriet Tubbleman" is a nod to Harriet Tubman, the African American abolitionist and Union spy during the American Civil War who, dubbed as "Moses," led many slaves to freedom via her Underground Railroad.

Damien's principal henchman is the idiotic, cockney-speaking crippled elf Tiny Tim (Sean Whalen, *Twister*), complete with crutch, who's a nod to the character of the same name in Dickens's *A Christmas Carol*.

At the North Pole, a sign outside reads "Santa's Village" with "of the Damned" scrawled in red beneath that, which is a nod to the film *Village of the Damned* (1960).

Although the film sported a two-million-dollar budget, it flopped at the box office, with a domestic gross total of approximately $82,000.

REVIEWS: According to the Rotten Tomatoes film review site, 52 percent of critics gave this movie a positive review. Metacritic gave it a score of 41/100 (mixed/average reviews).

Maitland McDonagh of *TV Guide*: "You don't have to be Jewish to love Jonathan Kesselman's uneven, profane and occasionally flat-out hilarious parody of vintage blaxploitation pictures, but it helps."

A.O. Scott of *The New York Times* (December 19, 2003): "...the movie, which would have worked brilliantly as a five-minute late-night comedy sketch, flogs its premise for nearly [90 minutes], generating too few laughs to justify the enterprise."

Matthew Gilbert of *The Boston Globe* (December 8, 2003): "...it's the only Jewsploitation [sic] film ever made.... This whimsical, wacked-out ethnic comedy is hysterical—if you're comfortable with rabid political incorrectness, that is … made with great affection and Mel Brooksian irreverence..."

PRODUCTION CREDITS—Writer and Director: Jonathan Kesselman. Producers: Josh Kesselman, Sofia Sondervan, and Lisa Fragner. Production Companies: Intrinsic Value Films, Comedy Central Films, Content Film, and Jericho Entertainment. Rating: R (abundant profanity, sexual references, and drug abuse). Genre: Comedy. Country: USA. Run Time: 85 min.

REFERENCES: Gilbert, Matthew. "'Hammer' Takes a Whimsical Whack at Jewish Stereotypes." *The Boston Globe*. http://archive.boston.com/ae/tv/articles/2003/12/08/hammer_takes_whimsical_whack_at_jewish_stereotypes/

The Hebrew Hammer. Box Office Mojo. http://www.boxofficemojo.com/movies/?id=hebrewhammer.htm

The Hebrew Hammer. Internet Movie Database. http://www.imdb.com/title/tt0317640/

Appearing as a cross between a pimp and a Hasidic Jew, Mordechai Jefferson Carver (Adam Goldberg, left), the Hebrew Hammer, is engaged in a battle against an evil Santa who would purge the world of Hanukkah and Kwanzaa. Here the Hammer pauses to encourage a young Jewish boy in *The Hebrew Hammer* (2003) (Comedy Central Films/Photofest).

The Hebrew Hammer. Metacritic. http://www.metacritic.com/movie/the-hebrew-hammer

The Hebrew Hammer. Rotten Tomatoes. http://www.rottentomatoes.com/m/hebrew_hammer/

The Hebrew Hammer. Velocity Home Entertainment, 2004. DVD Video.

McDonagh, Maitland. *The Hebrew Hammer. TV Guide.* http://www.tvguide.com/movies/the-hebrew-hammer/review/136088/

Scott, A.O. "When Hanukkah Is in Jeopardy, a Jewish Superman Gets the Call." *The New York Times.* http://movies2.nytimes.com/2003/12/19/movies/19HAMM.html

Wilson, Joanna. *Tis the Season TV: The Encyclopedia of Christmas-Themed Episodes, Specials and Made-for-TV Movies.* Akron, OH: 1701 Press, 2011.

Hercules Saves Christmas—2011
Television Movie

THREAT TO CHRISTMAS: Evil elf Rondo kidnaps Hercules for his magic collar in order to ruin Christmas.

HOW CHRISTMAS IS SAVED: Rondo and his minions are reduced to giggles.

SYNOPSIS AND COMMENTARY: Which would make a more interesting, albeit silly, story line: a talking pit bull (though his lips never move) named Hercules that saves Christmas or the mythological hero Hercules who saves Christmas in a time preceding Christianity? Whatever, in this case, the dog won out, and the film premiered on Animal Planet.

Two days before Christmas, Max Moogle (Anthony Robinson, *I'm in Love with a Church Girl*), a 12-year-old orphan, encounters Hercules (voiced by Luigi "Shorty" Rossi, *Pit Boss*), Santa's (George Maguire, *Flight Club*) elf-dog that is responsible for drawing up the naughty-and-nice list. By means of his magic collar, Hercules whisks Max to the North Pole, where he appears before Santa's kangaroo court of sorts. Having committed a series of childish misdeeds, Max has made the naughty list, but

Santa offers him a chance to redeem himself if he can spread the Christmas spirit to one dispirited, jobless man, Rick Wilder (Danny Arroyo, *Lethal Weapon 4*), by midnight on Christmas Eve. If the mission fails, Hercules will become an ordinary dog devoid of his powers. Only Max can see and hear Hercules, and together they not only enable Rick to find a job as a sales manager for Mr. Rosco (Marc McClure, *Apollo 13*), a really eccentric toy manufacturer, but they also become Rick's good friends. Rick gets the job over Helen Dunn (Mackenzie Phillips, *One Day at a Time*), a devious, deranged woman whom the bizarre, evil elf Rondo (Richard Van Vleet, *All My Children*) recruits to kidnap Hercules for his magic collar; without it, Hercules is powerless; with it, Rondo intends to ruin Christmas. Back at the North Pole on Christmas Eve, Max and Rick team up with elf Mickey (Dana Woods, **The Boy Who Saved Christmas**) in a faceoff against Rondo and his minions, defeating the latter by shooting them with "sticky belly laugh pellets." With Hercules and Christmas saved, Max receives two surprises on Christmas Day: Rick is to be his legal guardian, and Santa allows Hercules to become Max's very visible pet.

OTHER CAST: Kathy Garver (*Family Affair*) as Sister Augustus; Shorty Rossi as Brother Shorty; Brad Williams (*Life Is Short*) as elf Joseph; Arturo Gil (*Role Models*) as evil elf Remo; Ronald Clark (*Mirror Mirror*) as evil elf Rocky; Maggie VandenBerghe (*Aliens in the Attic*) as Sally; Carla Spindt as Mrs. Claus.

AWARDS: In 2012, this film received a Young Artist Award nomination for Best Performance in a TV Movie, Miniseries or Special–Leading Young Actor (Anthony Robinson).

INTERESTING TIDBITS: Just before meeting Max, Hercules announces his presence by howling, which prompts Max to mouth the phrase "WTF?"

A subplot focuses on a budding romance between Rick and Sally, the toy company's receptionist.

Rondo resembles the Joker, the pasty-faced villain in the *Batman* series.

Santa's elves are racially diverse dwarfs.

Producers Derek Zemrak and Leonard Pirkle respectively appear as the theater owner and a homeless man.

REVIEW: Brian Costello of *Common Sense Media* (March 26, 2013): "While there is a chance younger viewers will enjoy this movie and the wacky (if not outright bizarre) behavior of some of the adult characters, there is an equally good chance that older kids and parents will find this low-budget Christmas movie difficult to get through. While there needs to be more silly but sweet Christmas movies, this one lacked the budget and the talent to succeed."

PRODUCTION CREDITS—Writer: John Pizzo. Producers: Shorty Rossi, Derek Zemrak, and Leonard Pirkle. Director: Edward Hightower. Production Company: Zemrak-Pirkle Productions and Shortywood Productions. Rating: PG (brief language). Genre: Family. Country: USA. Run Time: 81 min.

REFERENCES: Costello, Brian. *Hercules Saves Christmas. Common Sense Media.* https://www.commonsensemedia.org/movie-reviews/hercules-saves-christmas

Hercules Saves Christmas. Amazon Instant Video at Amazon.com.

Hercules Saves Christmas. Internet Movie Database. http://www.imdb.com/title/tt2048854/

Holiday Hi-Jynx—October 5, 1998 (Japan); September 28, 1999 (USA)

Episode from the Japanese Anime Television Series *Pokémon*

THREAT TO CHRISTMAS: Members of Team Rocket capture Santa and steal his toys.

HOW CHRISTMAS IS SAVED: Ash Ketchum and his friends with a troupe of Santa's Jynx Pokémon subdue the villains.

SYNOPSIS AND COMMENTARY: An English abbreviation of the Japanese title *Poketto Monsuta* (*Pocket Monsters*), *Pokémon* is a TV series based on the *Pokémon* video games series and is part of the *Pokémon* franchise. Ongoing, the TV series boasts over 900 episodes since its inception in 1997. Whereas the number of characters is legion, the

Pokémon trainer and protagonist Ash Ketchum (center) from the *Pokémon* animated TV series, along with friends Misty (left) and Brock. Ash's Pikachu mouse-like mascot stands between him and Brock. In the episode "Holiday Hi-Jynx" (1998), the foursome take on villains Jessie, James, and Meowth the cat, who capture Santa and steal his toys (WB Television Network/Photofest).

principal protagonist of the anime series is Ash Ketchum (the last name is a play on "Gotta catch em all!"), a 10-year-old Pokémon trainer, whose adventures in the Pokémon universe frequently include friends such as Misty, also a 10-year-old Pokémon trainer, and Brock, a 15-year-old Pokémon breeder. Ash's mascot is a Pikachu, a species of Pokémon that's basically a mouse with electric powers used for defense against other Pokémon characters. Ash's principal antagonists are the trio of Jessie, James, and the cat Meowth, all bumbling thieves and members of Team Rocket, a criminal organization bent on world domination.

In "Holiday Hi-Jynx," Jessie plans to exact revenge on Santa for allegedly having "stolen" her best doll 10 years ago on Christmas Eve. As she, James, and Meowth rehearse a plan to capture Santa and steal his toys, Ash, Misty, Brock, and Pikachu encounter a Jynx (a blackfaced biped with long white hair and large lips, whose kiss causes a deep sleep), one of Santa's Pokémon creatures that substitute for elves. This Jynx has one of Santa's boots that it had been polishing when it got lost on an ice floe. Santa needs his boot, so Ash and friends head to the North Pole on a raft pulled by four Water Pokémon as Jessie and her troupe follow in a submarine in the shape of a giant, hideous fish.

When the Water Pokémon become exhausted, a Lapras (a large, blue sea creature endowed with mental telepathy that resembles a plesiosaur with a heavy, gray shell on its back) tows the raft the rest of the way. Just as they arrive, Jessie and crew emerge from the submarine and capture the Jynx, tie up Ash and friends with Santa, then order all the other Jynx to load the presents into the submarine. Revealed in a flashback, the Jynx had taken Jessie's broken doll to be repaired ten years ago, but Jessie, mistaking the Jynx for Santa, had lost faith, which prevented Santa from delivering her presents. Though she receives her mended doll, Jessie attempts to escape with the presents anyway, but Santa's Jynx troupe emit sound waves that force the submarine back and literally shake the presents out, whereupon the submarine explodes, blowing Jessie, James, and Meowth all the way back home. With Santa freed, he commences his rounds in a sleigh pulled by one flaming horse, not reindeer.

PRINCIPAL VOICES: Addie Blaustein as Meowth; Rachel Lillis as Misty, Jessie, and Jynx; Eric Stuart as Brock and James; Veronica Taylor as Ash; Ken Gates and Daniel Nicodème as narrators; Jayne Grand as Lapras; Ikue Ohtani as Pikachu; Michael Haigney as Charmander; Ed Paul and Alexander J. Rose as Santa. All the voice actors have worked on the *Pokémon* TV series.

AWARDS: In 2000, the series received a Blimp Award nomination for Favorite Cartoon.

INTERESTING TIDBITS: The terms "Jynx" and "Pokémon" serve as both singular and plural forms.

Although the story line certainly has no obviously religious implications, Santa's commencing his rounds in a sleigh drawn by a fiery horse is something of a nod to the biblical story of the prophet Elijah, who went up to heaven in a chariot and horses of fire (Second Kings 2:11).

This episode is now usually banned from circulation, because the Jynx, all black, are subservient to Santa and can say only one word repetitively: "Jynx, Jynx, Jynx." Although the episode is still available on DVD releases, it has been re-recorded with the Jynx in purple.

The pair of villains Jessie and James is a nod to the outlaw Jesse James.

REVIEW: *Common Sense Media*'s take on the series: "The often cute-and-cuddly Pokémon monsters appeal to kids as young as 4 or 5, but the subject matter—pitting monsters against each other using a multitude of attacks—may not be appropriate for them.... Characters strive to battle honorably, respect their elders, and care for their monsters, which partly balances the show's violent premise."

PRODUCTION CREDITS—Story: Satoshi Tajiri. Producers: Keisuke Iwata, Takayuki Yanagisawa, and Takemoto Mori. Director: Masamitsu Hidaka. Production Companies: 4 Kids Entertainment, Creatures, Game Freak, Nintendo, OLM-Animation Studio, Shogakukan, Summit Media Group, and TV Tokyo. Rating: TV-Y. Genres: Animation, Action, Comedy, Drama, Family. Country: Japan. Run Time: 22 min.

REFERENCES: "Holiday Hi-Jynx." In *Pokémon: Indigo League. Season 1, Episodes 53–79.* San Francisco: VIZ Media, 2008. DVD Video.
"Holiday Hi-Jynx." Internet Movie Database. http://www.imdb.com/title/tt0761093/
Pokémon. Common Sense Media. https://www.commonsensemedia.org/tv-reviews/pokemon
Pokémon. Internet Movie Database. http://www.imdb.com/title/tt0176385/
Pokémon. Web Site. http://www.pokevmon.com/us/
Wilson, Joanna. *Tis the Season TV: The Encyclopedia of Christmas-Themed Episodes, Specials and Made-for-TV Movies.* Akron, OH: 1701 Press, 2011.

Holiday Time—December 16, 2000

Episode from the Animated Television Series *Buzz Lightyear of Star Command*

THREAT TO CHRISTMAS: Evil Emperor Zurg steals Santa's chrono-disruptor and all traces of Christmas throughout the galaxy.

HOW CHRISTMAS IS SAVED: Santa resorts to his old-fashioned sleigh to deliver the gifts.

SYNOPSIS AND COMMENTARY: In outer space, Santa doesn't live at the terrestrial North Pole. He might live in a space castle, as in the

1959 movie ***Santa Claus***, or he might live in North Polaris, a giant space snow globe, as in Disney's *Buzz Lightyear* science-fiction series that ran for 65 half-hour episodes from 2000 to 2001 on UPN and ABC. The series followed the adventures of space ranger Buzz Lightyear, who was originally a protagonist in the *Toy Story* series of films. Other principal characters in the series included Princess Mira Nova, Buzz's second-in-command with red hair and blue skin; Booster Sinclair Munchapper, a huge red creature resembling a dinosaur from the planet Jo-ad (a play on the family name Joad from Steinbeck's *The Grapes of Wrath*); XR (experimental ranger), a short, sarcastic robot; LGMs (little green men), small, three-eyed aliens, some of whom worked as Santa's elves; and Emperor Zurg, the chief antagonist, who sought ways to destroy Star Command.

In "Holiday Time," when Zurg steals Santa's chrono-disruptor, a device that stops time and allows Santa to deliver all the presents in one night, Santa solicits Buzz's help. Instead, he, Mira, Booster, and XR initially dismiss the old gent as senile until Zurg steals all traces of Christmas throughout the galaxy, thus removing the galaxy's spirit of togetherness and hope. Using Santa's former device, an outdated hyper-speed accelerator, Buzz engages Zurg in battle, in which both the chrono-disruptor and hyper-speed accelerator are destroyed, whereupon Zurg believes he has defeated Santa and Christmas. Yet Santa has one last item, his old-fashioned sleigh that runs on belief (not reindeer). As the rangers express their belief, the sleigh powers up, but XR requires some additional coaxing, after which Santa and Buzz make the rounds together.

PRINCIPAL VOICES: Patrick Warburton (*Family Guy*) as Buzz and LGMs; Stephen Furst (*Animal House*) as Booster; Larry Miller (*The Nutty Professor*) as XR; Nicole Sullivan (*Rita Rocks*) as Mira; Wayne Knight (*Jurassic Park*)

Space ranger Buzz Lightyear, shown here as a protagonist in *Toy Story* (1995), comes to Santa's aid when Emperor Zurg removes all traces of Christmas throughout the galaxy in "Holiday Time" (2000), an episode from the animated TV series *Buzz Lightyear of Star Command*. Whereas *Toy Story* was computer animated, the *Buzz Lightyear* series was not (Walt Disney Pictures/Photofest).

as Zurg; Adam Carolla (*The Hammer*) as Commander Zeb Nebula; Earl Boen (*The Terminator*) as Santa.

AWARDS: In 2001, the *Buzz Lightyear* series won a Daytime Emmy for Outstanding Sound Editing Special Class; Daytime Emmy nomination for Outstanding Special Class Animated Program; Golden Reel nominations for Best Sounding Editing: Television Animated Series Sound and Television Animation Music.

NOTE: At the time of this writing, "Holiday Time" was not available on DVD or VHS but could be seen on YouTube.

REVIEW: Andrea Graham of *Common Sense Media* commented on the series: "…typical sci-fi adventure, filled with action sequences, quirky aliens, and … trademark Disney humor … a perfect example of how studios can beat a franchise to death in the pursuit of merchandising gold."

PRODUCTION CREDITS—Writer: Mark Palmer. Executive Producers: Mark McCorkle, Robert Schooley, and Tad Stones. Director: Victor Cook. Production Company: Walt Disney Television Animation. Rating: TV-Y7. Genres: Action, Adventure, Animation, Comedy, Family, Sci-Fi. Country: USA. Run Time: 30 min.

REFERENCES: Graham, Andrea. *Buzz Lightyear of Star Command. Common Sense Media.* https://www.commonsensemedia.org/tv-reviews/buzz-lightyear-of-star-command

"Holiday Time." Big Cartoon Database. http://www.bcdb.com/cartoon/28293-Holiday-Time

"Holiday Time." Internet Movie Database. http://www.imdb.com/title/tt1097809/

Wilson, Joanna. *Tis the Season TV: The Encyclopedia of Christmas-Themed Episodes, Specials and Made-for-TV Movies.* Akron, OH: 1701 Press, 2011.

Holidaze: The Christmas That Almost Didn't Happen—2006

Animated Television Special

THREAT TO CHRISTMAS: Santa is changing computers and can't retrieve his naughty-and-nice list.

HOW CHRISTMAS IS SAVED: Courtesy of Rusty the Reindeer, a formerly cynical kid repairs Santa's new computer.

SYNOPSIS AND COMMENTARY: If older viewers are willing to sit through the first 55 or so minutes of this hour-long film with a threadbare plot, they'll eventually realize that it is indeed a save-Christmas film. As long as children see that it's a cartoon, they won't care one way or another. This special features clay puppets in smooth, stop-motion animation resembling CGI quality.

The protagonist is Rusty the Reindeer, Rudolph's virtually unknown little brother, who desperately wants to find his place in and be an important part of Christmas, just like his famous sibling. But when it's not to be, Rusty leaves the North Pole for the Big City and joins Icons Anonymous, a church-sponsored support group for depressed holiday icons such as Candie the Easter Bunny; Mr. C, a grouchy Cupid; Albert, a neurotic Thanksgiving turkey; and Trick and Treat, two valley-girl-type Halloween ghosts. Candie is directing the church's Christmas play and casts Rusty as a camel. This also doesn't pan out, but there Rusty meets a cynical, unnamed kid who, also living in his older brother's shadow, believes in neither Christmas nor Santa, until he confirms online Rusty's description of Santa's "Naughty-N-Nice-O-Matic," a six-ton dinosaur of a computer that stores the naughty-n-nice list. Now a believer, the kid wants on Santa's nice list to get a special catcher's mask; for that, he must confess his belief either to any of Santa's deputized helpers (fake Santas) or to Santa himself before midnight on Christmas Eve, but the only fake Santa he knows is Kringle, a self-absorbed jerk who imagines himself a thespian. That leaves journeying to Santa via the postal service's "super hyper ultra mega rush delivery," and Rusty and the kid parachute down to the North Pole on Christmas Eve. There, the kid fixes Santa's new laptop computer that had given trouble in transferring all the files from the old Naughty-N-Nice-O-Matic. Without the list, Santa would have had to cancel Christmas.

PRINCIPAL VOICES: Jonathan Prince (*American Dreams*) as the narrator elf; Fred Savage (*The Wonder Years*) as Rusty; Fred Willard (*American Wedding*) as Santa and dogcatcher; Edie McClurg (*Frozen*) as Mrs. Claus; John O'Hurley (*Santa Barbara*) as Kringle; Gladys Knight (*Gladys Knight and the Pips*) as Candie; Paul Rodriguez (*Blood Work*) as Mr. C; Harland Williams (*Dumb and Dumber*) as Albert; Emily Osment (*Young and Hungry*) as Trick; Brenda Song (*The Social Network*) as Treat; twins Cole and Dylan Sprouse (*Grace Under Fire*) as the kid.

INTERESTING TIDBITS: The film is filled with references to its TV sponsors' commercial products, such as a family of three polar bears drinking Coca Cola; Mrs. Claus hosting an on-again-off-again cooking show where she prepares soup with her "secret" ingredients—Campbell's Soup—complete with the famous slogan, "Mmm mmm good!"; Wal-Mart; and Ask.com.

There's a veiled reference to the animated special ***Rudolph, the Red-Nosed Reindeer*** (1964) by mentioning "Herbie" the elf-dentist instead of "Hermey," the elf's name in the earlier special.

Several loosely connected subplots basically serve as filler material: a dogcatcher in the Big City mistakes Rusty (even with his antlers) for a stray dog and repeatedly tries to haul him to the pound; at the behest of Trick and Treat, bizarre, heavy metal bands attempt to write a Christmas song about Rusty (the answer to "Rudolph") without mentioning "Christmas," followed by *Holiday Icon*, a parody of *American Idol*, with Albert, Candie, and Mr. C. serving as judges; Albert's perpetually paranoid belief that people only see him as dinner; Kringle giving Rusty acting lessons in a restaurant while the chef chases Albert up and down with a meat cleaver.

All the characters exhibit exophthalmos (protrusion of the eyeballs), which begs the question: is there an epidemic of hyperthyroidism?

PRODUCTION CREDITS—Story: Peter Murietta and Jonathan Prince. Teleplay: Peter Murietta. Producer: Andi Copley. Director: David H. Brooks. Production Companies: Bix Pix Entertainment, Madison Road Entertainment, and Once upon a Frog Productions. Rating: Not rated. Genres: Animation, Comedy. Country: USA. Run Time: 60 min.

REFERENCES: *Holidaze: The Christmas That Almost Didn't Happen*. Big Cartoon Database. http://www.bcdb.com/cartoon/121727-Holidaze-The-Christmas-That-Almost-Didn't-Happen

Holidaze: The Christmas That Almost Didn't Happen. Internet Movie Database. http://www.imdb.com/title/tt0849447/

Holidaze: The Christmas That Almost Didn't Happen. Los Angeles: Porchlight Entertainment, 2007. DVD Video.

Holly and Hal Moose: Our Uplifting Christmas Adventure—December 2008

Computer-Animated Television Movie

THREAT TO CHRISTMAS: The elves urge Santa to cancel Christmas because of a major winter storm.

HOW CHRISTMAS IS SAVED: Two moose calves enable the reindeer to fly in the storm.

SYNOPSIS AND COMMENTARY: Dogs and cats have saved Christmas, so now it's time for a couple of anthropomorphic moose calves to have the honors. Desiring to be a reindeer and fly with Santa's team, young Hal Moose (wearing blinking Christmas lights in his antlers) believes that if he follows the Northern Lights from his home in the North, he will reach the North Pole. When his older sister Holly's back is turned, Hal heads off as a major winter storm approaches Santa's realm. Holly soon pursues and finds him, and after a few mishaps, they both slide down a long hill, crashing into Santa's team near his workshop. After proper introductions, Santa is initially skeptical about a moose flying with the reindeer, and the latter laugh themselves silly at such a notion, but at Mrs. Claus's suggestion, Holly makes herself useful in the toyshop, while Hal unsuccessfully practices flying in a wind tunnel in the flight training department. When the storm overtakes the North Pole, Santa's two weather elves urge him to cancel Christmas despite his optimism, whereupon little inventor Holly discovers that attaching fake moose antlers to the reindeer will give them more "lift" to combat the fierce winds. Santa is so pleased that he grants Hal's wish and invites him and Holly to fly with the team.

VOICES: Chiara Zanni (*X-Men 2*) as Holly; Sam Vincent (*Martin Mystery*) as Hal and Little Hal; Ron Halder (*Antitrust*) as Santa; Cathy Weseluck (*Dragon Ball Z*) as Mrs. Claus; Ian James Corlett (*Mega Man*) as Sol the elf and supervisor elf; Tabitha St. Germain (*Captain Flamingo*) as worker elf; Alan Marriott (*Planet 51*) as Donner and Blitzen; Kelly Metzger (*Hop the Twig*) as Stella; Meaghan Martin (*Camp Rock*) as Easton; Jonathan Morgan Heit (*Date Night*) as Weston; Jeff Tomlinson (*UFO Hunters*) as mighty elf; Bojan Tikvarovski (*Holly and Hal Moose: Our Uplifting Christmas Adventure*) as eye of storm.

INTERESTING TIDBIT: The story is based on characters from Build-A-Bear Workshop.

REVIEWS: Emily Ashby of *Common Sense*

Media (November 21, 2009): "…adorable characters, pleasant animation, and feel-good messages…. Hal, whose unbridled enthusiasm for adventure and fulfilling his dreams will ring true with kids. And Holly's devotion to her brother is an inspiring example of love and compassion for kids."

PRODUCTION CREDITS—Story: Maxine Clark. Screenplay: Cassie Wells and David B. Miller. Producers and Directors: David B. Miller and William J. Tomlinson. Production Company: Build-A-Bear Workshop Entertainment. Rating: Not rated. Genres: Animation, Family. Country: USA. Run Time: 50 min.

REFERENCES: Ashby, Emily. *Holly and Hal Moose: Our Uplifting Christmas Adventure. Common Sense Media.* https://www.commonsensemedia.org/movie-reviews/holly-and-hal-moose-our-uplifting-christmas-adventure

Holly and Hal Moose: Our Uplifting Christmas Adventure. Internet Movie Database. http://www.imdb.com/title/tt1717155/

Holly and Hal Moose: Our Uplifting Christmas Adventure. Level 33 Entertainment, 2011. DVD Video.

Wilson, Joanna. *Tis the Season TV: The Encyclopedia of Christmas-Themed Episodes, Specials and Made-for-TV Movies.* Akron, OH: 1701 Press, 2011.

Holly Jolly Jimmy—December 8, 2003

Episode from the Computer-Animated Television Series *The Adventures of Jimmy Neutron: Boy Genius*

THREAT TO CHRISTMAS: Jimmy's DNA tracker accidentally scrambles Santa's atoms.

HOW CHRISTMAS IS SAVED: Jimmy and gang initially deliver the presents, but Santa returns to take over when Jimmy fails.

SYNOPSIS AND COMMENTARY: The first

A scene from the animated feature science-fiction film *Jimmy Neutron: Boy Genius* (2001). From left: Carl Wheezer; Jimmy Neutron; pet robotic dog Goddard; and King Goobot V, Jimmy's archenemy and ruler of an alien race, the Yolkians. Whereas the former three characters appear in the episode "Holly Jolly Jimmy" (2003) from the animated TV series *The Adventures of Jimmy Neutron: Boy Genius*, Goobot does not (Nickelodeon Movies/Photofest).

spinoff to the animated feature science-fiction film *Jimmy Neutron: Boy Genius* (2001) and created by John A. Davis, the *Adventures* series ran on Nickelodeon for 119 episode segments from 2002 to 2006. The series, set in fictional Retroville, carried over principal characters from the feature film: Jimmy Neutron, a ten-year-old brainiac who used his scientific knowledge and inventions to bail him out of comic situations he brought on himself; Hugh and Judy Neutron, respectively Jimmy's dimwitted, pie-obsessed father and June Cleaver–type mother; hyperactive Sheen Estevez and nerdy, bespectacled Carl Wheezer, Jimmy's best friends; Cindy Vortex, Jimmy's blonde rival; Libby Folfax, Cindy's black friend; and Goddard, Jimmy's versatile, robotic dog.

During a Christmas-themed show-and-tell session at Jimmy's school, Jimmy opines that it is a scientific impossibility for Santa to deliver all the presents in one night and fit into slim chimneys; therefore, Santa is bogus. Jimmy's skepticism arose two years ago, when Santa had failed to deliver a core sample from a particular dwarf star, as Jimmy had requested, and that had spawned his unreasonable Santa-doesn't-exist-because-I-didn't-get-what-I-wanted attitude. Jimmy's DNA tracker receives a signal from part of a Santa snack left over from Sheen's previous Christmas, whereupon Sheen and Carl conclude that Jimmy's device is tracking Santa's DNA in the saliva on the snack. To prove it, they head to the North Pole. Meanwhile, as Cindy and Libby scheme to shoot a video to humiliate Jimmy, they unwittingly find themselves aboard Jimmy's rocket stuffed within his "hypercube" (a device appearing like a Rubik's cube that stores unlimited objects) as he, Carl, and Sheen zoom to the Arctic. Though he witnesses Santa's workshop, Jimmy's in big-time denial: to him it's just a glorified factory from which parents order toys, and the elves are all short people with misshapen ears. Trouble hits when Jimmy's overloaded DNA tracker scrambles Santa's atoms, whereupon Cindy and Libby, having escaped from the hypercube, arrive in the nick of time to video the Jimmy-ruined-Christmas disaster and deliver the footage to a TV station back in Retroville. Daddy Hugh's response to such news is to junk Christmas and invent a new pie-themed holiday called "Pule" (a composite of "Pie" and "Yule"), yet his pie give-away spree somehow just doesn't pan out. Reasoning that delivering all the presents using science will prove that Santa is bogus, Jimmy loads his hypercube, affixes a red navigational beacon to Goddard's nose (in the spirit of Rudolph), and proceeds with the deliveries in his rocket with pals Carl and Sheen, yet he forgets about the presents for Retroville. With time running out, Jimmy's rocket blows apart when given a light-speed blast; such failure supposedly proves that Santa is real. Having recovered his scrambled atoms, a most definitely real Santa rescues the three boys with his tractor beam (everybody's a techie now) and speeds his sleigh to deliver Retroville's presents (coal for Cindy and Libby) using one of Jimmy's warp modules. And Jimmy does receive that dwarf star sample; it had only taken two years to cool off.

PRINCIPAL VOICES: Debi Derryberry (*Aladdin*) as Jimmy; Jeffrey Garcia (*Happy Feet*) as Sheen; Rob Paulsen (*Animaniacs*) as Carl; Mark DeCarlo (*The Ant Bully*) as Hugh; Megan Cavanagh (*Junior*) as Judy; Carolyn Lawrence (*Resident Evil 4*) as Cindy; Crystal Scales (*Titan A.E.*) as Libby; Frank Welker (*Aladdin*) as Goddard; Andrea Martin (*Wag the Dog*) as teacher Ms. Fowl; Mel Brooks (*Blazing Saddles*) as Santa.

AWARDS: The *Adventures* series won Annie Awards for Outstanding Achievement and Outstanding Voice Acting (Jeffrey Garcia) (2004); Annie nominations for Outstanding Directing (2004 and 2005), Outstanding Voice Acting (Carolyn Lawrence, 2005), and Best Writing in an Animated TV Production (2006); won BMI Cable Awards (2003 and 2004); Blimp Award nominations for Favorite Cartoon (2006 and 2007); won Golden Reel Awards for Best Sound Editing in TV Animation (2004 and 2005); Vision Award nomination for Best Children's Series (2004); and WGA TV Award nomination for Best Animation (2004).

INTERESTING TIDBITS: "Holly Jolly Jimmy" is not only the first Nicktoon to be computer animated but also the first to be based on an existing film. The episode title is an obvious parody of the song title "A Holly Jolly Christmas" by Johnny Marks.

Jimmy Neutron's full name is James Isaac Neutron, which is a parody of Sir Isaac Newton, the English physicist and mathematician.

Jimmy's father's full name is Hugh Beaumont Neutron, which is a nod to Hugh Beaumont, who portrayed Ward Cleaver, Beaver's dad, in *Leave It to Beaver* (1957–1963).

Sheen Estevez is a nod to father-son actors Martin Sheen (Ramón Estévez) and Charlie Sheen (Carlos Estévez), and robotic dog Goddard is named after Dr. Robert Goddard, who is considered to be the father of the U.S. space program.

NOTE: Several DVD collections include selected *Adventures* episodes, but at the time of this writing, "Holly Jolly Jimmy" was not one of them, nor was the episode available on other media such as Amazon, Hulu, YouTube, or Netflix.

REVIEW: Joly Herman of *Common Sense Media* reviewed the series: "…a lot of yelling and some stereotyping … the program has a vaudeville element … the cadence of a slapstick Broadway show and the energy of Bugs Bunny … well-developed characters, humor, adventure, and a good sci-fi punch … superior viewing compared to other programs in its genre."

PRODUCTION CREDITS—Supervising Producer: Jed Spingarn. Director: Mike Gasaway. Production Companies: DNA Productions, O Entertainment, and Nickelodeon Animation Studios. Rating: TV-Y7. Genres: Animation, Adventure, Comedy, Family, Sci-Fi. Country: USA. Run Time: 25 min.

REFERENCES: *The Adventures of Jimmy Neutron: Boy Genius*. Internet Movie Database. http://www.imdb.com/title/tt0320808/

Herman, Joly. *The Adventures of Jimmy Neutron*. Common Sense Media. https://www.commonsensemedia.org/tv-reviews/the-adventures-of-jimmy-neutron

"Holly Jolly Jimmy." Big Cartoon Database. https://www.bcdb.com/cartoon/52032-Holly-Jolly-Jimmy

Wilson, Joanna. *Tis the Season TV: The Encyclopedia of Christmas-Themed Episodes, Specials and Made-for-TV Movies*. Akron, OH: 1701 Press, 2011.

Hoops and Yoyo Ruin Christmas—
November 25, 2011

Animated Television Short Film

THREAT TO CHRISTMAS: Hoops, Yoyo, and Piddles unwittingly upset a time-space continuum involving Santa.

HOW CHRISTMAS IS SAVED: Traveling back in time, the three work with a young Kris Kringle to get him back on track to fulfill his destiny as Santa.

SYNOPSIS AND COMMENTARY: Two characters featured on Hallmark Cards' animated greeting card and e-card lines are Hoops, a sarcastic pink cat, and Yoyo, a green rabbit, both of whose large heads are far out of proportion to their bodies. Created by Bob Holt and Mike Adair, both characters prefer coffee and various treats and are often seen in the company of their good friend Piddles, a highly educated, tiny blue mouse.

In *Ruin Christmas*, Hoops, Yoyo, and Piddles provide a new spin on the origin of Santa Claus. When Santa lands on their rooftop and is occupied, the three protagonists snoop around in the sleigh and accidentally become trapped therein when Santa resumes his route. As he passes through a time-space continuum (a worm hole) that allows him to deliver all the Christmas presents in one night, the three principals fall out, traveling centuries back in time, and crash into the abode of a skinny, nerdy, bespectacled stableboy named Kris Kringle in his early days as an amateur toymaker. Their dramatic entrance also wrecks the unique music box that he had created to enter the Royal Toy Contest. Now they must get Kris back on track to fulfill his destiny as Santa and begin by working together with him through the night to repair the toy. Next day at the Toymaker's Fair, when his creation dazzles a little girl who has never had a toy of her own, kind-hearted Kris gives her the toy and forgoes the contest. Back at the stable, Kris and the gang are surprised to see the same little girl waiting, whereupon she morphs into a lovely spirit who announces that, by his unselfish generosity to one child, Kris is worthy to become Santa Claus to all children. Having magically received all the traditional trappings of his role (reindeer sleigh, red suit, etc.), Kris takes to the skies through a worm hole, temporarily leaving Hoops, Yoyo, and Piddles behind, then returns as the timeless Santa Claus to transport them back to the present.

VOICES: Mike Adair (*Hoops and Yoyo's Haunted Halloween*) as Hoops; Bob Holt (*Hoops and Yoyo's Haunted Halloween*) as Yoyo; Bev Carlson (*Hoops and Yoyo's Haunted Halloween*) as Piddles; Michael Monken (*The Polar Express*) as Kris Kringle; Dave Parke (*Visible Scars*) as Santa; Pamela Morency (*Petrified*) as the spirit; Brooke Lloyd (*Hoops and Yoyo Ruin Christmas*) as little girl; Circus Szalewski (*The Rockville Slayer*) as snooty clerk and mean toymaker.

AWARDS: In 2012, this picture received Annie Award nominations for Directing, Production Design, and Best General Audience Animated TV Production.

REVIEW: Emily Ashby of *Common Sense Media* (November 25, 2011): "…it's always fun to mix in a fresh take on holiday stories, and Hoops and Yoyo don't disappoint with their interpretation of how Santa came to exist…. The sweet story inspires even as its colorful stars keep the audience in stitches with their antics and their observations about … everything around them."

PRODUCTION CREDITS—Writers: Mike Adair, Bob Holt, and Bev Carlson. Producer: Melinda Wunsch Dilger. Director: Tony Craig. Production Company: Pershing Road Productions. Rating: Not rated. Genres: Animation, Family. Country: USA. Run Time: 23 min.

REFERENCES: Ashby, Emily. *Hoops and Yoyo Ruin Christmas. Common Sense Media.* https://www.commonsensemedia.org/movie-reviews/hoops-yoyo-ruin-christmas

Hoops and Yoyo Ruin Christmas. Big Cartoon Database. http://www.bcdb.com/cartoon/138298-Hoops-Yoyo-Ruin-Christmas

Hoops and Yoyo Ruin Christmas. Hallmark, 2011. DVD Video.

Hoops and Yoyo Ruin Christmas. Internet Movie Database. http://www.imdb.com/title/tt2079513/

How Murray Saved Christmas—December 5, 2014

Animated Television Musical

THREAT TO CHRISTMAS: A new toy punches out Santa, who can't make his deliveries.

HOW CHRISTMAS IS SAVED: A grouchy Jewish deli owner fills in for Santa.

SYNOPSIS AND COMMENTARY: Based on *How Murray Saved Christmas* (2000) and *Santa Claustrophobia* (2002), children's books by Mike Reiss, this absolutely hilarious, offbeat musical utilizing rhyming dialogue is set in the town of Stinky Cigars, located north of the North Pole. There, a host of characters representing American holidays reside, such as George Washington, Abraham Lincoln, Columbus, the Easter Bunny, and others, including Santa Claus. On Christmas Eve, Santa inspects little Edison Elf's new invention (a nod to inventor Thomas Edison), a "jack-in-the-boxer" (a boxing glove replaces the clown head), and receives a hard punch in the face; suffering a concussion and manifesting bizarre behavior, he can't make his deliveries. After a round of singing, dancing, and generally whooping the crowd into a frenzy, Edison convinces everyone to help Santa, until arguments and brawls break out with slapstick antics like The Three Stooges ("Woo woo woo"). The only suitable person Edison trusts to fill in for Santa is Murray Weiner, a cranky, middle-aged, Jewish deli owner and former milkman, who's been a grouch since the day long ago when milkmen became obsolete, the annual Milkman Day Parade ended, and he told his love, Libby (the Statue of Liberty), to take a hike. Murray reluctantly assumes Santa's duties, which present various complications; for example, when Murray's pants accidentally drop down in front of a six-year-old kid, Murray exclaims, "I'm going to jail!" Meanwhile, Santa recovers and, upon discovering that his sleigh, suit, and gifts are missing, alerts the cops, then buys $8,000-worth of "garbage" gifts for "brats" at an all-night store, run by a Hindu with eight arms (a parody of Hindu gods). A much happier man for having taken Santa's role, Murray also delivers gifts to naughty children as well as to those of other religions and cultures. On returning home, a motorcycle cop would arrest Murray for "stealing Christmas" (a nod to the Grinch), but a quick round with Edison's jack-in-the-boxer silences him. And to top it off, Libby returns to Murray ("No one can carry a *torch* like me!").

PRINCIPAL VOICES: Jerry Stiller (*The King of Queens*) as Murray; Jason Alexander (*Seinfeld*) as Doc Holiday (without Wyatt Earp); Sean Hayes (*The Bucket List*) as Edison Elf; Dennis Haysbert (*The Unit*) as Baby New Year, the narrator; John Ratzenberger (*Cheers*) as Officer Bender; Kevin Michael Richardson (*Lilo and Stitch*) as Santa.

SONGS: Mike Reiss and Walter Murphy.

AWARDS: In 2015, this picture won the International Film Award Berlin for Best Animated Feature Film. It received a Primetime Emmy nomination for Outstanding Music and Lyrics for the song "You Gotta Believe" and an Annie nomination for Best Animated Special Production.

INTERESTING TIDBITS: Doc Holiday's idiotic diagnoses of Santa's condition include "superficial fractures of his little baby toesis" and "antisocial claustrophobic paranoid neurosis," both of which are parodies of "Supercalifragilisticexpialidocious" from *Mary Poppins*.

The ethnically diverse elves sing a variety of amusing songs stating, for example, that Santa runs a sweatshop operation and, therefore, the elves never miss a day of work because they have no health insurance; that Santa hires elves to work, because they are cheaper than the Chinese; and that Santa is a "jerk" because of the above and because he demands cash when he offers them hot chocolate.

There are nods to crooner Bing Crosby and Google when Edison researches Murray's background with the "Bingle" Internet search engine, and a nod to The Andrews Sisters, a vocal trio who often made appearances and recordings with Crosby. Here, they appear in WAC uniforms (Women's Army Corp during World War II) and emerge from a large milk bottle during a flashback scene of the Milkman Day Parade.

When the groundhog sees his shadow, he erroneously remarks that Spring is not far away. According to the old legend, however, there will be six more weeks of winter weather if the groundhog sees his shadow on Groundhog Day.

Murray cannot remember the names of Santa's reindeer. During one attempt, he calls out, "On, Dumbo, on, Jumbo, on, Mason and Dixon, on, Cosmo and Kramer and Richard M. Nixon!" Dumbo and Mrs. Jumbo were, respectively, a baby elephant and its mother in the Disney animated film *Dumbo* (1941). Note references to the Mason-Dixon line and a former U.S. president. Cosmo Kramer was a wacky character on the TV sitcom *Seinfeld* (1990–1998), played by Michael Richards. In a final attempt, Murray hollers, "On, Lipstick, on, Dipstick, on, Pixie and Dixie, on Kramden and Norton and Alice and Trixie!" Lipstick and Dipstick refer to a pair of lesbians in which the former is more feminine and the latter more masculine. Pixie and Dixie were mouse characters on the animated TV series *The Huckleberry Hound Show* (1958–1961). Ralph and Alice Kramden (played by Jackie Gleason and Audrey Meadows) with neighbors Ed and Trixie Norton (played by Art Carney and Joyce Randolph) were the principals on the TV sitcom *The Honeymooners* (1955–1970).

REVIEWS: According to the Rotten Tomatoes film review site, 50 percent of critics gave this film a positive review. Metacritic gave it a score of 60/100 (mixed/average reviews).

Rob Owen of the *Pittsburgh Post-Gazette* (December 4, 2014): "…it's a clever, funny hour that's written in rhyme with imaginative songs threaded throughout…. But as fun as this Christmas special may be for viewers who appreciate a twist on the usual, schmaltzy holiday cheer, that's the exact reason it may not become a holiday classic. It's too offbeat."

Patrick Kevin Day of the *Los Angeles Times* (December 5, 2014): "Strangely, despite Murray's obvious Jewish-ness, there's not one mention made of Hanukkah in this holiday town … despite chuckles here and there, the special's sensibility will probably hold more appeal for viewers closer to Murray's age than the boys and girls looking for something to watch and re-watch."

Robert Bianco of *USA Today* (December 5, 2014): "Many of the jokes are intentionally sent sailing above children's heads—and a few may not be appropriate for the very youngest. But with that exception, the very multicultural *Murray* is one of those rare holiday specials the entire family can enjoy for years to come."

PRODUCTION CREDITS—Writer: Mike Reiss. Producers: Claudia Katz and Lee Supercinski. Director: Peter Avanzino. Production Companies: Rough Draft Studios, Universal Animation Studios, Universal Television. Rating: Not rated. Genres: Adventure, Animation, Comedy, Family, Fantasy. Country: USA. Run Time: 42 min.

REFERENCES: Bianco, Robert. *How Murray Saved Christmas*. USA Today. http://www.usatoday.com/story/life-tv/2014/12/05/critics-corner-dec-5/19491885/

Day, Patrick Kevin. "'How Murray Saved Christmas' Skews Older." *Los Angeles Times*. http://www.touch.latimes.com/#section/-1/article/p2p-82189862/

How Murray Saved Christmas. Internet Movie Database. http://www.imdb.com/title/tt3816346/

How Murray Saved Christmas. Metacritic. http://www.metacritic.com/tv/how-murray-saved-christmas

How Murray Saved Christmas. Rotten Tomatoes. http://www.rottentomatoes.com/m/how_murray_saved_christmas

How Murray Saved Christmas. Universal City, CA: Universal Studios Home Entertainment, 2014. DVD Video.

Owen, Rob. "TV Review: 'How Murray Saved Christmas' Is a Rare, Irreverent Holiday Special." *Pittsburgh Post-Gazette*. http://www.post-gazette.com/ae/tv-radio/2014/12/04/TV-Review-Murray-is-a-rare-irreverent-Christmas-special/stories/201412040114

Reiss, Mike. *How Murray Saved Christmas*. Illustrated by David Catrow. New York: Price Stern Sloan, 2000.

_____. *Santa Claustrophobia*. Illustrated by David Catrow. New York: Price Stern Sloan, 2002.

How the Toys Saved Christmas

Also Known as *The Toys Who Saved Christmas*

August 28, 1996, Animated Feature Film (Italy)

October 21, 1997, Direct-to-Video Animated Movie (USA)

THREAT TO CHRISTMAS: Sick abed with a cold, Santa-surrogate Granny Rose cannot deliver her toys, and evil Mr. Grimm would sell her toys to those with the most cash.

HOW CHRISTMAS IS SAVED: The toys rebel and deliver themselves to deserving children, and Grimm receives his comeuppance.

SYNOPSIS AND COMMENTARY: Originally titled in Italy as *La freccia azzurra* (literally *The Blue Arrow*), this film is based on a children's book of the same title by Italian author Gianni Rodari, first published in 1954. The film is one of Italy's first principal productions to employ digital animation.

The original film adaptation, set in the 1930s, incorporates a figure from Italian folklore, the good witch *La Befana*, who rides about on her broom and delivers gifts to deserving children on the night of January 5, the eve of Epiphany. When illness prevents *La Befana* (voice of Lella Costa, *The Icicle Thief*) from making her rounds, her evil assistant, Scarafoni (voice of Dario Fo, *Joc de dos*), would accommodate only those willing to pay exorbitant sums for their children's toys. The toys, believing that they should match themselves with children to whom they would bring the greatest joy, escape and comb the city in search of appropriate recipients while riding on a model train designated as *The Blue Arrow*. Despite Scarafoni's numerous attempts to recapture them, the toys persevere, and intervention from *La Befana* herself ultimately succeeds in defeating the villain. In a subplot, the boy Francesco receives a special friend for Christmas, a puppy named Jingles.

In 1997, the film was brought to the USA with English dialogue. This version alters the story in several respects: the holiday setting is Christmas instead of Epiphany; *La Befana* becomes good witch Granny Rose (voice of Mary

Tyler Moore, *The Mary Tyler Moore Show*), who assists Santa Claus (voice of Neil Shee, *Toad Patrol*) in dispensing gifts; and Scarafoni becomes Mr. Grimm (voice of Tony Randall, *The Odd Couple*). Francesco becomes the orphan Christopher (voice of Michael Caloz, *Arthur*), whom two thieves frame for their bungled attempt to rob Granny Rose's toy shop. When Grimm fails to deliver her toys as she requested, Granny Rose, suffering from a cold, leaves her bed to make the rounds. Grimm is caught while attempting to abscond with her funds, and Christopher gets his puppy-friend Jingles (voice of Sonja Ball, *Arthur*).

Awards: In 1997, *La freccia azzurra* won the David di Donatello Award for Best Music as well as the Silver Ribbon and the Special Silver Ribbon from the Italian National Syndicate of Film Journalists, respectively, for Best Score and for an Animated Film Produced in Italy.

Interesting Tidbits: As a Santa-surrogate, Granny Rose abed with a cold smacks of other films in which Santa's cold precludes his making the deliveries: **Christmas Flintstone, A Flintstone Christmas**, and **The Year Without a Santa Claus.**

Reviews: Brian Costello of *Common Sense Media* (November 19, 2012): "[This film] is a delightful Christmas cartoon delivering timeless holiday themes of selfless giving and Christmas cheer overcoming greed.... Whereas many Christmas movies and cartoons can feel heavy-handed or even cynical, this should-be classic finds its own place in holiday fare."

Nancy Bouwens of The Dove Foundation: "Friendship, teamwork and the magic of the holiday season are woven throughout making this delightful viewing for families and children of all ages. We are happy to award this film the Dove 'Family-Approved' Seal."

Production Credits—Writers: Enzo d'Alò and Umberto Marino. English-Language Script: Shelly Altman. Producers: Maria Fares, Rolf Schmid, Vreni Traber, and Paul Thiltges. English Version Producer: Eve Chilton. Director: Enzo d'Alò. Production Companies: La Lanterna Magica (Italy), Fama Film (Switzerland), Monipoly Productions (Luxembourg). Rating: G. Genres: Animation, Adventure, Family, Fantasy. Countries: Italy, Switzerland, Luxembourg. Run Time: 78 min.

References: Bendazzi, Giannalberto. "La freccia azzurra (The Blue Arrow)." *Animation World Magazine*. http://www.awn.com/mag/issue1.10/articles/bendazziblue1.10.html

Bouwens, Nancy. *How the Toys Saved Christmas*. The Dove Foundation. http://www.dove.org/review/8927-how-the-toys-saved-christmas/

Costello, Brian. *How the Toys Saved Christmas. Common Sense Media*. https//www.commonsensemedia.org/movie-reviews/how-the-toys-saved-christmas

Crump, William D. *The Christmas Encyclopedia*. Third Edition. Jefferson, NC: McFarland, 2013.

La Freccia Azzurra. Big Cartoon Database. http://www.bcdb.com/cartoon/79549-La-Freccia-Azzurra

How the Toys Saved Christmas. Internet Movie Database. http://www.imdb.com/title/tt0122494/

How the Toys Saved Christmas. Santa Monica, CA: Lionsgate, 2014. DVD Video.

Rodari, Gianni. *La freccia azzurra*. 1954. Reprint. Illustrazioni di Maria Enrica Agnostinelli. Roma: Editori Riuniti, 1983. Italian language.

Wilson, Joanna. *Tis the Season TV: The Encyclopedia of Christmas-Themed Episodes, Specials and Made-for-TV Movies*. Akron, OH: 1701 Press, 2011.

Howdy Doody's Christmas—1951

Television Short Film

Threat to Christmas: Ugly Sam mistakenly believes that Santa is an escaped, bearded bandit and holds him captive at the North Pole.

How Christmas Is Saved: Howdy Doody, Buffalo Bob, and Clarabell the Clown rocket to the North Pole to save Santa.

Synopsis and Commentary: An icon in American children's television programming, *The Howdy Doody Show*, the creation of E. Roger Muir, ran for more than 2,500 episodes on NBC from 1947 to 1960. The star was Howdy Doody, a character first created and voiced on radio by Bob Smith. When Howdy was brought to television, puppeteer Frank Paris created a red-headed Howdy Doody marionette boy with 48 freckles, one for each of the then-48 states in the USA. Hosted by "Buffalo Bob" Smith in cowboy garb, the show featured a Western frontier setting with Howdy's name deriving from typical greetings "howdy doody" or "howdy do" or "how do," all variations of "How do you do?" Howdy received "plastic surgery" with a more appealing makeover by Velma Dawson, and that's the Howdy most people of that era remember. Along with a "peanut gallery" of some 40 children, the show featured a number of other puppets, such as Phineas T. Bluster and Flub-a-Dub, as well as human characters, the most notable of whom was Clarabell the Clown, originally played by Bob Keeshan (*Captain Kangaroo*), a mute who communicated by honking horns and squirting seltzer.

Three principals on *The Howdy Doody Show*, ca. 1956. From left: "Buffalo Bob" Smith, Howdy Doody, and Lew Anderson as Clarabell the Clown. *In Howdy Doody's Christmas* (1951), Bob Keeshan portrays Clarabell. NBC Television (collection of William D. Crump).

In *Howdy Doody's Christmas*, filmed in black and white, it's Christmas Eve near midnight, and while they wait for Santa's arrival, Howdy, Buffalo Bob, and Clarabell (Bob Keeshan) are decorating their Christmas tree with tinsel and strings of buttered popcorn. Clarabell sits and eats the popcorn, then hangs up his bottomless stocking on the mantel by pounding in the nail with his head. As the clock strikes 12, the three principals hide from Santa, but when he doesn't show up, they fly to the North Pole in a hokey rocket ship straight from the *Flash Gordon* series to investigate the trouble. At the North Pole, Ugly Sam (Dayton Allen, *The Deputy Dawg Show*), the world's worst wrestler (knocked in the head too many times), is holding Santa captive (actor not credited), having mistaken him for an escaped, bearded bandit. When the others arrive in Santa's darkened workshop, a slapstick altercation with Ugly Sam occurs involving lots of crashing, running around, and Howdy hollering "Aw, stop, everybody, stop!" Howdy frees Santa, and when the lights come up, Sam and Bob recognize each other, whereupon Santa gives Sam a mirror to admire his beautiful, ugly self, and Santa takes to the skies (in animation).

AWARDS: In 1949, *The Howdy Doody Show*

won a Peabody Award (NBC) and received Primetime Emmy nominations in 1953 and 1956 for Best Children's Program/Series.

PRODUCTION CREDITS—Writer, Producer, Director: all uncredited. Production Company: United World Films. Rating: G. Genre: Short. Country: USA. Run Time: 8.5 min.

REFERENCES: "Howdy Doody." Word Press. https://deepfriedhoodsiecups.wordpress.com/2011/01/20/1202011/

Howdy Doody's Christmas. Digiview Entertainment, 2006. DVD Video.

Howdy Doody's Christmas. Internet Movie Database. http://www.imdb.com/title/tt2586172/

Wilson, Joanna. *Tis the Season TV: The Encyclopedia of Christmas-Themed Episodes, Specials and Made-for-TV Movies.* Akron, OH: 1701 Press, 2011.

I Saw Stroker Killing Santa Claus—
December 4, 2005

(AKA *A Cold, Dead, White Christmas*)

Episode from the Animated Television Series *Stroker and Hoop*

THREAT TO CHRISTMAS: Santa dies after an assailant stabs him in the neck with poison.

HOW CHRISTMAS IS SAVED: Three ghosts in Dickensian fashion lead Stroker and Hoop backward and forward in time to save Santa.

SYNOPSIS AND COMMENTARY: Created by Casper Kelly and Jeffrey G. Olsen, this bizarre, adult-themed comedy series of only 13 episodes aired on Cartoon Network's Adult Swim from 2004 to 2005. Riddled with abundantly vulgar language (the strongest words were bleeped), the series revolved around the crime-solving adventures of two incompetent private detectives in Los Angeles, John Strockmeyer ("Stroker"), whom women regarded as a repulsive chauvinist, and his nerdy partner, Hoop Schwartz, whose disguises always failed. Often bailing them out of sticky situations was their vehicle C.A.R.R., a talking AMC Pacer with its own neurotic personality. Other principal characters included Double Wide, a mechanic addicted to pornography who created C.A.R.R.; Coroner Rick, who ran the county morgue and consistently cracked crude jokes about his "clients"; and Stroker's ten-year-old son Keith.

When the real Santa moonlights as a mall Santa to get the feel of the public, an assailant stabs him in the neck with a syringe containing an unknown poison, whereupon Stroker on the scene hauls Santa yet still living to Coroner Rick, who cannot provide an antidote. Stroker had retrieved a lottery ticket that the assailant had dropped while fleeing, and now when the latest lottery numbers appear on Rick's TV, Stroker is a winner. Abandoning the dying Santa, Stroker and Hoop head for the ski slopes, leaving C.A.R.R. behind as Santa, throwing up blood and green puke, trudges through deep L.A. *snow* to Stroker's house, where C.A.R.R. learns of his plight. Apparently on a run to find Stroker, C.A.R.R. with Santa aboard hits a tree and Santa dies. Bring in Dickens's *A Christmas Carol* laced with a bit of sci-fi. At the ski lodge, Stroker's former partner, Jermaine Washington, deceased for seven years (a nod to Jacob Marley), confronts him as the Ghost of Christmas Past and takes him back when Jermaine had been shot and killed, because Stroker had borrowed Jermaine's gun clip without telling him. Enter the Ghost of Christmas Present, who recounts Santa's death on the road, while the Ghost of Christmas Future reveals that the two detectives are now the neighborhood's destitute pariahs for letting Santa die. As Scrooge saw his own death, Stroker in present self kills his future self in a shootout. Jumping back to the present in a game of time travel with the ghosts, C.A.R.R. partners with the reindeer team to deliver the presents, but it rounds up Stroker and Hoop instead to get stiff Santa to the morgue after the sight of his corpse panics a little girl. While Rick diddles with Santa's brain and liver, Christmas Future whisks the detectives 15 years ahead to get the antidote from Rick, then back to the past to save Santa before he dies in C.A.R.R., then ahead again to the present. (Don't worry if none of it makes any sense.) With all the ghosts together, Stroker deduces their involvement in a lottery ring, Jermaine having poisoned Santa when the latter had become suspicious. Now

Santa, in a most un–Christmas-like display of revenge, shoots down all three ghosts in cold blood, (on this show they're vulnerable), plugs them several more times for spite, then pleads for another clip. This breaks the space-time continuum such that Stroker never won the lottery. Finding himself back home with Hoop, the latter urges him to get a Christmas goose instead. Cut to Stroker with son Keith and Hoop at a *turkey* farm, where viewers learn that the narrator has been a talking turkey that soon becomes the gang's Christmas dinner.

PRINCIPAL VOICES: Jon Glaser (*Human Giant*) as Stroker; Speed Levitch (*School of Rock*) as Hoop; Paul Christie (*Brother Bear*) as C.A.R.R.; Mary Birdsong (*The Descendants*) as Keith; Daran Norris (*The Replacements*) as Santa; Gary Anthony Williams (*End of Days*) as Coroner Rick, Jermaine, and Ghost of Christmas Present; and Eli Wallach (*The Magnificent Seven*) as the narrator.

INTERESTING TIDBITS: Obviously, this episode title is a play on the song title "I Saw Mommy Kissing Santa Claus," even though Stroker has nothing directly to do with Santa's death, except to abandon him.

In addition to allusions to *A Christmas Carol*, there are several other parodies here. The series itself is a parody of buddy cop shows like *Starsky and Hutch*, and C.A.R.R., somewhat resembling the Ford Torino in that particular series, is a parody of K.I.T.T., Michael Knight's talking car in the series *Knight Rider*. Moreover, "C.A.R.R." is a parody of "K.A.R.R.," K.I.T.T.'s antagonist. And the names of the two lead characters are nods to two action comedy films starring Burt Reynolds, *Stroker Ace* (1983) and *Hooper* (1978).

NOTE: At the time of this writing, this series was not available on DVD or VHS but could be seen at the Adult Swim Web Site at www.adultswim.com/videos/stroker-and-hoop.

REVIEWS: Melissa Camacho of *Common Sense Media* reviewed the series: "…this animated spoof includes strong sexual content, exaggerated gun violence, images of blood pouring out of bullet wounds, and lots of inappropriate language (though the strongest words are bleeped out). While adult fans may enjoy the way [the series] pokes fun at some of their old favorites, it's not meant for younger viewers."

PRODUCTION CREDITS—Writers: Casper Kelly and Jeffrey G. Olsen. Producer: Evan W. Adler. Directors: David Wachtenheim and Robert Marianetti. Production Companies: Williams Street, Turner Studios, and Studio B. Productions. Rating: TV-MA. Genres: Animation, Comedy. Country: USA. Run Time: 30 min.

REFERENCES: Camacho, Melissa. *Stroker and Hoop*. Common Sense Media. https://www.commonsensemedia.org/tv-reviews/stroker-and-hoop

I Saw Stroker Killing Santa Claus. Internet Movie Database. http://www.imdb.com/title/tt0876058/

Wilson, Joanna. *Tis the Season TV: The Encyclopedia of Christmas-Themed Episodes, Specials and Made-for-TV Movies*. Akron, OH: 1701 Press, 2011.

Ice Age: A Mammoth Christmas Special—November 24, 2011

Computer-Animated Television Short Film

THREAT TO CHRISTMAS: Prehistoric beasts accidentally ruin all of Santa's presents while trying to get one of their kind off the naughty list.

HOW CHRISTMAS IS SAVED: The beasts work together to make new presents.

SYNOPSIS AND COMMENTARY: Animals celebrating Christmas in prehistoric times? It may be hard to swallow, but with lots of imagination and make-believe, anything is possible. The *Ice Age* series of computer-animated films follow the adventures of talking, Paleolithic mammals and include the following principal protagonists: wooly mammoths Manny and Ellie; Sid, a ground sloth; Diego, a saber-toothed tiger; and Scrat, a saber-toothed squirrel.

In *Mammoth Christmas*, when Sid accidentally shatters Manny's Christmas rock heirloom while decorating a Christmas tree, an angry Manny announces that Sid is on Santa's naughty list, even though Manny doesn't really believe in Santa. Overhearing this confession,

Peaches, the mammoths' young daughter, heads to the North Pole along with Sid and twin 'possums Crash and Eddie to prove that Santa is real and to get Sid off the naughty list. En route, the four fall off a cliff during a snowy whiteout but are saved by Prancer the flying reindeer, who flies them to the North Pole. There, an army of mini-sloths turns them away, and during their retreat, Prancer accidentally creates an avalanche that destroys Santa's presents. Manny, Ellie, and Diego, out searching for Peaches, arrive on the scene just in time to share the blame for destroying Christmas (which, as usual, centers around the presents), but Manny and his friends redeem themselves by enlisting the help of the mini-sloths to fashion new presents. Prancer, unable to pull Santa's heavy sleigh alone, realizes he needs the seven other members of his family, and they all work as a team to become Santa's eight classic reindeer (evidently Rudolph didn't exist back then). With Christmas saved, Santa places everyone on his nice list.

PRINCIPAL VOICES: Ray Romano (*Everybody Loves Raymond*) as Manny; Queen Latifah (*Living Single*) as Ellie; John Leguizamo (*Ice Age*) as Sid; Denis Leary (*Ice Age*) as Diego; Chris Wedge (*Ice Age*) as Scrat; Ciara Bravo (*Big Time Rush*) as Peaches; Seann William Scott (*Role Models*) as Crash; Josh Peck (*Red Dawn*) as Eddie; T.J. Miller (*Cloverfield*) as Prancer; Billy Gardell (*Bad Santa*) as Santa.

AWARDS: In 2012, this film received a Golden Reel Award nomination for Best Sound Editing–Sound Effects, Foley, Dialogue and ADR Animation in Television.

INTERESTING TIDBIT: A brief subplot features Scrat's performing an ice ballet to Tchaikovsky's "Waltz of the Flowers" while attempting to capture a coveted acorn.

REVIEWS: Emily Ashby of *Common Sense Media* (November 21, 2011): "…the story does offer a new perspective on the origin of some timeless Christmas traditions…. While the plot … is a little predictable (who else but Sid could cause such chaos that he'd need the whole pack to help dig him out?), there are enough twists that long-time fans won't be bored."

Kevin Carr of *7M Pictures*: "Don't try to

A scene from *Ice Age* (2002), showing three principal characters. From left: Diego, a saber-toothed tiger; Sid, a ground sloth; and Manny, a wooly mammoth. They also star in *Ice Age: A Mammoth Christmas Special* (2011), along with two other principals: Ellie, the wooly mammoth, and Scrat, the saber-toothed squirrel (Twentieth Century–Fox Film Corporation/Photofest).

make too much sense from this film and how it fits into the chronology of the movies.... Just enjoy it with the established characters."

PRODUCTION CREDITS—Writers: Sam Harper and Mike Reiss. Producer: Andrea M. Miloro. Director: Karen Disher. Production Companies: Blue Sky Studios and Reel FX Creative Studios. Rating: G. Genres: Adventure, Animation, Family, Short. Country: USA. Run Time: 25 min.

REFERENCES: Ashby, Emily. *Ice Age: A Mammoth Christmas. Common Sense Media.* https://www.commonsnsemedia.org/movie-reviews/ice-age-a-mammoth-christmas

Carr, Kevin. *Ice Age: A Mammoth Christmas Special. 7M Pictures.* http://www.7mpictures.com/ice-age-a-mammoth-christmas-special-dvd-review

Crump, William D. *The Christmas Encyclopedia.* Third Edition. Jefferson, NC: McFarland, 2013.

Ice Age: A Mammoth Christmas Special. Beverly Hills, CA: 20th Century Fox Home Entertainment, 2011. DVD Video.

Ice Age: A Mammoth Christmas. Big Cartoon Database. http://www.bcdb.com/cartoon/138311-Ice-Age-A-Mammoth-Christmas

Ice Age: A Mammoth Christmas. Internet Movie Database. http://www.imdb.com/title/tt2100546/

I'm Dreaming of a White Ranger

November 25, 1995

Episode from the Live-Action Children's Television Series *Mighty Morphin' Power Rangers*

THREAT TO CHRISTMAS: Lord Zedd's minions take over the North Pole and force the elves to make toys that will brainwash children.

The Mighty Morphin' Power Rangers, ninja-type warriors with superpowers who defend the universe against alien invaders, shown here in *Mighty Morphin' Power Rangers: The Movie* (1995). From left: Adam (Johnny Yong Bosch), Billy (David Yost), Tommy (Jason David Frank), Kimberly (Amy Jo Johnson), Aisha (Karan Ashley), and Rocky (Steve Cardenas). These six Rangers also star in the TV series *Mighty Morphin' Power Rangers*, which includes the episode "I'm Dreaming of a White Ranger" (1995) (Twentieth Century–Fox Film Corporation/Photofest).

HOW CHRISTMAS IS SAVED: The Power Rangers overthrow Lord Zedd's forces (it couldn't be any other way).

SYNOPSIS AND COMMENTARY: Based on an adaptation of the Japanese children's television show *Kyoryu Sentai Zyuranger* and created by Haim Saban and Shuki Levy, *Mighty Morphin' Power Rangers* consisted of 145 half-hour episodes that ran on Fox Kids from 1993 to 1995 with numerous other incarnations in subsequent years. The series spawned a feature film, video games, comic books, and other merchandise. Pure sci-fi fantasy, the series focused on a group of high-school students hand-picked by their mentor Zordon, who enabled them to "morph" into ninja-type warriors with superpowers to defend the universe against a bunch of alien invaders and who piloted giant robots termed Zords (not unlike the all-terrain robot walkers of the *Star Wars* films). The Rangers' chief antagonists were the Darth Vader–like Lord Zedd, the space witch Rita Repulsa, the griffin-like Goldar, the skeleton Rito Revolto, and their monster henchmen.

While the Rangers host a politically correct event termed a "Holiday Pageant" for underprivileged children, Lord Zedd sends Rito Revolto and his minions to the North Pole to capture Santa and to force the elves to make hypnospins—spinning toys that brainwash children into doing Zedd's evil bidding. Zordon alerts the Rangers about the problem, but cautions that at the North Pole, their powers are useless. Zedd then orders Goldar to the scene to battle the Rangers, but since he and Rito also lack superpowers there, the Rangers defeat them in a snowball fight (rather innocuous compared to the martial arts fighting typically found in the series) and trip them so they can be rounded up together and zapped back to Zedd. The fracas puts Santa behind schedule, so the Rangers join the elves in making and packing the toys in time for Santa's rounds, then return to the children's party with a sack of gifts from Santa. The old gent also has gifts for Zedd and his cronies—a box full of hypnospin toys.

CAST: Amy Jo Johnson as Pink Ranger Kimberly; David Yost as Blue Ranger Billy; Johnny Yong Bosch as Black Ranger Adam; Karan Ashley as Yellow Ranger Aisha; Steve Cardenas as Red Ranger Rocky; Jason David Frank as Green/White Ranger Tommy; Robert von Fliss as Santa. All have worked on the *Power Rangers* series.

VOICES: Richard Wood as Alpha 5; Colin Phillips as Baboo; Robert Axelrod as Lord Zedd and Finster; Kerrigan Mahan as Goldar; Kurt Strauss as Ninjor; Barbara Goodson as Rita; Bob Pappenbrook as Rito; Michael J. Sorich as Squatt; Bob Manahan as Zordon.

AWARDS: The series received a Daytime Emmy nomination for Outstanding Single Camera Photography (1995) and IGN Summer Movie Award nominations for Best TV DVD or Blu-Ray (2012 and 2013).

INTERESTING TIDBITS: The Holiday Pageant is ecumenical in that a group of children sing three numbers with different "flavors": a secular Christmas song ("We Wish You a Merry Christmas"), a Hanukkah song ("O Hanukkah"), and a sacred Christmas song ("Silent Night"). Holiday symbols include a Christmas tree, Santa faces, and a large Star of David. Kwanzaa is not mentioned here.

REVIEWS: Andrea Graham of *Common Sense Media* reviewed the series: "*Power Rangers* is based on that flourishing formula of robots, martial arts, and sci-fi action that children—especially boys—find so intoxicating. While it has enjoyed years of success … the series is still iffy due to its violent nature … the show's focus tends to be on action and fighting."

David Johnson of *DVD Verdict* reviewed the series (November 26, 2012): "To this day, the Power Rangers have a stranglehold on kids' live-action television, which is ironic, because there's probably an excellent chance that your children currently have strangleholds on each other because of the Power Rangers.… Is [the series] ridiculous and corny? Of course it is … despite its propensity for cartoon violence, there's not an offensive strand of DNA in its make-up."

PRODUCTION CREDITS—Writers: Ron Milbauer and Terri Hughes. Producers: Ronnie Hadar and Jonathan Tzachor. Director: Douglas Sloan. Production Companies: MMPR Productions, Renaissance-Atlantic Films, Saban Entertainment, Toel Company. Rating: TV-Y7. Genres: Action, Adventure, Animation, Family, Fantasy, Sci-Fi. Countries: Japan and USA. Run Time: 21 min.

REFERENCES: Graham, Andrea. *Mighty Morphin' Power Rangers. Common Sense Media.* https://www.commonsensemedia.org/tv-reviews/mighty-morphin-power-rangers

"I'm Dreaming of a White Ranger." In *Mighty Morphin' Power Rangers: The Complete Series.* Los Angeles: Shout! Factory, 2012. DVD Video.

Johnson, David. *Mighty Morphin' Power Rangers: The Complete Series. DVD Verdict.* http://www.dvdverdict.com/reviews/powerrangerscomplete.php

Mighty Morphin' Power Rangers. Internet Movie Database. http://www.imdb.com/title/tt0106064/

Wilson, Joanna. *Tis the Season TV: The Encyclopedia of Christmas-Themed Episodes, Specials and Made-for-TV Movies.* Akron, OH: 1701 Press, 2011.

In the Nick of Time—
December 16, 1991

Television Movie

THREAT TO CHRISTMAS: Santa must find a replacement or Christmas is cancelled.

HOW CHRISTMAS IS SAVED: Santa chooses a dispirited journalist as his successor.

SYNOPSIS AND COMMENTARY: Instead of being immortal or at least serving for life, Santa follows some kind of mandate stipulating that he must choose a successor after serving at the North Pole for X number of years. In this case, Santa has reigned for 300 years and must now retire. Time has almost expired for Nicholas V (Lloyd Bridges, *Sea Hunt*), who discovers that he has only one week remaining to find a replacement, or Christmas will end. Whether Nick just forgot about the time or deliberately procrastinated until the last minute, we'll never know. Nick's trek takes him to New York City, where his magic powers vanish after 24 hours and his task becomes more difficult. He finds a friend in Freddy (Cleavon Little, *Blazing Saddles*), a watchman for a failing recreation center, and meets Ben Talbot (Michael Tucker, *L.A. Law*), a newspaper journalist whose depression over the loss of his wife has severely jeopardized his career. Nick's positive influence instills Ben with the Christmas spirit, and Ben takes steps

The typical Santa-must-find-a-replacement-or-Christmas-will-end film, *In the Nick of Time* (1991) features Lloyd Bridges (left) as Nicholas V (Santa), with Michael Tucker as Ben Talbot, a failing newspaper journalist who becomes Santa's replacement (NBC/MMG Photo Archives; collection of William D. Crump).

that effect a successful rescue of the recreation center. He is further inspired after learning of Nick's mission and, in the spirit of Francis P. Church ("Yes, Virginia, There Is a Santa Claus"), writes "The Great Santa Hunt," an article designed to produce the next Santa from the masses. On Christmas Eve, however, when Nick fails to remember a particular Christmas gift he had received as a child, it is the "sign" that Ben has been chosen as the next Santa. His first official act is to produce snow for Christmas.

NOTE: At the time of this writing, this film was not available on DVD or VHS and should not be confused with *Nick of Time* (1995), a political thriller film.

REVIEW: Ken Tucker of *Entertainment Weekly* gave this film a grade of B+ (December 13, 1991): "This happily sappy 'Disney Night at the Movies' production spends most of its two hours with gently comic scenes in which Santa tries to convince Tucker's character that he's the man for the job…. It's fun to see Bridges stroll through New York City and watch legions of rude people on every level of society become sweetly smiling softies."

PRODUCTION CREDITS—Story: Jon S. Denny. Teleplay: Maryedith Burrell, Rick Podell, and Michael Preminger. Producer: Michael Jaffe. Director: George Miller. Production Companies: Spectacor Films and Walt Disney Television. Rating: Not rated. Genres: Comedy, Family, Fantasy. Countries: Canada and USA. Run Time: 89 min.

REFERENCES: Crump, William D. *The Christmas Encyclopedia*. Third Edition. Jefferson, NC: McFarland, 2013.

In the Nick of Time. Internet Movie Database. http://www.imdb.com/title/tt0102113/

Tucker, Ken. *In the Nick of Time*. *Entertainment Weekly*. http://www.ew.com/article/1991/12/13/nick-time

Inspector Gadget Saves Christmas—
December 4, 1992

Animated Television Short Film

THREAT TO CHRISTMAS: Dr. Claw takes over the North Pole to make defective toys.

HOW CHRISTMAS IS SAVED: Inspector Gadget, niece Penny, and pet dog Brain foil Claw's scheme.

SYNOPSIS AND COMMENTARY: Dimwitted

A bionic bonehead, Inspector Gadget (right), often unwittingly requires the assistance of his young niece Penny (left) and pet dog Brain to solve his cases. All three star in *Inspector Gadget Saves Christmas* (1992) (LBS Communications/Photofest).

and dressed in a trench coat like Inspector Clouseau in *The Pink Panther* series and behaving like clueless Maxwell Smart in the *Get Smart* series, Inspector Gadget was an idiotic cyborg police detective and protagonist in a Canadian-French-Japanese-Taiwanese-American animated television series that ran for 86 half-hour episodes from 1983 to 1986. Gadget was so named, because he had any number of gadgets linked to his person that he could activate in a pinch by saying, "Go, go, gadget" plus the gadget's name. Though quite sure of himself, Gadget usually bungled his cases and solved them by sheer luck. His savvy niece Penny and pet dog Brain accompanied him on his capers and were primarily instrumental in effecting Gadget's "victories." Gadget's nemesis was Dr. Claw, a mysterious villain and leader of the evil organization MAD, whose face was never shown, and who performed his misdeeds with his ever-present pet, MAD Cat. Gadget received assignments from his boss, Chief Quimby of the Metro City Police Department. The animated series spawned other series, video games, and live-action films.

In *Christmas*, Dr. Claw gains access to Santa's toy factory disguised as the jolly ole elf and converts all the other elves to drones via mind-control devices, whereupon the elves capture the real Santa and drop him along with the reindeer into a cell below the North Pole (which begs the question: Why would the North Pole need cells underground?). With Santa out of the picture, the elves now fashion defective toys, for which Santa will be blamed, and Christmas will be ruined; that is, lousy presents beget a lousy Christmas. Alerted about the trouble, Gadget, Penny, and Brain find themselves at the North Pole, where Gadget's inability to tell one Santa from another gets him mangled in a machine and then tossed into the same cell where he mistakes the real Santa for Dr. Claw and "arrests" him. Meanwhile, as Gadget interrogates Santa using lines from "'Twas the Night Before Christmas," the elves trap Penny in a jack-in-the-box, and Brain manages to sneak the key to Santa's cell away from MAD Cat. But Gadget, mistaking Brain for one of Claw's minions, lassos him and Santa together, then runs out to help Claw/Santa load defective toys into the sleigh. Having sprung herself from the box, Penny, who totes around a computer manual for situations like this, uses information therein to deactivate the device that controls the elves as Claw/Santa is about to take off in his MAD mobile with the sleigh in tow. Just in the nick of time, Santa arrives to release the sleigh, the reindeer crack the ice behind Claw, which sends him and his vehicle floating away into the Arctic waters, and Chief Quimby parachutes in to congratulate the still-clueless Gadget.

VOICES: Don Adams (*Get Smart*) as Inspector Gadget; Frank Welker (*Aladdin*) as Brain, Dr. Claw, MAD Cat, Santa; Maurice LaMarche (*Futurama*) as Chief Quimby; Erica Horne (*On Location: The Roseanne Barr Show*) as Penny.

AWARDS: In 1993, this film received a Primetime Emmy nomination for Outstanding Animated Program (One Hour or Less).

INTERESTING TIDBITS: Even before they become drones, the elves might as well be clones, because they all look alike (that's such a familiar phrase).

While sitting on a mall Santa's knee and discussing his Christmas list, Gadget receives his assignment in the form of a note from Santa, who is Chief Quimby in disguise. Smacking of *Mission: Impossible*, the self-destructing note explodes in Quimby's face.

Inspector Gadget was the first animated TV series to be broadcast in stereo sound.

PRODUCTION CREDITS—Writers: Jack Hanrahan and Eleanor Burian-Mohr. Producer and Director: Chuck Patton. Production Company: DiC Enterprises. Rating: Not rated. Genres: Animation, Comedy, Family. Country: USA. Run Time: 23 min.

REFERENCES: *Inspector Gadget Saves Christmas*. Big Cartoon Database. http://www.bcdb.com/cartoon/47787-Inspector-Gadget-Saves-Christmas

Inspector Gadget Saves Christmas. Fort Mill, SC: Sterling Entertainment Group, 2004. DVD Video.

Inspector Gadget Saves Christmas. Internet Movie Database. http://www.imdb.com/title/tt0285225/

Lenburg, Jeff. *The Encyclopedia of Animated Cartoons*. Third Edition. New York: Facts on File, 2009.

Wilson, Joanna. *Tis the Season TV: The Encyclopedia of Christmas-Themed Episodes, Specials and Made-for-TV Movies*. Akron, OH: 1701 Press, 2011.

It Nearly Wasn't Christmas—1989

Television Movie

THREAT TO CHRISTMAS: Santa decides to quit, because the holiday is overrun with commercialism.

HOW CHRISTMAS IS SAVED: A little girl's letter and the end to a cross-country trek convince Santa that mankind still believes in him.

SYNOPSIS AND COMMENTARY: If eight-year-old Virginia O'Hanlon (of "Yes, Virginia, There Is a Santa Claus" fame) could still believe in Santa at that age, then so can eight-year-old Jennifer Baxter (Risa Schiffman, *Camp Cucamonga*), whose letter to Santa is a godsend. Plunged into the doldrums over Christmas commercialism and wallowing in self-pity—nobody cares about him anymore—Santa (Charles Durning, *Elmo Saves Christmas*) decides to quit, until he receives Jennifer's letter: all she wants is for her family to be together again for Christmas. This could have been just one of many routine Santa-reunites-the-family movies, except that here, a more positive Mrs. Claus (Beverly Rowland, *Halloween 4*) urges Santa not only to fulfill Jennifer's wish but to go into the outside world and see for himself how much people really do believe in him. Determined to see her musician-father Jeff (Wayne Osmond of the Osmond Brothers) in Los Angeles, Jennifer covertly hops a bus and joins a portly stranger whom she quickly deduces to be Santa in street dress. With the help of Philpot (Bruce Vilanch, *Get Bruce*), Santa's bumbling giant of a chief elf, the two begin a series of cross-country adventures which include: Santa's brief arrest as the unwitting accomplice of Napoleon (Ted Lange, *The Love Boat*), a black con artist; a stint in a hot-air balloon; Santa's winning $5,000 in a sleigh race to pay a poor farmer's mortgage; and reforming a workaholic executive who would force his employees to work on Christmas Day. Despite Jennifer's and her mother Laura's (Annette Marin, *Ladybugs*) happy reunion with Jeff, Santa still remains skeptical of mankind's basic goodness, until he suffers a near-fatal injury while preventing Napoleon (who with Laura had been pursuing Santa) from absconding with illicit raffle funds at a shopping mall. Santa's survival depends on people's believing in him, whereupon Jennifer's passionate plea to the rubberneckers saves Santa and Christmas.

SONG: "It Nearly Wasn't Christmas," performed by Wayne Osmond, written by Merrill Osmond, James A. Osmond, and Kurt Bestor.

INTERESTING TIDBITS: Jennifer's plea parallels that in J.M. Barrie's play *Peter Pan* (1904), when at Peter's behest, the audience applauds to indicate their belief in fairies, which saves the poisoned fairy Tinker Bell. A similar scenario is found in **The Elf Who Saved Christmas, Elmo's Christmas Countdown,** and **Raggedy Ann and Andy in the Great Santa Claus Caper**.

Santa is away from the North Pole in most of this movie, so there are no scenes of his workshop. Before he departs for the outside world, however, it's interesting to note that in his office, there are two separate desks for incoming mail: one for children's letters requesting gifts for themselves, the other for letters requesting gifts for others. To Santa's grief, the first desk is piled high and overflowing; the second desk is empty—until Jennifer's letter magically appears there.

This film should not be confused with another save-Christmas film with a similar title: **Nearly No Christmas**.

NOTE: At the time of this writing, this film was not available on DVD or VHS but could be seen on YouTube.

PRODUCTION CREDITS—Story: Stanley Isaacs, Golda David, and Alan Jay Glueckman. Teleplay: Golda David and Alan Jay Glueckman. Producers: Jon Ackelson and Mark Burdge. Director: Burt Brinckerhoff. Production

Company: Osmond Entertainment. Rating: Not rated. Genres: Adventure, Comedy. Country: USA. Run Time: 100 min.

REFERENCES: Crump, William D. *The Christmas Encyclopedia*. Third Edition. Jefferson, NC: McFarland, 2013.

It Nearly Wasn't Christmas. Internet Movie Database. http://www.imdb.com/title/tt0097601/

Wilson, Joanna. *Tis the Season TV: The Encyclopedia of Christmas-Themed Episodes, Specials and Made-for-TV Movies*. Akron, OH: 1701 Press, 2011.

It's a SpongeBob Christmas!—November 23, 2012

Musical Episode from the Animated Television Series *SpongeBob SquarePants*

THREAT TO CHRISTMAS: Plankton's jerktonium-laced fruitcake makes jerks of everyone and puts them on Santa's naughty list, while Plankton creates a robot to destroy Santa.

HOW CHRISTMAS IS SAVED: The antidote for being a jerk is a special song, and SpongeBob defeats the robot with tainted fruitcake.

SYNOPSIS AND COMMENTARY: Santa visits creatures at the bottom of the sea? That's no more bizarre than his visits to prehistoric people and creatures as in *The Flintstones* or *Ice Age*. Being a magical being, Santa needs no diving equipment in *SpongeBob SquarePants*, a popular, ongoing series created in 1999 by marine biologist and animator Stephen Hillenburg for Nickelodeon. Set in the underwater village of Bikini Bottom, the series revolves around the adventures of SpongeBob SquarePants, a square, yellow, anthropomorphic sea sponge who resembles an ordinary kitchen sponge, lives in a pineapple house, and works as a fry cook at the Krusty Krab Restaurant. Other principal characters include Patrick Star, a dimwitted starfish; Squidward Tentacles, a sarcastic octopus; Sandy Cheeks, a female squirrel-inventor who lives topside and wears a diving suit to visit SpongeBob; Mr. Krabs, a

Citizens of Bikini Bottom attend the grand opening of the Krusty Krab 2 Restaurant in *The SpongeBob SquarePants Movie* (2004), featuring SpongeBob (center) and Squidward Tentacles (second from left). SpongeBob and Squidward are two of several principals in the episode "It's a SpongeBob Christmas!" (2012) from the animated TV series *SpongeBob SquarePants* (Paramount/Photofest).

red crab who runs the Krusty Krab; Gary, SpongeBob's meowing pet snail; and principal antagonist Plankton, a copepod and owner of the rival Chum Bucket restaurant, who always tries to steal Krabs's secret recipe for Krabby Patties.

"SpongeBob Christmas" utilizes puppets in stop-motion animation. When Plankton grows weary of receiving coal every Christmas for being the biggest jerk in town, he discovers "jerktonium," an element that turns nice folks into jerks. Reasoning that he will look really good if everyone else is a jerk (surely Santa will give him the recipe for Krabby Patties), he laces fruitcake with jerktonium and tests it on an unwitting SpongeBob, but he is immune because of his tiny brain and huge heart. Plankton then frames SpongeBob by sending out a wind-up robot in his likeness to commit foul deeds. Meanwhile, SpongeBob dispenses the delicious but tainted fruitcake all over town, and as the number of jerks multiplies, so does the mayhem that ultimately ruins the Christmas parade. SpongeBob consults Sandy, who discovers that singing a song titled "Don't Be a Jerk, It's Christmas" is the antidote. All seems well until Santa announces that everyone except Plankton is on the naughty list for having been jerks and will receive coal, but all that is moot as the robot arrives to destroy Santa, whereupon SpongeBob destroys it by pelting it with tainted fruitcake. SpongeBob is finally exonerated when discovery of the robot's key inscribed with "Chum Bucket" points to Plankton as the culprit, who receives yet another bag of coal.

SONGS: "Santa Has His Eyes on Me" by Luke Brookshier and Eban Schletter, performed by Tom Kenny, Bill Fagerbakke, Carolyn Lawrence, and Mr. Lawrence; "Hot Fruitcake" by Marc Ceccarelli, performed by Tom Kenny; "Don't Be a Jerk, It's Christmas" by Tom Kenny and Andy Paley, performed by Tom Kenny, Crissy Guerrero, and Tracy De Nise.

PRINCIPAL VOICES: Tom Kenny as SpongeBob and his taste buds, Patchy the Pirate, Toyboy, and Postman; Bill Fagerbakke as Patrick and Frankie; Rodger Bumpass as Squidward and Johnny; Clancy Brown as Mr. Krabs and fake Santa; Carolyn Lawrence as Sandy; Mr. Lawrence as Plankton; Jill Talley as Karen; Lori Alan as Pearl; John Goodman (*Roseanne*) as Santa and imaginary Santa; Paul Tibbitt as Potty the parrot. All voice actors except John Goodman are known for their work on the *SpongeBob SquarePants* TV series.

AWARDS: In 2013, this episode won an Annie Award for Character Animation in an Animated Television or Other Broadcast Venue Production; Annie nominations for Directing and Character Animation in an Animated Television or Other Broadcast Venue Production and for Best Animated Television Production for Children; Golden Reel Award nomination for Best Sound Editing–Sound Effects, Foley, Dialogue and ADR Animation in Television; Special Award for a TV Series nomination at the Annecy International Animated Film Festival.

INTERESTING TIDBITS: Bikini Bottom first became aware of Christmas in the episode titled "Christmas Who?" (2000).

"SpongeBob Christmas" was the first episode in the series to be produced in stop-motion animation. Because it premiered on CBS, it was also the first episode of the series to air on a network other than on Nickelodeon. The basis for the episode itself was Kenny's and Paley's song "Don't Be a Jerk, It's Christmas," originally written in 2009.

In a nod to the stop-motion animated special *Santa Claus Is Comin' to Town* (1970), in which a mailman serves as the narrator, host Patchy the Pirate with Potty the Parrot hijacks a mail truck and gives the mailman the day off (gags him in the back) in order to narrate this episode.

Santa's freakish appearance caught the attention of one reviewer (see below).

REVIEWS: Will Brownridge of *The Film Reel* (December 3, 2012): "[The film is] plenty of fun, and the stop motion is incredibly well done. They just don't make very many good Christmas specials [anymore], so [this film] is a terrific addition."

Paul Mavis of *DVD Talk* (November 18, 2012): "Like any *SpongeBob* toon, [this film] has its share of expected juvenile silliness; throw-away jokes that are so stupid they make the kids groan and laugh at the same time ... possibly the grossest kids' movie Santa *ever*, with a bald head covered in liver spots, rubbery, grouper balloon lips, and baggy, goggling eyes that look like hard-boiled eggs."

PRODUCTION CREDITS—Writers: Luke Brookshier, Marc Ceccarelli, Derek Iversen, and Mr. Lawrence (Douglas Lawrence Osowski). Supervising Producer: Paul Tibbitt. Directors: Mark Caballero and Seamus Walsh. Production Companies: Nickelodeon Animation Studios, Screen Novelties, and United Plankton Pictures. Rating: Not rated. Genres: Animation, Comedy, Family, Fantasy. Country: USA. Run Time: 23 min.

REFERENCES: Brownridge, Will. "It's a SpongeBob Christmas (2012)—or—Never Eat Fruitcake." *The Film Reel*. http://www.the-filmreel.com/2012/12/03/its-a-spongebob-christmas-2012-or-never-eat-fruitcake/

"It's a SpongeBob Christmas!" Big Cartoon Database. http://www.bcdb.com/cartoon/139482-Its-A-SpongeBob-Christmas

"It's a SpongeBob Christmas!" Internet Movie Database. http://www.imdb.com/title/tt2476918/

"It's a SpongeBob Christmas!" Nickelodeon, 2012. DVD Video.

Lenburg, Jeff. *The Encyclopedia of Animated Cartoons*. Third Edition. New York: Facts on File, 2009.

Mavis, Paul. *SpongeBob SquarePants: It's a SpongeBob Christmas! DVD Talk*. http://www.dvdtalk.com/reviews/57569/spongebob-squarepants-its-a-spongebob-christmas/

It's a Very Merry Eek's-Mas—December 5, 1993

Episode from the Animated Television Series *Eek! The Cat*

THREAT TO CHRISTMAS: The reindeer and elves are on strike, Mrs. Claus has left, and Santa is abed with a broken leg. That's about as bad as it can get.

HOW CHRISTMAS IS SAVED: Eek the Cat, Elmo the brown-nosed reindeer, and Sharky the sharkdog pull duty for Santa.

SYNOPSIS AND COMMENTARY: If a dog isn't available to save Christmas, call a cat. Following in the footsteps of the famous feline Felix, the slapstick series *Eek! The Cat*, created by Savage Steve Holland and Bill Kopp, ran for 75 half-hour episodes (with several different title variations) on Fox Kids in the USA and on YTV in Canada from 1992 to 1997. With references to pop culture, the series followed the misadventures of Eek, a purple cat whose catchphrase was "Kumbaya!" and whose motto was "It never hurts to help," although with Eek, the situation at hand usually fell apart. Other principal characters included Eek's girlfriend Annabelle, an obese white cat, and Sharky the sharkdog, Annabelle's vicious guard dog that resembled a shark. Various celebrities in caricatures often made cameo appearances.

In "Eek's-Mas," anarchy is afoot at the North Pole as the reindeer and elves are on strike, and Mrs. Claus flies the coop, leaving behind a "Dear Santa" letter. And to top off a Merry Christmas, Santa slips and breaks his leg, whereupon Elmo, the brown-nosed reindeer and Santa's only ally, appears on a TV talk show (a nod to Larry King) to solicit help from viewers. With no calls forthcoming, Elmo is tossed from the station and runs into Eek and Sharky, who've had no luck searching for the whereabouts of Sharky's family. Surely Santa has the answer, and with Eek ever-willing to help someone who's down, the three head to the North Pole and finish making the toys, but the sleigh is too heavy to pull. The solution: confer with the Barbi Twins, two blonde bombshells who provide complex, scientific rigmarole about hitching the sleigh to a rocket (which shatters the stigma of dumb blondes). After two launch attempts, both of which annihilate Santa's house, Eek, Sharky, and Elmo zoom about, pouring out gifts from Santa's sack around the world, but the rocket is destroyed when they pause to help a little girl find her lost bunny, so it's back to pulling the sleigh again. As reporters cover the story, people congregate to pull, along with the repentant elves and reindeer, and Mrs. Claus has a change of heart. The reindeer assume their roles, the sleigh is aloft again, and when the job's done, the sleigh glides sans reindeer toward the island inhabited by Sharky's family. But they're shot down as a UFO, and Eek and Sharky crash into a stewing cauldron on the island, where Sharky is reunited with his family, and Eek wonders if he'll be invited for Christmas dinner (as sharks sprinkle salt on him).

Principal Voices: Bill Kopp (*Tom and Jerry Blast Off to Mars*) as Eek, Elves, Sky Hawk 1; William Shatner (*Star Trek*) as Santa; Bobcat Goldthwait (*God Bless America*) as Blitzen; Savage Steve Holland (*Better Off Dead*) as Elmo; Tawny Kitaen (*Bachelor Party*) as Annabelle; Anita Dangler (*The Goodbye Girl*) as Mrs. Claus; Sia and Shane Barbi (*Skin Trade*) as themselves, the Barbi Twins.

Awards: *Eek! The Cat* series won an Artios Award for Best Casting for Animated Voiceover (Alice Cassidy, 1994); Artios nominations for the same category and same person (1995 and 1996); Daytime Emmy nomination for Outstanding Writing in an Animated Program (1994).

Interesting Tidbits: Elmo, Eek, and Sharky fly a commercial airline to the North Pole, because Elmo's flying license (spelled here as "licence") is expired. Sharky spends the flight with his head in a barf bag, while Elmo is engrossed in the nudie magazine *Play Doe*.

When Sharky attempts to prevent the rocket from falling off a cliff, his heart grows several sizes larger (a nod to the Grinch).

Review: Bob Cannon of *Entertainment Weekly* reviewed *Eek! The Cat* (October 2, 1992): "…equal parts Garfield cuteness, Roger Rabbit adventure, and Mister Magoo mishaps … [the writers] inflict such an unhealthy *Tom and Jerry*-style pounding on their cute, fuzzy star that the show becomes a relentlessly sadistic workout…. Monty Python–like transitions between episodes are intriguing and inventive."

Production Credits—Writer: Savage Steve Holland. Producer: Jocelyn Hamilton. Director: John Halfpenny. Production Companies: Fox Children's Productions, Nelvana, and Savage Studios. Rating: Not rated. Genres: Animation, Comedy, Family. Countries: Canada and USA. Run Time: 22 min.

References: Cannon, Bob. *Eek! The Cat*. *Entertainment Weekly*. http://www.ew.com/article/1992/10/02/eek-cat

Eek! The Cat. Internet Movie Database. http://www.imdb.com/title/tt0103408/

"It's a Very Merry Eek's-Mas." Big Cartoon Database. http://www.bcdb.com/cartoon/33486-Its-A-Very-Merry-Eeks-mas

"It's a Very Merry Eek's-Mas." In *Eek! The Cat DVD Box Set Fox*. Available at DVDRare.com.

"It's a Very Merry Eek's-Mas." Internet Movie Database. http://www.imdb.com/title/tt0569392/

Wilson, Joanna. *Tis the Season TV: The Encyclopedia of Christmas-Themed Episodes, Specials and Made-for-TV Movies*. Akron, OH: 1701 Press, 2011.

It's a Wonderful Leaf—November 4, 1991

Episode from the Animated Television Series *Darkwing Duck*

Threat to Christmas: A disgruntled scientist recruits an army of Christmas trees to steal all the presents in town.

How Christmas Is Saved: Darkwing Duck foils the scientist amid slapstick mayhem.

Synopsis and Commentary: A rhapsody on a collection of parodies, *Darkwing Duck* spoofed such crime-fighting superheroes as the Shadow, Batman, the Lone Ranger, and others. A spinoff of Disney's *Duck Tales*, this series of 91 half-hour episodes ran on the Disney Channel, on ABC, and in syndication from 1991 to 1992. The series revolved around the adventures of anthropomorphic Darkwing Duck, bedecked in purple cape, mask, and broad-brimmed hat, whose secret identity by day was Drake Mallard (a parody of Kent Allard, real name of the Shadow in that series), an ordinary citizen of St. Canard (a parody of Gotham City). Other principals included his sidekick and pilot Launchpad McQuack and his spunky, nine-year-old adopted daughter Gosalyn (a play on "gosling"). One of the Fearsome Five supervillains, the scientist Dr. Reginald Bushroot was a green, duck/plant hybrid with a mop of purple hair who controlled plants.

Preliminary scenes in "Wonderful Leaf" depict crazed Christmas shoppers running amok amid sales. Weary of being treated like "last year's fruitcake," Bushroot decides to ruin

Christmas, first by provoking citizens at the mall to fight among themselves and attack the mall Santa, whom Bushroot frames for a series of misdeeds. Then using his power over plants, he recruits an army of Christmas trees to steal all the presents in St. Canard. Once Darkwing gets the scent, a good portion of the show involves high-speed chases between him and Bushroot with lots of slapstick and cartoon violence. All the mayhem finally ends when Darkwing redirects the water from a broken hydrant onto the trees, which freezes them, and Bushroot is arrested. And to add a bit of aw-ain't-that-nice sentiment, when the town's presents are returned to the respective recipients, those for the Muddlefoots, Gosalyn's neighbors, are missing, whereupon she gives her presents to them.

PRINCIPAL VOICES: Jim Cummings (*Shrek*) as Darkwing Duck and Herb Muddlefoot; Christine Cavanaugh (*Babe*) as Gosalyn; Terry McGovern (*Duck Tales*) as Launchpad McQuack; Dana Hill (*European Vacation*) as Tank Muddlefoot; Tino Insana (*Barnyard*) as Bushroot; Katie Leigh (*Despicable Me*) as Honker Muddlefoot; Susan Tolsky (*Madame's Place*) as Binkie Muddlefoot.

AWARDS: *Darkwing Duck* won an Annie Award for Voice Acting in the Field of Animation (Jim Cummings, 1992); Annie nomination for Best Animated Television Program (1992); Daytime Emmy nominations for Outstanding Animated Program (1992 and 1993), Outstanding Film Sound Mixing and Sound Editing (1992 and 1993), Outstanding Writing in an Animated Program (1992); Young Artist Award nomination for Outstanding New Animation Series (1992).

When the evil Bushroot commands all the Christmas trees to steal the gifts lying beneath them, Darkwing Duck goes undercover as Santa to save Christmas in "It's a Wonderful Leaf" (1991), an episode from *Darkwing Duck*. Riding atop Darkwing/Santa's sack is his little adopted daughter Gosalyn (Walt Disney Company/Globe Photos; collection of William D. Crump).

INTERESTING TIDBIT: Christmas is all about the presents, as Bushroot affirms when the trees have done their job: "Now that they've stolen all the presents, Christmas will be nothing but stale eggnog."

PRODUCTION CREDITS—Writers: John Behnke, Jim Peterson, and Rob Humphrey. Producer: James T. Walker. Production Company: Walt Disney Television Animation. Rating: TV-Y. Genres: Animation, Comedy, Family. Country: USA. Run Time: 30 min.

REFERENCES: *Darkwing Duck*. Internet Movie Database. http://www.imdb.com/title/tt0101076/

"It's a Wonderful Leaf." Big Cartoon Database. http://www.bcdb.com/cartoon/5686-Its-A-Wonderful-Leaf

"It's a Wonderful Leaf." In *Disney's Darkwing Duck: Volume 2*. Burbank, CA: Walt Disney Home Entertainment, 2007. DVD Video.

"It's a Wonderful Leaf." Internet Movie Database. http://www.imdb.com/title/tt0995945/

Wilson, Joanna. *Tis the Season TV: The Encyclopedia of Christmas-Themed Episodes, Specials and Made-for-TV Movies*. Akron, OH: 1701 Press, 2011.

Jingle Bell Rock—1995

Animated Television Short Film

THREAT TO CHRISTMAS: Santa is bankrupt and plans to cancel Christmas.

HOW CHRISTMAS IS SAVED: Buddy Elf and his friend Holly bail out Santa by winning a talent contest with Buddy's new song.

SYNOPSIS AND COMMENTARY: Little could Joseph Beal and James Boothe ever imagine that one day a cartoon would be based on their 1957 Christmas hit, "Jingle Bell Rock." Whatever, Santa is bankrupt, having placed too many people on the nice list, so he plans to cancel Christmas until his finances are back in the black. Buddy Elf believes that if he can sell his new song "Jingle Bell Rock" in Hollywood, the income will save Santa's finances—and Christmas. Buddy would audition for a spot on the TV show *Star Seekers*, but two other elves, Art and Richie, beat him to the draw with plans to keep any cash they win for themselves. Buddy then teams up to sing his song with Holly, the producer's niece, who initially will not perform when she learns that her uncle has rigged the show in her favor. Nevertheless, Buddy convinces her to go on with him and, as expected, they bring down the house, Art and Richie having cheated during their own performance. Christmas is back on, thanks to Buddy, who replaces Art as the new music supervisor at the North Pole, and Art and Richie are demoted to stable hands.

PRINCIPAL VOICES: Milton Berle (*The Milton Berle Show*) as TV producer Jerry Labello; Sam Khouth (*Martin Mystery*) as Buddy; Kathleen Barr (*ReBoot*) as Holly; Don Brown (*Dragon Ball Z*) as Art; Brian Drummond (*Dragon Ball Z*) as Richie.

INTERESTING TIDBITS: Two nods to the late rock performer Buddy Holly: Buddy Elf's guitar is named "Peggy Sue," a Buddy Holly classic, and the singing duo are introduced on the show as "Buddy and Holly."

PRODUCTION CREDITS—Story: Phil Harnage. Teleplay and Producers: Elana Lesser and Cliff Ruby. Director: Michael B. Hefferon. Production Company: DiC Productions. Rating: Not rated. Genre: Animation. Country: USA. Run Time: 24 min.

REFERENCES: *Jingle Bell Rock*. In *DiC Animated Christmas Blast*. Los Angeles: Shout! Factory, 2008. DVD Video.

Jingle Bell Rock. Internet Movie Database. http://imdb.com/title/tt1934292/

Wilson, Joanna. *Tis the Season TV: The Encyclopedia of Christmas-Themed Episodes, Specials and Made-for-TV Movies*. Akron, OH: 1701 Press, 2011.

Krampus—December 4, 2015

Feature Film

THREAT TO CHRISTMAS: The Germanic demon Krampus arrives to send a dysfunctional family to hell for losing the Christmas spirit.

HOW CHRISTMAS IS SAVED: Though Krampus dispatches the family to hell, they awaken *as if* from a dream and seemingly safe at home on Christmas morning.

SYNOPSIS AND COMMENTARY: In many areas of Europe on December 5, the eve of St. Nicholas's Day, men dressed as Bishop St. Nicholas in full clerical attire ride about cities on white horses, while children set our their shoes for the saint to fill with toys and treats overnight. Accompanying St. Nicholas is a personification of Satan, known, depending on the region, by a host of different names, one of which is "Krampus" that supposedly derives from a Germanic word meaning "claw." A hideous, horned, fur-clad demon with blackened face, dark beard, cloven hooves like a goat, long tail, and red, serpentine tongue, this antithesis of St. Nicholas growls, rattles chains (from the superstition of "binding the devil"), and sports a whip with which to "beat" naughty children and those ignorant of their catechism. Some characters tote bags or baskets in which they threaten to stuff and whisk away the little offenders. The demon Krampus is thought by some to derive from Odin, the wild king of the Norse gods; from the son of Hel, Norse goddess of the underworld; from Thor, Norse god of war and thunder; and by others from the so-called "Wild Man," a hairy beast-god of primordial civilizations.

Instead of accompanying St. Nicholas or Santa, the demon in the film *Krampus* arrives to send a dysfunctional, American family to hell, because their bickering has caused them to lose the Christmas spirit. Of Austrian heritage (where Krampus is well known), the primary family consists of Tom Engel (Adam Scott, *The Aviator*), wife Sarah (Toni Collette, *Muriel's Wedding*), teenage daughter Beth (Stefania LaVie Owen, *The Lovely Bones*), young son Max (Emjay Anthony, *Chef*), and the grandmother Omi (Krista Stadler, *Mobbing*). The terror begins three days before Christmas after the remainder of the family arrives for the holidays: Sarah's redneck sister and brother-in law with their obnoxious hellions and a sarcastic, hard-drinking aunt. Though Max still believes in Santa, his skeptical cousins taunt him mercilessly to the point that a vicious fight erupts at the dinner table, whereupon Max declares his hatred for Christmas. This brings on a freak blizzard that kills the power all over town and heralds the arrival of Krampus (Luke Hawker, *Avatar*). The remainder of the film chronicles Krampus's dispatching Max's family one member at a time with assistance from his minions, nightmarish versions of holiday icons. After Beth and a cousin disappear, Omi describes their executioner as the "shadow of St. Nicholas," who had spared her as a child in the Old Country after sending her family and town to hell when poverty had robbed them of the Christmas spirit. To remind others *not* to lose the Christmas spirit, Krampus had given her a little bauble inscribed with his name. But alas, even she is not immune and now succumbs to Krampus's wrath as he dispatches the rest of the family. Only Max is spared and receives a similar bauble. When he pleads with Krampus to return the others and take him instead, Krampus obliges by dropping Max screaming into the pit of hell—yet he awakens alive, whole, and seemingly safe at home on Christmas morning. Was it all just a bad dream? Opening gifts with his relatives, Max discovers his dreaded Krampus bauble, which silences the family as memories of the previous night flood their minds. The closing footage shows their house trapped within a snow globe that resides on a shelf in Krampus's domain, along with thousands of similar snow globes.

AWARDS: In 2015, this film won an International Film Music Critics Award for Best Original Score for a Comedy Film; a Golden Schmoes Award nomination for Best Horror Movie of the Year; a Rondo Hatton Classic Horror Award nomination for Best Movie. In 2016, the film received a Saturn Award nomination for Best Horror Film; an Empire Award nomination, UK, for Best Horror Film; Fangoria Chainsaw Award nominations for Best Wide-Release Film, Best Supporting Actress (Krista Stadler), Best Makeup/Creature FX; Horror Society Award Second Place for Best Horror Film; Young Artist Award nomination for Best Performance in a Feature Film, Leading Young Actor 11–13 (Emjay Anthony).

INTERESTING TIDBITS: The film's opening and closing scenes illustrate some real irony. As greedy Christmas shoppers in slow motion storm stores like maniacs—pushing, shoving, and brawling—Bing Crosby's mellow crooning fills the background with "It's Beginning to Look a Lot Like Christmas." Then the film closes with his popular rendition of "Santa Claus Is Coming to Town."

The engravings on Omi's and Max's Krampus baubles read "*Gruss vom Krampus*" (German, "Greetings from Krampus").

"Omi" is German for "Granny"; "Engel" is German for "angel."

As Omi bakes Christmas goodies, the program she's watching on TV is the black-and-white version of *A Christmas Carol* (1951), starring Alastair Sim.

A part of Central European alpine folklore

for at least a millennium, Krampus has been the central figure on *Krampusnacht*, (Krampus Night), a festival held on various nights in December but especially on December 5, the eve of St. Nicholas's Day. There, men dressed as Krampus accompany St. Nicholas figures and run through the streets terrorizing children.

With a budget of $15 million, this film earned $42.7 million in domestic box office sales and $18.8 million in foreign sales for a worldwide total of $61.5 million.

REVIEWS: According to the Rotten Tomatoes film review site, 66 percent of critics gave this film a positive review. Metacritic gave it a score of 49/100 (mixed/average reviews).

Darren Franich of *Entertainment Weekly* (December 3, 2015): "...full credit to director Michael Dougherty (*Trick 'r Treat*) because this is [a] great-looking movie, filled with freaky creature designs and a just-right mixture of practical effects and CGI."

A.O. Scott of *The New York Times* (December 3, 2015): "Occasionally funny, intermittently scary, but mostly hectic and sloppy, *Krampus* tries very hard to be a different kind of Christmas movie. It wants to have its store-bought fruitcake and eat it too, to satirize the meanness and materialism of holiday-observing Americans and also connect with the vaguely defined real meaning of the season."

Noel Murray of the *Los Angeles Times* (December 4, 2015): "...Dougherty's effects team is top-notch, and the movie takes unexpected chances with the style and the storytelling—including a beautiful stop-motion interlude."

Jeffrey M. Anderson of *Common Sense Media* (December 6, 2015): "...the monsters are menacing, but they also have a fun quality, not unlike those in the *Gremlins* movies. The movie sometimes gets lost in all its monster fights, but then the ominous, somewhat ambiguous ending ties everything together. *Krampus* may be too much for sensitive viewers, but lovers of alternative holiday viewing will rejoice."

PRODUCTION CREDITS—Writers: Todd Casey, Michael Dougherty, and Zach Shields. Producers: Michael Dougherty, Alex Garcia, Thomas Tull, and Jon Jashni. Director: Michael Dougherty. Production Companies: Legendary Pictures and Universal Pictures. Rating: PG-13 (horror, violence, terror, language, drug material). Genres: Comedy, Fantasy, Horror. Countries: USA and New Zealand. Run Time: 98 min.

REFERENCES: Anderson, Jeffrey M. *Krampus. Common Sense Media.* https://www.commonsensemedia.org/movie-reviews/krampus

Basu, Tanya. "Who Is Krampus? Explaining the Horrific Christmas Devil." *National Geographic.* http://news.nationalgeographic.com/news/2013/12/131217-krampus-christmas-santa-devil/

Crump, William D. *The Christmas Encyclopedia*. Third Edition. Jefferson, NC: McFarland, 2013.

Franich, Darren. "*Krampus*: EW Review." Entertainment Weekly. http://www.ew.com/article/2015/12/03/krampus-ew-review

Krampus. Box Office Mojo. http://www.moxofficemojo.com/movies/?id=krampus.htm

Krampus. Internet Movie Database. http://www.imdb.com/title/tt3850590/

Krampus. Metacritic. http://www.metacritic.com/movie/krampus

Krampus. Rotten Tomatoes. http://www.rottentomatoes.com/m/krampus/

Krampus. Universal City, CA: Universal Studios Home Entertainment, 2016. DVD Video.

Murray, Noel. "'Krampus' Kills It with Christmas Scares That Are All in Good Fun." *Los Angeles Times.* http://touch.latimes.com/#section/641/article/p2p-85233482/

Scott, A.O. "Review: In 'Krampus,' the Holiday Involves a Demonic Santa." *The New York Times.* http://www.nytimes.com/2015/12/04/movies/review-in-krampus-the-holiday-involves-a-demonic-santa.html?_r=0

Siefker, Phyllis. *Santa Claus, Last of the Wild Men.* Jefferson, NC: McFarland, 1997.

Taylor, Alan. "Krampus: Saint Nicholas' Dark Companion." *The Atlantic.* http://www.theatlantic.com/photo/2013/12/krampus-saint-nicholas-dark-companion/100639/

Last Chance for Christmas — December 6, 2015

Television Movie

THREAT TO CHRISTMAS: Prancer injures his hoof and cannot fly, and a business tycoon kidnaps Santa's reindeer.

HOW CHRISTMAS IS SAVED: Santa's stable master finds a replacement for Prancer and convinces the tycoon to release the other reindeer.

SYNOPSIS AND COMMENTARY: Here's quite a combination: romance and reindeer kidnapping reign in this Lifetime Channel movie. Four days before Christmas, reindeer Prancer develops a fractured hoof and cannot fly with Santa (Derek McGrath, *Doc*). Rather than cancel Christmas, Mrs. Claus (Jayne Eastwood, *The Santa Clause*) orders John Stockman (Gabriel Hogan, *Heartland*), the North Pole's socially inept stable master, to find a replacement. John's search takes him to a reindeer ranch in Alaska at a time when the no-nonsense proprietor, single mom and Santa skeptic Annie Miller (Hilarie Burton, *Solstice*), not only faces the inevitable holiday foreclosure but pressure from land tycoon and Scrooge surrogate Reginald Buckley (Tim Matheson, *Animal House*) to deed over her ranch. Annie sees John as just another Buckley or bank leech who's come to harass her, so the sparks initially fly. Yet an uncannily rapid romance develops between them over the next few days that's sealed when John wins the trust of Annie's eight-year-old daughter Madison (Lola Flanery, *Lavender*), whose pet reindeer Frankie would make a perfect replacement. When John doesn't move his tail fast enough to suit Mrs. Claus, she sends two elves to kidnap Frankie to the North Pole (while Santa runs around hyperventilating), but John, being the ethical poster boy, brings Frankie and the remaining reindeer team back to Annie's farm to convince her that Santa is real and desperately needs Frankie. Meanwhile, to intimidate Annie, Buckley's goons kidnap Santa's reindeer with Frankie on Christmas Eve, whereupon Annie probably considers castrating John, until Santa and Mrs. Claus arrive to intervene. In a showdown with Buckley, the Millers, the Clauses, and John learn that Buckley's negative Christmas spirit stems from childhood (seemingly the source of all Christmas humbugs) when his hovering, elitist parents had denied him the "dangerous" little sled that Santa had brought. Though Annie initially signs over the ranch, all the sappy, emotional turmoil generated affects Buckley such that he caves in and rips up the contract. The reindeer are freed, and Frankie takes his place among Santa's team.

INTERESTING TIDBITS: In movies that focus on Santa, it's virtually unthinkable that the Clauses would allow even one child to be disappointed at Christmas. But in this film, Mrs. Claus takes on a different persona by being ruthless enough to do whatever it takes to see that Santa runs on schedule, even if it means kidnapping (stealing) one little girl's reindeer. After all, to Mrs. Claus, the needs of the many outweigh the needs of the few, which also happens to be Spock's philosophy in a number of *Star Trek* films. John finds this highly unethical, given that Mrs. Claus is portrayed as running a virtual "crime syndicate" from the North Pole.

NOTE: At the time of this writing, this movie was not available on DVD or VHS but could be seen on Amazon Instant Video.

REVIEW: Andy Webb of *The Movie Scene*: "…think back to those westerns [that] you might have watched as a child, the ones where the stranger comes to town and helps a sweet woman who has inherited a ranch [and] has to deal with a devious businessman and a corrupt bank manager … the stranger and the woman end up falling in love … [this film] uses that old idea but smothers it in some magic Santa dust to make it a Christmas movie…"

PRODUCTION CREDITS — Writers: Mike Bell and Gary Yates. Producers: Deborah Marks and Steve Solomos. Director: Gary Yates. Production Companies: Automatic TV & Film and Lifetime. Rating: Not rated. Genres: Family, Fantasy, Romance. Countries: Canada and USA. Run Time: 87 min.

REFERENCES: *Last Chance for Christmas*. Internet Movie Database. http://www.imdb.com/title/tt5266444/

Webb, Andy. "Frankie the Other Reindeer." *The Movie Scene*. http://www.themoviescene.co.uk/reviews/last-chance-for-christmas-2015/last-chance-for-christmas-2015.html

The Last Christmas—April 17, 1997

Episode from the Animated Television Series *Bruno the Kid*

THREAT TO CHRISTMAS: An evil toymaker plants computer-chip bombs in Christmas toys.

HOW CHRISTMAS IS SAVED: Bruno and his partner are on the case and stop the toymaker in a most unconventional way.

SYNOPSIS AND COMMENTARY: Following in the footsteps of dashing British spy James Bond, the not-so-dashing *Bruno*, developed by Lance Raichert, ran in syndication for 36 half-hour episodes from 1996 to 1997. Bruno was a bald, bespectacled, ten-year-old boy and top spy for the secret peacekeeping organization GLOBE, which knew nothing of Bruno's real age, because he communicated via a computer-generated avatar of Bruce Willis. Bruno's partner was Jarlesburg (Jarly), a black Brit, while Harris, a spoof of Bond's "Q," supplied a load of spy-related gadgets.

In "The Last Christmas," the evil toymaker Klaus Von Claus desires to destroy Christmas, because everyone is too preoccupied with Christmas to recognize his birthday, which is also December 25. Spouting "I will not be ignored!" (a nod to Glenn Close in *Fatal Attraction*, 1987), Claus implants computer chips serving as bombs in two special lines of toys that, when activated, bring the toys to life. At midnight on Christmas Eve, the toys will detonate and destroy all who possess them. Receiving an alert from Claus about the impending disaster, GLOBE sets Bruno and Jarly on the case. When their snooping gets too close for comfort, Claus's goons attempt to murder them, but they escape using Harris's gadgets. The two spies trace the chips to Claus's toy factory in Canada, where Claus greets them with an army of toy soldiers and planes firing real bullets as well as with flying, fire-breathing toy dragons, but the spies prevail using slingshots and boomerangs. With seconds to spare, Bruno offers Claus a birthday present, Claus dissolves in tears, and Bruno destroys the computer controlling the bomb-toys. Following a bit of Christmas-is-all-about-giving-and-peace-on-earth philosophy from Bruno, Claus promises to mend his ways and make toys only for good. But first, he'll make a bunch of license plates in the slammer.

VOICES: Bruce Willis (*Die Hard*) as Bruno; Tony Jay (*Twins*) as Jarlesburg; Mark Hamill (*Star Wars*) as Harris. Other voices: Kath Soucie, John Bower, Frank Welker, Jennifer Hale, Earl Boen, Bronson Pinchot, Dave Coulier, Jeff Bennett.

INTERESTING TIDBITS: "Bruno" is Bruce Willis's nickname. Commenting about *Bruno the Kid: The Animated Move* (1997), a feature-length production that merely strung together the three-part episode "Bye Bye Jarly" from the half-hour show, *TV Guide* noted, "[Bruce Willis] first introduced Bruno as his alter ego in musical performances and thus dubbed his popular 1980s album *The Return of Bruno*."

PRODUCTION CREDITS—Teleplay: Bill Braunstein. Executive Producers: Phil Roman and Bruce Willis. Voice Director: Kris Zimmermen. Production Companies: Active Entertainment, Film Roman Productions, and Flying Heart. Rating: TV-Y. Genres: Action, Animation, Comedy. Country: USA. Run Time: 30 min.

REFERENCES: *Bruno the Kid: The Animated Movie. TV Guide*. http://www.tvguide.com/movies/bruno-kid-animated-movie/review/132289/

Bruno the Kid: The Last Christmas. Van Nuys, CA: Family Home Entertainment, 1997. VHS Video.

"The Last Christmas." Big Cartoon Database. http://www.bcdb.com/cartoon/33704-Last-Christmas

Wilson, Joanna. *Tis the Season TV: The Encyclopedia of Christmas-Themed Episodes, Specials and Made-for-TV Movies*. Akron, OH: 1701 Press, 2011.

The Librarians and Santa's Midnight Run—December 21, 2014

Episode from the Television Series *The Librarians*

The principal cast of the TV series *The Librarians*. From left: Cassandra Cillian (Lindy Booth), Jake Stone (Christian Kane), Col. Eve Baird (Rebecca Romijn), caretaker Jenkins (John Larroquette), and Ezekiel Jones (John Kim). In the episode "The Librarians and Santa's Midnight Run" (2014), the team rescues a kidnapped Santa from the clutches of the evil Dulaque and his deputy Lamia (Turner Network Television/Photofest).

THREAT TO CHRISTMAS: Members of the Serpent Brotherhood incapacitate and kidnap Santa.

HOW CHRISTMAS IS SAVED: Three librarians-in-training and their leader rescue Santa.

SYNOPSIS AND COMMENTARY: Developed by John Rogers for TNT, *The Librarians* is a spinoff of *The Librarian*, a series of three television movies that starred Noah Wyle (*ER*) as a newly hired Librarian for New York City's Metropolitan Public Library that secretly housed a number of rare and often magical artifacts. Ongoing since 2014, *The Librarians* focuses on the adventures of three librarians-in-training (LITs), all of whom receive promotions later in the series: Jake Stone (Christian Kane, *Leverage*), an Oklahoma cowboy proficient in art history; Cassandra Cillian (Lindy Booth, *Dawn of the Dead*), a mathematician and scientist with the gift of synesthesia; and Ezekiel Jones (John Kim, *The Pacific*), a world-class thief. Other principal characters: Col. Eve Baird (Rebecca Romijn, *X-Men*), a no-nonsense, counter-terrorism agent and the original Librarian's guardian, now tasked with protecting and training the new recruits; Jenkins (John Larroquette, *Night Court*), the group's cantankerous caretaker; Dulaque (Matt Frewer, *Max Headroom*), the principal antagonist and immortal leader of the Serpent Brotherhood; and Lamia (Lesley-Ann Brandt, *Lucifer*), Dulaque's deputy.

In this episode, Santa (Bruce Campbell, *Army of Darkness*), the immortal avatar of goodwill, neither sequesters himself at the North Pole making toys nor is he attired in traditional garb. Instead, Santa, clad in suit, tie, and beret, travels around the world throughout the year participating in acts of kindness and absorbing the goodwill so generated, which he then releases back to the world at midnight on Christmas Eve. Failure to do so would not only cancel Christmas, but all civilized societies would collapse. Desiring Santa's power and finding him working in a London soup kitchen, Dulaque and Lamia incapacitate him with a poisoned dart and kidnap him back to their local museum with plans to kill him at the magic hour. Thanks to Cassandra's photographic memory, Eve and Jake arrive to stall the two villains by carelessly playing with the latter's priceless artifacts while Cassandra and Ezekiel rescue Santa and escape up the chimney. Ezekiel dons Santa's talisman-beret to lead the villains further astray, but without his beret, Santa manifests different incarnations through various cultural time periods, while Ezekiel becomes quite annoyingly "Christmasy." Meanwhile, the villains steal Santa's sleigh, which requires him to journey to Alaska, where he will release his goodwill to the Aurora Borealis. The trek is fraught with a host of twists and turns for Santa, Eve, and the LITs, including their altercation with the villains aboard a transport plane en route to Alaska, with Dulaque falling out and the plane crashing in the Arctic. Taking shelter with the gang in a nearby hut, Santa, under the poison's influence, lacks the will to carry on, whereupon Eve, a Christmas skeptic, must ironically become Santa's temporary replacement, given that she was born on the last stroke of midnight at Christmas and is now the one most attuned to Christmas. Her mission only requires a second as her spirit sprints around the world, spreading the gift of hope to those in otherwise hopeless situations. On Christmas Day, while Santa recuperates, the LITs celebrate Eve's birthday as she quietly muses over her new outlook on Christmas.

AWARDS: *The Librarians* received Saturn Award nominations for Best Guest Performance in a TV Series (John Larroquette, 2015), Best Actress in a TV Series (Rebecca Romijn, 2015 and 2016), and Best Action/Thriller TV Series (2016).

INTERESTING TIDBITS: As the team discusses a strategy for rescuing Santa, Jenkins shows them a series of classic drawings by cartoonist Thomas Nast that depict Santa. Being a Christmas skeptic and certain that Santa does not exist, however, Eve refuses to call the jolly gent "Santa."

Eve can only tolerate Santa's saying "Ho Ho" and won't permit the third "Ho" in her presence.

Santa has a penchant for talking in the third person.

Other save-Christmas films in which Santa is kidnapped include ***The Boy Who Saved Christmas; The Elf and the Magic Key; The Glo Friends Save Christmas; The Great Santa Claus Switch; Santa Claus Conquers the Martians; Sonic Christmas Blast; Spinach Greetings; Tim Burton's The Nightmare Before Christmas;*** and ***Who Stole Santa?***

NOTE: At the time of this writing, this episode was available on DVD but in non–USA format (see references). However, it could be seen on such media as Amazon Instant Video and Hulu.

REVIEWS: According to the Rotten Tomatoes film review site, 71 percent of critics gave *The Librarians* series a positive review. Metacritic gave the series a score of 64/100 (generally favorable reviews).

Matt Roush of *TV Guide* reviewed the series (December 5, 2014): "...a delightful series version of its *Librarian* TV-movie franchise, mixing elements of Indiana Jones, *The Da Vinci Code* and even *Warehouse 13* in jaunty and fantastical capers extolling the power and allure, and sometimes danger, of magic."

Mary McNamara of the *Los Angeles Times* reviewed the series (December 5, 2014): "Unabashedly retro, with plenty of high- and low-tech silliness.... Action-packed with more than a little history and mythology thrown in ... one of those rare and wonderful shows that isn't out to change the television landscape, just make it a little more fun."

PRODUCTION CREDITS—Writers: Paul Guyot and John Rogers. Producer: Paul F. Bernard. Director: Jonathan Frakes. Production Company: Electric Entertainment. Rating: TV-14. Genres:

Action, Adventure, Comedy. Country: USA. Run Time: 42 min.

REFERENCES: *The Librarians.* Metacritic. http://www.metacritic.com/tv/the-librarians-2014

The Librarians. Rotten Tomatoes. https://www.rottentomatoes.com/tv/the-librarians/s01

"The Librarians and Santa's Midnight Run." In *The Librarians: The Complete Season One.* Newton, NSW, Australia: Icon Film Distribution Pty, 2014. PAL, non–USA format. DVD Video.

"The Librarians and Santa's Midnight Run." Internet Movie Database. http://www.imdb.com/title/tt4279086/

McNamara, Mary. "'The Librarians,' with Noah Wyle, Opens Fun New Chapter on TNT." *Los Angeles Times.* http://touch.latimes.com/#section/-1/article/p2p-82201626/

Roush, Matt. "Weekend TV: *Red Tent, One Child, Librarians.*" *TV Guide.* http://www.tvguide.com/news/weekend-tv-red-tent-1090423/

A Light in the Forest: The Legend of Holly Boy—October 28, 2003

Fantasy Film

THREAT TO CHRISTMAS: Reincarnated, an evil king and a witch seek to stamp out Holly Boy and other embodiments of Christmas.

HOW CHRISTMAS IS SAVED: Holly Boy ensures that the king receives his comeuppance, which in turn destroys the witch.

SYNOPSIS AND COMMENTARY: Black magic, sorcery, and pagan sentiment reign in this rather free adaptation of *The Legend of Holly Boy*, a children's book by Frank Latino, published in 1988. The film personifies several traditional holiday symbols as Christmas spirits or the embodiments of Christmas: mistletoe, pine tree, poinsettia, and holly, although mistletoe and poinsettia play very minor roles. Centuries ago in Europe, the evil King Otto (Edward Albert, *Guarding Tess*) and his minions sought to stamp out Christmas by executing Miss Mistletoe (Jessica Stone, *Play Dead*), the Pine Queen (Lindsay Wagner, *The Bionic Woman*), and Poinsettia Patty (Chelsey Cole, *View from the Top*). Though the immortal spirit Holly Boy (Christopher Khayman Lee, *Safe Harbor*) rescued them, a curse from Witch Hazel (Alexandra Ford, *Chaos Theory*) transformed Holly Boy into a stone statue that was brought to the USA. The curse could be broken only by great sadness, at which time Otto and the witch would be reincarnated and free again to pursue their destruction of Christmas. The curse is lifted in present-day Los Angeles when the new transfer student Brita (Danielle Nicolet, *Born Again Virgin*) mourns the recent deaths of her parents. Reincarnated with Holly Boy are Otto as land developer Ridgewell, who seeks to acquire the Holly Woods adjacent to Brita's school and then bury the school; Otto's darkling elf Hoiman (Michael Lee Gogin, *Critters*) as Principal Kemmel (Frank Bonner, *City Guys*); Witch Hazel as a beautiful hottie; and the Pine Queen as the teacher Ms. Audry, a positive influence in Brita's life. While Brita and her friend Gabriel (Christian Oliver, *Speed Racer*) strive to win the school's Christmas talent competition together, which would save the Holly Woods and the school, Holly Boy ensures that Otto, who again would sacrifice the Pine Queen/Ms. Audry, receives his comeuppance as a boar turned to stone which, upon exploding, destroys the witch. Thus, Christmas survives, because the various Christmas spirits or embodiments of the holiday remain alive and well.

INTERESTING TIDBITS: While the film's subtitle is appropriate, the principal title, *A Light in the Forest*, is a bit puzzling. Holly Boy's stone statue winds up in the Holly Woods, but there's no miraculous "light" as such that beams down to animate it; hence, the principal title is inexplicable. Moreover, it may lead to confusion with a Disney film titled *The Light in the Forest* (1958), which is an adaptation of a novel by Conrad Richter that has nothing to do with Christmas. Carol Lynley, who played Brita's grandmother here, also starred in the Disney production.

There's very little resemblance between the story in Frank Latino's book and what's portrayed in this film. In the book, items such as holly, mistletoe, poinsettia, and pine tree become anthropomorphic, Christian symbols of

Christmas through the intervention of an angel that evolves from the Star of Bethlehem when Jesus is born. As such, they also symbolize eternal life in Christ. Transformed from an oak tree, Otto the woodsman king denies the Nativity story as related by the four symbols and destroys them all, but in a battle with the forest animals, Otto plunges over a cliff, and the angel returns to reanimate the symbols. The secular film adaptation attributes no Christian symbolism to Holly Boy, Miss Mistletoe, Poinsettia Patty, or the Pine Queen; instead, they are the neutral embodiments of Christmas.

PRODUCTION CREDITS—Story: Frank Latino, Gary LoConti, and John Carol Buechler. Writer and Director: John Carol Buechler. Producers: Gary LoConti, Roger Mende, and Talieh Safadi. Production Companies: Holly Boy Productions, Blue Horizon International, and RGH Lions Share Pictures. Rating: PG (thematic elements and mild language). Genres: Drama, Fantasy. Country: USA. Run Time: 95 min.

REFERENCES: Latino, Frank. *The Legend of Holly Boy*. Illustrated by Jack B. Hood. Boca Raton, FL: Frank Latino, 1988.

A Light in the Forest: The Legend of Holly Boy. Encino, CA: Ardustry Home Entertainment, 2003. DVD Video.

A Light in the Forest: The Legend of Holly Boy. Internet Movie Database. http://www.imdb.com/title/tt0285292/

Wilson, Joanna. *Tis the Season TV: The Encyclopedia of Christmas-Themed Episodes, Specials and Made-for-TV Movies*. Akron, OH: 1701 Press, 2011.

Like Father, Like Santa—December 1, 1998

Television Movie

THREAT TO CHRISTMAS: In revolt, the North Pole postal division imprisons Santa and his estranged son.

HOW CHRISTMAS IS SAVED: Santa and son learn to cooperate together to put the Christmas spirit back into the postal division.

SYNOPSIS AND COMMENTARY: Who would ever guess that there would be strife within the Claus family, especially between father and son? Bitterly perceiving that his father, Santa Claus (William Hootkins, *Raiders of the Lost Ark*), had been too preoccupied with holiday commitments for a close, father-son relationship, Tyler Madison (Harry Hamlin, *L.A. Law*) had remained estranged from his father for years. Now a workaholic (the ole neglect-the-wife-and-kid routine definitely runs in the family) and ruthless toy magnate in competition with Santa, Tyler plans to steal his father's classified "Naughty or Nice" list in order to blackmail other toy enterprises. Tyler's scheme carries him to the North Pole on Christmas Eve, where he discovers that Santa's disgruntled, overworked postal personnel have launched a revolution by crowning chief postal worker Ambrose Booth (Roy Dotrice, *Beauty and the Beast*) as Snow King and incarcerating Santa and his elves. When Tyler is apprehended and tossed into the same cell with his father, the two learn to work together to save the North Pole and Christmas—and their family ties—by blasting the postal workers with rockets containing heavy doses of Christmas spirit. Tyler receives an epiphany about his family situation when he discovers a heartrending email (forget snail mail in this situation) from his own son Danny (Curtis Blanck, *Beverly Hills Ninja*) to Santa, pleading for the old gent to find and send his father back home for Christmas. Charles Brown's "Please Come Home for Christmas" wafting in the background would have been something of a nice touch.

NOTE: At the time of this writing, this film was not available on DVD, VHS, Amazon Instant Video, Hulu, or Netflix.

PRODUCTION CREDITS—Writer: Mark Valenti. Producers: Melissa Barrett and Robert J. Wilson. Director: Michael Scott. Production Companies: Carroll Newman Productions and Saban International N.V. Rating: Not rated. Genres: Family, Fantasy. Country: USA. Run Time: 105 min.

REFERENCES: Crump, William D. *The Christmas Encyclopedia*. Third Edition. Jefferson, NC: McFarland, 2013.

Like Father, Like Santa. Internet Movie Database. http://www.imdb.com/title/tt0181655/

Wilson, Joanna. *Tis the Season TV: The*

Encyclopedia of Christmas-Themed Episodes, Specials and Made-for-TV Movies. Akron, OH: 1701 Press, 2011.

Madeline at the North Pole—October 28, 2000

Madeline and Santa—November 4, 2000

Two Related Episodes from the Animated Television Series *The New Adventures of Madeline*

THREAT TO CHRISTMAS: The elves are sick with the flu at the North Pole and cannot finish making the toys.

HOW CHRISTMAS IS SAVED: Madeline and her classmates take over the toymaking, then Madeline carries on singlehandedly when her cohorts fall ill.

SYNOPSIS AND COMMENTARY: In 1939, Austrian author Ludwig Bemelmans published *Madeline*, the first of seven children's picture books about the adventures of the title character, the smallest of 12 little girls living in a boarding school in Paris. The book series spawned an animated television series of the same title that aired on the Family Channel for 20 episodes in 1993 and on ABC followed by the Disney Channel for 13 episodes in 1995 as *The New Adventures of Madeline*. The latter series resumed on the Disney Channel for 26 episodes in 2000–2001. In addition to Madeline, principal characters included the girls' teacher Miss Clavel and Lord Cucuface, chairman of the school's board of trustees. The episodes were narrated in rhyming dialogue.

In "Madeline at the North Pole," when warm weather promises no snow for Christmas, the little girls are so disappointed that Lord Cucuface takes them via ship to visit Santa's workshop at the North Pole. Trouble strikes when the elves all contract the flu, so it's up to the girls to finish making the toys in their stead; by Christmas Eve, however, even Miss Clavel, Lord Cucuface, and all the other girls except Madeline are sick as well. Madeline heroically completes the tasks and is rewarded by a personal visit from Santa, who presents her with his cap as a gift.

The story continues in "Madeline and Santa" as Madeline bakes traditional *bûche de Noël* (Yule log cakes) for her sick comrades. But when Santa swipes the cakes and gains too much weight to fit into chimneys, Madeline saves Christmas by accompanying Santa on his rounds and jumping down the chimneys to deliver the gifts.

PRINCIPAL VOICES: Andrea Libman (*Dragon Ball*) as Madeline; Christopher Gaze (*Cool Runnings*) as the narrator; Stephanie Louise Vallance (*Sonic Underground*) as Miss Clavel and Genevieve; Brittney Irvin (*The Vow*) as Nicole; Chantal Strand (*Barbie as Rapunzel*) as Danielle; Veronica Sztopa (*RV*) as Chloe; Michael Heyward as Pepito; French Tickner (*Double Jeopardy*) as Lord Cucuface.

AWARDS: The *Madeline* series won a Primetime Emmy for Outstanding Voice-Over Performance (Christopher Plummer, 1994); won a Daytime Emmy for Outstanding Children's Animated Program (2002); won a CableACE Award for Children's Programming Series–Six and Younger (1995); Daytime Emmy nomination for Outstanding Children's Animated Program (2001); two Humanitas Prize nominations for Children's Animation Category (1994).

The *New Adventures of Madeline* series received Daytime Emmy nominations for Outstanding Children's Animated Program (1996) and Outstanding Special Class Animated Program (1997); two Humanitas Prize nominations for Children's Animation Category (1996 and 2001).

INTERESTING TIDBIT: Of all the possible "disaster" themes that animated episodes could weave around saving Christmas, being sick with the flu at this time is probably the least likely to garner much viewer enthusiasm. Of course, with all others flat on their backs, Madeline has a greater opportunity to save Christmas singlehandedly. (One wonders, however, what the "WOW" level would have been had the North Pole been swept by something with more of a bite, like Ebola.) These two episodes perpetuate the everyone-sick-at-Christmas theme that was first evident in the 1990 TV special *Madeline's Christmas*. Another special with a similar theme is *A Flintstones*

Christmas Carol (1994); other save-Christmas films in which the flu hits the North Pole include *The Magic Sack of Mr. Nicholas, The Night B4 Christmas, Nine Dog Christmas, The Super Special Gift,* and *'Twas the Night.*

REVIEW: Erich Asperschlager of *DVD Verdict* reviews the DVD collection titled *Madeline's Christmas and Other Wintery Tales* (October 27, 2010), which include "Madeline at the North Pole," "Madeline and Santa," and three other tales. Ironically, despite the title, this collection does *not* include the TV special titled *Madeline's Christmas*: "*Madeline* distinguishes itself from other tiny tot fare with its easygoing charm. Maybe it's the European flair, maybe it's Christopher Plummer's laid back rhyming narration, but *Madeline* is a welcome break from the hyperactivity of modern kids' cartoons. Her holiday adventures don't have any high-speed sleigh chases or Battle of Gettysburg-esque snowball fights, and that's a good thing."

PRODUCTION CREDITS—Story: Judy Rothman Rofé. Teleplay: Betty G. Birney and Judy Rothman Rofé. Producer: Stan Phillips. Director: Judy Reilly. Production Company: DiC Enterprises. Rating: Not rated. Genre: Animation. Country: Canada and USA. Run Time: 23 min. each.

REFERENCES: Asperschlager, Erich. *Madeline's Christmas and Other Wintry Tales.* DVD Verdict. http://www.dvdverdict.com/reviews/madelineschristmas.php

Lenburg, Jeff. *The Encyclopedia of Animated Cartoons.* Third Edition. New York: Facts on File, 2009.

Madeline's Christmas and Other Wintery Tales. Los Angeles: Shout Factory, 2010. DVD Video.

The New Adventures of Madeline. Internet Movie Database. http://www.imdb.com/title/tt0262977/

Wilson, Joanna. *Tis the Season TV: The Encyclopedia of Christmas-Themed Episodes, Specials and Made-for-TV Movies.* Akron, OH: 1701 Press, 2011.

Magic Christmas Tree—December 19, 1964
Fantasy Film

THREAT TO CHRISTMAS: A boy uses one of his three wishes to have Santa all to himself.

HOW CHRISTMAS IS SAVED: After seeing how much the world grieves over a missing Santa, the boy uses his third wish to restore Santa to the world.

SYNOPSIS AND COMMENTARY: This obscure, amateurish "parable" about greed not only combines Halloween and Christmas, similar to the combination in *Tim Burton's The Nightmare Before Christmas* (far more professionally executed in the latter), but it also smacks of the "Jack and the Beanstalk" fairy tale. Instead of beans, there's a magic seed, a tree replaces the beanstalk, and there's a giant to boot.

The disheveled old crone Miss Finch (Valerie Hobbs) detains schoolboy Mark (Chris Kroesen) when she catches him spying on her allegedly haunted house on Halloween. She induces him to climb a tree to retrieve her black cat Lucifer, but Mark falls and is knocked unconscious. Up to this point, all the footage has been in black and white, but when Mark awakens, the story resumes in color. Now Mark sees that Miss Finch, decked in black with a pointed hat, is the witch he had supposed her to be. For retrieving Lucifer, the witch rewards Mark with a magic ring that contains a seed. If Mark plants the seed under the wishbone of a Thanksgiving turkey during the dark of the moon, a magic tree will appear that, when fully grown, will grant him three wishes. Mark does as instructed (twirling the ring three times on his finger and saying some magic words), and a little evergreen tree sprouts overnight that his dad (Dick Parish) cannot cut down. On Christmas Eve while his family is occupied with last-minute shopping, the now fully grown and sarcastically *talking* tree urges Mark to twirl the ring and speak the words as before, whereupon it vanishes and reappears in his house; repeating the ritual produces a fully decorated tree covered in tinsel. The same ritual gives Mark his first wish, to have absolute power for one hour, whereupon Mark creates havoc in his neighborhood with emergency vehicles and compels bakers to perform slapstick pie-throwing routines. One wasted wish leads to another that's worse, to have Santa all to himself. A startled Santa (actor not specified) appears and supposedly gives Mark all the toys he lists, but Santa is glued to his chair and cannot leave. Suddenly Mark is transported to a forest, where he runs into that giant (without the goose that lays golden eggs), the mythical incarnation of greed, who would keep Mark there, then reveals how much the grieving world is in chaos over the missing Santa. The giant allows a repentant Mark to return home, where his third wish is, of course, to have everything back as it was. The tree disappears and the film returns to black and white as Mark awakens in the arms of old Miss Finch, who rewards him with cookies and milk instead of a ring. The too-obvious lesson of the "parable": Be careful what you wish for!

INTERESTING TIDBITS: The film's opening and closing black-and-white segments and color dream segment are similar in style to those found in *The Wizard of Oz* (1939). As a witch, Miss Finch lacks a green sheen and, save for the black dress and hat, looks nothing like Margaret Hamilton's character in *Wizard*.

This is the only film that Richard C. Parish ever directed. Here, he also played Mark's dad. Spoofed on *RiffTrax*, the film is generally regarded as one of the worst holiday films ever made. That list would also include such save-Christmas films as **Santa and the Ice Cream Bunny** and **Santa Claus Conquers the Martians**.

REVIEWS: Dennis Schwartz of *Ozus' World Movie Reviews* (December 18, 2015): "Strictly amateur.... It's a stinker Christmas-themed fantasy film.... After seeing this mess, you will understand why Parish never directed again.... It has been rightfully called one of the worst and most depressing holiday films of all time.... Grade D."

PRODUCTION CREDITS—Screenplay: Harold Vaughn Taylor. Producer: Bruce Scott. Director: Richard C. Parish. Production Company: Holiday Pictures. Rating: Not rated. Genres: Family, Fantasy. Country: USA. Run Time: 60 min.

REFERENCES: *Magic Christmas Tree*. Internet Movie Database. http://www.imdb.com/title/tt0195039/

Magic Christmas Tree. New York: GoodTimes Home Video, 1992. VHS Video.

RiffTrax: Christmas with RiffTrax Featuring Magic Christmas Tree. San Diego: Legend Films, 2013. DVD Video.

Schwartz, Dennis. *Magic Christmas Tree. Ozus' World Movie Reviews*. http://homepages.sover.net/~ozus/magicchristmastree.html

Wilson, Joanna. *Tis the Season TV: The Encyclopedia of Christmas-Themed Episodes, Specials and Made-for-TV Movies*. Akron, OH: 1701 Press, 2011.

The Magic Sack of Mr. Nicholas—
November 14, 1987

Episode from the Animated Television Series *The Smurfs*

THREAT TO CHRISTMAS: The witch Chlorhydris swipes Santa's magic sack of toys before they can be delivered on Christmas Eve.

HOW CHRISTMAS IS SAVED: Unwittingly, Grouchy Smurf is the key to returning Santa's sack.

SYNOPSIS AND COMMENTARY: One of the most successful and longest-running Saturday morning cartoons in television history, *The Smurfs* aired on the NBC television network from 1981 to 1989. The creation of Belgian cartoonist Pierre "Peyo" Culliford, the Smurfs were blue, elfin characters "three apples high" who lived in mushroom-shaped houses and who first appeared as a comic strip in *Le Journal de Spirou* on October 23, 1958, where they were known as *Les Schtroumpfs*. A host of Smurf dolls and other merchandise followed, which inspired the television series after Fred Silverman, then-president of NBC, saw the pleasure that a Smurf doll brought to his daughter Melissa. Led by Papa Smurf, the more than 100 citizens of the sylvan Smurf Village bore names commensurate with personal characteristics: Brainy, Hefty, Handy, Grouchy, etc., with two female characters, Smurfette and tomboy Sassette. Serving as their principal nemeses were non–Smurf characters such as the evil wizard Gargamel, his young assistant Scruple, the diabolical cat Azrael, and the evil witch Chlorhydris, who strove to remove love from the world. The series featured 256 episodes (418 stories) and seven specials, one of the latter being **The Smurfs Christmas Spe-**

cial, discussed in this volume. The Smurfs were also featured in several animated theatrical releases, for example, *The Smurfs and the Magic Flute* (1976), *The Baby Smurf* (1984), *The Smurfs* (2011), *The Smurfs 2* (2013), and *Get Smurfy* (2017).

As in an earlier *Smurfs* episode, **Baby's First Christmas**, Gargamel and Chlorhydris are out to ruin Christmas. Again, Santa is known as Mr. Nicholas, and there is no mention of his residing at the North Pole. Although he is now blessed with eight flying reindeer, his troupe of green elves are all sick with the flu, whereupon Nicholas, needing assistance to wrap the presents, solicits the Smurfs' help via a message-bearing reindeer. The troubles escalate when Gargamel, having disguised himself as a snowman, stuffs a group of forest-trekking Smurfs into a sack, and Chlorhydris, having followed another group of Smurfs to Nicholas's abode, swipes his identical-appearing magic sack with Grouchy Smurf trapped inside. After a series of confusing, sack-switching routines between Gargamel and Chlorhydris, the two villains realize that Scruple now possesses the magic sack and has hidden it. Scruple's distraction over his "victory" allows Grouchy to escape with the sack and merrily slide downhill atop it all the way in the snow to Nicholas' residence, just in time for Christmas deliveries, thus foiling the two villains who had been in hot pursuit. As Nicholas with the Smurfs speeds away, he calls out the blessedly traditional greeting of "Merry Christmas."

PRINCIPAL VOICES: Lucille Bliss as Smurfette, William Callaway as Clumsy Smurf, Hamilton Camp as Greedy Smurf, June Foray as Jokey Smurf, Danny Goldman as Brainy Smurf, Amanda McBroom as Chlorhydris, Don Messick as Papa Smurf, Brenda Vaccaro as Scruple, Frank Welker as Hefty Smurf, Paul Winchell as Gargamel, and Alan Young as Farmer Smurf. All these voice-actors have worked on *The Smurfs* series.

AWARDS: *The Smurfs*—Emmy Awards for Outstanding Children's Entertainment Series (1983, 1984); Emmy nominations for Outstanding Animated Program (1985–1989); Humanitas Prize for Children's Animation Category (1987); Blimp Award nominations for Favorite Cartoon (1988, 1989).

INTERESTING TIDBITS: *The Smurfs* frequently utilized classical music in the background or for themes. Background music heard during this episode includes excerpts from Franz Liszt's *Piano Concerto No. 1* in E-Flat Major (when Gargamel is especially evil), and from the overture to Gioachino Rossini's opera *William Tell* (during high-spirited chase scenes).

Other save-Christmas films in which the flu hits the North Pole include **Madeline at the North Pole, The Night B4 Christmas, Nine Dog Christmas, The Super Special Gift**, and **'Twas the Night.**

PRODUCTION CREDITS—Writers: Alan Burnett and Tom Spath. Producers: Don Jurwich and Walt Kubiak. Directors: Bob Goe, John Kimball, Don Lusk, Jay Sarbry, Paul Sommer, and Ray Patterson (Supervising Director). Production Companies: Hanna-Barbera Productions and SEPP International, S.A. Rating: Not rated. Genres: Animation, Family, Fantasy. Countries: Belgium and USA. Run Time: 23 min.

REFERENCES: Crump, William D. *The Christmas Encyclopedia*. Third Edition. Jefferson, NC: McFarland, 2013.

"The Magic Sack of Mr. Nicholas." Big Cartoon Database. http://www.bcdb.com/cartoon/13832-Magic-Sack-Of-Mr-Nicholas

"The Magic Sack of Mr. Nicholas." In *The Smurfs: The Complete Seventh Season, Volume 2*. Amazon Instant Video.

"The Magic Sack of Mr. Nicholas." Internet Movie Database. http://www.imdb.com/title/tt1328401/

Lenburg, Jeff. *The Encyclopedia of Animated Cartoons*. Third Edition. New York: Facts on File, 2009.

Mallory, Michael. *Hanna-Barbera Cartoons*. Westport, CT: Hugh Lauter Levin Associates, 1998.

The Smurfs (TV Series). Wikipedia. http://en.wikipedia.org/wiki/The_Smurfs_(TV_series)

Wilson, Joanna. *Tis the Season TV: The Encyclopedia of Christmas-Themed Episodes,*

Specials and Made-for-TV Movies. Akron, OH: 1701 Press, 2011.

The Man Who Saved Christmas—
December 15, 2002

Television Movie

THREAT TO CHRISTMAS: During World War I, the government asks toymaker A.C. Gilbert to make munitions instead of toys at Christmastime and to endorse cancelling Christmas for the war effort.

HOW CHRISTMAS IS SAVED: Gilbert convinces the government that making toys boosts the country's wartime morale.

SYNOPSIS AND COMMENTARY: Taking time out from villains who wish to stick it to the North Pole, here's a biographical drama based on the career of Dr. Alfred Carlton ("A.C.") Gilbert (1884–1961), a medical doctor and highly respected American toy manufacturer who popularized the Erector Set and other educational toys (we can put Santa aside in this film but we still can't get away from the toys). Having successfully built Erector Sets along with munitions during World War I, Dr. Gilbert was literally acclaimed as "The Man Who Saved Christmas" in 1918.

Five years after founding the highly successful A.C. Gilbert Company in New Haven, Connecticut, Gilbert (Jason Alexander, *Seinfeld*), complying with a request from the National Defense Council, retools his factory in order to produce munitions instead of toys. His products are now the complete antithesis of what his factory once represented, and company morale is low. Seizing on an earlier statement that Gilbert had made to the effect that not producing toys would be like giving up Christmas, the Defense Council promotes such slogans as "Santa Claus wants you to give up Christmas," "Buy bonds, not toys," and "All we want for Christmas is our boys back home." In addition, Gilbert is expected to sell America's children on the idea with the slogan "A.C. Gilbert says, 'It's no time for toys, boys,'" and the newspapers hail Gilbert, America's number-one toy manufacturer at the time, as the man responsible for canceling Christmas. Burdened with the knowledge that his brother Frank (Ari Cohen, *Maps to the Stars*) is missing in action and the sudden news that a valued employee's son has been killed in action, Gilbert rebels against the national no-Christmas campaign. Armed with a host of his educational toys to display before the National Defense Committee, Gilbert heads to Washington, D.C., where he successfully delivers a passionate plea that Christmas not be cancelled, for doing so would allow the enemy to rob Americans of hope for a brighter future. The Council agrees that Gilbert should resume manufacturing his toys, which have the ability to stimulate children's imaginations toward creative goals. But in order to manufacture toys *and* fulfill outstanding munitions contracts, Gilbert conducts the former enterprise from his home. Shortly thereafter, Germany signs the armistice on November 11, 1918, ending the Great War. That Christmas is one of the happiest for Americans, but even more for the Gilbert family with the return home of brother Frank, injured but safe.

OTHER CAST: Kelly Rowan (*Hook*) as Gilbert's wife Mary; Ed Asner (*Lou Grant*) as his father Charles; Jayne Eastwood (*Hairspray*) as his mother Evelyn; Jake Brockman (*Camp Rock*) as his son Al, Jr.

AWARDS: In 2003, this picture received a Visual Effects Society Award nomination for Best Matte Painting in a Televised Program, Music Video, or Commercial; it also received a Gemini Award nomination for Best Digital Visual Effects.

INTERESTING TIDBITS: For some forty years after the war, A.C. Gilbert continued to make toys, which included Erector Sets, microscope and chemistry sets, American Flyer electric trains, Mysto Magic Exhibition Sets, and many others. At the time of his death, he held patents on more than 150 inventions. The first artificial heart pump was designed with Erector Set parts.

Though Santa plays no direct role here, the film still pushes the typical notion that no toys or presents means no Christmas.

REVIEWS: Anita Gates of *The New York Times* (December 13, 2002): "The film's first accomplishment is that Jason Alexander ... is so convincingly cherubic and sincere.... This is a slightly too sweet, slightly too familiar holiday story complete with ... an inspiring speech that melts the hearts of a chamberful of grumpy Washington politicians."

Terry Kelleher of *People* magazine (December 16, 2002): "Plot and characterization are rather thin. Gilbert conducts business with unbelievable benevolence, and his father ... goes from controlling tightwad to proud supporter in a twinkling. Still, Alexander's energetic performance may put you in the mood to pile presents under the tree."

PRODUCTION CREDITS—Story: Joe Maurer. Teleplay: Joe Maurer, Debra Frank, and Steve L. Hayes. Producer: Randi Richmond. Director: Sturla Gunnarsson. Production Companies: Alliance Atlantis Communications and Orly Adelson Productions. Rating: Not rated. Genre: Drama. Countries: Canada and USA. Run Time: 88 min.

REFERENCES: "Alfred Carlton Gilbert." Wikipedia. http://en.wikipedia.org/wiki/Alfred_Carlton_Gilbert

Crump, William D. *The Christmas Encyclopedia*. Third Edition. Jefferson, NC: McFarland, 2013.

Gates, Anita. "A Toy Maker Who's Rich, and Also Sweet and Good." The New York Times. http://www.nytimes.com/2002/12/13/movies/tv-weekend-a-toy-maker-who-s-rich-and-also-sweet-and-good.html

"Heart Pump Out of an Erector Set–Who Knew?" Connecticut History. http://connecticuthistory.org/heart-pump-out-of-an-erector-set-who-knew/

Kelleher, Terry. "Picks and Pans Review: *The Man Who Saved Christmas*." *People* magazine. http://www.people.com/archive/article/0,,20138731,,00.html

The Man Who Saved Christmas. Echo Bridge Home Entertainment, 2008. DVD Video.

The Man Who Saved Christmas. Internet Movie Database. http://www.imdb.com/title/tt0339343/

Wilson, Joanna. *Tis the Season TV: The Encyclopedia of Christmas-Themed Episodes, Specials and Made-for-TV Movies*. Akron, OH: 1701 Press, 2011.

Mary Engelbreit's The Night Before Christmas—November 9, 2004

Computer-Animated Short Film

THREAT TO CHRISTMAS: The mischievous fairy Implestik creates a star field to prevent Santa from delivering presents.

HOW CHRISTMAS IS SAVED: The mouse Gregory searches for the Fairy Queen to undo the spell.

SYNOPSIS AND COMMENTARY: Here's a different spin on the poem "The Night Before Christmas," adapted from a book version illustrated by American graphic artist and children's book illustrator, Mary Engelbreit. Kevin Kline reads the poem in its entirety, but after mama and papa have just settled down for a long winter's nap, the story focuses on Gregory, the curious house-mouse who overhears the mischievous fairy Implestik hatch a plan to create a star field that will hinder Santa from delivering any presents. According to the elder mouse Augustus, only another fairy can undo the spell, so Gregory must find the fairy circle in the woods. On the advice of an old owl he meets along the way, Gregory continues in the direction of the north star, where he will find the Enchanted Wood and the Fairy Queen. Implestik attempts to thwart a dejected Gregory, but Elliester, the Fairy of the Silver Mist, encourages him and takes him to the Enchanted Wood, where she battles Implestik, until the Fairy Queen emerges from a toadstool and upbraids Implestik for his pride and selfishness. Forgiving the repentant fairy, she endows him with Christmas spirit and removes the star field. At this point, the poem resumes—where papa hears the clatter of Santa's arrival—and proceeds to its conclusion as Gregory and his family take it all in.

VOICES: Kevin Kline (*Cry Freedom*) as Papa; Lee Tockar (*Johnny Test*) as Gregory; Chiara Zanni (*X-Men 2*) as Ms. Mouse; Sam Vincent (*Martin Mystery*) as Implestik; John Baldry (*Nilus the Sandman*) as Augustus; Dale Wilson (*Dragon Ball*) as the owl; Tabitha St. Germain (*Littlest Pet Shop*) as Elliester; Kathleen Barr (*Littlest Pet Shop*) as the Fairy Queen; French Tickner (*Double Jeopardy*) as Santa.

SONGS: Lyrics by William J. Schwartz and W. Tyler Schwartz. Songs by Sandra M. Levy Smith.

INTERESTING TIDBIT: Kline reads the last line of the poem as "Merry Christmas to all, and to all a good night." Actually, the last line is "*Happy* Christmas to all,..." etc. We're far more used to saying "Merry Christmas" than "Happy Christmas" (unless we're bent on being politically correct and saying "Happy Holidays"). Other save-Christmas films with the same error are *A Christmas Story* and *'Twas the Night.*

PRODUCTION CREDITS—Concept and Script: William J. Schwartz and W. Tyler Schwartz. Producers: Elizabeth Schwartz, William J. Schwartz, and W. Tyler Schwartz. Director: W. Tyler Schwartz. Production Companies: Mary Engelbreit Enterprises and Schwartz and Associates. Rating: Not rated. Genres: Animation, Family, Fantasy, Short. Country: USA. Run Time: 26 min.

REFERENCES: *Mary Engelbreit's The Night Before Christmas.* New York: GoodTimes Entertainment, 2004. DVD Video.

Wilson, Joanna. *Tis the Season TV: The Encyclopedia of Christmas-Themed Episodes, Specials and Made-for-TV Movies.* Akron, OH: 1701 Press, 2011.

Meet the Santas—December 17, 2005

Television Movie

THREAT TO CHRISTMAS: When Beth initially cancels her wedding to Nick Claus, there can be no Christmas without a Mrs. Claus.

HOW CHRISTMAS IS SAVED: Beth learns to trust her heart, marries Nick, and Christmas is back on.

SYNOPSIS AND COMMENTARY: Here's another Hallmark Channel romance goodie, the sequel to *Single Santa Seeks Mrs. Claus.* Having inherited the mantle of Santa Claus when his father retired last year, Nick Claus (Steve Guttenberg, *Police Academy*) must now marry his fiancée Beth Sawtelle (Crystal Bernard, *Wings*) on Christmas Eve. As time grows short, the pressures of selling her home and the prospect of duties as the future Mrs. Claus overwhelm Beth, whereupon she turns the wedding arrangements over to her Grinch of a socialite mother Joanna (Mariette Hartley, *One Life to Live*), who lacks the Christmas spirit. Joanna is not aware of Nick's real identity and feels that he is Beth's social inferior; hence, Joanna plans a much more extravagant wedding than the two had ever desired. Complicating Beth's situation is Mark (Roark Critchlow, *Mr. Deeds*), an old flame who is determined to rekindle their romance. An exasperated Beth ultimately folds to the mounting pressures and cancels the wedding, at which point the Christmas lights all over the world wink out, a sign that there can be no Christmas without a Mrs. Claus. At the last minute on Christmas Eve, Beth has a change of heart as she finally trusts her heart and marries Nick at her house, for no one but a Claus and the elves may enter the North Pole. As the couple kiss, Christmas lights wink back on, a sign that Christmas has been saved.

OTHER CAST: Dominic Scott Kay (*Charlotte's Web*) as Beth's young son Jake; John Wheeler (*Single Santa Seeks Mrs. Claus*) as Mr. Claus, the former Santa; Marcia Ann Burrs (*The Bling Ring*) as Mrs. Claus; Armin Shimerman (*Buffy the Vampire Slayer*) as Ernest, Santa's no-nonsense executive assistant.

INTERESTING TIDBIT: *Meet the Santas* broke the record set by its predecessor, posting the highest-ever ratings for a Hallmark Channel movie, scoring a 3.6 household rating, 2.5 million homes, and 4.65 million unduplicated persons.

NOTE: At the time of this writing, this film was not available on DVD or VHS but could be seen on YouTube.

REVIEWS: Andy Webb of *The Movie Scene* "[This film] is basically the same fun which [its predecessor] was, just with a different story. It does mean that if you are not in the Christmas spirit then it is going to be cheesy and painful, but for those feeling some Christmas love it should entertain."

Richard Scheib of *Moria Science Fiction, Horror and Fantasy Film Review*: "[This film] proves to be astonishingly traditional in its values. Everything, for instance, centres around how Christmas will fall apart if Santa isn't married, which does start to smack just a little too much of the evangelical Christian stipulation of no sex or unwed cohabitation before marriage."

[Author's Input]. Since Santa Claus is closely associated with Christmas, a decidedly *Christian* holiday, and since he is a positive role model, especially for children, then it's only fitting that Santa at least be depicted on film as upholding traditionally Christian values.

PRODUCTION CREDITS—Writer: Pamela Wallace. Producer: Albert T. Dickerson III and Jeff Kloss. Director: Harvey Frost. Production Companies: Hallmark Entertainment, Alpine Medien Productions, and Larry Levinson Productions. Rating: Not rated. Genre: Romance. Country: USA. Run Time: 96 min.

REFERENCES: Crump, William D. *The Christmas Encyclopedia*. Third Edition. Jefferson, NC: McFarland, 2013.

"Hallmark Channel Original Holiday Movie 'Meet the Santas' Becomes Network's Highest-Ever Rated Telecast." *The Futon Critic*. http://thefutoncritic.com/ratings/2005/12/20/hallmark-channel-original-holiday-movie-becomes-networks-highest-ever-rated-telecast-20141/20051220hallmark01/

Scheib, Richard. *Meet the Santas*. *Moria-Science Fiction, Horror and Fantasy Film Review*. http://moria.co.nz/fantasy/meetthesantas.htm

Webb, Andy. "Meet the Santas (2005)." *The Movie Scene*. http://www.themoviescene.co.uk/reviews/meet-the-santas/meet-the-santas.html

Wilson, Joanna. *Tis the Season TV: The Encyclopedia of Christmas-Themed Episodes, Specials and Made-for-TV Movies*. Akron, OH: 1701 Press, 2011.

Merry Madagascar—November 19, 2009

Computer-Animated Television Short Film

THREAT TO CHRISTMAS: Santa suffers amnesia when animals shoot him and the reindeer team down over Madagascar.

HOW CHRISTMAS IS SAVED: The animals on Madagascar take over Santa's route.

The four principals in the *Madagascar* series of computer-animated films, shown here in *Madagascar: Escape 2 Africa* (2008). From left: Melman the giraffe, Gloria the hippopotamus, Alex the lion, and Marty the zebra. In the TV short film *Merry Madagascar* (2009), they deliver the presents when Santa suffers amnesia (DreamWorks/Photofest).

SYNOPSIS AND COMMENTARY: The series of computer-animated *Madagascar* films follow the adventures of four animals in New York City's Central Park Zoo that are unexpectedly shipwrecked on the island of Madagascar: Alex the lion, Marty the zebra, Melman the giraffe, and Gloria the hippopotamus. Also shipwrecked are four penguins: Kowalski, Private, Skipper, and Rico.

In *Merry Madagascar*, Alex, Marty, Melman, and Gloria attempt to escape from Madagascar to New York in a hot-air balloon but are shot down by King Julien of the lemurs, who mistakes the balloon for the "red night goblin." As Julien explains, this latter entity appears annually in the night sky on the 24th of Julianuary (a holiday honoring Julien) and pelts them with coal. When the "goblin" appears soon thereafter, Alex and friends shoot him down, then realize their target was Santa and his reindeer. Santa suffers amnesia, whereupon the four animals volunteer to deliver the gifts, but when the reindeer refuse to cooperate without Santa, the four penguins serve as substitutes and use Santa's magic dust to fly. Leaving Santa, the reindeer, and the lemurs behind to celebrate Merry Julianuary, the eight animals bungle their way around the world with many crash-landings, and they nearly abandon the seemingly hopeless task until the joy of little Abby prompts them to plunge ahead. Meanwhile, Santa pulls Julien out of a funk by encouraging him to give gifts to the other lemurs. Discovering a shortage of magic dust, the eight animals in flight sacrifice a trip back to New York and instead return to Madagascar and crash into Santa, which restores his memory. With one bag of gifts remaining, Santa switches to a reserve tank of magic dust and flies away with the reindeer before the other animals can hop a ride back to New York. Stranded again on Madagascar, the animals nevertheless celebrate Christmas with Julien and the lemurs.

PRINCIPAL VOICES: All the cast previously had voice roles in *Madagascar* except where indicated: Ben Stiller as Alex; Chris Rock as Marty; David Schwimmer as Melman; Jada Pinkett Smith as Gloria; Tom McGrath as Skipper; Chris Miller as Kowalski; Christopher Knights as Private; Cedric the Entertainer as Maurice; Andy Richter as Mort; Danny Jacobs (*Madly Madagascar*) as King Julien; Willow Smith (*I Am Legend*) as Abby; Nina Dobrev (*Chloe*) as Cupid; Jim Cummings (*Mickey Mouse Clubhouse*) as Donner; Carl Reiner (*The Dick Van Dyke Show*) as Santa.

AWARDS IN 2010: Annie Award for Storyboarding in a Television Production; Annie Award nominations for Best Animated Television Production, Character Animation in a Television Production, Character Design in a Television Production, and Voice Acting in a Television Production (Danny Jacobs and Willow Smith).

INTERESTING TIDBITS: Rico the penguin has no speaking part.

Call a neurologist! Santa suffers amnesia in these other save-Christmas films: ***The Amazing World of Gumball: Christmas Episode; The Boy Who Saved Christmas; Miracle at the 34th Precinct; The Night Before the Night Before Christmas; Santa Who? The Search for Santa Paws;*** and ***Snow 2: Brain Freeze.***

REVIEWS: Emily Ashby of *Common Sense Media* (November 17, 2009): "The special is packed with the same character-based comedy that fans love, complete with a fresh target for the maniacal South Pole penguins: a 'polar' rivalry with Santa's North Pole reindeer ... there's a real attempt here to mix feel-good messages about generosity, caring, and compassion with the silly stuff..."

Brian Orndorf of *DVD Talk* (December 9, 2009): "While thinly plotted, [this film] contains an ample amount of Christmas cheer, supplemented by more traditional franchise highlights, including the self-centered madness of King Julien and the neurotic hysteria shared between our four heroes. The short throws a few needed curveballs, including an amusing rivalry between the South Pole penguins and the North Pole reindeer..."

Ben Simon of *Animated Views* (November 18, 2009): "...once we *do* get away from Julien and Madagascar, and the guys start their gift giving run, the pace is picked up no end, with much faster editing, funnier comedy and the pre-requisite warm Christmas spirit, which had been lacking until this point ... [we should] question why on Earth they didn't get the characters into this routine earlier as opposed to spending too much time with Julien."

PRODUCTION CREDITS—Writers: Eric Darnell, Tom McGrath, and David Soren. Producer: Joe M. Aguilar. Director: David Soren. Production Company: DreamWorks Animation. Rating: Not rated. Genres: Animation, Adventure, Comedy, Family. Country: USA. Run Time: 22 min.

REFERENCES: Ashby, Emily. *Merry Madagascar*. Common Sense Media. https://www.commonsensemedia.org/movie-reviews/merry-madagascar

Crump, William D. *The Christmas Encyclopedia*. Third Edition. Jefferson, NC: McFarland, 2013.

Merry Madagascar. Glendale, CA: DreamWorks Home Entertainment, 2011. DVD Video.

Merry Madagascar. Internet Movie Database. http://www.imdb.com/title/tt152630/

Orndorf, Brian. *Merry Madagascar*. DVD Talk. http://www.dvdtalk.com/reviews/41082/merry-madagascar/

Simon, Ben. *Merry Madagascar*. Animated Views. http://animatedviews.com/2009/merry-madagascar-tv-special

Wilson, Joanna. *Tis the Season TV: The Encyclopedia of Christmas-Themed Episodes, Specials and Made-for-TV Movies*. Akron, OH: 1701 Press, 2011.

Merry Wishmas—December 12, 2008

Episode from the Animated Television Series *The Fairly OddParents*

THREAT TO CHRISTMAS: When Timmy Turner doesn't get the gift he wanted for Christmas, he creates "Wishmas" and unwittingly puts Santa out of business.

HOW CHRISTMAS IS SAVED: Timmy convinces Santa to return to the North Pole and resume Christmas while stopping Jorgen Von Strangle from perpetuating Wishmas.

SYNOPSIS AND COMMENTARY: Imagine having your very own personal fairies to grant your every wish. It would be like experiencing Christmas every day ... almost. That's the case with *The Fairly OddParents*, an animated TV comedy series created by Butch Hartman for Nickelodeon, ongoing since 2001. The setting is the town of Dimmsdale with protagonist Timmy Turner, a ten-year-old boy neglected by his parents and left to the wiles of his evil babysitter Vicky, who delights in tormenting him. To make life easier, Timmy receives two fairy godparents, oddballs Wanda and Cosmo with their baby Poof, who grant all of Timmy's wishes, within reason. The catch is that his wishes usually backfire with comically disastrous consequences. Obviously, the title *Fairly OddParents* is a play on "fairy godparents."

In "Merry Wishmas," it's the day after Christmas. Timmy and his friends didn't get the gifts they wanted, so Timmy wishes for a sled, then has Cosmo and Wanda dress as mail carriers and deliver one-wish coupons around to his friends so they all get their wishes. When Vicky wishes for a million wishes, her mailbox pours out tons of wish coupons such that the kids' flood of wishes produces a mountain of toys in Dimmsdale, and "Wishmas" is born. Although such wishes overload the big wand in Fairy World and force Fairy King Jorgen Von Strangle to intervene, he sees much advantage if Wishmas replaces Christmas and if he as the Magic Mailman wish-bringer replaces Santa. After all, the fairies lend Santa their magic but never receive any credit. Wishmas soon puts Santa out of business, whereupon he and Mrs. Claus, along with the elves and reindeer, move into and commandeer the Turners' house, where all meals are milk and cookies, and it's up to Timmy to persuade Santa to return to the North Pole. As next year's Wishmas approaches, Timmy manages to incapacitate Jorgen long enough so that kids receive no wish coupons, and Santa restores Christmas after hearing lots of pitiful crying. But Santa faces two problems: he sold his sleigh to buy food and he made no toys all year. Not to worry, because Timmy's dad (who had wished himself into being Nog-Man, the champion of eggnog) offers his Nog-Mobile, the kids donate all the toys they had received from the previous Wishmas, and Santa is back in business with his reindeer.

PRINCIPAL VOICES: Tara Strong (*Ice Age*) as Timmy and Poof; Susanne Blakeslee (*Tangled*) as Wanda and Mrs. Turner; Daran Norris (*The Replacements*) as Cosmo, Mr. Turner, and Jorgen; Grey DeLisle (*The Replacements*) as Vicky, Mrs. Claus, and Tootie; Kevin Michael Richardson (*Lilo and Stitch*) as Santa; S. Scott Bullock (*The Ant Bully*) as the narrator.

AWARDS: *The Fairly OddParents* series has received a large number of awards and nominations, including Daytime and Primetime Emmys, Annies, and Golden Reels, among others.

INTERESTING TIDBITS: As Wishmas runs rampant and Timmy searches for anything Christmasy on TV, he finds a parody of a classic cartoon: the Grinch steals Wishmas.

The Fairly OddParents series is the second longest-running Nicktoon, the longest being *SpongeBob SquarePants*.

Check out the TV movie *A Fairly Odd Christmas*.

Timmy Turner (top) and his two fairy godparents, Cosmo (bottom left) and Wanda; all three are the principals in the animated TV series *The Fairly OddParents*. In the episode "Merry Wishmas" (2008), Timmy creates "Wishmas" and unwittingly puts Santa out of business (Nickelodeon/Photofest).

REVIEW: Betsy Wallace of *Common Sense Media*: "Timmy often learns a thing or two from his misguided wishes, but the focus here is on cartoon zaniness more than education…. Much like *SpongeBob SquarePants*, *The Fairly OddParents* can be fast-paced, raucous, and contain mature humor. [Cartoon violence] isn't unusual, though no one is ever hurt permanently."

PRODUCTION CREDITS—Writers: Butch Hartman, Scott Fellows, and Kevin Sullivan. Executive Producers: Butch Hartman, Fred Seibert, and Scott Fellows. Director: Ken Bruce. Production Companies: Billionfold, Frederator Studios, and Nickelodeon Productions. Rating: TV-Y7. Genres: Animation, Comedy, Family, Fantasy. Country: USA. Run Time: 25 min.

REFERENCES: Lenburg, Jeff. *The Encyclopedia of Animated Cartoons*. Third Edition. New York: Facts on File, 2009.

"Merry Wishmas." Big Cartoon Database. http://www.bcdb.com/cartoon/108004-Merry-Wishmas

"Merry Wishmas." In *The Fairly OddParents Season 6*. Amazon Instant Video.

"Merry Wishmas." Internet Movie Database. http://www.imdb.com/title/tt1632276/

Wallace, Betsy. *The Fairly OddParents*. *Common Sense Media*. https://www.commonsensemedia.org/tv-reviews/the-fairly-oddparents

Wilson, Joanna. *Tis the Season TV: The Encyclopedia of Christmas-Themed Episodes,*

Specials and Made-for-TV Movies. Akron, OH: 1701 Press, 2011.

Mickey Saves Santa—December 16, 2006
Episode from the Computer-Animated Television Series *Mickey Mouse Clubhouse*

THREAT TO CHRISTMAS: Santa's sleigh is stuck on top of a mountain with a broken harness.

HOW CHRISTMAS IS SAVED: Mickey and Donald Duck improvise a new harness from ribbons.

SYNOPSIS AND COMMENTARY: In this Disney series for preschoolers, ongoing since 2006, principal characters Mickey Mouse, Minnie Mouse, Donald Duck, Daisy Duck, Goofy, and Pluto interact with viewers to solve simple problems. From a computer "Mousekedoer," Mickey selects certain "Mouseketools" (one of which is always a mystery tool) needed to solve the current problem and downloads them to Toodles, a small, flying extension of the Mousekedoer.

In *Mickey Saves Santa*, it's Christmas Eve, and Santa is stranded atop Mistletoe Mountain with his reindeer team. When Mrs. Claus astride Dasher arrives at the clubhouse with a plea for help, Mickey downloads a spotlight, skis, and the mystery tool to Toodles, then he and Donald fly to the North Pole in their toon plane, lead by Mrs. Claus and Dasher. En route, they use the spotlight against poor visibility and the skis when they encounter deep snow. After ascending the mountain, Mickey and Donald discover only the reindeer team (without Rudolph), whereupon Mickey invites the viewers to join him in summoning Santa with the special Santa call: "Santa, Santa, Ho Ho Ho!" The old gent drops from a tree and explains that the sleigh's harness has snapped. Mickey quickly makes repairs with the mystery tool—a pair of ribbons—and Christmas is saved. Santa then returns Mickey and Donald to the clubhouse, where they and the gang enjoy Santa's gifts.

PRINCIPAL VOICES: Wayne Allwine (*Mickey's Christmas Carol*) as Mickey; Tony Anselmo (*Who Framed Roger Rabbit*) as Donald; Dee Bradley Baker (*American Dad!*) as Santa; Bill Farmer (*Toy Story*) as Goofy and Pluto; Tress MacNeille (*Animaniacs*) as Daisy and Mrs. Claus; Russi Taylor (*The Simpsons*) as Minnie; Corey Burton (*Aladdin*) as Ludwig Von Drake.

AWARDS: The series won a Behind the Voice Actors Award for Best Vocal Ensemble in a TV Series, Children's Educational (2014) as well as other BTVA nominations. The series also received Daytime Emmy nominations for Outstanding Directing (2008), Outstanding Pre-School Series (2011), Outstanding Performers (Bill Farmer 2011 and Dick Van Dyke 2015), and Outstanding Music Direction/Composition (2011); as well as Annie nominations for Best Animated TV Production (2010 and 2012).

INTERESTING TIDBITS: In a production that stresses the importance of getting Christmas presents, it's not surprising to hear Mrs. Claus exclaim, "If someone doesn't rescue Santa real soon, there won't be any Christmas this year!" The film sends the clear message that Santa *IS* Christmas; no Santa, no Christmas.

All through the episode, Donald is preoccupied with completing his yards-long Christmas list, and Mrs. Claus repeatedly counters his frequent temper tantrums by warning him to be nice, lest he not receive any presents.

REVIEWS: Larisa Wiseman of *Common Sense Media*: "…the series keeps the viewer's brain engaged almost continually—there's always something to count, find, identify, or compare. Mickey is constantly in your face (in a good way)—asking questions, acknowledging viewers' answers, cheering them on, and giving kudos for a job well done."

Paul Mavis of *DVD Talk* (November 11, 2006): "*Mickey Saves Santa and Other Mouseketales* is a sweet, light, funny little Christmas show that your preschoolers will undoubtedly love … not only is there nothing to worry about as far as content … but more importantly, the show actually helps the young viewer with early learning concepts such as problem solving, simple counting and mathematics, storytelling concepts and goal achievement."

PRODUCTION CREDITS—Writer and Producer: Leslie Valdes. Director: Rob LaDuca.

Production Company: Walt Disney Television Animation. Rating: TV-Y. Genres: Animation, Comedy, Family. Country: USA. Run Time: 25 min.

REFERENCES: Crump, William D. *The Christmas Encyclopedia*. Third Edition. Jefferson, NC: McFarland, 2013.

Mavis, Paul. *Disney's Mickey Mouse Clubhouse—Mickey Saves Santa and Other Mouseketales*. DVD Talk. http://www.dvdtalk.com/reviews/24987/disneys-mickey-mouse-clubhouse-mickey-saves-santa-and-other-mouseketales/

Mickey Saves Santa. Big Cartoon Database. http://www.bcdb.com/cartoon/95681-Mickey-Saves-Santa

Mickey Saves Santa. In *Mickey Mouse Clubhouse: Mickey Saves Santa and Other Mouseketales*. Burbank, CA: Buena Vista Home Entertainment, 2006. DVD Video.

Mickey Saves Santa. Internet Movie Database. http://www.imdb.com/title/tt1233028/

Wilson, Joanna. *Tis the Season TV: The Encyclopedia of Christmas-Themed Episodes, Specials and Made-for-TV Movies*. Akron, OH: 1701 Press, 2011.

Wiseman, Larisa. *Mickey Mouse Clubhouse. Common Sense Media*. https://www.commonsensemedia.org/tv-reviews/mickey-mouse-clubhouse

Miracle at the 34th Precinct—

November 27, 1993

Episode from the Animated Television Series *Bonkers*

THREAT TO CHRISTMAS: Santa falls from his sleigh during a blizzard over Hollywood and suffers amnesia.

HOW CHRISTMAS IS SAVED: Santa spontaneously recovers and restores a child's faith in him.

SYNOPSIS AND COMMENTARY: Following in the footsteps of the famous feline Felix the Cat, Bonkers D. Bobcat was the anthropomorphic bobcat protagonist in this series that ran for 65 half-hour episodes on the Disney Channel and in syndication from 1993 to 1994. A spinoff of Disney's *Raw Toonage* series and filled with slapstick comedy, the series featured the antics of Bonkers, a hyperactive, washed-up cartoon star who became a cop and the junior partner of Detective Lucky Piquel, a grim, fat slob. Other principal characters included Lucky's wife Dyl Piquel, child-genius daughter Marilyn, and Police Chief Leonard Kanifky.

With rookie toon-turned-cop Bonkers D. Bobcat (top) on the prowl, crime-fighting colleague Detective Lucky Piquel (bottom right) finds himself in some very unusual predicaments in the animated TV series *Bonkers*. When Santa suffers amnesia, elves recruit Lucky to take over while Bonkers pulls Santa together in the episode "Miracle at the 34th Precinct" (1993) (Walt Disney Company/MMG Photo Archives; collection of William D. Crump).

In "Miracle," Santa is out test-driving his sleigh two days before Christmas when he hits a massive blizzard over Southern California (amazing, huh?), falls out of the sleigh, crashes into the Hollywood apartment of Fall-Apart Rabbit (Bonkers' friend who falls apart at the drop of a hat), and suffers amnesia. Not realizing that his guest is Santa, Rabbit calls him "Jim" and entertains him by taking him water skiing during the blizzard. Meanwhile, elves Jingle and Bell report Santa missing, and Chief Kanifky assigns Bonkers and Lucky to the case. Should they not find Santa, the elves persuade Lucky to be a substitute (because of his expansive girth), and Lucky agrees for the sake of Marilyn, who has doubts about Santa's existence. While the two elves put Lucky through a Santa crash course (enduring gale-force winds from a giant fan and getting stuck in mock chimneys), Bonkers scours the neighborhood and finds a now-recovered Santa at Rabbit's place. Informed about Marilyn, Santa heads to Lucky's house with Bonkers just as Lucky/Santa and the elves land on the roof with the sleigh. The two Santas enter by different routes, and following their argument about who's the real Santa, Bonkers explains to a confused Marilyn that one is a back-up Santa, whereupon the real Santa reveals himself, yet Marilyn, still a believer, loves her Daddy/Santa more.

PRINCIPAL VOICES: Jim Cummings (*Shrek*) as Bonkers and Lucky; Earl Boen (*The Terminator*) as Chief Kanifky; Katie Leigh (*Despicable Me*) as Bell; Sherry Lynn (*Toy Story*) as Marilyn; Hal Smith (*The Andy Griffith Show*) as Santa; Beau Weaver (*Fantastic Four*) as Jingle; Frank Welker (*Aladdin*) as Fall-Apart Rabbit; April Winchell (*Antz*) as Dyl.

AWARDS: In 1993, *Bonkers* won Golden Reel Awards for Best Sound Editing–Television Animated Specials and Television Animation.

INTERESTING TIDBITS: The only "miracle" in this episode is that Santa isn't seriously injured any more than he is, given all the slapstick flying around.

Santa also suffers amnesia in other save-Christmas movies, such as **The Amazing World of Gumball: Christmas Episode; The Boy Who Saved Christmas; Merry Madagascar; The Night Before the Night Before Christmas; Santa Who? The Search for Santa Paws;** and **Snow 2: Brain Freeze**.

Of course, the episode title is a play on the title *Miracle on 34th Street*.

NOTE: At the time of this writing, this film was not available on DVD or VHS but could be seen on YouTube.

PRODUCTION CREDITS—Writer: Ralph Sanchez. Producer: Robert Taylor. Director: Roy Wilson. Production Company: Walt Disney Television Animation. Rating: TV-Y. Genres: Animation, Comedy, Family. Country: USA. Run Time: 27 min.

REFERENCES: "Miracle at the 34th Precinct." Big Cartoon Database. http://www.bcdb.com/cartoon/5614-Miracle-At-The-34th-Precinct

"Miracle at the 34th Precinct." Internet Movie Database. http://www.imdb.com/title/tt0529943/

Wilson, Joanna. *Tis the Season TV: The Encyclopedia of Christmas-Themed Episodes, Specials and Made-for-TV Movies*. Akron, OH: 1701 Press, 2011.

A Miser Brothers' Christmas—December 13, 2008

Animated Television Musical

THREAT TO CHRISTMAS: Santa injures his back and the North Wind schemes to usurp Santa's role.

HOW CHRISTMAS IS SAVED: The Miser Brothers learn to cease bickering long enough to deliver Santa's gifts.

SYNOPSIS AND COMMENTARY: Pagan gods dominate Christmas in this stop-motion-animation spinoff of the 1974 Rankin/Bass special, **The Year Without a Santa Claus**, as the Miser Brothers reprise their roles while ole Santa plays a secondary role here. At a reunion with her children (which include the two Tides, Lightning, Thunder, North Wind, and Earthquake), Mother Nature reveals that, should anything happen to Santa, then vain blowhard North Wind would take over, whereupon the latter sends two minions to sabotage Santa's new super sleigh. During a test run, Santa crashes near the Miser Brothers' territory, injures his back and takes to his bed, and the ever-feuding Misers receive the blame. Although their penance, so to speak, is to take Santa's place in the toy factory, their fighting, surreptitiously fueled by North Wind, precludes any productivity and continues until Christmas Eve, when Santa, having no recourse, is forced to take the reindeer team out to deliver the presents. North Wind attacks again, but the Misers perform a mid-air, sleigh-to-sleigh rescue and bring Santa back home, which earns the Misers a place on the Nice List. With Santa still incapacitated, the Miser Brothers finally learn to work together to perform Santa's gift-giving duties.

PRINCIPAL VOICES: Mickey Rooney (*National Velvet*) as Santa; George S. Irving (*Underdog*) as Heat Miser; Juan Chioran (*The Cheetah Girls*) as Snow Miser and Flakes; Catherine Disher (*Forever Knight*) as Mrs. Claus; Brad Adamson (*The Mummy Lives*) as North Wind; Patricia Hamilton (*Anne of Green Gables*) as Mother Nature; Susan Roman (*Heavy Metal*) as Tinsel.

SONGS: "Snow Miser" (music and lyrics respectively by Maury Laws and Jules Bass). Other songs by William Kevin Anderson and Sonia Levitin: "It's Christmas Time!"; "No Santa, Just Me!"; and "Brothers."

AWARDS: In 2009, this production received an Annie Award nomination for Best Animated Television Production Produced for Children.

INTERESTING TIDBITS: Mickey Rooney and George S. Irving reprise their roles from *The Year without a Santa Claus* (1974) at the respective ages of 88 and 86. Had Shirley Booth, Dick Shawn, and Rhoda Mann been available, they probably would have reprised their respective roles as Mrs. Claus, Snow Miser, and Mother Nature. Booth died in 1992, Shawn in 1987, and Mann in 2015. Rooney had also voiced for Santa in the Rankin/Bass production of *Santa Claus Is Comin' to Town* (1970).

Because this film was made 34 years after its predecessor, it is recommended that younger viewers first catch the 1974 *The Year without a Santa Claus* before watching *A Miser Brothers' Christmas* in order to have a better appreciation for the roles of Heat Miser and Snow Miser.

REVIEWS: Kari Croop of *Common Sense Media* (December 8, 2008): "[This film] is unlikely to become a Christmas classic that stands the test of time. The award-winning animation is stellar.... But the story loses major points for a convoluted plot involving Mother Nature, a failed assassination attempt, and mostly lackluster characters who fail to capture our hearts.... Without [the North Wind], *A Miser Brothers' Christmas* would be utterly skippable."

Rodney Figueiredo of *Animated Views* (December 25, 2009): "The characters are very entertaining in the original [*The Year without a Santa Claus*] so it was great to see them spotlighted in a new story. The story itself is standard Christmas fare with a message about brotherly love and family ... what makes the show worth the time is the special attention to detail in both the character animation and in the sets ... the songs are harmless and don't really detract from enjoying the show."

Ryan Cracknell of *Movie Views* (December 7, 2009): "[The film] pulls a *Terminator* and makes the bad guys good for the second spin ... has the look and feel of an old Rankin-Bass special with subtle effects that bring it into the modern computer age. The visual direction of the film is delightful to experience. All of the characters have a distinct look that works to define and enhance their portrayals."

PRODUCTION CREDITS—Writer: Eddie Guzelian. Producers: Lynda Craigmyle and Christine Davis. Director: Dave Barton Thomas. Production Companies: Warner Bros. Animation and Cuppa Coffee Studios. Rating: Not rated. Genres: Animation, Family. Countries: Canada and USA. Run Time: 45 min.

REFERENCES: Cracknell, Ryan. *A Miser Brothers' Christmas. Movie Views*. http://movieviews.ca/a-miser-brothers-christmas

Croop, Kari. *A Miser Brothers' Christmas. Common Sense Media*. https://www.commonsensemedia.org/movie-reviews/a-miser-brothers-christmas

Figueiredo, Rodney. *A Miser Brothers' Christmas. Animated Views*. http://animatedviews.com/2009/a-miser-brothers-christmas/

A Miser Brothers' Christmas. Big Cartoon Database. http://www.bcdb.com/cartoon/107730-Miser-Brothers-Christmas

A Miser Brothers' Christmas. Burbank, CA: Warner Home Video, 2009. DVD Video.

A Miser Brothers' Christmas. Internet Movie Database. http://www.imdb.com/title/tt1332026/

Wilson, Joanna. *Tis the Season TV: The Encyclopedia of Christmas-Themed Episodes, Specials and Made-for-TV Movies.* Akron, OH: 1701 Press, 2011.

Mr. St. Nick—November 17, 2002
Television Movie

THREAT TO CHRISTMAS: Playboy Nick St. Nick is reluctant to step into the shoes of his retiring father, King Nicholas XX, and be the new Santa Claus.

HOW CHRISTMAS IS SAVED: Powerful forces beyond his control drive Nick to become the new Santa.

SYNOPSIS AND COMMENTARY: This film joins those movies in which Santa reigns a finite number of years and then either voluntarily retires or is replaced. If no replacement can be found, there is no Christmas. In this instance, Santa reigns for one century and then retires, passing the torch to his reluctant son.

Having reigned as the Santa Claus of the twentieth century, King Nicholas XX (Charles Durning, *Elmo Saves Christmas*) must now pass the role to his son, Prince Nicholas St. Nicholas von Claus (Kelsey Grammer, *Cheers*), who prefers the name Nick St. Nick. Yet Nick's fast, playboy lifestyle in Miami Beach and his high-tech, nontraditional attitude toward Christmas so offend the North Pole that King Nicholas would defy tradition and continue as Santa Claus into the twenty-first century. Notwithstanding the rift between father and son, forces more powerful than they dictate that tradition *will* be upheld, lest there be no Christmas. Therefore, as the magic power and jovial spirit slowly depart from King Nicholas, those same attributes fall upon Nick, who eventually and predictably yields to his fate.

INTERESTING TIDBITS: Since this is a Hallmark production, there must be some romance afoot. Indeed, a subplot focuses on Nick's initial desire to wed Heidi (Elaine Hendrix, *The Parent Trap*), a sexy, local television personality-turned-con artist, who persuades an unwitting Nick to endorse a phony Christmas charity. After he overthrows Heidi's scheme to abscond with the charity's funds, Nick finds his queen for the North Pole in Lorena (Ana Ortiz, *Devious Maids*), his headstrong Venezuelan cook and housekeeper, the epitome of love and unquestioning faith.

REVIEWS: Robert Pardi of *TV Guide*: "Individual tolerance for cuteness will determine viewer reaction to this ... spin on the Santa legend.... Fans of TV star Grammer will get their fill of the fussy star's patented double takes in this good-natured Christmas comedy... [The writers] don't deliver much in the way of sparkling dialogue, but they put the characters through enough comically embarrassing situations to keep the merriment coming."

Sloan Freer of *Radio Times*: "For a festive TV movie, it's fun enough, but some suggestive jokes and unnecessary swearing mean it's best enjoyed by older family audiences." [In that case, it should have been rated PG.]

PRODUCTION CREDITS—Story: Maryedith Burrell and Matthew Jacobs. Teleplay: Maryedith Burrell, Debra Frank, and Steve L. Hayes. Producers: Camille Grammer, Tom Rowe, and Mary Anne Waterhouse. Director: Craig Zisk. Production Companies: Hallmark Entertainment and Mr. St. Nick, Inc. Rating: Not rated. Genres: Comedy, Fantasy. Countries: Canada and USA. Run Time: 100 min.

REFERENCES: Crump, William D. *The Christmas Encyclopedia.* Third Edition. Jefferson, NC: McFarland, 2013.

Freer, Sloan. *Mr. St. Nick. Radio Times.* http://www.radiotimes.com/film/mjmhv/mr-st-nick

Mr. St. Nick. Internet Movie Database. http://www.imdb.com/title/tt0325849/

Mr. St. Nick. Santa Monica, CA: Hallmark Home Entertainment, 2003. DVD Video.

Pardi, Robert. *Mr. St. Nick. TV Guide.* http://www.tvguide.com/movies/mr-st-nick/review/137178/

A Monster Christmas—January 1994
Movie from the Animated Video Series *Friendly Monsters*

THREAT TO CHRISTMAS: Santa becomes injured when one of Tom's monsters scares him.

HOW CHRISTMAS IS SAVED: Tom and his monsters take over for Santa.

SYNOPSIS AND COMMENTARY: Originally produced for British television, *A Monster Christmas* is one of three movies in the animated children's video series *Friendly Monsters*, the other two being *A Monster Easter* and *A Monster Holiday*. Featuring simple cel animation, the story line revolves around little boy Tom, whose companions are a group of benign "monsters" who live not only under his bed but in his closet, bathroom, dresser drawer, under the stairs, in his toy box, in the teapot, and out in the shed. The monsters appear in various colors as assorted blobs or reptiles with two or more eyes (some on stalks) and some with tails. Tom and his monsters solve crimes usually perpetrated by Moggie McNab.

It's Christmas Eve, and as Tom and his monsters settle into bed, Tom notices that purple monster Collin is missing, which prompts a search throughout the snowy neighborhood (all done without the knowledge of Tom's parents and despite all the racket the monsters create beforehand). Unable to find Collin, the gang returns to Tom's house to make Christmas pudding (so much for worrying about Collin). Meanwhile, Collin is out sledding and plops into Santa's *one-reindeer* sleigh pulled only by Rudolph (no mention of what happened to the other eight reindeer), whereupon Santa is scared so badly that he falls out, crashes down Tom's chimney, injures his foot, and cannot continue his route. Now it's up to Tom and his monsters to take over for Santa (Collin has turned up by now), so they either drop the presents via parachutes down chimneys or hand-deliver the presents themselves. During this time, Moggie McNab, disguised as a cat burglar, sneaks into Tom's house and, finding Santa recuperating in Tom's bed, kidnaps the old gent and is about to leave with him, when Tom and the monsters arrive, having delivered all the presents. Moggie is scared so badly that he flees right into the hands of two bumbling cops, who take him away, after which Tom, the monsters, and Santa all enjoy a Christmas Eve party.

VOICES: Rob Rackstraw, Emily Oldfield, and Martin Oldfield.

INTERESTING TIDBITS: Other films in which the presents are delivered via parachutes include ***Christmas Flintstone***, ***The Christmas Orange***, ***Christmas Present Time***, and ***The Super Special Gift***.

PRODUCTION CREDITS—Script: Phil Jackson. Producer: Heather Pedley. Director: Vincent James. Production Companies: Carrington Productions International, JWP Entertainment International, and Fat City Films. Rating: Not rated. Genres: Animation, Family. Country: United Kingdom. Run Time: 26 min.

REFERENCES: *Friendly Monsters: A Monster Christmas*. Internet Movie Database. http://www.imdb.com/title/tt2833108/

A Monster Christmas. Van Nuys, CA: Family Home Entertainment, 1996. VHS Video.

Wilson, Joanna. *Tis the Season TV: The Encyclopedia of Christmas-Themed Episodes, Specials and Made-for-TV Movies*. Akron, OH: 1701 Press, 2011.

Mrs. Santa Claus—December 8, 1996

Television Musical

THREAT TO CHRISTMAS: When Mrs. Claus takes the sleigh out for a spin, she becomes stranded in New York City, and a mean-spirited toymaker captures her reindeer.

HOW CHRISTMAS IS SAVED: Mrs. Claus fulfills the toymaker's childhood wish.

SYNOPSIS AND COMMENTARY: Mrs. Claus gets into mischief in this film while Santa takes a back seat. The year is 1910. Feeling neglected by her husband Santa (Charles Durning, *Elmo Saves Christmas*) each year during the Christmas rush, Mrs. Anna Claus (Angela Lansbury, *Murder, She Wrote*) yields to a whim and takes the reindeer sleigh out for a spin around the world six days before Christmas. She becomes trapped in the Big Apple after making an emergency landing in Manhattan's Lower East Side because of inclement weather, and Cupid is injured in the process. While Cupid recuperates, Anna, posing as a revolutionary Mrs. North, participates in a women's suffrage march and fights for better child labor laws after observing intolerable working conditions at the Tavish

Toy Company, which employs children. Outraged by Tavish's cheap toys and its motto, "It only has to last till Christmas," she succeeds in staging a citywide boycott of Tavish Toys. Augustus Tavish (Terrence Mann, *Critters*), seeking revenge, discovers Anna's true identity and captures her reindeer on Christmas Eve. But Tavish's desire to ruin Christmas stems from his having lost a prized Christmas teddy bear as a child. Anna discerns this and replaces the bear, Tavish reforms, and Anna returns to a more appreciative Santa just in time for Christmas Eve rounds.

AWARDS: In 1997, this film won a Primetime Emmy Award for Outstanding Hairstyling; Primetime Emmy nominations for Outstanding Art Direction, Outstanding Choreography, Outstanding Costume Design, and Outstanding Music and Lyrics (Jerry Herman, for the song "Mrs. Santa Claus"); Art Directors Guild Award nomination for Excellence in Television Production Design; Online Film and Television Association Award nominations for Best Music (Jerry Herman) and Best Actress (Angela Lansbury) in a Motion Picture or Miniseries.

SONGS: Music and lyrics by Jerry Herman. "Seven Days 'Til Christmas"; "Mrs. Santa Claus"; "Avenue A"; "A Tavish Toy"; "Almost Young"; "Suffragette March"; "We Don't Go Together At All"; "Whistle"; "Dear Mrs. Santa Claus"; "He Needs Me"; "The Best Christmas of All."

CHOREOGRAPHY: Rob Marshall.

INTERESTING TIDBIT: To cheer up a depressed Santa during his wife's absence, several of the elves perform a brief tumbling act to "We Need a Little Christmas," another holiday standard by Jerry Herman. Angela Lansbury first sang that song in the 1966 Broadway musical production of *Mame*, for which Herman also provided the music.

REVIEWS: *TV Guide*: "A toe-tapping delight, [this film] deftly puts its unique stamp on a Christmas legend ... [and] ... subtly slips in its messages about divergent cultures living in harmony and husbands learning to treat their spouses as equals."

Tony Scott of *Variety* (December 4, 1996): "Lansbury, taking up with secondary characters, dances and sings charmingly through Jerry Herman's tunes, some of which are not only in Herman's style, but are reminiscent of earlier works.

Out for a spin in the reindeer sleigh before Christmas, Mrs. Anna Claus (Angela Lansbury, left) ends up trapped in New York City where she leads a crusade for better social conditions in *Mrs. Santa Claus* (1996). Charles Durning shown here also stars as Santa (Hallmark Television/Photofest).

Generally, they're appealing and often clever, standard show songs.... Major contributor to the production is designer Hub Braden, whose whimsical North Pole décor and huge, musical comedy-style Lower East Side street scenes are impressive."

PRODUCTION CREDITS—Writer: Mark Saltzman. Producer: J. Boyce Harman, Jr. Director: Terry Hughes. Production Companies: Corymore Productions and Hallmark Entertainment. Rating: G. Genres: Comedy, Family, Fantasy, Musical. Country: USA. Run Time: 91 min.

REFERENCES: Crump, William D. *The Christmas Encyclopedia.* Third Edition. Jefferson, NC: McFarland, 2013.

Mrs. Santa Claus. Internet Movie Database. http://www.imdb.com/title/tt0117103/

Mrs. Santa Claus. Santa Monica, CA: Hallmark Home Entertainment, 2003. DVD Video.

Mrs. Santa Claus. TV Guide. http://www.tvguide.com/movies/mrs-santa-claus/review/132871/

Scott, Tony. *Mrs. Santa Claus.* Variety. http://variety.com/1996/tv/reviews/mrs-santa-claus-1200448162/#

Wilson, Joanna. *Tis the Season TV: The Encyclopedia of Christmas-Themed Episodes, Specials and Made-for-TV Movies.* Akron, OH: 1701 Press, 2011.

Mule-Tide Christmas (Olentzero eta iratxoen jauntxoa)

Also Known As *The Elf Who Stole Christmas* and *In the Land of Magic*

December 2, 2011

Computer-Animated Feature Film

THREAT TO CHRISTMAS: The mayor of a small mountain village cancels Christmas when an evil elf escapes from Santa's prison and wreaks havoc with the townspeople.

HOW CHRISTMAS IS SAVED: Young Andy and his friends launch a plan with Santa to capture the elf.

SYNOPSIS AND COMMENTARY: *Mule-Tide Christmas, The Elf Who Stole Christmas,* and *In the Land of Magic* are English-language titles for *Olentzero eta iratxoen jauntxoa* (Basque, literally *Christmas and Elves Lord*), a film from Spain with English dialogue based on Christmas customs from the Basque region of Spain. According to a popular story in Basque folklore, the ancient pagan figure Olentzero, a mountain-dwelling coal miner and equivalent of Santa Claus today, descends into villages on Christmas Eve with the good news that Christ is born. Abandoned at birth, Olentzero was raised by a woodland couple after a fairy brought him to them. He grew up a favorite of children and made toys for them, giving his life to save them in a time of calamity. The fairy bestowed immortality on Olentzero, and he returns each year during the time of the winter solstice with gifts for children. Over time, his annual mission acquired a Christmas theme. He is depicted as a plump, straw- or herb-stuffed doll wearing a regional beret, woolen socks and goatskin vest, and carrying a wine flask with frying pan. In Olentzero parades, men dress the part and are carried about on the shoulders of their comrades.

In this film, the Olentzero character is referred to as Santa who appears as a white-bearded old man otherwise dressed as above. There are no helper elves as such, no reindeer, and no sleigh. Signs and documents shown to viewers are in the Basque language. In a small village nestled in the Pyrenees Mountains, young Anje (Andy in English) becomes Santa's assistant at Christmastime and has the glorious task of mopping out Santa's workshop. But there's a caveat: he must not touch the little wooden cage on the shelf. To a kid, that's like saying, "Do it, do it!" That cage imprisons an evil little elf, the Basque version of the Grinch, who coaxes Andy to release him. Once out, the elf wreaks havoc all over town by stealing and ruining the Christmas decorations and causing much discord among the townspeople, who blame each other for all the mishaps. The elf glues the local priest to his chair and poisons other people, and the town is in such an uproar that the mayor cancels Christmas. Out searching for the elf with Napoleon (Napo), his wise-cracking "mule" sidekick (actually a donkey), Santa morphs into an owl (because if men see him as Santa, he will lose his magic) and locates the elf's stash of stolen decorations, which

Andy and his friends remove to the church belfry according to a plan to lure and capture the elf. On Christmas Eve, the elf storms the belfry and engages in a physical altercation with Santa, but Andy, after several cliff-hanger delays, manages to ring the large bell, which stuns the elf and allows Santa to trap him back into his little prison, and Christmas is back on.

PRINCIPAL VOICES (BASQUE): Joxe Ramón Argoitia (*Paper Birds*) as Olentzero/Santa; Itziar Urretabizkaia (*Flowers*) as Anje/Andy; Anjel Alkain (*Supertramps*) as Napoleon/Napo; and Kiko Jauregi as the elf.

PRINCIPAL VOICES (ENGLISH): Scott Schenberg; David Schifter; Steve Vernon; and Matthew Warzel.

INTERESTING TIDBITS: *The Elf Who Stole Christmas* is a much more accurate title. *Mule-Tide Christmas* appears on the cover of the English-language DVD and in the closing credits, whereas the opening credits display the title as *In the Land of Magic*. Confusing, yes?

REVIEW: Grace Montgomery of *Common Sense Media* (April 10, 2015): "The title is doubly misleading. First, the mule, who is billed as being the main character, is a small, annoying side character who doesn't add much to the plot … second … there's a decided lack of Christmas cheer…. The emphasis is mostly on people being mad at each other…"

PRODUCTION CREDITS—Screenplay: Beatriz Iso and Segundo Altolagirre. Producers: Eduardo Baringa and Karmelo Vivanco. Director: Gorka Vazquez. Production Companies: Baleuko S.L. and Talape. Rating: PG (some mild action and rude humor). Genres: Animation, Fantasy. Country: Spain. Run Time: 74 min.

REFERENCES: Crump, William D. *The Christmas Encyclopedia*. Third Edition. Jefferson, NC: McFarland, 2013.

Montgomery, Grace. *Mule-Tide Christmas*. Common Sense Media. https://www.commonsensemedia.org/movie-reviews/mule-tide-christmas

Mule-Tide Christmas. Fort Mill, SC: Phase 4 Films, 2014. DVD Video.

Mule-Tide Christmas. Internet Movie Database. http://www.imdb.com/title/tt4049534/

"Olentzero: The Basque Santa Claus." http://www.nabasque.org/old_nabo/NABO/Olentzero.htm

The Munsters' Scary Little Christmas—December 17, 1996

Television Movie

THREAT TO CHRISTMAS: A few days before Christmas, Grandpa accidentally conjures up Santa at the Munster home and can't return him to the North Pole.

HOW CHRISTMAS IS SAVED: The Munsters enable Santa to continue making toys at their home.

SYNOPSIS AND COMMENTARY: Spoofing the famous monsters from Universal Studios, *The Munsters* was a black-and-white television sitcom series of 70 half-hour episodes that ran on CBS from 1964 to 1966 with a couple of later spinoffs. In that time, the original series never produced a Christmas episode; 30 years later, the television movie brought back the same benign characters for Christmas but with a completely different cast. The principal, original cast included Fred Gwynne as Herman Munster, a spoof of Frankenstein's monster; Yvonne De Carlo as his vampire-wife Lily; Butch Patrick as their young werewolf-son Eddie; Al Lewis as Grandpa, a spoof of Count Dracula; and Beverley Owen and Pat Priest as Marilyn Munster, Lily's "normal" niece.

Christmas in Southern California just isn't the same as those back in Transylvania, which sported gloom and snow. Realizing that little Eddie Munster (Bug Hall, *The Little Rascals*) has the Christmas blues, the Munster family rallies to get him back into the Christmas spirit and plans a Christmas bash with monster friends from all over the world. Herman Munster (Sam McMurray, *Christmas Vacation*), short on holiday cash, seeks additional employment, while his wife Lily (Ann Magnuson, *Panic Room*) and Eddie enter the neighborhood home decorating contest. As Marilyn Munster (Elaine Hendrix, *The Parent Trap*) mails invitations, Grandpa (Sandy Baron, *Birdy*) unwittingly conjures up Santa Claus (Mark Mitchell, *Round the Twist*) and two elves while attempting to make snow. Unable to transport Santa back to the North Pole in time for Christmas Eve, the Munsters save the holiday by converting their home into a toy factory, but not before Santa's brief transformation into a portly fruitcake at the hands of the two elves, who had desired to cancel Christmas.

AWARDS: In 1997, the show received a Young Star Award nomination for Best Performance by a Young Actor in a Made-for-TV Movie (Bug Hall).

REVIEWS: Will Brownridge of *The Film Reel* (December 12, 2010): "[The actors] succeed in bringing the concept of the Munsters back to life and manage to cook up a story that keeps with the theme of the original show ... it's so freaking weird.... This is one that you have to see to believe..."

Ian Jane of *DVD Talk* (December 1, 2007): "...seeing other faces under the familiar [makeup] is, quite simply, weird... [The cast does] a decent job of impersonating their predecessors, but there are still too many differences that are too easily spotted for this to earn a get out of jail free card in that regard ... that lack of inseparable original cast members ... is hard to overlook."

PRODUCTION CREDITS—Based on characters created by Norm Liebmann and Ed Haas. Writers: Ed Ferrara and Kevin Murphy. Supervising Producer: Michael R. Joyce. Director: Ian Emes. Production Companies: Michael R. Joyce Productions, St. Clare Entertainment, and MCA Television Entertainment. Rating: Not rated. Genres: Comedy, Family, Sci-Fi. Country: USA. Run Time: 91 min.

REFERENCES: Brownridge, Will. *The Munsters' Scary Little Christmas*. The Film Reel. http://www.the-filmreel.com/2010/12/12/the-munsters-scary-little-christmas-1996-film-reel-review/

Crump, William D. *The Christmas Encyclopedia*. Third Edition. Jefferson, NC: McFarland, 2013.

Jane, Ian. *Munster's* [sic] *Scary Little Christmas*. DVD Talk. http://www.dvdtalk.com/reviews/31562/munsters-scary-little-christmas/

The Munsters' Scary Little Christmas. Internet Movie Database. http://www.imdb.com/title/tt0117109/

The Munsters' Scary Little Christmas. Universal City, CA: Universal Studios Home Entertainment, 2007. DVD Video.

Wilson, Joanna. *Tis the Season TV: The Encyclopedia of Christmas-Themed Episodes, Specials and Made-for-TV Movies*. Akron, OH: 1701 Press, 2011.

A Muppets Christmas: Letters to Santa—December 17, 2008

Television Musical Comedy

THREAT TO CHRISTMAS: The Muppets discover three letters to Santa that haven't been mailed.

HOW CHRISTMAS IS SAVED: The Muppets hand-deliver the letters to Santa at the North Pole.

SYNOPSIS AND COMMENTARY: It's not uncommon for movies to focus on saving Christmas for several individuals instead of the whole world, as Jim Henson's Muppets illustrate here. On Christmas Eve in New York City, the Muppets make a last-minute trek to the post office. Along with some cards, they intend to mail a letter to Santa from their young neighbor Claire (Madison Pettis, *Life with Boys*). Curiosity leads them into the sorting room, where a postal worker (Jesse L. Martin, *The Flash*) extols the virtues of the postal system in song, after which the Muppets create a bit of havoc and are ejected. Back home, they discover that during the melee at the post office, they not only failed to mail Claire's letter, but two other letters to Santa have fallen into their possession. By now, the post office is closed, so the Muppets seek other ways to get the letters to the North Pole, such as by UPS (United Pigeon Service) and through a couple of mobsters (Steve Schirripa and Tony Sirico of *The Sopranos*), but these methods fail. The only right thing to do is hand-deliver the letters personally to Santa (Richard Griffiths, *Harry Potter*), but only Kermit, Gonzo, Fozzie, Pepe, and Rizzo are willing to go. En route, they encounter several other celebrities in cameo appearances, including Whoopi Goldberg (*The View*) as a grumpy taxi driver; Nathan Lane (*The Lion King*) as Officer Meany of airport security; Uma Thurman (*Pulp Fiction*) as Joy, an

Several Muppet monsters all wrapped up in lights for the holidays in *The Muppets* (2011). From left: Fozzie Bear, Kermit the Frog, Miss Piggy, Gonzo, and Animal. In *A Muppets Christmas: Letters to Santa* (2008), Kermit, Gonzo, Fozzie, Pepe, and Rizzo take several unmailed letters to Santa at the North Pole (Walt Disney Studios Motion Pictures/Photofest).

oddball flight attendant at North Pole Airlines; New York City Mayor Michael Bloomberg as himself; Jane Krakowski (*30 Rock*) as Claire's mother; and supermodel Petra Nemcova (*Fashion News Live*) as Beaker's wish-girlfriend. Just missing their flight to the North Pole, the Muppets quintet nevertheless "wing it" by literally clinging in flight to the aircraft's wing and then jump off, crashing near Santa's abode, where they learn from an elf (Paul Williams, *Ishtar*) that Santa has already left. Hearing their song "I Wish I Could Be Santa Claus," the jolly gent returns to grant the wishes in the three letters: Officer Meany is removed from the naughty list, and Pepe becomes an opera singer. As for Claire, the movie ends with a parade of Muppets characters providing a Christmas party for her, which fulfills her wish, because all her human friends had left town for the holidays.

PRINCIPAL MUPPETS PERFORMERS: Steve Whitmire as Kermit, Rizzo, Statler, and Beaker; Dave Goelz as Gonzo, Waldorf, Dr. Bunsen Honeydew, and Zoot; Bill Barretta as Pepe, Swedish Chef, Rowlf, Dr. Teeth, Bobo, and Husband Pigeon; Eric Jacobson as Fozzie, Piggy, Animal, and Sam Eagle.

SONGS: Composed by Paul Williams: "Delivering Christmas"; "It's All About Heart"; "I Wish I Could Be Santa Claus"; and "My Best Christmas Yet."

AWARDS: In 2009, this program received a Primetime Emmy nomination for Outstanding Original Music and Lyrics (Paul Williams).

INTERESTING TIDBITS: The principal show runs about 45 minutes. Tacked on are another 10 minutes of outtakes and bloopers.

At Claire's party, there's a nod to Hanukkah as Zoot lights a menorah and says, "Shalom!"

REVIEWS: Emily Ashby of *Common Sense Media* (December 15, 2008): "Few other stuffed stars can rival the Muppets' unique blend of comedy, adventure, and musical accomplishment, and this special weaves themes like loyalty, friendship, and good will into a delightful, tune-filled tale..."

David Nusair of *Reel Film Reviews*: "The barrage of celebrity cameos ... [serves] no real purpose other than to pad out the almost unreasonably thin storyline ... the majority of the gags and jokes are of the grade-school variety..."

Jason Bailey of *DVD Talk*: "...since [Jim] Henson's untimely death in 1990 ... the genuine heart of the early Muppet pictures was replaced by syrupy, vanilla formula ... [this film] falls mostly into this realm ... mostly aimed squarely at young kids, without much to keep anyone else interested ... the Muppets are cute, the jokes are easy, and it has plenty of Christmas cheer. But older viewers, longing for the glory days of Muppet entertainment, won't find much of that here."

PRODUCTION CREDITS—Story and Teleplay: Hugh Fink, Scott Ganz, Andrew Samson, and Paul Williams. Producers: Martin G. Baker and Anthony Katagas. Director: Kirk R. Thatcher. Production Companies: The Muppets Studio and Walt Disney Studios. Rating: G. Genres: Comedy, Family, Musical. Country: USA. Run Time: 55 min.

REFERENCES: Ashby, Emily. *A Muppets Christmas: Letters to Santa*. Common Sense Media. https://www.commonsensemedia.org/movie-reviews/a-muppets-christmas-letters-to-santa

Bailey, Jason. *Muppets Christmas: Letters to Santa*. DVD Talk. http://www.dvdtalk.com/reviews/39980/muppets-christmas-letters-to-santa/

Crump, William D. *The Christmas Encyclopedia*. Third Edition. Jefferson, NC: McFarland, 2013.

A Muppets Christmas: Letters to Santa. Burbank, CA: Walt Disney Studios Home Entertainment, 2009. DVD Video.

A Muppets Christmas: Letters to Santa. Internet Movie Database. http://www.imdb.com/title/tt1292569/

Nusair, David. *A Muppets Christmas: Letters to Santa. Reel Film Reviews.* http://reelfilm.com/disfam7.htm#muppets

Wilson, Joanna. *Tis the Season TV: The Encyclopedia of Christmas-Themed Episodes, Specials and Made-for-TV Movies*. Akron, OH: 1701 Press, 2011.

Must Be Santa—December 12, 1999

Television Movie

THREAT TO CHRISTMAS: Santa is old, ill, and must be replaced lest the Christmas spirit be lost.

HOW CHRISTMAS IS SAVED: Santa passes his magic to an escaped felon.

SYNOPSIS AND COMMENTARY: Just like **Call Me Claus**, here's another find-a-new-Santa film that "steps out of the box," so to speak, in which the new Santa is black. Instead of employing elves, the North Pole operates on a heavenly, high-tech system of angelic assistants, primarily children, with the militaristic Tuttle (Dabney Coleman, *Nine to Five*) serving as chief operations officer. Realizing that Santa (Gerard Parkes, *Fraggle Rock*), whom Tuttle supervises, has become crippled and ill with age, Tuttle must find a replacement, lest the Christmas spirit be lost. Two days before Christmas, ailing Santa passes his magic to Floyd Court (Arnold Pinnock, *The Incredible Hulk*), a black, deadbeat father and petty criminal. Although Floyd finds living up to Santa's reputation challenging enough, given his previous lifestyle, he faces a seemingly greater challenge in resuming his role as father to his ten-year-old daughter Heather (Keenan MacWilliam, *The Saddle Club*), who believes that he's a failure. Through his Santa power, Floyd brings Heather to the North Pole where the two seem to bond, until Tuttle discovers that Floyd is an escaped felon and dismisses him. On the outside, Floyd makes a bet, which breaks his Santa vows, whereupon the eternal flame of Christmas is extinguished, causing a violent storm to erupt at the North Pole that endangers Heather. Tuttle gives his life to bring Heather to safety and the eternal flame is re-ignited, thus ending the storm. Believing that Heather needs him more than he needs to be Santa, Floyd would resign, yet Heather, knowing that her father truly has become Santa, bids him to fulfill his role to all children.

AWARDS IN 2000: A Gemini Award for Best Visual Effects; Gemini nominations for Best Direction, Best Performance by an Actress in a Leading Role (Deanna Milligan), and Best Photography in a Dramatic Program or Miniseries.

INTERESTING TIDBITS: As Floyd/Santa is making rounds in his sleigh that requires no reindeer, he states quite profoundly to Heather, "Santa Claus doesn't deliver presents like video games and Barbie dolls. He delivers this—spirit—all the ideas, all the good thoughts that have built up throughout the year at the North Pole. He makes people happy. He fills them with goodwill. He inspires little acts of kindness. This is what Santa has to give."

While the members of the North Pole are immortal angels, it is a prerequisite that all Santas be mortals so that they can be more in touch with the hopes and dreams of children.

Comedian and actor Joe Flaherty makes a cameo appearance as his *Second City Television* character "Count Floyd."

A strike of the Canadian Broadcasting Company's technicians in February 1999 temporarily interrupted film production, which resumed in May following a labor settlement.

The film features a budding, interracial romance between Floyd Court and Natalie Fairlie (Deanna Milligan, *Avalanche*), Tuttle's white, sugary assistant.

PRODUCTION CREDITS—Writer: Douglas Bowie. Producer: Robert Sherrin. Director: Brad Turner. Production Company: Canadian Broadcasting Corporation. Rating: G. Genres: Comedy, Drama, Fantasy. Country: Canada. Run Time: 91 min.

REFERENCES: Crump, William D. *The Christmas Encyclopedia*. Third Edition. Jefferson, NC: McFarland, 2013.

Must Be Santa. Internet Movie Database. http://www.imdb.com/title/tt0226194/

Must Be Santa. Toronto: Video Service Corp., 2000. DVD Video.

Wilson, Joanna. *Tis the Season TV: The Encyclopedia of Christmas-Themed Episodes, Specials and Made-for-TV Movies*. Akron, OH: 1701 Press, 2011.

My Friends Tigger and Pooh: Super Sleuth Christmas Movie—November 20, 2007

Direct-to-Video Animated Movie

THREAT TO CHRISTMAS: During a practice run with the reindeer on Christmas Eve, Santa loses his magic sack of toys in the snow. If it cannot be found in time, Santa will cancel Christmas.

HOW CHRISTMAS IS SAVED: The Super Sleuths rescue Holly, a little reindeer sent to find the sack, and accompany her back to the North Pole in the nick of time.

SYNOPSIS AND COMMENTARY: The characters found in the *Winnie the Pooh* children's books, first published in 1926 by British author Alan Alexander Milne (1882–1956), have appeared in a number of Disney animated television series and specials for children. Milne's principal, anthropomorphic characters were Winnie the Pooh, a small, gentle yet rather witless bear with a passion for honey; Tigger, the bouncing tiger; Eeyore, the moping, ever-complaining donkey; Kanga and Roo, a female kangaroo and her joey, respectively; Rabbit; Piglet; Owl; and Christopher Robin, a young boy modeled after Milne's son of the same name. All the animals lived in the 100-Acre Wood.

Disney's interactive television series *My Friends Tigger and Pooh*, on which *Super Sleuth Christmas Movie* is based, aired on the Disney channel from 2007 to 2010 and consisted of 87 episodes. For that series, Disney created Darby, a red-headed, six-year-old girl who led the problem-solving Super Sleuths and essentially replaced Christopher Robin, who rarely appeared in the series; and Buster, Darby's pet puppy. Also featured was Lumpy the Heffalump, a lavender, elephant-like character. In addition to problem-solving, this first computer-animated *Pooh* series encouraged teamwork, curiosity, and imagination.

In *Super Sleuth*, it's Christmas Eve, and as Lumpy and Roo frolic outside, they discover Santa's red sack buried in the snow. At the same time, they spy Holly, a young reindeer trapped in a thicket, and call the Super Sleuths (Darby, Tigger, Pooh, and Buster) to free her. Holly had returned from Santa's practice run to retrieve the sack, but she doesn't remember how to get back to the North Pole, whereupon all the characters become Super Sleuths and accompany Holly to her destination. Along the way, Darby encourages her group never to give up, for they otherwise would have abandoned the mission after enduring several mishaps. Eventually they come upon the Valley of the Snowmen, the entrance to the North Pole. The giant snowmen lined along the way spring to life and escort the Super Sleuths with the sack to Santa, just as he is about to cancel Christmas. Similar to a dog whistle, a reindeer whistle summons six reindeer who ready themselves for flight, and because Holly also heard the whistle, she is now flight-worthy and takes her place out front, along with Eeyore for "balance." The rest of the gang rides with Santa and deliver presents by dropping them from the sleigh like bombs into chimneys, a method identical to that seen in ***A Flintstone Christmas*** (1977).

SONGS: "Super Sleuths Theme" and "Think Think Think" by Brian Hohlfeld and Andy Sturmer; "Christmas Comes Tomorrow" by Nicole Dubuc and Andy Sturmer; "Time to Go (on a Trek Through the Snow)" and "Snowman Song" by Nicole Dubuc, Brian Hohlfeld, and Andy Sturmer.

PRINCIPAL VOICES: Chloe Moretz (*Hugo*) as Darby; Ken Sansom (*The Sting*) as Rabbit; Travis Oates (*Winnie the Pooh*) as Piglet; Peter Cullen (*Transformers*) as Eeyore; Max Burkholder (*Parenthood*) as Roo; Oliver Dillon (*The Sparticle Mystery*) as Lumpy; Mikaila Baumel (*Novel Romance*) as Holly; Kath Soucie (*Rugrats*) as Kanga; Tara Strong (*Ice Age*) as Vixen; Jim Cummings (*Shrek*) as Pooh, Tigger, and Snowman; Jeffrey Tambor (*Transparent*) as Santa; Randy Crenshaw, Dick Wells, and Bill Cantos as singing snowmen.

INTERESTING TIDBITS: Viewers will note that in this depiction, neither Holly nor Eeyore nor any of the other reindeer are in harness when they pull Santa's sleigh; evidently a harness isn't necessary when magic is involved. The author has not seen similar, harness-free reindeer-and-sleigh teams in animated or live-action productions.

Because Holly and her mother Vixen sport antlers, the question has arisen whether antlers are strictly seen in male reindeer. In an essay about reindeer, Jill Harness noted that, "In most deer species, only the male grows antlers, but that's not true for most reindeer ... older male reindeer lose their antlers in December.... That means Santa's [sleigh] either has to be pulled by young reindeer, constantly replaced as they start to age, or Santa's reindeer are female."

PRODUCTION CREDITS—Writers: Nicole Dubuc and Brian Hohlfeld. Story: Nicole Dubuc, Brian Hohlfeld, and Jeff Kline. Producer: Dorothy McKim. Director: Don MacKinnon. Production Company: Walt Disney Studios. Rating: Not rated. Genres: Animation, Kids and Family. Country: USA. Run Time: 44 min.

REFERENCES: Harness, Jill. "11 Things You Might Not Know About Reindeer." Mental Floss Web Site. http://mentalfloss.com/article/29470/11-things-you-might-not-know-about-reindeer

My Friends Tigger and Pooh. TV.com. http://www.tv.com/shows/my-friends-tigger-and-pooh/

My Friends Tigger and Pooh: Super Sleuth Christmas Movie. Burbank, CA: Walt Disney Home Entertainment, 2007. DVD Video.

My Friends Tigger and Pooh: Super Sleuth Christmas Movie. Internet Movie Database: http://www.imdb.com/title/tt1141984/

Pooh's Super Sleuth Christmas Movie. Big Cartoon Database. http://www.bcdb.com/cartoon/98636-Poohs-Super-Sleuth-Christmas-Movie

Wilson, Joanna. *Tis the Season TV: The Encyclopedia of Christmas-Themed Episodes, Specials and Made-for-TV Movies*. Akron, OH: 1701 Press, 2011.

My Little Pony: A Very Minty Christmas—October 25, 2005

Animated Movie in the Direct-to-Video Series *My Little Pony*

THREAT TO CHRISTMAS: The pony Minty accidentally destroys the candy cane beacon that leads Santa to Ponyville.

HOW CHRISTMAS IS SAVED: The ponies' love and concern for each other leads Santa to Ponyville.

SYNOPSIS AND COMMENTARY: This video series is just one of numerous products within the *My Little Pony* franchise, which began with a line of pony toys that Hasbro marketed primarily to girls in 1983. That line further inspired a host of animated specials, animated television series, animated theatrical films, comic books, and a musical. The video series boasts a large repertoire of talking female ponies, but only a small number of them appear as principal characters in any one title. Each pony possesses characteristic colors plus a "cutie mark," a unique symbol on her flank. The first video in this series, *Minty Christmas* includes the following principal characters: Minty—a complete klutz with a mint-green body, pink mane and tail, and three swirled mint candies cutie mark; Pinkie Pie—pink body, mane, and tail, and three balloons cutie mark; Rainbow Dash—sky-blue body, multicolored mane and tail, rainbow-on-clouds cutie mark, speaks with a British accent, and frequently says "Daahhling"; Star Catcher—winged with a white body, blue-white-pink mane and tail, and glittery pink heart cutie mark; and Thistle Whistle—also winged with a blue body, pink-and-yellow mane and tail, purple thistle flowers with butterfly cutie mark, and frequently whistles.

Each year on Christmas Eve, the ponies of the all-female Ponyville gather around their gigantic community Christmas tree to affix the traditional "Here Comes Christmas Candy Cane" tree topper, a glowing emblem that guides Santa to Ponyville. Overflowing with OCD, Minty absolutely *must* straighten the beacon, but when she reaches the tree top in a hot-air balloon and diddles with the Candy Cane, it falls and shatters. Believing that Santa will not come, Minty decides to be his replacement and covertly hangs her decorative socks like stockings on her friends' fireplaces. But when Pinkie discovers Minty prowling about, the latter confesses all, then sets out for the North Pole alone in a hot-air balloon (knocking over the community tree in the process) to guide Santa to Ponyville, and winged Thistle soon flies out to keep an eye on her. Minty's rash action alarms Pinkie, who alerts the town, and all the ponies form a balloon brigade to go after Minty. Though Thistle attempts to gain control of Minty's bouncing balloon, it snags on a limb and deflates with Minty and Thistle hanging perilously over an abyss, but the other ponies arrive in time to rescue them. The troupe treks on to the North Pole, only to find that Santa is out on his rounds, but Minty's heroic act to give her friends a happy Christmas touches them all, which otherwise eases their disappointment. Arriving back home, to their wonder, the tree and Candy Cane have been restored, and Minty's socks filled with gifts for everyone adorn the tree, thanks to Santa. It's not a glowing candy cane that brings Santa, they learn, but "the glow of everyone's love and concern for each other," which they claim is the true meaning of Christmas" (warm fuzzies with no religious implications). Santa leaves a note stating that he's so impressed with Minty's sock idea that he'd like to adopt it (which supplies a twist on the origin behind Santa's filling stockings).

PRINCIPAL VOICES: Chiara Zanni (*X-Men 2*) as Triple Treat; Tabitha St. Germain (*Littlest Pet Shop*) as Minty and Thistle; Kelly Sheridan (*Class of the Titans*) as Cotton Candy; Kathleen Barr (*ReBoot*) as Sweetberry and Cloud Climber; Janyse Jaud (*Maison Ikkoku*) as Pinkie; Venus Terzo (*Da Vinci's Inquest*) as Rainbow Dash and Sparkleworks; Lenore Zann (*X-Men*) as Star Catcher; Adrienne Carter (*The Book of Love*) as Sunny Daze.

SONGS: Music and lyrics respectively by Mark Watters and Lorraine Feather. "That's What I Love About Christmas" and "Nothing Says Christmas Like a New Pair of Socks" performed by Tabitha St. Germain; "The Magic of Christmas" performed by Lenore Zann.

INTERESTING TIDBITS: Fearing that Santa may not come, Pinkie voices the typically secular sentiment about Christmas: "Without Santa, there's no Christmas!" Only *after* Santa has gratified their materialistic desires, the ponies then reflect, seemingly as an afterthought, that there just might be other reasons for the season, even if they're not particularly religious.

REVIEWS: Carrie R. Wheadon of *Common Sense Media* (October 20, 2008): "...a very predictable story with characters that only young kids, especially girls, could love: pastel-colored prancing ponies with silly voices..."

David Johnson of *DVD Verdict* (October 24, 2008): "...for a reclusive, matriarchal hamlet like [Ponyville], the Yule-time season provides one of the few respites from pink and pastel saccharine living that the all-female ... population can look forward to. A lot of pressure then on Santa Claus to cough up the goods ... the moral of the story is to be quick to forgive your idiot friends ... or maybe it's not to screw around with stuff you're not supposed to..."

Mike Long of *DVD Talk* (October 25, 2005): "...[this film] is aimed squarely at the girls who play with and know the *My Little Pony* line of toys ... the story itself [is] incredibly simple and clichéd ... a plot that we've seen before, but once again, the target audience for this program will find it delightful."

PRODUCTION CREDITS—Writer: Jeanne Romano. Producers: Robert Winthrop, Cheryl McCarthy, Carol Monroe, Julia Bricklin, and Jeanne Romano. Director: Vic Dal Chele. Production Companies: Hasbro and SD Entertainment. Rating: G. Genres: Animation, Family, Fantasy. Country: USA. Run Time: 45 min.

REFERENCES: Johnson, David. *My Little Pony: A Very Minty Christmas. DVD Verdict.* http://www.dvdverdict.com/reviews/mintychristmas.php

Long, Mike. *My Little Pony: A Very Minty Christmas. DVD Talk.* http://www.dvdtalk.com/reviews/18254/my-little-pony-a-very-minty-christmas/

My Little Pony: A Very Minty Christmas. Hollywood: Paramount Pictures, 2005. DVD Video.

My Little Pony: A Very Minty Christmas. Internet Movie Database. http://www.imdb.com/title/tt0840350/

Wheadon, Carrie R. *My Little Pony: A Very Minty Christmas. Common Sense Media.* https://www.commonsensemedia.org/movie-reviews/my-little-pony-a-very-minty-christmas

Wilson, Joanna. *Tis the Season TV: The Encyclopedia of Christmas-Themed Episodes, Specials and Made-for-TV Movies.* Akron, OH: 1701 Press, 2011.

The Naughty List—November 12, 2013

Computer-Animated Direct-to-Video Movie

THREAT TO CHRISTMAS: Placed on Santa's naughty list, two unruly elves and a rebellious reindeer unwittingly shut down the North Pole with food poisoning.

HOW CHRISTMAS IS SAVED: The three principals learn to clean up their acts and work together to finish preparations for Christmas.

SYNOPSIS AND COMMENTARY: Capricious elf-brothers Winter and Snowflake find themselves on Santa's naughty list (their antics wreck the North Pole's Christmas tree), along with rebellious young reindeer Sparkle (her antics put Blitzen in a full-body cast), because they don't take their duties seriously and thereby put their own happiness above that of the world's children. Instead of flogging them, boiling them in oil, or executing them, a most jovial Santa sentences them to perform menial, unpleasant tasks, such as washing windows, cleaning restrooms, and mining coal for the naughty children. Even then, their rowdiness leads to more trouble. When finally assigned to kitchen duty, they manage to give the remaining elves, reindeer team, and even Santa food poisoning a few days before Christmas. With the North Pole incapacitated, it's up to Winter, Snowflake, and Sparkle to pull together to save the holiday. Sparkle rounds up three other reindeer who otherwise would not be qualified (two are decrepit and one is a baby) plus one drowsy moose to pull the sleigh, while Snowflake ultimately persuades Winter to stop cutting corners and stick to the business of finishing the toys. Prior to that, they're nearly annihilated by flying space laser toys out of control. At the last moment, Santa revives enough to make his journey as he and the misfit team take to the skies, led by Sparkle, and on Christmas morning after examining their stockings, the three principals pleasantly discover that they've been removed from the naughty list.

PRINCIPAL VOICES: Drake Bell (*High Fidelity*) as Snowflake; Sean Astin (*The Lord of the Rings*) as Winter; Naya Rivera (*Glee*) as Sparkle; Kyle Chandler (*Friday Night Lights*) as Santa; Matthew Lillard (*Scooby-Doo*) as the robot Tinsel.

AWARDS: In 2014, this film won a Behind the Voice Actors Award for Best Female Vocal Performance in a TV Special/Direct-to-DVD Title or Theatrical Short (Naya Rivera).

INTERESTING TIDBIT: With the exception of Winter and Snowflake, the other elves are clones of each other.

REVIEWS: Brian Costello of *Common Sense Media* (November 12, 2013): "[This film], in spite of the occasional moment of inappropriate bathroom humor, is mostly a cute and fun Christmas movie best enjoyed by young kids and anyone with a silly sense of humor … [imparts] lessons on traditional Christmas values such as selflessness and being 'nice' rather than 'naughty.'"

Dawn Hunt of *DVD Verdict* (December 1, 2013): "What real lesson are we expected to learn from movies like this? That if you go your own way and screw up something as long as you make it right in the end it's something to be praised and rewarded? No…. Winter, Snowflake, and Sparkle didn't learn respect for the Christmas traditions they tarnished…. They lose nothing and so learn nothing … a disappointing bit of fluff."

PRODUCTION CREDITS—Writers: Samantha Shear and Michael Shear. Producers: Susan Norkin and Heather Puttock. Directors: Gordon Crum and Jay Surridge. Production Companies: ARC Entertainment, Kickstart Productions Canada, Kickstart Productions USA, and Raindance Entertainment. Rating: Not rated. Genres: Animation, Comedy, Family. Countries: Canada and USA. Run Time: 46 min.

REFERENCES: Costello, Brian. *The Naughty List. Common Sense Media.* https://www.commonsensemedia.org/movie-reviews/the-naughty-list

Hunt, Dawn. *The Naughty List. DVD Verdict.* http://www.dvdverdict.com/reviews/naughtylist.php

The Naughty List. Internet Movie Database. http://www.imdb.com/title/tt3229036/

The Naughty List. Santa Monica, CA: ARC Entertainment, 2013. DVD Video.

Nearly No Christmas—1983

Television Movie

THREAT TO CHRISTMAS: When Santa's steam boiler blows a valve, his toy factory shuts down.

HOW CHRISTMAS IS SAVED: Santa takes a job as Father Christmas in a department store.

SYNOPSIS AND COMMENTARY: Though he's a bit eccentric, bumbling, and has trouble operating a simple telephone, Santa (Michael Haigh, *Mr. Wrong*) has enough on his mind producing enough Christmas toys for the world. But when he pushes his clown-faced steam boiler Rumbletum to deliver more speed to his factory's machines, Rumbletum blows a valve and production grinds to a halt. With Christmas around the corner, Santa has another problem: he's strapped for cash and cannot afford a new valve. Therefore, Santa heads out into the world to find a paying job and leaves his factory beneath the North Pole in the hands of Mrs. Claus (Mildred Woods, *Shark in the Park*) and the elves (racially diverse children from Ohakune School and Wellington Schools). Santa's either too jolly, too old, or too fat for most jobs, but those attributes finally land him a job as Father Christmas in a department store. The stipulation: he must visit with no less than 10,000 children. Meanwhile, the folks back home keep the factory temporarily running by rigging a series of bicycles as generators, thanks to the help of several young *penguins* (at the North Pole?), who join the elves in pedaling the bikes in shifts. But this rigorous activity eventually exhausts them, whereupon Mrs. Claus solicits help from the obnoxious King Penguin (John Bach, *The Lord of the Rings*), who loans out hundreds of his subjects for seven days in return for fish juice. However, when the king demands that his subjects return early, Mrs. Claus stalls for time by giving him a factory tour. Santa having completed his assignment by then, his grateful boss flies him over the North Pole, Santa parachutes down, crashes into his factory with the new valve just two days before Christmas, and Rumbletum and Christmas are saved.

INTERESTING TIDBITS: The natural habitat for penguins is the Southern Hemisphere and most certainly not the North Pole. Perhaps penguins appeared in this film because it is a product of New Zealand television and because penguins are found on the coast of New Zealand (as well as Antarctica and on the coast of other continents in the Southern Hemisphere). The "penguins" here were neither live animals nor computer-animated images but adults and children in silly penguin costumes.

Scenes of Santa's trek across the "Arctic" were filmed at the Turoa Ski Fields on Mt. Ruapehu in Tongariro National Park, New Zealand.

This film should not be confused with another save-Christmas film with a similar title: *It Nearly Wasn't Christmas*.

PRODUCTION CREDITS—Writer: John Banas. Producer: Dave Gibson. Director: Yvonne Mackay. Production Companies: Gibson Film Productions and Movie Makers. Rating: G. Genres: Family, Fantasy. Country: New Zealand. Run Time: 50 min.

REFERENCES: *Nearly No Christmas*. Internet Movie Database. http://www.imdb.com/title/tt0259459/

Nearly No Christmas. Roseland, NJ: Inspired Productions, licensed from Optik Film and Television, 2003. DVD Video.

O'Keeffe, Jillian. "Do Penguins Live at the North Pole?" eHow. http://www.ehow.com/facts_6972491_do-penguins-live-north-pole_.html

Wilson, Joanna. *Tis the Season TV: The Encyclopedia of Christmas-Themed Episodes, Specials and Made-for-TV Movies*. Akron, OH: 1701 Press, 2011.

The Night B4 Christmas—2003

Animated Television Short Film

THREAT TO CHRISTMAS: Flu hits the North Pole.

HOW CHRISTMAS IS SAVED: Elvin the elf-turned-rap-singer returns with friends to stave off the flu and make the toys.

SYNOPSIS AND COMMENTARY: Although this film's title is an obvious play on the title of the famous poem, and although it does feature rhyming dialogue, there is no other parallel between film and poem.

Three days into his job as an elf, Elvin is fired for trying to make the North Pole less traditional and more "hip." Aspiring to be a rap singer, he goes out into the world where as "Slim Shorty" he meets three new friends with a similar goal: Pup Daddy, a large, anthropomorphic dog; his girlfriend Jel-O; and Seamus, a gnome with an Irish accent. In Los Angeles, the four sign a contract with Mr. Saul, a record producer who enslaves them until their rap album tops the charts. As they're about to go on tour, Elvin learns that Santa has cancelled Christmas, because everyone at the North Pole is sick with a nasty flu. The selfishness and greed of Saul's little daughter Evilina, who plays with toys only once and throws them away, coupled with his memory of how good life had been at the North Pole, convince Elvin to postpone the tour and save Christmas. When Elvin attempts to leave, Saul imprisons him and the other three, but they escape, thanks to Seamus's lock-picking talents, and use Saul's and his guard dogs' lust for rich food to dodge them. Summoning the reindeer sleigh, Elvin and friends zoom back to the North Pole with Evilina as a stowaway. Seeing the wonder of Santa's workshop melts Evilina's heart, and while the others make more toys, she uses her late mother's herbal recipe to mix a foul-tasting potion against the flu that "smelled like manure" (watch out, big pharma), and soon Santa and the elves are back in business. Elvin becomes the chief elf, and this time Santa is more receptive to Elvin's non-traditional approach to Christmas.

PRINCIPAL VOICES: Aries Spears (*The Pest*) as Elvin; Chali 2Na (*Heartbreaker*) as Pup Daddy; Melique Berger (*Justice League*) as Jel-O; Steve Blum (*The BoxTrolls*) as Seamus and Mr. Saul; Dorothy Fahn (*Arc the Lad*) as Evilina; Earthquake (*Barnyard*) as Santa; Beau

Billingslea (*The American President*) as Elvin's Dad; Miron Willis as the narrator.

SONGS: "Elvin's Rap" by Sib Ventress, performed by Wolf "D"; "Night B4 Christmas" by Brian E. O'Neal, performed by Dr. Stank.

INTERESTING TIDBITS: Other save-Christmas films in which the flu hits the North Pole include **Madeline at the North Pole, The Magic Sack of Mr. Nicholas, Nine Dog Christmas, The Super Special Gift**, and **'Twas the Night**.

PRODUCTION CREDITS—Writer: Sib Ventress. Producer: Brian E. O'Neal. Directors: Tom Tataranowicz and Ron Myrick. Production Companies: Nite B4 Productions and Sunwoo Entertainment. Rating: Not rated. Genre: Animation. Country: USA. Run Time: 25 min.

REFERENCES: *The Night B4 Christmas*. Hollywood: Sunwoo Entertainment/UrbanWorks Entertainment, 2003. DVD Video.

The Night B4 Christmas. Internet Movie Database. http://www.imdb.com/title/tt0407043/

Wilson, Joanna. *Tis the Season TV: The Encyclopedia of Christmas-Themed Episodes, Specials and Made-for-TV Movies*. Akron, OH: 1701 Press, 2011.

The Night Before the Night Before Christmas—November 20, 2010

Television Movie

THREAT TO CHRISTMAS: Santa crashes the sleigh, suffers amnesia, and cannot deliver his presents.

HOW CHRISTMAS IS SAVED: A dysfunctional family pulls together to help Santa regain his memory and find the sack.

SYNOPSIS AND COMMENTARY: Hardly an original film, the basic themes here have been played out in other productions: workaholic parents who have no time for the holidays; offspring who feel neglected; Santa crashes his sleigh, falls off the roof, suffers amnesia, and loses his vitally precious, all-important, magic sack of toys. And we need not be rocket scientists to know that, regardless how Santa fares, *without the infernal presents, there can be no Christmas*. In this particular film, the dysfunctional parents are Wayne and Angela Fox (Rick Roberts, *Pontypool*, and Jennifer Beals, *Flashdance*); and the poor, neglected offspring are teenage daughter Hannah (Rebecca Williams, *Reviving Ophelia*) and adolescent son Toby (Gage Munroe, *Immortals*). Confused about the time, Santa (R.D. Reid, *Capote*) mistakenly leaves the North Pole on his rounds a night early and, following a mid-air accident, crashes his sleigh and reindeer into the Foxes' house, falls off the roof, suffers total amnesia, the sack turns up missing, and that's the way the ball bounces. Now the Fox family must set aside their personal worries and work as a team to help Santa regain his memory as well as retrieve the magic sack, lest Christmas be "cancelled." And even if you've never seen this movie, you *know* how everything turns out, because it's just too predictable.

AWARDS: In 2011, this picture received a Young Artist Award nomination for Best Performance in a TV Movie, Miniseries or Special–Leading Young Actor (Gage Munroe).

In 2010 it won a couple of "Yulies," spoof awards from *Entertainment Weekly*: Best Conspiracy Theory About Santa Claus (Hannah thought the entity crashing on her roof could be a brain-eating alien); and Outstanding Representation of Christmas Clichés in Two Minutes or Less (the film's final two minutes feature Santa granting a white Christmas and bellowing "Merry Christmas," a star affixed atop a Christmas tree, a dog with fake antlers, a kiss under the mistletoe, and the family Christmas photo).

INTERESTING TIDBITS: Santa suffers amnesia from various mishaps in other save-Christmas films, such as **The Amazing World of Gumball: Christmas Episode, The Boy Who Saved Christmas, Merry Madagascar, Miracle at the 34th Precinct, Santa Who?, The Search for Santa Paws,** and **Snow 2: Brain Freeze**.

PRODUCTION CREDITS—Writers: Jim Cruickshank and James Orr. Producer: Steve Solomos. Director: James Orr. Production Company: Muse Entertainment Enterprises. Rating: G. Genres: Family, Fantasy. Country: Canada. Run Time: 88 min.

REFERENCES: Crump, William D. *The Christmas Encyclopedia*. Third Edition. Jefferson, NC: McFarland, 2013.

The Night Before the Night Before Christmas. Internet Movie Database. http://www.imdb.com/title/tt1567140/

The Night Before the Night Before Christmas. Louisville, CO: Gaiam Americas, 2011. DVD Video.

Snierson, Dan. "The Third Annual Yulies: Let's Celebrate the Absurdity of Holiday TV Movies!" *Entertainment Weekly*. http://www.ew.com/article/2010/12/23/holiday-tv-movies-xmas-specials-yulies

The Night They Saved Christmas— December 13, 1984

Television Movie

THREAT TO CHRISTMAS: Oil prospectors blasting near the North Pole may unwittingly destroy Santa's abode.

HOW CHRISTMAS IS SAVED: Santa enlists the aid of a mother and her three children to convince the oil company to focus on a safer, alternate site.

SYNOPSIS AND COMMENTARY: Whereas run-of-the-mill bogeys that threaten Santa and the North Pole are mean-spirited, as in, for example, ***The Christmas That Almost Wasn't***, the oil company involved here has no clue that the real Santa Claus (Art Carney, *The Honeymooners*) and his elves dwell in an establishment that is hidden behind mountainous walls of ice. Matters become more urgent, because the blasting project is scheduled for Christmas Eve. When Ed (Paul Williams, who also composed the film's songs), Santa's emissary and chief elf, confronts company site manager and geologist Michael Baldwin (Paul Le Mat, *American His-*

Quakes from an oil company's blasting near North Pole City startle Santa (Art Carney, left), Claudia Baldwin (Jaclyn Smith), and her three children, David (Scott Grimes, right of Santa), C.B. (R.J. Williams), and Marianne (Laura Jacoby), in *The Night They Saved Christmas* (1984) (ABC/MMG Photo Archives; collection of William D. Crump).

tory X) with the problem, Michael dismisses Ed as a practical joke. Ed's appeal to Michael's initially skeptical wife Claudia (Jaclyn Smith, *Charlie's Angels*) convinces her to meet with Santa, whereupon she rides with Ed in a "reindeer zephyr," a self-propelled sleigh, to North Pole City, along with her three children, David (Scott Grimes), Marianne (Laura Jacoby), and C.B. (R.J. Williams). Not only do they become instant believers in awe of Santa's high-tech domain, which boasts a time decelerator device that allows Santa (who wears a hearing aid and has grown weary of hearing "Jingle Bells") to get around the world in one night and a worldwide language communicator/translator, but Santa also reveals the location of an abundant oil site farther away. Then it's a race against time to inform the oil company before it carries out the scheduled detonation, and Christmas is saved after all.

AWARDS: In 1985, this picture received an Emmy nomination for Outstanding Children's Program. In 1986, it won a Young Artist Award for Best Young Actress Starring in a Television Special or Miniseries (Laura Jacoby).

INTERESTING TIDBITS: The film slips in a bit of politically correct dialogue. When during a chat with Mrs. Claus (June Lockhart, *Lassie*, *Lost in Space*), C.B. recalls a cap pistol that he had received from Santa at a previous Christmas, she assures the boy that Santa has never brought any toy guns to children, because "Santa doesn't like guns." Perhaps a subtle pitch for gun control?

For the sake of authenticity, portions of the picture were filmed in Barrow, Alaska, and near the Arctic Circle.

PRODUCTION CREDITS—Teleplay: Jim Moloney and David Niven, Jr. Story: Jim Moloney, Rudy Dochtermann, and David, Niven, Jr. Producers: Robert Halmi, Sr., and David R. Kappes. Director: Jackie Cooper. Production Company: Sonar Entertainment, formerly RHI Entertainment. Rating: Not rated. Genre: Children's fantasy. Country: USA. Run time: 94 min.

REFERENCES: Crump, William D. *The Christmas Encyclopedia*. Third Edition. Jefferson, NC: McFarland, 2013.

The Night They Saved Christmas. Internet Movie Database: http://www.imdb.com/title/tt0087797/

The Night They Saved Christmas. New York: Cabin Fever Entertainment, 1992. VHS video.

Wilson, Joanna. *Tis the Season TV: The Encyclopedia of Christmas-Themed Episodes, Specials and Made-for-TV Movies*. Akron, OH: 1701 Press, 2011.

Nilus the Sandman: The Boy Who Dreamed Christmas—December 1, 1991 (Canada); December 10, 1991 (USA)

Precursor Special to the Television Series *Nilus the Sandman*

THREAT TO CHRISTMAS: Toymaster, Santa's robot, takes over operations at the North Pole and puts Santa out of work.

HOW CHRISTMAS IS SAVED: A young boy and the sandman eliminate Toymaster.

SYNOPSIS AND COMMENTARY: Created by Michael Fawkes, the *Nilus the Sandman* series consisted of 26 half-hour episodes that ran on The Family Channel from 1996 to 1998. In addition to *The Boy Who Dreamed Christmas*, two other *Sandman* specials preceded the series: the Halloween special *Monsters in the Closet* (1994) and the back-to-school special *The First Day* (1995). The series revolved around the sandman Nilus, who gave happy dreams to children coping with various difficulties. In the specials and the series, the dream segments were animated, whereas the opening and closing segments were live-action; the principal difference was that in the series, Nilus had two assistants, Blue the camel and Pearl the talking clam. *The Boy Who Dreamed Christmas* premiered in Canada and the USA respectively on CTV and The Disney Channel.

During the opening sequence, it's Christmas Eve, and as young Peter Fletcher (Zachary Bennett, *Cube Zero*) prepares for bed, his parents (Larysa Fenyn, *Shining Time Station*, and Chris Delaney, *The New Adventures of Mother Goose*) caution him not to be disappointed if Santa doesn't bring him everything on his list (which means, "You've asked for too much, kid!"). In the dream segment, Nilus whisks

Peter away in an oversized tennis shoe to the North Pole, where they discover that Santa is out of work. Because greedy children's demands for more toys had exceeded Santa's output, he created Toymaster, a robot in the form of an enormous jack-in-the-box-like clown to speed up production. But the Toymaster took over, built a highly computerized factory in a huge cavern beneath Santa's workshop, "retired" Santa, enslaved the elves, and replaced the sleigh and reindeer with a rocket plane. To restore the Christmas spirit and reduce Santa's workload, Peter uses Toymaster's computer to eliminate all but the top one or two items on children's wish lists (which causes corresponding factory hardware and toys to disappear), but an angry Toymaster scoots Peter and Nilus out of the control center on the bike that Peter had wanted. Peter jams the factory's control clock by ramming the bike into it, whereupon the whole factory explodes and destroys Toymaster. Now Santa and the elves are back to making and delivering toys the old-fashioned way, and when Santa departs on his rounds, Peter and Nilus ride along, which ends the dream. On Christmas morning, instead of finding a bike, Peter finds a wind-up toy locomotive in his stocking. After all, the bike had been ruined, and Santa had said that the locomotive was his favorite toy to make. So maybe Peter's nocturnal experience wasn't a dream after all!

VOICES: Long John Baldry (*Nilus the Sandman*) as Nilus; Frank Mackay (*Haven*) as Santa; Michael Fawkes (*A Child's Christmas in Wales*) as Toymaster; Elizabeth Rukavina (*The Boy in Blue*) as Mrs. Fletcher; Murray Cruchley (*Dead Ringers*) as Mr. Fletcher.

AWARDS IN 1993: Gemini nomination for Best Animated Program or Series; Certificate of Creative Excellence in Animation, Non-Computer, at the U.S. International Film and Video Festival.

AWARDS IN 1992: Silver Award, TV and Video Production, Animated, at Worldfest Houston; Second Prize, Best Animated Short, Chicago International Children's Film Festival; Certificate de Participation, *Cinanima* International Animation Film Festival, Portugal; Finalist, *Festival Film d'Animation pour la Jeunesse*, France; Finalist, Golden Sheaf Award; Award, Museum of Radio and Television's International Children's Film Festival.

INTERESTING TIDBIT: Co-producer and director Chris Delaney appears as Mr. Fletcher in the live-action segment, and series creator Michael Fawkes is the voice of Toymaster.

PRODUCTION CREDITS—Writer: Michael Mercer. Producers: Arnie Zipursky, Bruce Glawson, and Chris Delaney. Director: Chris Delaney. Production Companies: Delaney and Friends Cartoon Productions, Cambium Film and Video Productions, CTV Television Network, Téléfilm Canada, and The Ontario Film Development Corporation. Rating: Not rated. Genres: Animation, Family. Country: Canada. Run Time: 30 min.

REFERENCES: *The Boy Who Dreamed Christmas*. Big Cartoon Database. http://www.bcdb.com/cartoon/54857-Boy-Who-Dreamed-Christmas

Nilus the Sandman: The Boy Who Dreamed Christmas. Internet Movie Database. http://www.imdb.com/title/tt0158515/

Nilus the Sandman: The Boy Who Dreamed Christmas. Troy, MI: Video Treasures, 1991. VHS Video.

Wilson, Joanna. *Tis the Season TV: The Encyclopedia of Christmas-Themed Episodes, Specials and Made-for-TV Movies*. Akron, OH: 1701 Press, 2011.

Nine Dog Christmas—October 5, 2004

Direct-to-Video Animated Movie

THREAT TO CHRISTMAS: Santa's reindeer are sick with the flu.

HOW CHRISTMAS IS SAVED: Nine dogs become surrogate reindeer.

SYNOPSIS AND COMMENTARY: There's always a threat to Christmas whenever Santa is ill and cannot make his deliveries, as in ***Christmas Flintstone*** and ***The Year without a Santa Claus***. The threat is just as serious should the elves fall ill and cannot make the toys, as in ***Madeline at the North Pole*** and ***The Magic Sack of Mr. Nicholas***. And then at other times, the reindeer become ill and cannot pull the sleigh, as in ***'Twas the Night*** and this present film.

When all of Santa's nine reindeer, including Rudolph, contract the North Pole flu, elves Buzz and Agnes Ann must find replacements. Out in the world, they locate a truck carrying eight stray dogs that the criminal Pierre LeRond has captured for his traveling circus, but nearsighted Buzz initially mistakes them for reindeer and drives the truck back to the North Pole, where he puts the "reindogs" through training courses to be surrogate reindeer. The eight talking dogs are a variety of breeds: Snowplow, an English sheepdog with a British accent; Tank, a basset hound; Q.T. (a play on "Cutie"), a female cocker spaniel; Cheech, a Chihuahua with a Mexican accent; Chester, a boxer; Fetch, a mutt; MacGregor, a Scottish terrier with a Scottish accent; and No-Name, a bloodhound obsessed with going home. Meanwhile, LeRond and his grumpy bull terrier Frenchie follow the dogs to the North Pole and recapture them as they sleep, whereupon Agnes Ann launches a search to find them. When Frenchie learns that LeRond has lost the dogs in a bet to a man who would put them all, including Frenchie, to work in the mines, he turns against LeRond and leads Agnes Ann to the other dogs after saving her from a hungry polar bear. All nine dogs overpower LeRond and chase him off, then return with Agnes Ann to the North Pole where Buzz hitches them to the sleigh and enables them to fly with Christmas magic. After Santa completes his rounds, he finds good homes for all the dogs, then for lack of animal power, has his sleigh towed away.

PRINCIPAL VOICES: James Earl Jones (*The Lion King*) as the narrator; Scott Hamilton (*Blades of Glory*) as Buzz; Russi Taylor (*The Simpsons*) as Agnes Ann; Randy Rice (*Camp Blood*) as LeRond, Tiny, Chester, and Snowplow; Mitch Urban (*Blood Drive*) as Tank, Frenchie, and No-Name; Jeanine DiTomasso (*The Server*) as Q.T.; Keith Silverstein (*The Spectacular Now*) as Cheech and desk sergeant; Tom Garner (*Get Smart*) as MacGregor and Fetch; Pat Fraley (*Monsters, Inc.*) as Santa; Gill Ellis (*The Heat Chamber*) as the butcher.

SONGS: Written by Gary Morris and Matt Morris. "Up at the North Pole" (performed by Chuck Glass and Matt Morris); "Stick-to-It-Ive" (performed by Matt Morris); "Someone Like You" (performed by Lari White); "The Present" (performed by Gary Morris); "Nine Dogs Out & Santa's In" (performed by Matt Morris).

Other save-Christmas films in which the flu hits the North Pole include: ***Madeline at the North Pole, The Magic Sack of Mr. Nicholas, The Night B4 Christmas, The Super Special Gift***, and ***'Twas the Night***.

REVIEW: Dennis Prince of *DVD Verdict* (December 24, 2004): "…the story lacks any deep purpose other than a hopeful expectation of maybe turning a profit in the home DVD market … it's not a bad show, but it passes by without really lifting the spirit, much less raising an eyebrow of interest."

PRODUCTION CREDITS—Writers: Carter Crocker and Roy Wilson. Producers: Peter Keefe and Diane Woods Branco. Director: Ka Moon Song. Production Companies: KMC Films, Vitello Productions, Gary Morris Productions, Timeless Entertainment Productions, and JRS Properties. Rating: Not rated. Genres: Animation, Family. Country: USA. Run Time: 60 min.

REFERENCES: *Nine Dog Christmas*. Burbank, CA: Warner Home Video, 2004. DVD Video.

Nine Dog Christmas. Internet Movie Database. http://www.imdb.com/title/tt0439734/

Prince, Dennis. *Nine Dog Christmas*. DVD Verdict. http://www.dvdverdict.com/reviews/ninedogchristmas.php

Wilson, Joanna. *Tis the Season TV: The Encyclopedia of Christmas-Themed Episodes, Specials and Made-for-TV Movies*. Akron, OH: 1701 Press, 2011.

Noddy Saves Christmas—October 11, 2004

Direct-to-Video, Computer-Animated Short Film

THREAT TO CHRISTMAS: Santa's magical clock that stops time has malfunctioned and his reindeer sleigh has been stolen.

HOW CHRISTMAS IS SAVED: Noddy and Big Ears come to Santa's aid.

SYNOPSIS AND COMMENTARY: Between 1949 and 1963, British author Enid Blyton published a series of children's books, the first of which was *Noddy Goes to Toyland*. The protagonist of the series, Noddy was a little wooden boy who served as a self-employed cabby for Toyland and whose trademark was a blue hat with a sleigh bell. Other principal characters included Big Ears, a wise old bearded brownie and father-figure; Tessie Bear, Noddy's best friend; Bumpy Dog, Tessie's rambunctious, pet pooch; Mr. Plod, Toyland's only cop; and the mischievous goblins Sly and Gobbo, Toyland's villains. Commencing with *The Adventures of Noddy* (1955), the character has appeared in a host of different British television series until the present in stop-motion animation and computer animation.

In *Noddy Saves Christmas*, Noddy poses three classic questions that children have wondered about for centuries: (1) How does Santa deliver all those presents in one night? (2) How does Santa get all those presents into one bag? (3) How does Santa get down chimneys when he's so large? Noddy receives an answer to his first question when Santa visits Noddy and Big Ears at the latter's toadstool house, because Santa's magical clock will not stop time on demand. Stopping time is the only way Santa can deliver all those presents in one night. To repair the clock, Big Ears persuades Noddy to sacrifice the precious little bell on his hat, but Christmas still hangs in the balance, because Santa's reindeer team has now disappeared. The sleigh's tracks in the snow lead Noddy and Santa to Sly and Gobbo, the obvious culprits who stole the sleigh. Santa's shrinking potion gets those two out of his hair for the moment, which answers Noddy's second question: all the presents can fit into Santa's bag because he reduces them to tiny sizes. Santa then provides Noddy with a magical snowflake such that when he claps his hands, he and the bag are transported down chimneys or through keyholes, which answers Noddy's third question. So empowered, Noddy at Santa's insistence delivers all the presents to Toyland with assistance from reindeer Dasher on loan. Although they are unworthy, Sly and Gobbo also receive gifts, and to show their appreciation, they present Noddy with a little replacement bell for his cap on Christmas Day.

VOICES: A voice cast is not provided.

INTERESTING TIDBIT: Enid Blyton (1897–1968) wrote some 700 children's books that covered a very wide range of subjects, including adventure and mystery, circus and farm life, religion, animals, poetry, plays and songs, and retelling myths and legends. She is best remembered for her *Noddy*, *Secret Seven*, and *Famous Five* series.

PRODUCTION CREDITS—Writer: Jymn Magon. Producers: Len Dunne and Robert Winthrop. Director: Davis Doi. Production Companies: Wang Film Productions Co. Ltd., CGCG, Chorion Group Company, and Sabella Dern Entertainment. Rating: G. Genres: Animation, Short. Countries: United Kingdom and USA. Run Time: 26 min.

REFERENCES: The Enid Blyton Society. http://www.enidblytonsociety.co.uk/

Lenburg, Jeff. *The Encyclopedia of Animated Cartoons*. Third Edition. New York: Facts on File, 2009.

Noddy Saves Christmas. BBC Worldwide, 2004. DVD Video.

Noddy Saves Christmas. Internet Movie Database. http://www.imdb.cm/title/tt0495165/

Stoney, Barbara. *Enid Blyton: A Biography*. London: Hodder and Stoughton, 1974.

Northpole—November 15, 2014

Television Movie

THREAT TO CHRISTMAS: World apathy toward Christmas weakens the Northern Nights, which in turn reduce the elves' energy to make toys at the North Pole.

HOW CHRISTMAS IS SAVED: An elf, a boy, and two adults team together to restore the Christmas spirit to their town and thence to the entire world.

SYNOPSIS AND COMMENTARY: Here's an example of what can happen when the Christmas spirit goes viral. When families around the world become too busy to enjoy Christmas together, the situation wreaks havoc with the Northern Lights and the Cycle of Happiness, whereupon the elves at Northpole, Santa's sprawling North Pole domain, lack sufficient energy to make toys. In order to save Christmas, sugary young elf Clementine (Bailee Madison, *Good Witch*) collaborates with Kevin (Max Charles, *American Sniper*), a ten-year-old Christmas devotee, to convince his apathetic town to reinstate their beloved, century-old tree-lighting ceremony that the mayor has cancelled. Once Kevin gets his cynical, journalist-mom Chelsea (Tiffani Thiessen, *Saved by the Bell*) and his imaginative teacher Ryan (Josh Hopkins, *Cougar Town*) on board, they manage to share the importance of the season with the entire world. Chelsea's newspaper column about the importance of community connection especially at Christmastime goes viral, and not only does the town turn out for the tree-lighting ceremony, but the magic of the lights and the Christmas spirit spreads throughout the world, which restores the vitality of the Northern Lights. And since this is a Hallmark Channel movie, where romance reigns supreme, expect Chelsea and Ryan to pitch some woo.

OTHER CAST: Robert Wagner (*Hart to Hart*) as Santa; Jill St. John (*Diamonds Are Forever*) as Mrs. Claus; *American Idol* winner Candice Glover as Gospel singer Josephine.

AWARDS: In 2015, this film received a Directors Guild of Canada Craft Award nomination for Production Design–Television Movie/Miniseries.

INTERESTING TIDBIT: Check out the sequel, ***Northpole: Open for Christmas***.

REVIEWS: Renee Schonfeld of *Common Sense Media* (November 13, 2014): "Sweet film with magic, elves, romance, and holiday spirit…. Saving a town from greedy interests and bringing back the Christmas spirit aren't new concepts, but there's enough originality here to make it worth watching."

Mary McNamara from *Los Angeles Times* (November 15, 2014): "…undeniably a cookie-cutter tale…. After some initial conflict, the four [principal characters] come together in a sweet but not saccharine way to remind us of the importance of faith, hope, love, and snowball fights…. Which is, of course, almost always the best way to…. Save Christmas."

PRODUCTION CREDITS—Writers: Gregg Rossen and Brian Sawyer. Producer: Irene Litinsky. Director: Douglas Barr. Production Company: Muse Entertainment Enterprises. Rating: G. Genres: Family, Fantasy. Country: Canada. Run Time: 84 min.

REFERENCES: Crump, William D. *The Christmas Encyclopedia*. Third Edition. Jefferson, NC: McFarland, 2013.

McNamara, Mary. "Hallmark's 'Northpole' a Sweet Reminder of Holiday Spirit." *Los Angeles Times*. http://touch.latimes.com/#section/-1/article/p2p-81976970/

Northpole. Internet Movie Database. http://www.imdb.com/title/tt3595848/

Northpole. Santa Monica, CA: ARC Entertainment, 2014. DVD Video.

Schonfeld, Renee. *Northpole. Common Sense Media*. https://www.commonsensemedia.org/movie-reviews/northpole

Northpole: Open for Christmas—November 21, 2015

Television Movie

THREAT TO CHRISTMAS: One of Santa's "power stations" located in an old inn has lost its magic.

HOW CHRISTMAS IS SAVED: Elf Clementine and other secret elves at the inn instill the Christmas spirit in the inn's owner and some romance to boot, which revives the magic.

SYNOPSIS AND COMMENTARY: Bailee Madison reprises her role as the cute young elf Clementine in this sequel to ***Northpole*** (2014) from Hallmark (where romance reigns supreme). This time, her assignment from Santa (Donovan Scott, *Popeye*) is to renew the Christmas spirit in Mackenzie ("Mac") (Lori Loughlin, *Full House*), an estate appraiser from New York with "commitment problems," who has inherited her late aunt's property, the Northern Lights Mountain Inn in Vermont. Little does Mac know that the inn is one of several "power stations" along Santa's route that produces the magic that enables his sleigh to fly (apparently old-fashioned reindeer power needs help in the 21st century). Moreover, not only is her attorney an elf in disguise but so is a member of the inn's staff (his hair covers his pointed ears). Though the inn is in disrepair (and its magic *must* be restored by Christmas Eve), Mac has fond memories of it and her now-late Aunt Grace from childhood; nevertheless, she now has no use for the inn and plans to sell it. Enter Clementine who, along with local handyman Ian (Dermot Mulroney, *The Grey*) and his young daughter Jenny (Ava Telek, *Flowers in the Attic*), convince Mac to fix up the inn (which would boost the magic there), not to mention pitching a bit of ye ole woo between Mac and Ian (after all, it is a Hallmark movie). Complications arise when Mac receives a dream job offer overseas and signs a contract to sell the inn, despite having met Santa at Northpole, courtesy of Clementine, who reveals the inn's secret. At the last moment, Mac changes her mind and decides to stay at the inn, which has fortunately been sold to … well, with all those secret elves running around there, can't you guess who the new "owner" is—Ho Ho Ho?

INTERESTING TIDBIT: Aunt Grace's favorite Christmas ornament consists of a decorative snowflake that rapidly spins on a base when the Christmas magic is running at full power. When Mac first arrives at the Inn, the ornament is still; by show's end, it's spinning merrily away.

REVIEW: Felix Vasquez of *Cinema Crazed* (December 9, 2015): "[This film] embraces the positive messages of the Christmas spirit, and remembering our inner child, while also following a heroine who is always upbeat and smiling…. Madison keeps Clementine likable and admirable, and always pulls back enough to keep the character from feeling cloying or irritating."

PRODUCTION CREDITS—Story: Gregg Rossen and Brian Sawyer. Teleplay: Gregg Rossen, Brian Sawyer, Tippi Dobrofsky, and Neal Dobrofsky. Producer: Irene Litinsky. Director: Douglas Barr. Production Company: Muse Entertainment Enterprises. Rating: G. Genres: Family, Fantasy. Country: Canada. Run Time: 85 min.

REFERENCES: *Northpole: Open for Christmas*. Internet Movie Database. http://www.imdb.com/title/tt4843046/

Northpole: Open for Christmas. Santa Monica, CA: ARC Entertainment, 2015. DVD Video.

Vasquez, Felix. *Northpole: Open for Christmas* (2015). *Cinema Crazed*. http://cinema-crazed.com/blog/2015/12/09/northpole-open-for-christmas-2015/

Olive, the Other Reindeer—December 17, 1999

Computer-Animated Television Musical

THREAT TO CHRISTMAS: When Blitzen becomes injured in a test run, Santa plans to cancel his flight on Christmas Eve.

HOW CHRISTMAS IS SAVED: Believing that she is a reindeer instead of a dog, Olive manages to replace Blitzen.

SYNOPSIS AND COMMENTARY: One may have cause to worry about the mental stability of a pooch who thinks she's a reindeer, but that's just the case in this first animated Christmas special from the Fox Television Network, an adaptation of the children's book of the same title by American authors Vivian Walsh and J. Otto Seibold, published in 1997. In the book version, Olive, a female Jack Russell terrier who hears "Rudolph" sung on the radio, mishears the phrase "All of the other reindeer…" as "Olive, the other reindeer…" and believes that she must be a reindeer instead of a dog (perhaps in another world, she could have set a trans-species precedent with animals as the answer to the transgender craze with humans). Christmas Eve is at hand, so Olive hurries to the North Pole via *buses* to take her place with Santa's reindeer team. Secured in place by Comet, the largest reindeer, Olive proves quite a valuable addition, for she bails the team out of several mishaps along the way. Paralleling Rudolph, whose bright red nose guided Santa through a foggy Christmas Eve, Olive's keen sense of smell detects Mrs. Claus's cookies and guides the team home safely through the North Pole fog. For her reward, Olive receives a pair of reindeer antlers to wear and joins in the reindeer games.

The animated adaptation considerably alters and extends the plot to create virtually an entirely new story. An injured Blitzen prompts

Olive, the Other Reindeer

Santa to announce over the radio that his Christmas Eve flight may be cancelled, unless he can make do with "all of the other reindeer." Although Olive hears this correctly, her pet flea Fido misheard and convinces her that Santa instead said "Olive, the other reindeer." Believing that Santa has invited her to replace Blitzen, Olive heads to the North Pole via bus. Dogging (yeah, a pun) Olive along the way, a psychotic Scrooge of a mailman muttering "Christmas, bah, bug, and hum"—who begrudges Santa for having put him on the naughty list years ago and who detests delivering tons of Christmas mail—repeatedly attempts to foil Olive and her streetwise penguin friend Martini (who outwits the mailman more than once) with typical cartoon violence. Mailman's other antics include intimidating Santa with false hate mail from children and substituting Santa's bag of toys with a bag of junk mail. Flying with the reindeer team, Olive tracks the mailman's scent and retrieves Santa's bag with more cartoon shenanigans. Back in the skies and back on track with the book, when Santa's team runs into heavy fog, Olive smells her way back to the North Pole and Mrs. Claus's gingerbread cookies.

PRINCIPAL VOICES: Drew Barrymore (*E.T., the Extra-Terrestrial*) as Olive; Dan Castellaneta (*The Simpsons*) as the mailman; Joe Pantoliano (*Risky Business*) as Martini; Edward Asner (*The Mary Tyler Moore Show*) as Santa; Peter MacNicol (*Battleship*) as Fido; Tim Meadows (*Mean Girls*) as bus driver Richard Stands; Jay Mohr (*Saturday Night Live*) as Tim, Olive's master; Michael Stipe (*R.E.M.*) as Schnitzel, Blitzen's flightless cousin; Matt Groening (*The Simpsons*) as Arturo; Mitch Rouse (*Strangers with Candy*) as bar owner Round John Virgin/Comet; Tress MacNeille (*The Simpsons*) as Mrs. Claus.

SONGS: Music and lyrics respectively by

A psychotic mailman with a grudge against Santa and who detests delivering Christmas mail pesters Olive, a little female Jack Russell terrier. Believing that she's a reindeer, Olive successfully replaces an injured Blitzen on Santa's team in *Olive, the Other Reindeer* (1999) (Fox Network/Photofest).

Christopher Tyng and Steve Young: "The Days Still Remaining 'Til Christmas" (performed by Drew Barrymore); "Christmas (Bah, Bug and Hum)" (performed by Dan Castellaneta); "We're Not So Bad" (performed by Michael Stipe); "Merry Christmas After All" (performed by Big Bad Voodoo Daddy and Drew Barrymore).

AWARDS: In 2000, this production won two Annie Awards for Outstanding Achievement for Writing (Steve Young) and for Voice Acting by a Male Performer (Dan Castellaneta) in an Animated Television Production; and a Primetime Emmy nomination for Outstanding Animated Program (for Programming More Than One Hour).

INTERESTING TIDBITS: The special features several mondegreens—words or phrases that result from mishearing something said or sung: "all of the other reindeer" vs. "Olive, the other reindeer"; the character Richard Stands is a parody of "which it stands" from the United States Pledge of Allegiance; the character Round John Virgin is a parody of "round yon virgin" from "Silent Night."

Inside jokes and allusions to other films or works: Martini, having escaped the mailman's clutches, remarks that he is "shaken, not stirred" (nod to *James Bond* films); Round John Virgin's half-track is named *Polar Express* (nod to the book by Chris Van Allsburg); a sign for "Frostbite Falls" (nod to the animated TV series *Rocky and His Friends*, starring Rocky and Bullwinkle); a radio advertisement—"Tonight on Fox, the world's wildest mistletoe accidents."

As the reindeer team flies around the world, they distribute gifts to certain celebrities, including the Pope in the Vatican, Godzilla in Tokyo, and the hunchback Quasimodo in Paris's Notre Dame Cathedral. The clock face of Big Ben in London also sports "Rolexxx," the brand of junk watches that Martini is hawking when Olive meets him.

Other holidays receive nods: Santa's home sports a Hanukkah menorah on the roof; the bus driver Richard Stands bids Olive and Martini a "Happy Hanukkah"; and a radio commercial briefly mentions a pre–Ramadan clearance sale.

In a really clever utilization of the literary device *Deus ex machina* (Latin, "God from the machine," a character or item that enters the story and solves a seemingly unsolvable problem), Olive, imprisoned in the mailman's truck, opens a package addressed to her from "Deus ex machina" and uses the metal file found therein to escape.

Vivian Walsh and J. Otto Seibold have written and illustrated many children's books together, which include *Mr. Lunch Takes a Plane Ride*, *Mr. Lunch Borrows a Canoe*, and *Going to the Getty*, among others.

REVIEWS: Will Brownridge of *The Film Reel* (December 2, 2011): "The animation is a blend of 2D characters in a 3D world. It actually takes a second to get used to but ends up looking really great. I wish I could say the same thing about the characters themselves. Some of them just look really strange, with eyes on their noses or what looks like no nose at all.... Very cartoony and cute."

MaryAnn Johanson of *Flick Filosopher* (December 13, 2000): "...*Olive* comes to us via Matt Groening, and as with *The Simpsons*, there's often so much stuff going on that you need to go back to catch it all.... It's nowhere near as incisive or sharp as *The Simpsons*, but *Olive* is still highly amusing."

Eamonn McCusker of *The Digital Fix* (December 24, 2003): "Olive ... is laugh-out-loud funny ... kids will love the bright and colorful animation and the obvious slapstick but there's so much in the film for adults.... Kids would miss so much but then, even on a first viewing, so would adults as the jokes range from the obvious to the subtle and very clever..."

PRODUCTION CREDITS—Writer: Steve Young. Producer: Alex Johns. Director: Oscar Moore. Production Companies: Twentieth Century–Fox Television, Curiosity Company, DNA Productions, and Flower Films. Rating: Not rated. Genres: Animation, Comedy, Fantasy, Musical. Country: USA Run Time: 45 min.

REFERENCES: Brownridge, Will. "Olive, the Other Reindeer (1999)–or–Rudolph Is a Myth." *The Film Reel.* http://www.the-filmreel.com/

2011/12/02/olive-the-other-reindeer-1999-or-rudolph-is-a-myth/

Crump, William D. *The Christmas Encyclopedia*. Third Edition. Jefferson, NC: McFarland, 2013.

Johanson, MaryAnn: "Olive, the Other Reindeer (review)." *Flick Filosopher*. http://www.flickfilosopher.com/2000/12/olive-the-other-reindeer-review.html

Lenburg, Jeff. *The Encyclopedia of Animated Cartoons*. Third Edition. New York: Facts on File, 2009.

McCusker, Eamonn. *Olive, the Other Reindeer. The Digital Fix*. http://film.thedigitalfix.com/content/id/6348/olive-other-reindeer.html

Olive, the Other Reindeer. Beverly Hills, CA: Twentieth Century Fox Home Entertainment, 2003. DVD Video.

Olive, the Other Reindeer. Big Cartoon Database. http://www.bcdb.com/cartoon/55364-Olive-The-Other-Reindeer

Olive, the Other Reindeer. Internet Movie Database. http://www.imdb.com/title/tt0227173/

Walsh, Vivian, and J. Otto Seibold. *Olive, the Other Reindeer*. Illustrated by J. Otto Seibold. San Francisco: Chronicle Books, 1997.

Wilson, Joanna. *Tis the Season TV: The Encyclopedia of Christmas-Themed Episodes, Specials and Made-for-TV Movies*. Akron, OH: 1701 Press, 2011.

On Whiskers, On Lola, On Cheryl and Meryl—December 17, 2004

Episode from the Animated Television Series *Brandy and Mr. Whiskers*

THREAT TO CHRISTMAS: In a fit of anger, Brandy the mutt injures Santa, who cannot complete his rounds.

HOW CHRISTMAS IS SAVED: Brandy and Mr. Whiskers fill in for Santa.

SYNOPSIS AND COMMENTARY: Not quite like *Gilligan's Island*, two anthropomorphic animals who fell out of a cargo plane became stranded in the Amazon rainforest in this series, created by Russell Marcus, that ran for 39 episodes (77 segments) on the Disney Channel and Toon Disney from 2004 to 2006. The principal characters were pompous Brandy Harrington, a blonde, female mutt from the dog pound whom a wealthy family adopted in Palm Beach, Florida. Her annoying companion was Mr. Whiskers, a hyperactive white rabbit. Though she made friends of the local animals, Brandy always sought ways to escape back home to her pampered life.

In this episode, it's Christmas Eve, and Brandy is homesick for a lush, Florida Christmas, even without snow. Believing that she can hitch a ride back home with Santa, she prompts her friends to build a chimney for him and to decorate a local tree using fireflies for lights as a beacon. But when Santa arrives, Whiskers, afraid that Santa will eat him, attacks the old gent and drives him back to the sleigh. All packed and ready, Brandy pleads with Santa to take her along, but she's made the naughty list for being mean to Whiskers and receives a lump of coal. As Santa takes off, an enraged Brandy hurls the coal, which takes out the reindeer team, Santa injures his back, and he cannot complete his rounds. Not to worry, for Brandy and Whiskers hitch Lola Boa (a pink-and-purple-striped boa constrictor), Ed (a dimwitted otter), and Cheryl and Meryl (twin toucan sisters) to the sleigh, even though the latter is jet powered. Now as they zoom around the world, Brandy has the chance to ditch the route when she reaches her home, but the joy she's brought to children compels her to complete the mission. Returning to the rainforest, Brandy waxes philosophical about the purpose of Christmas—giving and sharing, not getting—but Santa takes off in a hurry and leaves her behind. If she's good for *another* year (the other animals laugh hysterically), Santa might take her home.

PRINCIPAL VOICES: Kaley Cuoco (*The Big Bang Theory*) as Brandy; Charles Adler (*Aladdin*) as Mr. Whiskers; Alana Ubach (*Pound Puppies*) as Lola; Sherri Shepherd (*The View*) as Cheryl and Meryl; Tom Kenny (*Adventure Time*) as Ed; Grey DeLisle (*The Replacements*) as Joey; Stephen Root (*Finding Nemo*) as Santa; André Sogliuzzo (*The Polar Express*) as Gaspar Le Gecko.

AWARDS: In 2005, *Brandy and Mr. Whiskers* won a Daytime Emmy for Outstanding Individual Achievement in Animation; Daytime Emmy nomination for Outstanding Original Song (for the main title song by Randy Petersen, Kevin Quinn, and Tim Heintz); Annie nominations for Storyboarding and Writing in an Animated Television Production.

NOTE: At the time of this writing, *Brandi and Mr. Whiskers* was not available on DVD or VHS, but this episode could be seen on YouTube.

REVIEW: Pam Gelman of *Common Sense Media*: "Despite all of the opportunity for interesting adventures provided by the colorful Amazon setting, *Brandy and Mr. Whiskers* plays on the same joke—she's a snob and he's a hapless sidekick. The story has been done before and with much more success."

PRODUCTION CREDITS—Writer: Russell Marcus. Line Producer: Natasha Kopp. Director: Timothy Björklund. Production Company: Walt Disney Television Animation. Rating: TV-Y. Genres: Animation, Comedy, Family. Country: USA. Run Time: 30 min.

REFERENCES: *Brandy and Mr. Whiskers*. Internet Movie Database. http://www.imdb.com/title/tt0423621/

Gelman, Pam. *Brandy and Mr. Whiskers*. Common Sense Media. https://www.commonsensemedia.org/tv-reviews/brandy-and-mr-whiskers

"On Whiskers, On Lola, On Cheryl and Meryl." Big Cartoon Database. http://www.bcdb.com/cartoon/151343-On-Whiskers-On-Lola-On-Cheryl-And-Meryl

"On Whiskers, On Lola, On Cheryl and Meryl." Internet Movie Database. http://www.imdb.com/title/tt0531307/

Wilson, Joanna. *Tis the Season TV: The Encyclopedia of Christmas-Themed Episodes, Specials and Made-for-TV Movies*. Akron, OH: 1701 Press, 2011.

Once Upon a Christmas—December 10, 2000

Television Movie

THREAT TO CHRISTMAS: Santa wants to retire because of mounting greed and materialism; if he does, his naughty daughter will take over and ruin Christmas.

HOW CHRISTMAS IS SAVED: Santa's nice daughter reforms one dysfunctional family as per Santa's stipulation.

SYNOPSIS AND COMMENTARY: Disheartened over the mounting greed and materialism that surrounds Christmas each year, Santa Claus (Douglas Campbell, *Strange Brew*) plans to retire, in which case his elder, naughty daughter Rudolfa (Mary Donnelly Haskell, *Going for Broke*) would take over and convert Christmas into a prank-filled "Christmas Fool's Day" (a combination of Christmas and April Fool's Day). Yet for the sake of his younger daughter, sugar-tempered Kristen (Kathy Ireland, *The Player*), Santa will withdraw the order if she can reform one naughty family by Christmas Eve. Kristen poses as an *au pair* for a dysfunctional family comprised of workaholic-widower Bill Morgan (John Dye, *The Perfect Weapon*) and his two bratty children, Kyle (James Kirk, *Two for the Money*) and Brittany (Kirsten Prout, *Social Nightmare*), with deadbeat brother-in-law John (Wayne Thomas Yorke, *A Boy's Life*), all of whom have lacked the Christmas spirit since the death of Bill's wife. Despite Rudolfa's attempts to sabotage Kristen at every turn, a romance develops between Kristen and Bill (which in the movies usually solves everything), and she trades her immortality to save Kyle during an outbreak of fire in an abandoned house. On Christmas Eve, Santa returns from a "vacation" just in time to prevent Rudolfa from zooming out in her jet sleigh and initiating her phony Christmas. As for the Morgan family, of course they were reformed, thanks to Kristen's patience and kindness.

INTERESTING TIDBITS: Kristen has a confidant at the North Pole, the lisping Tooth Fairy (Liz Torres, *Joe Dirt*), whose presence is otherwise noncontributory.

This film should not be confused with *Mickey's Once upon a Christmas*.

Check out the sequel, ***Twice Upon a Christmas***.

REVIEWS: Andy Webb of *The Movie Scene*: "[This] is one of those movies which is for children and only children because for adults it is painfully over the top and corny.... Everything about it feels like it is pantomime … from Rudolfa being evil to Kristin giving Mary Poppins a run for her money…"

David Parkinson of *Radio Times*: "Essentially, it's Scrooge without the ghosts, as Ireland sets out to reform workaholic John Dye and his neglected, but ghastly kids. Unexpectedly lively festive fodder."

PRODUCTION CREDITS—Writer: Steven H. Berman. Producers: Jon Carrasco, Deboragh Gabler, and Stephen Roseberry. Director: Tibor Takács. Production Companies: Ardent Productions, Legacy Filmworks, Lincoln Field Productions, Sterling/Winters Company Studios, and Viacom Productions. Rating: G. Genres: Drama, Family, Fantasy, Romance. Country: Canada. Run Time: 90 min.

REFERENCES: Crump, William D. *The Christmas Encyclopedia*. Third Edition. Jefferson, NC: McFarland, 2013.

Once upon a Christmas. Hollywood: Paramount Home Entertainment, 2006. DVD Video.

Once Upon a Christmas. Internet Movie Database. http://www.imdb.com/title/tt0242848/

Parkinson, David. *Once upon a Christmas*. *Radio Times*. http://www.radiotimes.com/film/cwbqh/once-upon-a-christmas

Webb, Andy. *Once upon a Christmas*. *The Movie Scene*. http://www.themoviescene.co.uk/reviews/once-upon-a-christmas-2000/once-upon-a-christmas-2000.html

Wilson, Joanna. *Tis the Season TV: The Encyclopedia of Christmas-Themed Episodes, Specials and Made-for-TV Movies*. Akron, OH: 1701 Press, 2011.

One Magic Christmas—November 22, 1985

Feature Film

THREAT TO CHRISTMAS: Oppressed with the cares of everyday life, Ginnie Grainger has become a Christmas skeptic. Such pessimism dampens her family's Christmas spirit.

A most dispirited Ginnie Granger (Mary Steenburgen) debates whether or not to mail her daughter's letter to Santa in *One Magic Christmas* (1985). The dark and somber setting reflects Ginnie's skepticism about Christmas (Walt Disney Productions; collection of William D. Crump).

HOW CHRISTMAS IS SAVED: The Christmas angel Gideon resorts to radical methods to restore Ginnie's Christmas spirit.

SYNOPSIS AND COMMENTARY: It's rather commonplace in Christmas movies for angels to be sent to earth to help those in dire straits. In some movies such as *It's a Wonderful Life* and **Unlikely Angel**, for example, the angels earn their wings upon completion of successful missions. In others, such as *The Bishop's Wife* and the present movie under consideration, the angels seem to have no motive other than the welfare of their charges. Angels ordinarily receive their assignments from heaven; with *One Magic Christmas*, however, it is Santa Claus himself (Jan Rubes, *Witness*) who sends the Christmas angel Gideon (Harry Dean Stanton, *Alien*), a gentle and rather shabby figure dressed in black with a broad-brimmed hat, on an annual mission to restore the Christmas spirit to one dispirited individual. This year his assignment is Ginnie Grainger (Mary Steenburgen, *The Proposal*), an overworked and underpaid grocery store clerk who, together with her jobless husband Jack (Gary Basaraba, *Fried Green Tomatoes*) and two young children, Abbie (Elisabeth Harnois, *Ten Inch Hero*) and Cal (Robbie Magwood, *One Magic Christmas*), must vacate their company home by January first. With only $5,000 to their names, Ginnie's pessimism faults an optimistic Jack's desire to give the kids a decent Christmas and sends a clear message that the kids shouldn't expect much from Santa. For Ginnie to see the tragedies that will unfold should she fail to find the Christmas spirit, Gideon removes everything precious to her: she's fired from her job, a gunman murders Jack during a bank holdup, and the gunman kidnaps her children who drown with him when his car crashes in a river. Having broken Ginnie, Gideon now begins to raise her spirits by first rescuing (perhaps resurrecting) her children. Although Gideon can do nothing about Jack, or so it seems, he whisks Abbie to the North Pole to visit Santa, a kindly man of rather frightening appearance, who retrieves a letter that young Ginnie had written when she was eight years old. Since only Ginnie's faith can bring Jack back, upon seeing that old letter, she remembers, and her faith in Christmas is restored, which prompts her simple act of kindness to the desperate man who otherwise would be driven to rob the bank with its ensuing domino effect. As Frank Thompson notes in *AMC Great Christmas Movies*, "Ginnie's happy ending comes with a profound message. Her deliverance has not come from a miracle but through the realization that the clichés of Christmas—charity, good will, faith, love—are in fact eternal truths, necessary for a fulfilling life."

AWARDS: In 1986, this picture received Genie Awards for Best Achievement in Sound Editing and Best Achievement in Overall Sound. It received Genie nominations for Best Motion Picture; Best Performance by an Actress in a Leading Role (Mary Steenburgen); and Best Achievements in Cinematography, Art Direction, and Costume Design. In 1987, it received a Young Artist Award Nomination for Exceptional Feature Film–Family Entertainment–Drama and for Exceptional Performance by a Young Actress Starring in a Feature Film–Comedy or Drama (Elisabeth Harnois).

INTERESTING TIDBITS: *One Magic Christmas* departs from the usual save-Christmas movies in that it does not uphold the receiving of presents as the focus of the holiday. As screenwriter Thomas Meehan noted, "This film is trying to distill the spirit of Christmas while attacking commercialism." Save for the ending, throughout the film the mood is dark, somber, and depressing, which reflects not only Ginnie's skepticism but symbolizes the heartache and despair that many families experience in real life and especially at Christmastime. That mood deepens when all the Christmas lights on Ginnie's street wink out, which heralds that Ginnie's trials, courtesy of Gideon, are about to commence. The scenario is similar to that in *It's a Wonderful Life* when, courtesy of the angel Clarence, the cessation of snowfall heralds that George Bailey had never been born. Likewise, the Christmas lights and snowfall return after Ginnie and George experience their respective epiphanies.

As Santa is depicted here as a god-like being who summons angels to do his bidding, so the North Pole becomes a kind of heaven for the deceased of the world. During Abbie's tour there, Santa goes about issuing greetings in multiple languages to his helpers who consist not of conventional elves but of good people from all nationalities who have passed on and now spend an eternity there making toys.

The film earned over $13.6 million at the box office.

REVIEWS: According to the Rotten Tomatoes film review site, 50 percent of critics gave this production a positive review.

Brian Costello of *Common Sense Media* (October 1, 2013): "'80s Christmas movie has depressing, intense scenes."

Roger Ebert of rogerebert.com (November 22, 1985): "This is a happy ending, but, boy, do we have to sweat for it ... [Harry Dean Stanton's angel] looks just like the kind of guy our parents told us never to talk to."

Janet Maslin of *The New York Times* (November 22, 1985): "But it is the ... depression that extends through most of the movie, that gives *One Magic Christmas* its realistic edge."

PRODUCTION CREDITS—Story: Phillip Borsos, Barry Healey, and Thomas Meehan. Writer: Thomas Meehan. Producer: Peter O'Brian. Director: Phillip Borsos. Production Companies: Walt Disney Pictures, Silver Screen Partners II, Northpole Picture Company of Canada, and Téléfilm Canada. Rating: G. Genres: Family, Fantasy. Countries: Canada and USA. Run Time: 89 min.

REFERENCES: Costello, Brian. *One Magic Christmas*. *Common Sense Media*. https://www.commonsensemedia.org/movie-reviews/one-magic-christmas

Crump, William D. *The Christmas Encyclopedia*. Third Edition. Jefferson, NC: McFarland, 2013.

Ebert, Roger. "Review: *One Magic Christmas*." http://www.rogerebert.com/reviews/one-magic-christmas-1985

Maslin, Janet. "'Magic Christmas' with Santa and Angel." *The New York Times*. http://www.nytimes.com/movie/review?res=9B00EFDD1138F931A15752C1A9639482608&partner=Rotten%2520Tomatoes

One Magic Christmas. Box Office Mojo. http://www.boxofficemojo.com/movies/?id=onemagicchristmas.htm

One Magic Christmas. Burbank, CA: Buena Vista Home Entertainment, 2004. DVD Video.

One Magic Christmas. Internet Movie Database. http://www.imdb.com/title/tt0089731/

One Magic Christmas. Rotten Tomatoes. http://www.rottentomatoes.com/m/one_magic_christmas/

Thompson, Frank T. *American Movie Classics Great Christmas Movies*. Dallas, TX: Taylor Publishing, 1998.

Wilson, Joanna. *Tis the Season TV: The Encyclopedia of Christmas-Themed Episodes, Specials and Made-for-TV Movies*. Akron, OH: 1701 Press, 2011.

Papa's Angels—December 3, 2000

Television Movie

THREAT TO CHRISTMAS: A grief-stricken father vows to cancel his family's Christmas celebration.

HOW CHRISTMAS IS SAVED: His children's little Christmas kindnesses turn the father around.

SYNOPSIS AND COMMENTARY: Here's a different kind of movie in which there's no threat to the North Pole or Santa; instead, a grief-stricken father vows to cancel his family's Christmas celebration. The movie is based on a novella of the same title, written by Collin Wilcox Paxton and Gary Carden, published in 1996, which in turn is based on Wilcox Paxton's play of the same title. Set in the Appalachian Mountains in the fall of 1935, the story is told from the perspective and in the local dialect of 12-year-old Becca Jenkins (Kimberley Warnat, *Silver Wolf*), who has been mute since birth.

After Becca's mother Sharon (Cynthia Nixon, *Sex and the City*) dies from tuberculosis a few weeks before Christmas, her father Grins (Scott Bakula, *Quantum Leap*) falls into a deep depression and withdraws his family from society. Grins, who loses all interest in former activities, spends lonely hours in the barn drinking and grieving, while Becca and her siblings—Hannah Rose (Jenny-Lynn Hutcheson, *Nightmare Street*); Alvin (Lachlan Murdoch, *The Santa Clause*); and John Neale (Brandon James Olson, *Replicant*)—no longer attend church or school. As Christmas approaches, their Grammy (Eva Marie Saint, *North by Northwest*) tells the children all about Yule log traditions and that their mother's spirit will return to them in the flames on Christmas Eve. A skeptic, Grins scoffs and vows there will be no Christmas celebrations, because they have nothing to celebrate, yet the children remain undaunted and feel that it's time to get on with their lives. Believing that Santa will bring their tree if nothing else, they retrieve their decorations from the attic on Christmas Eve, and Grins fires both barrels of his shotgun outside to scare Santa away. As Grins sleeps in his chair, the children quietly place in his lap the loving, simple gifts they have prepared, and upon awakening, he is moved to tears, especially after reading Becca's gift, a little journal she has kept since her mother died. When Grins realizes that his children have silently suffered much because of his neglect, he has a change of heart and celebrates the joy of Christmas with his family. As the Yule log blazes, Grins plays a new Christmas song on his guitar, and they all wish Momma a Merry Christmas.

AWARDS: In 2001, this film won a Young Artist Award for Best Family TV Movie; a Primetime Emmy nomination for Outstanding Music Composition; and an ASC Award nomination for Outstanding Achievement in Cinematography.

INTERESTING TIDBITS: According to ancient superstition, family ancestors supposedly became manifest in the glowing embers of the Yule log. Therefore, a libation of wine poured over the log beforehand honored their memories, and all who touched the log first purified themselves by washing their hands.

Collin Wilcox Paxton (1935–2009) was an actress best known for her portrayal of Mayella Violet Ewell in the film *To Kill a Mockingbird*. Her play *Papa's Angels* has had three successful stage productions. A storyteller, lecturer, and playwright, Gary Carden is the author of *Mason Jars in the Flood*, which won the Appalachian Writers Association Book of the Year prize. His plays include *The Raindrop Waltz*, *Land's End*, and *Birdell*, among others.

REVIEWS: Stuart Levine of *Variety*: "Promoting itself as a holiday tale…. *Angels* offers an underlying storyline of how the dead come back via a Yule log during Christmas that bookends the telepic. Though it adds a warm and fuzzy touch, it's not entirely necessary. This is a drama that could work any time of the year."

PRODUCTION CREDITS—Teleplay: Bill Cain. Producer: Edna Lishman. Director: Dwight H. Little. Production Companies: Bakula Productions, Columbia Broadcasting System, and Marian Rees Associates. Rating: PG (thematic events and mild language). Genre: Drama. Country: USA. Run Time: 83 min.

REFERENCES: Crump, William D. *The Christmas Encyclopedia*. Third Edition. Jefferson, NC: McFarland, 2013.

Levine, Stuart. *Papa's Angels. Variety*. http://variety.com/2000/tv/reviews/papa-s-angels-1200465126/#

Papa's Angels. Hollywood: Paramount, 2002. VHS Video.

Papa's Angels. Internet Movie Database. http://www.imdb.com/title/tt0263836/

Wilcox Paxton, Collin, and Gary Carden. *Papa's Angels*. Illustrated by Elsa Sibley. Novato, CA: New World Library, 1996.

Wilson, Joanna. *Tis the Season TV: The Encyclopedia of Christmas-Themed Episodes, Specials and Made-for-TV Movies*. Akron, OH: 1701 Press, 2011.

Prep and Landing: Naughty vs. Nice—December 5, 2011

Computer-Animated Television Short Film

THREAT TO CHRISTMAS: When a classified device from the North Pole falls into the hands of a computer hacker and malfunctions, it threatens to throw Christmas into chaos.

HOW CHRISTMAS IS SAVED: Exposing the hacker, the Prep and Landing team retrieves and repairs the device.

SYNOPSIS AND COMMENTARY: On Christmas

Eve, the elite team of elves known as "Prep and Landing" travels ahead of "The Big Guy" (Santa) and, with stealth, prepares millions of nice children's homes for his visit. But if the children have been naughty, the Coal Elf Brigade (elves responsible for delivering lumps of coal) comes into play. When the classified conduct calculator, dubbed the "fruitcake" (a device that determines who is naughty or nice), falls into the hands of a hacker known as "Jinglesmell1337," the Prep and Landing team of Wayne and Lanny is dispatched to the hacker's home to retrieve the device. Accompanying them is Noel, Wayne's estranged, younger brother and a burly member of the Coal Elf Brigade. Upon entering the hacker's home, the three fall prey to a booby trap that roughs them up a bit, and Lanny finds himself a captive in the hacker's room. Perpetrating all this mess is a kid named Grace Goodwin, who believes that her toddler brother had framed her, and now she seeks the fruitcake's password to remove herself from Santa's naughty list. Lanny hints to use the magic word "please," which naughty children never say, and Grace is off the naughty list, but the fruitcake then malfunctions, and the entire planet is in danger of winding up on the naughty list. After some squabbling among the two brothers over their childhood, their rift dissolves when Noel gives Wayne a gift that he had always wanted but never got, and their influence prompts Grace to appreciate her own brother. Then the brothers work together to fix the problem with the fruitcake. With the mission accomplished, Santa awards Wayne and Noel the title of "Elves of the Year."

PRINCIPAL VOICES: Dave Foley (*A Bug's Life*) as Wayne; Derek Richardson (*Hostel*) as Lanny; Rob Riggle (*The Hangover*) as Noel; Emily Alyn Lind (*Enter the Void*) as Grace; Sarah Chalke (*Scrubs*) as Magee; W. Morgan Sheppard (*The Prestige*) as The Big Guy.

AWARDS: In 2012, this film won a Primetime Emmy for Outstanding Individual in Animation (character designer Bill Schwab); Primetime Emmy nominations for Outstanding Voice-Over Performance (Rob Riggle) and Outstanding Music Composition; won Annie Awards for Character Animation, Character Design, Music, and Storyboarding in a Television Production; Annie nominations for Best General Audience Animated Television Production, Character Animation, Directing, Storyboarding, and Writing in a Television Production; a Visual Effects Society Award nomination for Outstanding Visual Effects in a Broadcast Special; a Young Artist Award nomination for Best Young Actress Performance in a Voice-Over Role (Emily Alyn Lind).

INTERESTING TIDBITS: This film is a sequel to the Disney computer-animated TV short *Prep and Landing* (2009).

Producer Dorothy McKim and writer-director Stevie Wermers-Skelton lend their voices as miscellaneous elves.

REVIEWS: Emily Ashby of *Common Sense Media* (December 5, 2011): "It's not easy to present a truly original Christmas story, but [this film] manages it with ease ... laugh-out-loud holiday special ... heartwarming messages about the ties that bind family and loved ones, even as their presence at the holidays can strike a nerve or two."

Morgan R. Lewis of *Morgan on Media* (December 9, 2011): "...reasonably fun ... like [*Prep and Landing*, 2009], there are little jokes thrown in for the adults.... Some of it is as simple as the obvious substitute swearing [such as 'Oh, frostbite!'], and some of it is going to go *way* over the heads of the children ... the voice actors do their jobs well enough that it's easy to believe that *this* character would have *that* voice and mannerisms ... the original [*Prep and Landing*] was slightly better in terms of plot ... both are definitely kid fare..."

PRODUCTION CREDITS—Writers and Directors: Kevin Deters and Stevie Wermers-Skelton. Additional Story: Robert L. Baird and Daniel Gerson. Producer: Dorothy McKim. Production Company: Walt Disney Animation Studios. Rating: G. Genres: Animation, Comedy, Short. Country: USA. Run Time: 22 min.

REFERENCES: Ashby, Emily. *Prep and Landing: Naughty vs. Nice. Common Sense Media.* https://www.commonsensemedia.org/movie-reviews/prep-and-landing-naughty-vs-nice

Crump, William D. *The Christmas Ency-*

clopedia. Third Edition. Jefferson, NC: McFarland, 2013.

Lewis, Morgan R. *Prep and Landing: Naughty vs. Nice*. Morgan on Media. https://morganrlewis.wordpress.com/2011/12/09/prep-landing-naughty-vs-nice/

Prep and Landing: Naughty vs. Nice. Big Cartoon Database. http://www.bcdb.com/cartoon/138299-Prep-Landing-Naughty-vs-Nice

Prep and Landing: Naughty vs. Nice. Burbank, CA: Buena Vista Home Entertainment, 2012. DVD Video.

Prep and Landing: Naughty vs. Nice. Internet Movie Database. http://www.imdb.com/title/tt2069885/

Pups Save Christmas—December 12, 2013

Episode from the Computer-Animated Television Series *PAW Patrol*

THREAT TO CHRISTMAS: Santa runs into a blizzard and crashes his sleigh.

HOW CHRISTMAS IS SAVED: The PAW Patrol comes to the rescue.

SYNOPSIS AND COMMENTARY: Here's an ongoing series for preschoolers created by Keith Chapman that first aired in 2013 on Nickelodeon in the USA and on TVOKids in Canada. Collectively known as the PAW Patrol who work on various rescue missions to protect the city of Adventure Bay, the protagonists consist of a team of talking pups of different breeds and skills: Marshall, a Dalmatian skilled as a fire-pup and medic; Rubble, an English bulldog, construction; Chase, a German shepherd, police dog/traffic cop/super spy; Rocky, mixed breed, eco skills; Zuma, a chocolate lab, lifeguard/diving skills; Skye, a cockapoo, pilot; Everest, a Siberian Husky, snow/mountain rescues; Tracker, a beagle, jeep driver; and the pack leader, Ryder, a tech-savvy boy, who invented Robo-Dog, a robot that drives the PAW Patroller.

Everest and Tracker were respectively added during the second and third seasons and do not appear in "Pups Save Christmas." As Santa approaches Adventure Bay on Christmas Eve, he runs into a strong blizzard, crashes the sleigh, loses the sack of presents, and his reindeer scatter. (What, Santa didn't suffer amnesia after the crash?) Santa calls the PAW Patrol for help, whereupon Ryder assigns the pups different tasks according to the tools and machines they operate: Rubble digs the sleigh out of the snow with his machine shovel; Rocky lifts the sleigh for repairs with his forklift; Skye with her helicopter, Zuma with his hovercraft, and Marshall with his fire truck round up and deliver the presents to Anchor Bay; and Chase rounds up the reindeer with his megaphone and net. Meanwhile, Santa is out looking for the magic Christmas star that fell off his sleigh; without it, the sleigh and reindeer cannot fly. (Santa and his team seem to have lost their inherent ability to fly in the 21st century and require a supply of magic from external sources, such as a star here and an old inn as seen in **Northpole: Open for Christmas**, for example.) The pups find the star attached to a cow flying about and entice her down with some hay, after which Santa is all set to resume his rounds.

PRINCIPAL VOICES: Owen Mason as Ryder; Devan Cohen as Rubble; Kallan Holley as Skye; Gage Munroe as Marshall; Stuart Ralston as Rocky; Tristan Samuel as Chase; Alex Thorne as Zuma. They all voice for the *PAW Patrol* series. The voice actor for Santa is not credited.

AWARDS: *PAW Patrol* received Young Artist Award nominations for Best Performance in a Voiceover Role: Kallan Holley (2013); Devan Cohen (2014); Berkley Silverman, Max Calinescu, Alex Thorne, and Christian Distefano (2015). Won Young Artist Awards for Best Performance in a Voiceover Role: Devan Cohen and Kallan Holley (2015). Won Joey Awards Vancouver for Young Actor Voiceover Role: Christian Distefano and Alex Thorne (2014); Christian Distefano, Berkley Silverman, Devan Cohen, and Max Calinescu (2015); Best Young Ensemble in a Voiceover Performance (2015). Joey nominations: Devan Cohen and Kallan Holley (2014); Alex Thorne and Elijha Hammill (2015). Annie Award nomination for Best General Audience Animated TV/Broadcast Production for Preschool Children (for episode "Pup Saves a MerPup," 2016).

REVIEWS: Emily Ashby of *Common Sense Media* reviews *PAW Patrol*: "Perhaps the show's best attribute is how it demonstrates the value of thoughtful problem-solving… [The pups] take a moment to collect their thoughts, identify the skills best suited to the job, and support each other's efforts, if only in verbal encouragement."

PRODUCTION CREDITS—Writer: Ursula Ziegler Sullivan. Executive Producers: Jennifer Dodge, Ronnen Harary, Keith Chapman, and Scott Kraft. Director: Jamie Whitney. Production Companies: Nickelodeon Productions and Spin Master Studios. Rating: Not rated. Genres: Animation, Comedy, Family. Countries: Canada and USA. Run Time: 23 min.

REFERENCES: Ashby, Emily. *PAW Patrol*. Common Sense Media. https://www.commonsensemedia.org/tv-reviews/paw-patrol

PAW Patrol. Internet Movie Database. http://www.imdb.com/title/tt3121722/

"Pups Save Christmas." Internet Movie Database. http://www.imdb.com/title/tt3367288/

"Pups Save Christmas." In *PAW Patrol: Winter Rescues*. Hollywood: Paramount Pictures, 2014. DVD Video.

Raggedy Ann and Andy in the Great Santa Claus Caper—November 30, 1978

Animated Television Short Film

THREAT TO CHRISTMAS: Alexander Graham Wolf plans to take over Santa's workshop and make a profit by selling toys sealed in plastic "Gloopstik."

HOW CHRISTMAS IS SAVED: Raggedy Ann and Andy persuade Wolf to change his greedy ways.

SYNOPSIS AND COMMENTARY: The world's best-known and most-adored rag dolls, Raggedy Ann and her brother Raggedy Andy were the creations of Johnny Gruelle (1880–1938), a cartoonist, illustrator, and author from Indianapolis, IN. A long-forgotten, family-made rag doll retrieved from his parents' home served as the inspiration for the Raggedy Ann dolls that Gruelle designed and patented in 1915. The P.F. Volland Company published Gruelle's collection *Raggedy Ann Stories* in 1918, and a series of *Raggedy Ann* children's books followed. *Raggedy Andy Stories* (1920) introduced Raggedy Ann's brother, Raggedy Andy. Possessing a candy heart, Raggedy Ann sported red yarn for hair and a triangle nose, whereas Raggedy Andy was clad in a sailor suit and hat. The characters have appeared in multiple media, including toys and animation.

In *Caper*, Alexander Graham Wolf, alias the Big Bad Wolf, decides to become Santa's new "partner" and put Christmas on a paying basis. While Santa and the reindeer are napping, Wolf invades Santa's workshop with his "Gloopstik" contraption and seals all the toys in a clear, unbreakable plastic that will preserve them forever. The catch is that now there's a price on all Christmas toys that children can neither play with nor touch. Discovering Wolf's plan, Comet the reindeer solicits the aid of Raggedy Ann, Raggedy Andy, and their dog Raggedy Arthur to foil Wolf. When Wolf seals Raggedy Arthur in Gloopstik, Raggedy Andy turns the tide and seals Wolf as well. Only the dolls' love liberates their dog from Gloopstik. To liberate a now-repentant Wolf, the dolls bid the audience to shout appropriate responses, which do the trick.

VOICES: June Foray (*The Smurfs*) as Raggedy Ann and Comet; Daws Butler (*The Jetsons*) as Raggedy Andy; Les Tremayne (*North by Northwest*) as Santa and Wolf.

INTERESTING TIDBITS: The scenario of audience participation parallels that in J.M. Barrie's play *Peter Pan* (1904), when at Peter's behest, the audience applauds to indicate their belief in fairies, which saves the poisoned fairy Tinker Bell. A similar scenario is found in **The Elf Who Saved Christmas, Elmo's Christmas Countdown,** and **It Nearly Wasn't Christmas.** Wolf also bears a striking resemblance to the character Wile E. Coyote, which animation director Chuck Jones created for Warner Bros.' *Looney Tunes* and *Merrie Melodies* series of animated cartoon shorts.

PRODUCTION CREDITS—Writer, Producer, and Director: Chuck Jones. Production Company: Chuck Jones Enterprises. Rating: G. Genres: Animation, Family. Country: USA. Run Time: 30 min.

REFERENCES: Hall, Patricia. *Johnny Gruelle: Creator of Raggedy Ann and Andy*. Gretna, LA: Pelican, 1993.

Raggedy Ann (right) and Raggedy Andy (left) share a moment with Alexander Graham Wolf in *Raggedy Ann and Andy in The Great Santa Claus Caper* (1978) (CBS/MMG Photo Archives; Collection of William D. Crump).

Lenburg, Jeff. *The Encyclopedia of Animated Cartoons*. Third Edition. New York: Facts on File, 2009.

Raggedy Ann and Andy in the Great Santa Claus Caper. Big Cartoon Database. http://www.bcdb.com/cartoon/63468-Raggedy-Ann-And-Andy-In-The-Great-Santa-Claus-Caper/

Raggedy Ann and Andy in the Great Santa Claus Caper. Internet Movie Database. http://www.imdb.com/title/tt1146440/

Raggedy Ann and Andy in the Great Santa Claus Caper. Charlotte, NC: UAV Home Video, 1993. VHS Video.

Wilson, Joanna. *Tis the Season TV: The Encyclopedia of Christmas-Themed Episodes, Specials and Made-for-TV Movies*. Akron, OH: 1701 Press, 2011.

Regular Show: The Christmas Special—December 3, 2012

Animated Television Short Film

THREAT TO CHRISTMAS: Quillgin the elf wants to destroy Christmas with his special gift-box.

HOW CHRISTMAS IS SAVED: Mordecai, Rigby, and The Park gang destroy the gift-box.

SYNOPSIS AND COMMENTARY: There's nothing at all "regular" about *Regular Show*, a wacky, animated television series created by J.G. Quintel for Cartoon Network, ongoing since 2010. Inspired by *The Simpsons* and *Beavis and Butt-Head*, Quintel based the series and its often bizarre characters on his life and experiences at California Institute for the Arts, particularly his student films. The series revolves around the adventures of mischievous, anthropomorphic protagonists Mordecai the blue jay and Rigby the raccoon, both of whom serve as groundskeepers for The Park but in reality excel as slackers. Other principal characters include their boss Benson, a hot-tempered, living gumball machine prone to fits of rage; Pops, an elderly but childlike man with features of a lollipop who believes that the lollipops he carries in his wallet are real money; Skips, an immortal yeti who skips rather than walks; Muscle Man, a short, obese, green-skinned man; and Hi Five Ghost, a small ghost and Muscle Man's brother with a hand extending from the top of his head. Skips, Muscle Man, and Hi Five Ghost all work as groundskeepers at The Park with Mordecai and Rigby.

In earlier events, Santa's chief toy designer, elf Quillgin, had used dark magic to create a giftbox that would grant anyone's wish. But when test runs turned the bearers evil, Santa nixed the idea and locked the box away. Seeking revenge and desiring to destroy Christmas, Quillgin blew up Santa's factory and escaped with the box in the reindeer sleigh. Using his invisibility cloak, rough-and-tumble Santa-cum-pony tail pursued on his flying snowboard and fought Quillgen in the sleigh, but the elf shot Santa, who fell out with the box and crashed into Skip's garage. Back to the present, Mordecai and Rigby find an injured Santa, whose identity they initially doubt, but they soon learn they must destroy the box, lest Quillgin find it. After the rest of the gang briefly fall prey to the box by opening it and fighting among themselves for possession, Skip leads them through rival East Pines Park to destroy the box in a lava pit within an abandoned mine shaft. En route, East Pines guards capture the gang on suspicion of their pulling a prank, and just as Benson's staff did, the East Pines staff initially fight for possession of the box. With Quillgin and his henchmen close by, however, the rival park manager Gene leads Benson's gang to the mine shaft with a warning that deadly booby traps lie ahead. Here the scenario is similar to that in *Indiana Jones and the Last Crusade* as the gang navigate perilous slides, spears in walls, floors that drop out when wrong tiles are pressed, and so forth. An armed Quillgin greets them at the lava pit, but an initially invisible Santa (who survived the shooting, thanks to his bullet-proof vest) is also there to disarm Quillgin. The elf counters with a grenade and grabs the box, but when Mordecai charges him, they fall into the pit with Rigby close behind. As they battle for the box—Quillgin wishing for a detonator, Rigby for an ice cream cone—Mordecai snatches the box, wishes up two flying snowboards for Rigby and himself as Quillgin plunges with the box to his death, and Christmas is saved.

PRINCIPAL VOICES: J.G. Quintel (*Regular Show*) as Mordecai and Hi Five Ghost; William Salyers (*Regular Show*) as Rigby; Sam Marin (*Regular Show*) as Benson, Pops, and Muscle Man; Mark Hamill (*Star Wars*) as Skips; Thomas Haden Church (*Sideways*) as Quillgin; Kurtwood Smith (*RoboCop*) as Gene the vending machine; Edward Asner (*The Mary Tyler Moore Show*) as Santa.

AWARDS: The series has won a Primetime Emmy and several BMI Film and TV Awards; it has received numerous nominations for BAFTA Awards, Annie Awards, and Emmys, among others.

INTERESTING TIDBITS: Periodically through the film, a running gag consists of derogatory remarks made about the hideous appearance of Benson's Christmas sweater.

Note the parallels between the two rival park managers: Benson, manager of The Park, is a living gumball machine, whereas Gene, manager of East Pines Park, is a living vending machine.

The series is known for using licensed music. For example, Brenda Lee singing "Rockin' Around the Christmas Tree" plays in the background at the Christmas party for The Park staff. Background music during the battle for the box in the lava pit consists of an excerpt from "Christmas Eve/Sarajevo 12/24" by Savatage, played by the Trans-Siberian Orchestra.

REVIEWS: Melissa Camacho of *Common Sense Media* reviewed the series: "…definitely creative, but some of the fantasy violence and mildly crude humor aren't appropriate for younger viewers … older viewers who are into creative animation will definitely appreciate the wit featured here."

Paul Mavis of *DVD Talk* reviewed the series (November 5, 2012): "*Regular Show* is a beautifully surreal, deadpan hilarious mixture of workplace sitcom and wild slacker/gamer flights of sci-fi fancy, frequently blown up to hysterical, epic proportions. A show kids instinctively adore, and one their parents can actually sit and watch (and laugh along) with them…"

PRODUCTION CREDITS—Writers: Sean Szeles, Kat Morris, Benton Connor, and Hilary Florido. Supervising Producer: Mike Roth. Directors: J.G. Quintel and Mike Roth. Production Company: Cartoon Network Studios.

Rating: PG (crude humor). Genres: Animation, Action, Adventure, Comedy, Family, Fantasy. Country: USA. Run Time: 23 min.

REFERENCES: Camacho, Melissa. *Regular Show. Common Sense Media.* https://www.commonsensemedia.org/tv-reviews/regular-show

Mavis, Paul. "Regular Show: The Best DVD In the World* (*at this moment in time)." *DVD Talk.* http://www.dvdtalk.com/reviews/57653/regular-show-best-dvd-in-the-world-at-this/

Regular Show. Internet Move Database. http://www.imdb.com/title/tt1710308/

Regular Show: The Christmas Special. In *Cartoon Network Holiday Collection.* Burbank, CA: Warner Home Entertainment, 2014. DVD Video.

Regular Show: The Christmas Special. Internet Movie Database. http://www.imdb.com/title/tt2526742/

The Reindeer Hunter—December 9, 1995

Episode from the Animated Television Series *Ace Ventura: Pet Detective*

THREAT TO CHRISTMAS: All of Santa's reindeer have been kidnapped.

HOW CHRISTMAS IS SAVED: Although Santa calls Ace Ventura for help, Santa ends up taking matters in hand himself.

SYNOPSIS AND COMMENTARY: Consisting of 39 episodes and running from 1995 to 2000, the *Ace Ventura* series was a spinoff from the 1994 live-action comedy film of the same title that starred Jim Carrey in the title role. As an animal detective, his task was to find the Miami Dolphins' mascot that had been abducted. Although Ace Ventura appeared as a caricature of Carrey in the series, he was voiced by Canadian actor Michael Hall (AKA Michael Daingerfield). A wacky private eye, Ace investigated cases of missing or abducted animals.

In "The Reindeer Hunter," as Santa delivers gifts in Miami, someone kidnaps all his reindeer, and Santa calls Ace for help. Certain that the culprit is among those on Santa's naughty list, Ace commences to question suspects amid slapstick shenanigans but only succeeds in having doors slammed in his face. He eventually discovers that the culprit is perfume magnate Atrocia Odora, who wants to extract the reindeer glands to perfect an age-reducing potion. Ace attempts a bumbling rescue but Odora's thugs overpower him, whereupon Santa arrives just in time with martial arts skills that subdue the thugs, and Odora is arrested for having a rare, albino alligator in captivity. So in reality, Santa really didn't need Ace at all.

PRINCIPAL VOICES: Michael Hall (*Nerds and Monsters*) as Ace; Dan Hennessey (*Inspector Gadget*) as Santa; Pam Hyatt (*The Story of Luke*) as Odora; Richard Binsley (*Cinderella Man*) as Spike; Vince Corraza (*Bride of Chucky*) as Shickadance; Al Waxman (*The Hurricane*) as Aguado; Bruce Tubbe (*Dogboys*) as Emilio; Bruce Hunter (*Good Will Hunting*) as Uwe; Ron Pardo (*PAW Patrol*) as Roy.

AWARDS: In 1997, the animated series received a Blimp Award nomination for Favorite Cartoon.

INTERESTING TIDBITS: This episode was the first in the *Ace Ventura* series. Beware of those DVD containers that state that only Rudolph is kidnapped. Instead, all of Santa's reindeer are kidnapped; Rudolph doesn't even appear in this cartoon.

PRODUCTION CREDITS—Writer: Duane Capizzi. Executive Producers: James G. Robinson and Gary Barber. Director: Dave Pemberton. Production Companies: Morgan Creek Productions, Nelvana, and Warner Bros. Television. Rating: TV-Y. Genres: Animation, Comedy, Family. Countries: Canada and USA. Run Time: 30 min.

REFERENCES: "The Reindeer Hunter." Big Cartoon Database. http://www.bcdb.com/cartoon-story/40952-Reindeer-Hunter

"The Reindeer Hunter." In *Ace Ventura, Pet Detective: The Animated Series.* Burbank, CA: Warner Home Video, 2006. DVD Video.

"The Reindeer Hunter." Internet Movie Database. http://www.imdb.com/title/tt0944252/

Wilson, Joanna. *Tis the Season TV: The Encyclopedia of Christmas-Themed Episodes, Specials and Made-for-TV Movies.* Akron, OH: 1701 Press, 2011.

Richie Rich's Christmas Wish—
November 3, 1998

Direct-to-Video Movie

THREAT TO CHRISTMAS: Blamed for an accident while delivering Christmas presents to orphans, Richie Rich wishes he'd never been born, whereupon he gets to see how miserable Christmas would be without his influence.

HOW CHRISTMAS IS SAVED: Richie and his friends must find the key element to operate a wishing machine so that Richie can reverse his wish.

SYNOPSIS AND COMMENTARY: Richard "Richie" Rich, Jr., the "poor little rich boy," the richest kid in the world, is a comic book character created by Alfred Harvey and Warren Kremer of Harvey Comics. Richie Rich first appeared in 1953 and went on to become Harvey Comics' most popular character that starred in more than 50 separate titles. A live-action film adaptation of the character, *Richie Rich* (1994) starred Macaulay Culkin in the title role, followed by a sequel, *Richie Rich's Christmas Wish*, starring David Gallagher (*7th Heaven*).

It's Christmas Eve, and Richie, a most benevolent and affable 12-year-old, sets forth on his annual mission to deliver presents to the children at the Richville Orphanage. His vehicle is a decorative, motorized sleigh, which his greedy cousin, Reggie Van Dough (Jake Richardson, *Clerks II*), has secretly sabotaged, so that the sleigh plunges into a ravine. Despite Richie's spotless reputation, the town erroneously blames him for ruining the orphans' Christmas, and Richie wishes that he had never been born. His wish is granted through a washing machine-turned-wishing machine, a wacky contraption invented by Professor Keenbean (Eugene Levy, *Bringing Down the House*), the Rich family's eccentric scientist-in-residence.

Here the picture takes on the ambiance of the film classics *It's a Wonderful Life* and *Back to the Future*. Without Richie's positive influence, the insufferable Reggie now dominates the town, which he renames Reggieville, and its citizens are reduced to utter poverty. Because the wishing machine works only on Christmas Eve and its power ends at midnight, Richie, together with his personal valet Cadbury (Keene Curtis, *Silver*) and friends, steal from the local museum a dinosaur wishbone that Keenbean needs to repair Reggie's malfunctioning wishing machine. Though briefly jailed for the deed, they escape, and Reggie threatens to cancel Christmas and cut off all city utilities if Richie is not captured by midnight. This atrocity angers the authorities, who back off. With the wishbone installed, Richie reverses his wish and returns to his own world of Christmas cheer, running through town yelling "Merry Christmas" to everyone, just like George Bailey.

OTHER CAST: Martin Mull (*Mr. Mom*) as Mr. Rich; Leslie Ann Warren (*Cinderella*) as Mrs. Rich; Richard Fancy (*The Girl Next Door*) as Mr. Van Dough; Marla Maples (*Executive Decision*) as Mrs. Van Dough; Michelle Trachtenberg (*Buffy the Vampire Slayer*), Blake Jeremy Collins (*The Little Rascals*), and Austin Stout (*Eight Crazy Nights*) as, respectively, Gloria, Freckles, and Pee Wee, Richie's friends; Kathleen Freeman (*The Blues Brothers*) as Miss Peabody; Richard Riehle (*The Search for Santa Paws*) as Sgt. Mooney; Don McLeod (*Hook*) as Irona, the fire-breathing robotic maid.

INTERESTING TIDBITS: This was Keene Curtis's final role (1923–2002). He died four years later at the age of 79.

For exterior scenes of the Rich Family's mansion, the film used the Langham Huntington Hotel and Spa in Pasadena, California.

Dollar, the Rich Family's pet dog, is a "Dollarmatian," a Dalmatian with dollar signs instead of spots.

REVIEW: *TV Guide*: "The story pays lip service to morals about 'responsibility' and the concept of 'noblesse oblige,' but the real message is revealed at the end, as the happy citizens of Richville gather around a Christmas tree and sing a carol, and the camera pans up to show a golden angel sitting atop the tree, holding a dollar sign in its hand."

PRODUCTION CREDITS—Story: Rob Kerchner and Jason Feffer. Screenplay: Mark Furey. Producer: Mike Elliott. Director: John Murlowski. Production Companies: Saban Entertainment and The Harvey Entertainment

Company. Rating: G. Genres: Comedy, Family. Country: USA. Run Time: 84 min.

REFERENCES: Crump, William D. *The Christmas Encyclopedia*. Third Edition. Jefferson, NC: McFarland, 2013.

Markstein, Don. "Richie Rich, the Poor Little Rich Boy." Toonopedia. http://www.toonopedia.com/richie.htm

Richie Rich's Christmas Wish. Burbank, CA: Warner Home Video, 2006. DVD Video.

Richie Rich's Christmas Wish. Internet Movie Database. http://www.imdb.com/title/tt0155110/

TV Guide. Richie Rich's Christmas Wish. http://www.tvguide.com/movies/richie-richs-christmas-wish/review/133736/

Wilson, Joanna. *Tis the Season TV: The Encyclopedia of Christmas-Themed Episodes, Specials and Made-for-TV Movies*. Akron, OH: 1701 Press, 2011.

Road to the North Pole—December 12, 2010

Episode from the Animated Television Series *Family Guy*

THREAT TO CHRISTMAS: Stewie seeks to kill Santa for snubbing him at the mall, then learns that Santa is dying from exhaustion.

HOW CHRISTMAS IS SAVED: Stewie and his dog Brian convince the world to request fewer Christmas gifts to lighten Santa's work load.

SYNOPSIS AND COMMENTARY: Imagine a one-year-old old hellion who, after a mall Santa snubs him, is determined to kill Santa in person at the North Pole. That's the kind of insanity that runs rampant in *Family Guy*, an adult sitcom created by Seth MacFarlane for the Fox Network, ongoing since 1999. Set in the fictional city of Quahog, RI, *Family Guy* lampoons American culture and revolves around the antics of the dysfunctional Griffin family: Peter the father, a lazy, obese, dimwitted alcoholic; Lois, his promiscuous wife; Meg, their 18-year-old daughter and social outcast; Chris, their obese,14-year-old son and younger version of his father; Stewie, their diabolical,

The dysfunctional Griffin family from the animated TV series *Family Guy*. From left: Meg, Peter, Lois, Stewie, pet dog Brian, and Chris. When a mall Santa snubs Stewie, the little hellion vows to kill Santa at the North Pole in the episode "Road to the North Pole" (2010) (Fox Broadcasting/Photofest).

one-year-old son, a genius with adult mannerisms who speaks with a British accent; and Brian, the family's anthropomorphic, talking dog, who smokes, drinks, and has yet to find employment as a writer. *Family Guy* is noted for its periodic "Road" episodes, parodies of the *Road* series of comic films starring Bing Crosby, Bob Hope, and Dorothy Lamour.

Believing that the mall Santa is the real deal, Stewie endures a two-hour wait in line with Brian, but when it's Stewie's turn, Santa ends his shift and blows the kid off. Enraged, Stewie vows to kill Santa and forces Brian to take him to the North Pole. Instead, Brian unsuccessfully attempts to fool Stewie with a trip to a Santa amusement park, where Stewie initially pulls a gun on the endlessly yammering dog, then hitches a ride with a trucker into Canada as Brian pursues. En route, Stewie causes a massive traffic pile-up that totals Brian's car when Stewie accidentally fires a flare gun in the truck, which catches fire and explodes. Never mind the accident victims. A ridiculous argument erupts between Brian, who claims that Santa isn't real, and Stewie, who claims that Santa is just as real as Elmo, SpongeBob, and Curious George, for example, after which the two acquire a snowmobile from a passing Canadian trucker amid dialogue that confuses AA with AAA. Having traveled many hours and the snowmobile having run out of gas, the two take shelter for the night in a deserted cabin, as instructed by the "Aurora Boreanaz" (a nod to David Boreanaz, *Bones*, whose live-action face appears in the Aurora Borealis). Stewie and Brian trudge the last leg of the journey on foot, only to discover that Santa's realm has degenerated into a dismal, polluted wasteland, having succumbed to the world's outrageous demands for more toys each year. The elves are now an inbred lot of mutated freaks; the reindeer, a group of feral, carnivorous monsters that devour exhausted elves who wander into the snow to die; and Santa is too old and sick to deliver the presents. This nightmare situation compels Stewie to fill in for Santa with Brian, but their mission ends at their first stop when Stewie wreaks bloody havoc on a troublesome family. So, the world goes without Santa and presents that year. To save future Christmases, Brian and Stewie appear on a TV news broadcast with an invalid Santa to plead that everyone request just one present each Christmas; otherwise, the world's greed will kill Santa. This do-with-less bit may be hard for Peter to swallow, whose motto is, "Christmas is about gettin'!" Nevertheless, he and the world comply, and by Christmas a year later, Santa and the North Pole are back in business.

SONGS: "All I Really Want for Christmas" and "Christmastime Is Killing Us." The former was originally a track titled "A Family Guy Christmas" in the album *Swallow My Eggnog*, released in 2001 by Los Angeles-area DJs Kevin and Bean of radio station KROQ. The latter song, written by Ron Jones, Seth MacFarlane, and Danny Smith, received a Grammy nomination for Best Song Written Specifically for a Motion Picture or for Television (2012).

PRINCIPAL VOICES: Seth MacFarlane (*Ted*) as Peter, Stewie, Brian, and Quagmire; Alex Borstein (*Ted*) as Lois; Seth Green (*The Italian Job*) as Chris; Mila Kunis (*Ted*) as Meg; Drew Barrymore (*E. T.: The Extraterrestrial*) as Brian's ex-girlfriend Jillian; Jon Benjamin (*Bob's Burgers*) as Carl; John G. Brennan (*Tara Road*) as Jewish pharmacist Mort Goldman; Carrie Fisher (*Star Wars*) as Peter's boss Angela; Karley Scott Collins (*Amish Grace*) as Abby; Will Ryan (*The Little Mermaid*) as Winnie the Pooh; John Viener (*Ted*) as Eeyore; Jennifer Tilly (*Liar Liar*) as Bonnie Swanson; Patrick Warburton (*Ted*) as Joe Swanson; Adam West (*Batman*) as Mayor Adam West; Bruce McGill as Santa. Ron MacFarlane, Seth's father, appears as the live-action narrator.

AWARDS: *Family Guy* has received a whole slew of awards and nominations, including Primetime Emmy Awards for Outstanding Voiceover Performance (Seth MacFarlane, 2000), Outstanding Music and Lyrics (2002), Outstanding Individual Achievement in Animation (storyboard artist Steve Fonti, 2007), and Outstanding Sound Mixing for a Comedy or a Drama Series (Half-Hour) and Animation (2011). Other awards include Annie Awards, BAFTA nominations, and People's Choice Award nominations, among many others.

INTERESTING TIDBITS: The opening credits provide brief nods to well-known holiday fare, such as *The Nutcracker, A Christmas Carol, How the Grinch Stole Christmas, Frosty the Snowman, Home Alone,* and *National Lampoon's Christmas Vacation.*

The series' craziness certainly extends to Christmas gifts as the Griffins and neighbors formulate their bizarre and excessive Christmas lists in song. For example, Peter lusts for actresses Jessica Biel and Megan Fox "wearing nothing but their socks" plus lunch with Michael Landon's ghost; Lois wants to party with two black guys in Mexico and some "blow" (cocaine, in case you've lived a sheltered life and didn't know); Stewie wants yellowcake uranium; neighbor Quagmire wants BDSM with cute Japanese girls who garrote and flagellate him until he faints; and the list goes wickedly on.

Christianity clashes with Islam as the bedbound, obviously delusional Santa states, "I'll be with Allah soon!"

It goes without saying that all the jokes and dark humor are too numerous to detail, but some of the most notable appear in cutaway scenes, for which *Family Guy* is noted. For example, Stewie believes Santa betrayed him, just as reality supposedly betrayed actor Gary Busey—cutaway to cartoon Busey gazing at the reflection of himself as a wildly crazed clown in a mirror.

Despite the twisted humor, some scenes are frankly quite graphic. For example, the carnivorous reindeer will not fly until Stewie whacks off a zombie elf's arm and dangles it in front of them on a fishing line, like the proverbial carrot before the horse.

There's even a nod to Hanukkah peppered with political correctness as Mort, sporting a picture of a menorah on his wall, declares in song that if anyone puts a Christmas tree in the public airport, "I will go to court and sue your [a**]," then yells, "Happy Holidays!"

REVIEWS: Todd VanDerWerff of *A.V. Club* (December 13, 2010): "…I liked the chance the episode took in making the North Pole a grim hellhole, at least initially. This was the sort of thing that could have gotten uncomfortable for the sake of making something cringe-y, but the way the episode kept piling more and more ridiculous horrors on top of each other kept the whole thing funny … a satisfying episode of *Family Guy* all around…"

Kate Moon of *TV Fanatic* (December 13, 2010): "While I normally have no problems about *Family Guy*'s shocking or offensive themes, I felt [a] bit disconcerted about the direction of this Christmas episode. Perhaps it was the way that the series stomped on something as innocent as Santa and his elves and twisted them all around. Or perhaps it was the cannibalistic [reindeer]. Whatever the specific reason, the irreverent nature of *Family Guy* seemed just a little too graphic for me this time around."

Will Brownridge of *The Film Reel*: "I just can't get enough of *Family Guy*. The humour [sic] is always funny and usually very dark. No subject matter seems off-limits and it's always well done, even if it is uncomfortable. It's the kind of funny that you don't always go around sharing with everyone just to be sure you don't offend them. Whenever Stewie and Brian are involved you know you'll get some great songs as well as the aftermath of a homicidal Stewie."

PRODUCTION CREDITS—Writers: Chris Sheridan and Danny Smith. Producers: Shannon Smith and Kara Vallow. Director: Greg Colton. Live-Action Sequences Director: Steve Beers. Production Companies: 20th Century Fox Television, Fox Television Animation, and Fuzzy Door Productions. Rating: TV-14. Genres: Animation, Comedy. Country: USA. Run Time: 44 min.

REFERENCES: Brownridge, Will. "Family Guy: Road to the North Pole (2010)." *The Film Reel.* http://www.the-filmreel.com/2010/12/14/family-guy-road-to-the-north-pole-2010-film-reel-reviews/

Family Guy. Internet Movie Database. http://www.imdb.com/title/tt0182576/

Moon, Kate. "Family Guy Review: 'Road to the North Pole.'" *TV Fanatic.* http://www.tv-fanatic.com/2010/12/family-guy-review-road-to-the-north-pole/

"Road to the North Pole." In *Family Guy. Volume 10.* 20th Century Fox Home Entertainment, 2012. DVD Video.

"Road to the North Pole." Internet Movie

Database. http://www.imdb.com/title/tt1710689/

VanDerWerff, Todd. "Donnie Fatso"/"The Road to the North Pole"/"For Whom The Sleigh Bell Tolls." *A.V. Club.* http://www.avclub.com/tvclub/donnie-fatsothe-road-to-the-north-polefor-whom-the-48927

Rudolph, the Red-Nosed Reindeer—
December 6, 1964

Television Special

THREAT TO CHRISTMAS: Santa plans to cancel Christmas because of a major winter storm.

HOW CHRISTMAS IS SAVED: Rudolph, with his nose so bright, is pleased to guide Santa's sleigh on Christmas Eve night.

SYNOPSIS AND COMMENTARY: In 1939, Robert L. May (1905–1976), seeking a Christmas promotional gimmick for the Montgomery Ward Company, created "Rudolph, the Red-Nosed Reindeer," a story about a little reindeer whom his peers taunted for his physical abnormality—a big, shiny red nose. But Rudolph's "deformity" became an asset in guiding Santa's sleigh through heavy fog on Christmas Eve. May's brother-in-law, songwriter John D. (Johnny) Marks (1909–1985), immortalized the little reindeer in a song by the same title that was released in 1949 and recorded by cowboy singing star Gene Autry. The Rudolph character has become a long-standing Christmas icon, the song a treasured Christmas standard. Both served as inspiration for this television special, which premiered on the *General Electric Fantasy Hour*, and for several animated sequels, including *Rudolph's Shiny New Year*, *Rudolph and Frosty's Christmas in July*, and ***Rudolph, the Red-Nosed Reindeer and the Island of Misfit Toys.***

Unpopular because of his glowing red nose, young Rudolph runs away from Christmas Town with a misfit elf, Hermey (various spellings include "Hermie" and "Hermy"), who aspires to be a dentist. Yukon Cornelius, a grizzled prospector, joins them in adventures that lead them to the Island of Misfit Toys, ruled by King Moonracer (a griffin-like lion with wings), and populated by toys rejected by their owners. Such toys include a white elephant with red spots, a train caboose with square wheels, a water pistol that squirts jelly instead of water, and others. Months pass. Convinced that Santa could find homes for these toys, Rudolph returns to Christmas Town, where he learns that the Abominable Snow Monster has captured Clarice, his doe friend, and his parents, who had been out looking for him. Rudolph tracks down the Monster, Cornelius incapacitates him, and Hermey pulls his teeth, which renders him docile. As Cornelius would say, Abominable is now a "humble Bumble." Only when a major winter storm sets in and Santa is about to cancel Christmas does Rudolph realize the true value of his red nose. Leading Santa's team of *seven* reindeer, Rudolph proves that even misfits can lead useful lives. Their first stop is to retrieve the Misfits from the Island of Misfit Toys.

MUSIC AND LYRICS: Johnny Marks

SONGS: "Rudolph, the Red-Nosed Reindeer," "A Holly Jolly Christmas," "Silver and Gold," "Jingle, Jingle, Jingle," "We Are Santa's Elves," "We're a Couple of Misfits," "There's Always Tomorrow," and "The Most Wonderful Day of the Year" (which should not be confused with "It's the Most Wonderful Time of the Year" by Eddie Pola and George Wyle). "Fame and Fortune," a duet with Rudolph and Hermey, was added in 1965 to replace "We're a Couple of Misfits," but by 2008, the "Fame" song was deleted and the "Misfits" song was back in, with additional cuts made for more commercial time.

PRINCIPAL VOICES: Billie Mae Richards (*Rudolph's Shiny New Year*) as Rudolph (credited as Billy Richards); Stan Francis (*Encounter*) as Santa and King Moonracer; Paul Kligman (*Hulk*) as Donner, Coach Comet, and Clarice's father; Burl Ives as narrator Sam the Snowman who also sings "Rudolph, the Red-Nosed Reindeer," "Silver and Gold," and "Holly Jolly Christmas"; Paul Soles (*The Score*) as Hermey; Janis Orenstein (*Festival*) as Clarice; Larry Mann (*The Sting*) as Yukon Cornelius; Peg Dixon (*Captain America*) as Mrs. Claus; Corrine Conley (*WolfCop*) as Mrs. Donner and Dolly (credited as Corine Conley); Carl Banas (*The Raccoons*) as Boss Elf, Spotted Elephant, and other toys; Alfie Scopp (*Fiddler on the Roof*) as reindeer Fireball and Charlie-in-the-Box.

INTERESTING TIDBITS: *Rudolph* was the first major animated feature for Rankin/Bass Productions. It has been telecast annually since 1964, premiering on the NBC network and thereafter on the CBS network since 1972, which makes it the longest-running, highest-rated Christmas television special of all time. Instead of conventional cel animation in which the characters are drawn, *Rudolph* utilizes a stop-motion method termed "Animagic," in which the characters consist of three-dimensional puppets that are moved about and filmed frame by frame. Rankin/Bass Productions would create a long series of animated television Christmas specials with Animagic.

During *Rudolph*'s original end-credits, an elf attaches little umbrellas to the toys and drops them from the sleigh (in ***Christmas Flintstone***, ***Christmas Present Time***, and ***A Monster Christmas***, they drop by parachute). However, the original ending does not show Santa retrieving the Misfits from the Island of Misfit toys, which leaves the impression that Santa did not fulfill his promise to find homes for them. A slew of complaints from viewers prompted a new scene for broadcasts in all subsequent years in which Santa's first stop was to pick up the Misfits on the Island; this required trimming a scene with Yukon Cornelius, who thought he had found a peppermint mine near Santa's abode.

During the opening credits, the copyright date places *Rudolph* back in the Middle Ages, because it is erroneously written as "MCLXIV"

Principal characters from the classic, animated TV special *Rudolph, the Red-Nosed Reindeer* (1964). Back row: Yukon Cornelius, Sam the Snowman, and Santa. Front row: Hermey the Elf, Rudolph, and the Head Elf (NBC/Photofest).

("1164"), instead of "MCMLXIV" ("1964"). Also, a sign in all-capital letters on a package is supposed to read, "BURL IVES SINGS": but it's written as "BURI IVES SINGS":

In 1998, *Rudolph* was remade as ***Rudolph, the Red-Nosed Reindeer: The Movie***.

Coincidence or not, *Rudolph* premiered on December 6, St. Nicholas's Day, which commemorates the death of St. Nicholas (?304–?345), the archbishop of Myra in Asia Minor.

REVIEWS: According to the Rotten Tomatoes film review site, 92 percent of critics gave this production a positive review.

James Poniewozik of *Time Magazine* (November 29, 2007): "All these years later, as a reminder that every oddball fits in somewhere, it still shines. You could even say it glows."

Colette DeDonato of *Common Sense Media* (November 3, 2006): "Old-school, heartwarming classic for all ages."

PRODUCTION CREDITS—Writer: Romeo Muller. Producers: Arthur Rankin, Jr., and Jules Bass. Director: Larry Roemer. Production Companies: Rankin/Bass Productions and Videocraft International. Rating: G. Genres: Animation, Adventure, Family. Countries: Japan and USA. Run Time: 51 min.

REFERENCES: Crump, William D. *The Christmas Encyclopedia.* Third Edition. Jefferson, NC: McFarland, 2013.

DeDonato, Colette. *Rudolph the Red-Nosed Reindeer. Common Sense Media.* https://www.commonsensemedia.org/movie-reviews/rudolph-the-red-nosed-reindeer

Goldschmidt, Rick. *The Enchanted World of Rankin/Bass.* Bridgeview, IL: Miser Bros. Press, 1997.

_____. *The Making of the Original Rankin/Bass Holiday Classic Rudolph the Red-Nosed Reindeer.* Bridgeview, IL: Miser Bros. Press, 2001.

Lenburg, Jeff. *The Encyclopedia of Animated Cartoons.* Third Edition. New York: Facts on File, 2009.

May, Robert L. *Rudolph, the Red-Nosed Reindeer.* Illustrated by Denver Gillen. Chicago: Montgomery Ward, 1939.

Poniewozik, James. *Time Magazine.* http://content.time.com/time/specials/2007/article/0,28804,1689075_1689089_1689106,00.html

Rudolph, the Red-Nosed Reindeer. Big Cartoon Database: http://www.bcdb.com/cartoon/27854-Rudolph-The-Red-Nosed-Reindeer

Rudolph, the Red-Nosed Reindeer. Internet Movie Database: http://www.imdb.com/title/tt0058536/

Rudolph, the Red-Nosed Reindeer. New York: Sony Wonder, 2005. DVD Video.

Rudolph, the Red-Nosed Reindeer. Rotten Tomatoes: http://www.rottentomatoes.com/m/1017962-rudolph_the_rednosed_reindeer/

Werts, Diane. *Christmas on Television.* Westport, CT: Praeger, 2006.

Wilson, Joanna. *Tis the Season TV: The Encyclopedia of Christmas-Themed Episodes, Specials and Made-for-TV Movies.* Akron, OH: 1701 Press, 2011.

Rudolph, the Red-Nosed Reindeer and the Island of Misfit Toys—October 30, 2001

Computer-Animated Direct-to-Video Musical

THREAT TO CHRISTMAS: The mysterious Toy Taker steals Santa's toys.

HOW CHRISTMAS IS SAVED: Rudolph and his friends capture and unmask the Toy Taker.

SYNOPSIS AND COMMENTARY: The animated television special **Rudolph, the Red-Nosed Reindeer** (1964) introduced audiences to the Island of Misfit Toys, a place populated with odd toys, such as a kite with acrophobia, a piggy bank without a slot, a plane that couldn't fly, and a boomerang that didn't return when thrown. That same island is the principal setting for this *Rudolph* sequel, and the computer animation simulates the stop-motion puppet-action that was featured in the original Rankin-Bass production.

Rudolph, his doe-friend Clarice, misfit elf-turned-dentist Hermey, prospector Yukon Cornelius, and Abominable Snow Monster Bumbles all reprise their roles to save Christmas from another bogey. This time, it's the mysterious Toy Taker, who hypnotizes toys the world over with tunes played on his magic flute, then transports them to his blimp flying overhead. Sailing back home after fixing King Moonracer's tooth, Hermey and Rudolph encounter a storm that blows them to Castaway Cove, a region ruled by Queen Camilla where broken toys are mended, and Rudolph considers having his nose fixed, but not yet. Back in Christmas Town, when word arrives that the Toy Taker has robbed Santa's warehouse as well as Castaway Cove, Rudolph and all of his companions disguise themselves as toys and wait for the Toy Taker on the Island of Misfit Toys. As expected, he strikes, sucks up everyone into his transport tube except the enormous Bumbles, and an altercation erupts on the blimp, whereupon Toy Taker bails out and dashes into Cornelius's Peppermint Mine with Rudolph and

Clarice in hot pursuit. After an extended chase in mine carts (reminiscent of the scene in *Indiana Jones and the Temple of Doom*), Toy Taker is cornered, just as Santa, Mrs. Claus, and the remaining principals arrive to unmask the villain. Instead of a fiend, the Toy Taker is nothing more than Mr. Cuddles, a ragged little teddy bear on stilts, who had been a Christmas gift to a little boy years ago and had become disheartened when the boy grew up. So, Cuddles set out to ensure that other toys would never suffer as he did. Courtesy of Queen Camilla, Cuddles receives a makeover and becomes a Christmas present for the little daughter of the same man who had once had him in years past. Of course, Cuddles returns all the stolen toys, and Rudolph decides that no one will ever change his nose.

SONGS: "Rudolph, the Red-Nosed Reindeer" by Johnny Marks (performed by Tony Bennett). Other original songs by Bruce Roberts and Diana B (with performers in parentheses): "Beyond the Stars" (Clark Anderson); "Keep Your Chin Up" (Kathleen Barr and Scott McNeil); "The Island of Misfit Toys" (Bruce Roberts, Kathleen Barr, and Scott McNeil); "Beautiful Like Me" (Shawn King and Bruce Roberts); "The Toy Taker" (Bruce Roberts); "Mr. Cuddles" (Bruce Roberts); "The Best Christmas Ever" (Shawn King, Scott McNeil, Garry Chalk, Bruce Roberts, Nick Di Fruscia, Diana Bulgarelli, and David Tobocman).

PRINCIPAL VOICES: Richard Dreyfuss (*Jaws*) as narrator Scoop the Snowman; Jamie Lee Curtis (*Halloween*) as Queen Camilla; Richard Moranis (*Ghostbusters*) as Toy Taker/Mr. Cuddles; Kathleen Barr (*ReBoot*) as Rudolph and Mrs. Claus; Scott McNeil (*Dragon Ball Z*) as Hermey, Cornelius, and Coach Comet; Garry Chalk (*Godzilla*) as Santa and Bumbles; Elizabeth Carol Savenkoff (*Watchtower*) as Clarice; Colin Murdock (*Altitude*) as King Moonracer.

AWARDS: In 2001, this picture received the following Video Premiere Award nominations: Best Animated Character Performance (Jamie Lee Curtis and Bill Kowalchuk), Best Animated Video Premiere Movie, Best Original Score, and Best Original Song ("Beyond the Stars" and "Beautiful Like Me").

REVIEW: Andy Webb of *The Movie Scene*: "[This film] is made for very young children ... the CGI animation is rudimentary ... [while] the story has charm the whole cheapness of the effects really pulls it down ... even the youngest of children will find the simplistic animation a little bit cheesy."

PRODUCTION CREDITS—Story: Kevin Hopps. Writer: Michael Aschner. Producer and Director: Bill Kowalchuk. Production Companies: A Cayre Brothers Presentation, Goodtimes Entertainment, GT Merchandising and Licensing Corp., Golden Books Family Entertainment, and Tundra Productions. Rating: Not rated. Genres: Animation, Comedy, Family, Musical. Country: USA. Run Time: 74 min.

REFERENCES: Crump, William D. *The Christmas Encyclopedia*. Third Edition. Jefferson, NC: McFarland, 2013.

Rudolph, the Red-Nosed Reindeer and the Island of Misfit Toys. Internet Movie Database. http://www.imdb.com/title/tt0293913/

Rudolph, the Red-Nosed Reindeer and the Island of Misfit Toys. New York: GoodTimes Entertainment, 2001. DVD Video.

Webb, Andy. *Rudolph, the Red-Nosed Reindeer and the Island of Misfit Toys. The Movie Scene*. http://www.themoviescene.co.uk/reviews/rudolph-and-the-red-nosed-reindeer-2001/rudolph-and-the-red-nosed-reindeer-2001.html

Wilson, Joanna. *Tis the Season TV: The Encyclopedia of Christmas-Themed Episodes, Specials and Made-for-TV Movies*. Akron, OH: 1701 Press, 2011.

Rudolph, the Red-Nosed Reindeer: The Movie—October 16, 1998

Animated Feature Film/Musical

THREAT TO CHRISTMAS: Having shut off the North Pole by closing her bridge, ice queen Stormella sends a howling blizzard to ruin Santa and Christmas.

HOW CHRISTMAS IS SAVED: Rudolph convinces Stormella to be "nice" and leads Santa's team through the storm.

SYNOPSIS AND COMMENTARY: Utilizing traditional cel animation, this musical remake of the 1964 television special adds a few twists to the original story line. Rudolph's peers still jeer at his red nose, except for Zoey, who replaces Clarice as his doe friend, and the wicked ice queen Stormella replaces the Abominable Snow Monster as Santa's nemesis. When Santa refuses to hand over Boone and Doggle, the two elves who accidentally ruin Stormella's ice garden, she closes her bridge, which isolates the North Pole, then promises to bury Santa's operation in ice if anyone crosses the bridge. Humiliated at the reindeer games, Rudolph runs away from Christmas Town as before and befriends Slyly, a Jersey-talking, albino Arctic fox, and Leonard the polar bear, who replace Hermey the elf and Yukon Cornelius. Stormella imprisons Zoey in an ice cave for having crossed the bridge while searching for her beau, and Rudolph learns of her predicament through new characters Aurora, Sparkle, Glitter, and Twinkle, the four tiny Sprites of the Northern Lights, who teach him how to use his bright nose to save Zoey. As the blizzard rages, an altercation with Stormella at her ice castle permits Rudolph to save her from toppling off a cliff, for which she in gratitude grants him one wish. But instead of asking for a normal nose, he merely asks her to "be nice." She complies, yet the blizzard is beyond her control and Santa is about to cancel Christmas, until Rudolph returns and goes down in history.

PRINCIPAL VOICES: Eric Pospisil (*Stellaluna*) as younger Rudolph; Kathleen Barr (*ReBoot*) as older Rudolph and Twinkle; John Goodman (*Roseanne*) as Santa; Whoopi Goldberg (*Call Me Claus*) as Stormella; Debbie Reynolds (*Singin' in the Rain*) as Mrs. Claus, Mitzi (Rudolph's mother), and Mrs. Prancer; Bob Newhart (*Elf*) as Leonard; Eric Idle (*Life of Brian*) as Slyly; Richard Simmons (*Sweatin' to the Oldies*) as Boone; Alec Willows (*Air Waves*) as Doggle and Prancer; Lee Tockar (*Johnny Test*) as Ridley (Stormella's butler), Milo, and Vixen; Garry Chalk (*Watchmen*) as Blitzen; Christopher Gray (*Fear*) as Arrow and Donner; Vanessa Morley (*Masterminds*) as young Zoey; Myriam Sirois (*Ranma ½*) as older Zoey and Glitter; Elizabeth Carol Savenkoff (*Watchtower*) as Aurora and Zoey's mother; Cathy Weseluck (*Ranma ½*) as Sparkle; Colin Murdock (*Altitude*) as Comet; David Kaye (*Ranma ½*) as Cupid; Paul Dobson (*Ranma ½*) as Dasher; Terry Klassen (*Ranma ½*) as Dancer.

Santa has a moment with Rudolph in *Rudolph, the Red-Nosed Reindeer: The Movie* **(1998) (Goodtimes Entertainment/Photofest).**

ORIGINAL MUSIC AND LYRICS: Michael Lloyd and Al Kasha.

SONGS AND (PERFORMERS): "Rudolph, the Red-Nosed Reindeer" by Johnny Marks (Clint Black); "Christmas Town" (The Pointer Sisters); "Santa's Family" (John Goodman); "It Could Be Worse" (Eric Idle); "What About His Nose" (cast); "Wonderful Christmastime" by Paul McCartney (Wings); "Show Me the Light (Love Theme)" (Michael Lloyd and Debby Lytton Lloyd); "We Can Make It" (Johnny Tillotson, Tommy Roe, and Brian Hyland); "I Hate Santa Claus" (Carmen Twillie); "Show Me the Light (Love Theme)" (Bill Medley and Jennifer Warnes); "The Sprites' Songs" (Debby Lytton Lloyd).

AWARDS: In 1999, this film received a Golden Reel Award nomination for Best Sound Editing in an Animated Feature and a Young Artist Award nomination for Best Animated Family Feature.

INTERESTING TIDBITS: The elf population in Santa's workshop is an integrated society with racial diversity, as are the four Sprites. Male and female elves of varying ages are equally represented.

Blatant discrimination is afoot during the reindeer games. Rudolph wins the sleigh race, despite the cheating of reindeer Arrow, a bully who vies for Zoey's affection, yet Rudolph is disqualified because his red nose supposedly "distracted" other competitors. A spineless Santa yields to the bigoted judges.

The film bombed at the box office, earning approximately $113,000 compared to its ten-million-dollar budget.

REVIEWS: According to the Rotten Tomatoes film review site, 40 percent of critics gave this production a positive review.

Todd McCarthy of *Variety* (October 19, 1998): "…bland as the lowest-end Saturday morning cartoons … will be palatable only to the very youngest of viewers."

Lawrence Van Gelder of *The New York Times* (October 16, 1998): "…plodding, though well-intended lesson in nasal tolerance may divert very young and indiscriminating audiences."

PRODUCTION CREDITS—Writer: Michael Aschner. Producer and Director: Bill Kowalchuk. Production Companies: Golden Books Family Entertainment, Cayre Brothers Productions, GoodTimes Entertainment, and Tundra Productions. Rating: G. Genres: Animation, Adventure, Family. Countries: Canada and USA. Run Time: 83 min.

REFERENCES: Crump, William D. *The Christmas Encyclopedia*. Third Edition. Jefferson, NC: McFarland, 2013.

Lenburg, Jeff. *The Encyclopedia of Animated Cartoons*. Third Edition. New York: Facts on File, 2009.

McCarthy, Todd. "Review: *Rudolph, the Red-Nosed Reindeer: The Movie*." Variety. http://variety.com/1998/film/reviews/rudolph-the-red-nosed-reindeer-the-movie-1117487795/#

Rudolph, the Red-Nosed Reindeer: The Movie. Big Cartoon Database. http://www.bcdb.com/cartoon/25029-Rudolph-The-Red-Nosed-Reindeer-The-Movie/

Rudolph, the Red-Nosed Reindeer: The Movie. Internet Movie Database. http://www.imdb.com/title/tt0137201/

Rudolph, the Red-Nosed Reindeer: The Movie. New York: GoodTimes Entertainment, 2001. DVD Video.

Rudolph, the Red-Nosed Reindeer: The Movie. Rotten Tomatoes. http://www.rottentomatoes.com/m/rudolph_the_red_nosed_reindeer_the_movie/

Van Gelder, Lawrence. "Different but Determined to Beat the Christmas Rush." *The New York Times*. http://www.nytimes/library/film/101698rudolph-film-review.html

Wilson, Joanna. *Tis the Season TV: The Encyclopedia of Christmas-Themed Episodes, Specials and Made-for-TV Movies*. Akron, OH: 1701 Press, 2011.

Santa and the Ice Cream Bunny—1972

Feature Film

THREAT TO CHRISTMAS: Santa's sleigh becomes stuck in the sand on a beach in Florida.

HOW CHRISTMAS IS SAVED: The Ice Cream Bunny comes to Santa's rescue.

SYNOPSIS AND COMMENTARY: Given the title above, if viewers have the ole feeling that this is a bizarre children's fantasy film with a threadbare plot, they would be correct. A few days before Christmas, Santa (Jay Clark AKA Jay Ripley) takes the reindeer sleigh out for a test run and becomes stuck in the sand in Florida, the hot climate having induced the reindeer to bolt and return to the North Pole. In Santa's absence at the North Pole, several children posing as elves diddle with toys and incoherently sing "tra-la-la-la-la" about his not being there. Santa summons the local children (including Tom Sawyer and Huck Finn who float in on a raft and do nothing but observe from a distance), who attach a host of different beasts to the sleigh (dog, pig, mule, sheep, cow, horse, and even a man in a gorilla suit). When the sleigh still won't budge, Santa encourages the children to "believe" (in something), then launches into "Thumbelina," a fairy tale by Hans Christian Andersen, which has absolutely nothing to do with Christmas. Here, consuming most of the run time (over one hour), the film inserts *Thumbelina* (1970), an otherwise failed film starring Shay Garner as the title character and directed by Barry Mahon (*Fanny Hill Meets Lady Chatterly*, *Cuban Rebel Girls*, *The Diary of Knockers McCalla*) as an advertisement for Pirates World, a now-defunct Florida theme park where *Thumbelina* and *Bunny* were filmed. Following the tale, the children grab the Ice Cream Bunny (sans ice cream and looking more like a huge, white Easter Bunny sporting an oversized animal costume) from Pirates World, who enters the picture at the last minute driving an antique fire truck. As he takes Santa away, presumably back to the North Pole, the sleigh disappears.

INTERESTING TIDBITS: Alternate prints of *Santa and the Ice Cream Bunny* have Santa telling the story of "Jack and the Beanstalk," also adapted by Barry Mahon.

Much footage is wasted on Santa's bemoaning his predicament, falling asleep, wiping the sweat from his brow (eventually he does remove his coat), and frying his retinas by looking directly at the sun.

The elves and beach children are only credited as a group: "Kids" from Ruth Foreman's Pied Piper Playhouse. One of them, Kim Nicholas (the blonde elf kissing a Raggedy Ann doll), would later star in several films, such as *Limbo* (1972), *Impulse* (1974), and *Black Sunday* (1977). Also not credited is the narrator, Dorothy Green.

Compare the description of the film above with the text of its promotional advertisement: "The amazing story of Santa in big trouble … and his exciting rescue by the daring Ice Cream Bunny…. It's breathtaking, fun for all." Perhaps the PR department was a wee bit overzealous.

Opening in 1967 in Dania, Florida, Pirates World was a buccaneer theme park that was developed by Recreation Corporation of America. It did well until Walt Disney World opened in 1971, and by 1973, Pirates World was bankrupt; it did not operate beyond 1975.

Santa and the Ice Cream Bunny has been lampooned on RiffTrax.

REVIEWS: Critics generally consider this movie to be such a farce that it has become a cult classic.

Tim Brayton of *Antagony and Ecstasy* (April 6, 2015): "…its execution is at places so determinedly bereft of even the most limited, accidental filmmaking talent that it doesn't seem right to call the resultant object an actual work of cinema."

Fred Belden of *AllMovie*: "…there isn't even a token nod to the usual homilies of the season (good will toward men, importance of family, etc.), making [the film] as crass a Christmas exploitation as there ever was, an interesting but utterly insulting failure."

Scott W. Davis of *Moviocrity* (December 22, 2014): "…the strangest Christmas film…. It's a cheapie and the whole film is actually a cheat … it's one thing to read [about the film] and another to see it."

PRODUCTION CREDITS—Writer: Not credited. Executive Producer: C.T. Robertson. Director: R. Winer. Production Company: R & S Film Enterprises. Rating: G. Genres: Fantasy, Family. Country: USA. Run Time: 96 min.

REFERENCES: Belden, Fred. *Santa and the Ice Cream Bunny. AllMovie*. http://www.allmovie.com/movie/santa-and-the-ice-cream-bunny-v42829/review

Brayton, Tim. "Santa on the Beach." *Antagony and Ecstasy*. http://antagonie.blogspot.com/2015/04/santa-on-beach.html

Davis, Scott W. "Jingle Bell Schlock!:Non-Traditional Christmas Films You May Have Missed (Part 2 of 4)." *Moviocrity*. http://moviocrity.com/2014/12/22/jingle-bell-schlock-2/

Duralde, Alonso. *Have Yourself a Movie Little Christmas*. New York: Limelight Editions, 2010.

"Pirates World." Florida's Lost Tourist Attractions. http://www.lostparks.com/piratesw.html

RiffTrax: Santa and the Ice Cream Bunny. Legend Films, 2011. DVD Video.

Santa and the Ice Cream Bunny. Internet Movie Database. http://www.imdb.com/title/tt0138074/

Wilson, Joanna. *Tis the Season TV: The Encyclopedia of Christmas-Themed Episodes, Specials and Made-for-TV Movies*. Akron, OH: 1701 Press, 2011.

Santa, Baby!—December 17, 2001

Animated Television Movie

THREAT TO CHRISTMAS: Santa breaks his leg while skiing.

HOW CHRISTMAS IS SAVED: A struggling songwriter and his daughter deliver Santa's presents.

SYNOPSIS AND COMMENTARY: In 1953, Joan Javits, Philip Springer, and Tony Springer wrote "Santa Baby," a song that has now become a Christmas classic. Intended for a seductive, female singer, the blatantly materialistic lyrics detail the mind-boggling Christmas list of a kept woman in exchange for her sole affections. The song was first recorded and made popular by the African American pop singer Eartha Kitt. This animated production is *very* loosely based on that song and is the first Rankin/Bass holiday special to feature an all-African American cast, which includes Eartha Kitt.

When little Dakota rescues the nearly frozen Melody Birdsong, a magical Christmas partridge, she receives one wish. But rather than use it on herself, Dakota bestows it upon her father Noel, a songwriter who needs a hit song (which is *not* "Santa Baby" but "Heart and Soul of Christmas") to overcome his creative slump. As the wish unfolds, Noel and Dakota make Christmas Eve rounds for Santa (who broke his leg while skiing), find Christmas homes for animals from a local shelter, and bring the spirit of a soulful Christmas to their otherwise economically depressed neighborhood.

PRINCIPAL VOICES: Gregory Hines (*The Cotton Club*) as Noel; Kianna Underwood (*Little Bill*) as Dakota; Patti LaBelle (*The Patti LaBelle Show*) as Melody Songbird; Vanessa Williams (*Ugly Betty*) as Alicia; Eartha Kitt (*The Wolf of Wall Street*) as Emerald; Tom Joyner (*The Tom Joyner Show*) as Mr. Sweet.

AWARDS: In 2003, this production received a nomination from the Writers Guild of America for Animation.

INTERESTING TIDBITS: To give Noel inspiration for his song, Melody compels him to dress in a Santa suit and ring the collection bell on the street as well as perform various acts of charity around the neighborhood. Her nickname for him in this capacity is "Santa, Baby."

Noel's hit song, "Heart and Soul of Christmas," is by Glen Roven and Gary Haase.

PRODUCTION CREDITS—Teleplay: Peter Bakalian and Suzanne Collins. Producer: Peter Bakalian. Director: Lee Dannacher. Production Company: Rankin/Bass Productions. Rating: G. Genres: Animation, Family. Country: USA. Run Time: 60 min.

REFERENCES: Crump, William D. *The Christmas Encyclopedia*. Third Edition. Jefferson, NC: McFarland, 2013.

Lenburg, Jeff. *The Encyclopedia of Animated Cartoons*. Third Edition. New York: Facts on File, 2009.

Santa, Baby! Internet Movie Database. http://www.imdb.com/title/tt0358103/

Santa, Baby! New York: Hart Sharp Video, 2001. DVD Video.

Wilson, Joanna. *Tis the Season TV: The Encyclopedia of Christmas-Themed Episodes, Specials and Made-for-TV Movies*. Akron, OH: 1701 Press, 2011.

Santa Baby—December 10, 2006

Television Movie

THREAT TO CHRISTMAS: Santa suffers a heart attack a month before Christmas.

HOW CHRISTMAS IS SAVED: Santa's daughter

leaves the real world and returns to the North Pole to take over for him.

SYNOPSIS AND COMMENTARY: When Santa (George Wendt, *Cheers*) suffers a heart attack one month before Christmas (it's ironic that a seemingly immortal Christmas icon would be depicted as having health problems), the North Pole summons his daughter, Mary Class (Jenny McCarthy, *The View*), to return home from the outside world. A successful business executive, Mary seizes the opportunity to modernize the family business and save Christmas, but in doing so, she turns the North Pole upside down. For example, a toy-making machine replaces the elves, cookie breaks are eliminated, and the mail room becomes a data-processing center. The sudden changes overwhelm the simple-minded elves and morale declines, despite the fact that production is at an all-time high. Meanwhile, a renewed relationship with her childhood boyfriend Luke Jessup (Ivan Sergei, *The Break-Up*) and a business proposal from her current boyfriend-assistant Grant Foley (Tobias Mehler, *Carrie*) to build a mall next to the North Pole (which would bring tourists and chaos to the previously secret location of Santa's workshop) put spice and complexity into Christmas. Eventually, Mary learns that Daddy-Santa's old-fashioned Christmas traditions far outweigh ruthlessly cold efficiency.

INTERESTING TIDBITS: Originally airing on the ABC Family channel, this film boasted more than 4.7 million viewers at the time, which made it the most-watched original movie for that channel. Without a doubt, Ms. McCarthy provided the principal incentive for watching this film.

This film should not be confused with the animated television production **Santa, Baby!** (2001).

Check out the sequel, ***Santa Baby 2: Christmas Maybe***.

REVIEWS: Emily Ashby of *Common Sense Media* (November 19, 2007): "...full of snowy scenery, chipper elves, twists on Christmas tradition and lore (the religious aspect of the holiday isn't addressed), and holiday spirit ... themes of love, forgiveness, and respect."

Adam Buckman of the *New York Post* (October 17, 2007): "So why's the movie titled *Santa Baby*? ... it might have something to do with sexpot/pinup girl Jenny McCarthy.... I guess she's Santa's 'baby' ... [the film bears] similarities to many of the dozens of made-for-TV Christmas movies ... so wholesome that buxom Jenny bares no cleavage whatsoever..."

PRODUCTION CREDITS—Writers: Garrett Frawley and Brian Turner. Producers: Tom Cox, Craig McNeil, Murray Ord, and Jordy Randall. Director: Ron Underwood. Production Companies: "Mary Christmas" Filmproduktions [sic] and Alberta Film Entertainment. Rating: PG (mild language and sensuality). Genres: Comedy, Fantasy. Countries: Canada, Germany, and USA. Run Time: 89 min.

REFERENCES: Ashby, Emily. *Santa Baby*. Common Sense Media. https://www.commonsensemedia.org/movie-reviews/santa-baby

Buckman, Adam. "Santa's Kid: Wendt and McCarthy Dole Out Some Christmas Cheer." *New York Post*. https://web.archive.org/web/20090112151120/http://www.nypost.com/seven/12092006/tv/santas_kid_tv_adam_buckman.htm

Crump, William D. *The Christmas Encyclopedia*. Third Edition. Jefferson, NC: McFarland, 2013.

Santa Baby. Internet Movie Database. http://www.imdb.com/title/tt0772185/

Santa Baby. Santa Monica, CA: Lionsgate, 2007. DVD Video.

Wilson, Joanna. *Tis the Season TV: The Encyclopedia of Christmas-Themed Episodes, Specials and Made-for-TV Movies*. Akron, OH: 1701 Press, 2011.

Santa Baby 2: Christmas Maybe—December 13, 2009

Television Movie

THREAT TO CHRISTMAS: Suffering a late-life crisis, Santa forsakes his duties at the North Pole while a disgruntled elf plots to take over Christmas.

HOW CHRISTMAS IS SAVED: Santa's daughter returns to the North Pole to battle the interloper.

SYNOPSIS AND COMMENTARY: In this sequel

to ***Santa Baby*** (2006), Jenny McCarthy (*The View*) reprises her role as Mary Class, Santa's (Paul Sorvino, *Goodfellas*) platinum-blonde-bombshell daughter, who once again leaves her business enterprises in the lower 48 and returns home to the North Pole to save Christmas when Santa suffers a late-life crisis. Weary of his responsibilities, Santa has abandoned his workshop in preference for such pursuits as jazz music and golf. In his absence, Phoebe (Kelly Stables, *The Exes*), a disgruntled little elf, disguises herself as the ambitious newcomer Teri, who sows discord in the workshop with an intent to take over Christmas as the next Santa. As the two women battle for control, Teri not only thwarts Mary's efforts to put the workshop back on track by organizing an elf strike, but she also competes for Luke (Dean McDermott, *Chopped Canada*), Mary's boyfriend. Feeling guilty about abandoning the world's children, Santa eventually decides to resume his position on Christmas Eve, whereupon Teri incapacitates Santa and Mrs. Claus (Lynne Griffin, *Strange Brew*) by tying them up and boxing them in a crate. When Mary discovers Phoebe's ruse, the latter dashes off in the sleigh with what she assumes to be the sack of toys while hollering, *"Christmas is mine!"* Mary with Luke and Santa (yes, he escapes) track her to a little house, where Phoebe destroys the sack, which contained only cookies, not toys. Though Santa is most forgiving, time runs short, so Santa and daughter divide up the reindeer team and take off in two separate sleighs on Christmas rounds.

Interesting Tidbits: At Teri's prompting, the elves confront Mary with a list of demands in the following order: a 20 percent pay raise; being paid at all (yes, they put the cart before the horse); a store in which to spend money; a credit union; Monopoly money; cookies with sprinkles on the top *and* bottom; hats with cups for hot cocoa; trampolines at each work station; jetpacks; and a pet chipmunk for each elf. There are more demands, but at that point, Mary rips up the list, and the elves go on strike.

At its first airing on the ABC Family Channel, this film ranked as cable's number one telecast in its time period, pulling in 3.8 million viewers. Ms. McCarthy did it again, just as she did in this film's predecessor.

Reviews: Emily Ashby of *Common Sense Media* (December 13, 2009): "…blend of comedy, holiday spirit, and family-friendly messages. Rare instances of salty language and some mild sexual references … lovely scenery, jolly elves, and imaginative spin on traditional Christmas folklore."

Robert Lloyd of the *Los Angeles Times* (December 12, 2009): "Like its predecessor, it is clever and charming, if, apparently, anti-union."

Production Credits—Writers: Garrett Frawley and Brian Turner. Producers: Tom Cox, Craig McNeil, Murray Ord, and Jordy Randall. Director: Ron Underwood. Production Companies: Alberta Film Entertainment and Well Done Productions. Rating: Not rated. Genres: Comedy, Fantasy. Countries: Canada and USA. Run Time: 85 min.

References: "ABC Family Original Movie, 'Santa Baby 2: Christmas Maybe,' Ranks As Cable's No. 1 Telecast in Its Time Period." *The Futon Critic*. http://www.thefutoncritic.com/ratings/2009/12/15/abc-family-original-movie-santa-baby-2-christmas-maybe-ranks-as-cables-no-1-telecast-in-its-time-period-33847/20091215abcfamily01/

Ashby, Emily. *Santa Baby 2: Christmas Maybe. Common Sense Media.* https://www.commonsensemedia.org/movie-reviews/santa-baby-2-christmas-maybe

Crump, William D. *The Christmas Encyclopedia*. Third Edition. Jefferson, NC: McFarland, 2013.

Lloyd, Robert. "5 New Christmas Tales on Cable Neatly Tied Up with a Bow." *Los Angeles Times*. http://articles.latimes.com/2009/dec/12/entertainment/la-et-christmas12-2009dec12

Santa Baby 2: Christmas Maybe. Internet Movie Database. http://www.imdb.com/title/tt1361330/

Santa Baby 2: Christmas Maybe. Louisville, CO: Gaiam Americas, 2010. DVD Video.

Wilson, Joanna. *Tis the Season TV: The Encyclopedia of Christmas-Themed Episodes, Specials and Made-for-TV Movies*. Akron, OH: 1701 Press, 2011.

Santa Buddies: The Legend of Santa Paws—November 24, 2009

Direct-to-Video Film

THREAT TO CHRISTMAS: The Christmas Icicle at the North Pole is quickly melting, because too many people in the world have lost the true meaning of Christmas. A total meltdown would put an end to Christmas.

HOW CHRISTMAS IS SAVED: Santa Paws and the Buddies bring the Christmas spirit to a wretched dogcatcher and fill in for Santa's reindeer who lack the magic to pull his sleigh.

SYNOPSIS AND COMMENTARY: Christmas goes to the dogs with no dog in the manger in this adventure film, the fourth in the *Air Buddies* series, which is a spinoff from the *Air Bud* franchise, begun in 1997. The principal character in *Air Bud* is Buddy, a golden retriever that plays sports. The *Air Buddies* series, begun in 2006, focuses on the adventures of Buddy's five talking puppies collectively known as the "Buddies": Rosebud, the sister; Buddha, who meditates; Budderball, a glutton; Mudbud, who enjoys rolling in dirt; and B-Dawg, the rapper.

Deep in a cave at the North Pole lies the Christmas Icicle, an entity from which Santa (George Wendt, *Cheers*) and his elves (a mix of dwarves and young adults) draw their magical powers. Santa and his Great Pyrenees, Paws, are especially worried about the Icicle's melting because too many people in the world have become materialistic and neither believe in the true meaning of Christmas nor in Santa. Should the Icicle melt to nothing, Christmas will end. Meanwhile, Paws's son Puppy Paws has become disillusioned with the North Pole and has no desire to advance to his father's position. Wishing to be a normal puppy and believing that he could best learn from Budderball, who landed on Santa's naughty list for gobbling up a Thanksgiving turkey, Puppy flees the North Pole and journeys to the Air Buddies' hometown in Fernfield, Washington. There, he interacts with them in a series of misadventures and is captured and thrown into the dog pound by the ruthless dogcatcher Stan Cruge (Christopher Lloyd, *Back to the Future*), who has hated Christmas since his childhood, because Santa didn't bring him a puppy. From the North Pole, Santa sends Eli the elf (Danny Woodburn, *Mirror Mirror*) and his elf-dog Eddy, a Jack Russell terrier, to Fernfield to find Puppy. They and the Air Buddies not only rescue Puppy, who has experienced his own epiphany about the true meaning of Christmas, but also instill Cruge with the Christmas spirit, which is to give to those in need. Although the Christmas Icicle is on the mend, the reindeer are still powerless to fly, whereupon the Buddies save Christmas by pulling the sleigh with Puppy Paws taking Santa's role, led by B-Dawg who gains a "Rudolph" nose, thanks to the magic crystal in Puppy's collar.

DOG VOICES: Tom Bosley (*Happy Days*) as Santa Paws (this was Bosley's final role before his death on October 19, 2010); Field Cate (*Space Buddies*) as Buddha; Tim Conway (*McHale's Navy*) as Deputy Sniffer, a bloodhound; Chris Copploa (*Postal*) as Comet the Reindeer; Josh Flitter (*License to Wed*) as Budderball; Skyler Gisondo (*Vacation*) as B-Dawg; Zachary Gordon (*Diary of a Wimpy Kid*) as Puppy Paws; Richard Kind (*Inside Out*) as Eddy; Kaitlyn Maher (*The Search for Santa Paws*) as Tiny, a Yorkshire terrier; Liliana Mumy (*The Santa Clause 2*) as Rosebud; and Ty Panitz (*Super Buddies*) as Mudbud.

AWARDS: In 2010, this picture received a Young Artist Award nomination for Best Performance in a DVD film (Gig Morton).

In 2009, this film won a "Yulie," a spoof award from *Entertainment Weekly* for Tastiest Christmas Cookie Calamity. Dan Snierson: "Puppy Paws uses his magic powers to transform a tray of unattended plain cookies into multi-colored treats; then he gobbles them up and ducks out as the unhappy chef returns, in the process accidentally framing his friend, [Budderball]."

INTERESTING TIDBIT: Check out the prequel, ***The Search for Santa Paws.***

REVIEWS: According to the Rotten Tomatoes film review site, 20 percent of critics gave this production a positive review.

David Nusair of *Reel Film Reviews* (November 26, 2009): "…immediately establishes itself as a pointless and downright interminable family comedy that's almost entirely lacking in elements designed to appeal to older viewers."

Brian Orndorf of *DVD Talk* (November 25, 2009): "It's a tidy story but never remarkable, and a few burp jokes reveal disconcerting limitations to the goodwill of the film."

Sierra Filucci of *Common Sense Media* (November 23, 2009): "Popular puppy series adds a cheery holiday message."

PRODUCTION CREDITS—Writers and Producers: Anna McRoberts and Robert Vince. Director: Robert Vince. Production Companies: Walt Disney Pictures, Keystone Entertainment, and Santa Buddies Productions. Rating: G. Genres: Adventure, Family. Countries: Canada and USA. Run Time: 88 min.

REFERENCES: Crump, William D. *The Christmas Encyclopedia*. Third Edition. Jefferson, NC: McFarland, 2013.

Filucci, Sierra. *Santa Buddies. Common Sense Media*. https://www.commonsensemedia.org/movie-reviews/santa-buddies

Nusair, David. *Santa Buddies. Reel Film Reviews*. http://reelfilm.com/disfam7.htm#santa

Orndorf, Brian. *Santa Buddies: The Legend of Santa Paws. DVD Talk*. http://www.dvdtalk.com/reviews/38360/santa-buddies/

Santa Buddies. Rotten Tomatoes. http://www.rottentomatoes.com/m/santa_buddies/

Santa Buddies: The Legend of Santa Paws. Burbank, CA: Walt Disney Home Entertainment, 2009. DVD Video.

Santa Buddies: The Legend of Santa Paws. Internet Movie Database: http://www.imdb.com/title/tt1328875/

Santa Buddies: The Legend of Santa Paws. Official Web Site: http://buddies.disney.com/santa-buddies

Snierson, Dan. "The Third Annual Yulies: Let's Celebrate the Absurdity of Holiday TV Movies!" *Entertainment Weekly*. http://www.ew.com/article/2010/12/23/holiday-tv-movies-xmas-specials-yulies

Santa Claus—1959

Feature Film

THREAT TO CHRISTMAS: The devil Lucifer sends the demon Pitch to earth to sabotage Santa's gift-giving spree.

HOW CHRISTMAS IS SAVED: Water from a fire hose sends Pitch on the run.

SYNOPSIS AND COMMENTARY: In a classic, albeit bizarre, battle between good and evil, Santa (José Elías Moreno) teams up with Merlin (Armando Arriola "Arriolita"), his magician-in-residence (the same Merlin who was the sidekick to King Arthur), against the demon Pitch (José Luis Aguirre "Trotsky"), stereotypically clad all in red with horns and tail. Residing not at the North Pole but in a castle in outer space with a host of gadgets, Santa observes the goings-on down on Earth via a telescope with a built-in, retractable snake-like device that sports an "eye," similar to that used by the Martian invaders in *War of the Worlds*. Instead of elves, groups of young children from 16 nations or regions around the world assist Santa, who accompanies them on an organ during a snowfall as they sing traditional, non–Christmas songs peculiar to their respective cultures. Equipped with magic sleeping dust, a flower that produces invisibility (both courtesy of Merlin), and a key that unlocks all doors (courtesy of the castle blacksmith), Santa heads to earth on Christmas Eve in a toy sleigh with four mechanized, wind-up reindeer, from which contraption he descends by a rope ladder and enters homes either via doors or chimneys. Meanwhile, although Pitch on Earth tempts several children to do evil, most of them resist, except for three incorrigible little brothers, whom Santa rewards with lumps of coal in their shoes. Subplots revolve around Lupita (Lupita Quezadas), an impoverished little girl whom Santa has never visited, whom Pitch torments through dreams of macabre dancing rag dolls that tempt her to steal, and whom Santa rewards for her ultimate piety; and poor little rich boy Billy (Antonio Días Conde hijo), whom Santa reunites with his neglectful parents via a "cocktail of remembrance." Failing to sabotage Santa sufficiently, Pitch convinces Billy's family through dreams that Santa is an intruder, whereupon they summon the police, the fire department, the Red Cross, and all manner of other authorities for a full-scale circus of Christmas mayhem. Caught in the spraying water from the fire department, Pitch rapidly sizzles in smoke and departs,

Santa (José Elías Moreno) rebukes the demon Pitch (José Luis Aguirre "Trotsky") for trying to ruin Christmas in *Santa Claus* (1959) (K. Gordon Murray Productions/Photofest).

which smacks of the demise of the Wicked Witch of the West in *The Wizard of Oz*. The film ends on a religious note with the following printed message: "Blessed are they who believe for they shall see God. Peace on Earth good will toward men. Merry Christmas."

AWARDS: Received a Golden Gate Award at the San Francisco International Film Festival for Best International Family Film (1959).

INTERESTING TIDBITS: Originally released in Mexico, *Santa Claus* came to the land of the free and the home of the brave in 1960 via American film producer K. Gordon Murray, whose penchant was to obtain the rights to foreign films (chiefly Mexican fairy tales), redub the dialogue into English, and repackage them for American audiences. For his efforts, Murray was dubbed "King of the Kiddie Matinee." In the English-language version of *Santa Claus*, Murray provides narration under the name of Ken Smith.

To illustrate that *Santa Claus* was produced during an era not influenced by political correctness, the children's song sequences at the beginning show half-clad African children sporting bones in their hair of all things and dancing to drums.

An episode of *Mystery Science Theater 3000* lampooned *Santa Claus* on Christmas Eve, 1993, after which Pitch (there played by Paul Chaplin) became a recurring character on the show.

Before Pitch goes topside to wreak havoc with Santa, he and other demons perform a dance in hell and are surrounded by a group of figures in white robes and hoods who bear a striking resemblance to members of the Ku Klux Klan.

Despite its bizarre story line and the fact that most American critics consider it to be one of the worst Christmas movies ever made, *Santa Claus* has become the equivalent of *It's a Wonderful Life* in many Spanish-speaking countries, where it is telecast annually.

REVIEWS: *Cool Cinema Trash* (November 30, 2008): "Words cannot express the severity of holiday weirdness on display in *Santa Claus* (1959), a children's fantasy that mixes religious and secular traditions into an intoxicating brew that is sure to leave even the strongest bad movie fan with an unforgettable holiday hangover."

Alonso Duralde in *Have Yourself a Movie Little Christmas*: "After your first exposure to *Santa Claus*, watch out: Its crazy energetic pull will have you going back for just one more look (because the last time you couldn't quite believe your own eyes)…"

PRODUCTION CREDITS—Writers: Adolfo Torres Portillo and René Cardona. Producer: Guillermo Calderón Stell. Director: René Cardona. Production Company: Cinematográfica Calderón S.A. Rating: Not rated. Genres: Comedy, Family, Fantasy. Country: Mexico. Run Time: 94 min.

REFERENCES: Duralde, Alonso. *Have Yourself a Movie Little Christmas*. New York: Limelight Editions, 2010.

Rose, Michael. "Weird Christmas: 'Santa Claus' (1959)." Mysterious Universe. http://mysteriousuniverse.org/2013/12/weird-christmas-santa-claus-1959/

Santa Claus. Cool Cinema Trash. http://www.coolcinematrash.com/cctmovies/santa-claus/

Santa Claus. Internet Movie Database. http://www.imdb.com/title/tt0053241/

Santa Claus. VCI Entertainment, 2011. DVD Video.

Wilson, Joanna. *Tis the Season TV: The Encyclopedia of Christmas-Themed Episodes, Specials and Made-for-TV Movies*. Akron, OH: 1701 Press, 2011.

The Santa Claus Brothers—December 14, 2001

Computer-Animated Television Movie

THREAT TO CHRISTMAS: Snorkel the head elf plans to get rid of Santa's three sons and be the new Santa who turns a profit.

HOW CHRISTMAS IS SAVED: Snorkel's plans only succeed in getting him demoted when Santa decides not to retire.

SYNOPSIS AND COMMENTARY: Santa is thinking of retiring, but he's not sure that his sons, 150-year-old triplets Daryl (a party animal), Roy (obsessed with numbers), and Mel (always plays with toys), are ready to take over, because they still don't know the true meaning of Christmas. So what has dear old dad been teaching his boys for the last 150 years—the art of eating cookies and milk, the proper inflections to give "Ho Ho Ho," or how to keep the elves from forming a union? To see which son would be a worthy replacement, Santa sends them out into the world early on Christmas Eve to *Santa* Monica, CA, because that name may give them some inspiration; the one who learns the meaning of Christmas and is the first to return by nightfall will be the successor. It they fail, then Snorkel the head elf will take over temporarily. But Snorkel, desiring to be the new Santa permanently who would turn a profit, schemes to oust the sons and separately gives each one a cock-and-bull version of the true meaning of Christmas: to Mel, it's the perfect toy; to Daryl, the perfect party; and to Roy, the perfect number. Having never driven dad's new reindeer sleigh before, the sons crash it onto Santa Monica beach and go their separate ways, while elf Busby, a stowaway, hides it so that the sons cannot return to the North Pole. As expected, the three learn nothing about Christmas using Snorkel's bogus tips, but when Santa finds them as the deadline approaches (Santa also having crashed his old sleigh onto the beach, thanks to Snorkel's sabotage), the sons discover that they had unwittingly given joy, the true meaning of Christmas (without religious implications), to everyone they had encountered, despite their own selfish pursuits. Busby takes them all back home in the new sleigh, Snorkel is demoted, and Santa decides that Christmas will be better off if he remains on the job after all.

PRINCIPAL VOICES: Bryan Cranston (*Breaking Bad*) as Santa; Caroline Rhea (*The Perfect Man*) as Mrs. Claus; Harland Williams (*Half Baked*) as Daryl; Richard Kind (*A Bug's Life*) as Roy; Kevin McDonald (*Epic Movie*) as Mel; Joe Flaherty (*Happy Gilmore*) as Snorkel.

AWARDS: In 2002, this film won a Daytime Emmy for Outstanding Individual in Animation (Michael Bedard, production designer).

PRODUCTION CREDITS—Writers: Jon Cooksey and Ali Marie Matheson. Producer: Pam Lehn. Director: Mike Fallows. Production Companies: Film Roman Productions, Nelvana, Sitting Duck Productions, and YTV. Rating: Not rated. Genres: Animation, Family, Fantasy. Countries: Canada and USA. Run Time: 47 min.

REFERENCES: *The Santa Claus Brothers*. Internet Movie Database. http://www.imdb.com/title/tt0307410/

The Santa Claus Brothers. Our Time Family Entertainment and Nelvana Ltd, 2004. DVD Video.

Wilson, Joanna. *Tis the Season TV: The Encyclopedia of Christmas-Themed Episodes, Specials and Made-for-TV Movies*. Akron, OH: 1701 Press, 2011.

Santa Claus Conquers the Martians

Also Known As *Santa Claus Defeats the Aliens*

November 14, 1964

Feature Film

THREAT TO CHRISTMAS: Desiring that their children should learn to have fun like the children on Earth, Martians kidnap Santa and take him to their planet to set up a toy factory.

HOW CHRISTMAS IS SAVED: One Martian learns to portray Santa so well that the Martians release the real Santa back to Earth just in time for Christmas Eve.

SYNOPSIS AND COMMENTARY: In most save-Christmas movies, the bogeys involved usually threaten to shut down or destroy Santa's operation at the North Pole, but in the present film, Santa is packed off to Mars.

Because Martian children are not permitted to laugh or play, they amuse themselves by watching television shows from Earth about Santa Claus. Noting this in his own children, Bomar ("Boy Martian," Chris Month, *The Doctors and the Nurses*) and Girmar ("Girl Martian," Pia Zadora, *Hairspray*), Martian ruler Kimar ("King Martian," Leonard Hicks, *Route 66*) consults Chochem the Ancient One (Carl Don, *Ransom*), who advises that Mars should have its own Santa Claus figure. Kimar takes this advice literally and heads to Earth with his officers, but when a plethora of street Santas only confuses them, they kidnap Billy and Betty (Victor Stiles and Donna Conforti), two young siblings who direct the Martians to the North Pole, and a most cooperative Santa (John Call, *Fearless Fagan*) is whisked away to the red planet. Now with assistance from Billy and Betty, Santa sets up an automated toymaking factory on Mars and turns out products that please their captors except for Officer Voldar (Vincent Beck, *Vigilante*), who opposes the whole business because, in his opinion, Santa and toys will only steer the Martians away from their warlike legacy. Voldar unsuccessfully attempts to murder Santa and the two Earth children on several occasions as well as sabotage the factory and is finally arrested for his treachery. Meanwhile, because Kimar's excessively enthusiastic (if not dimwitted) assistant Dropo (Bill McCutcheon, *Steel Magnolias*) emulates Santa perfectly, Dropo becomes the new Martian St. Nick, and Santa returns to Earth with Billy and Betty.

INTERESTING TIDBITS: Over the years, this picture has received consistently dismal reviews and is featured in Medved and Dreyfuss's *The Fifty Worst Films of All Time*, a book that alphabetically lists the 50 worst sound films ever made. *Martians* is the only Christmas film vilified in that book.

Three members of the principal cast came from the Broadway stage: John Call (Santa) and Victor Stiles (Billy) from the original Broadway company of *Oliver*, where Call's role was Dr. Grimwig and Stiles's role was initially one of Fagin's boys and later the title role; Donna Conforti (Betty) from Meredith Willson's *Here's Love*, a musical adaptation of *Miracle on 34th Street*, in which she was a little Dutch girl.

This is the first film to depict a Mrs. Claus, played by Doris Rich, and child actress Pia Zadora, who sang the theme song "Hooray for Santy Claus" (by Roy Alfred and Milton Delugg), made her screen debut here as Girmar.

The opening credits spell "Costume Designer" as "Custume Designer."

The film, shot in ten days in an old airport

Though he's been kidnapped, Santa (John Call) brings Christmas and happiness to the humanoid alien beings of Mars in *Santa Claus Conquers the Martians* (1964). With Santa are Earth children, Betty (Donna Conforti, far left) and Billy (Victor Stiles, far right); and hokey Martians, Girmar (Pia Zadora, third from left), Dropo (Bill McCutcheon), Bomar (Chris Month), and Kimar (Leonard Hicks) (Embassy Pictures Corp. Collection of William D. Crump).

hangar-turned-studio on an estimated budget of $200,000, has been lampooned on *Mystery Science Theater 3000* and by *Cinematic Titanic*. Among all that could be riffed would especially be the robot Torg, which is little more than someone attired in a glorified Halloween costume, and the person in a polar bear suit, who lunges at the two Earth children en route to Santa's abode.

Other save-Christmas films in which Santa is kidnapped include **The Boy Who Saved Christmas; The Elf and the Magic Key; The Glo Friends Save Christmas; The Great Santa Claus Switch; The Librarians and Santa's Midnight Run; Sonic Christmas Blast; Spinach Greetings; Tim Burton's The Nightmare Before Christmas**; and **Who Stole Santa?**

REVIEWS: According to the Rotten Tomatoes film review site, 25 percent of critics gave this film a positive review.

TV Guide: "This is, without exaggeration, one of the single worst films ever made, which hasn't prevented it from becoming a cult classic ... amateurish production and worthless acting..."

Ryan Cracknell of *Movie Views* (December 15, 2003): "...like a car accident unfolding before your eyes, it's impossible to look away even if only to see how just bad it can get."

Will Brownridge of *The Film Reel* (December 20, 2009): "...so bad it's good. And it really is bad, but the kind of bad that brings back fuzzy warm memories of long forgotten movies.... Quite a convincing portrayal [of

Santa] if I've ever seen one, but it's his complete disregard for anything bad happening that is so funny."

Alonso Duralde in *Have Yourself a Movie Little Christmas*: "…few celluloid stinkers reach the depths of *Santa Claus Conquers the Martians*, a movie that combines a loony high-concept plot … condescending film-making … and a thoroughly pervasive sense of inanity."

PRODUCTION CREDITS—Story: Paul L. Jacobson. Screenplay: Glenville Mareth. Producer: Paul L. Jacobson. Director: Nicholas Webster. Production Company: Jalor Productions. Rating: Not rated. Genres: Comedy, Family, Science Fiction. Country: USA. Run Time: 81 min.

REFERENCES: Brownridge, Will. *Santa Claus Conquers the Martians. The Film Reel.* http://www.the-filmreel.com/2009/12/20/santa-claus-conquers-the-martians-film-reel-reviews/

Cracknell, Ryan. *Santa Claus Conquers the Martians. Movie Views.* http://www.movieviews.ca/santa-claus-conquers-the-martians

Crump, William D. *The Christmas Encyclopedia.* Third Edition. Jefferson, NC: McFarland, 2013.

Duralde, Alonso. *Have Yourself a Movie Little Christmas.* New York: Limelight Editions, 2010.

Medved, Harry, and Randy Dreyfuss. *The Fifty Worst Films of All Time (and How They Got That Way).* New York: Popular Library, 1978.

Santa Claus Conquers the Martians. Internet Movie Database. http://www.imdb.com/title/tt0058548/

Santa Claus Conquers the Martians. Narberth, PA: Alpha Video, 2004. DVD Video.

Santa Claus Conquers the Martians. Rotten Tomatoes. http://www.rottentomatoes.com/m/santa_claus_conquers_the_martians/

Santa Claus Conquers the Martians. TV Guide. http://www.tvguide.com/movies/santa-claus-conquers-the-martians/review/116767/

Wilson, Joanna. *Tis the Season TV: The Encyclopedia of Christmas-Themed Episodes, Specials and Made-for-TV Movies.* Akron, OH: 1701 Press, 2011.

Santa Claus: The Movie—November 27, 1985

Feature Film

THREAT TO CHRISTMAS: B.Z., an evil toy magnate, plans to put an end to Santa and take over Christmas.

HOW CHRISTMAS IS SAVED: B.Z. falls victim to his own greedy scheme.

SYNOPSIS AND COMMENTARY: Sometime in the distant past, master wood-carver Claus (David Huddleston, *Blazing Saddles*) and his wife Anya (Judy Cornwell, *Keeping Up Appearances*) perish in a blizzard while delivering Christmas toys to children in their village and find themselves the expected immortals in a magical, polar world of toymaking Vendequm, better known as elves. According to the Ancient Elf (Burgess Meredith, *Grumpy Old Men*), Claus, thereafter dubbed "Santa Claus," has fulfilled the prophecy of a childless "Chosen One" (not quite a messiah), an artisan sent to deliver the elves' gifts of toys to the world's children on Christmas Eve. As centuries pass and Santa enters the twentieth century, he chooses an assistant, Patch (Dudley Moore, *Arthur*), an elf bent on modernizing the workshop with automated technology. But Patch loses his position because his assembly lines produce inferior toys, whereupon he journeys out into the world and unwittingly falls into the hands of a greedy New York City toy magnate, B.Z. (John Lithgow, *3rd Rock from the Sun*), whom a Senate subcommittee has investigated for marketing cheap, dangerous toys. Desiring to create something special that will restore Santa's faith in him, Patch produces the "Puce Pop," a lollipop that, when eaten, allows the consumer to walk on air, which takes the world by storm that Christmas. Santa, seemingly outdone, questions whether children will ever need him anymore. Intending to take over Christmas, B.Z. persuades a clueless Patch to alter his candy invention so that people can fly, but two children overhear B.Z.'s scheme: his young step-niece Cornelia (Carrie Kei Heim, *The Parent Trap II*) and Joe (Christian Fitzpatrick, *Vice Versa*), a homeless street urchin whom Cornelia and Santa have befriended.

Santa (David Huddleston) comforts homeless street urchin Joe (Christian Fitzpatrick) during a moment in *Santa Claus: The Movie* (1985) (TriStar Pictures. Collection of William D. Crump).

"Thank You, Santa," all by Henry Mancini and Leslie Bricusse.

INTERESTING TIDBITS: Whereas Santa's fictitious origins are explored in such animated films as *Santa Claus Is Comin' to Town* (1970), *The Story of Santa Claus* (1996), and *The Life and Adventures of Santa Claus* (1985 and 2000), *Santa Claus: The Movie* is the first live-action film to do the same.

The movie is clearly divided into two sections. The first reveals Santa's origins, his appearance at the North Pole as an immortal, his immense and complex workshop (which cost two million dollars to build) manned by numerous elves, and his Christmas treks over the centuries. The second focuses more on B.Z.'s manipulating Patch to undermine Santa, who fades somewhat into the background but makes a comeback at the end to rescue those in trouble. Contributing little to the story line (save for Cornelia's alerting Santa of B.Z.'s scheme) is the subplot involving the children Cornelia and Joe, who seem to have been included as afterthoughts. It's as if the powers

Discovering that the new candy will explode if overheated, Cornelia writes to Santa for help, her letter magically disappearing up the chimney in British fashion and reappearing on Santa's hearth, as do all letters addressed to Santa. Meanwhile, Patch finds Joe imprisoned in his basement, courtesy of B.Z., and the two, unaware of the sugary danger, head to the North Pole in Patch's jet sleigh full of explosive candy. En route, as expected, the sleigh overheats and the candy explodes, but Santa and Cornelia, pursuing and executing the "super-dooper-looper" maneuver with the reindeer, overtake and rescue the other two. While Joe finds a new home with Santa, B.Z., attempting to escape from the law by eating the new candy, floats away into outer space and oblivion.

SONGS: "Every Christmas Eve," "Making Toys," "It's Christmas Again," "Patch! Natch!"

at hand realized that a Santa movie needed children somewhere along the line, so a couple were added. Rhetorical question: Could those two characters have been developed to be more than incidental?

In 1985, because it was not politically correct to use dwarves in the roles of elves, full-sized people (albeit a bit short) served in that capacity in this movie.

Budgeted at $50 million, this film earned less than half of that in domestic gross sales of $23.7 million.

REVIEWS: According to the Rotten Tomatoes film review site, only 17 percent of critics gave this film a positive review.

Vincent Canby of *The New York Times* (November 27, 1985): "It has the manner of a listless musical without any production numbers. From the appearance of the toys that the elves turn out, this Santa's workshop must be the world's largest purchaser of low-grade plywood. Even the sleigh-flying scenes aren't great."

Roger Ebert of rogerebert.com (November 27, 1985): "...the central weakness ... is its lack of real conflict.... The movie needs a super-Scrooge.... The good thing about the movie is the special effects ... little kids will probably like most of this movie."

TV Guide: "Moore is saddled with silly dialogue, Lithgow chews up the scenery, and Huddleston is about as believable as the cheery Santa Claus as Vlad the Impaler might have been."

Despite the negative reviews, *Santa Claus: The Movie* has become a popular standard in the repertoire of Christmas films.

PRODUCTION CREDITS—Story: David Newman and Leslie Newman. Screenplay: David Newman. Producers: Ilya Salkind and Pierre Spengler. Director: Jeannot Szwarc. Production Companies: Calash Corporation, GGG, Santa Claus Productions Ltd., and TriStar Pictures. Rating: PG (mild profanity). Genres: Adventure, Family, Fantasy. Countries: United Kingdom and USA. Run Time: 107 min.

REFERENCES: Canby, Vincent. *Santa Claus: The Movie. The New York Times.* http://www.nytimes.com/movie/review?res=9400EEDB1E38F934A15752C1A963948260&partner=Rotten%2520Tomatoes

Crump, William D. *The Christmas Encyclopedia.* Third Edition. Jefferson, NC: McFarland, 2013.

Duralde, Alonso. *Have Yourself a Movie Little Christmas.* New York: Limelight Editions, 2010.

Ebert, Roger. *Santa Claus: The Movie.* http//www.rogerebert.com/reviews/santa-claus-the-movie-1985

Santa Claus: The Movie. Box Office Mojo. http://www.boxofficemojo.com/movies/?id=santaclausthemovie.htm

Santa Claus: The Movie. Internet Movie Database. http://www.imdb.com/title/tt0089961/

Santa Claus: The Movie. Santa Monica, CA: Lionsgate, 2010. DVD Video.

Santa Claus: The Movie. TV Guide. http://www.tvguide.com/movies/santa-claus-the-movie/review/126008/

Thompson, Frank T. *American Movie Classics Great Christmas Movies.* Dallas, TX: Taylor Publishing, 1998.

Vinge, Joan D. *Santa Claus the Movie Storybook.* New York: Grosset and Dunlap, 1985.

Wilson, Joanna. *Tis the Season TV: The Encyclopedia of Christmas-Themed Episodes, Specials and Made-for-TV Movies.* Akron, OH: 1701 Press, 2011.

The Santa Clause—November 11, 1994
Feature Film

THREAT TO CHRISTMAS: Santa dies when he falls off a roof on Christmas Eve.

HOW CHRISTMAS IS SAVED: A divorced father unwittingly becomes the next Santa Claus through the power of the "Santa Clause."

SYNOPSIS AND COMMENTARY: Santa is sometimes depicted as retiring and passing the mantle from one person to the next after a long period of time, as in *Ernest Saves Christmas* and *In the Nick of Time*. But can Santa Claus ever really die? While we usually think of Santa as being immortal, some movies depict him as coming close to death, as in *It Nearly Wasn't Christmas* and *The Search for Santa Paws*. In *The Santa Clause*, the first installment in the trilogy of the same name, however, Santa takes a fatal tumble off Scott Calvin's (Tim Allen, *Home Improvement*) roof on Christmas Eve (or at least we're left with the impression that Santa has expired). As Scott watches, Santa's body vanishes, leaving only the red-and-white suit behind. A card inside requests that the finder don the suit and mount the reindeer sleigh on the roof; the reindeer will do the rest. Complying, Scott and his son Charlie (Eric Lloyd, *Jesse*) resume Christmas Eve rounds, where Scott finds that the suit enables him to change his shape to enter any home magically through any sort of entrance. Returning with the reindeer sleigh back to the North Pole, Scott learns from chief elf Bernard (David Krumholtz, *Numbers*) that, by wearing the late Santa's suit, he has now become Santa Claus, according to a microscopic clause written on the aforementioned card, known as the "Santa Clause." Through the following year, Scott assumes Santa's physical qualities by rapidly gaining weight and developing a full, white beard that instantly reappears despite repeated shavings. Scott's evolving appearance and Charlie's frequent, bizarre tales about the North Pole cause Charlie's mother Laura (Wendy Crewson, *The Good Son*) and his psychiatrist-stepfather Dr. Neil Miller (Judge Reinhold, *Fast Times at Ridgemont High*) to revoke Scott's visitation privileges with Charlie. Despite this restriction, the boy again accompanies Scott on Christmas Eve rounds, which forces Laura, who mistakenly believes that Scott has kidnapped her son, to summon the law. Although Scott is arrested while performing Santa duties, Charlie and a squad of elves with "attitude" liberate him from jail. Returning Charlie to his mother, Scott-Santa, true to character, also returns good for evil, so to speak, by providing gifts that Laura and Neal had always wanted as children but never received: a "Mystery Date" game for Laura and an Oscar Mayer Wiener whistle for Neal. In return, Laura arranges unlimited visitation privileges between Santa and Charlie.

AWARDS IN 1995: People's Choice Award for Favorite Comedy Motion Picture and a BMI Film Music Award; Saturn Award nominations for Best Fantasy Film and Best Make-Up; a Blimp Award nomination for Favorite Movie Actor (Tim Allen); MTV Movie Award nominations for Best Breakthrough Performance and Best Comedic Performance (both to Tim Allen); Young Artist Award nominations for Best Family Motion Picture Comedy and Best Performance by a Young Actor Co-Star (Eric Lloyd).

INTERESTING TIDBITS: Check out the two sequels, *The Santa Clause 2: The Mrs. Clause* (2002) and *The Santa Clause 3: The Escape Clause* (2006).

Santa also falls from a roof in *Santa Claws* (2014) and becomes a jailbird in *Ernest Saves Christmas* (1988).

The Santa Clause was filmed in Toronto, as was another Christmas classic, *A Christmas Story* (1983).

With a budget of $22 million, *The Santa Clause* earned nearly $145 million in domestic box office sales and $45 million overseas for a worldwide total of nearly $190 million. It was clearly the most profitable film of the trilogy. *The Santa Clause 2* earned a worldwide total of nearly $173 million; *The Santa Clause 3*, nearly $111 million.

REVIEWS: According to the Rotten Tomatoes film review site, 75 percent of critics gave this film a positive review. Metacritic gave it a score of 57/100 (mixed/average).

Jeff Shannon of *The Seattle Times* (November 11, 1994): "This is Allen's movie debut.... There's an effortless quality to his humor, but it's also got a quietly urgent edge to it..."

Kevin Thomas of the *Los Angeles Times* (November 11, 1994): "...there's real edge to this picture, yet it doesn't cut out the youngsters who will find so much to embrace in this genuinely imaginative work with its amazing special effects ... [it] is a Christmas picture for the frequently splintered families of the hard-driving '90s."

Rita Kempley of *The Washington Post* (November 11, 1994): "Aimed at kids, but written with parents in mind, 'The Santa Clause' balances the sugar with the spice, which Allen sprinkles on just right."

Charles Cassady, Jr., of *Common Sense Media* (October 7, 2005): "Some parents may be disappointed that this movie overlooks the religious significance of Christmas in favor of present-giving and childhood wish-fulfillment, but the movie ends on an appropriate note of good will and reconciliation."

PRODUCTION CREDITS—Writers: Leo Benvenuti and Steve Rudnick. Producers: Robert F. Newmyer, Brian Reilly, and Jeffrey Silver. Director: John Pasquin. Production Companies: Walt Disney Pictures, Hollywood Pictures, and Outlaw Productions. Rating: PG (few crude moments). Genres: Comedy, Drama, Family. Country: USA. Run Time: 97 min.

REFERENCES: Cassady, Charles, Jr. *The Santa Clause. Common Sense Media.* https://www.commonsensemedia.org/movie-reviews/the-santa-clause

Crump, William D. *The Christmas Encyclopedia*. Third Edition. Jefferson, NC: McFarland, 2013.

Duralde, Alonso. *Have Yourself a Movie Little Christmas*. New York: Limelight Editions, 2010.

Fleischer, David. "Reel Toronto: *The Santa Clause*." *Torontoist* (December 7, 2010). http://torontoist.com/2010/12/reel_toronto_the_santa_clause/

Kempley, Rita. *The Santa Clause*. *The Washington Post*. http://www.washingtonpost.com/wp-srv/style/longterm/movies/videos/thesantaclausepgkempley_a0a49b.htm

The Santa Clause. Box Office Mojo. http://www.boxofficemojo.com/movies/?id=santa-clause.htm

The Santa Clause. Burbank, CA: Walt Disney Home Entertainment, 2002. DVD Video.

The Santa Clause. Internet Movie Database. http://www.imdb.com/title/tt0111070

The Santa Clause. Metacritic. http://www.metacritic.com/movie/the-santa-clause/critic-reviews

The Santa Clause. Rotten Tomatoes. http://www.rottentomatoes.com/m/santa_clause/

Shannon, David. "Allen Delivers Belly Laughs in Amusing 'Santa Clause.'" *The Seattle Times*. http://community.seattletimes.nwsource.com/archive/?date=19941111&slug=1941324

Thomas, Kevin. "Movie Review: Allen's 'Santa Clause' Delivers the Goods." *Los Angeles Times*. http://articles.latimes.com/1994-11-11/entertainment/ca-61429_1_santa-clause

Thompson, Frank T. *American Movie Classics Great Christmas Movies*. Dallas, TX: Taylor Publishing, 1998.

Wilson, Joanna. *Tis the Season TV: The Encyclopedia of Christmas-Themed Episodes, Specials and Made-for-TV Movies*. Akron, OH: 1701 Press, 2011.

The Santa Clause 2: The Mrs. Clause—
November 1, 2002

Feature Film

THREAT TO CHRISTMAS: The discovery of the "Mrs. Clause" reveals that Santa must take a wife by Christmas Eve or Christmas will end.

HOW CHRISTMAS IS SAVED: Santa takes a wife by Christmas Eve (as if there were an alternative).

SYNOPSIS AND COMMENTARY: In this sequel to *The Santa Clause* (1994), principal cast members in the original movie reprise their roles. Two problems initially plague Santa/Scott Calvin (Tim Allen): one, an exceedingly minute clause discovered within the "Santa Clause" requires that Santa take a wife by Christmas Eve, or Christmas will be history; hence, the new clause is termed the "Mrs. Clause." Santa has already begun the "desantafication" process: his broad waistline is shrinking, his magical powers are waning, and his full, white beard soon disappears. The second problem: Santa's teenage son Charlie (Eric Lloyd) winds up on the "Naughty List," and Santa must re-enter human society to investigate, which prompts a visit from the Council of Legendary Figures: Mother Nature (Aisha Tyler, *Ghost Whisperer*), Father Time (Peter Boyle, *Everybody Loves Raymond*), Cupid (Kevin Pollak, *A Few Good Men*), the Easter Bunny (Jay Thomas, *Cheers*), the Tooth Fairy (Art LaFleur, *The Sandlot*), and the Sandman (Michael Dorn, *Star Trek: The Next Generation*). During Santa's absence from the North Pole, a life-size Toy Santa action figure (Tim Allen) oversees the toy production. Frustrated about his father, Charlie is at constant odds with his school principal, Carol Newman (Elizabeth Mitchell, *Lost*), a cold, cynical, yet beautiful woman who has no time for Christmas frivolities and will not tolerate holiday spirit among the student body. Predictably (perhaps even desperately), Scott pursues a relationship with bah-humbug Carol that blossoms on the night of the faculty Christmas party where, though it dangerously drains his magic, Scott learns that Carol acquired her sour Christmas attitude in childhood, when her parents dropped the Santa-is-a-myth bomb. Scott further saves the party from total apathy by whipping up gifts that the faculty members had individually cherished as children (much like he did with Laura and Neil in the first film). This consumes all of Scott's magic, yet Carol is overwhelmed and in love. On Christmas Eve, Toy Santa, deciding that too many children have been naughty, orders lumps of coal for everyone and produces an army of giant, toy soldiers to enforce his edict, then heads out with the reindeer team.

Scott/Santa finds a way back home, courtesy of the Tooth Fairy, who responds when Charlie's little half-sister Lucy (Liliana Mumy, *Cheaper by the Dozen*) loses a tooth, and who also brings Charlie (he sacrifices a tooth) and Carol to the North Pole. Mounting Chet, an inexperienced little buck with lots of "crash time," Santa zooms wildly ahead to overtake Toy Santa as the elves battle the toy soldiers below. With victory in hand, with minutes to spare, and with Mother Nature officiating, Santa and Carol are married, whereupon Santa promptly regains his weight and beard. In the final scenes, as Santa and his team speed away, reindeer Comet, having stuffed himself with too much Christmas candy, languishes in the sleigh while Chet, giggling hysterically through the night, takes his place.

OTHER CAST: Wendy Crewson as Laura Miller, Scott's ex-wife; Judge Reinhold as Dr. Neil Miller, Laura's second husband; David Krumholtz as Bernard the arch-elf; Spencer Breslin as Curtis the elf and Keeper of the Handbook of Christmas; Danielle Woodman as Abby the elf; Bob Bergen as the voice of reindeer Comet; Kath Soucie as the voice of reindeer Chet.

AWARDS IN 2003: Won a BMI Film Music Award; Saturn Award nomination for Best Fantasy Film; Phoenix Film Critics Society Award nomination for Best Live Action Fantasy Film; Young Artist Award nomination for Best Performance in a Feature Film–Supporting Young Actor (Eric Lloyd).

INTERESTING TIDBITS: With a budget of $65 million, *The Santa Clause 2* earned about $139 million at domestic box offices and nearly $34 million overseas for a worldwide total of nearly $173 million. *The Santa Clause* earned a worldwide total of nearly $190 million; *The Santa Clause 3*, nearly $111 million.

Santa, the Easter Bunny, the Tooth Fairy, and the Sandman also team up with Jack Frost in the animated feature film *Rise of the Guardians* (2012), in which they battle the evil spirit Pitch Black, who launches an attack against Earth. The setting is Easter, however, not Christmas.

REVIEWS: According to the Rotten Tomatoes film review site, 55 percent of critics gave this film a positive review. Metacritic gave it a score of 48/100 (mixed/average).

A.O. Scott of *The New York Times* (November 1, 2002): "…captures the true spirit of the holiday. It's mildly sentimental, unabashedly consumerist (with anything-but-subliminal advertisements for McDonald's hamburgers and Nestlé candy stuck inside), studiously inoffensive and completely disposable."

Paul Clinton of *CNN* (October 21, 2002): "The scenery, props, and costumes are all way over the top. But the film has no pretensions other than being exactly what it is: a sweet, slickly manufactured tale for the whole family, a holiday diversion cut to fit everyone from 6 to 60."

James Berardinelli of *ReelViews*: "The special effects are bad enough to be embarrassing. When compared to the imaginative majesty of Whoville in Ron Howard's *How the Grinch Stole Christmas*, Santa's North Pole looks nothing short of cheesy… [The film] is entirely inoffensive, so it makes for perfect family fare—but only if the children are young enough to be indiscriminating about what they're seeing."

C.W. Nevius of the *San Francisco Chronicle* (November 1, 2002): "There are plots, subplots and sidetracks. It's a love story, a father-son bonding tale, and … a slam-bang knockout finish featuring body-slamming Santas. Come for the cute little elves; stick around for the high-speed sleigh crash."

PRODUCTION CREDITS—Story and characters: Leo Benvenuti and Steve Rudnick. Screenplay: Ken Daurio, Ed Decter, Cinco Paul, Don Rhymer, and John J. Strauss. Producers: Robert F. Newmyer, Brian Reilly, and Jeffrey Silver. Director: Michael Lembeck. Production Companies: Walt Disney Pictures, Outlaw Productions, and Boxing Cat Films. Rating: G. Genres: Comedy, Family, Fantasy. Country: USA. Run Time: 104 min.

REFERENCES: Berardinelli, James. "*Santa Clause 2*, The (United States, 2002)." *ReelViews*. http://www.reelviews.net/reelviews/santa-clause-2-the

Clinton, Paul. "Review: 'Santa Clause 2' Pleasant Confection." *CNN*. http://www.cnn.

com/2002/SHOWBIZ/Movies/10/31/review.santa.clause2/index.html

Crump, William D. *The Christmas Encyclopedia*. Third Edition. Jefferson, NC: McFarland, 2013.

Nevius, C.W. "Allen All Over Map in 'Santa Clause 2.'" *San Francisco Chronicle*. http://www.sfgate.com/bayarea/nevius/article/Allen-all-over-map-in-Santa-Clause-2-2757905.php

The Santa Clause 2. Burbank, CA: Walt Disney Home Entertainment, 2003. DVD Video.

The Santa Clause 2. Internet Movie Database. http://www.imdb.com/title/tt0304669

The Santa Clause 2. Metacritic. http://www.metacritic.com/movie/the-santa-clause-2

The Santa Clause 2. Rotten Tomatoes. http://www.rottentomatoes.com/m/the_santa_clause_2/

Scott, A.O. "Santa Cheers Up a School and Marries the Principal." *The New York Times*. http://www.nytimes.com/2002/11/01/movies/01CLAU.html

Wilson, Joanna. *Tis the Season TV: The Encyclopedia of Christmas-Themed Episodes, Specials and Made-for-TV Movies*. Akron, OH: 1701 Press, 2011.

The Santa Clause 3: The Escape Clause—November 3, 2006

Feature Film

THREAT TO CHRISTMAS: Desiring a holiday devoted to himself, Jack Frost plans to take over the North Pole.

HOW CHRISTMAS IS SAVED: Santa uses the same trickery on Jack Frost that Frost used on him to set things right.

SYNOPSIS AND COMMENTARY: While his wife Carol (Elizabeth Mitchell, *Frequency*) awaits the birth of their first child in this third and final installment of *The Santa Clause* trilogy, Santa/Scott Calvin (Tim Allen) faces a malicious competitor in icy Jack Frost (Martin Short, *Jungle 2 Jungle*), who devises a plan to upstage Santa, take over the North Pole, and change Christmas to "Frostmas." Utilizing a snow globe, Jack tricks Santa into evoking the powerful "Escape Clause," which propels the two back in time twelve years ago to the point when Scott first became Santa. This time, Jack dons the red suit and becomes Santa instead, and the scenario that follows parallels *It's A Wonderful Life*, which portrays what life would be like if Scott were not Santa: Jack converts the North Pole into a highly commercialized tourist attraction where rich parents must pay handsomely for their little hellions to be on the Nice List. After Scott discovers a way to pull the same trick on Jack via a snow globe to set things right, the two head back in time once again with Scott now commandeering the Santa suit, and with two hours to spare before Santa/Scott must begin his Christmas Eve rounds, Carol gives birth to "Buddy Claus."

OTHER CAST: Spencer Breslin as Curtis the elf and Eric Lloyd as Charlie Calvin.

AWARDS FOR 2007: Won a BMI Film Music Award; Razzie Award nominations for Worst Actor (Tim Allen), Worst Excuse for Family Entertainment, Worst Sequel, Worst Screen Couple (Allen and Short), Worst Supporting Actor (Short); and a Young Artist Award nomination for Best Young Ensemble in a Feature Film.

INTERESTING TIDBITS: To placate Carol, who is homesick and sick of being pregnant, Scott stages a family reunion at the North Pole by inviting not only her bickering parents, Sylvia and Bud Newman (Ann-Margret, *Bye Bye Birdie*, and Alan Arkin, *The Heart Is a Lonely Hunter*), but also his ex-wife Laura (Wendy Crewson), her psychiatrist-husband Neil (Judge Reinhold), and their daughter Lucy (Liliana Mumy), the latter three reprising their roles as in the previous film. But because Scott is not ready to spring the fact that he is Santa to his in-laws, he disguises the North Pole to look like he operates a Canadian toymaking business. Also reprising their roles to deal with Jack Frost are members of the Council of Legendary Figures: Mother Nature (Aisha Tyler), Father Time (Peter Boyle), the Easter Bunny (Jay Thomas), Cupid (Kevin Pollak), the Tooth Fairy (Art LaFleur), and the Sandman (Michael Dorn).

Santa, the Easter Bunny, the Tooth Fairy, and the Sandman also team up with Jack Frost in the animated feature film *Rise of the*

Desiring to change Christmas to "Frostmas," icy Jack Frost (Martin Short, left) uses a snow globe to trick Santa/Scott Calvin (Tim Allen) into evoking the powerful "Escape Clause" in *The Santa Clause 3: The Escape Clause* (2006) (Walt Disney Pictures/Photofest).

Guardians (2012), in which they battle the evil spirit Pitch Black, who launches an attack against Earth. The setting is Easter, however, not Christmas.

With a budget of $12 million, *The Santa Clause 3* earned $84.5 million in domestic box office sales and nearly $26.3 million overseas for a worldwide total of nearly $111 million. *The Santa Clause* earned a worldwide total of nearly $190 million; *The Santa Clause 2*, nearly $173 million.

REVIEWS: According to the Rotten Tomatoes film review site, only 15 percent of critics gave this film a positive review. Metacritic gave it a score of 32/100 (generally unfavorable).

Ty Burr of *The Boston Globe* (November 4, 2006): "At one point, Jack Frost gains control of Santa's workshop and turns it into a Las Vegas-style theme park—supposedly a hideous inversion of Christmas values. So blandly commercialized is the movie's vision of the holiday that you can hardly tell the difference."

David Nusair of *Reel Film Reviews* (November 3, 2006): "...there's little doubt that the Santa Clause series has finally run out of steam. *The Santa Clause 3*—more often than not—comes off as an entirely superfluous piece of work, recycling the themes and plot points of its predecessors."

Justin Chang of *Variety* (November 2, 2006): "Not unlike the shiny snow globe at its center, [this film] is a thing of consummate craftsmanship, a smoothly engineered and fundamentally lifeless object that's nevertheless capable of giving even the grinchiest moviegoers a brief attack of the warm-and-fuzzies."

Maitland McDonagh of *TV Guide*: "Contrary to what filmmaker Michael Lembeck appears to believe, distractions like busy set design, cartoon special-effects noises and farting reindeer can't hide a thin yet overly complicated plot that will bore children and adults alike."

PRODUCTION CREDITS—Characters: Leo Benvenuti and Steve Rudnick. Writers: Ed Decter and John J. Strauss. Producers: Robert F. Newmyer, Brian Reilly, and Jeffrey Silver. Director: Michael Lembeck. Production Companies: Walt Disney Pictures, Boxing Cat Films, Outlaw Productions, and Santa Frost Productions. Rating: G. Genres: Adventure, Comedy, Family. Country: USA. Run Time: 97 min.

REFERENCES: Burr, Ty. "This 'Clause' Has Cheer but Lacks Laughs." *The Boston Globe.* http://www.boston.com/ae/movies/articles/2006/11/04/this_clause_has_cheer_but_lacks_laughs/

Chang, Justin. "Review: 'The Santa Clause 3: The Escape Clause.'" *Variety.* http://variety.com/2006/film/markets-festivals/the-santa-clause-3-the-escape-clause-1200512234/#

Crump, William D. *The Christmas Encyclopedia.* Third Edition. Jefferson, NC: McFarland, 2013.

McDonagh, Maitland. *The Santa Clause 3: The Escape Clause. TV Guide.* http://www.tvguide.com/movies/the-santa-clause-3-the-escape-clause/review/283881/

Nusair, David. *The Santa Clause 3: The Escape Clause. Film Reel Reviews.* http://www.reelfilm.com/santacls.htm#santa3

The Santa Clause 3. Box Office Mojo. http://www.boxofficemojo.com/movies/?id=santaclause3.htm

The Santa Clause 3. Burbank, CA: Walt Disney Home Entertainment, 2007. DVD Video.

The Santa Clause 3. Internet Movie Database. http://www.imdb.com/title/tt0452681/

The Santa Clause 3. Metacritic. http://www.metacritic.com/movie/the-santa-clause-3-the-escape-clause

The Santa Clause 3. Rotten Tomatoes. http://www.rottentomatoes.com/m/santa_claus_3/

Wilson, Joanna. *Tis the Season TV: The Encyclopedia of Christmas-Themed Episodes, Specials and Made-for-TV Movies.* Akron, OH: 1701 Press, 2011.

Santa Claws—November 4, 2014

Direct-to-Video Movie

THREAT TO CHRISTMAS: Santa falls off a roof, passes out, and cannot deliver his presents.

HOW CHRISTMAS IS SAVED: Three kittens take over for Santa and pilot the sleigh.

SYNOPSIS AND COMMENTARY: In some save-Christmas movies in which Santa becomes incapacitated (or is killed), other humans take over, as in *The Santa Clause* and *A Flintstone Christmas*, for example; in others, animals save Christmas with dogs heretofore predominating, as in *The Dog Who Saved Christmas* and *Hercules Saves Christmas*. Not to be outdone, cats are now entering the fray with such movies as *Felix the Cat Saves Christmas* and this specimen, *Santa Claws* (note the intended pun). Despite the jumbled plot, cat lovers and children will appreciate the film; dog lovers, perhaps not so much.

It's Christmas Eve, but single-mom Julia (Nicola Lambo, *Last Life*) is not celebrating because, as she informs her young son Tommy (Ezra James Colbert, *The Mindy Project*), Christmas is overly commercialized and Santa is a myth. Drawing the line when Julia would put his three pet kittens up for adoption, Tommy boxes them up with a note for Santa to take care of them. When Santa (John P. Fowler, *Santa Claws*), who is highly allergic to cats, falls off Tommy's roof in a fit of sneezing and passes out, the reindeer draft kittens Hairball, Mittens, and Patches to take over the deliveries. The high-tech sleigh, complete with a GPS, is now at the mercy of three playfully cute and witless kitties, who manage to create chaos during deliveries, lose the reindeer, and crash the sleigh in the frozen North. With remote assistance from Tommy's Santa-crazed, computer-hacking neighbor, Mr. Bramble (Evan Boymel, *Salesgirl*), the fearless felines forge ahead in the sleigh under rocket power with only a few hours remaining until sunrise, by which time all the presents must be delivered, as the GPS image Tinsel (Erica Duke, *Bikini Spring Break*) warns, lest children riot in the streets and the North Pole becomes a *CAT*astrophe. Meanwhile, sanity returns to the picture as Santa, having recovered at Tommy's house, turns philosopher and, performing a few feats of magic, makes a believer of Julia again who had once believed but had denied him for 30 years, because her friends had mercilessly teased her for unsuccessfully trying to prove his existence at the time. In turn, she had denied Tommy the joy of Christmas rather than see him suffer for believing as she had. According to Santa, "Christmas isn't about proof or evidence, it's about sharing in that experience and spreading the joy," which, along with the North Pole, elves, reindeer, and Mrs. Claus, would all be in danger if he were to give the world absolute proof of his existence.

PRINCIPAL ANIMAL VOICES: Jordan Bielsky (*Intelligence*) as Patches; Lauren Elizabeth Hood (*Hunger*) as Mittens; Quinn Ljoka (*Santa Claws*) as Hairball; Marguerite Insolia (*The Muse*) as Maisy, the kittens' mother; Dylan Vox (*The Lair*) as Prancer; and James Kondelik (*Age of Tomorrow*) as Donner.

INTERESTING TIDBIT: In an early scene with Santa eating cookies, the studio camera can be seen in a mirror. A similar incident occurred in *A Christmas Carol* (1951) with Alastair Sim: as Scrooge frolics around on Christmas morning, a stage technician can be seen in a mirror—twice.

PRODUCTION CREDITS—Screenplay: Anna Rasmussen. Producer: David Michal Latt. Director: Glenn R. Miller. Production Company: The Asylum. Rating: PG (brief sexual innuendo). Genres: Family, Fantasy. Country: USA. Run Time: 86 min.

REFERENCES: *Santa Claws*. Internet Movie Database. http://www.imdb.com/title/tt3922810/

Santa Claws. Official Web Site: http://www.theasylum.cc/product.php?id=259

Santa Claws. Universal Sony Pictures, 2014. DVD Video.

The Santa Incident—December 9, 2010
Television Movie

THREAT TO CHRISTMAS: Santa and his reindeer team are mistaken for a UFO and shot down.

HOW CHRISTMAS IS SAVED: Santa, along with an elf posse and two children, outwit government agents bent on capturing the jolly man.

SYNOPSIS AND COMMENTARY: When Santa (James Cosmo, *Braveheart*) and his reindeer team unwittingly cross into a government no-fly zone, they are mistaken for an unidentified aircraft, shot down by the Air National Guard, and Santa suffers a skull fracture. Two children, Daniel (Scott Graham, *The Cabin*) and his sister Sophia (Ali Lyons, *Planet Cosmo*), rescue Santa and, together with their mother Joanna (Ione Skye, *Wayne's World*), nurse him back to health. While awaiting his elf posse, Santa occupies himself with odd jobs around town and sets up a secret factory to make toys from everyday materials. Meanwhile, two bumbling Homeland Security agents, Erickson (Greg Germann, *War Games*) and Cunningham (Sean McConaghy, *Gypsy Cops!*), are tracking Santa's ground activities under the notion that he is an alien life form and a threat to national security. It's a race to see if the elves will arrive in time to rescue their boss before the agents destroy all of Santa's good work.

INTERESTING TIDBITS: Subplots revolve around Daniel and Sophia missing their father who had abandoned the family, their mother's loneliness, and a possible budding relationship between Joanna and Hank (Jonathan Kerrigan, *Diana*), the town sheriff.

The filming location is County Dublin, Ireland. Therefore, most of the principals in this movie are of Irish or Scottish descent.

REVIEWS: Scott Rolfe of The Dove Foundation: "This is a fun, light-hearted romp that will have your family laughing along with Santa as he thwarts the Government agent[s'] plans. There is a bit of slapstick violence but nothing too rough. Due to some mild language issues, we have awarded [this film] our Dove 'Family-Approved' Seal for ages 12 and over."

Andy Webb of *The Movie Scene*: "As an adult, [this film] is a hard slog of a movie which dishes out some Christmas movie clichés but ignores the most important ingredient, Christmas Magic. But then [this film] is really a movie made for young children who won't be put off by bad acting, cliché ideas and will hopefully warm to James Cosmo as Santa Claus, although at times he sounds more like Captain Birdseye [the advertising mascot for the Birds Eye frozen food brand] than the jolly old fellow."

Paul Pritchard of *DVD Verdict* (November 1, 2011): "Younger children should ... get a kick out of the movie, thanks mostly to James Cosmo's impressive turn as Santa, which is full of warmth, making [this film] worthy of consideration.... Even the most forgiving of audiences will find it hard to deny the distinct lack of Christmas magic here. Maybe it's the sunny locales, the fact that Santa fails to sport his famous red outfit until the very end, or the plot's emphasis on the agents out to capture St. Nick..."

PRODUCTION CREDITS—Writer: Jeffrey Scott Simmons. Producer: Susan Mullen. Director: Yelena Lanskaya. Production Companies: RHI Entertainment, Parallel Film Productions, MNG Films, and the Government of Ireland. Rating: Not rated. Genres: Comedy, Family. Countries: Ireland and USA. Run Time: 88 min.

REFERENCES: Crump, William D. *The Christmas Encyclopedia*. Third Edition. Jefferson, NC: McFarland, 2013.

Pritchard, Paul. *The Santa Incident*. DVD Verdict. http://www.dvdverdict.com/reviews/santaincident.php

Rolfe, Scott. *The Santa Incident*. The Dove Foundation. http://www.dove.org/review/8856-the-santa-incident/

The Santa Incident. In *Family Holiday Collection*. Universal City, CA: Vivendi Entertainment, 2012. DVD Video.

The Santa Incident. Internet Movie Database. http://www.imdb.com/title/tt1761007/

Webb, Andy. *The Santa Incident* (2010). *The Movie Scene*. http://www.themoviescene.co.uk/reviews/the-santa-incident-2010/the-santa-incident-2010.html

Santa, Jr.—December 6, 2002
Television Movie
THREAT TO CHRISTMAS: The West Coast of the USA may have no Christmas when Santa's son, "Santa, Jr.," is mistakenly arrested as a burglar.

HOW CHRISTMAS IS SAVED: Junior captures the real burglar, exonerates himself, and learns what the Christmas spirit is all about.

SYNOPSIS AND COMMENTARY: Needing to relieve some of his Christmas burden, Santa has assigned his son, Chris Kringle, Jr. (Nick Stabile, *Sunset Beach*), to cover the West Coast of the USA. But Chris, ambivalent about Christmas, begins his gift-giving routine two days beforehand, because he doubts that he can complete his assignment in one night. He lands in San Diego at a time when a Santa impersonator is burglarizing homes, and Chris is arrested instead by police detectives Bedford (Judd Nelson, *The Breakfast Club*) and Potter (George Wallace, *The Ladykillers*). Despite being in custody, the burglaries continue, yet no one believes Chris's story about someone having stolen his identity, and his case is postponed until the holidays are over. Until then, Chris remains under house arrest in the home of his public defender, Susan Flynn (Lauren Holly, *What Women Want*), who shunned Christmas after her parents died. Meanwhile, the elf Stan (Ed Gale, *The Polar Express*), who has followed Chris since he left the North Pole, rummages through trash cans to make emergency gifts, because the police have confiscated Chris's bag. The bag contains an endless supply of gifts that the detectives and Susan distribute to children. That and Chris's knowledge of children, his iPod containing the naughty/nice list, and his transformation of Susan's sterile home into a Christmas wonderland help to revive Susan's Christmas spirit. When the Santa burglar strikes Susan's house, Chris overpowers him and, after a lengthy series of twists and turns, hands him over to Bedford and Potter. From these events, Chris acquires a deep appreciation for his father's work and a sense of responsibility toward those who would be saddened if he failed them. Thus, Chris learns that the Christmas spirit is going the extra mile for people with nothing to gain and possibly something to lose.

INTERESTING TIDBITS: The names of Bedford and Potter are nods to *It's a Wonderful Life*, which is set in the fictional town of Bedford Falls; there, Mr. Potter runs the bank.

Although the film is not rated, it should be rated as TV-14 or PG because of mild language.

Since this film is a Hallmark production, it's no surprise to see a budding romance develop between Susan and Bedford.

The film first aired on December 6, which is St. Nicholas's Day.

PRODUCTION CREDITS—Writer: Marc Hershon. Producers: Kevin Bocarde, Kyle Clark, and Wendy Winks. Director: Kevin Connor. Production Companies: Alpine Medien Productions, Hallmark Entertainment, and Larry Levinson Productions. Rating: Not rated. Genres: Comedy, Fantasy, Romance. Country: USA. Run Time: 100 min.

REFERENCES: Crump, William D. *The Christmas Encyclopedia*. Third Edition. Jefferson, NC: McFarland, 2013.

Santa, Jr. Internet Movie Database. http://www.imdb.com/title/tt0338410/

Santa, Jr. New York: GoodTimes Entertainment, 2003. DVD Video.

Wilson, Joanna. *Tis the Season TV: The Encyclopedia of Christmas-Themed Episodes, Specials and Made-for-TV Movies*. Akron, OH: 1701 Press, 2011.

Santa Mouse and the Ratdeer—2000

Animated Television Short Film

THREAT TO CHRISTMAS: Santa Mouse crashes his sleigh in the woods and the exasperated ratdeer walk off the job.

HOW CHRISTMAS IS SAVED: The little mouse Rosie uses the gifts that she had intended for her family to help Santa Mouse get back on track.

SYNOPSIS AND COMMENTARY: Rodents apparently have their own version of the North Pole with Santa Mouse at the helm and rats or "ratdeer" substituting for reindeer, according to this adaptation of the 1998 children's book of the same title by Thacher Hurd. It's Christmas Eve, but at the home of Rosie the little mouse, things aren't so merry: her big sister

When his six ratdeer balk at pulling a run-down sleigh and grumble about wearing fake antlers, Santa Mouse (far right) gives them a pep-talk in *Santa Mouse and the Ratdeer* (2000), an animated adaptation of the book of the same title by Thacher Hurd (Fox/Photofest).

Molly, skeptical about Santa Mouse, feels that the holidays are too stressful; Dad is frustrated over diddling with the Christmas tree lights; and Mom, worn out from baking, burns her cookies. Too bad that Rosie's Christmas enthusiasm doesn't apply to Santa Mouse's *six* ratdeer (Blunder, Basher, Lousy, Loopy, Bugsy, and Twizzlebum), who are also in a foul mood, bickering and complaining about the fake antlers they wear, the snowy night, and this and that. To make matters worse, Santa Mouse is forced to buy another sleigh, because the Easter Squirrel (not Bunny) had borrowed the original sleigh and had never returned it (and Santa Mouse apparently had never demanded it back). On Santa Mouse's meager budget, he settles for buying a worthless pile of junk that the ratdeer laugh to scorn. It's just not Santa Mouse's night, because he loses his map during the flight and crashes the sleigh in the woods. Exasperated, the ratdeer walk off the job, and when they show up at Rosie's house, she welcomes them with mugs of hot chocolate (that were intended as her present to Mom) and boosts their waning Christmas spirit in song. Revived, the team fetches Santa Mouse back to Rosie's, where she uses a hair dryer (her present to Molly) to dry Santa's beard, then loans Santa a toolbox (her present to Dad) to fix the sleigh, and the team resumes their flight in much better spirits, though Santa Mouse loses the map again. On Christmas morning, despite her family's guarded reactions to their "used" presents, the best gift is being all together as a family, though Santa Mouse had left a special gift for Rosie.

PRINCIPAL VOICES: Emily Hart (*Sabrina, the Animated Series*) as Rosie; Melissa Joan Hart (*Sabrina, the Teenage Witch*) as Molly; Sudsy Clarke (*Beauty's Revenge*) as Santa Mouse; Phil Hayes (*Unforgiven*) as Basher; Saffron Henderson (*Dragon Ball Z*) as Blunder; Peter Kelamis (*Big Eyes*) as Bugsy and Easter Squirrel; Scott McNeil (*Dragon Ball Z*) as Loopy and French Foreman; Alistair Abell (*Dragon Ball Z*) as Lousy; Colin Murdock (*Altitude*) as Twizzlebum; Ellen Kennedy (*Dragon Ball Z*) as Mom; John Payne (*Duets*) as Dad and Honest Weasel.

SONG: "Christmas Is the Best Time of the Year" by Jai Winding and Dean Stefan; lead vocal by Jamie Cronin.

INTERESTING TIDBIT: Emily Hart and Melissa Joan Hart are sisters.

NOTE: At the time of this writing, this film was not available on DVD or VHS but could be seen on YouTube.

PRODUCTION CREDITS—Writer: Dean Stefan. Producer: Michael van der Bos. Director: Chris Bartelman. Production Companies: Sony Music Entertainment and Studio B Productions. Rating: Not rated. Genres: Animation, Family. Country: Canada. Run Time: 27 min.

REFERENCES: Hurd, Thacher. *Santa Mouse and the Ratdeer*. New York: HarperCollins, 1998.

Santa Mouse and the Ratdeer. Internet Movie Database. http://www.imdb.com/title/tt0267906/

Santa Paws 2: The Santa Pups—
November 20, 2012
Direct-to-Video Musical

THREAT TO CHRISTMAS: A young boy's wish threatens to wipe out the Christmas spirit all over the world.

HOW CHRISTMAS IS SAVED: The boy retracts his wish and restores the Christmas spirit through the magic of the Santa Pups' crystal.

SYNOPSIS AND COMMENTARY: Crystal magic reigns once again in this sequel to ***The Search for Santa Paws*** (2010), featuring Santa Paws's four new puppies—Noble, Jingle, Charity, and Hope—who not only talk but demonstrate their singing talents. And for variety, this time Santa (Pat Finn, *Dude, Where's My Car?*) appears only briefly with Santa Paws. Both remain at the North Pole while Mrs. Claus (Cheryl Ladd, *Charlie's Angels*) takes the reindeer sleigh to Pineville, USA, the town possessing the most Christmas spirit, to find a new ambassador for the Santa Cause (no, not *The Santa Clause*). Desiring to prove that they are ready for their own magic crystals, the four Santa pups steal Eddy the Elf-Dog's crystal and stow away in the sleigh. In Pineville, while Mrs. Claus befriends a melancholy widower (George Newbern, *Justice League*) and his two children, perpetually

Santa Paws's four new Great Pyrenees puppies, Noble, Jingle, Charity, and Hope, who talk, sing, and help to restore the Christmas spirit with their magic crystal in *Santa Paws 2: The Santa Pups* (2012) (Walt Disney Studios Home Entertainment/Photofest).

Christmasy Sarah (Kaitlyn Maher, *The Search for Santa Paws*) and Carter (Josh Feldman, *Do Over*), the Pups unwittingly abuse the crystal by indiscriminately granting Christmas wishes. Carter, despondent over the recent loss of his mother, wishes for the Christmas spirit everywhere to end, which spawns a citywide epidemic of the bah-humbugs that spreads beyond Pineville and threatens the world with a pandemic known as "Christmas flu." As conditions worsen, Mrs. Claus is jailed for illegally stabling the reindeer (a predicament usually reserved for Santa) and performs a rock number there with the Bright Sisters (Ali Hillis, Jennifer Elise Cox, and Audrey Wasilewski); the Santa Pups land in the pound as "strays" and lose their crystal to the dogcatcher; and the Christmas Icicle at the North Pole (the source of crystal magic) begins to melt as worldwide Christmas spirit wanes. Dog-friend Baxter (a Schnauzer mix) springs the Pups, and chief elf Eli (Danny Woodburn, *Mirror Mirror*) with elf-dog Eddy (a Jack Russell terrier) again journeys from the North Pole to rescue a Claus member by staging a jailbreak the old-fashioned way—by pulling the wall down. Sarah, whose eternal Christmas spirit immunized her from the Christmas flu, performs a rendition of "O Holy Night" over the radio that revives Pineville's Christmas spirit; Carter, retracting his earlier wish, restores the Christmas spirit to the world through the magic of the Pups' crystal; and Mrs. Claus now has two Christmas ambassadors in Sarah and Carter.

ANIMAL VOICES: Tom Everett Scott (*That Thing You Do!*) as Santa Paws; Bonnie Somerville (*Holiday Engagement*) as Mrs. Paws; Aidan Gemme (*Tomorrowland*) as Noble; Tatiana Gudegast (*Super Buddies*) as Hope; G. Hannelius (*Den Brother*) as Charity; Marlowe Peyton (*Candybar*) as Jingle; Richard Kind (*Inside Out*) as Eddy; Diedrich Bader (*Office Space*) as Comet; Chris Coppola (*Postal*) as Dancer; Josh Flitter (*License to Wed*) as Brutus, a bulldog; Trevor Wright (*Shelter*) as Baxter.

AWARD: Won a Young Artist Award for Best Performance in a TV Movie, Miniseries or Special–Leading Young Actor (Josh Feldman, 2013).

ORIGINAL SONGS: "The Santa Pups Are Coming" (by Brahm Wenger and John M. Rosenberg); "Time to Celebrate Christmas" (by Brahm Wenger); "Hark the Herald Angels Sing" (by Sam Cardon); "Deck the Hall" (by Margaret Dorn, Linda Lawley, and Danny Pelfrey); "My Blue Christmas" (by Brahm Wenger and John M. Rosenberg); "Jingle Bell Postcard" (by Andrea Wittgens); "Christmas Cold" (by Brahm Wenger); "Holman's Christmas Cookies" (by Brahm Wenger); "Sing Hallelujah" (by Brahm Wenger); "Christmas Is More" (by Brahm Wenger and Justin K. Long).

INTERESTING TIDBITS: Another film in which Mrs. Claus takes the sleigh out for a pre–Christmas spin is **Mrs. Santa Claus** (1996), starring Angela Lansbury.

While Santa, Mrs. Claus, and other North Pole characters vary in the *Santa Paws* series, which is a spinoff of the *Air Buddies* series, the two constant characters are chief elf Eli and his elf-dog Eddy, who appear in **Santa Buddies, The Search for Santa Paws**, and **Santa Paws 2**.

This is one of very few otherwise "secular" Christmas movies that mentions the birth of Christ, as Sarah sings in "O Holy Night." Another film, **Angels Sing**, features Willie Nelson's rendition of "Silent Night."

REVIEW: Sandie Angulo Chen of *Common Sense Media* (November 14, 2012): "Holiday musical with adorable puppies will amuse kids…. The Santa pups and young characters learn the real meaning of Christmas isn't stuff but a spirit of service and love."

PRODUCTION CREDITS—Writers: Philip Fracassi, Anna McRoberts, and Robert Vince. Producers: Anna McRoberts and Robert Vince. Director: Robert Vince. Production Companies: Walt Disney Pictures and Key Pix Productions. Rating: G. Genres: Adventure, Family. Country: USA. Run Time: 88 min.

REFERENCES: Chen, Sandie Angulo. *Santa Paws 2: The Santa Pups. Common Sense Media.* https://www.commonsensemedia.org/movie-reviews/santa-paws-2-santa-pups

Santa Paws 2: The Santa Pups. Burbank, CA: Walt Disney Studios Home Entertainment, 2012. DVD Video.

Santa Paws 2: The Santa Pups. Internet Movie Database. http://www.imdb.com/title/tt2414212/

Santa Switch—December 7, 2013
Television Movie

THREAT TO CHRISTMAS: When an unemployed travel agent thinks he can do a better job than Santa, the jolly gent puts him in charge to teach him a lesson about priorities.

HOW CHRISTMAS IS SAVED: Knowing what the outcome will be, Santa steps back in just in the nick of time to keep Christmas from collapsing.

SYNOPSIS AND COMMENTARY: As if Christmas weren't stressful enough, unemployment, separation from your spouse, and trying to win back your family whom you've neglected are almost more than most folks can take. That's the situation with Dan (Ethan Erickson, *Jawbreaker*), an unemployed travel agent whose year-long separation from wife Linda (Anne Dudek, *Covert Affairs*) is about to end in divorce. To top it all, Linda's boss Trevor (Steve Valentine, *Crossing Jordan*) is putting the moves on her. But Dan is certain that he can win back Linda and their two children, Sally (Annie Thurman, *Dark Skies*) and Joe (Griffin Cleveland, *The Gambler*), by impressing them with many extravagant gifts. When Dan blames all his troubles on Christmas and vows that he could do a better job than Santa, the big guy himself (Donovan Scott, *Matchmaker Santa*), disguised as the elderly gent Kris, confronts Dan in a bar, puts him in charge of the whole Christmas shebang, and leaves on vacation. Santa's executive assistant Eddie (Sean Astin, *The Lord of the Rings*) attempts to guide Dan in his new role, but Dan spends so much time zapping back and forth between the North Pole and his family in the lower 48 that all parties suffer. Just as pulling off Christmas seems an impossibility, Santa returns, knowing that Dan would create a shambles. But Santa also knew that Dan needed to have everything in his life that he *thought* he wanted, only to realize that he already had everything that he really *needed*. So Santa resumes his role, and Dan returns a changed man to give all of himself and his love to his family. By the way, Linda rips up the divorce papers.

INTERESTING TIDBITS: When Eddie utters a Jewish exclamation, he explains that he's a Hanukkah elf on his father's side. That would mean Eddie's a Christmas elf on his mother's side.

The racially diverse elves are paid in cookies, not cash. Dan has the Midas touch of Christmas, but instead of everything turning into gold, it turns into something Christmasy. For example, when he attempts to prepare a romantic dinner for Linda, the lobster he cooks becomes fruitcake and the champagne becomes eggnog. Even the recording of romantic music by Frank Sinatra becomes traditional Christmas carols.

NOTE: At the time of this writing, this film was not available on DVD or VHS but could be seen on YouTube.

PRODUCTION CREDITS—Story: Rod Spence. Teleplay: Rod Spence, Gregg Rossen, and Brian Sawyer. Producer: Lincoln Lageson. Director: David Cass, Jr. Production Company: Larry Levinson Productions. Rating: Not rated. Genre: Family. Country: USA. Run Time: 90 min.

REFERENCES: *Santa Switch*. Hallmark Channel. http://www.hallmarkchannel.com/santa-switch/about

Santa Switch. Internet Movie Database. http://www.imdb.com/title/tt2639488/

The Santa Trap—December 13, 2002

Television Movie

THREAT TO CHRISTMAS: A little girl captures Santa in her home, then her father has him arrested as an intruder.

HOW CHRISTMAS IS SAVED: Santa escapes with the help of the police chief's young son and a team of elves.

SYNOPSIS AND COMMENTARY: The hot climate of the American Southwest and lack of snow may not deter little Judy Emerson's (Sierra Abel, *Halley's Comet*) Christmas spirit, but when brother Mike (Brandon Michael De-Paul, *Blue Streak*) declares that Santa Claus is a myth, she draws the line. To prove that Santa is real to skeptics like Mike and her parents, Bill and Molly (Robert Hays, *Cat's Eye*, and Shelley Long, *Cheers*), Judy constructs an elaborate trap on Christmas Eve, that involves an electric train, golf balls, a bowling ball, the family's cat, a Hula-Hoop, and a ceiling fan (rather smacks of *Home Alone*). Although she successfully captures Santa (Dick Van Patten, *Eight Is Enough*), Bill has the jolly old gent arrested as an intruder in disguise. Later that night, when strange noises lead Bill to discover a team of reindeer waiting on the roof, his doubts vanish, and he rushes to free Santa from jail. Instead, bumbling deputies release Max (Stacy Keach, *The Bourne Legacy*), a rough-and-tumble biker, who has persuaded Santa to exchange clothes with him. Santa escapes with the assistance of little Brian (Paul Butcher, *Over the Hedge*), son of the police chief (Corbin Bernsen, *L.A. Law*). The police soon find Max at the Emersons' house, where he is holding the entire family hostage, including Santa. With Christmas hanging in the balance, Santa temporarily foils the law, which allows Max time to visit his mother in the hospital, while Mike and Judy gladly deliver to hospitalized children those gifts that Santa had marked for the Emersons. Santa again dodges incarceration, this time with the assistance of Elf Ranger One (Martin Klebba, *Jurassic World*), a specialist sent from the North Pole. As Santa and his sleigh speed skyward, the magical moment makes believers of all witnesses, and Molly receives a most unusual gift to make her holiday more Christmasy—snow.

INTERESTING TIDBIT: Amanda Pays (*Leviathan*), real-life wife of Corbin Bernsen, portrays Brian's mom, Doris.

PRODUCTION CREDITS—Writers: Steve Jankowski and John Shepphird. Producer: Steve Jankowski. Director: John Shepphird. Production Company: Tag Entertainment. Rating: Not rated. Genres: Comedy, Family. Country: USA. Run Time: 92 min.

REFERENCES: Crump, William D. *The Christmas Encyclopedia*. Third Edition. Jefferson, NC: McFarland, 2013.

The Santa Trap. Internet Movie Database. http://www.imdb.com/title/tt0347938/

The Santa Trap. New York: GT Media, 2007. DVD Video.

Wilson, Joanna. *Tis the Season TV: The Encyclopedia of Christmas-Themed Episodes, Specials and Made-for-TV Movies*. Akron, OH: 1701 Press, 2011.

Santa vs. the Snowman—1997

Animated Television Special

THREAT TO CHRISTMAS: A Snowman battles Santa for control of Christmas.

HOW CHRISTMAS IS SAVED: A simple act of goodwill from Santa earns a buddy in the Snowman.

SYNOPSIS AND COMMENTARY: There's war at the North Pole! It's not exactly the Battle of Armageddon, just Santa and a mute, lonely Snowman and their respective armies going head-to-head for control of Christmas. Having observed Santa's operation and fixating on the love that children bestow on him, a jealous Snowman launches "Project Blizzard" by dressing as Santa and creating a vast army of snow minions from ice cubes, along with giant igloo robot walkers that shoot snowballs. Santa counters with elves riding rocket-propelled reindeer, guns squirting hot chocolate, and hot gingerbread men to melt the snow minions. Despite Santa's final coup—a colossal nutcracker whose heat ray melts the Snowman's monstrous snow beast—the Snowman escapes in a sleigh full of ice toys that melt or shatter when children receive them. Santa pursues and replaces the ice toys with real ones, then surprises the Snowman by returning good for evil, so to speak: he gives the Snowman a little flute to replace the one he had initially swiped from the North Pole but had dropped while evading Santa's elf-guards. Such goodwill bonds Santa and the Snowman in friendship.

PRINCIPAL VOICES: Jonathan Winters (*The Smurfs 2*) as Santa; Ben Stein (*The Fairly OddParents*) as Spunky the Elf; Victoria Jackson (*Saturday Night Live*) as Communications Elf; Don LaFontaine (*Fillmore!*) as the narrator; Mark DeCarlo (*Jimmy Neutron: Boy Genius*) as Flippy.

AWARDS: In 1998, the television special won a Lone Star Film and Television Award for Best Animation; in 2003, the 3-D version won a Golden Reel Award for Best Sound Editing in a Special Venue Film.

INTERESTING TIDBITS: This short film is the creation of Steve Oedekerk, who produced *Jimmy Neutron: Boy Genius* (2001) and wrote *The Nutty Professor* (1996) and *Patch Adams* (1998). Originally a computer-animated television special, it was remade in 3-D format and presented as *Santa vs. the Snowman 3D* in IMAX theaters during the holiday seasons from 2002 to 2006, after which time its worldwide gross box office sales totaled nearly $10.4 million.

Gliding across the snow without legs, the Snowman somewhat resembles Frosty with a black top hat; unlike Frosty, however, the hat does not animate the Snowman, nor does he sport a corncob pipe or say, "Happy Birthday!"

Santa's elves are bizarre little creatures blessed not only with the usual pointed ears but also with pointed, upturned noses that give them the appearance of miniature rhinoceroses.

The entire polar battle, especially the giant igloo robot walkers, spoofs *Star Wars: Episode V–The Empire Strikes Back* (1980) with its AT-AT devices.

The 3-D version includes several "blooper" outtake scenes at the end that further contribute to the slapstick.

REVIEWS: According to the Rotten Tomatoes film review site, 81 percent of critics gave the 3-D version a positive review. Metacritic gave it a score of 62/100 (generally favorable).

Stephen Holden of *The New York Times* (November 1, 2002): "…after all the toys and doodads have been stripped away, this is a children's war movie… [It] isn't a movie you should try to make sense of. It is best appreciated as an immersion in a three-dimensional toyland outfitted with enough whimsical gadgetry to fill a thousand playrooms."

Desson Thomson of *The Washington Post* (November 26, 2004): "Although there may be too much implied militarism for some parents (the snowmen and the elf army fire at each other with weaponry that blasts heat or shoots chocolate sauce, and there are some 'Star Wars'-like walking igloos), this is a sweet-natured film for the very young."

Marjorie Baumgarten of *The Austin Chronicle* (November 13, 2002): "The movie's self-defense posture has become more timely than ever, although be warned that the sound of Santa hollering, 'Attack, attack!' might be disconcerting to some of his believers."

PRODUCTION CREDITS—Screenplay and director: John A. Davis. Producers: Steve Oedekerk, Paul Marshal, John A. Davis, and Keith Alcorn. Production Companies: DNA Productions and O Entertainment. Rating: Not rated. Genres: Animation, Short, Comedy, Family. Country: USA. Run Time: 32 min.

REFERENCES: Baumgarten, Marjorie. "Santa vs. the Snowman 3D." *The Austin Chronicle.* http://www.austinchronicle.com/calendar/film/2002-11-13/141652/

Holden, Stephen. "A War Rages During the Season of Good Will." *The New York Times.* http://www.nytimes.com/2002/11/01/movies/01SNOW.html

Lenburg, Jeff. *The Encyclopedia of Animated Cartoons.* Third Edition. New York: Facts on File, 2009.

Santa vs. the Snowman. Big Cartoon Database. http://www.bcdb.com/cartoon/64423-Santa-Vs-The-Snowman

Santa vs. the Snowman 3D. Internet Movie Database. http://www.imdb.com/title/tt0337714/

Santa vs. the Snowman. Metacritic. http://www.metacritic.com/movie/santa-vs-the-snowman

Santa vs. the Snowman (2002). Rotten Tomatoes. http://www.rottentomatoes.com/m/santa_vs_the_snowman/

Santa vs. the Snowman. Universal City, CA: Universal, 2004. DVD Video. Includes 2-D and 3-D versions with 3-D glasses for the latter.

Thomson, Desson. "Here Comes 'Santa' in 3-D." *The Washington Post.* http://www.washingtonpost.com/wp-dyn/articles/A10117-2004Nov24.html

Wilson, Joanna. *Tis the Season TV: The Encyclopedia of Christmas-Themed Episodes, Specials and Made-for-TV Movies.* Akron, OH: 1701 Press, 2011.

Santa Who?—November 19, 2000
Television Movie

THREAT TO CHRISTMAS: During a pre–Christmas spin in the sleigh, Santa tumbles out and suffers amnesia.

HOW CHRISTMAS IS SAVED: A skeptical newsman, his girlfriend, and her young son work to restore Santa's memory in time for Christmas.

SYNOPSIS AND COMMENTARY: While out on a pleasure ride with the reindeer to take his mind off rampant Christmas commercialism, Santa (Leslie Nielsen, *All I Want for Christmas*) falls from his sleigh and suffers complete amnesia a few days before Christmas. On the scene is Peter Albright (Steven Eckholdt, *Message in a Bottle*), an ambitious, skeptical, television news reporter in desperate need of a catchy, holiday story. By coincidence, Peter's girlfriend, single-mom Claire Dreyer (Robyn Lively, *Savannah*), needs a Santa for her department store, and "Nick" gets the job, at which he is most profoundly adept. Peter then seizes the opportunity to run a series of ads that bid viewers to identify the kind old gent and reunite him with his family for Christmas. Orphaned as a child, Peter now scorns Christmas, yet he finds himself teaching Nick all he knows about the holiday on professional advice that, by recalling familiar items, Nick may regain his memory. Together Peter and Claire's little boy Zack (Max Morrow, *The Christmas Shoes*) review stories, carols, and classic Christmas movies with Nick, but nothing rings a bell until Peter discovers a letter in Nick's coat that he had written to Santa 25 years ago while at the orphanage. Whereas the discovery does the trick with Nick's memory and makes a true believer of Peter, Zack had never doubted Nick for one moment.

AWARDS: In 2001, this picture received a Saturn Award nomination for Best Single Genre Television Presentation; Young Artist Award nominations for Best Family TV Movie/Pilot/Mini-Series–Network and Best

Performance in a TV Movie (Comedy)–Supporting Young Actor (Max Morrow).

INTERESTING TIDBITS: This picture illustrates the tradition of sending letters to Santa by burning them. Most prevalent in England, letters written to Father Christmas are believed to receive favor if they burn quickly; otherwise, they must be rewritten. In *Santa Who?*, Sister Greta (Laura de Carteret, *Dawn of the Dead*) at the orphanage had unwittingly "mailed" Peter's letter by tossing it into the fire, and Peter, feeling betrayed, had hated Christmas from that time. Since the setting for this film is the United States, Sister Greta had probably intended to destroy Peter's letter; nevertheless, Santa had received it.

Worried over Santa's absence, one of the elves expresses the typically materialistic sentiment regarding Santa's link to Christmas: "What if we can't find him? … We'll have to cancel Christmas!"

To show more racial diversity, Santa's chief elf Max (Tommy Davidson, *Partners in Crime*) is black. Other films featuring a white Santa and a black chief elf include ***The Boy Who Saved Christmas*** and ***Spike: The Elf That Saved Christmas***.

Leslie Nielsen also portrays Santa in *All I Want for Christmas* (1991).

Santa really needs a neurologist, because he also suffers amnesia in other save-Christmas movies, such as ***The Amazing World of Gumball: Christmas Episode, The Boy Who Saved Christmas, Merry Madagascar, Miracle at the 34th Precinct, The Night Before the Night Before Christmas, The Search for Santa Paws***, and ***Snow 2: Brain Freeze***.

PRODUCTION CREDITS—Based on an unpublished story by Chad S. Hoffman and Robert Schwartz. Teleplay: Debra Frank and Steve L. Hayes. Producer: Frank Siracusa. Director: William Dear. Production Companies: American Broadcasting Company, Gleneagle Productions, and Hearst Entertainment Productions. Rating: G. Genres: Comedy, Fantasy. Country: USA. Run Time: 92 min.

REFERENCES: Crump, William D. *The Christmas Encyclopedia*. Third Edition. Jefferson, NC: McFarland, 2013.

Santa Who? Burbank. CA: Buena Vista Home Entertainment, 2001. DVD Video.

Santa Who? Internet Movie Database. http://www.imdb.com/title/tt0251382/

Wilson, Joanna. *Tis the Season TV: The Encyclopedia of Christmas-Themed Episodes, Specials and Made-for-TV Movies*. Akron, OH: 1701 Press, 2011.

Santa-Witch—July 27, 1957

Episode Short from the Animated Television Series

The Gumby Show

THREAT TO CHRISTMAS: Santa is sick and cannot deliver his presents.

HOW CHRISTMAS IS SAVED: Pokey the pony summons a witch to take over for Santa.

SYNOPSIS AND COMMENTARY: Created by Art Clokey, the Gumby character was portrayed in stop-motion animation as a green, clay, humanoid creature that was featured on television's *The Howdy Doody Show* (1955–1956) and was the subject of several television series for a total of 234 episodes: *The Gumby Show* (NBC, 1956–1957), syndicated revival (1962–1968), and *Gumby Adventures* (1988); a feature film, *Gumby: The Movie* (1995); and other media. Other principal characters in the series included Gumby's parents, Gumbo and Gumba; sister Minga; sidekick Pokey, a talking, orange pony; Prickle, a yellow dinosaur; and Goo, a blue flying mermaid. Gumby and friends experienced a considerable diversity of adventures.

In "Santa-Witch," Gumby does not appear. Instead, Pokey walks into the pages of a storybook to escape the Christmas rush in a toy store and finds himself at the North Pole, where he witnesses a sick Santa being carted out from Santa City on a dog sled. It's Christmas Eve, but rather than see Christmas cancelled, Pokey summons his friend Witty Witch to help. Because the reindeer won't pull the sleigh without Santa, Witty attaches a series of broomsticks to the sleigh, and away she flies cackling and dressed as Santa, along with Pokey and his friend Sybil the seal. If a house has no chimney, Witty simply enters by way of magic. When her hag-face unwittingly scares the wits out of a young brother and sister who are snooping about (the girl faints and the boy crashes through a wall to escape), Pokey gives her a Santa mask and beard to wear for the rest of the route.

PRINCIPAL VOICES: Art Clokey (*Davey and Goliath*) as Pokey; Ginny Tyler (*Davey and Goliath*) as Witty Witch.

INTERESTING TIDBITS: In the series, a common sequence has Gumby walking into a book and experiencing the world within. In "Santa-Witch," Pokey does the same thing in place of Gumby.

The brother and sister whom Witty Witch scares are virtually identical to the characters Davey Hansen and his sister Sally in *Davey and Goliath*, another clay-animated children's television series created by Art Clokey.

Check out **Scrooge Loose**, another *Gumby* save-Christmas cartoon.

PRODUCTION CREDITS— Writer, Producer, and Director: Art Clokey. Production Company: Clokey Productions and NBC. Rating: G. Genres: Animation, Comedy, Family. Country: USA. Run Time: 6 min.

REFERENCES: *The Gumby Show*. Internet Movie Database. http://www.imdb.com/title/tt0050022/

"Santa-Witch." Big Cartoon Database. http://www.bcdb.com/cartoon/23464-Santa-Witch

"Santa-Witch." In *Christmas with Gumby*. New York: GoodTimes Home Entertainment, 2003. DVD Video.

Wilson, Joanna. *Tis the Season TV: The Encyclopedia of Christmas-Themed Episodes, Specials and Made-for-TV Movies*. Akron, OH: 1701 Press, 2011.

Santabear's High Flying Adventure—
December 24, 1987

Animated Television Short Film

THREAT TO CHRISTMAS: Holding a grudge

Gumby (right) with his horse-pal Pokey from the TV series *The Gumby Show* (1957). **In the episode "Santa-Witch" (1957), Pokey persuades Witty Witch to fill in for a sick Santa with her series of broomsticks-turned-reindeer (NBC/Photofest).**

against Santa, Bullybear steals a bag of presents intended for the South Pole and would deliver them all broken, thus ruining Santa's reputation.

HOW CHRISTMAS IS SAVED: Santabear and his friend Missy thwart Bullybear.

SYNOPSIS AND COMMENTARY: *Santabear* was a series of collectible bear dolls and related products launched in 1985 by the Dayton-Hudson Corporation (now Macy's), at the time America's fourth largest general merchandise retailer, based in Minneapolis, Minnesota. The Santabear dolls, though discontinued after 2007, prompted the production of two animated stories for television, *Santabear's First Christmas* (1986), which was not a save-Christmas film, and its sequel, *Santabear's High Flying Adventure*, with adaptations into children's books.

Santabear is a little polar bear who acquired his name when Santa had brought him on board to be his assistant in the first story. Now as the two fly together over the South Pole on Christmas Eve, Santa doubts that the inhabitants there really believe in him, but instead of landing and finding out for himself, he commissions Santabear to parachute down and deliver a bag of presents for him while he continues his route. There, Santabear not only meets Missy, a little orphan bear-turned-pilot tinkering with her airplane, but he contends with Bullybear, once one of Santa's assistants who turned bad and was fired. Now out for revenge, Bullybear absconds with the bag of presents and intends to deliver them all broken, thus ruining Santa's reputation. Missy and Santabear chase Bully in her plane, but when it crashes, Bully switches clothes with Santabear, and it's the latter whom the penguin cops jail in an igloo for theft. Upon hearing Santabear's singing, Missy stages a jailbreak with her plane, after which Santabear chases Bully over the rooftops, and the two end up without their meager clothes just as Santa returns for Santabear. Because the two little bears look alike, Santa makes the distinction by asking them to explain the meaning of Christmas. To Bully, it's all about getting presents; to Santabear, it's giving presents, "especially those you can't wrap." Both bears learn that everyone is responsible for his actions, whereupon Bully tries to escape but receives his comeuppance in jail. And Santa's special gift to Missy is to take her on as an assistant just like Santabear.

PRINCIPAL VOICES: John Malkovich (*Empire of the Sun*) as Santa; Bobby McFerrin (*Jarhead*) as Santabear and Bullybear; Kelly McGillis (*Top Gun*) as Missy. Other voices: Glenne Hedley (*Don Jon*) and Dennis Hopper (*Speed*).

SONGS: Music and lyrics respectively by Felix Cavaliere and Lenore Kletter. "Out of the Blue" and "Bear in Mind" sung by Felix Cavaliere.

PRODUCTION CREDITS—Writer: Lenore Kletter. Producers: Mark Sottnick, Michael Sporn, and Joel Tuber. Director: Michael Sporn. Production Companies: Dayton-Hudson Corporation and Rabbit Ears Productions. Rating: Not rated. Genres: Animation, Family. Country: USA. Run Time: 23 min.

REFERENCES: Crump, William D. *The Christmas Encyclopedia*. Third Edition. Jefferson, NC: McFarland, 2013.

Kletter, Lenore. *Santabear's High Flying Adventure*. Minneapolis: Santabear Books, 1987.

Mikus, Kim. "Santabear Collectors Ho-Ho-Horrified." *Daily Herald* (November 9, 2007). http://prev/dailyherald.com/story/?id=73641

Santabear's High Flying Adventure. Internet Movie Database. http://www.imdb.com/title/tt0242850/

Santabear's High Flying Adventure. Stamford, CT: Vestron Video, 1988. VHS Video.

Wilson, Joanna. *Tis the Season TV: The Encyclopedia of Christmas-Themed Episodes, Specials and Made-for-TV Movies*. Akron, OH: 1701 Press, 2011.

Santa's Apprentice (*L'Apprenti Père Noël*)—November 24, 2010 (France); November 10, 2011 (Australia)

Animated Feature Film

THREAT TO CHRISTMAS: Facing mandatory retirement, Santa must train an apprentice to be his successor, lest the magic of Christmas end. Santa is arrested on kidnapping charges, and his magic ball falls into the wrong hands. Can it get any worse than that?

HOW CHRISTMAS IS SAVED: Santa finds a worthy candidate, convinces the cops of his innocence, and saves his magic ball when his apprentice fails to wrestle it from a young villain.

SYNOPSIS AND COMMENTARY: Based on the animated television series *SantApprentice*, a French-German-Irish production that ran for 50 episodes in 2006, *Santa's Apprentice* features a similar plot. According to the North Pole's "rules," each Santa faces mandatory retirement after he has served for 178 years and must take on a young apprentice to train as his successor (never mind that in the Santa mythos, there is only one such jolly gent who is immortal). The selection must be made by December 24, lest the magic of Christmas melt away. The apprentice must be an orphan boy named Nicholas with a pure heart (sorry, ladies, but tradition here holds that each Santa shall be a male, not as in a film like *Call Me Claus* that depicts the new Santa as female). Consulting their magic globe, the Council of Retired Santas finds its next Nicholas in an orphanage in Sydney, Australia, and when on Christmas Eve Santa brings seven-year-old Nicholas Barnsworth back to the North Pole, the orphanage reports him as missing. Over the next year, Santa provides instruction in climbing down chimneys, controlling the reindeer sleigh, making toys, and the like, then shares his best secret, a magic ball that shrinks and enlarges objects. But should it break, Christmas magic would disappear forever. There's a bit of trouble when Nicholas, desiring to impress Santa, builds a firecracker toy that accidentally sets fire to all the presents and incinerates Santa's beard. Though he makes mistakes, Nicholas is indispensable, for when Santa's memory begins to fail, the boy urges Santa to remember with his heart, which does the trick. During their route on Christmas Eve, they return to Nicholas's former orphanage, where the cops arrest Santa on kidnapping charges, but when his magic ball falls into the hands of the resident bully, Nicholas's former nemesis, Christmas really is in jeopardy. This boy, Nicholas Grincroch, holds a grudge because Santa had chosen the good Nicholas over him and creates havoc by shrinking some orphans and their teacher with the ball. The two boys wrestle for it, but just when the ball slips away and would have been lost, Santa retrieves it, having convinced the authorities of his innocence. Realizing that bully Nicholas needs a father figure, Santa promises to spend some time with him. As for good Nicholas, Santa passes his magic ball to him as they finish their route, and the boy becomes the new Santa.

PRINCIPAL VOICES (USA VERSION): Michael Sorich (*Castle in the Sky*) as Santa; Cole Sand (*Minions*) as Nicholas Barnsworth; Mary Pat Gleason (*Basic Instinct*) as Beatrice Lovejoy; Andrew Morris (*Psychonauts*) as Humphrey; Gabe Eggerling (*The Kicks*) as Nicholas Grincroch; Cristina Pucelli (*Monsters University*) as Felix; Bailey Gambertoglio (*Mulberry Stains*) as young Beatrice; Richard Tatum (*The Break Up*) as Waldorf.

AWARDS: At the Annecy International Animated Film Festival in France in 2011, this film won the special UNICEF Award and received a Cristal Award nomination for Best Feature. In 2016, it received a Golden Reel nomination for Best Sound Editing in Direct-to-Video Animation. In 2012, Nerida Tyson-Chew's music score was nominated for Film Score of the Year at the APRA-AGSC Australian Screen Music Awards.

INTERESTING TIDBITS: Just as the retiring Santa and his ever-loyal assistant, Beatrice Lovejoy, are close friends (no indication of a Mrs. Claus here), so Nicholas and the young Beatrice at the orphanage who takes a shine to him will become close friends (or perhaps more), for at the end, she accompanies him and the retired Santa back to the North Pole. But it appears that she could be a stowaway.

The film is basically a remake of the TV series with a few minor changes. For example, Nicholas's best friend in the series is Michael; in the film, it's Felix. Whereas the apprenticeship in the series is 15 years, it's only one year in the film.

NOTE: As of December 2015, this film was available on Netflix USA.

REVIEWS: According to the Rotten Tomatoes film review site, 80 percent of critics gave this film a positive review.

Brian Costello of *Common Sense Media* (January 14, 2016): "…a thoughtful and creative take on the familiar Christmas themes of Santa, toy-making [at] the North Pole, and the Christmas spirit of giving. There are moments of silliness, but there are also more serious messages, such as when Santa, instead of giving a bully his 'just desserts,' employs empathy to explain to the boy why he lashes out at everyone around him."

Andrew L. Urban of *Urban Cinefile*: "…the story is easy to follow, with simple, old-fashioned animation to match…. Good-hearted, well-meaning and innocuous, [the film] also has a couple of messages, one involving the bully and his need for parental love as a way to correct [his] nasty behavior."

PRODUCTION CREDITS—Writer: Alexandre Reverend. Producers: Clément Calvet and

Avrill Stark. Director: Luc Vinciguerra. Production Companies: Gaumont-Alphanim, Avrill Stark Entertainment, Flying Bark Productions, Cartoon Saloon, Orange Cinéma Séries, Centre National de la Cinématographie et de l'Image Animée, and Bord Scannán na hÉireann/Irish Film Board. Rating: G. Genres: Animation, Comedy. Countries: Australia, France, Ireland. Run Time: 80 min.

REFERENCES: Costello, Brian. *Santa's Apprentice. Common Sense Media.* https://www.commonsensemedia.org/movie-reviews/santas-apprentice

Santa's Apprentice. Chatswood, New South Wales, Australia: Paramount Home Entertainment (Australasia), 2012. DVD Video. PAL, Region 4. Non-USA Format.

Santa's Apprentice. Internet Movie Database. http://www.imdb.com/title/tt1754455/

Santa's Apprentice. Rotten Tomatoes. http://www.rottentomatoes.com/m/santas_apprentice/reviews/

Santa's Apprentice. Web Site. https://web.archive.org/20140126020757/http://www.santasapprentice.com.au

Urban, Andrew L. *Santa's Apprentice. Urban Cinefile.* http://www.urbancinefile.com.au/home/view.asp?a=18248&s=Reviews

Santa's Christmas Crash—1994

Animated Television Short Film

THREAT TO CHRISTMAS: Santa crashes his sleigh in the Sahara Desert.

HOW CHRISTMAS IS SAVED: Desert children repair the sleigh and make gifts for American children.

SYNOPSIS AND COMMENTARY: Here's a little production for French television originally titled *Le Père Noël et les enfants du désert* (*Santa and the Desert Children*), based on a children's book of the same title by Jacques Venuleth, published in 1992. While performing his rounds on Christmas Eve, Santa dozes in his sleigh during a blizzard and crash-lands his team of *two* reindeer in the Sahara Desert. There he meets several desert children, and when they ask what Christmas is, the reindeer and Santa mention presents, parties, stockings hanging up and boots arranged by the fireplace to receive gifts (obviously, no religious significance is attached). When the children next ask why he has never visited them, Santa replies that he delivers gifts only to American children, that the desert is outside his territory, and that he doesn't know who's supposed to deliver in their area. (That's ironic, considering the Santa mythos, which holds that he delivers to good children all around the world). Despite this snub, the desert children desire to help Santa, so they repair his sleigh and make new but very simple toys to replace those that were lost in the blizzard. An especially prized gift is a snake (probably a cobra) in a basket with an accompanying flute; it's a gift Santa can't possibly use. The reindeer aren't fit to fly, so the children attach Momo the camel to the sleigh, and Santa is off, dressed in a desert robe. He returns at daybreak with Tommy and Julie, two American siblings who collected gifts from their friends to thank the desert children for all their kindness.

PRINCIPAL VOICES (ENGLISH VERSION): French Tickner, Terry Klassen, David Kaye, Andrea Libman, Marcus Turner, Tony Sampson, and Christopher Turner.

INTERESTING TIDBITS: According to traditional French custom, children place their shoes near the hearth, near the crèche, or beneath the Christmas tree on Christmas Eve for *Père Noël* to fill with treats.

Check out another animated save-Christmas production for French TV, *Santa's Christmas Snooze.*

PRODUCTION CREDITS—Screenplay: Gilles Gay. Producer: Odile Limousin. Director (English Version): Sarah-Anne Dafoe. Production Companies: France 3, FIT Productions, La Fabrique, and The Ocean Group (English Version). Rating: Not rated. Genres: Animation, Family, Fantasy, Short. Country: France. Run Time: 26 min.

REFERENCES: *Santa's Christmas Crash.* Van Nuys, CA: Family Home Entertainment, 1994. VHS Video.

Venuleth, Jacques. *Le Père Noël et les enfants du désert.* Illustrated by Jean-Luc Serrano. [Toulouse]: Milan, 1992. French language.

Santa's Christmas Snooze—1994

Animated Television Short Film

THREAT TO CHRISTMAS: Grouchy Bear Magician places a spell on Santa that puts him to sleep.

HOW CHRISTMAS IS SAVED: When Bear has a change of heart but cannot undo the spell, he solicits help from Walrus, his mentor.

SYNOPSIS AND COMMENTARY: Here's another production for French television originally titled *Le Père Noël et le magicien* (*Santa and the Magician*). The setting is a mountain village populated by assorted anthropomorphic animals. When Strella the bat informs her grouchy companion, Bear Magician, that Santa is far more popular than he is, Bear seeks a magic spell that will ruin Christmas. Bear first forms a clay effigy of Santa and sticks a pin between two vertebrae, but when that fails, he next mixes a sleeping potion and sprinkles it over the effigy, which also fails. Finally, Bear tromps to Santa's home in the village (not at the North Pole), pours the powder down the chimney, and Santa falls asleep. His helpers, who consist of mice, not elves, attempt to rouse him with loud noises without success as word of Bear's foul deed spreads through the village. Bear has a change of heart and decides to awaken Santa when he encounters a young badger weeping because this would have been the little one's first Christmas. But when Bear discovers that the angry mice have destroyed his magic book and that he cannot undo the spell, he solicits help from his mentor the Walrus, Master of Magic, who provides an antidote to sprinkle over Santa. As expected, Santa awakens, and because it's Christmas Eve, Bear makes further amends by using his magic to finish the toys, and he, Santa, and Strella all deliver the presents.

PRINCIPAL VOICES (ENGLISH VERSION): French Tickner, Janyse Jaud, Ward Perry, Crystaleen O'Bray, Terry Klassen, and Robert O. Smith.

INTERESTING TIDBITS: Learning about Santa's problem, a squirrel voices the typical sentiment about where the focus of Christmas really lies by exclaiming, "Christmas won't happen because the Bear Magician put Santa to sleep!"

Santa travels through the sky in a sleigh pulled by *two* reindeer.

Check out another animated save-Christmas production for French TV, *Santa's Christmas Crash*.

PRODUCTION CREDITS—Screenplay: Martine Beck. Producer: Odile Limousin. Director: Sarah-Anne Dafoe (English Version). Production Companies: EVA Entertainment, FIT Productions, France 3 (FR 3), La Fabrique, and The Ocean Group (English Version). Rating: Not Rated. Genres: Animation, Family, Fantasy, Short. Country: France. Run Time: 26 min.

REFERENCES: *Santa's Christmas Snooze*. Internet Movie Database. http://www.imdb.com/title/tt2180515/

Santa's Christmas Snooze. Van Nuys, CA: Family Home Entertainment, 1994. VHS Video.

Santa's Little Helpers—October 7, 2014

Animated Direct-to-Video Short Film

THREAT TO CHRISTMAS: When Mrs. Claus adopts Tom Cat, his and Jerry Mouse's brawling destroys Santa's sleigh and the presents.

HOW CHRISTMAS IS SAVED: Tom and Jerry work together to make repairs, then make sure that a little girl receives a puppy that Santa accidentally left behind.

SYNOPSIS AND COMMENTARY: In 1940, cartoon giants William Hanna and Joseph Barbera created the *Tom and Jerry* series of theatrical animated cartoon shorts for MGM Studios. Featured in typical cat-and-mouse combative scenarios, the title characters Tom Cat and Jerry Mouse also enjoyed appearances in a number of movies and animated television series. One of the latter, *The Tom and Jerry Show* (computer-enhanced to simulate traditional full cel animation), has been ongoing on Cartoon Network and Teletoon since 2014 with *Santa's Little Helpers* being the Christmas special of that series.

Desiring a home of his own, Tom writes a letter to Santa to that effect but succeeds in mailing himself to the North Pole on Christ-

To save his canary friend, Jerry Mouse (left) has just knocked out Tom Cat's teeth with a hammer in *Kitty Foiled* (1948) from the *Tom and Jerry* series of animated cartoon shorts. Their classic cat-and-mouse antics are a prime feature in the short film *Santa's Little Helpers* (2014) (CBS/Photofest).

mas Eve, where he masquerades as a poor lost animal and induces Mrs. Claus to adopt him. Jerry and his little nephew Tuffy already have a good life as residents in Santa's workshop, so when Tom arrives, Jerry's not about to tolerate an interloper and attempts to boot Tom out, which prompts continuous mayhem. From toy soldiers firing bullets at Jerry, to Jerry shooting Tom in the face with a pop gun, to their wrecking Santa's Christmas tree, and finally to Jerry's rocket aimed at Tom that instead blows up Santa's sleigh and all the presents, the two just about ruin Christmas. To save the holiday, they work together to rebuild the toys and repair the sleigh, but after Santa takes off, the two discover that the puppy Jingles, a gift for a little girl named Cindy, has been left behind. Rather than see her disappointed, Jerry and Tuffy lay a guilt trip on reluctant Tom to join in and deliver the puppy themselves. Despite lacking a sleigh and reindeer, the problem is solved when Jingles' snacking on reindeer food enables him to fly, and Tom becomes a fur-ball "sleigh." The gang delivers Jingles via chimney just before dawn after first going to the wrong house and nearly being eaten alive by a vicious dog. For their unselfish spirit of giving, Santa makes them official Christmas elves.

PRINCIPAL VOICES: Nickie Bryar (*The Super Holidays*) as Cindy; Mark Hamill (*Star Wars*) as Santa; Edie McClurg (*Frozen*) as Mrs. Claus; Kath Soucie (*Rugrats*) as Tuffy; Rick Zieff (*Mississippi Burning*) as angel and devil Tom.

INTERESTING TIDBITS: Tom and Jerry rarely spoke in the original series; they do not speak in this film.

REVIEWS: Back in the era of classic, theatrical cartoon shorts before political correctness swept the land, audiences thoroughly enjoyed the slapstick "violence" of those cartoons, because no characters were ever seriously hurt or killed, no matter how many times they were "shot" or blown up with dynamite or bashed in the head with a brick. Slapstick comedy was very much in vogue, and audiences understood that it was not reality. Today, however, not everyone views those classic cartoons or their remakes with the same enthusiasm, as the following review of *The Tom and Jerry Show* by Emily Ashby of *Common Sense Media* illustrates: "…leans heavily on the legacy of the original series for its central relationship between the cat and the mouse, and their combative exchanges don't miss a beat following the example of the classic … little more than a series of violent encounters between two frenemies, neither of whom ever faces consequences for his actions … the messages they send your kids are concerning."

David Hinckley of the *New York Daily News* provides a totally different take on the same show (April 8, 2014): "Cartoon Network revives the warring cat and mouse, preserving the slapstick that's made them a success…. This latest incarnation does nothing to disturb what's clearly been a winning formula…. It's an old-school cartoon, more interested in zany slapstick and pancaking its characters than in delivering witty asides or pop-culture allusions for grownups … these guys haven't aged a day, physically or in mind-set…"

PRODUCTION CREDITS—Writers: Jim Praytor and Robert Zappia. Producers: Ashley Postlewaite and Darrel Van Citters. Director: Darrel Van Citters. Production Companies: Renegade Animation, Turner Entertainment, Warner Bros. Animation. Rating: G. Genres: Animation, Adventure, Comedy, Family. Country: USA. Run Time: 22 min.

REFERENCES: Ashby, Emily. *The Tom and Jerry Show*. *Common Sense Media*. https://www.commonsensemedia.org/tv-reviews/the-tom-and-jerry-show

Hinckley, David. "*The Tom and Jerry Show*: TV Review." *New York Daily News*. http://www.nydailynews.com/entertainment/tom-jerry-show-tv-review-article-1.1749853

Lenburg, Jeff. *The Encyclopedia of Animated Cartoons*. Third Edition. New York: Facts on File, 2009.

Tom and Jerry: Santa's Little Helpers. Internet Movie Database. http://www.imdb.com/title/tt5033328/

Tom and Jerry: Santa's Little Helpers. Turner Entertainment and Warner Bros. Entertainment, 2014. DVD Video.

Santa's Magic Crystal—November 18, 2011

Also Known As *The Magic Crystal*

Also Known as *The Elf That Rescued Christmas*

Computer-Animated Feature Film

THREAT TO CHRISTMAS: Santa's evil twin brother steals a magic crystal that enables Santa to deliver all the presents in one night.

HOW CHRISTMAS IS SAVED: The orphan boy Yotan and his friends brave many perils to retrieve the crystal.

SYNOPSIS AND COMMENTARY: In order to explain how Santa can deliver millions of presents in one night, some Santa films feature devices that stop time or that propel the old gent at astronomical speeds. The explanation in this film from Finland and Belgium, originally titled *Maaginen kristalli* (*Magic Crystal*), is quite innovative in that the device is a magic crystal that enables Santa to clone himself hundreds of times, thus producing a whole army of identical Santas who deliver around the world. But the crystal falls into the hands of Santa's evil twin brother Basil, who would usurp Santa and, instead of delivering gifts, would bring the world's children to Mount Korvatunturi (Santa's fell in Lapland according to Finnish folklore) to teach them obedience and discipline, which they all lack. Because only someone with a pure heart can remove the crystal from its secure environment, Basil compels Yotan, a young orphan boy who heads Santa's nice list, to steal the crystal. And because only a pure-hearted person can return the crystal, Santa enlists Yotan's aid, along with the boy's friend Jiffy (a squirrel with long ears like a rabbit), as well as elves Jaga, Didi, and Alpo, plus a strong-arm reindeer. Their efforts to get the crystal back involve evading Basil's robotic minions, a number of high-speed chases in jet sleighs, aerial battles with Basil, who first captures and imprisons Jaga and Didi, then Yotan, with the latter's rescue by Jiffy, Alpo, and the reindeer. When Jaga and Didi are trapped in a cage at one point, Basil lowers them toward an active volcano's lava bed beneath his fortress, which is reminiscent of a scene in *Indiana Jones and the Temple of Doom*. Predictably, magic stars enable those two to escape. Although Basil uses the crystal to duplicate himself on Christmas Eve, Yotan induces them all to squabble among themselves as a distraction, and when Yotan obtains the crystal, Basil's duplicates disappear, and his fortress falls in ruins.

PRINCIPAL VOICES (ENGLISH VERSION): Joe Carey (*The Ark*) as Santa; Kyle E. Christensen (*Graceland*) as Yotan; David Dreisen (*The Magic Crystal*) as Grouch; C.J. Fam (*Special Skills*) as Didi; Clarissa Humm (*Clarissa's World*) as Jaga; Lisa Kent (*The Magic Crystal*) as Jiffy; Michael Mena (*Powers*) as Smoo; Gerald Owens (*Big Trouble*) as Basil; Mathew Wetcher (*The Magic Crystal*) as Alpo; Santtu Karvonen (*Gloriously Wasted*) as the reindeer.

INTERESTING TIDBITS: When Jiffy first meets Yotan and asks what Christmas is all about, Yotan provides the typically secular answer: families get together to decorate a tree, exchange presents, have a special dinner, and Santa brings presents to all the good children. He mentions nothing about the religious aspects of Christmas.

While Yotan and Jiffy hide in a mail bag, note that it contains many letters addressed to Lapland, presumably to Santa.

In stereotypical portrayals, the "good guys" wear white hats and "bad guys" wear black hats; here, Santa's beard is white, while Basil's is black.

The alternate title *The Elf That Rescued Christmas* is not quite accurate in that the protagonist Yotan is a human boy, not an elf. The three elves who assist him are incidental to the story line.

REVIEWS: Brian Costello of *Common Sense Media* (March 21, 2014): "Finnish Christmas adventure has some cartoonish violence.... As often happens with computer-animated movies made in Europe, the biggest concern for North American audiences is trying to comprehend what exactly is happening, as some of the characters and dialogue seem lost in translation … the central story line is engaging enough for younger kids…"

Richard Cross of *20/20 Movie Reviews*: "[This film] never tries to resurrect within us that sense of wonder we felt at Christmas, choosing instead to try [to] tap into today's kids' fascination with gadgets and technology … importance of family … [is] secondary to a host of flashy, high-tech adventures…. The characters are pretty bland, thanks to a standard of animation which falls short of the standards set by the likes of Pixar."

PRODUCTION CREDITS—Screenplay: Thomas Wipf, Bob Swain, Dan and Nuria Wicksman, Allesandro Liggieri, Kurt Weldon, and Antii Haikala. Producers: Mikael Wahlforss and Mark Mertens. Director: Antii Haikala. Production Companies: Epidem, Araneo, Skyline Entertainment, Casa Kafka Pictures, Grid Animation, Le Tax Shelter du Gouvernement Fédéral de Belgique, Umedia, uFilm. Rating: Not rated. Genres: Animation, Adventure, Comedy, Family, Fantasy. Countries: Belgium and Finland. Run Time: 80 min.

REFERENCES: Costello, Brian. *Santa's Magic Crystal*. Common Sense Media. https://www.commonsensemedia.org/movie-reviews/santas-magic-crystal

Cross, Richard. *The Elf That Rescued Christmas*. 20/20 Movie Reviews. http://www.2020-movie-reviews.com/reviews-year/2011-movie-reviews/elf-rescued-christmas-2011-movie-review/

The Magic Crystal. Internet Movie Database. http://www.imdb.com/title/tt0986361/

Santa's Magic Crystal. Fort Mill, SC: KaBOOM! Entertainment, 2013. DVD Video.

Santa's Magic Toy Bag—December 1983
Television Short Film

THREAT TO CHRISTMAS: When elf apprentice Sherman washes Santa's magic toy bag, it shrinks and loses its magic powers.

HOW CHRISTMAS IS SAVED: Sherman creates another toy bag that has the same magic, because he learns to believe in himself.

SYNOPSIS AND COMMENTARY: Created by

Paul Fusco, who brought the popular sitcom *Alf* to television, *Santa's Magic Toy Bag* features similar hand puppets. Though it aired initially on Showtime, it has remained fairly obscure.

Sherman is a young elf apprentice right out of elf school who is determined to be one of Santa's finest. But Sherman, though very likeable, is a total klutz. He's been working at the North Pole for two weeks, and already he's been transferred around to just about every department, because he can't seem to fit in. For example, he creates bizarre toys (one of which is an electric kite with a fan and two miles of cord), doesn't file children's letters properly, unwittingly tosses 500 letters into the trash bin (they're retrieved from the incinerator at the last moment), and in the kitchen with Mrs. Claus, he bakes candy canes and adds stripes to gingerbread men. But a most patient Santa next assigns Sherman the task of guarding his magic toy bag on Christmas Eve. Seeing a smudge thereon, Sherman washes the bag, which shrinks and loses its magic powers; yes, Sherman has done it again. Not yet willing to throw in the towel, Sherman fashions a new toy bag by decorating one of the mail sacks. Not only is Santa pleased, but the bag actually is endowed with magic powers, because Sherman *believed* it would turn out that way; he believed in the magic of Christmas. For his reward, Sherman becomes an official elf and rides with Santa on his route.

PUPPET PERFORMERS: Lisa Buckley, Bob Fappiano, Rich Schellbach, and Paul Fusco.

INTERESTING TIDBITS: Just as Paul Fusco was the voice of Alf, he's also Santa's voice here.

Repeatedly through the show, there's a reference to a "Paul" from New Haven, CT, whose letters always present Santa and crew with new challenges. This year, he requests an electric kite for Christmas. This is a nod to Paul Fusco, who was born and raised in New Haven.

To console himself for his mistakes, Sherman often has one-sided conversations with his "companion" Danny, a jack-in-the-box clown on his bedside table. Perhaps Sigmund Freud would have had a field day with that.

REVIEWS: Renee Schonfeld of *Common Sense Media* (October 16, 2014): "Puppets, songs, and good cheer combine with a sweet story.... Messages about the magic of Christmas and developing one's skills and self-confidence are gently and humorously delivered."

Morgan R. Lewis of *Morgan on Media* (December 22, 2014): "It's your standard 'believe in yourself' moral lesson TV special.... It has the charm of the old Rankin-Bass stop-motion specials, only in a different medium.... If it had been released to a wider audience to begin with, it would be easy to see this becoming a cult-classic special, even if not a universal favorite."

PRODUCTION CREDITS—Writers: Paul Fusco and Troy Cabral. Producer: Paul Fusco. Director: James Field. Production Company: Imagicom Productions. Rating: Not rated. Genre: Family. Country: USA. Run Time: 28 min.

REFERENCES: Lewis, Morgan R. *Santa's Magic Toy Bag*. Morgan on Media. https://morganrlewis.wordpress.com/2014/12/22/santas-magic-toy-bag

Santa's Magic Toy Bag. Internet Movie Database. http://www.imdb.com/title/tt0185107/

Santa's Magic Toy Bag. San Diego: Legend Films, 2014. DVD Video.

Schonfeld, Renee. *Santa's Magic Toy Bag*. Common Sense Media. https://www.commonsensemedia.org/movie-reviews/santas-magic-toy-bag

Save the Reindeer—December 8, 2006

Episode from the Animated Television Series *Wonder Pets!*

THREAT TO CHRISTMAS: Santa's baby reindeer is stranded on thin ice, and his team needs her to fly.

HOW CHRISTMAS IS SAVED: The Wonder Pets travel to the North Pole to save the reindeer.

SYNOPSIS AND COMMENTARY: Created by Josh Selig, *Wonder Pets!* consisted of 42 half-hour episodes that ran on Nickelodeon and Nick Jr., from 2006 to 2013. By day, the protagonists were three pets in an elementary school classroom: Linny, a female guinea pig; Tuck, a male turtle; and Ming-Ming, a female duckling. When school was out, the caped trio sprang into action upon receiving calls to res-

The three principal characters from the animated TV series *Wonder Pets!* save baby animals around the world. From left: Linny, a female guinea pig; Ming-Ming, the female duckling; and Tuck, a male turtle, characters created utilizing photo-puppetry. By saving Santa's baby reindeer, the team save Christmas in the episode "Save the Reindeer" (2006) (Nickelodeon/Photofest).

cue baby animals in various parts of the world. Their principal mode of transportation was the "flyboat," a flying contraption that consisted of a red disc, four wheels, two felt marker caps for rocket boosters, and a sail. The episode format and animation were unusual in that the characters sang much of the dialogue, similar to opera, and animators utilized photos of real animals to create the characters (termed photo-puppetry) while other objects were drawn in conventional fashion.

In "Save the Reindeer," shortly after school dismisses on Christmas Eve (apparently no two-week vacation there), the Wonder Pets receive a call on their tin-can-and-string "phone" that Santa's baby reindeer needs to be rescued. She is to lead the team of six other adult reindeer, and Santa cannot make his rounds without her. Zooming to the North Pole in their flyboat, the Pets persuade a husky puppy to pull their vehicle over the snow until they locate the baby reindeer. The animal is stranded on cracking ice, so Ming-Ming, sacrificing her new Christmas sweater, fashions a sling to grab the reindeer moments before the ice falls through. By the way, the baby had run away because she had doubted her ability to lead Santa's team. After a pep talk from the Pets and back at Santa's workshop, baby hasn't the energy to pull the sleigh until Linny sacrifices her stalk of Christmas celery to fortify baby, and Santa's team takes off. Back at the school, Santa rewards Linny and Ming-Ming by replacing the gifts that they had sacrificed during the rescue, and Tuck receives a new snow globe to replace the one that Ming-Ming had accidentally broken.

PRINCIPAL VOICES (ALL CHILDREN): Sofie Zamchick as Linny; Teala Dunn as Tuck; Danica Lee as Ming-Ming; Steven Rebollido as the baby reindeer. These voice actors are all known for working on the *Wonder Pets!* series.

AWARDS: The series received Annie nominations for Best Directing and Writing (2010) and Best Music (2011) in a TV Production; Primetime Emmys for Outstanding Music Direction/Composition (2008–2012), Performer (Eartha Kitt, 2010), Children's and Animation Original Song (2010); Primetime Emmy nominations for Outstanding Performer (Danica Lee, 2007, 2008), Directing (Jennifer Oxley, 2008), Pre-School Children's Series (2009, 2010, 2012, 2014), Original Song and Sound Editing (2009), Music Direction/Composition (2011, 2014), Performer (Steven Tyler, 2011), Writing (2012, 2014).

INTERESTING TIDBITS: At the beginning, as the unseen children leave school, viewers hear their holiday greetings of "Happy Kwanzaa" and "Happy Hanukkah," in addition to "Merry Christmas." The politically correct teacher, however, wishes them "Happy Holidays."

At the beginning, the Pets sing that Christmas Eve is the longest night of the year. It surely must seem to be the longest night that children endure while waiting for Christmas Morning, but the Winter Solstice, December 21 or 22, not Christmas Eve, is actually *the* longest night of the year.

Linny expresses a politically correct, neutral sentiment about the holiday: "Christmas isn't about presents; it's about being together and helping others," a sentiment that is neither materialistic nor religious. Never mind that at the beginning, the Pets enthusiastically discuss opening *presents* before they receive the rescue call.

Ming-Ming pronounces all her Rs as Ws; for example, "Gweat pwesent! Can I twy it? It's Chwistmas!" Cute!

Linny receives a stalk of "imported" celery for Christmas. Lest kids rush off to feed tons of celery to their pet guinea pigs, the Internet article "Can Guinea Pigs Eat Celery?" warns that, "All those strings that we peel off celery stalks ... also wreak havoc on a guinea pig's teeth, throat, and intestinal tract. It's best to think of celery as an 'accent' to your guinea pigs' daily salad, served in small quantities."

REVIEW: Pam Gelman of *Common Sense Media*: "[The series], which combines adventure, an exemplary model of teamwork in action, and interesting information about different animals in our world, is a brilliant addition to the world of children's television."

PRODUCTION CREDITS—Head Writer: Billy Aronson. Producer: Tone Thyne. Director: Jennifer Oxley. Production Company: Little Airplane Productions. Rating: TV-Y. Genres: Animation, Family. Country: USA. Run Time: 24 min.

REFERENCES: "Can Guinea Pigs Eat Celery?" Guinea Pig Connection. http://guineapigconnection.typepad.com/pig_notes/2007/02/can_guinea_pigs.html

Gelman, Pam. *The Wonder Pets! Common Sense Media*. https://www.commonsensemedia.org/tv-reviews/the-wonder-pets

Lenburg, Jeff. *The Encyclopedia of Animated Cartoons*. Third Edition. New York: Facts on File, 2009.

"Save the Reindeer." In *Wonder Pets! Season 1*. New York: Viacom International, 2015. DVD Video.

Wilson, Joanna. *Tis the Season TV: The Encyclopedia of Christmas-Themed Episodes, Specials and Made-for-TV Movies*. Akron, OH: 1701 Press, 2011.

Wonder Pets! Internet Movie Database. http://www.imdb.com/title/tt0775407/

Saving Christmas—November 14, 2014

Also Known As *Kirk Cameron's Saving Christmas*

Feature Film

THREAT TO CHRISTMAS: When people believe that Christmas traditions have pagan origins, they take Christ out of Christmas.

HOW CHRISTMAS IS SAVED: By showing that Christmas traditions have a biblical basis, Kirk Cameron puts Christ back in Christmas.

SYNOPSIS AND COMMENTARY: The more any film focuses on Christianity and faith-based subjects, the more likely the critics will bristle, for God and Jesus are not politically correct subjects in any media. Such is the case with *Saving Christmas* (see the reviews below), in which the protagonist, evangelical Christian

Kirk Cameron (*Left Behind*), utilizes comedy and the Bible to put Christ back in Christmas.

In his opening monologue, Cameron lists everything he loves about Christmas, from cookies, lights, and the tree, to presents, stockings, and hot chocolate, then notes that there are two groups of Christmas naysayers: those who urge Christmas aficionados to keep their celebrations quiet without public display, and those who hold that because all Christmas traditions are "bad," they should be thrown out. Apparently Cameron's movie brother-in-law, ironically named Christian here (Darren Doane, *Godmoney*), resides somewhere in the latter camp, for at the annual family Christmas party hosted by his real-life sister, Bridgette Ridenour, Cameron learns that Chris, having left the party to sit alone in his car, is all in a funk over what he sees as rampant commercialism and supposedly the pagan origins that surround Christmas. As far as he's concerned, the traditions that we observe have strayed far from the true origins of Christmas, for none of those traditions are found in the Bible. Joining Chris in his car for the bulk of the movie, Cameron rejects the pagan origins and instead explains how those traditions actually *do* have a biblical basis (even though the Bible does not explicitly mention them as such). For example, the swaddling clothes in which Baby Jesus was wrapped and the burial spices of frankincense and myrrh presented at the Nativity foreshadowed Jesus' death on the cross, after which He was anointed with spices and wrapped for burial. Bypassing any biblical symbolism of the Wise Men's gold, Cameron next links the Christmas tree with those in the Garden of Eden. Whereas the first Adam (no mention of Eve) "stole" and ate the forbidden fruit from the Tree of Good and Evil, Jesus, the last "Adam," paid the final price by putting the Fruit of Himself back onto the metonymic tree of the cross with His own death so that mankind could finally partake of the "fruit" from the Tree of Life. Santa Claus sprang from Nicholas, the fourth-century bishop of Myra and later canonized, who defended the faith to preserve the doctrine of the divinity of Christ. When one sees presents, one sees the "skyline" of the New Jerusalem or heaven, in the center of which stands the Tree of Life, adorned with Fruit and Light made available by the conquering blood of Jesus to all who believe. Even toy soldiers represent King Herod's soldiers, who would have killed Baby Jesus; though He was spared in infancy, Jesus became the ultimate Warrior Who conquered death. Therefore, reasons Cameron, since God took on a *material* body, "it's right that our holiday is marked with material things." Armed with new insight, Chris has by now returned to the party, where the "God Squad Dance Crew" perform to a hip-hop version of "Angels We Have Heard on High." Along with the end credits, the final ten minutes consist of comical blooper outtakes.

Awards: In 2015, this film won Razzie Awards for Worst Picture, Worst Actor (Cameron), Worst Screenplay, and Worst Screen Combo. It received Razzie nominations for Worst Supporting Actress (Bridgette Ridenour) and Worst Director.

Interesting Tidbits: Matt Mauney of the *Orlando Sentinel* (December 5, 2014) noted that, "according to the Internet Movie Database, Kirk Cameron's 'Saving Christmas' is the worst film of all time." It received a popular rating of 1.3 stars/10 stars, making it the lowest-rated film on the IMDb's list of the Bottom 100 Films at the time.

According to Peter Holley of *The Washington Post* (December 8, 2014), Cameron attributed the dismal ratings to "'haters,' 'pagans,' and an atheist conspiracy that was allegedly hatched on Reddit." Holley further noted that, "The 'Duck Dynasty' gang endorsed the film. As did the Dove Foundation, Christian author and speaker Jay Younts and Ben Carson, among others."

With a budget of only $500,000, the film grossed about $2.8 million at the box office; hence, it was deemed a "success," despite the miserable reviews.

Reviews: According to the Rotten Tomatoes film review site, no critics gave this film a positive review. Metacritic gave it a score of 18/100 (overwhelming dislike).

Sandie Angulo Chen of *Common Sense Media* (November 20, 2014): "The most surprising thing about this movie is that Cameron isn't taking on or debating the secular humanists ... as [Cameron] sees it, God wants [believers] to spend lavishly on one another, party hard, and go full Pinterest-mode on decorations every Christmas ... those within the faith community who'd rather focus on charity and austerity are just party-pooping curmudgeons..."

Michael O'Sullivan of *The Washington Post* (November 14, 2014): "The one sales pitch that's hardest to buy is Cameron's insistence that there's nothing wrong with the materialistic focus of Christmas. His characterization of Jesus as a 'material' gift to us from God—evidence, he claims, that God *wants* us to shop—should offend anyone who balks at placing the Christ Child on the same scale as a $25 gift card."

Penny Walker of *The Arizona Republic* (November 13, 2014): "A well-intentioned defense of the trappings of Christmas makes a few interesting points but uses such poor logic throughout most of the film that it won't win any converts.... Beyond the leaps in logic, the most troubling part of this film is that it just feels like a defense of the excess of Christmas."

Alonso Duralde of *The Wrap* (November 14, 2014): "It's an 80-minute jeremiad aimed at other Christians who don't celebrate Christmas exactly the way Kirk Cameron does.... Director Doane offers no storytelling pizzazz; the lighting is careless, the pacing is deadly, the occasional stabs at comedy fall flat ... [the film] has nothing to share that Linus Van Pelt didn't already say better [in] *A Charlie Brown Christmas*."

PRODUCTION CREDITS—Writers: Darren Doane and Cheston Hervey. Producers: Darren Doane, Raphi Henley, Ankara Rosser, and David Shannon. Director: Darren Doane. Production Companies: Camfam Studios, Liberty University, Provident Films, and XDX2. Rating: PG (thematic elements). Genre: Comedy. Country: USA. Run Time: 80 min.

REFERENCES: Chen, Sandie Angulo. *Kirk Cameron's Saving Christmas.* Common Sense Media. https://www.commonsensemedia.org/movie-reviews/kirk-camerons-saving-christmas

Duralde, Alonso. "'Saving Christmas' Review: Kirk Cameron's Ho-Ho-Hum Holiday Revisionism." *The Wrap.* http://www.thewrap.com/saving-christmas-review-kirk-cameron-darren-doane-faith-based/

Holley, Peter. "Kirk Cameron Says 'Kirk Cameron's Saving Christmas' Is the Target of an Atheist Conspiracy." *The Washington Post.* https://www.washingtonpost.com/news/arts-and-entertainment/wp/2014/12/08/kirk-cameron-says-kirk-camerons-saving-christmas-is-the-target-of-an-atheist-conspiracy/

Kirk Cameron's Saving Christmas. Box Office Mojo. http://www.boxofficemojo.com/movies/?id=savingchristmas.htm

Kirk Cameron's Saving Christmas. Metacritic. http://www.metacritic.com/movie/kirk-camerons-saving-christmas/critic-reviews

Kirk Cameron's Saving Christmas. Rotten Tomatoes. http://www.rottentomatoes.com/m/kirk_camerons_saving_christmas/

Mauney, Matt. "Kirk Cameron's 'Saving Christmas' Officially Worst Movie in IMDb History." *Orlando Sentinel.* http://touch.orlandosentinel.com/#section/-1/article/p2p-82198415/

O'Sullivan, Michael. "'Kirk Cameron's Saving Christmas' Movie Review." *The Washington Post.* https://www.washingtonpost.com/goingoutguide/movies/kirk-camerons-saving-christmas-movie-review/2014/11/14/75c17f10-6c1e-11e4-9fb4-a622dae742a2_story.html

Saving Christmas. Internet Movie Database. http:///www.imdb.com/title/tt4009460/

Saving Christmas. Franklin, TN: Provident Films, 2015. DVD Video.

Walker, Penny. "Review: Earnest 'Saving Christmas' Leaves Logic Behind." *The Arizona Republic.* http://www.azcentral.com/story/entertainment/movies/2014/11/12/review-earnest-saving-christmas-leaves-logic-behind/18914449/

Saving Santa—November 5, 2013

Computer-Animated Direct-to-Video Musical

THREAT TO CHRISTMAS: An evil delivery magnate invades the North Pole to learn Santa's secret of delivering presents around the world in one night.

HOW CHRISTMAS IS SAVED: Bernard D. Elf goes back in time to set matters right.

SYNOPSIS AND COMMENTARY: How does

Santa deliver all those presents around the world in one night? Good people have asked that question over the centuries as have naughty folks, and none is naughtier than Neville Baddington, a middle-aged mama's-boy who runs Quickest Airborne Delivery with his domineering, son-bashing mother Vera. If Baddington can discover Santa's secret, he'll be able to usurp Santa and have the world's fastest delivery service. Invading the North Pole by air after a power glitch accidentally reveals Santa's classified location, Baddington and his commandos capture Santa, who has revealed his secret—a time globe built into the sleigh—to Bernard D. Elf, an imaginative yet error-prone little inventor known as the Reindeer Poop Shoveler but who prefers the more distinguished title of Director of Droppings. After twice traveling back in time prior to Baddington's invasion, where Bernard only succeeds in uselessly chasing his other two incarnations around the North Pole and where viewers observe events repeated from different vantage points, Bernard finally retrieves his recently invented Christmas memory machine to extract Baddington's childhood memories that he had forgotten. In one, mama had destroyed a letter he had written to Santa inquiring about how presents were delivered and, having never received a reply, Baddington had kept a grudge ever since. With this memory restored, Baddington becomes a changed man, and to prevent mama from overriding him, he erases her memory with Bernard's memory-erasing device, after which Bernard is promoted from stable elf to an inventor at Santech, Santa's think-tank.

PRINCIPAL VOICES: Martin Freeman (*The Hobbit*) as Bernard D. Elf; Tim Curry (*The Rocky Horror Picture Show*) as Baddington; Noel Clarke (*Doctor Who*) as Agent Snowy (whose name is rather ironic, given that he seems to be the only black elf in the whole realm); Tim Conway (*The Carol Burnett Show*) as Santa; Pam Ferris (*Matilda*) as Mrs. Claus; Ashley Tisdale (*High School Musical*) as Shiny; Joan Collins (*Dynasty*) as Vera; Nick Guest (*USA High*) as Blitzen.

SONGS: Original songs and music by Grant Olding. "A Christmas Wish" (performed by Benjy Norman); "Prospects" (performed by Martin Freeman); "An Elf Like Me" (performed by Martin Freeman); "Do or Die" (performed by Ashley Tisdale and Martin Freeman); "Swingle Bells" (parody of "Jingle Bells," additional lyrics by Grant Olding); "12 Days of Elevator Muzak" (parody of "The 12 Days of Christmas," additional lyrics by Grant Olding); "Some Kind of Miracle" (by Klaus Badelt, Mark Yaeger, Rachel Dahl, Jessica Burgan, Megan Bodul, and Vince Walker, performed by Ashley Tisdale).

INTERESTING TIDBIT: Through the song "Do or Die," Shiny, Bernard's love-interest, encourages a discouraged Bernard to think of a plan to rout Baddington, to think of the impact on children if there were no Santa. While her song is quite upbeat, it nevertheless sends the clear, materialistic implication that without the fun, merriment, and presents associated with Santa, Christmas would be essentially meaningless.

REVIEWS: According to the Rotten Tomatoes film review site, only 20 percent of critics gave this film a positive review.

Jen Johans of *Film Intuition* (November 1, 2013): "…*Saving Santa* is a charming, if utterly forgettable new stocking stuffer that's at least colorful and quirky enough to hold the attention span of the little ones…"

Amon Warmann of *CineVue* (November 2013): "…it's a fairly watchable jaunt that's high on Christmas spirit but short on originality … makes no bones about which market it's aiming for, with an opening song about belief in Santa bookended by a 'sweet, eh?' for good measure … destined to be another cog in the endless yuletide movie machine."

Renee Schonfeld of *Common Sense Media* (June 5, 2014): "…an engaging, pleasant family-viewing experience … not a landmark achievement in computer animation … not super-inventive or super-funny … vocal performances are first rate and there are nice messages about becoming our best selves and the wondrousness of childhood memories."

Jennifer Tate of *View London* (November 27, 2013): "Voiced by a recognisable [sic] cast, Saving Santa is a pleasant and well-timed festive animation, but its unsophisticated storyline, general lack of humor and substandard soundtrack ultimately let it down."

PRODUCTION CREDITS—Story: Antony Nottage. Screenplay: Ricky Roxburgh. Producers: Terry Stone, Nick Simunek, and Carolyn Bennett. Directors: Leon Joosen and Aaron Seelman. Production Companies: Gateway Films, Prana Animation Studios, and Prana Studios. Rating: Not rated. Genres: Animation, Adventure, Comedy, Family, Fantasy, Musical. Countries: United Kingdom, India, USA. Run Time: 83 min.

REFERENCES: Johan, Jen. "*Saving Santa* (2013)." *Film Intuition*. http://reviews.filmintuition.com/2013/11/SavingSanta2013.html

Saving Santa. Beverly Hills, CA: Anchor Bay Entertainment, 2013. DVD Video.

Saving Santa. Internet Movie Database. http://www.imdb.com/title/tt2204315/

Saving Santa. Rotten Tomatoes. http://www.rottentomatoes.com/m/saving_santa/

Schonfeld, Renee. *Saving Santa*. *Common Sense Media*. https://www.commonsensemedia.org/movie-reviews/saving-santa

Tate, Jennifer. *Saving Santa*. *View London*. http://www.viewlondon.co.uk/films/saving-santa-film-review-56490.html

Warmann, Amon. "Film Review: 'Saving Santa.'" *CineVue*. http://www.cine-vue.com/2013/11/film-review-saving-santa.html

A Scooby-Doo! Christmas—December 13, 2002

Also Known As *Ho! Ho! Horrors!*

Special from the Animated Television Series *What's New, Scooby-Doo?*

THREAT TO CHRISTMAS: A Headless Snowman prevents the town of Winter Hollow from celebrating Christmas.

HOW CHRISTMAS IS SAVED: Scooby-Doo

Something or someone has the gang of Mystery, Inc. really spooked in the animated TV series *Scooby-Doo, Where Are You!* From left: Scooby-Doo, Shaggy Rogers, Velma Dinkley, Daphne Blake, and Fred Jones. The gang investigate the "Headless Snowman" in the special *A Scooby-Doo! Christmas* (2002) from the series *What's New, Scooby-Doo?* (Hanna-Barbera Productions/Photofest).

and the gang unmask the culprit and restore Christmas to Winter Hollow.

SYNOPSIS AND COMMENTARY: Imagine a goofy, cowardly Great Dane foodie who ironically served as the mascot for an outfit bent on solving supernatural-related mysteries. That's Scooby-Doo, who first appeared in the Hanna-Barbera animated TV series *Scooby-Doo, Where Are You!* on CBS from 1969 to 1970. The ninth of multiple incarnations of the *Scooby-Doo* franchise, the *What's New* series ran on the WB Network for 43 half-hour episodes from 2002 to 2006. Although *What's New* was a modernized version of the *Where Are You!* series, it revived the original's formulaic version, in which Mystery, Inc., comprised of four teenagers (Fred Jones, Daphne Blake, Velma Dinkley, and beatnik Shaggy Rogers), solved "mysterious" incidents perpetrated by nothing more than humans in monster/ghost costumes.

En route to a friend's condo on a snowy Christmas Eve, the Scooby gang become stranded in Winter Hollow, a small New England town where a "Headless Snowman," a creature known for throwing its head, has prevented the residents from celebrating Christmas for many years. Each Christmas, the townsfolk gather at the local inn to escape the Snowman, who destroys the chimneys of homes. According to Professor Higginson, a local historian, the Snowman is supposedly the ghost of Blackjack Brody, a 19th-century highwayman who had robbed a Seamus Fagan of his gold but who had succumbed to a blizzard. When Brody was found buried within a snowman, he was covered in chimney soot. While the Scooby gang ponder the mystery and consider several suspects, the growling Snowman chases them around town, until Fred, Velma, and Daphne set a series of heat lamps along the road as a trap. Pursuing Shaggy and Scooby, the Snowman plunges into the heat wave and melts, revealing the culprit as Professor Higginson, a descendant of Seamus Fagan, whose gold Brody had hidden in a chimney as gold bricks. Instead of jail, Higginson receives forgiveness for his misdeeds (after all, it is Christmas), whereupon he donates the newly discovered gold to the town (which would cover the cost of much damage), and Christmas returns to Winter Hollow.

VOICES: Casey Kasem (*Ghostbusters*) as Shaggy; Frank Welker (*Aladdin*) as Scooby, Fred, and the Headless Snowman; Mindy Cohn (*The Facts of Life*) as Velma; Grey DeLisle (*The Replacements*) as Daphne; James Belushi (*Red Heat*) as innkeeper Asa Buckwald; Mark Hamill (*Star Wars*) as Tommy's father; Kathy Kinney (*Scrooged*) as Sheriff Ellen Perkins; Daryl Sabara (*Spy Kids*) as Tommy; Peter Scolari (*The Polar Express*) as Professor Higginson; M. Emmet Walsh (*Blade Runner*) as Jeb.

SONGS: "Christmas Fright" by Jeff Martin, performed by Rich Dickerson; "Santa Claus, Santa Claus" by Rich Dickerson and Gigi Meroni, performed by Heavy Trevy; "Merry Christmas Day" by Rich Dickerson, performed by Julia Fordham and Jonathan Rice.

AWARDS: In 2003, the *What's New, Scooby-Doo?* series received a Daytime Emmy nomination for Outstanding Performer in an Animated Program (Mindy Cohn).

INTERESTING TIDBITS: Winter Hollow and the Headless Snowman are obvious nods to *The Legend of Sleepy Hollow*. The name first considered for the New England town was Christmas Hollow.

As the Snowman melts, he hollers, "I'm melting, I'm melting, oh what a world!" which is a nod to the demise of the Wicked Witch of the West in *The Wizard of Oz*.

Near the end, Asa declares Professor Higginson as "the richest man in town," which is a nod to the character George Bailey in *It's a Wonderful Life*.

A Scooby-Doo! Christmas was the first prime-time holiday television special in the *Scooby-Doo* franchise.

REVIEW: Sarah Wenk of *Common Sense Media* reviewed the *What's New* series: "Silly mysteries with harmless mayhem.... Only very young children might find the show's puzzles and monsters frightening ... [scary situations] are quickly resolved, and the scariness quotient is low."

PRODUCTION CREDITS—Writers: John Collier, George Doty IV, Jim Krieg, and Ed Scharlach. Producer: Chuck Sheetz. Director: Scott Jeralds. Production Companies: Warner Bros. Animation and Television, Cartoon Network, and Hanna-Barbera Productions (copyright owners). Rating: TV-Y7. Genres: Animation, Comedy, Family, Mystery. Country: USA. Run Time: 21 min.

REFERENCES: King, Susan. "Christmas in the Eyes of Children: Scooby-Doo Gets His First Holiday Special, and the Networks Unwrap a Sleigh Full of Seasonal Gifts for Young Viewers." *Los Angeles Times*. http://articles.latimes.com/2002/dec/08/news/tv-coverstory8

A Scooby-Doo Christmas. Big Cartoon Database. http://www.bcdb.com/cartoon/59682-Scooby-Doo-Christmas

A Scooby-Doo Christmas. Bonus episode in *What's New, Scooby-Doo? The Complete Third Season*. Burbank, CA: Warner Home Video, 2008. DVD Video.

A Scooby-Doo Christmas. Internet Movie Database. http://www.imdb.com/title/tt0747083/

Wenk, Sarah. *What's New, Scooby-Doo? Common Sense Media*. https://www.commonsensemedia.org/tv-reviews/whats-new-scooby-doo

Scrooge Loose—1963

Episode from the Animated Television Series *The Gumby Show*

THREAT TO CHRISTMAS: Scrooge escapes from *A Christmas Carol* and replaces Santa's gifts with rocks.

HOW CHRISTMAS IS SAVED: Gumby makes sure that Scrooge is all tied up.

SYNOPSIS AND COMMENTARY: Created by Art Clokey, the Gumby character was portrayed in stop-motion animation as a green, clay, humanoid creature that was featured on television's *The Howdy Doody Show* (1955–1956) and was the subject of several television series for a total of 234 episodes: *The Gumby Show* (NBC, 1956–1957), syndicated revival (1962–1968), and *Gumby Adventures* (1988); a feature film, *Gumby: The Movie* (1995); and other media. Other principal characters in the series included Gumby's parents, Gumbo and Gumba; sister Minga; sidekick Pokey, a talking, orange pony; Prickle, a yellow dinosaur; and Goo, a blue flying mermaid. Gumby and friends experienced a considerable diversity of adventures.

In "Scrooge Loose," Gumby and Pokey respectively act as Sherlock Holmes and Dr. Watson, complete with their stereotypical hats. Playing with his telescope, Gumby observes Ebenezer Scrooge escape from Dickens's book *A Christmas Carol*. After exclaiming "Bah, humbug!" a few times too many, Scrooge pushes a bunch of toys off the shelf with a tractor, then enters a book of stories about Santa, where he finds himself outside Santa's workshop on Christmas Eve and would ruin Christmas by replacing Santa's toys with rocks. Gumby ties up Scrooge and stuffs him into a bag, but while Gumby searches for Santa, the jolly gent, seeing what he thinks is a misplaced bag of toys, hoists it onto his sleigh and takes off. "Instead of Christmas, it's April Fool's Day for Santa," laughs Pokey when he and Gumby discover the error. Gumby counters with, "You mean it's December Dopeys' Day for us!" Some kid will "get" Scrooge for Christmas.

PRINCIPAL VOICES: Dallas McKinnon (*Daniel Boone*) as Gumby; Art Clokey (*Davey and Goliath*) as Pokey.

INTERESTING TIDBITS: In the series, a common sequence has Gumby walking into a book and experiencing the world within.

Check out **Santa-Witch**, another *Gumby* save-Christmas cartoon.

PRODUCTION CREDITS—Writer, Producer, and Director: Art Clokey. Production Company: Clokey Productions and NBC. Rating: G. Genres: Animation, Comedy, Family. Country: USA. Run Time: 6.5 min.

REFERENCES: *Gumby*. Web Site. http://www.gumbyworld.com/

The Gumby Show. Internet Movie Database. http://www.imdb.com/title/tt0050022/

"Scrooge Loose." In *Christmas with Gumby*. New York: GoodTimes Home Entertainment, 2003. DVD Video.

Wilson, Joanna. *Tis the Season TV: The Encyclopedia of Christmas-Themed Episodes, Specials and Made-for-TV Movies*. Akron, OH: 1701 Press, 2011.

Search for Rudolph—December 25, 2002

Episode from the Computer-Animated Television Series *The Shapies*

THREAT TO CHRISTMAS: Rudolph, Santa's lead reindeer, is missing.

HOW CHRISTMAS IS SAVED: The Shapies commence a bedroom-wide search for Rudolph.

SYNOPSIS AND COMMENTARY: Created by Mark Traynor, *The Shapies* was a series for preschoolers that ran on Australian television for 27 half-hour episodes in 2002 and on PBS Kids in the USA. The Shapies was the name of a toy-box rock band that consisted of ten different geometrically shaped characters who came to life and emerged from a toy box into the bedroom of a young boy named Zach whenever he wasn't around. The members of this adventurous band were: Bob Oblong, the leader; Paul the Ball, the group clown; Tammy Triangle, the athlete; Rex the Rectangle, a drum-playing dog; Sarah Circle; Sally Cylinder, the vain member; Sammy Square, the smartest member; Starry Star, the sweetest member; Perry Pyramid; Connie Cone, the youngest member. Other principal characters included Mirror Man, a sometime-narrator whose face appeared in the bedroom mirror when Zach departed, and Mr. Boo, a bald villain and the Shapies' principal antagonist. The Shapies' ultimate goal was to become the most popular band in the world.

In "Rudolph," it's Christmas Eve and Zach is decorating his bedroom tree. When he leaves, the Shapies are all agog at seeing a toy Santa and his reindeer sleigh nearby. Introducing the Shapies to his *nine* reindeer, Santa discovers that Rudolph is missing, whereupon Santa laments that there will be no Christmas if Rudolph isn't around to light the way. While Bob, Sally, and Paul conduct their own search for Rudolph elsewhere, the others try to get Starry to the top of the tree as a lookout. Their attempts at building a tower by climbing up each other's shoulders, flying Starry in a toy plane then her parachuting down to the tree, and her climbing a ladder from a toy fire truck all fail. Bob, Sally, and Paul also return empty-handed, having chased a red glow that originated from Mr. Boo. By now, Santa is despondent and bawling, but then a rattling among a stack of presents reveals the missing Rudolph, and Santa is ready for his rounds. When Zach soon returns, the Shapies become lifeless and are hung on Zach's tree as ornaments, with Starry at the top.

PRINCIPAL VOICES: Tony Bellette, Jane U'Brien, Bonnie Fraser, Joanne Moore, and Declan Steele.

SONGS: Composed by Mark Traynor, Brian White, and Ken McLean. Vocals by Meika Robertson, Rob Robertson, and Belinda Rowe.

INTERESTING TIDBITS: Whereas in most Santa movies the traditional eight reindeer pull his sleigh, this film is one of few that include Rudolph as the ninth and lead reindeer.

Throughout the film, the Shapies express their hope of finding Rudolph so that they will get their presents. Only near the end when Rudolph turns up, seemingly as an afterthought, they suddenly remember that there's another side to Christmas, even if it's not entirely religious. As Santa reminds them, "Goodwill and Christmas spirit is [sic] what Christmas is all about."

Notice that Zach is dressed in a short-sleeve shirt and short pants. Since the setting is Australia, Christmas there is a summertime holiday.

NOTE: At this writing, this production was not available on DVD or VHS but could be seen on Amazon Instant Video.

PRODUCTION CREDITS—Writer and Director: Mark Traynor. Producer: Wes Tatters. Production Company: Light Knights Productions. Rating: Not rated. Genres: Animation, Adventure, Comedy, Family, Musical. Country: Australia. Run Time: 24 min.

REFERENCES: *The Shapies*. Internet Movie Database. http://www.imdb.com/title/tt0343305/

The Shapies. Website. http://www.shapies.tv/

The Search for Santa Paws—November 23, 2010

Direct-to-Video Musical

THREAT TO CHRISTMAS: Santa suffers amnesia and becomes gravely ill in New York City.

HOW CHRISTMAS IS SAVED: Puppy Paws, orphans, and a magic crystal save Santa.

SYNOPSIS AND COMMENTARY: The magic of crystal amulets reigns along with loveable, talking pooches in this prequel to *Santa Buddies: The Legend of Santa Paws* (2009). Although it is the fifth film in the *Air Buddies* spinoff series, the five Buddies puppies are not featured here.

While birthday partying, Santa (Richard Riehle, *Office Space*) receives news about the death of Mr. Hucklebuckle, an old friend and proprietor of a toy shop in New York City. The news comes with a canine plush toy, Hucklebuckle's last gift to Santa. To ease their boss's grief, the elves, via the magic of the Christmas Icicle, transform the toy into a live, Great Pyrenees puppy that Santa names Paws. Because Hucklebuckle's shop had been a source for the Christmas spirit, much of which has now waned, Santa and Paws journey to the Big Apple to revive the city. Hit by a taxi, Santa suffers amnesia and is separated from Paws, and a street bum robs him of his magic crystal, the source of his immortality. Calling himself "Bud," Santa lands a job as the in-house Santa for the old toy shop, which Hucklebuckle's grandson James (John Ducey, *Jonas*) now operates with wife Kate (Bonnie Somerville, *Bedazzled*), and sales skyrocket. Meanwhile, Paws teams up with three wise-cracking dogs to search for Santa: Haggis, a Scottish terrier; Rasta, a reggae puli; and T-Money, a bulldog. In a subplot, Paws buddies up with orphans Quinn (Kaitlyn Maher, *Santa Buddies*), who keeps the Christmas spirit, and Willamina (Madison Pettis, *Life with Boys*), a cynic who feels she will never be adopted. Both live in a girls' foster home run by Ms. Stout (Wendi McLendon-Covey, *Blended*), an evil woman who hates Christmas, locks the kids in the basement for punishment, and incinerates their toys. When Stout removes Paws's amulet, he becomes a stuffed toy again, and Quinn rescues him from an eternity in the incinerator. Now mortal, Santa falls gravely ill, whereupon head elf Eli (Danny Woodburn, *Santa Buddies*) and his elf-dog Eddy, a Jack Russell terrier (both reprising their roles from *Santa Buddies*), join forces with the orphans to smuggle Santa from the hospital. Though revived with his amulet, Paws once again becomes a toy when he sacrifices the amulet to save Santa yet receives life anew from the Christmas Icicle, which transforms him into a live adult Great Pyrenees that Santa renames Santa Paws. To complete the happiness, James and Kate, otherwise childless, adopt Quinn and Willamina, and Ms. Stout gets the boot.

ANIMAL VOICES: Zachary Gordon (*Diary of a Wimpy Kid*) as Puppy Paws; Mitchel Musso (*Monster House*) as Santa Paws; Jason Connery (*Night Skies*) as Haggis; Josh Flitter (*License to Wed*) as T-Money; Christopher Massey (*Zoey 101*) as Rasta; Richard Kind (*Inside Out*) as Eddy the Elf-Dog; Diedrich Bader (*Ice Age*) as Comet; Michael Deyermond (*Californication*) as Dancer.

SONGS: "Tinker Time" (by Brahm Wenger, John Rosenberg, and Justin Long); "Friends for Life" (by Brahm Wenger and Greg Prechel); "Who Will Sing to Me?" (by Brahm Wenger); "I Do Believe in Christmas" (by Brahm Wenger and John Rosenberg); "Why Don't I Believe?" (by Brahm Wenger); "It's That Wonderful Time of the Year" (by Brahm Wenger); "Love Is in Your Heart" (by Brahm Wenger).

AWARDS: In 2011, this picture received a Young Artist Award nomination for Best Performance in a DVD Film–Young Actress (Melody B. Choi).

INTERESTING TIDBITS: Santa employs elves who are a mix of young adults and dwarves of different races and ethnicities.

Santa eventually may need a neurologist, because he also suffers amnesia in other save-Christmas movies, such as *The Amazing World of Gumball: Christmas Episode; The Boy Who Saved Christmas; Merry Madagascar; Miracle at the 34th Precinct; The Night Before the Night Before Christmas; Santa Who?* and *Snow 2: Brain Freeze*.

If you're really into Christmas doggies, check out the sequel, *Santa Paws 2: The Santa Pups*.

REVIEWS: Hannah Goodwyn of The Christian Broadcasting Network: "[An] issue parents may have is the film's focus on the magical power of crystals that sustain Claus and Paws' lives... [The film] does present a good Christmas message of giving and friendship."

Kevin Carr of *7M Pictures*: "The film is cheesy, yes, but not too cheesy to enjoy with the kids ... the adult actors look like they're having fun rather than just collecting a paycheck."

Will Brownridge of *The Film Reel* (December 2, 2010): "...there is way too much going on in this movie ... there's almost no room to have dogs in a movie that's supposed to be about dogs.... Everything is just terribly sad here."

Joly Herman of *Common Sense Media* (November 10, 2010): "Kids will love Santa's puppy, but watch out for sad moments ... the movie's themes of loss, neglect, and abandonment might be too intense for very young or sensitive children.... There are also mixed messages about the 'true' meaning of Christmas (loot or love?)..."

PRODUCTION CREDITS—Writers and Producers: Anna McRoberts and Robert Vince. Director: Robert Vince. Production Companies: Walt Disney Pictures, Keystone Entertainment, Key Pix Productions, and Santa Paws Productions. Rating: G. Genres: Adventure, Family, Fantasy. Countries: Canada and USA. Run Time: 96 min.

REFERENCES: Brownridge, Will. *The Search for Santa Paws. The Film Reel.* http://www.thefilmreel.com/2010/12/02/the-search-for-santa-paws-2010-film-reel-reviews/

Carr, Kevin. *The Search for Santa Paws. 7M Pictures.* http://www.7mpictures.com/the-search-for-santa-paws-blu-ray-review/

Crump, William D. *The Christmas Encyclopedia*. Third Edition. Jefferson, NC: McFarland, 2013.

Goodwyn, Hannah. *The Search for Santa Paws.* The Christian Broadcasting Network. http://www.cbn.com/entertainment/screen/the-search-for-santa-paws

Herman, Joly. *The Search for Santa Paws. Common Sense Media.* https://www.commonsensemedia.org/movie-reviews/the-search-for-santa-paws

The Search for Santa Paws. Burbank, CA: Walt Disney Home Entertainment, 2010. DVD Video.

The Search for Santa Paws. Internet Movie Database. http://www.imdb.com/title/tt1544572/

The Secret World of Santa Claus
(*Le Monde secret du Père Noël*)—1997
Animated Television Series

THREAT TO CHRISTMAS: Two trolls persistently strive to thwart Santa's Christmas preparations through 26 episodes.

HOW CHRISTMAS IS SAVED: Santa, with assistance from his three elves, always manages to stay a few steps ahead of the trolls.

SYNOPSIS AND COMMENTARY: Most save-Christmas films that focus on Santa are set one or two days before the big guy makes his annual deliveries, when some bogey or other catastrophe gets in his way. In this Canadian-French children's series created by Olivier Brémond, Pascal Breton, and Annabelle Perrichon using simple animation, however, Santa faces assorted challenges in all of the 26 half-hour episodes that explore his Christmas preparations throughout the year. A few challenges are rather petty, but the toughest ones are courtesy of his neighbors, two trolls bent on ruining Christmas: the grizzled Gruzzlebeard, who sports a bald, pointed head and refers to Santa as either "that red-suited sap" or "bulb nose," and his lackey Dudley, who resembles a typically small elf. Santa also is rather nonconventional in that he works with only three elves: Thoren (the only female), who flies and can become invisible; Jordi, who can morph into any creature; and the apprentice Guilfi. There are as many reindeer: Rudolph, his aging father Donner, and Blitzen. Balbo the polar bear serves as Santa's assistant. The following paragraphs briefly summarize the episodes.

1. "La Perle Magique du Père Noël" ("The Magic Pearl"). When Gruzzlebeard and Dudley smash Santa's toymaking machine (which explains the paucity of elves) and its pearl, Santa and the gang find a replacement pearl in a cave, but first they must battle the Abominable Snowman and a large bat.

2. "Les Douze Travaux du Père Noël" ("The 12 Labors of Santa"). The Santa Claus Society recertifies Santa for another 100 years after he passes their rigorous, 12-part examination, but not before Gruzzlebeard and Dudley try to trip him up.

3. Les Petits Génies" ("Little Geniuses"). Troublemaking twin brothers hack into Santa's gift database and change the information such that they would receive all of Santa's presents.

4. "Rodolphe A Disparu" ("Rudolph Is Missing"). Santa must retrieve Rudolph when at Gruzzlebeard's prompting, he runs away and gives himself as a present to a little Inuit boy who wants a reindeer for Christmas.

5. "L'Enfant des Etoiles" ("The Star Child"). Santa delivers a pony to a boy living with his family on a space station while shrinking Gruzzlebeard to prevent him from sabotaging the sleigh.

6. "Un Noël pour Léon" ("Leon's Christmas"). Because of a lost letter, Santa never retrieved little Leon's dog that ran away, and Santa must deal with Leon's all-children-must-boycott-Santa campaign.

7. "Un Cadeau pour Deux" ("A Present for Two"). As the richest kid in the world (not Richie Rich here), Alex is bored with every toy, so Santa presents a gift to Alex's girlfriend that will benefit them both, a bicycle built for two.

8. "Super Lapin" ("Super Rabbit"). When Frank berates his younger brother Randy for having a rabbit doll, Santa creates a "Super Rabbit" video game that interests Frank. Since the game includes a Super Rabbit doll, Frank embraces it and leaves Randy alone.

9. "Porte-Bonheur" ("The Lucky Charm"). When a figure skater loses her lucky charm, she performs poorly, whereupon Santa supplies her with a fake charm that gives her the confidence to win, despite Gruzzlebeard's cheating antics.

10. "Tapis Volant" ("The Flying Carpet"). A little boy desires a flying carpet for Christmas and for his archaeologist-father to return home from work in the Middle East. Gruzzlebeard tampers with Santa's phone lines such that thieves from the father's archaeological site capture the elves for ransom.

11. "Les Mémoires du Père Noël" ("Santa Claus' Memoirs"). Upon being interviewed by a news reporter, Santa describes his greatest adventure, which is the tale of King Arthur, Excalibur, and the stone, in which Gruzzlebeard is on hand to cause mischief.

12. "La Baguette Magique" ("The Magic Wand"). When a little girl requests a magic wand to shorten her long nose, Gruzzlebeard gives her a tainted wand that turns people into animals, and Santa receives the blame.

13. "Le Garçon qui Voulait Redevenir Petit" ("The Boy Who Wished to Be Little Again"). Being small, Dudley wants to be taller, and David, jealous because his baby sister receives more parental attention, wants to be smaller. Dudley steals Santa's machine that fulfills their wishes, but Santa must alter his size to save David, who's been reduced to the size of a bug.

14. "Un Cadeau pour le Père Noël" ("A Present for Santa"). While the local children ponder over a suitable present to give Santa, Gruzzlebeard unleashes two termites that destroy Santa's special-occasions suit with magic powers (sounds more like those termites were cross-bred with moths). The elves and Balbo find materials for a new suit in the Forest of the Trolls, where Balbo surrenders his fur as payment, and the children give Santa a hot-air balloon. As payback, the elves flying aloft return the termites to Gruzzlebeard, whose house is demolished.

15. "Le Congrès de Noël" ("The Christmas Conference"). Every 100 years (perhaps to celebrate passing that awful test), Santa transforms the North Pole into a sunny paradise and invites his magical friends, one of whom is La Befana, a benevolent, broomstick-riding witch and Santa's Italian counterpart who brings gifts to good children on Epiphany, January 6. Santa intervenes when Gruzzlebeard kidnaps her and sabotages the Conference's games, then Santa and friends create a flight suit that enables a young boy to fly back home.

16. "Histoires de Trolls" ("The Story of the Trolls"). When two children request information about elves, Santa details their origins as opposed to the trolls, whereupon the elves

create an animated, 3-D book. Gruzzlebeard sabotages the book, which causes trolls to pour forth who threaten to ruin Santa's workshop.

17. "Le Noël de Geignard" ("Christmas for Dudley"). Gruzzlebeard works Dudley to the point that the latter covertly requests a robot to do his chores. The elves create a robot behind Santa's back, but it runs amok and siphons all the North Pole's electricity.

18. "Le Retour du Père Noël" ("The Return of Santa Claus"). Gruzzlebeard's sabotage of Jordi's teleportation device sends Santa and the elves to the year 2222, where no one celebrates Christmas and Gruzzlebeard rules all. After diddling with time, the foursome return to a point just before the sabotage to stop Gruzzlebeard.

19. "La Grande Petite Fille" ("The Tall Little Girl"). Moved by a little's girl's desire to be taller so she can play on her school's basketball team, the elves disobey Santa and provide her with a potion that turns her into a giant. Akin to *Attack of the 50-Foot Woman* (1958), the girl wreaks havoc with her city and Santa must intervene.

20. "L'Ours en Peluche" ("The Teddy Bear"). When the elves harass Balbo about his clumsiness, he gives himself to a boy who wants a bear-sized teddy bear for Christmas. Gruzzlebeard aims to hypnotize Balbo into telling him all about Santa, but he, Balbo, and the boy end up in a lake with their lives at risk, requiring Santa to intervene.

21. "On A Volé Noël" ("Stolen Christmas"). Taking revenge for having never received presents from Santa (because he never wrote Santa), a boy dresses as Santa, informs the post office to divert all Santa-letters to his private mansion, robs stores of their toys and frames Santa who is arrested, then returns to the North Pole with the elves. There, the toy-making machine creates pills that transform the impostor into a monster, but Santa escapes, saves the elves and, true to form, forgives the malefactor.

22. "La Révolte des Jouets" ("Havoc in Toyland"). Gruzzlebeard wreaks havoc with Santa's workshop when the former's magic powder brings the toys to life and they begin to explore. As Santa and the elves strive to restore order, Gruzzlebeard attempts to thwart Santa by trapping him in bubble gum.

23. "Une Bouteille À la Mer" ("Message in a Bottle"). When Gruzzlebeard intercepts a distress letter to Santa in a bottle from an island boy whose parents have been turned to stone by a Christmas-hating witch, he and Dudley are eager to investigate. Santa attempts to intervene but is also turned to stone, whereupon the elves must reverse the witch's spell.

24. "Balthazar Ne Sait Pas ce qu'il Veut" ("Balthazar Can't Make Up His Mind"). Little boy Balthazar changes his mind 64 times about the Christmas gift he wants and sends as many letters to Santa, who pays the boy a visit with the elves. By chance the rare Arctic squirrel Hoppy is with them, and Balthazar finally settles for him. But when a taxidermist captures Hoppy with plans to sell him as a prize scarf, Santa puts a cork in that.

25. "La Nuit la Plus Longue" ("The Longest Night"). It's now Christmas Eve as Santa commences his run with Thoren and Jordi, while Gruzzlebeard shifts his stop-Santa antics into high gear. He incapacitates Guilfi and Balbo back at the workshop by trapping the former in a pumpkin cage and serving "funny honey" laced with a mickey to the latter, then damages Santa's master time-stopping clock such that time runs backward to the dinosaur age. Interrupting their deliveries to return to the site of future North Pole City to free Guilfi and dodging hungry beasts, Santa and elves travel through the timeless gate to the cavern housing the master clock to effect repairs, then fast-forward to the present and freeze time once again. Gruzzlebeard, after an unsuccessful attempt to trap them in the cavern, is kept at bay as Dudley and Balbo pelt him with snowballs, while Santa and elves continue their run.

26. "Les Secrets du Père Noël" ("Santa Claus' Secrets"). Santa and elves continue their run from the previous episode, but Gruzzlebeard and Dudley are back to damaging the master time-stopping clock again, this time with Gruzzlebeard's guitar and amplifiers blasting away. Meanwhile, one Santa-secret is that

he can gain entrance to homes by animating children's toys therein with magic dust and having the toys admit him. With time running again, Santa races to finish his deliveries while facing more challenges, such as persuading hungry jackals in the desert to pull his sleigh from quicksand; evading a panther, crocodiles, and piranhas in a rain forest; and having storks relieve the exhausted reindeer on the sleigh. Gruzzlebeard uses trickery to trap Santa and elves in a glass cage on his last stop in Greenland, but Guilfi uses his then-unknown telekinetic power to free them, which earns him the title of Master Elf. The villains having received their just desserts, Santa reveals his last secret—making a French *bûche de Noël* (Yule log cake)—and the elves present him with a globe showing pictures of all the kids to whom he has given smiles.

PRINCIPAL VOICES (ENGLISH VERSION): Tony Robinow (*Martyrs*) as Santa; Teddy Lee Dillon (*Animal Crackers*) as Guilfi; Thor Bishopric (*Young Robin Hood*) as Jordi; Anick Mattern as Thoren; Michael Rudder (*Animal Crackers*) as Dudley; Marc Camacho (*Animal Crackers*) as Gruzzlebeard; Ian Finlay (*The Terminal*) as Donner; Gary Jewel (*How the Toys Saved Christmas*) as Blitzen; A.J. Henderson (*Young Robin Hood*) as Balbo; Bruce Dinsmore (*Arthur*) as Rudolph.

INTERESTING TIDBITS: To enable themselves to move through stopped time, Santa and the elves consume a special syrup, which Gruzzlebeard and Dudley also covertly obtain. However, there's no evidence that the reindeer receive this potion, which is a bit ironic, since all other animals and humans are frozen in time. Balbo likewise is denied the syrup, because he doesn't accompany Santa on his run.

Santa is able to pack more than two billion presents in his sleigh via a magical "bottomless treasure chest of presents." His other option would have been a bottomless sack.

NOTE: At the time of this writing, all 26 episodes of this series could be seen on Amazon Instant Video.

PRODUCTION CREDITS—Writers: Stéphane Cabel, Sandro Agenor, J. Gasiorowski, Christopher Assefi, Olivier Marvaud, Olivier Nicolas, Sophie Decoisette, J.R. Francois, A. Monrigal, Christophe Poujol, A. Rees, and J.M. Rudnicki. Executive Producers: Olivier Brémond and Pascal Breton. Directors: Jean-Louis Bompoint, Christian Choquet, and Prakash Topsy. Production Companies: France 3, Marathon Productions, and CinéGroupe. Rating: Not rated. Genres: Animation, Family. Countries: Canada and France. Run Time: 23 min. per episode.

REFERENCES: *The Secret World of Santa Claus.* Big Cartoon Database. https//www.bcdb.com/cartoons/Other_Studios/M/Marathon_Studio/The_Secret_World_of_Santa_Claus

The Secret World of Santa Claus. Internet Movie Database. http://www.imdb.com/title/tt0302145/

Wilson, Joanna. *Tis the Season TV: The Encyclopedia of Christmas-Themed Episodes, Specials and Made-for-TV Movies.* Akron, OH: 1701 Press, 2011.

Single Santa Seeks Mrs. Claus—2004

Television Movie

THREAT TO CHRISTMAS: As the new Santa, Nick has a year to take a wife, or it's the end of Christmas.

HOW CHRISTMAS IS SAVED: Nick must convince Beth that Santa is no myth.

SYNOPSIS AND COMMENTARY: If it's a television Christmas movie that involves romance and marriage, chances are it premiered on the Hallmark Channel, which happens to be true for *Single Santa*. In this case, there's also a save-Christmas theme lurking beneath.

Santa (John Wheeler, *Meet the Santas*) is retiring and his son Nick (Steve Guttenberg, *Police Academy*) will assume the mantle of Santa Claus on December 26. There are two strict requirements that must be fulfilled: Nick must marry on Christmas Eve of next year and his new wife must also believe in Santa. While reviewing a list of suitable candidates, Nick treks to Los Angeles to inspect the marriageable ladies, but none of them seem interested until he meets Beth Sawtelle (Crystal Bernard, *Wings*), a young, workaholic widow whose job as an advertising executive leaves her little time to spend with her young son Jake (Dominic Scott Kay, *Charlotte's Web*). When Nick successfully coaches a little girl with her lines on the set where Beth is shooting a Christmas toy commercial, she is impressed and persuades Nick to portray Santa in a series of holiday commercials. Predictably, Beth and Nick become quite attracted to one another, yet because Beth is skeptical about Santa and the North Pole, there can be no nuptials unless Nick can convince her that Santa is no myth.

AWARDS: In 2005, this picture received a Young Artist Award nomination for Best Performance in a TV Movie, Miniseries or Special–Leading Young Actor (Dominic Scott Kay).

INTERESTING TIDBITS: That Santa must take a wife or it's the end of Christmas smacks of **The Santa Clause 2**.

Check out the sequel, **Meet the Santas**, another Hallmark Channel romance goodie.

REVIEW: Matthew M. Foster of *Foster on Film*: "…as wholesome and inoffensive as a Christmas card. It is also as exciting and original…. There's even a crippled child who has nothing to do with the story, but he shows up because what tugs at those heart strings better than a kid in a wheelchair succeeding at sports? … a movie with no strong negatives, but no compelling positives either. It just lays there."

Richard Scheib of *Moria Science Fiction, Horror and Fantasy Film Review* had a considerably different view: "[This film] comes out as a thinly disguised parable about Christian belief with the name of Santa substituted for that of Jesus—the film's ultimate message is about having faith in things one cannot see and about how the happiest thing in life should be a traditional nuclear family."

PRODUCTION CREDITS—Writer: Pamela Wallace. Producers: Brian J. Gordon and Erik Olson. Director: Harvey Frost. Production Companies: Hallmark Entertainment, Alpine Medien Productions, Larry Levinson Productions, and MAT IV. Rating: Not rated. Genre: Romance. Countries: Germany and USA. Run Time: 85 min.

REFERENCES: Crump, William D. *The Christmas Encyclopedia*. Third Edition. Jefferson, NC: McFarland, 2013.

Foster, Matthew M. *Single Santa Seeks Mrs. Claus*. Foster on Film. http://fosteronfilm.com/holidays/xmas/singlesanta.htm

Scheib, Richard. *Single Santa Seeks Mrs. Claus*. Moria Science Fiction, Horror and Fantasy Film Review. http://moria.co.nz/fantasy/single-santa-seeks-mrs-claus-2004-htm

Single Santa Seeks Mrs. Claus. Internet Movie Database. http://www.imdb.com/title/tt0413900/

Single Santa Seeks Mrs. Claus. New York: GoodTimes Entertainment, 2005. DVD Video.

Wilson, Joanna. *Tis the Season TV: The Encyclopedia of Christmas-Themed Episodes, Specials and Made-for-TV Movies*. Akron, OH: 1701 Press, 2011.

Small Town Santa—October 14, 2014

Direct-to-Video Movie

THREAT TO CHRISTMAS: A group of people's circumstances in a small town portend an unhappy Christmas.

HOW CHRISTMAS IS SAVED: Santa manages to get himself thrown in jail in order to work some subtle Christmas magic.

SYNOPSIS AND COMMENTARY: Here's a different kind of save-Christmas movie in which no one is trying to shut down the North Pole or hold Santa hostage. Instead of bringing just toys, Santa brings a truly happy Christmas to a number of dispirited people in a small town in Michigan. Christmas Eve couldn't be a more grinchy time for Sheriff Rick Langston (Dean Cain, *Out of Time*): he's at odds with his ex-wife Diane (Janet Caine, *A Dog for Christmas*), he hardly ever sees their teenage daughter Kara (Mandalynn Carlson, *Sibilance*), the new job that was awaiting him in the big city has fallen through, and life in a small town without crime is stifling. The evening takes a different turn when Rick jails a white-bearded old intruder claiming to be Santa (Paul Hopper, *Beauty Queen*), who had suddenly appeared in Rick's home. Santa shares a cell with Raynor (Mark Boyd, *Consideration*), a failed real estate broker-turned-town-drunk. In addition to Rick and Raynor, other folks who will benefit from Santa's "magic" include newcomer Lucy Hart (Christine Lakin, *You Again*), a single mom with teenage daughter Alana (Sophie Bolen, *The Christmas Bunny*), who seek a new start in life; Deputy Tom Brookfield (Joel Paul Reisig, *Win by Fall*), who can't find the hot new Commando Dutch action figure that his little son wants and whose boozy mother-in-law Sylvia (Teri Lee, *Young Harvest*) despises him; and Joe Harold (James Cowans, *Crossover*), an elderly black man who's been estranged from his son. Santa first upbraids Rick for being a lousy husband and a fair father and further recognizes that Rick and Lucy each want love, so the matchmaking between the two begins. Alana finds the friend she needs in Kara at the church Christmas pageant, which they ruin by frolicking about in costume as the unscripted head and tail of an idiotic cow. Santa's subtle magic works more wonders when Rick sentences a teen boy who had egged Joe's home to shovel the snow from Joe's sidewalk all winter. Joe learns that the boy's father is unemployed and hires the father to manage his store. Joe in turn organizes a group who show their appreciation to Rick for staying on as sheriff, because the town loves him and needs him (a powerful incentive to stay). Diane and her Spanish boyfriend then miraculously receive tickets to Spain and hurry off, so Kara will spend Christmas with Rick after all, and an anonymous "friend" (you know who) calls Joe's son to arrange a reunion with his father. Upon his release, Santa leaves his bag behind; inside is a new suit for Raynor, whom Santa had inspired to clean up his act, and there are also *two* Commando Dutch figures, which Rick delivers to Tom at the latter's Christmas party. Santa may have spent most of his time in jail during this film, but everyone got his/her wish.

AWARDS: This film won a Jury Award at the Uptown Film Festival for Best Original Score (2013); it also won a Young Artist Award for Best Performance in a Film for DVD (Mandalynn Carlson, 2015).

INTERESTING TIDBITS: Raynor deliberately gets himself arrested by stealing the Baby Jesus figure from the church, because he needs a warm place to spend Christmas. The scenario is similar to that in the Christmas episode from *The Andy Griffith Show* (December 19, 1960), in which the lonely old merchant Ben Weaver commits a series of petty crimes so he can land in jail and participate in the festivities at the court house.

The fictitious Commando Dutch action figure is a nod to Arnold Schwarzenegger, who starred in the film *Commando* (1985) and played the role of "Dutch" in the film *Predator* (1987).

REVIEW: Tracy Moore of *Common Sense Media* (December 1, 2014): "…a family-friendly movie with positive messages about the redemptive spirit of the holidays … [and] about the serendipity of little miracles, letting go of grudges, and making the connections with others that are so difficult to do the rest of the year…"

PRODUCTION CREDITS—Writer: David Higlen. Producers: Joel Paul Reisig, Cort Johns, and Paula Fornier. Director: Joel Paul Reisig. Production Company: Be Your Own Hollywood. Rating: PG (mild thematic elements and some rude humor). Genre: Comedy. Country: USA. Run Time: 86 min.

REFERENCES: Moore, Tracy. *Small Town Santa*. Common Sense Media. https://www.commonsensemedia.org/movie-reviews/small-town-santa

Small Town Santa. Internet Movie Database. http://www.imdb.com/title/tt2766790/

Small Town Santa. Screen Media, 2014. DVD Video.

The Smurfs Christmas Special—
December 13, 1982

Animated Television Movie

THREAT TO CHRISTMAS: Gargamel plots with a malevolent stranger to destroy the Smurfs' Christmas and Smurf Village.

HOW CHRISTMAS IS SAVED: A Smurf song of goodness and love drives the evil away.

SYNOPSIS AND COMMENTARY: One of the most successful and longest-running Saturday morning cartoons in television history, *The Smurfs* aired on the NBC television network from 1981 to 1989. The creation of Belgian cartoonist Pierre "Peyo" Culliford, the Smurfs were blue, elfin characters "three apples high" who lived in mushroom-shaped houses and who first appeared as a comic strip in *Le Journal de Spirou* on October 23, 1958, where they were known as *Les Schtroumpfs*. A host of Smurf dolls and other merchandise followed, which inspired the television series after Fred Silverman, then-president of NBC, saw the pleasure that a Smurf doll brought to his daughter Melissa. Led by Papa Smurf, the more than 100 citizens of the sylvan Smurf Village bore names commensurate with personal characteristics: Brainy, Hefty, Handy, Grouchy, etc., with two female characters, Smurfette and tomboy Sassette. Serving as their principal nemeses were non–Smurf characters such as the evil wizard Gargamel, his young assistant Scruple, the diabolical cat Azrael, and the evil witch Chlorhydris, who strove to remove love from the world. The series featured 256 episodes (418 stories) and seven specials. The Smurfs were also featured in several animated theatrical releases, for example, *The Smurfs and the Magic Flute* (1976), *The Baby Smurf* (1984), *The Smurfs* (2011), *The Smurfs 2* (2013), and *Get Smurfy* (2017).

In *The Smurfs Christmas Special*, Gargamel interrupts the Smurfs' happy Christmas Eve celebrations by striking a bargain with a malevolent, cloaked stranger bent on revenge. Gargamel will kidnap and deliver two human children, William and Gwenevere, who have survived a sleighing accident, in return for which Gargamel will receive a magic scroll that will allow him to destroy Smurf Village. Meanwhile, the Smurfs out trekking through the forest rescue the children from a pack of vicious wolves, and Gargamel, searching for the children, meets their uncle, who offers a large reward for their return. After overpowering the Smurfs and children and delivering the latter to the stranger, Gargamel dispatches Smurf Village with the scroll, then plots to double-cross the stranger and collect the reward. The stranger, anticipating a betrayal, captures Gargamel and holds him along with the children in a ring of fire when the Smurfs arrive. The only spell that will cancel the stranger's powerful magic is a Smurf chorus of "Goodness Makes the Badness Go Away," which everyone sings, including Gargamel. The stranger vanishes in a fit of rage, the children forgive Gargamel's evil intentions and return home with their uncle, and the Smurfs return to a leveled

The Smurfs are "up a tree" in the best way as they decorate their Christmas tree. Bottom: Smurfette. Middle: Handy Smurf and Papa Smurf. Top: another Smurf. In *The Smurfs Christmas Special* (1982), the Smurfs prevent Gargamel from ruining their Christmas (NBC/Photofest).

village. Undaunted, the Smurfs proceed with their holiday celebrations, for the blowing of a Smurf trumpet miraculously restores their village directly.

PRINCIPAL VOICES: Rene Auberjonois (*The Patriot*) as the stranger; Lucille Bliss (*The Smurfs*) as Smurfette; Danny Goldman (*The Smurfs*) as Brainy Smurf; David Mendenhall (*Centurions*) as William; Don Messick (*The Smurfs*) as Papa Smurf and Azrael; Alexandra Stoddart (*Not Until Today*) as Gwenevere; and Paul Winchell (*The Smurfs*) as Gargamel.

AWARDS: *The Smurfs*—Emmy Awards for Outstanding Children's Entertainment Series (1983, 1984); Emmy nominations for Outstanding Animated Program (1985–1989); Humanitas Prize for Children's Animation Category (1987); Blimp Award nominations for Favorite Cartoon (1988, 1989). *The Smurfs Christmas Special* received a Primetime Emmy nomination for Outstanding Animated Program (1983).

INTERESTING TIDBITS: Santa Claus and his reindeer do not appear in this special. Instead, after Papa Smurf rescues the two children in the forest, they mistake him for the jolly toymaker and refer to him as Santa for the remainder of the story.

This production was the first of three *Smurfs* Christmas specials. In the other two, *'Tis the Season to Be Smurfy* (TV movie, 1987) and *The Smurfs: A Christmas Carol* (direct-to-video, 2011), "saving" Christmas was not the primary focus.

The Smurfs frequently utilized classical music in the background or for themes. Background music heard during this special includes excerpts from the following: first movement of Franz Schubert's *Symphony No. 8* in B Minor ("Unfinished"), first movement of Pyotr Tchaikovsky's *Symphony No. 6* in B Minor ("Pathetique"), and the fifth movement of Hector Berlioz's *Symphonie Fantastique*.

PRODUCTION CREDITS—Story: Gerard Baldwin, Peyo, and Yvan Delcorte. Teleplay: Len Janson and Chuck Menville. Producer and Director: Gerard Baldwin. Production Companies: Hanna-Barbera Productions and SEPP International, S.A. Rating: Not rated. Genres: Animation, Family, Fantasy. Countries: Belgium and USA. Run Time: 24 min.

REFERENCES: Crump, William D. *The Christmas Encyclopedia*. Third Edition. Jefferson, NC: McFarland, 2013.

Lenburg, Jeff. *The Encyclopedia of Animated Cartoons*. Third Edition. New York: Facts on File, 2009.

Mallory, Michael. *Hanna-Barbera Cartoons*. Westport, CT: Hugh Lauter Levin Associates, 1998.

The Smurfs (TV Series). Wikipedia. http://en.wikipedia.org/wiki/The_Smurfs_(TV_series)

The Smurfs Christmas Special. Big Cartoon Database. http://www.bcdb.com/cartoon/13932-Smurfs-Christmas-Special

The Smurfs Christmas Special. In *The Smurfs Holiday Celebration*. Burbank, CA: Warner Home Video, 2011. DVD Video.

The Smurfs Christmas Special. Internet Movie Database. http://www.imdb.com/title/tt1177949/

The Smurfs Christmas Special. Wikia Christmas Specials. http://christmas-specials.wikia.com/wiki/The_Smurfs%27_Christmas_Special

Wilson, Joanna. *Tis the Season TV: The Encyclopedia of Christmas-Themed Episodes, Specials and Made-for-TV Movies*. Akron, OH: 1701 Press, 2011.

Snow—December 13, 2004

Television Movie

THREAT TO CHRISTMAS: One of Santa's reindeer has been captured and the other seven reindeer will not fly without him.

HOW CHRISTMAS IS SAVED: Santa travels to California to rescue his reindeer.

SYNOPSIS AND COMMENTARY: It's rather odd to see a 21st-century Santa Claus who is nerdy, skinny, and beardless, but that's the case here because the North Pole has a new, young Santa (Tom Cavanagh, *The Flash*), who has assumed the role from his father. Three days before Christmas, Santa discovers that Buddy, a new member of his reindeer team, has been captured in the wild and taken to a zoo in San Ernesto, CA. It's crucial to rescue Buddy, for the other reindeer will not fly with only seven members. Stepping through his magic mirror and using the name "Nick Snowden" as an alias, Santa appears in San Ernesto where he becomes acquainted with Sandy Brooks (Ashley Williams, *Montana Sky*), the lonely zookeeper who would make an ideal Mrs. Claus (make book on that). Complicating matters is the big-game hunter Buck Seger (Patrick Fabian, *The Last Exorcism*), who has his own designs on Sandy. Buck had captured Buddy and now plans to sell him for a large sum because of his special skills. Rescuing Buddy requires the help of Hector (Bobb'e J. Thompson, *Role Models*), a sarcastic, street-savvy black kid who lives at the boarding house where Sandy also resides. Santa had been teaching Buddy to fly, and the latter learns well enough to dodge Buck's tranquilizer darts and fly into Santa's mirror that returns him to the North Pole. In a fit of anger, Buck receives his comeuppance by accidentally impaling himself with a dart and passing out.

INTERESTING TIDBITS: Buck's nickname for Sandy is "Bobcat" (the film provides no explanation—perhaps it's a step beneath "Hellcat"), and he refers to all reindeer as "meatloaf." Sandy's general reaction to Buck's persistent advances is, "Ewww!"

Santa mentions having eight reindeer, so Buddy apparently replaces one. Did one of the traditional eight reindeer (no mention of Rudolph here) die or retire? The film doesn't elaborate further.

This North Pole sports no elves.

Check out the sequel, ***Snow 2: Brain Freeze***.

REVIEW: Nancy Davis Kho of *Common Sense Media* (October 13, 2008): "There is virtually no mention of religious significance of the holiday. The film is a paean to the magic of secular Christmas, and the characters are motivated to good actions because of the holiday's importance ... filled with sight gags of surreptitious reindeer antics and narrow escapes from discovery by Nick to keep kids laughing."

PRODUCTION CREDITS—Writer: Rich Burns. Producer: Kevin Lafferty. Director: Alex Zamm. Production Company: Rockingham Productions. Rating: Not rated. Genres: Comedy, Fantasy. Countries: Canada and USA. Run Time: 90 min.

REFERENCES: Crump, William D. *The Christmas Encyclopedia*. Third Edition. Jefferson, NC: McFarland, 2013.

Kho, Nancy Davis. *Snow. Common Sense Media*. https://www.commonsensemedia.org/movie-reviews/snow

Snow. Internet Movie Database. http://www.imdb.com/title/tt0425468/

Snow. Louisville, CO: Gaiam, 2008. DVD Video.

Snow 2: Brain Freeze—December 14, 2008
Television Movie

THREAT TO CHRISTMAS: Santa takes a tumble and suffers amnesia after going through his magic mirror.

HOW CHRISTMAS IS SAVED: Wife Sandy, Buddy the reindeer, and some friends jog Santa's memory in time for Christmas.

SYNOPSIS AND COMMENTARY: Similar to its predecessor ***Snow*** (2004), this sequel also begins three days before Christmas a year later. The North Pole is hectic, and Santa, AKA Nick Snowden (Tom Cavanagh, *The Flash*), has forgotten about the promise he made to spend an early Christmas with his new bride Sandy (Ashley Williams, *Montana Sky*). An argument erupts, after which Santa heads to the city via his magic mirror but falls in the process and suffers amnesia. Through Galfrid (Jonathan Holmes, *Nightwatching*), the keeper of Santa's instruction book, Sandy learns that Nick will regain his memory and the Christmas magic only if he firmly believes that he is Santa; it is not sufficient for anyone to tell him the truth. Therefore, Sandy, Buddy the reindeer, a street urchin named Ryan (Alexander Conti, *Dog Pound*), and friends from the Order of the Caribou set out to jog Nick's memory in time for Christmas. Complicating matters again is big-game hunter Buck Seger (Patrick Fabian, *The Last Exorcism*), still putting the moves on Sandy, who pretends to help her but only wishes to keep Nick incapacitated and extract his secrets for personal gain. But it's Buck's turn to suffer amnesia when he receives a taste of the magic mirror, courtesy of Buddy, and Sandy hints at a very special announcement by presenting Nick with a very tiny Santa suit.

AWARDS: In 2009, this picture received a Young Artist Award nomination for Best Supporting Young Actor (Alexander Conti).

INTERESTING TIDBITS: *Snow* and *Snow 2* demonstrate a few parallels. Both feature a smart-alecky kid who helps Nick. In the former, it's the street-savvy Hector (Bobb'e J. Thompson) who lives in the boarding house; in the latter, it's the street kid Ryan (Alexander Conti). In both, Santa spends most of his time away from the North Pole, but when he's there, the action takes place primarily in the reindeer barn, not his workshop. Elves are absent in both films.

Other save-Christmas films in which Santa suffers amnesia include *The Amazing World of Gumball: Christmas Episode, The Boy Who Saved Christmas, Merry Madagascar, Miracle at the 34th Precinct, The Night Before the Night Before Christmas, Santa Who?* and *The Search for Santa Paws.*

REVIEW: Nancy Davis Kho of *Common Sense Media* (December 10, 2008): "Repeated messages about the importance of faith, belief, and trust during the holidays ... is as family-friendly as the original movie ... the romance between Santa and Mrs. Claus is surprisingly sweet. There's no depiction of the holiday's religious aspects."

PRODUCTION CREDITS—Writer: Rich Burns. Producers: Tom Cox, Craig McNeil, Murray Ord, and Jordy Randall. Director: Mark Rosman. Production Companies: The Alberta Film Development Program of the Alberta Foundation for the Arts and WalkingDistance [*sic*] Productions. Rating: Not rated. Genres: Comedy, Fantasy. Countries: Canada and USA. Run Time: 84 min.

REFERENCES: Crump, William D. *The Christmas Encyclopedia.* Third Edition. Jefferson, NC: McFarland, 2013.

Kho, Nancy Davis. *Snow 2: Brain Freeze. Common Sense Media.* https://www.commonsensemedia.org/movie-reviews/snow-2-brain-freeze

Snow 2: Brain Freeze. Internet Movie Database. http://www.imdb.com/title/tt1334278/

Snow 2: Brain Freeze. Louisville, CO: Gaiam, 2009. DVD Video.

Wilson, Joanna. *Tis the Season TV: The Encyclopedia of Christmas-Themed Episodes, Specials and Made-for-TV Movies.* Akron, OH: 1701 Press, 2011.

Snuffy, the Elf Who Saved Christmas— 1991

Animated Television Musical

THREAT TO CHRISTMAS: The Sandman's sleeping sand accidentally puts all the elves to sleep before their work is finished on Christmas Eve.

HOW CHRISTMAS IS SAVED: Snuffy the aged elf is not too old to be of value in a pinch.

SYNOPSIS AND COMMENTARY: Here's a cartoon that should be dedicated to senior citizens (and senior elves) who believe there is no purpose to their lives anymore. It's Christmas Eve, and Snuffy, the oldest elf at the North Pole, is under the impression that Santa and the other elves no longer need him, that he's too old to be of any help. While Snuffy is out tending to the reindeer in the barn, the Sandman drops by with a bag of sleeping sand to make the dolls' eyes close. Nursing a cold, elf foreman Virgil sneezes into the bag, blowing the sand all over the workshop, and the elves fall asleep, yet only half the toys are finished (the pessimist would say that half are unfinished). Remembering that Santa had said he was not to be disturbed before midnight, Snuffy takes the bull (or in this case the reindeer) by the horns (antlers here) and puts the reindeer to work such that all the toys are ready by midnight. Having labored so hard to load Santa's bag and hoist it onto the sleigh, Snuffy is bushed and falls asleep at the bag before hitching up the reindeer as Santa had requested. Arriving on the scene and thinking that Snuffy can't do the job, Santa is about to retire him when the other elves awaken and realize that Snuffy was responsible for finishing the toys and saving Christmas. The reindeer corroborate the story, and Snuffy becomes a hero who rides with Santa to deliver the gifts.

VOICES: Country singer Bobby Goldsboro as Snuffy, Santa, Sandman, and Virgil; Christie Westmoreland as Mitzi and Brandy.

SONGS: All were written and sung by

Bobby Goldsboro: "Where Do You Go?"; "Just a Little Pinch of Sand"; "Snuffy's Goodbye Song"; "Elves' Work Song"; "Snuffy's Theme."

INTERESTING TIDBITS: Bobby Goldsboro's audio recording, *Bobby Goldsboro Presents Snuffy, the Elf Who Saved Christmas*, was released in 1992 on the Kid Rhino label.

This film should not be confused with the live-action production titled **The Elf Who Saved Christmas.**

PRODUCTION CREDITS—Story and Dialogue: Bobby Goldsboro. Producer: Charlie Rose. Director: Dan Peeler. Production Company: Peeler-Rose Productions. Rating: Not rated. Genres: Animation, Short. Country: USA. Run Time: 22 min.

REFERENCES: *Bobby Goldsboro Presents Snuffy, the Elf Who Saved Christmas.* Santa Monica, CA: Kid Rhino, 1992. Audiocassette recording.

Snuffy, the Elf Who Saved Christmas. Internet Movie Database. http://www.imdb.com/title/tt4863946/

Snuffy, the Elf Who Saved Christmas. Van Nuys, CA: Family Home Entertainment, 1992. VHS Video.

Wilson, Joanna. *Tis the Season TV: The Encyclopedia of Christmas-Themed Episodes, Specials and Made-for-TV Movies.* Akron, OH: 1701 Press, 2011.

Sonic Christmas Blast—November 24, 1996

Animated Television Short Film

THREAT TO CHRISTMAS: Dr. Robotnik kidnaps Santa and steals all the presents in the world.

HOW CHRISTMAS IS SAVED: Sonic the Hedgehog uses his supersonic speed to defeat Robotnik, retrieve the presents, and deliver them around the world.

SYNOPSIS AND COMMENTARY: In 1993, the children's animated TV series *Adventures of Sonic the Hedgehog* ran in first-run syndication for 65 half-hour episodes, based on the *Sonic the Hedgehog* video game series produced by Sega. Set on the planet Mobius, the animated series revolved around Sonic (a blue, anthropomorphic hedgehog who could move at supersonic speeds) and his sidekick Miles "Tails" Prower (a little fox with two tails) as they consistently kept the evil Dr. Ivo Robotnik and his incompetent henchbots, Scratch (a humanoid, robotic rooster) and Grounder (a stocky teal machine with tank tracks for feet and drills that replaced his hands and nose), from taking over the planet. Though it aired three years after the series ended, *Sonic Christmas Blast* was the *Adventures* series' Christmas special.

It's Christmas Eve as Robotnik, bent on taking over the holiday, kidnaps Santa and then sends a robotic Santa out to the unsuspecting citizens of Robotropolis to announce that because he is retiring, his replacement will be "Robotnik Claus" (Robotnik in a Santa suit). The big difference is that instead of children receiving presents as usual, they must now *give* presents to Robotnik Claus or face dire consequences. To facilitate this, Robotnik builds a multitude of chimneys that will allow the citizens to deliver the presents as Santa did. Arriving in Robotropolis for some Christmas shopping, Sonic and Tails find that all the stores are empty, Robotnik's henchbots having stolen all the presents from there and from Santa's workshop, and after a tussle with Scratch and Grounder, Sonic learns where Robotnik holds Santa captive. Though Sonic quickly defeats the SWATbots (Robotnik's army) who guard Santa, the latter despairs because Robotnik still possesses all the world's presents. Yet Sonic's oddly designed ring enables him to achieve ultimate velocity when he passes three tests of skill: climb a certain mountain, snowboard down that mountain, and ride a bicycle through dangerous territory. So enabled, Sonic retrieves all the millions of stolen presents and zips around the world at super speed to deliver them without the assistance of Santa or reindeer, after which Santa is so impressed that he actually does retire and dubs Sonic as the new "Sonic Claus."

PRINCIPAL VOICES: Jaleel White (*Family Matters*) as Sonic; Chris Turner (*Air Bud*) as Tails; Long John Baldry (*Nilus the Sandman*) as Robotnik; Phil Hayes (*Unforgiven*) as Scratch; Garry Chalk (*Watchmen*) as Grounder; Jay Brazeau (*Watchmen*) as Santa.

Macy's Thanksgiving Day Parade showcases a Sonic the Hedgehog balloon. In *Sonic Christmas Blast* (1996), Sonic delivers the presents when Santa is kidnapped (NBC/Photofest).

INTERESTING TIDBITS: Whereas each episode of the TV series ended with a "Sonic Sez" segment that provided lessons about such subjects as alcohol abuse and personal safety, that segment did not appear in *Sonic Christmas Blast*.

Similar to *The Smurfs* series, which frequently utilized classical music in the background or for themes, the *Adventures of Sonic the Hedgehog* series and its Christmas special featured recurring excerpts of "In the Hall of the Mountain King" from Edvard Grieg's *Peer Gynt Suite* No. 1.

Other save-Christmas films in which Santa is kidnapped include *The Boy Who Saved Christmas; The Elf and the Magic Key; The Glo Friends Save Christmas; The Great Santa Claus Switch; The Librarians and Santa's Midnight Run; Santa Claus Conquers the Martians; Spinach Greetings; Tim Burton's The Nightmare Before Christmas*; and *Who Stole Santa?*

REVIEWS: Emily Ashby of *Common Sense Media* reviewed the TV series: "...moves at a frantic pace and features loud exchanges between its two main characters, one of whom aims to destroy the other. Parents might not be thrilled to hear their kids emulating some of the show's language [mostly name-calling]... or a main character's manipulative control over his assistants ... the series emphasizes positive themes for kids about personal safety and interpersonal relationships."

Michael Rubino of *DVD Verdict* reviewed the TV series (August 8, 2007): "Each episode plays out like a ripoff of the Warner Bros. Road Runner cartoons... [Robotnik] and his goons use a series of schemes and contraptions to try [to catch Sonic and Tails] ... they never work.... Guilty of being dated, contrived, and bloated with chili dog jokes."

PRODUCTION CREDITS—Writers: Reed Shelly and Bruce Shelly. Executive Producers: Andy Heyward, Robby London, and Michael Maliani. Director: Blair Peters. Production Companies: DiC Enterprises and Sega of America. Rating: Not rated. Genres: Animation, Action, Comedy. Country: USA. Run Time: 20 min.

REFERENCES: Ashby, Emily. *The Adventures of Sonic the Hedgehog. Common Sense Media.* https://www.commonsensemedia.org/tv-reviews/the-adventures-of-sonic-the-hedgehog

Rubino, Michael. *Adventures of Sonic the Hedgehog. DVD Verdict.* http://www.dvdverdict.com/reviews/adventuressonichedgehog.php

Sonic Christmas Blast. Internet Movie Database. http://www.imdb.com/title/tt0770807/

Sonic Christmas Blast. NCircle Entertainment, 2003. DVD Video.

Wilson, Joanna. *Tis the Season TV: The Encyclopedia of Christmas-Themed Episodes, Specials and Made-for-TV Movies.* Akron, OH: 1701 Press, 2011.

Spike: The Elf That Saved Christmas—
December 26, 2008

Computer-Animated Television Movie

THREAT TO CHRISTMAS: Santa's mailbag is accidentally stashed in the penguins' fish bank, and polar bears kidnap Santa's reindeer.

HOW CHRISTMAS IS SAVED: Spike and his friends retrieve the mailbag and thwart the reindeer-nappers.

SYNOPSIS AND COMMENTARY: Here's a film of two episodes from France with English dialogue. In the first episode, simply titled "Spike," Spike is an elf recruit newly arrived at Santa's workshop beneath the North Pole ice. Although it's a week before Christmas, Santa takes his annual pre–Christmas vacation and leaves chief elf Raymon in charge until Christmas Eve. When no one is willing to make the long journey to get Santa's mail, Spike volunteers, but on his return trip through Ping Ville, the penguins' capital, the birds mistake the mailbag for a bag of fish and stash it in their well-guarded fish bank. If Santa doesn't receive all the children's letters, Christmas is as good as cancelled, but Spike and Raymon surreptitiously bypass the bank's complex security system and break in. Greedy polar bears Tony and Vito, bent on stealing the fish, pursue and subdue the two elves, then suck all the bags from the bank with a giant vacuum hose. Though Spike escapes, Tony, double-crossing Vito, leaves him and Raymon locked in the vault and flees in a hot-air balloon. Pursuing in a flying sled, Spike and his penguin-friend Paco disable the balloon which crashes, and Tony is captured. Those in the vault are released, the fish bags are saved, and the mailbag is returned to a grateful Santa, who invites Spike and Raymon to accompany him on his Christmas rounds.

The second episode, titled "Spike 2," opens a year later as Tony finishes his one-year sentence of community service in Santa's workshop, and Santa again takes his pre–Christmas vacation. This time, Tony's mom uses a submarine to kidnap Santa's *four* reindeer, and she and Tony demand all the fish in Ping Ville's fish bank as ransom. Spike, chief elf Raymond (notice the different spelling from the first episode), Paco the penguin, and Spike's reporter-cousin Dorothy collectively appeal to Ping Ville, but when that city denies their request, Spike, Paco, and Dorothy confront Tony's mom in Teddy Ville, an Old West–type town inhabited by polar bears, resulting in a series of high-speed chases on snowmobiles. Captured, the three join the reindeer as Tony, piloting a giant robot, lumbers off to steal Ping Ville's fish. Having always wanted to fly and having received a sprinkling of magic dust from the flying reindeer, Paco effects their escape, and the group flies to Ping Ville astride the reindeer where Spike, following another battle, defeats Tony by removing the robot's giant battery. In the ensuing calm, Dorothy, pushing for gender equality, urges Santa to allow female elves to work with him. When Santa agrees, numerous female elves surprise him by removing their "male" disguises.

VOICES: Alexis Tomassian (*Papyrus*) as Spike; Barbara Tissier (*Godard's Passion*) as Dorothy; Med Hondo (*Antilles sur Seine*) as chief elf Raymon (first episode); Daniel Kamwa (*Notre fille*) as chief elf Raymond (second episode, different spelling); Michel Mella (*Pif and Hercules*) as Paco and Vito; Gilbert Levy (*Cours toujours*) as Tony; Sarah Roussel (*L'enchanteur*) as La Mamma; Laurent Morteau (*The Jungle Bunch: The Movie*) as seagull/reporter; David Vincent (*Spike*) as guardian bouli; Richard Duval as Santa.

INTERESTING TIDBITS: Although Santa is portrayed as white, his elves are racially diverse, with chief elf Raymon/Raymond being black. Other films featuring a white Santa and a black chief elf include **The Boy Who Saved Christmas** and **Santa Who?**

Reindeer are also kidnapped in **The Reindeer Hunter**.

REVIEW: Renee Schonfeld of *Common Sense Media* (November 30, 2014): "Cute animation, likeable characters … and funny situations should keep kids engaged. Although there is some stereotyping—the bad guys are comically Italian—and an old-fashioned take on women's rights in the workplace is explored, it's all handled cleverly with a touch of whimsy.… Best for kindergarten and primary-grade viewers…"

PRODUCTION CREDITS—Writers for Both Episodes: David Alaux, Eric Tosti, and Jean-François Tosti. Producers for First Episode: Jean-François Tosti and Patrice Masini. Producer for Second Episode: Jean-François Tosti. Directors for Both Episodes: David Alaux and Eric Tosti. Production Companies: Région Midi-Pyrénées, Master Image Programmes, and TAT Productions. Rating: G. Genres: Animation, Adventure. Country: France. Run Time: 71 min.

REFERENCES: Schonfeld, Renee. *Spike. Common Sense Media*. https://www.commonsensemedia.org/movie-reviews/spike

Spike: The Elf That Saved Christmas. Amarillo, TX: Anderson Digital, 2013. DVD Video.

Spike. Internet Movie Database. http://www.imdb.com/title/tt2279287/

Spinach Greetings—1960

Short Film in the Animated Television Series *Popeye the Sailor*

THREAT TO CHRISTMAS: The Sea Hag kidnaps Santa and destroys his presents.

HOW CHRISTMAS IS SAVED: Popeye rescues Santa (a rather simple solution).

SYNOPSIS AND COMMENTARY: Created by Elzie Crisler Segar, the character Popeye first appeared in the King Features comic strip *Thimble Theater*, which was highly popular during the 1930s and was renamed *Popeye* in the 1970s. Fleischer Studios adapted *Thimble Theater* into the *Popeye* series of cartoon shorts from 1933 to 1942, when Paramount took control and produced the series until 1957. *Popeye* cartoons also appeared in various television incarnations from King Features Syndicate (1960–62) and Hanna-Barbera Productions (1978–82 and 1987–88). Eating a can of spinach for superhuman strength whenever he ran into trouble, Popeye was known for his muscular forearms tattooed with anchors, a corncob pipe, his rough voice, and his abysmal English

Spinach Greetings

grammar and pronunciation (e.g., "I eats me spinach"; "That's a myskery"). Popeye often battled his arch rival Bluto (Brutus in the King Features Syndicate television series) for the affection of sweetheart Olive Oyl.

It's Christmas Eve as Popeye recites "The Night Before Christmas" to little Swee'pea while Olive and Wimpy listen. Spying on them from outside, the green Sea Hag, despising all the happiness that Santa brings, dispatches her buzzard Bernard to kidnap Santa from his jet plane flying overhead (no sleigh or reindeer here). Back at her hideout, the Hag hogties Santa, then smashes his toys and burns them in her fireplace as Santa weeps. Meanwhile, when Santa's jet crashes in Popeye's yard, a buzzard's feather in the wreckage leads Popeye to suspect the Sea Hag. Sneaking into her hideout, Popeye attempts to free Santa, but Bernard slams him against the wall. Popeye whips out his spinach, and the bird ends up as a "turkey" buzzard on a platter suitable for Christmas dinner, after which the Hag shoves Popeye down into a pit of alligators, but he simply makes suitcases out of them. Defeated, the Hag falls on the floor in a tantrum. Back at Popeye's place, Santa resumes his rounds, his jet and presents somehow having been completely restored. That's the advantage of cartoons: the inexplicable doesn't have to be explained.

PRINCIPAL VOICES: Jack Mercer as Popeye; Mae Questel as Olive and the Sea Hag. Both voice actors worked on the *Popeye the Sailor* TV series.

INTERESTING TIDBITS: Other save-Christmas movies in which Santa is kidnapped include *The Boy Who Saved Christmas; The Elf and the Magic Key; The Glo Friends Save Christmas; The Great Santa Claus Switch; The Librarians and Santa's Midnight Run; Santa Claus Conquers the Martians; Sonic Christmas Blast; Tim Burton's The Nightmare Before Christmas*; and *Who Stole Santa?*

Popeye and his can of strength-building spinach are inseparable, as shown in this ad art for the *Popeye the Sailor* series of cartoon shorts, ca. 1940s. In the episode "Spinach Greetings" (1960), Popeye rescues Santa from the Sea Hag (Paramount Pictures/Photofest).

REVIEW: Randy Miller III of *DVD Talk* reviewed *Popeye: The 1960s Animated Classics Collection, Volume One* (June 2, 2013): "Viewers more familiar with the Fleischer shorts ... will be taken aback by the much less fluid animation featured in these six-minute adventures. [The] extremely limited TV budget and production time constraints are obvious culprits ... but visual handicaps aside, most audiences will become used to its particular look soon enough."

PRODUCTION CREDITS—Writer and Director: Seymour Kneitel. Executive Producer: Al Brodnax. Production Company: King Features Syndicate. Rating: Not rated. Genres: Animation, Comedy. Country: USA. Run Time: 5.5 min.

REFERENCES: Crump, William D. *The Christmas Encyclopedia*. Third Edition. Jefferson, NC: McFarland, 2013.

Miller, Randy III. *Popeye: The 1960s Animated Classics Collection, Volume One. DVD Talk.* http://www.dvdtalk.com/reviews/61168/popeye-the-1960s-animated-classics-collection-volume-one/

Popeye the Sailor. Internet Movie Database. http://www.imdb.com/title/tt0145628/

Spinach Greetings. In *Popeye the Sailor: The 1960s Classics, Volume One*. Burbank, CA: Warner Home Video, 2013. DVD Video.

Wilson, Joanna. *Tis the Season TV: The Encyclopedia of Christmas-Themed Episodes, Specials and Made-for-TV Movies*. Akron, OH: 1701 Press, 2011.

Spot's Magical Christmas—September 11, 1995

Animated Television Special

THREAT TO CHRISTMAS: Two of Santa's reindeer have "lost" Santa's big, red sleigh.

HOW CHRISTMAS IS SAVED: Spot the puppy dog finds the sleigh that the reindeer just couldn't.

SYNOPSIS AND COMMENTARY: In 1980, British freelance graphic designer Eric Hill (1927–2014) published *Where's Spot?* his first children's lift-the-flap picture book about a playful little yellow puppy that he initially conceived to amuse his young son Christopher. That led to a whole series of more than 60 *Spot the Dog* books that served as reading primers not only for preschoolers but for adults as well. A number of audio books, sound books, books with plush toys, and other merchandise followed. Spot, so named for a brown spot on his body and tail, also starred with his family and friends in several animated television series that aired sporadically on the BBC from 1987 to 2001: *The Adventures of Spot, It's Fun to Learn with Spot*, and *Spot's Musical Adventures*. *Spot's Magical Christmas* was one of two television specials and was the only Christmas special.

Out in the snow, Spot encounters two of Santa's reindeer who have "lost" Santa's big red sleigh (as if something that large could ever be lost, but since this is a magical story, there's no need to belabor the issue). As they describe their plight, the male and female reindeer launch into a tango and emphatically declare in song that without the sleigh there will be no Christmas Day. Spot agrees to help the reindeer and makes inquiries of his neighborhood friends (Helen the hippopotamus, Tom the alligator, and Steve the monkey) who, of course, haven't seen the sleigh, which provides the opportunity for all of them to search together while spending much time frolicking in the snow. At last, Spot spots the sleigh in the woods and tracks down the two reindeer, who reward him with an aerial ride in the sleigh and a very brief tour of Santa's workshop, where all the elves are miniature bears.

PRINCIPAL VOICES: Ryan O'Donahue as Spot; Corey Burton; Tress MacNeille; and Jim Cummings.

INTERESTING TIDBITS: In contrast to the television series, which provided narration without the characters moving their lips, there is no narration in *Spot's Magical Christmas*. The characters move their lips and are voiced separately.

Because the female reindeer in this cartoon sports antlers, the question has arisen whether antlers are strictly seen in male reindeer. In an essay about reindeer, Jill Harness noted that, "In most deer species, only the male grows antlers, but that's not true for most reindeer ... older male reindeer lose their antlers in December.... That means Santa's [sleigh] either has to be pulled by young reindeer, constantly replaced as they start to age, or Santa's reindeer are female."

Spot's Magical Christmas should not be confused with another children's animated production, ***Dot and Spot's Magical Christmas Adventure***, the principal characters of which are also dogs, which has no relationship to the Eric Hill series of books.

PRODUCTION CREDITS—Writer: David McKee. Producer: Clive Juster. Director: Leo Nielsen. Production Company: King Rollo Films Ltd. Rating: Not rated. Genres: Animation, Family, Short. Country: United Kingdom. Run Time: 26 min.

REFERENCES: *The Adventures of Spot.* Toon hound. http://www.toonhound.com/spot.htm

Harness, Jill. "11 Things You Might Not Know About Reindeer." Mental Floss Web Site: http://mentalfloss.com/article/29470/11-things-you-might-not-know-about-reindeer

Hill, Eric. *Spot's Magical Christmas.* New York: Putnam, 1995.

Lenburg, Jeff. *The Encyclopedia of Animated Cartoons.* Third Edition. New York: Facts on File, 2009.

Spot the Dog. Wikipedia. https://en.wikipedia.org/wiki/Spot_the_Dog

Spot's Magical Christmas. Big Cartoon Database. http://www.bcdb.com/cartoon/117877-Spots-Magical-Christmas

Spot's Magical Christmas. BBC Home Entertainment, 2010. DVD Video.

Wilson, Joanna. *Tis the Season TV: The Encyclopedia of Christmas-Themed Episodes, Specials and Made-for-TV Movies.* Akron, OH: 1701 Press, 2011.

The Super Special Gift—December 5, 2008

Episode Segment from the Animated Television Series

Wow! Wow! Wubbzy!

THREAT TO CHRISTMAS: Santa's elves are all sick with the "fruitcake flu."

HOW CHRISTMAS IS SAVED: Wubbzy heads to the North Pole to seek a super special gift for his friend and ends up filling in for the elves.

SYNOPSIS AND COMMENTARY: Taking inspiration from a story written by his niece Viviana Ogawa, Bob Boyle created a little storybook for preschoolers titled *The Tail of Flopsy, Mopsy, and Ted*. Perhaps because Flopsy and Mopsy were far more associated with characters in Beatrix Potter's *The Tale of Peter Rabbit*, Boyle's characters were renamed Wubbzy, Widget, and Walden for the animated series, that ran on Nickelodeon for 52 half-hour episodes (104 segments) from 2006 to 2010. As befitting preschoolers, the animation was quite elementary with anthropomorphic characters rendered as if they had been drawn by preschoolers. Thus, the titular character Wubbzy, a childlike male yellow gerbil who loved to play, sported a nearly square body with two stubby ears, two black eyes, a round nose, a tail bent several times, two hands with four fingers each, and two rounded feet. His penchant for exclaiming, "Wow! Wow!" when excited found its way into the series' title. Wubbzy lived in the whimsical world of Wuzzleburg along with his best friends, Widget, a pink, female rabbit and mechanical whiz; Walden, a purple, bookish male wallaby with dark glasses; and Daizy, an aqua-green female dog.

When on Christmas Eve Wubbzy learns that Daizy wants the gift of a real rainbow, he consults with Widget and Walden, neither of whom know how to make that phenomenon, but Walden suggests that Santa could probably help. Thus begins Wubbzy's circuitous trek to the North Pole in one night. During his route, he passes by a Frenchman drinking a beverage, an Egyptian dancing beside the pyramids, a lone man on a small island, and an Inuit boy catching a small fish in a block of ice. Now hang on, because there's a reason behind this tedium that will become apparent. In the North, do-gooder Wubbzy befriends a benign Abominable Snowman by retrieving his lost car keys (though his car had run out of gas) and receives directions to Santa's abode. He then befriends a frantic mother penguin (so out of place at the North Pole) by finding her lost baby who's chowing down a huge candy cane, and in return she ferries him on an ice floe across a lake to Santa's workshop. There, Wubbzy renders more service by helping Santa load and deliver his presents, because all the elves are abed with the "fruitcake flu." Perhaps that's the North Pole's term for *measles*, since the elves are covered in red spots. During

Santa's route, the presents parachute down into chimneys of homes, and there's a TV for the lone islander, a giant cup of tea/coffee (perhaps spiked with some spirits) for the Frenchman, a huge fish in a block of ice for the Inuit boy, and a gas pump for the Abominable Snowman; a gift for the Egyptian is not shown. The route finished, Santa hands Wubbzy a "super special gift" and departs, but because Wubbzy had never queried Santa about Daizy's rainbow, he passes the gift on to her instead. Santa had known that making Daizy happy was all that Wubbzy wanted, for Santa's gift is indeed a rainbow.

PRINCIPAL VOICES: Grey De Lisle (*The Replacements*) as Wubbzy and mother penguin; Tara Strong (*Ice Age*) as Daizy and polar bear; Lara Jill Miller (*Gimme a Break!*) as Widget; Carlos Alazraqui (*Happy Feet*) as Walden, Abominable Snowman, and Santa.

AWARDS: *Wow! Wow! Wubbzy!* received Annie nominations for Best Animated Television Production and Best Production Design in an Animated Television Production in 2007; won a Daytime Emmy for Outstanding Individual in Animation (Bob Boyle) in 2008; and received Third Place at the Kids First! Film Festival in 2009.

INTERESTING TIDBITS: Like other episodes in the series, this episode originally consisted of two 15-minute segments: "A Great and Grumpy Holiday," which did not involve saving Christmas, and "The Super Special Gift."

Early in the segment, Daizy remarks that Christmas is all about helping others (without religious implications), which Santa later confirms after Wubbzy proves himself a good "Christmas Samaritan" to the jolly gent and others.

Santa's team consists of only Rudolph (with an exaggerated nose) and two other reindeer.

Other save-Christmas films in which presents parachute down include **Christmas Flintstone, The Christmas Orange, Christmas Present Time**, and **A Monster Christmas**.

Other save-Christmas films in which the flu hits the North Pole include **Madeline at the North Pole, The Magic Sack of Mr. Nicholas,** *The Night B4 Christmas, Nine Dog Christmas*, and *'Twas the Night*.

REVIEW: Larisa Wiseman of *Common Sense Media* reviewed the series: "Characters learn the importance of friendship, responsibility, sharing, listening, compromising, and helping and appreciating others ... the storylines are simple, engaging, and funny, and the characters are cute and energetic. Unfortunately, it is likely that some young viewers will be bored by the flat visuals..."

PRODUCTION CREDITS—Writer: Suzanne Collins. Executive Producers: Bob Boyle, Susan Miller Lazar, Fred Seibert, Kent Price, and Jay Fukuto. Directors: Steve Daye and Ron Crown. Production Companies: Hibbert Ralph Animation Ltd., Bolder Media for Boys and Girls, Chalkline Productions, Film Roman Productions, IDT Entertainment, Six Point Harness, and Starz Media. Rating: TV-Y. Genres: Animation, Family. Country: USA. Run Time: Approx. 15 min.

REFERENCES: "The Super Special Gift." In *Wubbzy's Christmas Adventure*. Beverly Hills, CA: Anchor Bay Entertainment, 2009. DVD Video.

Wilson, Joanna. *Tis the Season TV: The Encyclopedia of Christmas-Themed Episodes, Specials and Made-for-TV Movies*. Akron, OH: 1701 Press, 2011.

Wiseman, Larisa. *Wow! Wow! Wubbzy! Common Sense Media*. https://www.commonsensemedia.org/tv-reviews/wow-wow-wubbzy

Wow! Wow! Wubbzy! Internet Movie Database. http://www.imdb.com/title/tt0762067/

The Swan Princess Christmas—
November 6, 2012

Computer-Animated Direct-to-Video Musical

THREAT TO CHRISTMAS: Resurrected, an evil sorcerer would destroy Christmas in a kingdom.

HOW CHRISTMAS IS SAVED: Princess Odette, Prince Derek, and their friends foil the sorcerer.

SYNOPSIS AND COMMENTARY: Fashioned from Russian folk tales, Tchaikovsky's *Swan Lake* ballet is the story of Odette, a beautiful princess whom the evil sorcerer Von Rothbart transforms into a swan. A series of *Swan Princess* animated fantasy films further capitalized on the *Swan Lake* theme, commencing in 1994 with the theatrical release of *The Swan Princess* in traditional, two-dimensional animation. Four direct-to-video sequels followed: *The Swan Princess: Escape from Castle Mountain* (1997); *The Swan Princess: The Mystery of the Enchanted Kingdom* (1998); *The Swan Princess Christmas* (2012); and *The Swan Princess: A Royal Family Tale* (2014). The latter two of the sequels were the products of computer animation.

In *Christmas*, Princess Odette and Prince Derek, young newlyweds, spend the holidays at the castle of his mother, Queen Uberta. Though deceased with his spirit imprisoned in a large chest at the castle, Rothbart, bent on being resurrected and destroying Christmas in the kingdom, compels a black cat named Number 9 (for nine lives) to steal the royal Christmas tree's star, whereupon Derek searches the castle for it. Opening the chest, he unwittingly releases Rothbart's ghost, who casts little spells that cause much discord and ill will in the kingdom. Discovering that wind chimes weaken Rothbart (the answer to the vampire and the cross), Odette and Derek deck the castle with them, but the sorcerer compels the hag Bridgit to remove them. Meanwhile, because the festivities include musical performances, the spell creates a rift between the queen and Lord Rogers such that they launch a heated competition between themselves. Though Uberta had bidden Odette to stage her own musical number, the latter invites a group of young orphans to sing "Christmas Is the Reason," then she induces the queen and Rogers to bestow gifts and food to the poor, which break Rothbart's spell. Not to be outdone, Rothbart casts another spell on one of the electric light bulbs (a recent innovation at the castle) from the royal Christmas tree; when the tree is lit at the castle's Christmas Eve party, the tree bursts into flames, and Rothbart returns as living flesh and blood who steals the queen's crown and zaps Odette away to his lair at Swan Lake. There, his magic transforms her into a white swan imprisoned among roots, and when the moonlight touches her wings, she will become a golden, swan-shaped Christmas ornament. Derek arrives to battle Rothbart, who morphs into the hideous "Great Animal" from the original film (wolf's head, bat's body, eagle's feet, lizard's tail) and mortally wounds Derek. But Odette's singing "The Season of Love" annihilates Rothbart in flames (which breaks the swan spell on her), revives Derek, and restores the royal Christmas tree. Because each ornament on that tree represents centuries of goodness, the newest ornament to be added honors Odette and Derek.

PRINCIPAL VOICES: Elle Deets (*Soul Eater*) as Odette; Summer Anela Eguchi as Odette's singing voice; Yuri Lowenthal (*Big Hero 6*) as Derek; Michaelangelo as Derek's singing voice; Sean Wright (*Hot Shots!*) as Rothbart; Jennifer Miller (*The Swan Princess Christmas*) as Queen Uberta; Joseph Medrano (*Decisions*) as Lord Rogers; David Lodge (*Tomb Raider*) as Number 9; Catherine Lavin (*The Swan Princess Christmas*) as Bridgit; James Arrington (*The Swan Princess*) as Chamberlain; Clayton James (*Parables of Jesus*) as Jean-Bob; Gardner Jaas (*The Swan Princess Christmas*) as Puffin; Doug Stone (*Ninja Scroll*) as Speed.

SONGS: "Season of Love" (end credit) by Vassal Benford, Byron Stanfield, and Michaelangelo, performed by Anna Graceman; "Season of Love" (show version) by Vassal Benford, Jeremy Lubbock, Clive Romney, and Michaelangelo; "Christmas Is the Reason" by Jared F. Brown, performed by Shauna Madinah; "Far Longer Than Forever" by Lex De Azevedo. Christmas carol standards include "Jingle Bells," "Deck the Halls," "Hark! The Herald Angels Sing," "Jolly Old St. Nicholas," "Angels We Have Heard on High," "God Rest You Merry Gentlemen," "Joy to the World," "Here We Come A-Caroling," "Away in a Manger," "The 12 Days of Christmas," "O Christmas Tree," "Silent Night," and "We Wish You a Merry Christmas."

INTERESTING TIDBITS: Three of Odette's animal friends from the original film appear in this sequel: Jean-Bob, a *French frog* (now there's fodder for a riff); Puffin, an Irish puffin; and

Speed, a turtle. Although they provide a bit of comic relief, their presence is not crucial to the story line.

While there is something of a medieval, Old World flavor in the setting and the characters' appearances, the music is very much that of the 21st century. The majority of the musical numbers, including the Christmas carol standards, are presented with a rock beat.

REVIEWS: S. Jhoanna Robledo of *Common Sense Media* (March 31, 2014): "… lacks the charms of the original tale … tries to merge a standard-ish sequel, featuring another dastardly plot from the couple's nemesis Rothbart, with a wholesome find-the-real-meaning-of-Christmas lesson. The result feels forced, with plot elements bolted together, including some uninspired musical numbers and a few plot twists that seem to come from nowhere."

Clark Douglas of *DVD Verdict* (November 24, 2014): "…a completely insignificant story about what characters from a much better film are doing in their downtime. Any magic *The Swan Princess* contained (not that it had a whole lot) is gone, as a host of wheezy gags and irritating musical numbers join forces to deliver a pretty insufferable 84 minutes of kiddie-themed entertainment."

Princess Odette and Prince Derek are lovers in *The Swan Princess* (1994), a timeless tale of romance and adventure. In *The Swan Princess Christmas* (2012), they are newlyweds who, with their friends, foil an evil sorcerer bent on destroying Christmas (Nest Entertainment and New Line Cinema/MMG Photo Archives; collection of William D. Crump).

PRODUCTION CREDITS—Story: Richard Rich and Brian Nissen. Screenplay: Brian Nissen. Producers: Richard Rich, Seldon O. Young, and Jared F. Brown. Director: Richard Rich. Production Companies: Crest Animation Productions, Nest Family Entertainment, and Sony Pictures Entertainment. Rating: PG (scary moments). Genres: Animation, Adventure, Fantasy, Musical. Countries: India, South Korea, USA. Run Time: 84 min.

REFERENCES: Douglas, Clark. *The Swan Princess Christmas*. DVD Verdict. http://www.dvdverdict.com/reviews/swanprincesschristmas.php

Lenburg, Jeff. *The Encyclopedia of Animated Cartoons*. Third Edition. New York: Facts on File, 2009.

Robledo, S. Jhoanna. *The Swan Princess Christmas*. Common Sense Media. https://www.

commonsensemedia.org/movie-reviews/the-swan-princess-christmas

The Swan Princess Christmas. Culver City, CA: Sony Pictures Home Entertainment, 2012. DVD Video.

The Swan Princess Christmas. Internet Movie Database. http://www.imdb.com/title/tt1984279/

A Tale of Two Santas—December 23, 2001
Episode from the Animated Television Series *Futurama*

THREAT TO CHRISTMAS: The homicidal Robot Santa returns to terrorize *New* New York.

HOW CHRISTMAS IS SAVED: Despite the robot, the old spirit of Christmas is still alive because *fear*, not love, brings everyone together at this time.

SYNOPSIS AND COMMENTARY: In this Christmas sequel to *Xmas Story*, Robot Santa is back again at Xmastime to terrorize *New* New York in the 31st century, the setting of *Futurama*. Created by Matt Groening (*The Simpsons*), *Futurama* aired on the Fox Network and then Comedy Central for 140 half-hour episodes between 1999 and 2013. The series revolved around the adventures of Philip J. Fry, a dimwitted pizza delivery boy from New York City who, having been cryogenically frozen in 2000, was revived in 2999 to become a delivery boy with Planet Express, an interplanetary delivery company. Other principal characters included Turanga Leela, a purple-haired, female cyclops and captain of the Planet Express ship; Bender Rodriguez, a foul-talking, boozing robot and Fry's best friend; Professor Hubert Farnsworth, Fry's 160-year-old distant nephew and Planet Express founder; Dr. John Zoidberg, a lobster-like alien; Amy Wong, a Planet Express intern; and Hermes Conrad, Planet Express's Jamaican accountant.

As *New* New York prepares for another Xmas as Christmas is now called, a news broadcast features the head of the Xmas Safety Council, Walter Cronkite's head in a jar, who warns about the imminent arrival of Robot Santa. Clips from last Xmas depict Santa's mayhem. But Fry, Leela, and Bender head right into Santa's maw as the Professor sends them on a mission to deliver letters to Santa who's stationed on Neptune, not the North Pole. Learning that kids beg Santa to spare them from havoc, Fry is determined to bring back the old traditional ways of Christmas. Landing on Neptune in destitute Jolly Junction, the gang solicit help from bluish, out-of-work elves, who hide them in the mail bag and sneak them into Santa's Death Fortress. There, Leela unsuccessfully attempts to foil Santa with a logical paradox, namely that since he destroys the naughty and since he is also naughty, then he should destroy himself. But Santa, immune to paradox and responding with a rocket launcher and gunfire, chases them out. When Santa would prevent their flight by restraining their space ship, the exhaust melts the ice around Santa, who sinks up to his neck and freezes. Bender then takes over as the "good" Santa, the elves resume their toymaking, and Bender heads back to earth in Robot Santa's mechanical reindeer sleigh on Christmas Eve, where he's mistaken for Robot Santa. Arrested for "crimes against humanity," he endures a court trial on Xmas Day (which smacks of *Miracle on 34th Street*) and sentenced to death by magnetic dismemberment. Leela and Fry rush to Neptune to bring Santa back to exonerate Bender, but after he's cut from the ice, Santa erupts with more gunfire, forcing Leela and Fry to escape back to earth; unknown to them, Santa rides piggyback. When the Planet Express gang unsuccessfully attempt to stall Bender's execution by posing as Santas (Zoidberg posing as Jesus) to fool the mayor-turned-executioner, Robot Santa crashes in with the usual gunfire and frees Bender, who becomes Santa's willing accomplice in a super Xmas rampage. The city is in flames, and though the Planet Express gang huddle in fear, Fry realizes that, in an oddball way, the old spirit of Christmas still exists: instead of love, *fear* brought people together. The episode concludes with Santa warning Bender: "Play Santa again, and I'll kill you next year!" Then Santa kicks Bender off the sleigh into the flames below. Merry Xmas!

PRINCIPAL VOICES: Billy West (*Futurama*) as Fry, Farnsworth, Zoidberg, and Judge Ron

Whitey; Katey Sagal (*Married ... with Children*) as Leela; John DiMaggio (*Futurama*) as Bender and Robot Santa; Tress MacNeille (*The Simpsons*) as Linda, Vyolet, and Petunia; Maurice LaMarche (*Frozen*) as Morbo the alien anchorman, Hyper-Chicken, and Robot Devil; Coolio (*Bad Teacher*) as Kwanzaa-bot; Phil LaMarr (*Pulp Fiction*) as Hermes; David Herman (*Idiocracy*) as the mayor; Lauren Tom (*Bad Santa*) as Amy; Frank Welker (*Aladdin*) as Walter Cronkite's head.

AWARDS: *Futurama* has received a slew of awards, the most notable of which are Primetime Emmys for Outstanding Individual Achievement in Animation (2000, 2001), Outstanding Animated Program Less Than One Hour (2002, 2011), Outstanding Voice-Over Performance (Maurice LaMarche, 2011, 2012), and other Emmy nominations; Annie Awards for Outstanding Achievement in Directing (2000, 2003), Writing (2001, 2014), Voice Acting (John DiMaggio, 2001), Best General Audience Animated TV/Broadcast Production (2014), and other Annie nominations.

INTERESTING TIDBITS: This episode, the title of which obviously parodies the title of Dickens's novel *A Tale of Two Cities*, was originally slated to air in December 2000; it was postponed a year because of the episode's violence.

The courthouse is named "Famous Original Ray's Superior Courthouse," which is a parody of Famous Original Ray's Pizza in New York City.

The episode satirizes Kwanzaa. Bender solicits help in making Xmas deliveries from the Kwanzaa-bot, a robot that is too busy handing out the traditional Kwanzaa book titled *What the Hell Is Kwanza?* (spelled with one "a" at the end). The cover depicts two confused black people in African garb shrugging their shoulders. Kwanzaa-bot has been pitching that book for 647 years, but people are *still* clueless about Kwanzaa. While most save-Christmas movies do not mention Kwanzaa, another one that does is **Save the Reindeer**.

As prison guards lead Bender to his execution, they walk the "last mile" on a green floor with one guard chanting, "Deactivated robot walking!" This is a parody of a scene in *The Green Mile* (1999), in which the sadistic guard Percy chants, "Dead man walking!" when the death house receives a new prisoner.

There's irony in the name Jolly Junction on Neptune, since the town is a wasteland, thanks to Robot Santa. Jolly Junction is also a parody of two fictional towns in other animated Christmas specials: January Junction in *Jack Frost* (1979) and Junctionville in **'Twas the Night Before Christmas** (1974).

When Bender takes over as the good Santa and the Neptunian elves resume making toys, a conveyor belt in the workshop has three speeds: slow, fast, and Lucy. The third speed refers to a classic scene in "Job Switching" (September 15, 1952), an episode from *I Love Lucy*, in which Lucy and Ethel work in a chocolate factory against a ridiculously speeding conveyor belt.

Robot Santa gives Rudolph a nod after freeing Bender when he asks, "Bender, won't you join my slaying tonight?"

Robot Santa's "Ho Ho Ho" resembles that by the demonic department store Santa who terrorizes Ralphie Parker in *A Christmas Story* (1983).

REVIEWS: Metacritic gave *Futurama* a score of 72/100 (generally favorable reviews).

Ken Tucker of *Entertainment Weekly* reviewed *Futurama* (April 2, 1999): "Groening, deeply influenced by the paranoid fantasies of writer Philip K. Dick, the dystopian surrealism of the Firesign Theatre, and every cornball sci-fi movie, creates an airy atmosphere ripe for satirizing our love of computer technology."

John Levesque of the *Seattle Post-Intelligencer* reviewed *Futurama*: "...smart but not pointy-headed, satirical but not annoying. It's the hallmark of Groening and his people: sly, subversive humor delivered with such who-me? guiltlessness that it's hard not to like."

PRODUCTION CREDITS—Writer: Bill Odenkirk. Producers: Bill Odenkirk, Eric Kaplan, Brian J. Cowan, and Claudia Katz. Director: Ron Hughart. Production Companies: The Curiosity Company, 20th Century Fox Television, and Rough Draft Studios. Rating: TV-14.

Genres: Animation, Comedy, Sci-Fi. Country: USA. Run Time: 22 min.

REFERENCES: *Futurama*. Internet Movie Database. http://www.imdb.com/title/tt0149460/

Futurama. Metacritic. http://www.metacritic.com/tv/futurama/critic-reviews

Levesque, John. *Futurama. Seattle Post-Intelligencer* (March 26, 1999).

"A Tale of Two Santas." In *Futurama: The Complete Collection 1999–2009*. Beverly Hills, CA: 20th Century Fox Home Entertainment, 2009. DVD Video.

"A Tale of Two Santas." Internet Movie Database. http://www.imdb.com/title/tt0584429/

Tucker, Ken. *Futurama. Entertainment Weekly*. http://www.ew.com/article/1999/04/02/futurama

Wilson, Joanna. *Tis the Season TV: The Encyclopedia of Christmas-Themed Episodes, Specials and Made-for-TV Movies*. Akron, OH: 1701 Press, 2011.

The Three Dogateers—November 18, 2014
Direct-to-Video Movie

THREAT TO CHRISTMAS: Shortly before Christmas, two robbers break into a house and steal all the presents.

HOW CHRISTMAS IS SAVED: The house's three dogs pursue the robbers and retrieve the presents with Santa's help.

SYNOPSIS AND COMMENTARY: Christmastime robbers break into a house. Dogs foil robbers and save Christmas. But instead of the dogs setting all kinds of booby traps, as in ***The Dog Who Saved Christmas***, the dogs in *The Three Dogateers*, also known as *The Three Dogateers Save Christmas*, pursue the robbers when they leave the scene. The story revolves around three small, white, talking lap-dogs living under the same roof. Their leader, the mutt Arfamis, speaks with a Spanish accent and wildly imagines himself and his two companions—Barkos, a foodie with a Southern accent, and Wagos, a female Maltese—as the swashbuckling guards of their master's "castle" with roles similar to those of the Three Musketeers, or in this case, Dogateers. Two days before Christmas, their master Matt (the "king" to Arfamis) (Dean Cain, *Lois and Clark*) suddenly leaves town on urgent business while his dogs remain at home alone—with no food. That night, when two robbers steal all the Christmas presents in the house including the tree, the three dogs stow away in the crooks' van and vow to retrieve and return the presents. Thus begins an adventure that takes the dogs into the desert, where the crooks ditch them, after which they search for a way to The Mall (as advertised all over TV) where they'll get help from Santa. They're dogged (yes, pun) by a maniacal dogcatcher with a German accent (Bill Oberst, Jr., *Deadly Revisions*), who chases them all through the desert, because he needs just three more dogs to set the world's record for the most dogs captured in one year. The dogs end up hot-wiring a car and heading to The Mall with the dogcatcher in hot pursuit, which generates much cartoon mayhem, such as dodging a speeding train; the dogcatcher isn't that lucky. Arriving at The Mall, when the dogs spot the crooks selling their presents in the parking lot, Arfamis induces a mall cop to chase away the thieves, while the other two dogs hunt down the mall Santa (Richard Riehle, *Office Space*). Intuiting that the presents belong to the dogs and discovering their address, mall Santa piles the dogs, presents, and tree into his little red car and heads for their home—with the dogcatcher (covered in casts and bandages) in pursuit again, producing more cartoon mayhem. Although the dogcatcher initially overpowers mall Santa and captures the dogs, Wagos picks the locks on their cages, mall Santa overpowers the dogcatcher, and the gang arrives home in time to redecorate Matt's house before he returns. Now is the "Santa" who helps the dogs just a mall Santa or is he the real deal? Answer: As Santa heads down the road in his little red car, greeting Christmas with backfires, he zooms into the sky and away.

ANIMAL VOICES: Jesse Baget (*Mischief Night*) as Arfamis and Barkos; Danielle Judovits (*Toy Story*) as Wagos; Stephen Cedars (*Snatchers*) as prairie dog.

INTERESTING TIDBITS: Surely viewers

caught the puns in the Dogateers' names: *Arfamis*, *Barkos*, and *Wagos*.

In the scene with the dogs driving a car, Arfamis steers, while the other two operate the gas and brake pedals (fortunately, the car is an automatic).

REVIEWS: Renee Schonfeld of *Common Sense Media* (November 14, 2014): "…plenty of feather-brained, over-the-top villains and slapstick action. Stereotypes abound; discussions about body odor and farts announce a reliance on easy and expected laughs … a lot of screen time on dogs frolicking, dogs running through the desert, and a dog driving a car while on the run. Other than Santa Claus, there's nary a human in the story that rises above the lowest level of goofy humor."

Kevin Matthews of *For It Is Man's Number* (December 27, 2014): "…aimed squarely at kids. Movements and quirks are exaggerated, with most of the adults appearing onscreen shown to be stumbling, bumbling figures obviously needing help from, or to be outsmarted by, the three dogs … some amusing verbal gags, a few ill-timed farts … the dogs are cute."

PRODUCTION CREDITS—Writers: Jesse Baget and Lisa Baget. Producers: Jesse Baget, Lisandro Novillo, and Phillip B. Goldfine. Director: Jesse Baget. Production Company: Hollywood Media Bridge. Rating: Not rated. Genres: Comedy, Family. Country: USA. Run Time: 88 min.

REFERENCES: Matthews, Kevin. *The Three Dogateers. For It Is Man's Number.* http://foritismansnumber.blogspot.co.uk/2014/12/the-three-dogateers-2014.html

Schonfeld, Renee. *The Three Dogateers. Common Sense Media.* https://www.commonsensemedia.org/movie-reviews/the-three-dogateers

The Three Dogateers. Internet Movie Database. http://www.imdb.com/title/tt3179402/

The Three Dogateers. RLJ Entertainment, 2014. DVD Video.

Tim Burton's The Nightmare Before Christmas—October 29, 1993
Animated Motion Picture Musical

THREAT TO CHRISTMAS: Jack Skellington, the Pumpkin King of Halloween Town, kidnaps Santa and unwittingly wreaks havoc with Christmas.

HOW CHRISTMAS IS SAVED: Jack rescues Santa from the bogeyman's clutches.

SYNOPSIS AND COMMENTARY: Utilizing 227 three-dimensional puppets in stop-motion animation, *Nightmare* is based on a poem of the same title that director, producer, writer, and actor Tim Burton wrote in 1982 while working as an animator for Disney Studios. He drew inspiration from two animated television specials, **Rudolph, the Red-Nosed Reindeer** and **How the Grinch Stole Christmas,** as well as from the poem "A Visit from St. Nicholas," to create a dual celebration of his two favorite holidays, Halloween and Christmas. Here, Jack parallels the Grinch, and Jack's red-nosed ghost dog Zero parallels Rudolph.

As expected, Jack Skellington's subjects in Halloween Town consist of a host of ghouls, vampires, and other typically frightful creatures. Weary of creating the same screams and nightmares each year, Jack longs for something more meaningful. Wandering through a forest, he comes upon several trees with doors fashioned in various holiday symbols that are alien to him: an Easter egg, a Thanksgiving turkey, and a Christmas tree. He opens the latter door and plummets into a magical world of snow, toys, and Santa Claus—in short, Christmas Town. Anxious to share Christmas with Halloween Town, he returns with simple toys and commissions everyone in his domain to duplicate them as well as create a Santa suit, reindeer, and sleigh. Their efforts are anything but Christmasy, for their limited imaginations are capable of producing only fiendish toys with fangs and a coffin sleigh with skeletal reindeer. Overcome with the desire to participate in Christmas, Jack decides to usurp Santa's role on Christmas Eve. To get Santa temporarily out of the way, Jack orders three mischievous creatures, Lock, Shock, and Barrel, to kidnap the jolly old elf. These creatures deliver Santa to Oogie Boogie, the bogeyman. Sally, a female version of the Frankenstein monster created by Dr. Finklestein, senses that Jack is completely out of his element and conjures up a fog that almost puts a halt to Jack's midnight ride, until Zero, his red-nosed ghost dog, leads the skeletal team skyward in the spirit of Rudolph, the Red-Nosed Reindeer. As Jack disperses his toys, they wreak havoc by chasing and attacking children while Jack, spotted as an impostor, is shot from the sky by ground artillery. With Christmas nearly a disaster, Jack realizes that attempting to venture beyond his realm was a serious error. Just as Oogie Boogie is about to dispatch Santa, Jack returns to his role as Pumpkin King and frees Santa in time to save Christmas.

PRINCIPAL VOICES: Chris Sarandon (*Fright Night*) as Jack speaking; Danny Elfman (*Corpse Bride*) as Jack singing and Barrel; Catherine O'Hara (*Home Alone*) as Sally and Shock; William Hickey (*Prizzi's Honor*) as Dr. Finkelstein; Glenn Shadix (*Beetlejuice*) as Mayor of Halloween Town; Paul Reubens (*Pee-wee's Playhouse*) as Lock; Ken Page (*Dreamgirls*) as Oogie Boogie; Ed Ivory (*Nine Months*) as Santa.

AWARDS: In 1994, this picture won Saturn Awards for Best Fantasy Film and Best Music; won Annie Awards for Best Individual Achievement for Artistic Excellence and for Creative Supervision in the Field of Animation; won Blimp Award for Favorite Movie; Academy Award nomination for Best Visual Effects; Saturn Award nominations for Best Director and Best Special Effects; Annie Award nomination for Best Animated Film; Golden Globe Award nomination for Best Original Score in a Motion Picture; Hugo Award nomination for Best Dramatic Presentation; Young Artist Award nomination for Outstanding Family Motion Picture in Action/Adventure; Grammy Award nomination for Best Album for Children. In 2011, it won the International Film Music Critics Award for Best Archival Release of an Existing Score.

Sally (left), a female version of the Frankenstein monster created by Dr. Finkelstein, and Jack Skellington, the Pumpkin King of Halloween Town, share a moment in *Tim Burton's The Nightmare Before Christmas* (1993) (Touchstone Pictures; collection of William D. Crump).

MUSIC AND LYRICS: Danny Elfman

SONGS: "Overture," "Opening," "This Is Halloween," "Jack's Lament," "Doctor Finklestein/In the Forest," "What's This?" "Town Meeting Song," "Jack and Sally Montage," "Jack's Obsession," "Kidnap the Sandy Claws," "Making Christmas," "Nabbed," "Oogie Boogie's Song," "Sally's Song," "Christmas Eve Montage," "Poor Jack," "To the Rescue," "Finale," "Reprise," "Closing," "End Title."

INTERESTING TIDBITS: *Nightmare* was the first stop-motion animated feature to be converted entirely to 3-D and was re-released in that format in 2006. With a budget of $18 million, domestic box office sales reached approximately $50 million; total gross sales have exceeded $75 million.

Other save-Christmas films in which Santa is kidnapped include *The Boy Who Saved Christmas; The Elf and the Magic Key; The Glo Friends Save Christmas; The Great Santa Claus Switch; The Librarians and Santa's Midnight Run; Santa Claus Conquers the Martians; Sonic Christmas Blast; Spinach Greetings*; and *Who Stole Santa?*

REVIEWS: According to the Rotten Tomatoes film review site, 94 percent of critics gave this production a positive review.

Roger Ebert of rogerebert.com (October 22, 1993): "[Burton] has made a world here that is as completely new as the worlds we saw for the first time in such films as *Metropolis, The Cabinet of Dr. Caligari* or *Star Wars*."

Richard Corliss of *Time Magazine* (October 11, 1993): "A sweet and scary treat ... spins a fun-house fantasy for two holidays."

John Hartl of *The Seattle Times* (October 22, 1993): "Visually a macabre knockout, this 75-minute fantasy boasts some of the wittiest, most vigorous stop-motion animation effects in the history of the process."

Desson Howe of *The Washington Post* (October 22, 1993): "This brilliant combination of stop-motion animation, three-dimensional sets and superbly imaginative graphics, brings animation to new peaks."

PRODUCTION CREDITS—Story: Tim Burton. Adaptation: Michael McDowell. Screenplay: Caroline Thompson. Producers: Tim Burton and Denise DiNovi. Director: Henry Selick. Production Companies: Touchstone Pictures, Skellington Productions, Tim Burton Productions, and Walt Disney Pictures. Rating: PG (some frightening images). Genres: Animation, Kids and Family, Science Fiction and Fantasy. Country: USA. Run time: 75 min.

REFERENCES: Burton, Tim. *The Nightmare Before Christmas*. New York: Disney Press, 1993.

Corliss, Richard. *Time Magazine*. http://content.time.com/time/magazine/article/0,9171,979351,00.html?promoid-googlep

Crump, William D. *The Christmas Encyclopedia*. Third Edition. Jefferson, NC: McFarland, 2013.

Duralde, Alonso. *Have Yourself a Movie Little Christmas*. New York: Limelight Editions, 2010.

Ebert, Roger. "Review: *Tim Burton's The Nightmare Before Christmas*." http://www.rogerebert.com/reviews/tim-burtons-the-nightmare-before-christmas-1993

Hartl, John. "An Animation Dream—'Nightmare Before Christmas' Is Visual Treat, but It Lacks Vision." *The Seattle Times*. http://community.seattletimes.nwsource.com/archive/?date=19931022&slug=1727371

Howe, Desson. *The Nightmare Before Christmas*. *The Washington Post*. http://www.washingtonpost.com/wp-srv/style/longterm/movies/videos/thenightmarebeforechristmaspghowe_a0b003.htm

Lenburg, Jeff. *The Encyclopedia of Animated Cartoons*. Third Edition. New York: Facts on File, 2009.

The Nightmare Before Christmas Official Web Site. http://movies.disney.com/the-nightmare-before-christmas

The Nightmare Before Christmas. Rotten Tomatoes. http://www.rottentomatoes.com/m/nightmare_before_christmas

The Nightmare Before Christmas. Wikipedia. https://en.wikipedia.org/wiki/The_Nightmare_Before_Christmas

Thompson, Frank. *Tim Burton's The Nightmare Before Christmas: The Film, the Art and the Vision*. New York: Hyperion, 2002.

Tim Burton's The Nightmare Before Christmas. Big Cartoon Database. http://www.bcdb.com/cartoon/23389-Nightmare-Before-Christmas

Tim Burton's The Nightmare Before Christmas. Box Office Mojo. http://www.boxofficemojo.com/movies/?id=nightmarebeforechristmas.htm

Tim Burton's The Nightmare Before Christmas. Burbank, CA: Walt Disney Home Entertainment, 2010. DVD Video

Tim Burton's The Nightmare Before Christmas. Internet Movie Database. http://www.imdb.com/title/tt0107688/

Wilson, Joanna. *Tis the Season TV: The Encyclopedia of Christmas-Themed Episodes, Specials and Made-for-TV Movies*. Akron, OH: 1701 Press, 2011.

The Town Christmas Forgot—November 25, 2010

Television Movie

THREAT TO CHRISTMAS: Flagging economy crushes the Christmas spirit in a small, backwoods town.

HOW CHRISTMAS IS SAVED: A big-city family pulls the town out of its Christmas doldrums.

SYNOPSIS AND COMMENTARY: Charles and Annie Benson (Rick Roberts, *Traders*, and Lauren Holly, *Picket Fences*) with their children Trish (Torri Webster, *Life with Boys*) and Nolan (Azer Greco, *Really Me*) are bound for a ski resort a few days before Christmas when their car breaks down during a blizzard. They take refuge in Nowhere, a remote mining town in Colorado that lacks the Christmas spirit and is dying because the mine has closed. Samantha (Stephanie Belding, *Watchmen*), the owner of the local café, attempts to boost everyone's spirits by organizing a talent pageant on Christmas Eve, despite objections from her mayor-husband that the town cannot afford such a luxury. The simplicity of life in Nowhere (compared to the Bensons' lives ruled by digital technology) and the plight of the people capture the Bensons' hearts, and they lend a helping hand: Annie offers dancing tips for the pageant, Trish whips a teen rock band into shape, Nolan persuades the grumpy owner of the toy store to portray Santa, and banker Charles agrees to loan Nowhere the capital to build ski lifts that will revive the town's economy.

INTERESTING TIDBIT: Azer Greco is Lauren Holly's real-life son.

REVIEWS: Andy Webb of *The Movie Scene*: "…a fun, feel-good bit of Christmas fluff [that] doesn't try to moralise [sic] over the despair of struggling small towns … unoriginal and intentionally cheesy…"

Sloan Freer of *Radio Times*: "[The Bensons are] laughably able to solve all the stereotyped residents' woes with their big-city ways. Events are goofy and idealistic—from a cartoonish Holly cheesily choreographing the local yuletide pageant to her obnoxious teen daughter … teaching a high-school band how to rock—as they rush towards their predictably convenient conclusion. Naturally, the materialistic clan also ends up transformed…"

PRODUCTION CREDITS—Writer: Jim Makichuk. Producer: Marek Posival. Director: John Bradshaw. Production Company: Chesler/Perlmutter Productions. Rating: Not rated. Genres: Drama, Family. Country: Canada. Run Time: 85 min.

REFERENCES: Crump, William D. *The Christmas Encyclopedia*. Third Edition. Jefferson, NC: McFarland, 2013.

Freer, Sloan. *The Town Christmas Forgot*. *Radio Times*. http://www.radiotimes.com/film/ns972/the-town-christmas-forgot

The Town Christmas Forgot. Internet Movie Database. http://www.imdb.com/title/tt1720276/

The Town Christmas Forgot. New York: Cinedigm Home Entertainment, 2014. DVD Video.

Webb, Andy. *The Town Christmas Forgot*. *The Movie Scene*. http://www.themoviescene.co.uk/reviews/the-town-christmas-forgot/the-town-christmas-forgot.html

The Town Santa Forgot—December 3, 1993

Also Known As *The Town That Santa Forgot*

Animated Television Short Film

THREAT TO CHRISTMAS: Because of an oversight, Santa has never visited the impoverished town of Jeremy Creek.

HOW CHRISTMAS IS SAVED: Santa mistakes a whopping letter from greedy boy Jeremy Creek for that from all the children in the town of Jeremy Creek and gives his presents to the town instead of the boy.

SYNOPSIS AND COMMENTARY: Just hearing a kid's letter to Santa read on television can produce a story. When Charmaine Severson heard the *Tonight* show's Johnny Carson read one such letter from a kid who wanted "everything" for Christmas, she was inspired to write *Jeremy Creek*, a rhyming tale about a greedy little boy. Her story was published in a number of Sunday magazines and was adapted as the animated film, *The Town Santa Forgot*.

When his two young grandchildren seem overly concerned about having their Christmas wishes fulfilled, a grandfather teaches them the moral "It's better to give than to receive" through a rhyming "true story" about Jeremy Creek. The epitome of the spoiled brat, little Jeremy has a seemingly insatiable lust for toys and more toys. But instead of politely asking for them, he acquires each new toy by throwing tantrums that can be heard for miles until his parents and relatives fulfill his wishes. He has far more toys than other children, yet Jeremy refuses to share them, and eventually his parents decide that he will have no more toys. Undaunted, Jeremy then turns to Santa, but instead of waiting until Christmas to submit his list, Jeremy begins in June. Upon completion, his list is half a mile long. When Jeremy's bulky list reaches the North Pole, twelve elves are required to unfurl it, and a bewildered Santa surmises that such a list naming virtually every toy imaginable could only have come from an entire town, not one person. Searching the map, Santa not only discovers a town by the name of Jeremy Creek, but it is a town that he has never previously visited. Thus on Christmas Eve, Santa delivers all the toys on the list to delighted little boys and girls in the town of Jeremy Creek, while little boy Jeremy Creek throws another tantrum for having received no Christmas toys. On Christmas morning, a television news broadcast carries an interview with a grateful little girl from town Jeremy Creek, who expresses appreciation to the unknown person who wrote Santa on their behalf and thus brought untold happiness to all the children of her impoverished town. When Jeremy realizes that his greed had unwittingly been turned into good, his heart melts to the core, and the experience molds him into a generous person. As the lesson ends and the scene pans away from the grandfather's house, the wind blows the snow off the mailbox to reveal the name "J. Creek." What the audience should garner from that should be obvious.

Armed with a net, selfish little Jeremy Creek lies in wait for Santa, as if he's about to snare the old gent and capture all the presents in *The Town Santa Forgot* (1993) (Hanna-Barbera/Photofest).

PRINCIPAL VOICES: Dick Van Dyke (*The Dick Van Dyke Show*) as the narrator and old Jeremy Creek; Miko Hughes (*Pet Sematary*) as young Jeremy Creek; Troy Davidson (*Fine Things*) as the grandson; Ashley Johnson (*The Avengers*) as the granddaughter; Melinda Peterson (*Barrier Device*) as Mrs. Creek; Phil Proctor (*Toy Story*) as Mr. Creek; Hal Smith (*The Andy Griffith Show*) as Santa.

AWARDS: In 1994, this film received a Primetime Emmy nomination for Outstanding Animated Program (One Hour or Less).

INTERESTING TIDBITS: Raised in the United Kingdom, the now-American author Charmaine Severson wrote *Jeremy Creek* as the first of several children's rhyming tales, which also included *Listening for Christmas, Freddie Bemoan, The Socks of Farloo,* and *The Itsallmine Twins,* among others. She also published *The I Hate to Camp Book* (1973).

REVIEW: Will Brownridge of *The Film Reel* (December 20, 2103): "…teaches its lessons in a way that young kids will enjoy, without getting too sappy about it. The message of giving rather than getting is an important one that is often overlooked during the holidays, especially for kids … the rhyming nature of the script makes it feel a lot like a Dr. Seuss special. That's also going to make it appeal to kids…"

PRODUCTION CREDITS—Teleplay: Glenn Leopold. Producer: Davis Doi. Director: Robert Alvarez. Production Company: Hanna-Barbera Productions. Rating: Not rated. Genres: Animation, Family. Country: USA. Run Time: 23 min.

REFERENCES: Brownridge, Will. *The Town Santa Forgot. The Film Reel.* http://www.thefilmreel.com/2013/12/20/review-town-santa-forgot-1993-naughty-nice/

Crump, William D. *The Christmas Encyclopedia.* Third Edition. Jefferson, NC: McFarland, 2013.

Lenburg, Jeff. *The Encyclopedia of Animated Cartoons.* Third Edition. New York: Facts on File, 2009.

Severson, Charmaine. Web Page. http://charmaineseverson.com/home

The Town Santa Forgot. In *Hanna-Barbera Christmas Classics Collection.* Burbank, CA: Warner Home Video, 2012. DVD Video.

The Town Santa Forgot. Internet Movie Database. http://www.imdb.com/title/tt0356140/

The Town That Banned Christmas—
November 2006

Also Known As *A Merry Little Christmas*
Feature Film

THREAT TO CHRISTMAS: Town authorities ban Christmas observances when the annual home decorating contest degenerates into a street brawl.

HOW CHRISTMAS IS SAVED: A human behaviorist and an attorney convince the mayor to reinstate Christmas.

SYNOPSIS AND COMMENTARY: Similar to *Battle of the Bulbs* (2010), neighbors become rivals in a home Christmas decorating contest; the primary difference is that city officials don't ban Christmas in *Bulbs*. Norbert Bridges (Matt McCoy, *Abominable*), a human behaviorist, settles into the small town of Greenlawn to collect new material for his latest book project titled *A Merry Little Christmas: A Study in Pluralistic Ignorance.* Norbert, who doesn't care much for Christmas, is studying how people behave during the holidays and uses the town's annual home Christmas decorating contest as a springboard to stir up competition between the residents. Discovering that his neighbor and contest organizer Donnie Manning (Adam Ferrara, *Rescue Me*) is the obsessed, self-proclaimed "King of Christmas" who has won the contest for the past ten years, Norbert goads Donnie into a decorating frenzy, and the "fever" quickly envelops the town as a bitter spirit of one-upmanship replaces the spirit of Christmas. Donnie's noisy construction of a bizarre, lighted version of the Leaning Tower of Pisa prompts the neighbors to seek an injunction against him, and the situation escalates on the final night of the contest when the judges, unable to name a winner, award prizes to all the participants. Horrified, Donnie grabs the trophy for himself, a fistfight erupts, and Donnie and Norbert are jailed, along with other brawlers. It's nutty enough that city officials retaliate by banning all traces of Christmas in town and confiscating everyone's decorations, but there's more idiocy when the police arrest Norbert's son Kevin (Hunter Gomez, *National Treasure*) and Donnie's daughter Holly (Christa B. Allen, *Revenge*) on a charge of "committing the act of Christmas" (he gives her a gift and she accepts it). To undo this mess, Norbert and his tranquilizer-popping attorney Humphrey (Anthony Mangano, *The Dictator*) conduct some "research" and, behind closed doors, somehow convince the mayor to reinstate Christmas (the film leaves many loose ends here). A year later, Norbert's book is a best seller.

INTERESTING TIDBIT: This film was produced with a considerably low budget of approximately $200,000. One usually gets what one pays for. See Review.

REVIEW: Andy Webb of *The Movie Scene*: "…this movie doesn't even feel like a movie[;] it feels like a group of actors got together to make a home movie version of a story a friend wrote in the hope that some studio would see the potential and commission a proper movie to be made … the writing and in particular the humor [are] also lacking…"

PRODUCTION CREDITS—Writer: P.J. McIlvaine. Producers: Angelo Santomauro and Mike Forman. Directors: Karl Fink and John Dowling, Jr. Production Companies: AMLC Productions and On Point Productions. Rating: PG (mild thematic elements and language). Genres: Comedy, Family. Country: USA. Run Time: 85 min.

REFERENCES: Crump, William D. *The Christmas Encyclopedia*. Third Edition. Jefferson, NC: McFarland, 2013.

The Town That Banned Christmas. Internet Movie Database. http://www.imdb.com/title/tt0496411/

The Town That Banned Christmas. Peace Arch Home Entertainment, 2008. DVD Video.

Webb, Andy. *A Merry Little Christmas*. The Movie Scene. http://www.themoviescene.co.uk/reviews/a-merry-little-christmas-2006/a-merry-little-christmas-2006.html

A Town Without Christmas—December 16, 2001

Television Movie

THREAT TO CHRISTMAS: A town on the brink of bankruptcy lacks the Christmas spirit and a young girl considers suicide.

HOW CHRISTMAS IS SAVED: The angel Max intervenes.

SYNOPSIS AND COMMENTARY: Sometimes a town in the doldrums needs a bit of divine intervention to revive its Christmas spirit. Feeling alone, alienated, and fearing that her parents are planning a divorce, nine-year-old Megan McBride (Isabella Fink, *Fever Pitch*), under the pseudonym of "Chris," writes a passionate letter asking Santa to intervene. The letter, which suggests that she may commit suicide on Christmas Eve, receives national attention as media representatives storm the community of Seacliff, Washington, in search of the child. Among them is M.J. Jensen (Patricia Heaton, *The Middle*), a television reporter whose past emotional trauma has left her hardnosed and cynical of love. Believing that the letter is a hoax, she reluctantly collaborates with David Reynolds (Rick Roberts, *Traders*), a struggling writer, who has returned to his hometown to investigate a set of mysterious paintings that he received from an anonymous artist. Supernatural forces are at work, for the paintings portray scenes of events that will shortly transpire in Seacliff and that ultimately lead M.J. and David to identify Megan as "Chris." Megan claims that her friend Max (Peter Falk, *Columbo*) prompted her to send the letter, and that it is he who is the artist. Her story reminds David of also having felt alienated when he was a boy. As a foster child, he had run away at Christmastime, had fallen asleep in the snowy woods, and he would have succumbed to the elements, had a mysterious lumberjack not rescued him. By a series of deductions, David concludes that Max was also that "lumberjack." In reality, Max is an unconventional angel who has been sent to bring peace to Megan's troubled household, to initiate romance between David and a love-starved M.J., and to instill the Christmas spirit in the people of Seacliff (the town is on the brink of bankruptcy because a new dam has ruined the salmon fishing industry there). David is indispensable in reviving Seacliff's holiday spirit, for when a power failure threatens to cancel the annual Christmas Eve pageant, he arrives with 2,000 candles, courtesy of Max. And by Christmas Eve, M.J. is a changed woman. After learning Megan's plight and seeing the hope and joy of Christmas in Seacliff's citizens despite their difficulties, M.J. refuses to exploit the "Chris" hoax to boost news ratings and instead turns a live broadcast of the pageant into a heart-warming human-interest story.

INTERESTING TIDBITS: This production was the first of three that featured Peter Falk (1927–2011) as Max, the mischievous angel. The other two, which did not focus on saving Christmas, were *Finding John Christmas* (2003) and *When Angels Come to Town* (2004).

A Town without Christmas was the most popular TV movie of the 2001–2002 season, originally broadcast on CBS.

PRODUCTION CREDITS—Writer: Michael J. Murray. Producers: Stephanie Gaines, Ken Gross, and Michael Mahoney. Director: Andy Wolk. Production Companies: Daniel H. Blatt Productions and Viacom Productions. Rating: Not rated. Genres: Drama, Family. Country: USA. Run Time: 90 min.

REFERENCES: Crump, William D. *The Christmas Encyclopedia*. Third Edition. Jefferson, NC: McFarland, 2013.

"Peter Falk Television." Web Site. http://peterfalk.com/TELEVISION.htm

A Town without Christmas. Internet Movie Database. http://www.imdb.com/title/tt0290321/

A Town without Christmas. Lexington, KY: CBS Studios, 2014. DVD Video.

Wilson, Joanna. *Tis the Season TV: The Encyclopedia of Christmas-Themed Episodes, Specials and Made-for-TV Movies*. Akron, OH: 1701 Press, 2011.

The Toy That Saved Christmas—
October 1996

Episode from the Computer-Animated Direct-to-Video Series *VeggieTales*

THREAT TO CHRISTMAS: A greedy toymaker encourages the Veggie children to believe that Christmas is only about getting more toys.

HOW CHRISTMAS IS SAVED: When a come-to-life doll discovers that Christmas is all about the birth of Jesus and about giving, not getting, he and his Veggie friends spread the word.

SYNOPSIS AND COMMENTARY: In 1993, Phil Vischer and Mike Nawrocki created *VeggieTales*, an on-going, Christian-based series of videos for children that present stories with biblical and moral themes, often with humorous references to pop culture. The characters, who have since appeared in a number of incarnations, including feature films, television series, video games, and stage productions, consist of a group of anthropomorphic fruits and vegetables who live together on a kitchen countertop. Each video tale ends with the following signature sign-off: "Remember, God made you special and He loves you very much." However, to maintain religious neutrality, episodes that air on NBC are edited and end with a simple, "Good-bye."

In the first 17 minutes of this episode, Bob the Tomato and Larry the Cucumber host a TV show titled *The Veggie Tales Christmas Spectacular*, which is filler material that has nothing to do with the principal program. When they cannot locate the film to be shown, they fill the time with several vignettes, beginning with Junior Asparagus, a child dressed as a shepherd who sings the carol "While By My Sheep" from the Holy Land (his sheep "Baaa" in tune on the repetitive phrases). Larry then follows with his original song "Oh Santa" in the show's Silly Song segment, in which a bank robber, a crazed Viking, and an IRS agent crash the scene, after which Archibald Asparagus delivers his rendition of the carol "Ring, Little Bells." By this time, the film canister, initially mistaken for a pizza (only vegetable brains would make that mistake), is located and *Toy* begins.

It's Christmas Eve as Grandpa George the Green Onion tells his little granddaughter Annie a bedtime story about Wally Nezzer the Zucchini, a greedy toy manufacturer in Dinkletown who hooks children to the materialistic side of Christmas through his TV commercials. Nezzer's new line of dolls, "Buzz-Saw Louie," comes equipped with a working buzz saw in his right arm, and when his nose is pushed, Louie says, "Christmas is when you get stuff! You need more toys!" As Nezzer planned, Louie takes the town by storm, and the kids whine and beg for even more Christmas toys. But one Louie doll comes to life and, believing there must be more to Christmas than just toys, escapes from the factory to find out. When on Christmas Eve he encounters Bob, Larry, and Junior, they're soon wondering what Christmas means and seek an answer from wise old Grandpa George, who reads a contemporary account of the Nativity story from the Gospel of Luke in the Bible. Since God gave His only Son Jesus to the world (a nod to John 3:16), Christmas is about giving, not getting. The foursome are so impressed that they sneak into Nezzer's TV studio and broadcast the Christian meaning of Christmas to all the other Veggies. An enraged Nezzer hogties them all to a sled and is about to send them through a tunnel into a ravine when several Veggie families intervene. Although Nezzer melts when he receives a teddy bear as a gift from little Laura Carrot, the sled with the foursome accidentally takes off, whereupon Nezzer and his penguin workers race to save them from the ravine, but the tide turns, thanks to Louie, and he and the penguins end up saving Nezzer from a bad fate. Nezzer and the other Veggies celebrate Christmas together, and Louie puts his buzz saw to good use as a furniture manufacturer in Dinkletown.

PRINCIPAL VOICES: Dan Anderson as Dad Asparagus; Lesley Benodin as Li'l Pea; Kristin Belgen as Laura; Ken Cavanagh as Louie; Bridget Miller as Ma Grape; Mike Nawrocki as Larry; Lisa Vischer as Junior and Mom Asparagus; Phil Vischer as Bob, Grandpa George, Nezzer, Mr. Lunt, Pa Grape, Scallion, Dad Carrot, Dad Pea, and Mercy Pea; Shelby Vischer as Annie. Voices for "Oh Santa" Silly Song segment: Mike Nawrocki and Phil Vischer. All the voice actors have worked on *VeggieTales*.

SONGS: "Can't Believe It's Christmas" and "Grumpy Kids" by Phil Vischer. "Oh Santa" by Mike Nawrocki and Phil Vischer.

INTERESTING TIDBITS: The two carols in the opening segment, "While by My Sheep" ("Als ich bei meinen Schafen wacht") and "Ring, Little Bells" (Kling, Glöckchen"), both hail from Germany. The former is a traditional carol believed to date to 1500. Because phrases in the verses and refrain are repeated, it is also known as the "Echo Carol" and "How Great My Joy." The lyrics for the latter carol were written by Karl Enslin (1819–1875); the musical setting is believed by some to be a German traditional folk tune and by others to have been written by Benedikt Widmann (1820–1910) in 1884.

REVIEW: K.J. Dell Antonia of *Common Sense Media* reviewed the *VeggieTales* series: "…some of these TV episodes aren't the same 'VeggieTales' you'll find on DVD and video—they're a newly edited version. The morals remain as strong and clearly (if not subtly) presented as ever, but the biblical verses and stories are gone. It's also worth noting that the main characters always seem to be male…. The lessons at the hearts of these [TV] episodes are the kind that should be palatable to viewers of any—or no—religious persuasion."

PRODUCTION CREDITS—Writer: Phil Vischer. Producer: Chris Olsen. Director: Phil Vischer and Chris Olsen. "Oh Santa" Silly Song segment written and directed by Mike Nawrocki. Production Company: Big Idea Productions. Rating: Not rated. Genres: Animation, Comedy, Family. Country: USA. Run Time: 46 min.

REFERENCES: Crump, William D. *The Christmas Encyclopedia*. Third Edition. Jefferson, NC: McFarland, 2013.

Dell Antonia, K.J. *VeggieTales. Common Sense Media.* https://www.commonsensemedia.org/tv-reviews/veggietales

Lutz, Wilhelm. *Frohe Weihnacht: eine Sammlung von 40 der bekanntesten Weihnachtslieder.* Mainz: Schott, 1946. German language.

The Toy That Saved Christmas. Burbank, CA: Warner Home Video, 2002. DVD Video.

The Toy That Saved Christmas. Internet Movie Database. http://www.imdb.com/title/tt0284614/

VeggieTales. Internet Movie Database. http://www.imdb.com/title/tt0865856/

VeggieTales. Web Site: http://veggietales.com

Weber-Kellermann, Ingeborg, and Hilger

Schallehn. *Das Buch der Weihnachtslieder.* 10th Edition. Zurich: Atlantis, 2003. German language.

Wilson, Joanna. *Tis the Season TV: The Encyclopedia of Christmas-Themed Episodes, Specials and Made-for-TV Movies.* Akron, OH: 1701 Press, 2011.

The Tree That Saved Christmas—November 30, 2014

Television Movie

THREAT TO CHRISTMAS: A family in Vermont faces foreclosure on their Christmas tree farm.

HOW CHRISTMAS IS SAVED: An aspiring writer returns to her hometown to save her family's heritage.

SYNOPSIS AND COMMENTARY: It has no arms, no legs, it can't walk around, nor can it speak, yet a Christmas tree is supposed to "save" Christmas. Really? We'll see. Twenty years after she rescued a scrubby, Charlie Brown–like fir tree from the chain saw, Molly Logan (Lacey Chabert, *A Royal Christmas*), an aspiring writer-turned-assistant to a New York City publisher, learns that her family's 200-year-old Christmas tree farm in Vermont faces foreclosure. By coincidence (or not), the same tree now fully grown ends up at the residence of Walter (Jim Thorburn, *The Possession*), her widowed boss. Recognizing her "Molly tree" and seeing the circumstances as some kind of omen (as if the tree had come calling for her), Molly actually hauls the tree all the way back to Vermont for a final family Christmas. There, tensions rise when she discovers that her former boyfriend Lucas (Corey Sevier, *Immortals*) not only works at his father's bank, which is handling the foreclosure, but he's also negotiating with a development company to transform the Logan property into a golf resort. And of course, Lucas is all hot to rekindle their romance. Together with her brother Ryan (Matt Anderson, *Tomorrowland*), Molly urges the city council to save the property by declaring it a historic landmark. When her presentation goes viral, Walter, seemingly attracted to Molly, arrives with his two young daughters, who have previously bonded with Molly as something of a surrogate mother. Amid all the raging hormones and escalating emotions, the council declares the Logan house a landmark, but it will be moved into town as a museum, while the land will still become the golf resort, and tempers flare. On Christmas Eve, as the Logans, Walter and daughters, and Lucas (who by now has quit the bank) all mournfully gather for what would seem to be the final Christmas at the tree farm, Walter the hero reaches into his deep pockets at the 11th hour, so to speak, and becomes the Logans' guarantor of their mortgage.

AWARDS: In 2015, this film won a Platinum Remi Award for Independent Theatrical Feature Films and Videos, Action/Adventure, at WorldFest Houston; a Joey Award nomination for Best Actress in a Made-for-TV/Straight-to-Video Feature, Leading Role, Age 6–10 years (Yasmeene Ball) at the Joey Awards, Vancouver; and a Young Artist Award nomination for Best Performance in a TV Movie, Miniseries or Special, Leading Young Actress (Olivia Steele Falconer).

INTERESTING TIDBITS: Molly and Lucas initially fell into jobs that neither really desired: Molly had aspired to be a writer but instead became Walter's "gofer" at his New York publishing house, while Lucas had set his sights on photography but ended up at his father's bank. Seeing the unfair deal that his father works with the city council against the Logans, Lucas resigns to become a photographer, despite his father's objections. Having read some of Molly's Christmas stories that she kept in a journal, Walter realizes her immense talent and agrees to publish them in an anthology.

Does the once-scrubby Christmas tree actually "save" Christmas? Not in the strictest sense, which makes the film's title a bit inaccurate. The news about her parents' financial plight is incentive enough for Molly to return to Vermont, so the tree's appearance at Walter's residence where Molly serves as holiday decorator is more of a coincidence, unless supernatural forces are at work. After all, the tree does "shake" itself there as if to get Molly's attention. That's about as "spooky" as it gets. So let's give credit where credit is due: it's *Walter* who really saves the Logan family's Christmas here.

Viewers are left hanging in that Walter expects Molly to return to New York after Christmas, yet she states that she went to New York to find her dream when that dream had been in Vermont all along. So, does she stay or does she go?

NOTE: At the time of this writing, this film was not available on DVD or VHS but could be seen on Amazon Instant Video.

REVIEW: From *Movie Guide*: "[The film] keeps to a moral worldview, interjected with Christian faith elements … plot is unique [with] plenty of twists … though the path of the story becomes somewhat predictable … there are times where [the acting] seems shallow and contrived.… In order to make the story work, the writers jumped a few hurdles too quickly [near the end], not allowing for a more natural evolution of character and plot development."

PRODUCTION CREDITS—Writer: Michael J. Murray. Producer: Harvey Kahn. Director: David Winning. Production Companies: Farm Road Productions and Front Street Pictures. Rating: Not rated. Genre: Drama. Countries: Canada and USA. Run Time: 88 min.

REFERENCES: *The Tree That Saved Christmas*. Internet Movie Database. http://www.imdb.com/title/tt3579250/

The Tree That Saved Christmas. Movie Guide. https://www.movieguide.org/reviews/the-tree-that-saved-christmas.html

The Trolls and the Christmas Express—December 9, 1981

Animated Television Short Film

THREAT TO CHRISTMAS: A group of pesky trolls sabotage the North Pole and incapacitate Santa's reindeer.

HOW CHRISTMAS IS SAVED: Santa convinces the trolls to work with him and the elves to deliver the presents via the *Christmas Express*.

SYNOPSIS AND COMMENTARY: Bent on ruining Christmas, six ugly trolls led by Troglo infiltrate Santa's village disguised as elves on the first of December. Distinguishing elves from trolls is rather easy: whereas the elves have short pointed ears and are happy, the trolls consistently scowl and their pointed ears are much longer. Initially the trolls become keepers of the reindeer, then covertly use their mischievous magic to sabotage the toys all month long; for example, they cause lion dolls to bark, dog dolls to meow, and other toys to appear as assorted monstrosities. The clueless elves merely use their good magic to restore the toys, however, and fail to smell a rat. Two days before Christmas, Troglo concocts a plan that will surely prevent Santa from delivering the presents: he and the other trolls engage the reindeer in an all-night session of raucous singing and dancing such that by morning, the reindeer are too bushed to pull the sleigh. The elves solve the problem by loading the presents on the *Christmas Express*, the North Pole's train, for which they magically lay down tracks out of Santa's village. But in a last-ditch effort to thwart Santa, the trolls re-route the tracks back to the village, at which time their cover is blown. Playing amateur psychologist, Santa learns that the trolls carry a grudge because they are disliked, then informs them that they were once a happy part of the Christmas season, as a line from "Deck the Halls" illustrates: "*Troll* the ancient Yuletide carol…" (yes, it's a huge stretch). This mollifies the trolls, and Santa convinces them to join the elves in laying tracks for the *Christmas Express* all around the world. (Never mind how they'll lay tracks across the oceans; after all, anything is possible in a cartoon.)

VOICES: Narrated by Roger Miller (*Into the Wild*); Hans Conried (*The Hobbit*) as Troglo. Other Voices: Paul Soles, Len Carlson, Billie Mae Richards, and Carl Banas.

SONGS: Music by Hagwood Hardy; lyrics by Beryl Friesen; "The Christmas Express" performed by Roger Miller; "The Elves' Song"; "The Trolls' Song."

INTERESTING TIDBITS: The name "Troglo" could be a nod to "troglodyte," a prehistoric person who lived in caves. Today, "troglodyte" refers to a barbarian, heathen, savage, or person with crude manners and habits.

PRODUCTION CREDITS—Story: Mel Waskin and Bill Walker. Screenplay: Mel Waskin. Producers: Beryl Friesen and W.H. Stevens, Jr. Director: John R. Gaug. Production Companies: Titlecraft, Pooled Film Services, Atkinson Film Arts, and Coronet Films. Rating: Not rated. Genres: Animation, Family. Country: Canada. Run Time: 30 min.

References: Lenburg, Jeff. *The Encyclopedia of Animated Cartoons*. Third Edition. New York: Facts on File, 2009.

The Trolls and the Christmas Express. Big Cartoon Database. http://www.bcdb.com/cartoon/95211-Trolls-And-The-Christmas-Express

The Trolls and the Christmas Express. Internet Movie Database. http://www.imdb.com/title/tt1054055/

The Trolls and the Christmas Express. Phoenix Learning Group, 2008. Manufacture-on-Demand DVD-R Video.

Wilson, Joanna. *Tis the Season TV: The Encyclopedia of Christmas-Themed Episodes, Specials and Made-for-TV Movies*. Akron, OH: 1701 Press, 2011.

'Twas the Fight Before Christmas—
October 7, 2003

Television Special from the Animated Series

The Powerpuff Girls

Threat to Christmas: Spoiled rich kid Princess Morbucks deceives Santa by changing the naughty and nice lists so that she receives superpowers and all other kids get coal for Christmas.

How Christmas Is Saved: The Powerpuff Girls fight it out with Princess to overcome her deceit.

Synopsis and Commentary: Created by Craig McCracken, *The Powerpuff Girls* ran on Cartoon Network from 1998 until 2005 and consisted of 78 half-hour episodes (136 segments). Set in a city with the hardly unique name of Townsville, the series revolved around the crime-fighting adventures of three kindergartners who were produced when Professor Utonium (a play on plutonium) mixed sugar, spice, and everything nice, plus the accidentally added Chemical X, an ingredient that endowed the girls with assorted superpowers (flying, X-ray vision, super strength, super senses, etc.): Blossom, the redheaded leader, whose signature color was pink and who could freeze objects with her breath; Bubbles, a pigtailed blonde, whose signature color was blue and who could emit supersonic waves with her voice; and dark-haired Buttercup, whose signature color was green but had no unique superpower. The characters appeared in various incarnations, including video games, a feature film, and licensed merchandise; the series was revived in 2016 on Cartoon Network.

In *Fight*, the bratty rich kid Princess Morbucks (a play on "more bucks") is certain that daddy will have Santa to make her a Powerpuff Girl (with all the special accouterments), but when they reject her because she is perpetually naughty, Princess flies her private jet to the North Pole and sneaks in to check Santa's lists. Discovering that she is the *only* kid in the world who made the naughty list, she changes the list headings so that now *she* is the only nice kid and all others are naughty. Santa apparently is gullible (or senile) enough not to notice the change, because he delivers coal to all the world's children, including the Powerpuffs, and gives Princess the superpowers she requested. An appalled Bubbles, using X-ray vision, confirms the coal in other kids' stockings in town, whereupon the trio heads to the North Pole to inquire of Santa, but Princess confronts them and vows to tell Santa that the Powerpuffs are bent on destroying his workshop because he branded them as naughty. Thus begins a high-speed race to the North Pole with the adversaries fighting each other all the way until the four crash into the workshop, wreck the sleigh, and scatter the reindeer. When Santa is reluctant to believe Princess's accusations, she throws a tantrum, viciously insults Santa, and promises that daddy will build a parking lot over the workshop. An irate Santa, realizing her deception, cancels her superpowers and places her on the Permanent Naughty List. There's still time to rectify the coal problem, so the Powerpuffs throw Princess in jail and deliver presents to all the good children in Santa's place.

Principal Voices: Cathy Cavadini (*The Powerpuff Girls*) as Blossom; Tara Strong (*The Fairly OddParents*) as Bubbles; E.G. Daily (*Ru-*

Professor Utonium (far right) confers with his three Powerpuff Girls in *The Powerpuff Girls Movie* (2002). From left: Bubbles, Blossom, and Buttercup. In *'Twas the Fight Before Christmas* (2003), the Powerpuff Girls rectify Princess Morbucks's scheme to place all the world's children on Santa's naughty list (Warner Bros Pictures/Photofest).

grats) as Buttercup; Jennifer Hale (*Wreck-It Ralph*) as Princess; Tom Kane (*The Wild Thornberrys*) as Utonium; Mike Bell (*Turbo*) as Santa; Tom Kenny (*SpongeBob SquarePants*) as the narrator.

AWARDS: In 2004, *Fight* received a Primetime Emmy nomination for Outstanding Animated Program (One Hour or More). The series has received numerous awards, including two Primetime Emmys, two Annies, four Primetime Emmy nominations, seven Annie nominations, one Kids Choice Award nomination, and six Online Film and Television Association Award nominations.

INTERESTING TIDBITS: Throughout the film, the narrator provides allusions to the poem "'Twas the Night Before Christmas" in rhyming dialogue.

During their fight, each time the Powerpuffs score a hit on Princess, she screams, "No fair!"

Utonium may be able to whip up three extraordinary girls from kitchen ingredients, but he can't get his Christmas tree lights to work.

Buttercup tops her "Gimme" list for Santa with a Red Ryder Carbine Action 200-Shot Range Model Air Rifle (a BB gun), which is a nod to Ralphie Parker in *A Christmas Story* (1983). Princess follows with, "You'll shoot your eye out!"

Townsville's mayor wants a *Pony Puffs My Little Mare* doll for Christmas, which is a nod to the *My Little Pony* toy line from Hasbro.

The logo on Santa's cup reads "Old Nick," which is an archaic term for the Devil. After all, "Santa" is an anagram for "Satan."

Santa's workshop sports boxes of "Betty Wetty" dolls, which is a nod to "Betsy Wetsy," a line of drink-and-wet dolls first produced by the Ideal Toy Company in 1934.

The other names on Santa's Permanent Naughty List include Bill McCracken (after series creator Craig McCracken); Ryan Faust (after co-writer/director Lauren Faust); Adolph Schickelgruber (actually Schicklgruber, Adolf Hitler's alleged "original" name); and Stephen Fonti (the storyboard artist for the episode "Catastrophe").

Santa gives a nod to Rudolph when he asks, "Powerpuff Girls with your streaks so bright, won't you deliver the Christmas gifts tonight?"

REVIEWS: Marc Bernardin of *Entertainment Weekly* reviewed the series (June 2, 2000): "With spot-on pop-culture acumen ... and an unparalleled sense of fun, this Cartoon Network series is blisteringly creative in the most unassuming way."

Peter Marks of *The New York Times* reviewed the series (April 16, 2000): "*The Powerpuff Girls* is the most popular original series on [Cartoon Network], its tongue-in-cheekiness reflecting ... a sensibility that goes in heavily for the sort of playful satire that can appeal as much to a viewer of 37 as 7."

Joly Herman of *Common Sense Media* reviewed the series: "...cute, highly stylized series thrills the senses with its strange characters, funny situations, and lots of lowbrow humor. The message throughout is that violence is fun..."

PRODUCTION CREDITS—Story: Lauren Faust, Craig Lewis, Craig McCracken, and Amy Keating Rogers. Writers: Lauren Faust and Craig Lewis. Producer: Chris Savino. Director: Lauren Faust. Production Company: Cartoon Network Studios. Rating: TV-Y7. Genres: Animation, Family, Sci-Fi. Country: USA. Run Time: 45 min.

REFERENCES: Bernardin, Marc. *The Powerpuff Girls. Entertainment Weekly.* http://www.ew.com/article/2000/06/02/powerpuff-girls

Davin, Eric Leif. "Hitler Never Really Was Schicklgruber." Letters to the Editor. *The New York Times* (May 6, 1990). http://www.nytimes.com/1990/05/06/opinion/l-hitler-never-really-was-schicklgruber-016390.html

Herman, Joly. *The Powerpuff Girls. Common Sense Media.* https://www.commonsensemedia.org/tv-reviews/the-powerpuff-girls

Marks, Peter. "TELEVISION/RADIO; "Now Mom and Dad Are Going Cartoon-Crazy, Too." *The New York Times.* http://www.nytimes.com/2000/04/016/arts/television-radio-now-mom-and-dad-are-going-cartoon-crazy-too.html?pagewanted=2

The Powerpuff Girls: 'Twas the Fight Before Christmas. Burbank, CA: Warner Home Video, 2003. DVD Video.

The Powerpuff Girls: 'Twas the Fight Before Christmas. Internet Movie Database. http://www.imdb.com/title/tt0391404/

"'Twas the Fight Before Christmas (Powerpuff Girls)." Christmas Specials Wiki. http://christmas-specials.wikia.com/wiki/%27Twas_the_Fight_Before_Christmas_(Powerpuff_Girls)

Wilson, Joanna. *Tis the Season TV: The Encyclopedia of Christmas-Themed Episodes, Specials and Made-for-TV Movies.* Akron, OH: 1701 Press, 2011.

'Twas the Night—December 7, 2001
Television Movie

THREAT TO CHRISTMAS: Santa falls and is knocked unconscious after a computer glitch causes his high-tech sleigh to veer off course.

HOW CHRISTMAS IS SAVED: A con artist and his teenage nephew take over for Santa.

SYNOPSIS AND COMMENTARY: While fleeing from three angry thugs whom he has swindled in a scam on Christmas Eve, con artist Nick Wrigley (Bryan Cranston, *Breaking Bad*) steals a Santa suit to disguise himself and escapes to his brother John's (Barclay Hope, *Paycheck*) home. The evening's festivities are short-lived when, as physicians, John and his wife Abby (Torri Higginson, *The English Patient*) are called out to handle an epidemic of "reindeer flu," so Nick remains to look after his niece Kaitlin (Brenda Grate, *Odessa*) and nephews Peter (Rhys Williams) and Danny (Josh Zuckerman, *Surviving Christmas*). Overhead, Santa (Jefferson Mappin, *Unforgiven*), who carries a device that stops time and alters the size of objects, is traveling in a new, high-tech sleigh because the reindeer are all sick with the flu. When Nick's laptop accidentally jams the sleigh's computer, Santa loses control, lands on John's roof, and is knocked unconscious when he wanders indoors, trips, and falls while trying to escape. With Christmas hanging in the balance, Nick delivers the presents and Danny pilots the sleigh, until he discovers that Nick has been robbing the homes they visit. Feeling betrayed, Danny abandons his uncle and crashes the sleigh upon arriving back home, where a recovered Santa, Kaitlin, and Peter have been waiting. The sleigh's hard drive is badly damaged, and Kaitlin, the computer genius, cannot repair it. After Nick regains the children's faith by dispatching the same three thugs who had arrived to threaten them and Santa, Kaitlin wires Nick's laptop to the sleigh, and Santa flies away to finish his rounds. On Christmas morning as the family gathers to open gifts, Nick discovers that Santa had brought him the electric guitar he had always wanted since childhood but had never received, because he had always been on the naughty list.

AWARDS IN 2002: A Directors Guild of America Award for Outstanding Directorial Achievement in Children's Programs; a Young Artist Award for Best Supporting Young Actress (Brenda Grate); an ALMA Award nomination for Outstanding Performance in a Comedy Special (Los Lobos); and Young Artist Award nominations for Best Family TV Movie or Special and Best Leading Young Actor (Josh Zuckerman).

INTERESTING TIDBITS: A scene at the end shows the last line of the poem "'Twas the Night Before Christmas" that incorrectly reads, "Merry Christmas to all, and to all a good night." Actually, the last line is "*Happy* Christmas to all…," etc. We're far more used to saying "Merry Christmas" than "Happy Christmas" (unless we're bent on being politically correct and saying "Happy Holidays"). Other save-Christmas films with the same error are *A Christmas Story* and *Mary Engelbreit's The Night Before Christmas.*

Other save-Christmas films in which the flu hits the North Pole include *Madeline at the North Pole, The Magic Sack of Mr. Nicholas, The Night B4 Christmas, Nine Dog Christmas,* and *The Super Special Gift.*

NOTE: At the time of this writing, this film was not available on DVD or VHS but could be seen on Amazon Instant Video.

PRODUCTION CREDITS—Story: Jim Lincoln and Dan Studney. Teleplay: Jim Lincoln, Dan Studney, and Jenny Tripp. Producer: Kevin Lafferty. Director: Nick Castle. Production Companies: 'Twas Productions, Adam Productions, and the Disney Channel. Rating: G. Genres: Comedy, Family. Country: USA. Run Time: 84 min.

REFERENCES: Crump, William D. *The Christmas Encyclopedia.* Third Edition. Jefferson, NC: McFarland, 2013.

'Twas the Night. Internet Movie Database. http://www.imdb.com/title/tt0282223/

Wilson, Joanna. *Tis the Season TV: The Encyclopedia of Christmas-Themed Episodes, Specials and Made-for-TV Movies.* Akron, OH: 1701 Press, 2011.

'Twas the Night Before Bumpy—December 19, 1995

Musical Comedy Special from the Animated Television Series

Bump in the Night

THREAT TO CHRISTMAS: Mr. Bumpy travels to the North Pole to steal Santa's bag of gifts.

HOW CHRISTMAS IS SAVED: By accident, the gifts fall out of Santa's bag to appropriate recipients.

SYNOPSIS AND COMMENTARY: Running for two seasons on ABC (1994–1995), this series featured clay puppets in stop-motion animation. It was created by Ken Pontac and David Bleiman and consisted of 65 segments in 27 half-hour episodes. The setting was the bedroom of a ten-year-old boy with protagonist Mr. Bumpy, a small, green monster with purple warts and with bulging eyes on stalks like a crab who lived under the boy's bed (a kid's classic bedtime terror) and ate dirty socks and dust bunnies. Other principal characters included Squishington, a blue-blob monster with no feet who lived in a toilet tank; Molly Coddle, a Frankensteinian-type rag doll-turned-comfort doll; Destructo, a toy robot who saw himself as a cop and a stickler for rules; and Closet Monster, who consisted of a pile of the boy's clothes (again, personifying a kid's bedtime terror).

In *Night Before Bumpy*, greedy Bumpy lays traps for Santa in order to grab his bag of presents, but when the traps all blow up in Squishy's face, Bumpy heads to the North Pole and promises Squishy feet from Santa's bag if he will come along. Taking a highly circuitous route, the two wind up in a tropical jungle where General Juaquin Guasanito Sin Manos, an earthworm with no hands, would draft them into his army, until Bumpy promises him hands from Santa's bag if he will tunnel through to the North Pole. This gets them to Stonehenge, where Bumpy promises the hummingbird Doris a jetpack from the bag if she will fly him and Squishy to the North Pole. Crashing there, Bumpy and Squishy navigate through Santa's high-security facility, protected by an army of "snowjers" (snowmen soldiers with candy-cane guns that shoot snowballs) and drill-sergeant elves. Finding a secret passage to the bag, Bumpy evades a series of booby traps in the bag room, but when he removes the bag from its perch, a huge Santa-boulder chases him until he's outside at the sleigh (a nod to the famous scene in *Raiders of the Lost Ark*, 1981). Bumpy takes off in the sleigh with Squishy hanging on in back as they dodge the snowjers' candy-cane cruise missiles and as presents fall from the bag into chimneys and other locales around the world. Thus, Juaquin and Doris respectively receive their bionic hands and jetpack. The sleigh ultimately crashes into the Christmas pageant that Molly is directing, where all the remaining presents save one go to everybody else. Since Squishy didn't get his feet, he gets the last gift, which is almost as good—a tap-dancing noisemaker. And Bumpy does get one gift, a dirty sock with a hole, courtesy of the Closet Monster.

Songs: Jim Latham, Ken Pontac, and David Bleiman.

Principal Voices: Jim Cummings (*Shrek*) as Mr. Bumpy; Rob Paulsen (*The Mask*) as Squishy; Gail Matthius (*Bobby's World*) as Molly; Cheech Marin (*Nash Bridges*) as Juaquin; Danny Mann (*Babe*) as Phil Silverfish (a play on the actor Phil Silvers); Valery Pappas (*Ghostbusters II*) as Shane; Jennifer Darling (*Aladdin*) as Sia.

Awards: In 1995, *Bump in the Night* received an Annie nomination for Voice Acting in the Field of Animation (Jim Cummings as Mr. Bumpy).

Interesting Tidbits: During the Christmas pageant, several monsters crash the scene with a tribute to Hanukkah by singing "The Dreidel Song" followed by music to "Hava Nagila."

During a pep-talk to his snowjers, a drill-sergeant elf asks, "Will you do your duty?" then follows with, "When you stick your hand in a glob of slush that only seconds before was Frosty's face, you'll know what to do!" That's a nod to the introductory soliloquy to *Patton* (1970), starring George C. Scott in the title role.

As the elves prepare to launch the candy-cane cruise missiles, one of them says, "I'll round up the usual suspects," a nod to a famous line in *Casablanca* (1942).

The film is peppered throughout with parodies of traditional Christmas carols.

Santa does not appear in this film.

Review: Victor Valdivia of *DVD Verdict* (May 26, 2010): "*Bump in the Night* is a cut above most kid shows, mainly because the humor is far more ambitious and the animation more endearing ... enjoyable and entertaining ... deserves to be rediscovered by animation fans looking for something new."

Production Credits—Writer: Jeremy Cushner. Executive Producers: David Bleiman, Ken Pontac, and Patricia Rose Duignan. Directors: Ken Pontac and David Bleiman. Production Companies: Danger Productions and Greengrass Productions. Rating: TV-Y. Genres: Animation, Comedy, Family. Country: USA. Run Time: 64 min.

References: *Bump in the Night*. Internet Movie Database. http://www.imdb.com/title/tt0162796/

Bump in the Night: 'Twas the Night Before Bumpy. Dallas, TX: NCircle Entertainment, 2008. DVD Video.

'Twas the Night Before Bumpy. Big Cartoon Database. http://www.bcdb.com/cartoon/47753-Twas-The-Night-Before-Bumpy

'Twas the Night Before Bumpy. Internet Movie Database. http://www.imdb.com/title/tt1443787/

Valdivia, Victor. *Bump in the Night: The Complete Series. DVD Verdict*. http://www.dvd-verdict.com/reviews/bumpinthenight.php

Wilson, Joanna. *Tis the Season TV: The Encyclopedia of Christmas-Themed Episodes, Specials and Made-for-TV Movies*. Akron, OH: 1701 Press, 2011.

'Twas the Night Before Christmas—
December 8, 1974

Animated Television Special

THREAT TO CHRISTMAS: Santa rejects all letters from a town when its newspaper publishes a letter that slanders him.

HOW CHRISTMAS IS SAVED: A young mouse fixes the magical clock that he had unwittingly broken and its music lures Santa back to the town.

SYNOPSIS AND COMMENTARY: The story line is arranged around the poem "'Twas the Night before Christmas," with narration that includes the entire poem over the course of the action. When Santa rejects letters from Junctionville because its newspaper published an anonymous, slanderous letter about him, clockmaker Joshua Trundle builds a clock with magic chimes that will lure Santa to town on Christmas Eve. But during a trial run, the clock performs poorly, thanks to the tinkering of young, inquisitive Albert Mouse, who only wanted to see how its mechanism worked. Nevertheless, Joshua's reputation as a clockmaker is tarnished, and the mayor will not permit him to repair the clock. Father Mouse soon discovers that it was his own know-it-all son Albert who anonymously wrote the letter bashing belief in Santa, because he doesn't believe in anything he cannot see. After learning the degree of sadness there will be if Santa continues to ignore Junctionville, Albert fixes the clock with the aid of a book by Copernicus, and Santa arrives to everyone's happiness.

VOICES: Narrated and sung by Joel Grey (*Cabaret*) as Joshua and by George Gobel (*The George Gobel Show*) as Father Mouse; Tammy Grimes (*The Last Unicorn*) as Albert; John McGiver (*Midnight Cowboy*) as the mayor. Other voices: Robert McFadden, Allen Swift, Pat Bright, Christine Winter, Scott Firestone, and The Wee Winter Singers.

SONGS: "Give Your Heart a Try"; "Even a Miracle Needs a Hand"; "Christmas Chimes Are Calling (Santa, Santa!)." Music by Maury Laws; lyrics by Jules Bass.

REVIEWS: Nancy Davis Kho of *Common Sense Media* (November 20, 2007): "... tackles the notion of believing in Santa head-on, and may be a little risky for kids who are struggling with that notion."

Kevin Carr of *7M Pictures*: "...a charming adaptation of the original ... poem, working a story around it very smoothly ... the freshness and charm that this special has makes its overused story acceptable."

Randall Cyrenne of *An-

There's excitement in Junctionville when rumors fly that Santa Claus doesn't exit. A mouse receptionist at the North Pole substation takes a call from Junctionville about why Santa returned all the town's letters in '*Twas the Night Before Christmas* (1974) (CBS/MMG Photo Archives; collection of William D. Crump).

imated Views (December 8, 2010): "The story is as slight as can be, but it is undeniably charming. The plot is somewhat original, and the story's sentiments are worthwhile.... All the songs are cheery and nicely arranged..."

PRODUCTION CREDITS—Writer: Jerome Coopersmith. Producers and Directors: Arthur Rankin, Jr., and Jules Bass. Production Company: Rankin-Bass Productions. Rating: G. Genres: Animation, Family. Country: USA. Run Time: 24 min.

REFERENCES: Carr, Kevin. *'Twas the Night Before Christmas. 7M Pictures.* http://www.7mpictures.com/twas-the-night-before-christmas-dvd-review/

Crump, William D. *The Christmas Encyclopedia.* Third Edition. Jefferson, NC: McFarland, 2013.

Cyrenne, Randall. *'Twas the Night Before Christmas: Remastered Deluxe Edition. Animated Views.* http://animatedviews.com/2010/twas-the-night-before-christmas-remastered-deluxe-edition/

Kho, Nancy Davis. *'Twas the Night Before Christmas. Common Sense Media.* https://www.commonsensemedia.org/movie-reviews/twas-the-night-before-christmas

Lenburg, Jeff. *The Encyclopedia of Animated Cartoons.* Third Edition. New York: Facts on File, 2009.

'Twas the Night Before Christmas. Burbank, CA: Warner Home Video, 2010. DVD Video.

'Twas the Night Before Christmas. Internet Movie Database. http://www.imdb.com/title/tt0208654/

Wilson, Joanna. *Tis the Season TV: The Encyclopedia of Christmas-Themed Episodes, Specials and Made-for-TV Movies.* Akron, OH: 1701 Press, 2011.

Twice Upon a Christmas—December 8, 2001

Television Movie

THREAT TO CHRISTMAS: Santa's older daughter sells pieces of the North Pole around the world to ruin Christmas.

HOW CHRISTMAS IS SAVED: Santa's younger daughter convinces the world to "return" the pieces of the North Pole by believing in Santa and Christmas.

SYNOPSIS AND COMMENTARY: Most of the principals from *Once Upon a Christmas* reprise their roles in this sequel; a new face portrays Santa (Matthew Walker, *Night at the Museum*). It's a year later as Bill Morgan (John Dye) and his fiancée Kristen Claus (Kathy Ireland), Santa's younger daughter, plan Christmas nuptials. Having surrendered her immortality to save Bill's son Kyle (James Kirk), Kristen now has no memory of her past, so Bill, Kyle, daughter Brittany (Kirsten Prout), and Uncle John (Wayne Thomas Yorke) all set about to help Kristen find her roots. Meanwhile at the North Pole, Kristen's evil older sister Rudolfa (Mary Donnelly Haskell) is once again up to her old tricks to get rid of Santa and take over. This time, she slowly begins to dismantle the North Pole by selling pieces of it worldwide via TV commercials. In its place, Rudolfa conspires with Donald Trump (Sean Allen, *First to Die*) to build a huge hotel and casino. Bill's children order several items, one of which is a doll that Santa had given to Kristen when she was a child. Seeing this doll restores Kristen's past memory, whereupon she takes the two children to the ruined North Pole (once Bill believes, he soon follows) and thwarts Rudolfa by issuing a televised plea worldwide for all people to "return" their pieces of the North Pole by believing in Santa and Christmas. And as expected, Bill and Kristen are married on Christmas Day.

INTERESTING TIDBITS: Once Kristen regains her memory and realizes what Rudolfa is doing, she expresses the typical sentiment about what really drives Christmas: "How can there be Christmas if there's no North Pole?"

This film should not be confused with *Mickey's Twice upon a Christmas.*

REVIEWS: Kevin Matthews of *For It Is Man's Number* (December 21, 2012): "...the tone of the movie is exactly the same as its predecessor ... potential for boredom to set in as these characters had, essentially, completed a more interesting arc in the first film ... [the sequel] at least has the good grace not to move the goalposts or to try [to] run off in an entirely different direction ... a Christmas cookie sequel to a Christmas cookie first film..."

PRODUCTION CREDITS—Writer: Steven H. Berman. Producers: Jon Carrasco, Deboragh Gabler, and Stephen Roseberry. Director: Tibor Takács. Production Companies: Ardent Productions, Legacy Filmworks, and Viacom Productions. Rating: Not rated. Genres: Drama, Family, Fantasy, Romance. Country: Canada. Run Time: 90 min.

REFERENCES: Crump, William D. *The Christmas Encyclopedia*. Third Edition. Jefferson, NC: McFarland, 2013.

Matthews, Kevin. *Twice Upon a Christmas* (2001). *For It Is Man's Number.* http://foritismansnumber.blogspot.co.uk/2012/12/twice-upon-a-christmas-2001.html

Twice upon a Christmas. Hollywood: Paramount Home Entertainment, 2006. DVD Video.

Twice upon a Christmas. Internet Movie Database. http://www.imdb.com/title/tt0298580/

Wilson, Joanna. *Tis the Season TV: The Encyclopedia of Christmas-Themed Episodes, Specials and Made-for-TV Movies*. Akron, OH: 1701 Press, 2011.

Uncle Grandpa: Christmas Special—December 4, 2014

Episode from the Animated Television Series *Uncle Grandpa*

THREAT TO CHRISTMAS: Santa breaks his leg on Christmas Eve.

HOW CHRISTMAS IS SAVED: Uncle Grandpa and friends deliver the presents.

SYNOPSIS AND COMMENTARY: If ever there was a suitable series for an idiotic animated Christmas episode, it would be *Uncle Grandpa*. Created by Peter Browngardt for Cartoon Network, the series consisted of 156 11-minute cartoons that ran from 2013 to 2016. The series revolved around Uncle Grandpa, a mustached, snaggle-toothed, clownish figure with a rectangular head and propeller hat, who traveled around in a recreational vehicle (RV), and whose goal as the "uncle" and "grandpa" of everyone in the world was to guide children with problems through a series of misadventures. Grandpa's companions were Belly Bag, a talking red fanny pack of gadgets; Pizza Steve, a talking slice of pepperoni pizza; Mr. Gus, a green dinosaur and Grandpa's bodyguard; and Giant Realistic Flying Tiger, a rainbow-farting, static photographic cutout of a tiger and Grandpa's "steed" that communicated by roaring and rolling its eyes.

In part one of this two-part episode, Grandpa manages to overcome the grudge against his *brother* Santa when, thanks to the Abominable Snowman, he crashes his RV into Santa's workshop on Christmas Eve. Having recently broken his leg in a bowling ball accident, Santa cannot deliver the presents, yet unsympathetic Grandpa blames Santa as his reason for hating Christmas. In a flashback to 1983, Grandpa and Santa had performed a rap routine duo for a talent competition that had gone sour and Grandpa had became a laughingstock. Steve and Gus convince a reluctant Grandpa to fill in for his brother, whereupon he dons an absurd outfit of holly leaves, night-vision glasses, and a reindeer skull for a cap. With Tiger pulling the sleigh, Grandpa and gang receive instructions from Santa via radio. As expected, their initial stops produce crashes, fires, and mayhem (Steve despises the gluten-free raisin cookies with fat-free almond milk). Ignoring Santa's warning, Grandpa becomes the prisoner of naughty kid Sally, who "collects" living holiday icons: Easter Bunny, St. Patrick's Day leprechaun, Thanksgiving Day turkey, Veteran's Day velociraptor, etc. Grandpa escapes, thanks to Santa's instructions in rap, and attributes his freedom to "the influential power of hip-hop." Grandpa advises that in order to move forward, you must let go of the past, which prompts Sally to release all the holiday icons. Grandpa indeed saves Christmas, but it takes him until Spring to finish delivering the presents.

Part two is a parody of *It's a Wonderful Life*, in which Grandpa, ruining Christmas Eve dinner and desiring to launch himself into outer space, sees what life would be like without him, courtesy of Lawrence, his guardian lobster.

PRINCIPAL VOICES: Peter Browngardt (*Chowder*) as Uncle Grandpa; Eric Bauza (*Xi-*

aolin Chronicles) as Belly Bag; Adam DeVine (*Pitch Perfect*) as Pizza Steve; Grey DeLisle-Griffin (*The Replacements*) as Sally; Kevin Michael Richardson (*Lilo and Stitch*) as Mr. Gus; Bob Joles (*Puss in Boots*) as Santa.

AWARDS: In 2014, *Uncle Grandpa* won a Primetime Emmy for Outstanding Individual in Animation, a Primetime Emmy nomination in 2010 for Outstanding Short-Format Animated Program, and an Annie nomination in 2016 for Outstanding Achievement in Voice Acting (Kevin Michael Richardson).

INTERESTING TIDBIT: Although there's no specific mention of Hanukkah as such, in part two, a fully lit menorah is quite conspicuous on a table near the Christmas tree in Grandpa's RV.

NOTE: At the time of this writing, this episode was not available on DVD or VHS but could be seen on Amazon Instant Video in Season Two.

REVIEW: Emily Ashby of *Common Sense Media* reviewed the series: "[*Uncle Grandpa* is] another example of Cartoon Network's proclivity for bizarre, grotesque, but ultimately enticing cartoons. His moniker is a joke within itself, since he's the comical extension of the stereotypical crazy uncle, but his gags take the old 'Pull my finger' crack to new heights…. It's not exactly appetizing, and he's a little nuts, but it's the kind of wacky humor that, for better or worse, is sure to draw crowds."

PRODUCTION CREDITS—Writers: Mike Chilian and Ryan Kramer. Story: Kelsy Abbott, Tom Kauffman, Peter Browngardt, Audie Harrison, and Casey Alexander. Producer: Rossitza Likomanova. Animation Directors: Robert Alvarez and Randy Myers. Production Companies: Cartoon Network Studios and Rough Draft Studios. Rating: TV-PG. Genres: Animation, Comedy, Fantasy. Country: USA. Run Time: 30 min.

REFERENCES: Ashby, Emily. *Uncle Grandpa*. Common Sense Media. https://www.commonsensemedia.org/tv-reviews/uncle-grandpa

Uncle Grandpa. Internet Movie Database. http://www.imdb.com/title/tt3042608/

"Uncle Grandpa: Christmas Special." Big Cartoon Database. https://www.bcdb.com/cartoon/167098-Christmas-Special-Part-1

Unlikely Angel—December 17, 1996

Television Movie

THREAT TO CHRISTMAS: A grieving, dysfunctional family hasn't celebrated Christmas in several years.

HOW CHRISTMAS IS SAVED: In order to get her wings, a deceased lounge singer returns to earth to turn the family around and revive their Christmas spirit.

SYNOPSIS AND COMMENTARY: Dolly Parton (*A Smoky Mountain Christmas*) stars as Ruby Diamond, a brassy lounge singer who has led a less-than-virtuous life. Shortly before Christmas, she is killed in an automobile accident and finds that the gates of paradise are closed to her. Yet St. Peter (Roddy McDowall, *Planet of the Apes*) has hope for her redemption and sends her back to earth to help a dysfunctional family. Ruby has the week before Christmas in which to turn the family around, with midnight on Christmas Eve as the deadline. Two other stipulations: she must tell no one the purpose of her mission, and she must have no romantic affairs (at which she had been rather proficient in life). If she is successful, she will earn her wings. Failure is not an option. Ruby (with wig and cleavage) literally drops from the sky and becomes a nanny to the grieving family of Ben Bartilson (Brian Kerwin, *The Help*), a widower who, following the loss of his wife two years ago, has buried himself in his job, ignored his 14-year-old daughter Sarah (Allison Mack, *Smallville*) and eight-year-old son Matt (Eli Marienthal, *American Pie*), and shunned Christmas celebrations altogether. With such depression hanging over them, the family is adrift without purpose or direction, and Ruby must not only help them find the Christmas spirit but each other again. In such a predictable movie, of course Ruby gets her wings by subtly reviving beloved Christmas traditions that draw the family together (despite their initial objections), by succeeding in a bit of matchmaking between Ben and his business associate Allison (Maria del Mar, *The Christmas Shoes*), and by locating Matt when he runs away on Christmas Eve. As the film ends, Ruby celebrates by joining the heavenly choir to sing the "Hallelujah Chorus."

SONGS: Any film with Dolly Parton always features an original song or two: "Unlikely Angel" and "What'cha Trying to Do to Me?" both written and performed by Dolly Parton.

INTERESTING TIDBITS: Throughout the film, St. Peter periodically reminds Ruby of her goal by appearing as a priest, a bell-ringing street Santa, a man in a picture, a man walking his dogs, the host of a nightclub floor show, and a hotel desk clerk.

On Christmas Morning, Allison tops the Bartilsons' tree with an angel figure that resembles Ruby.

REVIEW: Danél Griffin of *Film As Art*: "As a conventional Christmas film, it never misses a note. It's sweet, overly sentimental, and teary-eyed…. The music swells when it's supposed to. There are plenty of warm-fuzzies to go around. Snow falls at just the right time … it is so fluffy that it is completely forgettable. The whole exercise works so well and routinely, it is almost offensive in its inoffensiveness."

PRODUCTION CREDITS—Story: Katherine Ann Jones. Teleplay: Liz Coe and Robert L. Freedman. Producer: Jonathan Bernstein. Director: Michael Switzer. Production Companies: Sandollar Productions and The Kushner-Locke Company. Rating: Not rated. Genres: Comedy, Family. Country: USA. Run Time: 95 min.

REFERENCES: Crump, William D. *The Christmas Encyclopedia*. Third Edition. Jefferson, NC: McFarland, 2013.

Griffin, Danél. *Unlikely Angel. Film As Art*. http://uashome.alaska.edu/~dfgriffin/website/unlikelyangel.htm

Unlikely Angel. Internet Movie Database. http://www.imdb.com/title/tt0118048/

Unlikely Angel. Las Vegas, NV: Hollywood Entertainment, 2005. DVD Video.

Wilson, Joanna. *Tis the Season TV: The Encyclopedia of Christmas-Themed Episodes, Specials and Made-for-TV Movies*. Akron, OH: 1701 Press, 2011.

A Very Barry Christmas—2005

Animated Television Movie

THREAT TO CHRISTMAS: In a freak accident, Santa and his look-alike double, Barry from the Australian outback, switch places.

HOW CHRISTMAS IS SAVED: Barry and his motley team of "adopted" animals deliver the gifts around the world.

SYNOPSIS AND COMMENTARY: This film features clay puppets in stop-motion animation in a Santa switcheroo. With the exception of his yellow mustache, Barry Buckley, a failed wild animal tour guide in the Australian outback, is the spitting image of Santa, which is the heart of the problem here. While out on a trial run with reindeer Nutmeg, who wants to join Santa's team, an aerial mishap tosses Santa from his sleigh down Barry's chimney and propels Barry into the sleigh and thence back to the North Pole. There, Mrs. Claus coerces Barry to fill in for Santa, but when at a press conference Barry accidentally destroys the naughty-and-nice list, he vows to give presents to everyone, naughty or nice. Having gorged on cookies and milk, the reindeer are too incapacitated to fly, whereupon Mrs. Claus has no choice but to send Barry and Nutmeg back to retrieve Santa in Australia. Meanwhile, the food-obsessed animals that Barry has "adopted," Nigel the crocodile, Lilly the boxing kangaroo, Walter the thespian platypus, and Simon the narcoleptic koala bear, refuse to accept that Santa is the real McCoy and instead believe that it's poor Barry who has lost his mind. Santa's woes continue when the police detain him for insanity but, using Christmas magic, he escapes and becomes lost in the outback, where he encounters Warrun the Aborigine who flies him back to the North Pole in his biplane. Because Barry and Nutmeg crash the sleigh at Barry's establishment, they convert an old truck into a sleigh pulled by Barry's animals and led by Nutmeg (who gets her wish of sorts), then head out to deliver the presents around the world. After a successful run, they arrive back at the North Pole as Santa parachutes in and makes a pitch for Barry's Down-Under Winter Wonderland.

PRINCIPAL VOICES: Roy Billing (*The Dish*) as Barry; Colin Mochrie (*Whose Line Is It Anyway?*) as Santa; Shannon Lawson (*Fitzgerald*) as Mrs. Claus; Gail Knight (*Blue Heelers*) as

Lilly; Michael Lamport (*Rescue Mediums*) as Walter; Aaron Pedersen (*Mystery Road*) as Warrun; Jim Pike (*Cappuccino*) as Nigel; Jacqueline Pillon (*Man of the Year*) as Nutmeg; Phil Williams (*Max Payne*) as Dasher; Deanna Aubert (*A Very Barry Christmas*) as Miss Hollyjolly; Stewart Horsley (*Sex After Kids*) as Douglas Fur the polar bear (a play on the Douglas fir tree).

INTERESTING TIDBIT: There's a nod to the now-late "Crocodile Hunter" Steve Irwin (1962–2006) as Nigel watches him in caricature wrestling a crocodile on television.

REVIEW: Tracy Moore of *Common Sense Media* (October 3, 2013): "Offbeat Santa mix-up has goofy humor, lots of teamwork … a silly take on the behind-the-scenes effort required to pull off Christmas…. Kids will enjoy the talking crocodile and kangaroo, the fun Claymation, the accents, and the mayhem, and parents will find a gag or two in the Australian humor amusing."

PRODUCTION CREDITS—Writer: Brendan Russell. Producer: Loretta VanHart. Director: Andrew Horne. Production Company: Cuppa Coffee Studios. Rating: Not rated. Genres: Animation, Comedy. Country: Canada. Run Time: 45 min.

REFERENCES: Moore, Tracy. *A Very Barry Christmas*. *Common Sense Media*. https://www.commonsensemedia.org/movie-reviews/a-very-barry-christmas

A Very Barry Christmas. Internet Movie Database. http://www.imdb.com/title/tt0920894/

A Very Barry Christmas. Toronto: Ka-BOOM Entertainment, 2005. DVD Video.

Wilson, Joanna. *Tis the Season TV: The Encyclopedia of Christmas-Themed Episodes, Specials and Made-for-TV Movies*. Akron, OH: 1701 Press, 2011.

A Very CatDog Christmas—November 30, 1999

Episode from the Animated Television Series *CatDog*

THREAT TO CHRISTMAS: Santa cancels Christmas when CatDog sell themselves to a rich rabbit as his bratty niece's Christmas present.

HOW CHRISTMAS IS SAVED: When CatDog learn that Christmas is not all about getting "stuff," Santa restores the holiday.

SYNOPSIS AND COMMENTARY: Conjoined human twins are unusual enough, but imagine a hybrid of a dog and a cat, "brothers," joined at the abdomen with two heads, two sets of front paws, no hind legs, and no tail. That's the case with CatDog, the protagonists in this series, created by Peter Hannan for Nickelodeon, that ran for 68 half-hour episodes from 1998 to 2005. Whereas Cat was cultured and refined, Dog was dopey and uncouth. The two lived in Nearburg, a town populated by anthropomorphic animals and a few humanoids.

In "CatDog Christmas," when bratty preschooler Rancine Rabbit spots CatDog at the mall and screams that she wants them for Christmas (despite having everything else under the sun), her rich uncle Rancid Rabbit entices the twins with a wad of cash. Believing that Cat will finally get his dream sports car and Dog an unlimited supply of bones, they sell themselves to Rancid. This act greatly angers Santa who cancels Christmas, because he believes the Christmas spirit is dead. All over the world, Christmas decorations and lights disappear, and the angry citizens of Nearburg storm the streets in search of CatDog as the perpetrators. Realizing they are now Rancine's prisoners, CatDog, missing their former holiday traditions, repent and manage to escape back to their home, only to find that some of the citizens are waiting to pulverize them. But when Dog informs them that Christmas isn't about getting "stuff" but about being and sharing with family, that Christmas is in the heart, and that not even Santa can really cancel Christmas, Santa reverses his decision and Christmas is back on, because the spirit of Christmas is alive and well (despite the absence of religious implications).

PRINCIPAL VOICES: Jim Cummings (*Shrek*) as Cat; Tom Kenny (*Adventure Time*) as Dog; Carlos Alazraqui (*Happy Feet*) as Winslow, Lube, bratty kid; Billy West (*Futurama*) as Rancid Rabbit, Randolph, Sunshine, neon Santa; Maria Bamford (*Adventure Time*) as Shriek, Mrs. Claus, Rancine; Dwight Schultz

(*Chowder*) as Squirrel; Brian Doyle Murray (*Groundhog Day*) as Santa.

AWARDS: The *CatDog* series received an Annie nomination for Outstanding Writing in an Animated Television Production (1998) and Blimp Award nominations for Favorite Cartoon (1999 and 2000).

REVIEWS: Sarah Wenk of *Common Sense Media* reviewed the *CatDog* series: "The focus is on looniness, silliness, and out-of-control antics, with very little in the way of redeeming qualities. This can be just the ticket for some kids, although the bizarreness of the concept is enough to leave most parents shaking their heads."

PRODUCTION CREDITS—Writer: Andrew Gottlieb. Executive Producer: Peter Hannan. Production Company: Peter Hannan Productions. Rating: TV-Y. Genres: Animation, Comedy, Family. Country: USA. Run Time: 24 min.

REFERENCES: *CatDog*. Internet Movie Database. http://www.imdb.com/title/tt0154061/

"A Very CatDog Christmas." Big Cartoon Database. http://www.bcdb.com/cartoon/34564-Very-CatDog-Christmas

"A Very CatDog Christmas." In *CatDog: Season 2 Part 2*. Los Angeles: Shout! Factory, 2012. DVD Video.

"A Very CatDog Christmas." Internet Movie Database. http://www.imdb.com/title/tt1430880/

Wilson, Joanna. *Tis the Season TV: The Encyclopedia of Christmas-Themed Episodes, Specials and Made-for-TV Movies*. Akron, OH: 1701 Press, 2011.

A Very Wompkee Christmas—November 2003

Direct-to-Video Computer-Animated Movie

THREAT TO CHRISTMAS: The Wompkees face a double humbug of a Christmas when they run out of Wompberries and the ice witch Iglora schemes to bury their village in ice.

HOW CHRISTMAS IS SAVED: Little Wompkee Twig and her cohorts melt Iglora and the ice fairies.

SYNOPSIS AND COMMENTARY: The year 1994 marked the arrival of the Wompkees, created by Paul Conway "Con" Fullam, a career musician, and his wife Maura Clarke, a recording artist. Furry, elfin-like creatures with infantile faces and with huge ears resembling butterfly wings that enabled them to fly, the Wompkees lived in the magical Wompkee Wood and thrived on a diet exclusively of purple Wompberries that also powered their village. Serving as positive role models for children, the Wompkees first appeared as plush toys that spawned a book-and-tape combo, *The Wompkee's First Grand Adventure* (1994) by Mark Medford; subsequently, they appeared in their first movie, *A Very Wompkee Christmas*. Although there may have been other Wompkees living within their realm, the featured characters included matriarch Gran, inventor Hummer, athlete Daisy, adventurous Scout, hefty Buster who lusted after Wompberries, and brave little Twig.

Although the setting is Christmas Eve as the Wompkees prepare for their festival, the holiday takes a back seat when the Wompkees discover that they're out of Wompberries. Their nemesis, the evil ice witch Iglora, had sent her ice fairies to steal the Wompberries to power her "ice device," because she intends to freeze the entire Wompkee Wood by morning. By coincidence (or not), the only source of Wompberries is a bush that grows right beside Iglora's lair on a mountaintop, yet because the bush will not yield its berries to her or her pet mongrel Woofus, her ice fairies steal them from the Wompkees instead. For some inexplicable reason, the Wompkees apparently have collected the berries without interference from Iglora in times past, but it's a different situation now that it's Christmas Eve when Iglora is on the warpath. Hummer, Daisy, Scout, and Buster encounter various difficulties as they attempt to climb the mountain, while Woofus coaxes naïve little Twig (who had set out on a mission by herself) to pick the berries for him. She unwittingly distracts the witch in the lair with her sweetness and childish games, while the other Wompkees fill their buckets and then whisk Twig back to Wompkee Wood. Enraged, Iglora sends her fairies back to steal more berries as her ice device sends a raging storm upon the

Wompkees, but this time Twig, learning to fly for the first time (thus fulfilling her Christmas wish), summons her companions, and their rapid spinning generates heat that melts Iglora and her ice fairies. That's not exactly like the demise of the Wicked Witch of the West in *The Wizard of Oz*, but close enough. Having saved Christmas and Wompkee Wood, Twig has the honor of placing the star atop the community Christmas tree.

PRINCIPAL VOICES: Alice Playten (*Legend*) as Buster; Kelli Rabke (*Necessary Parties*) as Daisy; Mary Elaine Monti (*Aunt Louisa*) as Gran and Iglora; Fred Newman (*Gremlins*) as Hummer and Woofus; Chris Phillips (*Max Payne*) as Scout; Lynne Lambert (*The Charmkins*) as Twig.

SONGS: "Christmas Eve in Wompkee Wood" by Paul Conway Fullam, sung by the Wompkee Chorus; "Iglora's Song" by Michael McInnis and Paul Conway Fullam, sung by Kym Dakin; "Christmas Wishes" by Paul Conway Fullam, sung by Pam Merritt and the Wompkee Chorus; "When Your Heart Is Ready" by Paul Conway Fullam, sung by Maura Clarke and Dan Merrill.

INTERESTING TIDBITS: Because of the story's rather sedate action (an extended berry-picking mission without high-speed sleigh chases or zip-bang martial arts fighting), it could have been compressed more readily into a half-hour time slot rather than the one hour allotted.

Preschoolers would probably identify the Wompkees as cute, fuzzy butterflies, because their ears remarkably resemble butterfly wings.

Santa and his trappings do not appear here, and Christmas itself, much less saving it, barely receives a nod. In fact, the principal story line would have suffered no significant compromise had Christmas not been mentioned at all.

PRODUCTION CREDITS—Story: Con Fullam and Maura Clarke. Writers: Peter Hunziker and Cynthia Riddle. Executive Producers: Mike DeVitto, Con Fullam, and Scott Guy. Director: Mike DeVitto. Production Companies: Deos Animation Studios and Wompkee. Rating: G. Genres: Animation, Family. Country: USA. Run Time: 54 min.

REFERENCES: Smyka, Mark. "Wompkee Started As a Toy." Kidscreen. http://kidscreen.com/1996/06/01/17076–19960601/

A Very Wompkee Christmas. Internet Movie Database. http://www.imdb.com/title/tt0934605/

A Very Wompkee Christmas. New York: Sony Wonder, 2003. DVD Video.

Wilson, Joanna. *Tis the Season TV: The Encyclopedia of Christmas-Themed Episodes, Specials and Made-for-TV Movies*. Akron, OH: 1701 Press, 2011.

When Santa Fell to Earth (*Als der Weihnachtsmann vom Himmel fiel*)—November 24, 2011

Feature Film

THREAT TO CHRISTMAS: When the evil Santa, Gerold Goblynch, takes over the great Christmas Council in Christmas Land, Niklas Julebukk, the last true Santa, escapes and loses his reindeer Twinklestar.

HOW CHRISTMAS IS SAVED: Two children help Niklas to find Twinklestar and put an end to Goblynch.

SYNOPSIS AND COMMENTARY: Bogeys have taken over Santa's realm again in this German production dubbed in English, which is an adaptation of the children's novel *Als der Weihnachtsmann vom Himmel fiel* by German author Cornelia Funke, originally published in 1994.

Funke's story provides a new twist to the Santa mythos. Santa is not just one person but a group of gift-givers governed by the Great Christmas Council in Christmas Land, equivalent to the North Pole. In the original setup, elves made the toys, angels listened to children's Christmas wishes then delivered the toys to the Santas, and the Santas delivered the gifts to the kids. All that changed when a corrupt Santa, Waldemar Wichteltod (Volker Lechtenbrink, *The Bridge*), and his army of nutcrackers gained control and turned the gift-giving season into an ultra-commercial enterprise based on greed. No longer requiring elves and angels, Wichteltod processed all but one reindeer into salami and zapped seven Santas into ice figures save one. The last remaining true Santa, the youthful and beardless Niklas Julebukk

(Alexander Scheer, *Eight Miles High*), escaped with two elves—Flybeard (Rufus Beck, *The Nutcracker and the Mouseking*) and Spillbeard (Konrad Wipp, *Endspiel*), and two little angels—Matilda (Christine Urspruch, *The Slurb*) and Emmanuel (Charly Hübner, *Ladykracher*)—in a gypsy caravan wagon pulled by Twinklestar, the last reindeer on earth. While flying in a freak storm of Wichteltod's conjuring, Twinklestar bolted, Niklas and wagon crashed into a small town, and now he's on the run from Wichteltod's henchmen. There Niklas convinces Ben (Noah Kraus, *The Lost Brother*), a young boy newly arrived in town and working through his own personal problems, to help him find the missing Twinklestar, who is invisible (except for his droppings) in the outside world. Ben turns to his classmate Charlotte (Mercedes Jadea Diaz, *Vicky the Viking*), a Christmas skeptic since her father abandoned the family at Christmastime a year ago, and it is her dog that sniffs out Twinklestar in a department store. In return for their help, Niklas foolishly allows the two kids to venture beyond his magic white door in the wagon into the now-dangerous Christmas Land to gather snow to win a bet with a school bully; as expected, Niklas winds up saving the kids from the menacing nutcrackers. Tipped off that Wichteltod is in town, Ben and Charlotte warn Niklas, but the villain kidnaps the three back to Christmas Land, where they battle the nutcrackers and remove Wichteltod's boots. With this significant move, he freezes into an ice figure after being bootless for 24 seconds, whereupon Niklas, the rightful Santa, reclaims Christmas Land.

AWARDS: In 2011, this film won the People's Choice Award at the Dubai International Film Festival, and in 2012, it received a White Elephant Special Award nomination at the Munich Film Festival (Mercedes Jadea Diaz and Noah Kraus).

INTERESTING TIDBITS: Given that this is a German film, it's ironic that the young Santa's surname here and in the German book version is "Julebukk," which is a Scandinavian term for "Yule Goat." The figure of the Yule Goat hearkens back to pre–Christian times with the worship of the Scandinavian god Thor, who rode through the skies in a chariot pulled by two goats. With the advent of Christianity, in time Father Christmas/Santa was depicted as riding on a Yule Goat. To that end, this film closes with Niklas riding on Twinklestar through the skies, which is a nod to the ancient Yule Goat.

The film and book differ somewhat in that the English version of the book translates the true Santa's name as Niklas Goodfellow; English versions of book and film change Wichteltod to Gerold Goblynch; and in the German version of the book, Wichteltod turns the other Santas to chocolate instead of ice.

The film does not explain the fate of the other missing elves whom Wichteltod had thrown out of Christmas Land, which leaves the impression that Niklas will carry on with only one reindeer, two elves as his toymakers, and two little angels to hear children's Christmas wishes.

The name "Wichteltod" is a combination of two German words, *Wichtel* (imp) and *Tod* (death).

REVIEWS: Joachim Kurz of *Kino-Zeit* (German language): "There is a little action, edifying morals, and skillful exchange between real and animated elements and sweet child actors. But the real strength of the film is Alexander Scheer, who appears as a freaky, student version of the benevolent and white-bearded Santa Claus, a soothing counterpoint to the sweetness and stickiness that children's Christmas stories can portray" (adapted from Google Translate).

Ronny Dombrowski of *Cinetastic* (German language, October 12, 2011): "Both children display playfulness, fun in their roles, and plenty of Christmas spirit. Their interaction with Alexander Scheer is outstanding. From countless Christmas movies that come out every year, this is probably one of the craziest. Funny, entertaining, and absolutely appropriate" (adapted from Google Translate).

PRODUCTION CREDITS—Script: Benjamin Biehn, Robin Getrost, and Uschi Reich. Producers: Uschi Reich and Bernd Krause. Director: Oliver Dieckmann. Production Companies: Bavaria Film, Wega Film, Kiddinx Filmproduktion, and Zweites Deutsches Fernsehen. Rating:

PG (mild peril and some language). Genres: Comedy, Family, Fantasy. Country: Germany. Run Time: 107 min.

REFERENCES: Crump, William D. *The Christmas Encyclopedia.* Third Edition. Jefferson, NC: McFarland, 2013.

Dombrowski, Ronny. *Als der Weihnachtsmann vom Himmel fiel. Cinetastic.* http://www.cinetastic.de/2011/10/als-der-weihnachtsmann-vom-himmel-fiel/

Funke, Cornelia. *Als der Weihnachtsmann vom Himmel fiel.* Illustrated by Regina Kehn. Hamburg: Dressler, 1994. (German language).

Kurz, Joachim. *Als der Weihnachtsmann vom Himmel fiel. Kino-Zeit.* http://www.kino-zeit.de/filme/als-der-weihnachtsmann-vom-himmel-fiel

When Santa Fell to Earth. Beverly Hills, CA: Anchor Bay Entertainment, 2014. DVD Video.

When Santa Fell to Earth. Internet Movie Database. http://www.imdb.com/title/tt http://www.imdb.com/title/tt1794725

Who Stole Santa?—1996

Episode from the Animated Direct-to-Video/Television Series *The Oz Kids*

THREAT TO CHRISTMAS: Two fiendish Agwas kidnap Santa.

HOW CHRISTMAS IS SAVED: The Oz kids and an elf rescue Santa.

SYNOPSIS AND COMMENTARY: Based on the *Oz* children's books by L. Frank Baum and the MGM film *The Wizard of Oz* (1939), this series consisted of 26 episodes that aired on ABC in 1996. The story line revolved around the adventures of the original *Oz* characters' children: Dot and Neddie Hugson, children of Dorothy and Zeb; Boris and Bela, children of the Cowardly Lion; Tin Boy, son of the Tin Woodman; Scarecrow, Jr.; Jack Pumpkinhead, Jr.; Andrea, daughter of Glinda the Good Witch; Frank, the Wizard's son; and Toto, Jr. They all lived in the Emerald City in Oz or its environs.

Jack and Andrea do not appear in *Who Stole Santa?* At the kids' urging a few weeks before Christmas, Dorothy relates the story of Santa's origins, which is a brief synopsis of Baum's novel, *The Life and Adventures of Santa Claus* (1902). Here, as in the novel, Santa lives in the Laughing Valley, not at the North Pole, and when two fiendish Agwas take their revenge by kidnapping Santa because he had defeated them in years past, his chief elf (no elves in the novel) turns to the Oz kids for help. They accompany the elf through the Laughing Valley to the castle atop a snowy cliff where the Agwas have imprisoned Santa. Along the way, they dodge the Wheelers (three pesky guys with wheels on all four limbs), avoid an avalanche, and escape from a cracked ice bridge. But the Agwas capture Boris and throw him in a cell with Santa, where the two learn that the Agwas are miserable and therefore want everyone else to be the same. Toto steals the keys while the Agwas sleep, and after nearly losing the keys in a lake, the gang escapes in a wooden sled that Tin Boy had fashioned, which precipitates the obligatory high-speed chase downhill with the Agwas in hot pursuit. When the sled crashes, the route includes hopping from ice floe to ice floe, and after a series of twists and turns, the Agwas disappear over a waterfall. The Oz kids enjoy a meal at Santa's house (Boris fixated on food all through the story but rejected the Agwas' stinking slop), after which they return to the Emerald City with a Christmas tree in tow.

PRINCIPAL VOICES: Marc Allen Lewis (*Playing by Heart*) as Santa; Eric Lloyd (*The Santa Clause*) as Neddie; Julianne Michelle (*Awakened*) as Dot; Bradley Pierce (*Jumanji*) as Boris; Shayna Fox (*Congo*) as Bela; Benjamin Salisbury (*Captain Ron*) as Tin Boy; Jonathan Taylor Thomas (*The Lion King*) as Scarecrow, Jr.; Alex Zuckerman (*Hook*) as Frank; Erika Schickel (*The Runestone*) as Dorothy. Voices for the Agwas, the Wheelers, and Santa's chief elf are not credited.

INTERESTING TIDBITS: The character of Frank is a nod to author L. Frank Baum and to Frank Morgan, who played the wizard in the 1939 film.

Other save-Christmas films in which Santa is kidnapped include **The Boy Who Saved Christmas; The Elf and the Magic Key; The Glo Friends Save Christmas; The Great Santa Claus Switch; The Librarians and Santa's**

Midnight Run; Santa Claus Conquers the Martians; Sonic Christmas Blast; Spinach Greetings; and *Tim Burton's The Nightmare Before Christmas*.

PRODUCTION CREDITS—Writer: Willard Carroll. Producer: John Bush. Directors: Bert Ring, Rhoydon Shishido, and David Teague. Production Companies: Canal+ Distribution, Hyperion Pictures, Meldac Corporation, and Wang Film Productions. Rating: Not rated. Genres: Animation, Fantasy. Country: USA. Run Time: 44 min.

REFERENCES: Baum, L. Frank. *The Life and Adventures of Santa Claus*. Illustrated edition with pictures by Mary Cowles Clark. New York: Greenwich House, 1983.

Who Stole Santa? Hollywood: Paramount, 1996. VHS Video.

Who Stole Santa? Internet Movie Database. http://www.imdb.com/title/tt0118162/

A Wish for Wings That Work—December 18, 1991

Animated Television Short Film

THREAT TO CHRISTMAS: Santa crashes his sleigh in a lake.

HOW CHRISTMAS IS SAVED: Though he cannot fly, Opus the penguin proves his worth by hauling the sleigh back to shore, which is quite a simple way to save Christmas.

SYNOPSIS AND COMMENTARY: Sometimes a film title alone provides no immediate clue that the subject is about Christmas, let alone saving Christmas. That applies to the film under consideration here, until we examine the revealing subtitle of the children's book from which the film is adapted: *A Wish for Wings That Work: An Opus Christmas Story* by the Pulitzer Prize-winning American cartoonist Berkeley Breathed, published in 1991, airing on CBS that same year. Most of the characters in the film and book are in turn based on those from Breathed's two comic strips, *Bloom County* and *Outland*. The protagonists are Opus, a penguin addicted to herring with a large nose like a puffin who lives away from his natural environment in Middle America and whose body parts (like his nose and buttocks) sometimes fall off; and his friend Bill, an orange, virtually mute and disheveled tabby cat who exists in a persistently near-catatonic state.

On Christmas Eve, Opus finally composes his letter to Santa in which he requests some useful wings with which to fly, then outlines the trying events of his day as if Santa were a participating confidant: the three ducks who mock him for attempting to fly; the bizarre personalities of those in his support group, Earthbound Birds Anonymous; a pig with a French accent who insists he's a rhinoceros; a cross-dressing cockroach; and his failed attempt at being an "aeronautic vigilante" when the makeshift balloon he creates crashes, thanks to Bill's clumsiness. That night, Opus dreams of piloting and crash-landing a DC-3 airplane amid black-and-white footage from the film *Lost Horizon* (1937), at which point the same three mocking ducks awaken him for help, because Santa has crashed his sleigh in a lake. The water being too frigid for the ducks and Opus being more adapted for such temperatures, he dives in and hauls the sleigh to shore, after which Santa praises his courage, rewards him with his own cap, and leaves him with the thought that he's still special even if he can't fly. Though Santa doesn't provide the wings that Opus wants, the appreciative duck population makes up for it by carrying Opus in flight on Christmas Day.

PRINCIPAL VOICES: Michael Bell (*Rugrats*) as Opus; Joe Alaskey (*Forrest Gump*) as Truffles and ducks; John Byner (*Wishmaster*) as Bill; Tress MacNeille (*The Simpsons*) as the chicken; Andrew Hill Newman (*Nobody's Perfect*) as Santa; Robin Williams (*Jumanji*) as the kiwi; Alexaundria Simmons as Ronald-Ann; Frank Welker (*Aladdin*) as Santa; Dustin Hoffman (*The Graduate*) as the cockroach.

INTERESTING TIDBITS: When Santa and his reindeer first appear in flight before his sleigh crashes, viewers should recognize the background music as the familiar theme from the film *The Magnificent Seven* (1960), which was also the theme for Marlboro cigarette commercials in the 1970s and 80s. Had the film been aimed at adult audiences, one might have expected to see Santa and team make their entrance to that music while puffing on cancer sticks.

Ironically, though Breathed wrote the special and was its executive producer, he was disappointed overall with the results and cited unspectacular ratings, his humor that wasn't meant for television, his lack of writing experience, and a director who was in over his head. Breathed, who had originally wanted Sterling Holloway for the voice of Opus, further quipped that DVD or VHS copies of the special belonged in the rubbish pail and that by taking speed, one could better enjoy the special.

For their voice roles, Robin Williams was credited as "Sudy Nim" (a play on "pseudonym"), while Dustin Hoffman was not credited.

REVIEWS: Will Brownridge of *The Film Reel* (December 14, 2015): "It shares a great message, but it wraps it up in a special that is completely different than the usual holiday fare, making this one a must-see..."

David Cornelius of *DVD Talk* (November 12, 2007): "...too disjointed in its episodic ramblings ... for all its problems, [the film] maintains a certain charm ... in fits and spurts, the whole thing is pretty darn funny, even if it never completely adds up."

PRODUCTION CREDITS—Writer: Berkeley Breathed. Producer: Peggy Regan. Director: Skip Jones. Production Companies: Amblin Television, Universal Cartoon Studios, and Universal Television. Rating: Not rated. Genres: Animation, Comedy, Family. Country: USA. Run Time: 22 min.

REFERENCES: Breathed, Berkeley. *A Wish for Wings That Work: An Opus Christmas Story*. Boston: Little, Brown, 1991.

Brownridge, Will. "Review: A Wish for Wings That Work (1991)—or—Rainbow Wigs and Penguins." *The Film Reel*. http://www.thefilmreel.com/2015/12/14/review-a-wish-for-wings-that-work-1991/

Cornelius, David. "Opus N' Bill in A Wish for Wings That Work." *DVD Talk*. http://www.dvdtalk.com/reviews/31365/opus-n-bill-in-a-wish-for-wings-that-work/

Opus N' Bill in A Wish for Wings That Work. Universal City, CA: Universal Studios Home Entertainment, 2007. DVD Video.

Wilson, Joanna. *Tis the Season TV: The Encyclopedia of Christmas-Themed Episodes, Specials and Made-for-TV Movies*. Akron, OH: 1701 Press, 2011.

A Wish for Wings That Work. Internet Movie Database. http://www.imdb.com/title/tt0103272/

A Wish for Wings That Work. Wikipedia. https://en.wikipedia.org/wiki/A_Wish_for_Wings_That_Work

Xmas Story—December 19, 1999

Episode from the Animated Television Series *Futurama*

THREAT TO CHRISTMAS: A homicidal Robot Santa terrorizes *New* New York in the year 3000.

HOW CHRISTMAS IS SAVED: Robot Santa is about to blow when his belly shakes like a bowl full of nitroglycerin, so the gang at Planet Express seal him in a chimney to contain the blast.

SYNOPSIS AND COMMENTARY: In those save-Christmas movies that focus on Santa, the jolly gent and his realm usually need to be saved from various bogeys. But imagine a scenario in which Santa *IS* the bogey from whom Christmas must be saved. That's the case here with "Xmas Story," but to be more specific, it's not the real Santa who's the bogey but an evil, Robot Santa who terrorizes *New* New York in the 31st century, the setting of *Futurama*. Created by Matt Groening (*The Simpsons*), *Futurama* aired on the Fox Network and then Comedy Central for 140 half-hour episodes between 1999 and 2013. The series revolved around the adventures of Philip J. Fry, a dimwitted pizza delivery boy from New York City who, having been cryogenically frozen in 2000, was revived in 2999 to become a delivery boy with Planet Express, an interplanetary delivery company. Other principal characters included Turanga Leela, a purple-haired, female cyclops and captain of the Planet Express ship; Bender Rodriguez, a foul-talking, boozing robot and Fry's best friend; Professor Hubert Farnsworth, Fry's 160-year-old distant nephew and Planet Express founder; Dr. John Zoidberg, a lobster-like alien; Amy Wong, a Planet Express intern; and Hermes Conrad, Planet Express's Jamaican accountant.

This is Fry's first Christmas (now called Xmas) in the year 3000, and it's just not the same as it was a millennium ago. For example, only Xmas palm trees are available, even in snowy weather, since pine trees are extinct. Realizing that Leela is just as lonely as he is, Fry ventures out to get her a special gift on Xmas Eve, but the gang cautions him to be back by sundown, lest he fall victim to the homicidal Robot Santa. A robot company had created this replacement for Santa in the year 2801 as a better way to determine who had been naughty and nice, but a malfunction had raised the robot's standards such that he now seeks to kill everyone for being naughty (apparently dispensing coal is passé). While Fry rejects presents like an electric snail and stink lizards and settles for a parrot that escapes, Bender hangs around a shelter for down-and-out robots in need of booze to keep functioning. Fry risks his life to chase down the parrot, but after Leela saves him, the Robot Santa attacks them in his flying, mechanical reindeer sleigh with a ray gun, grenades, and missiles (no nuclear device?). Bender and a group of homeless robots (having returned from committing a robbery) flee with Fry and Leela to the Planet Express building, where Robot Santa crashes down the chimney and threatens them with all manner of physical depravities, his belly shaking with "Ho Ho Ho" like a bowl full of nitroglycerin. With an explosion imminent, the gang shove Robot Santa into the chimney and seal it as he rockets into the skies. Bender serves Xmas dinner—the parrot as road kill—and the gang sing "Santa Claus Is Gunning You Down" (a parody of "Santa Claus Is Coming to Town"). As the end credits roll, Robot Santa vows to be back next Xmas.

PRINCIPAL VOICES: Billy West (*Futurama*) as Fry, Farnsworth, and Zoidberg; Katey Sagal

A host of characters from the animated TV series *Futurama*. Standing from left: Lt. Kif Kroker; Dr. John Zoidberg; Hermes Conrad; Philip J. Fry; Turanga Leela; robot Bender Rodriguez; Lord Nibbler; the villain "Mom" (whose butt Bender is pinching); Walt, Larry, and Igner, Mom's sons and henchmen; Prof. Farnsworth. Foreground: Capt. Zapp Brannigan and Amy Wong. In the episode "Xmas Story" (1999), Fry and his friends face a homicidal Robot Santa that terrorizes *New* New York (Fox Network/Photofest).

(*Married ... with Children*) as Leela; John DiMaggio (*Adventure Time*) as Bender; Phil LaMarr (*Pulp Fiction*) as Hermes; Lauren Tom (*Bad Santa*) as Amy; John Goodman (*Roseanne*) as Robot Santa; Tress MacNeille (*The Simpsons*) as Tinny Tim; Maurice LaMarche (*Frozen*) as Morbo, the alien anchorman. Guest star: Conan O'Brien as his talking head in a jar.

AWARDS: *Futurama* has received a slew of awards, the most notable of which are Primetime Emmys for Outstanding Individual Achievement in Animation (2000, 2001), Outstanding Animated Program Less Than One Hour (2002, 2011), Outstanding Voice-Over Performance (Maurice LaMarche, 2011, 2012), and other Emmy nominations; Annie Awards for Outstanding Achievement in Directing (2000, 2003), Writing (2001, 2014), Voice Acting (John DiMaggio, 2001), Best General Audience Animated TV/Broadcast Production (2014), and other Annie nominations.

INTERESTING TIDBITS: The episode satirizes homeless shelters. Whereas in real life the homeless are often alcoholics who seek a decent meal at such shelters, in this episode, the homeless robots flock to the shelters for booze in order to keep functioning.

A scene at the robot shelter provides a parody of two characters in Dickens novels. The little crippled robot Tinny Tim (a parody of Tiny Tim in *A Christmas Carol*) begs for a sip of booze from the proprietor (a parody of orphan Oliver Twist's begging for more gruel from Mr. Bumble the beadle in *Oliver Twist*).

The Alien Overlord and Taylor store that Fry visits is a parody of Lord and Taylor in New York City, the oldest luxury department store in North America.

While Robot Santa chases Fry, Leela, and the robots around town, Zoidberg presents Amy with a set of combs, but she had sold her hair to a wigmaker to buy a set of combs for Hermes, who in turn had sold his hair to buy a set of combs for Zoidberg, who ends up with two different colors of hair. This scenario is an obvious nod to O. Henry's short story "The Gift of the Magi."

Robot Santa's "Ho Ho Ho" resembles that by the demonic department store Santa who terrorizes Ralphie Parker in *A Christmas Story* (1983). In fact, the title "Xmas Story" is a parody of that film title.

An initially tranquil scene of children ice skating on a pond is a nod to similar winter scenes in the *Peanuts* TV specials, especially *A Charlie Brown Christmas*. The difference is that when Bender, snow-skiing off course, plunges from a cliff and smashes the ice, all the kids receive a dunking (no mention of drownings or hypothermia, though).

Bender receives an Xmas card from his "mother," the machine that built him, referring to him as Son #1729. This is a reference to the "Hardy–Ramanujan number" after British mathematician G.H. Hardy and Indian mathematician Srinivasa Ramanujan. The number 1729 is the smallest number expressible as the sum of two cubes in two different ways: $1^3 + 12^3 = 1729$ or $9^3 + 10^3 = 1729$ (see the reference for further details).

In an article dated May 26, 2016, *Rolling Stone* ranked *Futurama* as number 30 out of the 40 best TV science fiction TV shows of all time.

Check out the Christmas sequel, **A Tale of Two Santas**.

REVIEWS: Metacritic gave *Futurama* a score of 72/100 (generally favorable reviews).

Joly Herman of *Common Sense Media* reviewed *Futurama*: "…this series' content can be unpredictable, it's not meant for younger kids. The language can be crass, there are allusions to sex, characters drink and make drug references, and there is some cartoon violence. In general, characters don't cross the line when it comes to disrespecting each other, which would put the show into a more menacing sci-fi genre. Instead, this is a successful comedy that keeps you wanting more."

David Bianculli of the *New York Daily News* reviewed *Futurama*: "'Futurama,' like 'The Simpsons,' is a multi-layered, full-family treat: silly and goofy-looking enough to hook the kids, and subtle and sarcastic enough to charm their parents."

PRODUCTION CREDITS—Writer: David X. Cohen. Producers: J. Stewart Burns, Bill Odenkirk, Jane O'Brien, Brian J. Cowan, and

Claudia Katz. Director: Peter Avanzino. Production Companies: The Curiosity Company, 20th Century Fox Television, and Rough Draft Studios. Rating: TV-14. Genres: Animation, Comedy, Sci-Fi. Country: USA. Run Time: 22 min.

REFERENCES: Adams, Sam, Sean T. Collins, David Fear, et al. "40 Best Science Fiction TV Shows of All Time." *Rolling Stone*. http://www.rollingstone.com/tv/lists/40-best-science-fiction-tv-shows-20160526

Bianculli, David. "Futurama." *New York Daily News* (March 26, 1999).

Futurama. Internet Movie Database. http://www.imdb.com/title/tt0149460/

Futurama. Metacritic. http://www.metacritic.com/tv/futurama/critic-reviews

"Hardy–Ramanujan Number." Wolfram Math World. http://mathworld.wolfram.com/Hardy-RamanujanNumber.html

Herman, Joly. *Futurama*. Common Sense Media. https://www.commonsensemedia.org/tv-reviews/futurama

Wilson, Joanna. *Tis the Season TV: The Encyclopedia of Christmas-Themed Episodes, Specials and Made-for-TV Movies*. Akron, OH: 1701 Press, 2011.

"Xmas Story." In *Futurama: The Complete Collection 1999–2009*. Beverly Hills, CA: 20th Century Fox Home Entertainment, 2009. DVD Video.

The Year Scroogenip Swiped Christmas—December 12, 1987

Episode Segment from the Animated Television Series *Hello Kitty's Furry Tale Theater*

THREAT TO CHRISTMAS: Catnip portrays Scrinchnip, a composite of Scrooge and the Grinch, who desires to ruin Christmas.

HOW CHRISTMAS IS SAVED: The kindness of Hello Kitty and her friends persuades Scrinchnip to change her ways.

SYNOPSIS AND COMMENTARY: Created in 1974 by Yuko Shimizu and produced by the Japanese company Sanrio, the character *Hello Kitty* launched a global marketing phenomenon. Among other merchandise, the anthropomorphic, white female Japanese bobtail feline with a red bow was featured in several animated television incarnations, one of which was *Hello Kitty's Furry Tale Theater* that ran on CBS and TV Osaka for 13 episodes (each with two 11-minute segments) in 1987. The series revolved around Hello Kitty and her friends as they performed parodies of classic fairy tales and stories on stage. Other principal cast members included Mama, Papa, Grandma, and Grandpa Kitty; Tuxedo Sam, the penguin stage manager; My Melody, a little female rabbit with a red hood covering her ears; Chip, a white seal; Catnip, a green female Siamese cat; and Grinder, a dimwitted bulldog. Kitty or another character opened each episode segment with, "Once upon a meow…"

In this obvious parody of *Dr. Seuss' How the Grinch Stole Christmas* with a nod to *A Christmas Carol*, Catnip portrays Scrinchnip, a composite of Scrooge and the Grinch (no one portrays Jacob Marley, ghosts, or Tiny Tim, however). Despising the holiday, Scrinchnip attempts to identify those items that comprise Christmas and ruin them. She first destroys bows and wreaths, then steals the town's decorations and lights, followed by all the citizens' Christmas trees. Lastly, after Santa Paws (portrayed by Grinder) passes through town, Scrinchnip dressed as Santa pops down chimneys and proceeds to steal all the presents. But My Melody (portraying Cindy Lou Who) catches her in the act, whereupon the wily feline claims that she's replacing wrong presents with the correct ones. When the town awakens to no presents on Christmas Day, Grandma wisely admonishes the dispirited Kitty and friends that presents aren't necessary, because the best part of Christmas is giving. Heartened, the gang serenade the townspeople with secular carols and even surprise Scrinchnip with a little gift. Having never received such kindness before, she wonders (as did the Grinch) that maybe there's more to Christmas than presents, trees, decorations, and lights (while conveniently omitting any religious implications), which prompts her to haul all the stolen paraphernalia back into town in her sleigh as everyone rejoices.

PRINCIPAL VOICES: Tara Charendoff (*Ice Age*) as Hello Kitty; Carl Banas (*Rocket Robin*

Hood) as Grandpa; Elizabeth Hanna (*Beetlejuice*) as Grandma; Len Carlson (*Shyness*) as Papa; Cree Summer Francks (*Inspector Gadget*) as Catnip; Greg Morton (*Police Academy: The Series*) as Grinder; Sean Roberge (*In the Mouth of Madness*) as Tuxedo Sam; Mairon Bennett (*Lantern Hill*) as My Melody; Noam Zylberman (*Last Train Home*) as Chip.

NOTE: At the time of this writing, this episode was not available on DVD or VHS but could be seen on Hulu. Whereas the e-video displays the title as "How Scrinchio Stole Xmas," the title within the episode itself is "The Year Scroogenip Swiped Christmas."

PRODUCTION CREDITS—Writer: Phil Harnage. Producer and Director: Michael Maliani. Production Companies: DiC Enterprises, MGM/UA Television, and the Sanrio Company. Rating: TV-Y. Genres: Animation, Comedy, Family, Fantasy. Countries: Canada, Japan, and USA. Run Time: 11 min.

REFERENCES: *Hello Kitty's Furry Tale Theater.* Internet Movie Database. http://www.imdb.com/title/tt0092368/

Sanrio Web Site. http://www.sanrio.com/

The Year Without a Santa Claus—
December 10, 1974

Animated Musical Television Special

THREAT TO CHRISTMAS: Suffering from a cold and believing that no one cares anymore about Christmas, Santa decides to ditch Christmas and take a vacation.

HOW CHRISTMAS IS SAVED: Feeling that Santa needs a Christmas holiday of his own, children of the world flood the North Pole with gifts, whereupon Santa decides that he doesn't need a holiday after all.

SYNOPSIS AND COMMENTARY: Santa often cancels Christmas in save-Christmas movies because he's either ill (as if an immortal like him could ever become sick) or he feels unappreciated because he believes no one gives a hoot about Christmas, a sentiment that the crotchety old doctor who examines Santa only fuels: "Nobody cares a hoot or holler for you or Christmas!" In this TV special that features stop-motion puppets (Animagic animation), all of the above apply to Santa. Rather than disappoint children, Mrs. Claus sends two bumbling elves, Jingle and Jangle Bells, out into the world to round up some Christmas spirit. Riding baby reindeer Vixen, they settle on Southtown, U.S.A., a small Southern town, where Vixen, disguised as a dog, is tossed into the pound and suffers from the hot weather. The two elves befriend a young boy, Ignatius Thistlewhite, and although the three petition the skeptical mayor to release Vixen, he will do so only if the elves can work the seemingly impossible: create a snowfall for Christmas. On their behalf, Mrs. Claus initially petitions the two warring weather warlocks, Snow Miser and Heat Miser, and, getting nowhere with them, finally pleads with Mother Nature, who orders her two weather "sons" to compromise, whereupon Southtown gets its snow. Santa arrives in street dress to rescue Vixen as news breaks that children of the world are giving Santa his own Christmas holiday and are flooding the North Pole with gifts. With so much Christmas spirit still alive, Santa decides to make his deliveries after all.

VOICES: Shirley Booth (*Hazel*) as Mrs. Claus/narrator; Mickey Rooney (*National Velvet*) as Santa; Dick Shawn (*The Producers*) as Snow Miser; George S. Irving (*Underdog*) as Heat Miser; Bob McFadden (*The Life and Adventures of Santa Claus*) as Jingle Bells; Bradley Bolke (*Tennessee Tuxedo and His Tales*) as Jangle Bells; Rhoda Mann (*The ABC Saturday Superstar Movie*) as Mother Nature; Ron Marshall (*The Easter Bunny Is Comin' to Town*) as Mr. Thistlewhite; Colin Duffy (*The Land of Hope*) as Ignatius; Christine Winter (*'Twas the Night Before Christmas*) as girl singing "Blue Christmas"; The Wee Winter Singers as the Chorus.

SONGS: Christmas standards featured: "Blue Christmas"; "Here Comes Santa Claus"; "Sleigh Ride." Other original lyrics and music by Maury Laws and Jules Bass: "The Year Without a Santa Claus"; "I Could Be Santa Claus"; "I Believe in Santa Claus"; "It's Gonna Snow Right Here in Dixie"; "The Snow Miser Song"; "The Heat Miser Song."

INTERESTING TIDBITS: Initially shocked that Santa wants to stay abed rather than make his Christmas Eve rounds, Mrs. Claus ex-

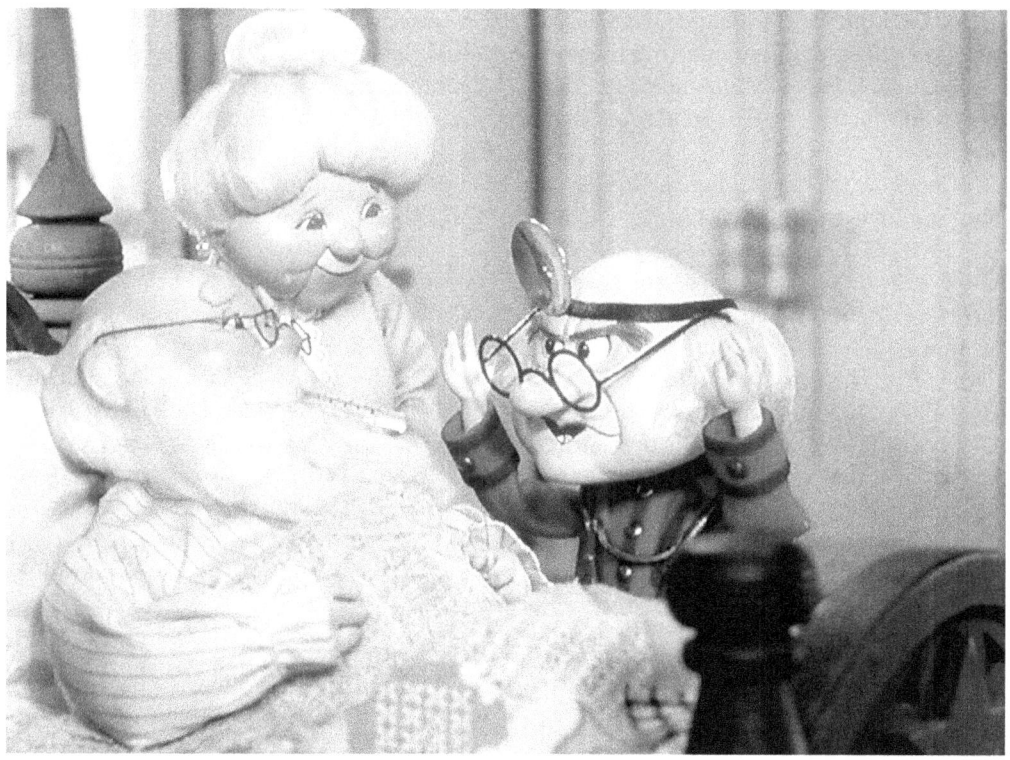

When Santa falls ill and his crabby doctor makes matters worse by declaring that no one cares about Santa or Christmas, Mrs. Claus sends two elves out to round up some Christmas spirit in *The Year Without a Santa Claus* **(1974) (ABC/Photofest).**

presses the typical, materialistic sentiment rampant in most Santa-oriented Christmas movies: "If Santa stayed home, why, there'd be no Christmas!" To that are added the "pagan" influences of the two weather warlocks, Snow Miser and Heat Miser, along with Mother Nature (see also Reviews below).

According to Mother Nature's compromise, Heat Miser permits one day of snow in Southtown, and Snow Miser permits one day of spring weather at the North Pole. The snowfall occurs, but there's no follow-up about the spring weather.

This special was partly based on the children's book (a narrative poem) of the same title by American author Phyllis McGinley, published in 1957. The scenarios involving Vixen's pound experience, Snow Miser, Heat Miser, and Mother Nature were not part of the original story and were appended to the special.

A writer of children's books and poems about the positive elements of suburban life, Phyllis McGinley (1905–1978) was elected a member of the National Academy of Arts and Letters in 1955. She won the Pulitzer Prize for Poetry in 1961 and received the Laetre Medal from the University of Notre Dame in 1964. McGinley is probably best remembered for her book *The Year Without a Santa Claus*.

For their specials, Rankin/Bass Productions routinely used the voices of well-established actors and other celebrities in order to introduce them to younger audiences. Mickey Rooney and George S. Irving reprised their respective voice roles as Santa and Heat Miser for the animated television special ***A Miser Brothers' Christmas*** (2008). Rooney had also voiced for Santa in the Rankin/Bass production of *Santa Claus Is Comin' to Town* (1970).

The Year Without a Santa Claus was Shirley Booth's last filmed acting project; she died in 1992.

Other films in which Santa or his surrogate suffers a cold and cannot deliver the presents include: *Christmas Flintstone, A Flintstone Christmas*, and *How the Toys Saved Christmas*.

Check out the live-action remake, starring John Goodman as Santa (2006).

REVIEWS: In her review of several Rankin/Bass Christmas specials, MaryAnn Johanson of *Flick Filosopher* (January 4, 2005) noted the pagan elements in *Santa Claus Is Comin' to Town* (1970) as well as in *The Year Without a Santa Claus*: "...Kris [Kringle] and the hottie schoolmarm's 'wedding,' which happens without benefit of clergy as they 'marry' each other under the trees of the wintry forest, with all the animals and the [Winter] Warlock in attendance. Very pagan.... What I remember most about [this] is always always [sic] the Snow Miser and the Heat Miser—those warring warlocks of weather; heh, more pagan stuff..."

Paul Mavis of *DVD Talk* (October 17, 2007): "...a sweet story that young children will respond to over thirty years after its original broadcast."

PRODUCTION CREDITS—Writer: William Keenan. Producers and Directors: Arthur Rankin, Jr., and Jules Bass. Production Company: Rankin/Bass Productions. Rating: Not rated. Genres: Animation, Comedy, Family, Fantasy, Musical. Country: USA. Run Time: 51 min.

REFERENCES: Crump, William D. *The Christmas Encyclopedia*. Third Edition. Jefferson, NC: McFarland, 2013.

Goldschmidt, Rick. *The Enchanted World of Rankin/Bass*. Bridgeview, IL: Miser Bros. Press, 1997.

Johanson, MaryAnn. "Rudolph the Red-Nosed Reindeer, Santa Claus Is Comin' to Town, The Year without a Santa Claus, Rudolph's Shiny New Year (review)." *Flick Filosopher*. http://www.flickfilosopher.com/2005/01/rudolph-the-red-nosed-reindeer-santa-claus-is-comin-to-town-the-year-without-a-santa-claus-rudolphs-shiny-new-year-review.html

Lenburg, Jeff. *The Encyclopedia of Animated Cartoons*. Third Edition. New York: Facts on File, 2009.

Mavis, Paul. "The Year Without a Santa Claus: Deluxe Edition." *DVD Talk*. http://www.dvdtalk.com/reviews/31039/year-without-a-santa-claus-deluxe-edition-the/

McGinley, Phyllis. *The Year Without a Santa Claus*. Illustrated by Kurt Werth. New York: J.B. Lippincott, 1957.

Wilson, Joanna. *Tis the Season TV: The Encyclopedia of Christmas-Themed Episodes, Specials and Made-for-TV Movies*. Akron, OH: 1701 Press, 2011.

The Year Without a Santa Claus. Burbank, CA: Warner Home Video, 2010. DVD Video.

The Year Without a Santa Claus. Big Cartoon Database. http://www.bcdb.com/cartoon/27859-Year-Without-A-Santa-Claus

The Year Without a Santa Claus. Internet Movie Database. http://www.imdb.com/title/tt0072424/

The Year Without a Santa Claus—
December 11, 2006

Television Special

THREAT TO CHRISTMAS: Santa is sick—sick and tired of mounting commercialism at the North Pole, that is—and decides to throw in the towel.

HOW CHRISTMAS IS SAVED: Elves Jingle and Jangle find some Christmas spirit in Iggy Thistlewhite in South Town.

SYNOPSIS AND COMMENTARY: Children will find Santa (John Goodman, *Roseanne*) anything but the jolly icon of Christmas festivities in this live-action remake of the 1974 Rankin/Bass stop-motion-animated special. Santa has become nothing more than a depressed pitchman for bizarre, 21st-century toys cranked out by SantaCo, a huge toy conglomerate at the North Pole overseen by chief elf Sparky (Chris Kattan, *Saturday Night Live*), whose interests lie in keeping up with the times and making profits. Down in South Town, ten-year-old Iggy Thistlewhite (Dylan Minnette, *Goosebumps*) is trying to revive holiday spirit by organizing a citywide Christmas Festival, which catches the attention of two elves, white Jingle (Ethan Suplee, *Without a Paddle*) and black Jangle (Eddie Griffin, *Undercover Brother*), whom Santa pursues to bring back to the North Pole.

In other departures from the animated version, Iggy, not Santa, springs Vixen from the pound and pines for more quality time with his workaholic mayor-father (Robert C. Treveiler, *Prisoners*), who is bent on modernizing South Town; Iggy, not the mayor, asks Santa for a Christmas snowfall in South Town; Santa, not Mrs. Claus (Delta Burke, *Designing Women*), negotiates the deal for snow between weather gods Heat Miser (Harvey Fierstein, *Independence Day*) and Snow Miser (Michael McKean, *Whatever Works*); Sparky as "Extreme Santa" (in cape and green tights), convinced that Santa has jumped ship, is all too eager to take control; Mother Nature (Carol Kane, *Carnal Knowledge*) briefly appears to shush her two feuding sons long enough for Santa to question them on the whereabouts of Jingle and Jangle; and in a brief scene at the end, the North Pole enjoys one day of Spring.

SONG: "Snow Miser" music and lyrics respectively by Maury Laws and Jules Bass.

AWARDS: In 2007, this production received a Directors Guild of America Award nomination for Outstanding Directorial Achievement in Children's Programs and a Golden Reel Award nomination for Best Sound Editing in Television: Long Form–Dialogue and Automated Dialogue Replacement.

INTERESTING TIDBITS: Sparky voices the typically materialistic view of Christmas: "Everyone knows there's no Christmas without Santa Claus!"

While Jangles ponders Santa's decision to cancel Christmas, he surfs snippets of Christmas classics on his hand-held TV: *The Year Without a Santa Claus* (1974) and *National Lampoon's Christmas Vacation* (1989), then considers that if he and Jingles lose their jobs, his dentist-cousin on the Island of Misfit Toys might hire them as assistants, which alludes to *Rudolph, the Red-Nosed Reindeer* (1964). More surfing brings up a cameo of self-help therapist Dr. Laura (Laura Schlessinger), who offers ways to dispel negative attitudes.

Courtesy of the Abominable Snowman,

Heat Miser (Harvey Fierstein, middle) clowns around during a ridiculous boxing match with Snow Miser (Michael McKean, right) while Santa (John Goodman) observes in *The Year Without a Santa Claus* (2006) (NBC/Photofest).

Santa receives a DVD of Hercules (cameo of the now-late fitness guru Jack LaLanne) pitching Mythopolis, a retirement community for aging mythical figures that piques Santa's interest. Also appearing in cameo is Carson Kressley (*Queer Eye*) as the elf costumer.

Having always been on the naughty list, a skeptical dog catcher informs Santa that he's still waiting for a BB gun, whereupon Santa fires back, "You'll shoot your eye out…. *OUCH!*" an obvious allusion to *A Christmas Story* (1983).

Whereas the spelling is "Southtown" in the animated version, it's "South Town" in the live-action version.

Media sources sometimes confuse the actors playing the roles of Jingle and Jangle, erroneously crediting Eddie Griffin as Jingle and Ethan Suplee as Jangle. The film's opening credits, however, list Griffin as Jangle and Suplee as Jingle.

REVIEWS: Critics were a tad unkind. Paul Mavis of *DVD Talk* (December 18, 2006): "The film is filled with trendy references to the evils of commercializing Christmas … the producers' solution for that distressing trend [is to show] a seriously damaged Santa [who] pushes people around, threatens them, and even hits them … hot blonde chicks in skimpy outfits gyrating behind…. Heat Miser … the drunken dog catcher *[lifts] up his shirt in front of a small boy*, showing his motto ['Life's 2 short 4 paper work'] tattooed on his belly (how did *anyone* think that was appropriate?)."

Emily Ashby of *Common Sense Media* (December 5, 2006): "The religious aspect of Christmas is absent from the plot." [That's generally par for the course in the majority of save-Christmas movies.] "Despite boasting such a stellar cast, [the film] is a disappointing mix of slow plot, poor writing, and subpar visual effects…. Families with tweens and teens might enjoy the character-based humor [here], but if your kids are little, they'll probably be turned off by the grumpy, sarcastic Santa and general lack of holiday spirit that exists for most of the show."

PRODUCTION CREDITS—Story and teleplay: Tom Martin and Larry Wilson. Producers: Gideon Amir and Robert J. Wilson. Director: Ron Underwood. Production Companies: The Wolper Organization and Warner Bros. Television. Rating: Not rated. Genres: Comedy, Family, Fantasy. Country: USA. Run Time: 85 min.

REFERENCES: Ashby, Emily. "The Year Without a Santa Claus." *Common Sense Media*. https://www.commonsensemedia.org/movie-reviews/the-year-without-a-santa-claus

Mavis, Paul. "The Year Without a Santa Claus." *DVD Talk*. http://www.dvdtalk.com/reviews/25691/year-without-a-santa-claus-the/

McGinley, Phyllis. *The Year Without a Santa Claus*. Illustrated by Kurt Werth. New York: J.B. Lippincott, 1957.

Wilson, Joanna. *Tis the Season TV: The Encyclopedia of Christmas-Themed Episodes, Specials and Made-for-TV Movies*. Akron, OH: 1701 Press, 2011.

The Year Without a Santa Claus. Burbank, CA: Warner Home Video, 2006. DVD Video.

The Year Without a Santa Claus. Internet Movie Database. http://www.imdb.com/title/tt0828465/

Appendix: Categories of Reasons for Saving Christmas Matched to the Films

(Some films fall into more than one category)

Aliens Threaten Santa (3)

Gotta Catch Santa Claus (TV Movie)
"Holiday Time" (Episode from *Buzz Lightyear of Star Command*)
Santa Claus Conquers the Martians (Feature Film)

Aliens Threaten the Earth (1)

"The Christmas Invasion" (Episode from *Doctor Who*)

Animals Threaten Santa (2)

The Flight Before Christmas (Feature Film)
The Guild of Thespian Puppets Save Christmas (Short Film)

Atheist Wrecks Christmas (1)

Christmas with a Capital C (Direct-to-Video)

Christmas Cancelled for War Effort (1)

The Man Who Saved Christmas (TV Movie)

Christmas Commercialism (8)

"The Gift" (Episode from *Kingdom under the Sea*)
It Nearly Wasn't Christmas (TV Movie)
Once Upon a Christmas (TV Movie)
Saving Christmas (Feature Film)
The Toy That Saved Christmas (Direct-to-Video)
"A Very CatDog Christmas" (Episode from *CatDog*)
When Santa Fell to Earth (Feature Film)
The Year Without a Santa Claus (2006, TV Special)

Christmas Countdown Disrupted (1)

Elmo's Christmas Countdown (TV Special)

Christmas Decorations or Presents Lost or Stolen (18)

Casper's Haunted Christmas (Direct-to Video)
The Christmas Angel: A Story on Ice (TV Movie)
Christmas Rescue (TV Short Film)
Dr. Seuss' How the Grinch Stole Christmas (1966, TV Special)
Dr. Seuss' How the Grinch Stole Christmas (2000, Feature Film)
The Dog Who Saved Christmas (TV Movie)
The Dog Who Saved Christmas Vacation (TV Movie)
The Dog Who Saved the Holidays (Direct-to-Video)
"Gekko Saves Christmas" (Episode from *PJ Masks*)
The Great Toy Robbery (Short Film)
"Holiday Hi-Jynx" (Episode from *Pokémon*)
"It's a Wonderful Leaf" (Episode from *Darkwing Duck*)
Mule-Tide Christmas (Feature Film)
My Little Pony: A Very Minty Christmas (Direct-to-Video)

319

Rudolph, the Red-Nosed Reindeer and the Island of Misfit Toys (Direct-to Video)
Sonic Christmas Blast (TV Short Film)
The Three Dogateers (Direct-to Video)
"'Twas the Night Before Bumpy" (Episode from *Bump in the Night*)
"The Year Scroogenip Swiped Christmas" (Episode from *Hello Kitty's Furry Tale Theater*)

Christmas Every Day (1)

Elmo Saves Christmas (TV Special)

Christmas Presents Destroyed (5)

The Christmas Conspiracy (Short Film)
Ice Age: A Mammoth Christmas Special (TV Short Film)
Santabear's High Flying Adventure (TV Movie)
Santa's Little Helpers (Direct-to-Video)
"Spinach Greetings" (Episode from *Popeye the Sailor*)

Christmas Spirit Lost (17)

An Angel for Christmas (Direct-to-Video)
Angels Sing (Feature Film)
Beauty and the Beast: The Enchanted Christmas (Direct-to-Video)
Cancel Christmas (TV Movie)
A Christmas Snow (Direct-to-Video)
A Christmas Visitor (TV Movie)
Krampus (Feature Film)
Northpole (TV Movie)
Northpole: Open for Christmas (TV Movie)
One Magic Christmas (Feature Film)
Papa's Angels (TV Movie)
Santa Buddies: The Legend of Santa Paws (Direct-to-Video)
Santa Paws 2: The Santa Pups (Direct-to-Video)
Small Town Santa (Direct-to-Video)
The Town Christmas Forgot (TV Movie)
A Town Without Christmas (TV Movie)
Unlikely Angel (TV Movie)

Christmas Traditions in Jeopardy (7)

Buster and Chauncey's Silent Night (Direct-to-Video)
The Christmas Candle (Feature Film)
A Light in the Forest: The Legend of Holly Boy (Fantasy Film)
Saving Christmas (Feature Film)
The Swan Princess Christmas (Direct-to-Video)
The Town That Banned Christmas (Feature Film)
A Very Wompkee Christmas (Direct-to-Video)

Cynicism and Disbelief with Bad Consequences (2)

The Christmas Path (TV Movie)
Krampus (Feature Film)

Electronics Problems (2)

Holidaze: The Christmas That Almost Didn't Happen (TV Special)
Prep and Landing: Naughty vs. Nice (TV Movie)

Elves, Reindeer or North Pole on Strike/Revolution (3)

"It's a Very Merry Eek's-Mas" (Episode from *Eek! The Cat*)
Like Father, Like Santa (TV Movie)
Santa Mouse and the Ratdeer (TV Movie)

Financial Problems/Poverty (8)

Booky and the Secret Santa (TV Movie)
Christmas Comes but Once a Year/True Boo (Theatrical Shorts)
The Christmas Angel (Short Film)
The Christmas Miracle (Short Film)
The Town Christmas Forgot (TV Movie)
The Town Santa Forgot (TV Short Film)
A Town Without Christmas (TV Movie)
The Tree That Saved Christmas (TV Movie)

Ghost/Monster Prevents Christmas Celebrations (1)

A Scooby-Doo! Christmas (TV Special from *What's New, Scooby-Doo?*)

Holiday Argument (1)

"The All Nighter Before Christmas" (Episode from *The Penguins of Madagascar*)

Inclement Weather (8)

The Bears Who Saved Christmas (TV Short Film)
A Christmas Adventure from a Book Called Wisely's Tales (Direct-to-Video)
Felix the Cat Saves Christmas (Direct-to-Video)
"Flicker Saves Christmas" (Episode from *Handy Manny*)
Holly and Hal Moose: Our Uplifting Christmas Adventure (TV Movie)
"Pups Save Christmas" (Episode from *PAW Patrol*)
Rudolph, the Red-Nosed Reindeer (TV Special)
Rudolph, the Red-Nosed Reindeer: The Movie (Feature Film)

Letters Not Mailed to Santa (2)

A Christmas Story (TV Short Film)
A Muppets Christmas: Letters to Santa (TV Comedy)

Mechanical Problems (1)

Nearly No Christmas (TV Movie)

Neglected Christmas (1)

The City That Forgot About Christmas (TV Short Film)

North Pole Suffers If Presents Aren't Delivered (1)

Arthur Christmas (Feature Film)

Prospectors' Interference (1)

The Night They Saved Christmas (TV Movie)

Reindeer Kidnapped, Missing or in Trouble (9)

A Christmas Adventure from a Book Called Wisely's Tales (Direct-to-Video)
Last Chance for Christmas (TV Movie)
Mrs. Santa Claus (TV Movie)
"The Reindeer Hunter" (Episode from *Ace Ventura: Pet Detective*)
"Save the Reindeer" (Episode from *Wonder Pets!*)
"Search for Rudolph" (Episode from *The Shapies*)
Snow (TV Movie)
Spike: The Elf That Saved Christmas (TV Movie)
The Trolls and the Christmas Express (TV Short Film)

Robot Santa Terrorist (2)

"A Tale of Two Santas" (Episode from *Futurama*)
"Xmas Story" (Episode from *Futurama*)

Santa Bankrupt (1)

Jingle Bell Rock (TV Short Film)

Santa Becomes a Vampire (1)

"Billy and Mandy Save Christmas" (Episode from *The Grim Adventures of Billy and Mandy*)

Santa Bewitched (5)

"Baby's First Christmas" (Episode from *The Smurfs*)
Magic Christmas Tree (Fantasy Film)
Mary Engelbreit's The Night Before Christmas (Short Film)
The Munsters' Scary Little Christmas (TV Movie)
Santa's Christmas Snooze (TV Short Film)

Santa Dies/Dying (6)

The Christmas Dragon (Direct-to-Video)
"For Whom the Sleigh Bell Tolls" (Episode from *American Dad!*)
The Hebrew Hammer (Feature Film)
"I Saw Stroker Killing Santa Claus" (Episode from *Stroker and Hoop*)
"Road to the North Pole" (Episode from *Family Guy*)
The Santa Clause (Feature Film)

Santa in Court (3)

The Case for Christmas (TV Movie)
The Christmas Orange (TV Movie)

Appendix

Grandma Got Run Over by a Reindeer (TV Movie)

Santa Kidnapped (10)

The Boy Who Saved Christmas (TV Movie)
The Elf and the Magic Key (TV Movie)
The Glo Friends Save Christmas (TV Short Film)
The Great Santa Claus Switch (TV Special)
"The Librarians and Santa's Midnight Run" (Episode from *The Librarians*)
Santa Claus Conquers the Martians (Feature Film)
Sonic Christmas Blast (TV Short Film)
"Spinach Greetings" (Episode from *Popeye the Sailor*)
Tim Burton's The Nightmare Before Christmas (Feature Film)
"Who Stole Santa?" (Episode from *The Oz Kids*)

Santa Loses His Magic Powers (2)

A Country Christmas (Direct-to-Video)
Mr. St. Nick (TV Movie)

Santa Mistaken for a UFO (1)

The Santa Incident (TV Movie)

Santa Mistaken for an Intruder (3)

Santa, Jr. (TV Movie)
The Santa Trap (TV Movie)
Small Town Santa (Direct-to-Video)

Santa Must Find a Successor (6)

Call Me Claus (TV Movie)
Ernest Saves Christmas (Feature Film)
In the Nick of Time (TV Movie)
Mr. St. Nick (TV Movie)
Must Be Santa (TV Movie)
Santa's Apprentice (Feature Film)

Santa Must Take a Wife (3)

Meet the Santas (TV Movie)
The Santa Clause 2: The Mrs. Clause (Feature Film)
Single Santa Seeks Mrs. Claus (TV Movie)

Santa/Other Protagonist Crashes the Sleigh (24)

"Anti-Claus Is Coming to Town" (Episode from *Big Wolf on Campus*)
Beethoven's Christmas Adventure (Direct-to-Video)
Christmas Comes to Pac-Land (TV Short Film)
"Christmas Present Time" (Episode from *Tickety Toc*)
A Christmoose Story (Feature Film)
The ChubbChubbs Save Xmas (Short Film)
A Country Christmas (Direct-to-Video)
"Diego Saves Christmas!" (Episode from *Go, Diego, Go!*)
Dot and Spot's Magical Christmas Adventure (Direct-to-Video)
Get Santa (Feature Film)
Hoops and Yoyo Ruin Christmas (TV Short Film)
"It's a Very Merry Eek's-Mas" (Episode from *Eek! The Cat*)
Merry Madagascar (TV Short Film)
"Miracle at the 34th Precinct" (Episode from *Bonkers*)
A Miser Brothers' Christmas (TV Movie)
The Night Before the Night Before Christmas (TV Movie)
"Pups Save Christmas" (Episode from *PAW Patrol*)
The Santa Claus Brothers (TV Movie)
Santa Claws (Direct-to-Video)
Santa Mouse and the Ratdeer (TV Movie)
Santa's Christmas Crash (TV Short Film)
"'Twas the Night Before Bumpy" (Episode from *Bump in the Night*)
When Santa Fell to Earth (Feature Film)
A Wish for Wings That Work (TV Short Film)

Santa Quits or Is Put Out of Business (7)

The Christmas Orange (TV Movie)
The Elf Who Saved Christmas (TV Movie)
It Nearly Wasn't Christmas (TV Movie)
"Merry Wishmas" (Episode from *The Fairly OddParents*)
"Nilus the Sandman: The Boy Who Dreamed Christmas" (Episode from *Nilus the Sandman*)

The Year Without a Santa Claus (1974, TV Special)
The Year Without a Santa Claus (2006, TV Special)

Santa Retaliates Against Slander (1)

'Twas the Night Before Christmas (TV Special)

Santa, Santa Surrogate, Elves or Reindeer Are Sick, Injured or Incapacitated (36)

"The Amazing World of Gumball: Christmas Episode" (Episode from *The Amazing World of Gumball*)
"A Barnyard Christmas Special" (Episode from *Back at the Barnyard*)
"Christmas Flintstone" (Episode from *The Flintstones*)
The ChubbChubbs Save Xmas (Short Film)
A Fairly Odd Christmas (TV Movie)
A Flintstone Christmas (TV Special)
"Holly Jolly Jimmy" (Episode from *The Adventures of Jimmy Neutron: Boy Genius*)
How Murray Saved Christmas (TV Movie)
How the Toys Saved Christmas (Direct-to-Video)
"It's a Very Merry Eek's-Mas" (Episode from *Eek! The Cat*)
Last Chance for Christmas (TV Movie)
"The Librarians and Santa's Midnight Run" (Episode from *The Librarians*)
"Madeline at the North Pole/Madeline and Santa" (Episodes from *The New Adventures of Madeline*)
Merry Madagascar (TV Short Film)
"Miracle at the 34th Precinct" (Episode from *Bonkers*)
A Miser Brothers' Christmas (TV Movie)
A Monster Christmas (From the Video Series *Friendly Monsters*)
The Naughty List (Direct-to-Video)
The Night B4 Christmas (TV Short Film)
The Night Before the Night Before Christmas (TV Movie)
Nine Dog Christmas (Direct-to-Video)
Olive, the Other Reindeer (TV Movie)

"On Whiskers, On Lola, On Cheryl and Meryl" (Episode from *Brandy and Mr. Whiskers*)
"Road to the North Pole" (Episode from *Family Guy*)
Santa, Baby! (2001, TV Movie)
Santa Baby (2006, TV Movie)
Santa Claws (Direct-to-Video)
Santa Who? (TV Movie)
"Santa-Witch" (Episode from *The Gumby Show*)
The Search for Santa Paws (Direct-to-Video)
Snow 2: Brain Freeze (TV Movie)
Snuffy, the Elf Who Saved Christmas (TV Short Film)
"The Super Special Gift" (Episode from *Wow! Wow! Wubbzy!*)
'Twas the Night (TV Movie)
"Uncle Grandpa: Christmas Special" (Episode from *Uncle Grandpa*)
The Year Without a Santa Claus (1974, TV Special)

Santa Switches Roles with Someone Else (3)

Santa Switch (TV Movie)
The Great Santa Claus Switch (TV Special)
A Very Barry Christmas (TV Movie)

Santa's Magic Trappings Lose Their Powers (1)

Santa's Magic Toy Bag (TV Short Film)

Santa's Magic Trappings Lost or Stolen (9)

"The Action Elves Save Christmas Eve" (Episode from *The Backyardigans*)
"Anti-Claus Is Coming to Town" (Episode from *Big Wolf on Campus*)
Beethoven's Christmas Adventure (Direct-to-Video)
Christmas Is Here Again (Direct-to-Video)
"The Magic Sack of Mr. Nicholas" (Episode from *The Smurfs*)
My Friends Tigger and Pooh: Super Sleuth Christmas Movie (Direct-to-Video)
Noddy Saves Christmas (Direct-to-Video)

Santa's Magic Crystal (Feature Film)
Spot's Magical Christmas (TV Special)

Sleigh Stuck in Sand or Snow (3)

"Diego Saves Christmas!" (Episode from *Go, Diego, Go!*)
"Mickey Saves Santa" (Episode from *Mickey Mouse Clubhouse*)
Santa and the Ice Cream Bunny (Feature Film)

Sleigh Taken from North Pole by Someone Other Than Santa (2)

The Elf Who Didn't Believe (TV Movie)
Mrs. Santa Claus (TV Movie)

Supernatural Problems (2)

Santa Claus (1959, Feature Film)
The Smurfs Christmas Special (TV Movie)

Time Disturbance (1)

Hoops and Yoyo Ruin Christmas (TV Short Film)

Villains Attempt to Sabotage or Take Over the North Pole (29)

The Boy Who Saved Christmas (TV Movie)
"Christmas Con Carne" (Episode from *Evil Con Carne*)
"Christmas Evil" (Episode from *Robotboy*)
Christmas in Cartoontown (Direct-to-Video)
Christmas Rescue (TV Short Film)
The Christmas That Almost Wasn't (Feature Film)
"A Doomed Christmas" (Episode from *T.U.F.F. Puppy*)
Fred Claus (Feature Film)
A Freezerburnt Christmas (TV Short Film)
The Great Santa Claus Switch (TV Special)
Hercules Saves Christmas (TV Movie)
"Holiday Hi-Jynx" (Episode from *Pokémon*)
Howdy Doody's Christmas (TV Short Film)
"I'm Dreaming of a White Ranger" (Episode from *Mighty Morphin' Power Rangers*)
Inspector Gadget Saves Christmas (TV Short Film)
"Nilus the Sandman: The Boy Who Dreamed Christmas" (Episode from *Nilus the Sandman*)
Once Upon a Christmas (TV Movie)
Raggedy Ann and Andy in the Great Santa Claus Caper (TV Short Film)
Santa Baby 2: Christmas Maybe (TV Movie)
The Santa Claus Brothers (TV Movie)
Santa Claus: The Movie (Feature Film)
The Santa Clause 3: The Escape Clause (Feature Film)
Santa vs. the Snowman (TV Special)
Saving Santa (Direct-to-Video)
The Secret World of Santa Claus (TV Series)
The Trolls and the Christmas Express (TV Short Film)
'Twas the Fight Before Christmas (TV Special from *The Powerpuff Girls*)
Twice Upon a Christmas (TV Movie)
When Santa Fell to Earth (Feature Film)

Villains Put Characters on Santa's Naughty List (1)

"It's a SpongeBob Christmas!" (Episode from *SpongeBob SquarePants*)

Villains Sabotage Presents (3)

"The Last Christmas" (Episode from *Bruno the Kid*)
"Scrooge Loose" (Episode from *The Gumby Show*)
Regular Show: The Christmas Special (TV Short Film)

Villains Threaten Orphans' Christmas (1)

Bratz Babyz Save Christmas: The Movie (Direct-to-Video)

A Wish Gone Bad (1)

Richie Rich's Christmas Wish (Direct-to-Video)

Index

Abbott, Kelsy 302
Abel, Jonathan 103
Abel, Sierra 237
Abell, Alistair 234
Abrams, Rita 107
Abreu, Laura 68
A.C. Gilbert Company 155
Ace Ventura: Pet Detective 201, 321
Ackelson, Jon 136
"Action Elves" 4
The Action Elves Save Christmas Eve 3, 323
Adair, Mike 122, 123
Adam (biblical character) 252
Adams, Don 135
Adamson, Brad 165
Addante, David 44
Addante, Shylah 44
Adkins, Trace 67
Adler, Charlie 17, 42, 104, 190
Adler, Evan W. 129
Adorf, Mario 63
The Adventures of Felix 88, 89
The Adventures of Jimmy Neutron: Boy Genius 120, 121, 122, 323
The Adventures of Noddy 185
Adventures of Sonic the Hedgehog 270, 271
The Adventures of Spot 275
Agenor, Sandro 263
Aguilar, Joe M. 160
Aguirre, José Luis 217, 218
Ahrens, Lynn 27
Air Bud 216
Air Buddies 216, 236, 259
Alan, Lori 138
Alaskey, Joe 309
Alaux, David 273
Alazraqui, Carlos 91, 277, 304
Alban, Carlo 82
Albert, Edward 149
Albright, Landry 72
Alcorn, Keith 239
Alexander, Casey 302
Alexander, David 30
Alexander, Jason 124, 155
Alf 249
Alfred, Roy 220
Alkain, Anjel 170
"All Because of Me" 51
"All I Really Want for Christmas" 204
All I Want for Christmas 240

"All I Want for Christmas Is You" 82
The All Nighter Before Christmas 4, 320
Allard, Kent 140
Allen, Christa B. 289
Allen, Dayton 127
Allen, Sean 300
Allen, Tim 224, 225, 226, 228, 229
Allwine, Wayne 162
"Almost Christmas Day" 84
"Almost Young" 168
Als der Weihnachtsmann vom Himmel fiel 306
"Als ich bei meinen Schafen wacht" 291
Altiere, Daniel 21
Altiere, Steven 21
Altman, Shelly 126
Altolagirre, Segundo 170
Alvarez, Robert 42, 288, 302
"Amazing Grace" 9
The Amazing World of Gumball: Christmas Episode 6, 25, 159, 164, 180, 240, 259, 269, 323
American Dad! 95, 96, 321
American Flyer trains 155
American Idol 119, 186
Amir, Gideon 318
Amritraj, Ashok 25, 80
Amundsen, Tom 31
Anasti, Tedd 14
Andersen, Hans Christian 35, 212
Anderson, Clark 209
Anderson, Dan 291
Anderson, Jeffrey M. 144
Anderson, Matt 292
Anderson, William Kevin 165
The Andrews Sisters 124
The Andy Griffith Show 265
An Angel for Christmas 8, 320
Angelou, Maya 81
Angels Sing 9, 236, 320
"Angels We Have Heard on High" 252, 278
Angiulli, Anthony 111
Animagic 207, 314
Animal Planet 113
Ann-Margret 228
Anne of Green Gables 23, 106
Anselmo, Tony 162
Antarctica 6, 179
Antebi, Cary 109
Anthon, Curt 103

Anthony, Emjay 143
Anti-Claus Is Coming to Town 10, 322, 323
L'Apprenti Père Noël 242
Arcelus, Sebastian 68
Argoitia, Joxe Ramón 170
Arkin, Alan 228
Armstrong, Curtis 20
Arnesen, Finn 45
Arnold, Michael William 75
Arnold, Tom 21, 27
Aronson, Billy 251
Arrington, James 278
Arriola, Armando 217
Arroyo, Danny 114
Arthur Christmas 11–13, 321
Artzi, Ami 54
"As Long As There's Christmas" 19
Aschner, Michael 209, 211
Asfur, Anthony 34
Ashby, Emily 7, 16, 44, 55, 74, 75, 78, 84, 86, 88, 91, 101, 119, 123, 130, 159, 173, 196, 197, 214, 215, 247, 272, 302, 318
Ashley, Karan 131, 132
Ashmore, Aaron 60
Asner, Ed 50, 155, 188, 200
ASPCA 21
Asperschlager, Erich 106, 152
Assefi, Christopher 263
Astin, Sean 178, 236
Atencio, Luke 37
Atoms, Maxwell 21, 22, 41
Attack of the 50-Foot Woman 262
Auberjonois, Rene 267
Aubert, Deanna 304
August Burns Red (band) 97
Austin, Jake T. 68
Autry, Gene 206
Avanzino, Peter 125, 313
Avellán, Elizabeth 10
"Avenue A" 168
"Away in a Manger" 278
Axelrod, Robert 132
Axlerod, David 82
Axton, Hoyt 64

"Baby Jesus Is Born" 29
The Baby Smurf 14, 154, 266
Baby's First Christmas 13, 154, 321
Bach, John 178
Back at the Barnyard 15, 16, 323
Back to the Future 81, 202

Index

The Backyardigans 3, 323
Badelt, Klaus 254
Bader, Diedrich 235, 259
Baget, Jesse 282, 283
Baget, Lisa 283
"La Baguette Magique" 261
Bailey, Brennan 75
Bailey, Jason 173
Baird, Robert L. 196
Bakalian, Peter 213
Baker, Avion 3
Baker, Carly 92
Baker, Dee Bradley 91, 97, 162
Baker, Leigh Allyn 16
Baker, Martin G. 173
Bakker, Daan 63
Bakula, Scott 194
Baldry, Long John 156, 183, 270
Baldwin, Alec 98
Baldwin, Daniel 61, 98
Baldwin, Gerard 14, 267
Baldwin, Stephen 98
Baldwin, William 98
Ball, Marcia 9
Ball, Sonja 126
Ball, Yasmeene 292
Bally Midway Manufacturing Company/Namco, Ltd. 40
"Balthazar Can't Make Up His Mind" 262
"Balthazar Ne Sait Pas ce qu'il Veut" 262
Bamford, Maria 304
Banas, Carl 206, 293, 313
Banas, John 179
Baniszewski, Dick 103
Banks, Elizabeth 98
Bannon, Mark 100
Bannon, Michael 100
Baranski, Christine 72
Barasch, Nicholas 3
Barber, Gary 201
Barbera, Joseph 46, 58, 95, 245
Barbera, P.J. 34
Barbi, Shane 140
Barbi, Sia 140
Barbi Twins 139, 140
Bargiel, Jeremy 22
Bargiel, Nina 22
Barinaga, Eduardo 170
Barker, Mike 95
Barnhart, Jennifer 84
Barnholtz, Barry 74, 75, 76
A Barnyard Christmas Special 15–17, 323
Barnyard: The Original Party Animals 15
Baron, Sandy 170
Barr, Douglas 186, 187
Barr, Kathleen 33, 34, 142, 156, 176, 209, 210
Barrett, Brendon Ryan 33
Barrett, Melissa 150
Barretta, Bill 172
Barrie, J.M. 81, 84, 136, 198
Barrymore, Drew 188, 189. 204
Bartelman, Chris 234
Basaraba, Gary 193
Bass, Jules 165, 208, 299, 300, 314, 316, 317

Bastian, Larry 29
Bastien, Charles E. 92
Bates, Kathy 50, 98
Bathory, Melissa 8
Batman (series) 114
Battle of the Bulbs 288
Baum, L. Frank 102, 308
Baumel, Mikaila 175
Baumgarten, Marjorie 239
Bauza, Eric 301
Baxter, Meredith 60
Baynham, Peter 13
Beach, Andrea 29, 67
Beach, John 47
Beal, Joseph 142
Beals, Jennifer 180
Bean, Charlie 45
"Bear in Mind" 242
The Bears Who Saved Christmas 17, 321
Beaumont, Hugh 122
"Beautiful Like Me" 209
Beauty and the Beast 19
Beauty and the Beast: The Enchanted Christmas 2, 18–20, 320
Beavis and Butt-Head 199
Beck, Jerry 107
Beck, Martine 245
Beck, Rufus 307
Beck, Sarah 63
Beck, Vincent 220
Bedard, Michael 220
Beers, Heather 43
Beers, Steve 205
Beethoven (film series) 20
Beethoven, Ludwig van 7, 20
Beethoven's Christmas Adventure 20–21, 51, 102, 322, 323
La Befana 125, 261
The Beggar Maiden 35
Behnke, John 141
Bela, Dalila 88
Belden, Fred 212
Belding, Stephanie 286
Belgen, Kristin 291
Bell, Dorla 26
Bell, Drake 87, 88, 178
Bell, Michael 14, 309
Bell, Mike 145, 295
La Belle et la Bête 19
Belle's Magical World 19
Bellette, Tony 258
Belushi, James 256
Bemelmans, Ludwig 151
Benford, Vassal 278
Benjamin, Jon 204
Bennett, Carolyn 255
Bennett, Jeff 5, 16, 19, 77, 146
Bennett, Jeff Glen 78
Bennett, Mairon 314
Bennett, Tony 209
Bennett, Zachary 182
Benodin, Lesley 291
Benrubi, Abraham 66
Benson, Jay 29
Benson, Ray 9
Benson, Robbie 19
Benvenuti, Leo 225, 227, 230
Berardinelli, James 227

Bergen, Bob 227
Berger, Anna 111
Berger, Melique 179
Bergman, Mary Kay 17
Berkenpas, Deb 51
Berle, Milton 142
Berlioz, Hector 267
Berman, Steven H. 192, 301
Bernard, Crystal 157, 263
Bernard, Paul F. 148
Bernardin, Marc 296
Berner, Geoff 54
Berney, Lou 10
Bernsen, Corbin 237
Bernstein, Gregory 29
Bernstein, Jonathan 303
Bernstein, Sara 29
"The Best Christmas Ever" 209
"The Best Christmas of All" 168
Bestor, Kurt 136
Betsy Wetsy dolls 295
Betty Boop 39
"Beyond the Stars" 209
Bianchi, Stephanie 104
Bianco, Robert 125
Biancolli, Amy 13
Bianculli, David 312
Biehn, Benjamin 307
Biel, Jessica 205
Bieling, Raban 63
Bielsky, Jordan 231
Big Bad Voodoo Daddy (performer) 189
Big Wolf on Campus 10, 322, 323
Billing, Roy 303
Billingslea, Beau 180
Billy and Mandy Save Christmas 2, 21–23, 90, 321
Binsley, Richard 201
Bird, Brian 29
Birdsong, Mary 129
Birney, Betty G. 152
Bishopric, Thor 263
The Bishop's Wife 193
Bizzarro, Michelle 103, 104
Björklund, Timothy 191
Black, Clint 211
Black, Don 19
Blakeslee, Susanne 88, 161
Blanc, Mel 45, 94
Blanchard, Rachel 31
Blanck, Curtis 150
Blanford, Josh 43
Blanford, Sarah 43
Blaustein, Addie 116
Blazer, Judy 27
Bleiman, David 297, 298
Blessed, Brian 7
Bliss, Lucille 14, 94, 154, 267
Blok, Lourens 64
Bloom, George Arthur 105
Bloom County 309
Bloomberg, Michael 172
Blu, Sue 107
The Blue Arrow 125
"Blue Christmas" 314
Blum, Steve 179
Blye, Garry 8
Blyton, Enid 185
Boakye, Kwesi 7

Bobby Goldsboro Presents Snuffy, the Elf Who Saved Christmas 270
Bobo, Jonah 3
Bocarde, Kevin 233
Bocquelet, Ben 6, 7
Bodul, Megan 254
Bodyfelt, Kirk 65
Boen, Earl 78, 117, 146, 164
Boerner, Heather 70
Bogush, Beth 4
Bolen, Sophie 265
Bolke, Bradley 314
Bollen, Roger 91, 92
Bompoint, Jean-Louis 263
Bond, Timothy 31
Bonkers 163, 322, 323
Bonner, Frank 149
Bookbinder, Ben 72
Booky and the Secret Santa 23–24, 320
Boone, Larry 67
Booth, Lindy 147
Booth, Shirley 165, 314, 315
Boothby, Ian 33
Boothe, James 142
Boreanaz, David 204
Borsos, Phillip 194
Borstein, Alex 204
Bosch, Johnny Yong 131, 132
Bosley, Tom 90, 216
Bosze, Michael 100
Bourne, Larz 39
Bourque, Andre 24
"Une Bouteille À la Mer" 262
Bouvard, Laurence 44
Bouwens, Nancy 126
Bowen, Bob 97
Bower, John 146
Bowie, Douglas 174
The Boy Who Saved Christmas 7, 24–25, 79, 100, 105, 109, 148, 159, 164, 180, 221, 240, 259, 269, 272, 273, 274, 285, 308, 322, 324
"The Boy Who Wished to Be Little Again" 261
Boyd, Linda 34
Boyd, Mark 264
Boyle, Bob 276, 277
Boyle, Peter 226, 228
Boyle, Susan 37
Boymel, Evan 230
Braden, Hub 169
Bradshaw, John 30, 286
Bram Stoker's Dracula 22
Branco, Diane Woods 184
"Brand New Kind of Christmas Song" 94
Brandt, Lesley-Ann 147
Brandy and Mr. Whiskers 190, 323
Bratz Babyz Save Christmas: The Movie 25–26, 324
Braunstein, Bill 146
Bravo, Ciara 130
Brayton, Timothy 19, 212
Brazeau, Jay 26, 270
Brazzi, Rossano 58, 59, 60
Breathed, Berkeley 309, 310
Breeze, Byron 84
Breitkopf, Kyle Harrison 101
Brémond, Olivier 260, 263

Brennan, John G. 204
Breslin, Spencer 227, 228
Breton, Pascal 260, 263
Bricklin, Julia 177
Bricusse, Leslie 223
Bridges, Chris "Ludacris" 98
Bridges, Lloyd 133, 134
Briggs, Christopher 10
Bright, Pat 299
Brill, Fran 84, 109
Brinckerhoff, Burt 136
Britton, Connie 9
Broadbent, Jim 12, 101, 102
Brockman, Jake 155
Brodnax, Al 275
Brook, David 67
Brooklyn Youth Chorus 84
Brooks, David H. 119
Brooks, Eric 67
Brooks, Garth 29
Brooks, Kix 67
Brooks, Mel 112, 121
Brooks, Randy 107
Brooks and Dunn (singing group) 67
Brookshier, Luke 138, 139
"Brothers" (song) 165
Brown, Charles 150
Brown, Clancy 97, 138
Brown, Don 53, 142
Brown, Jared F. 278, 279
Brown, Kimberly 47
Browngardt, Peter 301
Brownridge, Will 51, 74, 75, 76, 138, 171, 189, 205, 221, 260, 288, 310
Bruce, Ken 78, 161
Brunetti, Laurie John 26
Bruno the Kid 146, 324
Bruno the Kid: The Animated Move 146
Bruzzesse, Gianna 3
Bryan, Michelle 78
Bryar, Nickie 246
bûche de Noël 151, 263
Buckley, Lisa 249
Buckman, Adam 214
Buechler, John Carol 150
Buffy the Vampire Slayer 11
Build-A-Bear Workshop 119
Bulgarelli, Diana 209
Bullock, S. Scott 161
Bump in the Night 297, 298, 320, 322
Bumpass, Rodger 138
Burdge, Mark 136
Burgan, Jessica 254
Burian-Mohr, Eleanor 135
Burke, Delta 317
Burkholder, Max 175
Burnett, Alan 154
Burns, J. Stewart 312
Burns, Rich 268, 269
Burr, Ty 229
Burrell, Maryedith 134, 166
Burrs, Marcia Ann 157
Burton, Adam 21, 41
Burton, Corey 162, 275
Burton, Hilarie 145
Burton, Tim 283, 285
Busey, Gary 205

Bush, John 309
Buster, Jacob 43
Buster and Chauncey's Silent Night 26–28, 320
Butcher, Paul 237
Buteyn, Dina 6
Butler, Daniel 84
Butler, Daws 58, 198
Buza, George 31
Buzz Lightyear of Star Command 116, 117, 319
Byner, John 309

Caballero, Mark 139
Cabel, Stéphane 263
Cabot, Sebastian 66
Cabral, Troy 249
Cade, Sherry Hackney 51
"Un Cadeau pour Deux" 261
"Un Cadeau pour le Père Noël" 261
Cain, Bill 195
Cain, Dean 31, 34, 74, 75, 76, 264, 282
Caine, Janet 264
Calabrese, Russell 22
California Institute for the Arts 199
Califra, John 84
Calinescu, Max 197
Call, John 220, 221
Call Me Claus (film) 28–30, 173, 243, 322
"Call Me Claus" (song) 29
Callaway, William 14, 154
Calo, Nancy 90
Caloz, Michael 126
Calvet, Clément 45, 243
Camacho, Marc 263
Camacho, Melissa 129, 200
Cameron, Cody 64, 65
Cameron, Kirk 251, 252, 253
Cameron, Patsy 14
Camp, Hamilton 14, 154
Campbell, Bruce 147
Campbell, Douglas 191
"Can Santa Be Black?" 28
Canadian Broadcasting Corporation 174
Canby, Vincent 223
Cancel Christmas 30, 320
Cannon, Bob 140
"Can't Believe It's Christmas" 291
Canterbury, Chandler 9
Cantos, Bill 175
Canuel, Erik 11
Capizzi, Duane 201
Carden, Gary 194
Cardenas, Steve 131, 132
Cardon, Sam 236
Cardona, René 219
Carey, Joe 248
Carey, Mariah 72
Carlson, Bev 123
Carlson, Len 293, 314
Carlson, Mandalynn 264, 265
Carmichael, Caitlin 67
Carney, Art 108, 109, 124, 181
"Carol of the Bells" 83, 97
Carolla, Adam 117
Carpenter, Edwin L. 31, 60, 62, 67, 76

Index

Carr, Kevin 130, 260, 299
Carrara-Rudolph, Leslie 84
Carrasco, Jon 192, 301
Carrey, Jim 71, 72, 73, 201
Carroll, Willard 309
Carson, Ben 252
Carson, Johnny 286
Carter, Adrienne 176
Carter, Tim 84
Carteret, Laura de 240
Cartoon Network 6, 21, 42, 44, 128, 199, 245, 247, 294, 296, 301, 302
Casablanca 298
Casado, Desiree 82
The Case for Christmas 30–31, 321
Casey, Todd 144
Cashman, Shaun 22
Casper 32
Casper the Friendly Ghost 31, 38, 39, 89
Casper's Haunted Christmas 30, 31–33, 39, 319
Cass, David, Jr. 237
Cassady, Charles, Jr. 225
Cassidy, Alice 140
Castaneda, Rickie 31
Castellaneta, Dan 188, 189
Castle, Aimée 10
Castle, Nick 297
CatDog 304, 319
Cate, Field 216
categories of reasons for saving Christmas 319–324: aliens threaten Santa or Earth 319; animals threaten Santa 319; atheist wrecks Christmas 319; Christmas cancelled/war effort 319; Christmas commercialism 319; Christmas countdown disrupted 319; Christmas decorations/presents lost/stolen 319; Christmas every day 320; Christmas presents destroyed 320; Christmas spirit lost 320; Christmas traditions in jeopardy 320; cynicism/disbelief, bad consequences 320; electronics problems 320; elves/reindeer/North Pole on strike/revolution 320; financial problems/poverty 320; ghost/monster 320; holiday argument 320; inclement weather 321; letters not mailed to Santa 321; mechanical problems 321; neglected Christmas 321; North Pole suffers 321; prospectors' interference 321; reindeer kidnapped/missing/in trouble 321; robot Santa terrorist 321; Santa bankrupt/bewitched/dies/dying 321; Santa/elves/reindeer sick/injured/incapacitated 323; Santa finds successor 322; Santa in court 321, 322; Santa kidnapped 322; Santa loses powers 322; Santa mistaken for intruder/UFO 322; Santa must marry 322; Santa quits 322, 323; Santa slandered 323; Santa switched 323; Santa trappings lose power 323, 324; Santa vampire 321; sleigh crashes 322; sleigh stuck 324; sleigh taken 324; supernatural problems 324; time disturbance 324; villains 324; wish gone bad 324
Cavadini, Cathy 294
Cavaliere, Felix 242
Cavallari, Megan 46
Cavanagh, Ken 291
Cavanagh, Megan 121
Cavanagh, Tom 267, 268
Cavanaugh, Christine 141
Ceccarelli, Marc 138, 139
Cecconi, Mike 110
Cedars, Stephen 282
Cedric the Entertainer (performer) 159
Chabert, Lacey 292
Chaffee, Winnie 47
Chali 2Na (performer) 179
Chalk, Garry 209, 210, 270
Chalke, Sarah 196
Chambers, Munro 20
Chandler, Kyle 178
Chaney, Lon, Jr. 10
Chang, Justin 229
Chankin, James 62
Chaplin, Paul 218
Chapman, Keith 197, 198
Charendoff, Tara 313
Charles, Max 186
A Charlie Brown Christmas 69, 70, 253, 312
Charmed 11
Chase, Gary 107
Chase, Harry 68
Chase, Thomas 78
Chele, Vic Dal 177
Chen, Sandie Angulo 99, 236, 252
Cherry, John 86
Cheynet, Justine 101
Chialtas, George 68
Chilian, Mike 302
Chilton, Eve 126
Chin, Tiffany 36
Chioran, Juan 165
Choi, Jin 106
Choi, Melody B. 259
Choquet, Christian 263
Christensen, Kyle E. 248
Christianson, Paul 90
Christie, Paul 129
A Christmas Adventure from a Book Called Wisely's Tales 33, 34, 321
Christmas and Elves Lord 169
The Christmas Angel 34–36, 52, 320
The Christmas Angel: A Family Story 36
The Christmas Angel: A Story on Ice 36–37, 319
"Christmas (Bah, Bug and Hum)" 189
The Christmas Candle 37–38, 320
A Christmas Carol 28, 51, 59, 112, 128, 129, 143, 205, 231, 257, 312, 313
"Christmas Chimes Are Calling (Santa, Santa!)" 299
"Christmas Cold" 236
Christmas Comes but Once a Year 38–39, 320
Christmas Comes to Pac-Land 39–41, 322
"Christmas Comes Tomorrow" 175
Christmas Con Carne 41–42, 324
"The Christmas Conference" 261
The Christmas Conspiracy 42–43, 320
The Christmas Dragon 43–44, 321
"Christmas Eve in Wompkee Wood" 306
"Christmas Eve Montage" 284
"Christmas Eve/Sarajevo 12/24" 200
"Christmas Every Day" 81
Christmas Evil 44–45, 324
"The Christmas Express" 293
Christmas Flintstone 45–46, 53, 55, 95, 126, 167, 183, 207, 277, 316, 323
"Christmas for Dudley" 262
"Christmas Fright" 256
Christmas in Cartoontown 46–47, 324
"Christmas in Oberndorf" 27
The Christmas Invasion 47–50, 319
Christmas Is 66
Christmas Is Here Again (film) 50–52, 323
"Christmas Is Here Again" (song) 51
"Christmas Is More" 236
"Christmas Is the Best Time of the Year" 234
"Christmas Is the Reason" 278
The Christmas Miracle 35, 52–53, 320
The Christmas Orange 46, 53–54, 55, 167, 277, 321, 322
The Christmas Path 54, 320
Christmas Present Time 46, 55, 167, 207, 277, 322
Christmas Rescue 55–56, 319, 324
A Christmas Snow 56–57, 320
"The Christmas Song" 29
A Christmas Story (cartoon) 57–58, 94, 157, 297, 321
A Christmas Story (film) 16, 22, 90, 96, 225, 281, 295, 312, 318
The Christmas That Almost Wasn't 58–60, 181, 324
"Christmas Town" 211
A Christmas Visitor 60–61, 320
"Christmas, Why Can't I Find You?" 72
"A Christmas Wish" 254
"Christmas Wishes" 306
Christmas with a Capital C (film) 61–62, 319
"Christmas with a Capital C" (song) 61
Christmas with a Capital C—Snow: The Deluxe Edition 61
Christmas with the Kranks 9
"Christmastime Is Here" 9
"Christmastime Is Killing Us" 204
A Christmoose Carol 63
A Christmoose Story 62–64, 322
The ChubbChubbs! 64, 65

The ChubbChubbs Save Xmas 64–65, 322, 323
Church, Francis P. 134
Church, Thomas Haden 200
Church of St. Nicholas 26
Ciminera, Michael 74, 75, 76
Cinematic Titanic 221
The City That Forgot About Christmas 65–66, 321
Clarabell the Clown 127
Clark, Jay 212
Clark, Kyle 233
Clark, Maxine 120
Clark, Oliver 47, 85
Clark, Ronald 114
Clark, Spencer Treat 47
Clarke, Cam, 16, 78, 107
Clarke, Maura 305, 306
Clarke, Noel 48, 254
Clarke, Sudsy 234
Clary, Jennifer 43
Clash, Kevin 81, 84
Claybourne, Doug 86
Cleveland, Griffin 236
Clinton, Bill 82
Clinton, Paul 227
Clinton, Roger, Jr. 98
Clokey, Art 240, 241, 257
Close, Glenn 146
Coduri, Camille 48
Coe, Liz 303
Cohen, Ari 155
Cohen, David X. 312
Cohen, Devan 197
Cohn, Marjorie 88
Cohn, Mindy 256
Colbert, Ezra James 230
A Cold, Dead, White Christmas 128
Cole, Chelsey 149
Coleman, Dabney 173
Coleman, Townsend 27
Collette, Toni 143
Colliander, Helen 31
Collier, Ken 256
Collins, Blake Jeremy 202
Collins, Joan 254
Collins, Karley Scott 204
Collins, Suzanne 213, 277
Collision, Phil 49
Color Classics 38
Colton, Greg 205
"Come, Come All Ye Whos" 72
Comedy Central 280, 310
Commando 265
Compo, Alexandria 111
Conde, Antonio Días 217
Coney Island, Donna 47
Conforti, Donna 220, 221
"Le Congrès de Noël" 261
Conley, Corrine 206
Connery, Jason 259
Connick, Harry, Jr. 9
Connor, Benton 200
Connor, Kevin 233
Connor, Kit 102
Conried, Hans 293
Conti, Alexander 268, 269
Conway, Tim 216, 254
Cook, Victor 118
Cooke, Wendy 79, 80

Cooksey, Jon 220
Coolio (artist) 281
Cooper, Jackie 182
Coopersmith, Jerome 300
Copley, Andi 119
Coppola, Chris 216 235
Corden, Henry 94
Corlett, Ian James 119
Corliss, Richard 285
Cornelius, David 310
Cornwell, Judy 222
Corraza, Vince 201
Corwin, Carol 17
Cosmo, James 231, 232
Costa, Lella 125
Costello, Brian 114, 126, 178, 194, 243, 248
Coulier, Dave 90, 146
A Country Christmas 66–67, 322
Cowan, Brian J. 281, 312
Cowans, James 265
Cox, Jennifer Elise 235
Cox, Tom 214, 215, 269
Cox, Tony 87, 112
crackers (noisemakers) 48
Cracknell, Ryan 86, 165, 221
Craig, Tony 123
Craigmyle, Lynda 165
Cranston, Bryan 219, 296
Crenshaw, Randy 175
Crewson, Wendy 225, 227, 228
Cricks, Lisa 36
Critchlow, Roark 157
Crocker, Carter 184
Cronin, Jamie 234
Cronkite, Walter 280
Croop, Kari 165
Crosby, Bing 124, 143, 204
Cross, Richard 248
Crow, Sheryl 84
Crown, Ron 277
Crowther, Bosley 59
Cruchley, Murray 183
Cruickshank, Jim 180
Crum, Gordon 178
Cuck, Louis J. 22, 42
Culkin, Macaulay 202
Cullen, Peter 41, 175
Culliford, Pierre "Peyo" 13, 153, 265, 267
Cummings, Jim 16, 27, 141, 159, 164, 175, 275, 298, 304
Cuoco, Kaley 190
Curl, Tiffany 84
Curley, Sean 3
Curry, Tim 19, 254
Curtis, Jamie Lee 209
Curtis, Keene 202
Curtis, Tony 98
Cushner, Jeremy 298
"A Cut Above the Rest" 19
Cyrenne, Randall 299

Dafoe, Sarah-Anne 244, 245
Daguanno, Brianna 101
Dahl, Rachel 254
Daily, E.G. 294
Daingerfield, Michael 201
Dakin, Kym 306
d'Alò, Enzo 126

Dalton, Devyn 88
Daly, Chris 103
Dangler, Anita 140
Dannacher, Lee 213
Darkwing Duck 140, 141, 319
Darling, Jennifer 298
Darnell, Eric 160
Daurio, Ken 227
Davenport, Madison 51
Davey and Goliath 241
David, Golda 136
Davidson, Tommy 240
Davidson, Troy 288
Davies, Russell T. 49
Davin, Christian 45
Davis, Chip 36
Davis, Christine 165
Davis, John A. 121, 239
Davis, Scott W. 212
Davis, Warwick 101
Dawber, Pam 17
Dawson, Velma 127
Day, Patrick Kevin 124
Daye, Steve 277
"The Days Still Remaining 'Til Christmas" 189
Dayton-Hudson Corporation 241
Dean, Laura 47
Dear, William 240
"Dear Mrs. Santa Claus" 168
De Azevedo, Lex 278
DeCarlo, Mark 121, 238
De Carlo, Yvonne 170
"Deck the Hall" 236
"Deck the Halls" 16, 278, 293
Decoisette, Sophie 263
Decter, Ed 227, 230
DeDonato, Colette 208
Deets, Elle 278
Degas, Rupert 44
DeKorte, Paul 58
Delaney, Chris 182
DeLaurentis, Ray 78, 88
Delcorte, Yvan 267
Delgado, Emilio 82
DeLisle, Grey 22, 42, 77, 91, 161, 190, 256, 277, 302
"Delivering Christmas" 172
Dell Antonia, K.J. 291
del Mar, Maria 302
Delugg, Milton 220
DeMarcus, Jay 67
De Nise, Tracy 138
Denny, Jon S. 134
DePaul, Brandon Michael 237
DeRosa, Francesca 61
Derryberry, Debi 78, 121
de Souza, Steven E. 106
Deters, Kevin 196
Détresse et Charité 34–36
Deus ex machina 189
Devane, William 60
DeVilliers, David 43
DeVine, Adam 302
De Vita, Christian 101
DeVitto, Mike 306
Devji, Qayam 26
Deyermond, Michael 259
Diana B (artist) 209
Diaz, Joey 74, 75, 76

Index

Diaz, Mercedes Jadea 307
Dick, Andy 111
Dick, Philip K. 281
Dickens, Charles 28, 51, 59, 63, 112, 128, 281, 312
Dickerson, Albert T., III 158
Dickerson, Rich 256
Dieckmann, Oliver 307
Diego Saves Christmas! 67–69, 322, 324
Di Fruscia, Nick 209
Dilger, Melinda Wunsch 123
Dillon, Oliver 175
Dillon, Teddy Lee 263
DiMaggio, John 5, 16, 281, 312
"Dino the Dinosaur" 45
DiNovi, Denise 285
Dinsmore, Bruce 263
Disher, Karen 131, 165
Disney, Walt 89
Disney Channel 91, 140, 151, 163, 174, 182, 190
Disney Junior 91, 101
Disney Studios 283
Distefano, Christian 197
Distress and Charity 35
DiTomasso, Jeanine 184
Dixon, Peg 206
"Do or Die" 254
"Do You Hear What I Hear?" 84
Doane, Darren 252, 253
Dobkin, David 99
Dobrev, Nina 159
Dobrofsky, Neal 187
Dobrofsky, Tippi 187
Dobson, Michael 34
Dobson, Paul 34, 210
Dochtermann, Rudy 182
"Doctor Finklestein/In the Forest" 284
Dr. Otto and the Riddle of the Gloom Beam 85
Dr. Seuss' How the Grinch Stole Christmas! (1966) 69–71, 283, 313, 319
Dr. Seuss' How the Grinch Stole Christmas (2000) 71–73, 227, 319
Dr. Stank (performer) 180
Doctor Who 47, 48, 319
Dodd, Cathal J. 105
Dodge, Jennifer 198
Doduk, Alex 107
The Dog Who Saved Christmas 73–74, 75, 76, 230, 282, 319
The Dog Who Saved Christmas Vacation 74–76, 319
The Dog Who Saved Easter 74, 75, 76
The Dog Who Saved Halloween 74, 75, 76
The Dog Who Saved Summer 74, 75, 76
The Dog Who Saved the Holidays 74, 75, 76–77, 319
Doi, Davis 185, 288
Dombrowski, Ronny 307
Don, Carl 220
Donnelly, Sean 80
Donovan, Elisa 73, 75, 76
"Don't Be a Jerk, It's Christmas" 138

"Don't Fall in Love" 19
Doohan, James 105
A Doomed Christmas 77–78, 324
Dora the Explorer 68
Doran, Cory 105
Dorn, Margaret 236
Dorn, Michael 42, 226, 228
Dot and Spot's Magical Christmas Adventure 78–79, 276, 322
Dotrice, Roy 150
Doty, George IV 256
Dougherty, Michael 144
Douglas, Buddy 85
Douglas, Clark 279
"Les Douze Travaux du Père Noël" 261
Dowie, Fran 34
Dowling, John, Jr. 289
DreamWorks Classics 32
"The Dreidel Song" 298
Dreisen, David 248
Dreyfuss, Richard 209
Drummond, Brian 26, 142
Dubuc, Nicole 175
Ducey, John 259
Duck Dynasty 252
Duck Tales 140
Dudek, Anne 236
Dufau, Oscar 14
Duffy, Colin 314
Duignan, Patricia Rose 298
Duke, Erica 230
Dumbo 124
Dunamis 104
Duncan, Felicity 55
Dunn, Teala 250
Dunne, Len 185
Duralde, Alonso 219, 222, 253
Durbin, Erik 97
Durning, Charles 81, 136, 166, 167, 168
Duval, Richard 273
Dye, John 191, 192, 300

Eagles, Greg 22
Earthquake (performer) 179
Eastwood, Jayne 145, 155
"Easy to Dream" 51
Eaton, Timothy 23
Eaton's Santa Claus Parade 23
Ebbie 28
Eberson, Sharon 49
Ebert, Roger 194, 224, 285
"Echo Carol" 291
Eckholdt, Steven 239
The Ed Sullivan Show 108, 109
Edelman, Gregg 27
Ederveen, Arjan 63
Edison, Thomas 123
Edmonson, Kat 9
Eek! The Cat 139, 322, 323
Eggerling, Gabe 243
Eguchi, Summer Anela 278
Eisenloeffel, Eva 64
elf 1, 12, 20, 22, 24–26, 28, 30, 34, 43, 46, 50, 64, 79–81, 83, 84, 88, 94, 97, 98, 102, 105, 107, 108, 109, 112, 113, 114, 118, 119, 122, 123, 124, 136, 142, 148, 149, 169, 170, 172, 179, 185, 186, 196, 198, 199, 200, 205, 207, 211, 212, 214, 215, 219, 224, 227, 228, 231, 232, 235, 237, 238, 240, 247, 248, 249, 253, 259, 260, 263, 269, 272, 298, 308, 316, 318, 321–324
The Elf and the Magic Key 25, 79, 81, 105, 109, 148, 221, 272, 274, 285, 308, 322
"An Elf Like Me" 254
The Elf That Rescued Christmas 247, 248
The Elf Who Didn't Believe 79–80, 324
The Elf Who Saved Christmas 79, 80–81, 84, 136, 198, 270, 322
The Elf Who Stole Christmas 169, 170
Elfman, Danny 284
"An Elf's Work Is Never Done" 46
Elijah (biblical character) 116
Ellingson, Annlee 10
Elliott, Mike 202
Ellis, Gill 184
Elmo & Patsy (performers) 107
Elmo Saves Christmas 81–83, 320
Elmo's Christmas Countdown 81, 82, 83–85, 136, 198, 319
elves 1–4, 8, 11, 14, 22, 24, 25, 43, 45, 56, 77, 80, 81, 85, 86, 88, 95, 97, 98, 108, 114, 115, 117, 119, 121, 124, 131, 132, 135, 139, 140, 142, 145, 150, 151, 160, 163, 164, 168, 169, 170, 173, 177, 178, 181, 184, 185, 186, 187, 196, 204, 205, 212, 214, 215, 216, 217, 222, 223, 224, 225, 227, 231, 237, 238, 240, 245, 246, 247, 248, 259, 260, 261, 262, 263, 268, 269, 270, 275, 276, 280, 281, 287, 293, 298, 306, 307, 308, 314, 315, 316
The Elves' Song" 293
"Elves' Work Song" 270
"Elvin's Rap" 180
Emes, Ian 171
"Enchanted Christmas" 19
"L'Enfant des Etoiles" 261
Engelbreit, Mary 156
Enslin, Karl 291
Epiphany 125, 261
Erector Set 155
Erickson, Ethan 236
Ernest Goes to Africa 86
Ernest Goes to Camp 85
Ernest Goes to Jail 86
Ernest Goes to School 86
Ernest in the Army 86
Ernest Rides Again 86
Ernest Saves Christmas 85–87, 224, 225, 322
Ernest Scared Stupid 86
Es ist ein Elch entsprungen 62
Estévez, Carlos 122
Estévez, Ramón 122
Evans, Josh Ryan 72
Eve (biblical character) 252
"Even a Miracle Needs a Hand" 299
"Every Christmas Eve" 223
"Every Day Can't Be Christmas" 82
"Everybody Glo" 104

Evil Con Carne 21, 41, 324
Ewaniuk, Jacob 101
Extreme Makeover: Home Edition 84

Fabian, Patrick 268
Fagerbakke, Bill 138
Fahn, Dorothy 179
A Fairly Odd Christmas 87–88, 161, 323
A Fairly Odd Movie: Grow Up, Timmy Turner! 87
The Fairly OddParents 87, 160, 161, 322
Fairman, Elly 55
"Faith (Gracie's Song)" 103, 104
Falconer, Olivia Steele 88, 292
Falk, Peter 289, 290
Fallows, Mike 220
Fam, C.J. 248
"Fame and Fortune" 206
Family Channel 151, 182, 214, 215
Family Guy 95, 97, 203, 323
"A Family Guy Christmas" 204
Famous Original Ray's Pizza 281
Famous Studios 32
Fancy, Richard 202
Fappiano, Bob 249
"Far Longer Than Forever" 278
Fares, Maria 126
Farmer, Bill 162
Fatal Attraction 146
Father Christmas 43, 44, 52, 56, 101, 102, 178, 240, 307
Faust, Lauren 295, 296
Fawkes, Michael 182, 183
Feather, Lorraine 176
"Feels Like Christmas" 107
Feffer, Jason 202
Feifer, Michael 74, 75, 76
Feinstein, Mara 82
Feiss, Dave 65
Feldman, Josh 235, 236
Feline Follies 88
Felix the Cat 88, 139, 163
Felix the Cat Saves Christmas 88–90, 230, 321
Felix the Cat Shatters the Sheik 89
"Felix the Cat Theme" 90
Fell, Sarah 7
Fellows, Scott 161
Fenyn, Larysa 182
Fernandez, Peter 47
Ferrara, Adam 288
Ferrara, Ed 171
Ferraro, Christine 83
Ferris, Pam 254
Fiddler on the Roof 111
Field, James 249
Fierstein, Harvey 81, 317
Figueiredo, Rodney 165
Filipenko, Cindy 54
Filippi, Nick 6
Filucci, Sierra 106, 217
Finding John Christmas 290
Fink, Hugh 173
Fink, Isabella 289
Fink, Karl 289
Finlay, Ian 263
Finn, Pat 234

Firesign Theater 281
Firestone, Scott 299
The First Day 182
"The First Nowell" 38
Fischer, Jeff 97
Fisher, Carrie 204
Fisher, Jim 108
The Fitzerino Singers 27
Fitzpatrick, Christian 222, 223
Fitzsymons, Patrick 92
Flaherty, Joe 174, 219
Flaherty, Stephen 27
Flanery, Lola 145
Flash Gordon (series) 127
Flatman, Barry 31
Fleischer, Dave 39
Fleischer, Max 38, 39
Fleischer Studios 38, 273
Fleming, John 30
Flicker Saves Christmas 90–92, 321
The Flight Before Christmas 92–93, 319
A Flintstone Christmas 46, 58, 93–95, 126, 175, 230, 316, 323
The Flintstones 45, 46, 93, 94, 137, 323
A Flintstones Christmas Carol 151, 152
Fliss, Robert von 132
Flitter, Josh 216, 235, 259
Florido, Hilary 200
"The Flying Carpet" 261
Flynn, Michael 43
Fo, Dario 125
Fogelman, Dan 99
Foley, Dave 196
Folkmann, Jason 61
Follows, Megan 23
Fonti, Stephen 204, 295
For Whom the Bell Tolls 97, 321
"For Whom the Sleigh Bell Tolls" 95–98
Foray, June 70, 154, 199
Ford, Alexandra 149
Ford, Colin 51
Fordham, Julia 256
Foreman, Ruth 212
Forman, Mike 289
Fornier, Paula 265
Foster, Allen 17
Foster, Jon 7
Foster, Liz 9
Foster, Matthew M. 264
Foster, Warren 46
14 Karat Soul (performers) 82
Fowler, John P. 230
Fox, Jack 29
Fox, Megan 205
Fox, Shayna 308
Fox, Sonny 59
Fox Kids 132, 139
Fox Network 95, 187, 203, 280, 310
Foxx, Jamie 84
Fracassi, Philip 236
Fragner, Lisa 112
Frakes, Jonathan 148
Fraley, Pat 184
Francis, Andrew 34
Francis, Stan 206
Francks, Cree Summer 314

Francks, Don 8
Francois, J.R. 263
Franich, Darren 144
Frank, Debra 156, 166, 240
Frank, Jason David 131, 132
frankincense 252
Fraser, Bonnie 258
Frawley, Garrett 214, 215
Frazier, Harry 79, 80
La freccia azzurra 125
Fred Claus 11, 98–100, 324
Fredericks, Roger 33
Freedman, Ian 54
Freedman, Robert L. 303
Freeman, Kathleen 202
Freeman, Martin 254
Freer, Sloan 166, 286
A Freezerburnt Christmas 25, 100, 324
Freilich, Jeff 21
Freud, Sigmund 249
Freund, Mandy 64
Frewer, Matt 147
The Friendly Ghost 32
Friendly Monsters 166, 167, 323
"Friends for Life" 259
Friesen, Beryl 293, 294
Frost, Harvey 158, 264
Frost, Kristen 4
Frost, Robert 83
Frostmas 228, 229
Frosty (snowman character) 9, 53, 64, 238, 298
Frosty the Snowman 205
The FTC Singers 90
Fukuto, Jay 277
Fullam, Paul Conway "Con" 305, 306
Funke, Cornelia 306
Furey, Mark 202
Furst, Stephen 117
Fusco, Paul 249
Futterman, Nika 91
Futurama 280, 310, 311, 321

Gabler, Deboragh 192, 301
Gagné, Christian 11
Gaines, Stephanie 290
Gale, Ed 232
Galeota, Cathy 68
Galindo, Rudy 36
Gallagher, David 202
Gallagher, Teresa 7
Gambertoglio, Bailey 243
Gant, Charles 102
Ganz, Scott 173
Garcia, Alex 144
Garcia, Jeffrey 16, 121
"Le Garçon qui Voulait Redevenir Petit" 261
Gardell, Billy 130
Garden of Eden 252
Gardner, Joan 66
gargon 36
Garner, Shay 212
Garner, Tom 184
Garrett, Brad 17, 51
Garth Brooks and the Magic of Christmas: Songs from Call Me Claus 29

Garver, Kathy 114
Gasaway, Mike 122
Gasiorowski, J. 263
Gates, Anita 155
Gates, Ken 116
Gaug, John R. 294
Gauger, Jon 107
Gay, Gilles 244
Gaynor, Gloria 90
Gaze, Christopher 151
Geffen, Marco van 63
Geisel, Theodor Seuss 69, 70
Geiss, Tony 82, 83
Gekko Saves Christmas 100–101, 319
Gelman, Pam 191, 251
Gemme, Aidan 235
General Electric Fantasy Hour 206
Genzlinger, Neil 10, 13
Germann, Greg 231
Gerson, Daniel 196
Gerstell, Ellen 78
Get Santa 20, 101–103, 322
Get Smart (series) 135
Get Smurfy 14, 154, 266
Getrost, Robin 307
Geurs, Karl 26
Ghali, Stacie 104
Ghostly Trio 32, 39
Giamatti, Paul 98, 99
Gibbon, Mark 88
Gibson, Charles 83
Gibson, Dave 179
Gibson, Henry 17
Gifford, Chris 68
The Gift 103–104, 105, 319
"The Gift of the Magi" 312
Gil, Arturo 114
Gilbert, Alfred Carlton 155
Gilbert, Matthew 112
Gildemeister, Christopher 62
Gilder, Sean 48
Gillet, Rachel 35
Gilligan's Island 190
Gillmor, Don 53
Gilvezan, Dan 17
Gisondo, Skyler 216
Gitelson, Rick 91, 92
"Give Your Friends an Easter Egg for Christmas" 82
"Give Your Heart a Try" 299
Glaser, Jon 129
Glass, Chuck 184
Glawson, Bruce 183
Gleason, Jackie 124
Gleason, Mary Pat 243
Glen, Edward 8
The Glo Friends 104
The Glo Friends Save Christmas 25, 79, 104–105, 109, 148, 221, 272, 274, 285, 308, 322
Glover, Candice 186
Glueckman, Alan Jay 136
Gnolfo, Richard 74, 75, 76
Go, Diego, Go! 67, 322, 324
Go Fish (band) 61
Gobel, George 299
"God Rest You Merry Gentlemen" 278
God Squad Dance Crew 252
Goddard, Robert 122
Goe, Bob 154
Goelz, Dave 172
Gogin, Michael Lee 149
gold 252
Gold, Martha 103, 104
Goldberg, Adam 111, 113
Goldberg, Dana 63
Goldberg, Jake 3
Goldberg, Marcy 26
Goldberg, Whoopi 28, 171, 210
The Golden Compass 97
Goldfine, Phillip B. 283
Goldman, Danny 14, 154, 267
Goldman, Paul D. 60
Goldsboro, Bobby 269, 270
Goldsmith, David 46
Goldthwait, Bobcat 140
Gomez, Hunter 289
"Good Things Come in Small Packages" 46
Goodchild, George 78
Goodman, John 138, 210, 211, 312, 316, 317
Goodman, Tommy 104
Goodson, Barbara 132
Goodwyn, Hannah 259
Gordon, Barry 41
Gordon, Brian J. 264
Gordon, George 14
Gordon, Zachary 64, 216, 259
gorgon 36
Gotta Catch Santa Claus 104, 105–107, 319
Gottfried, Gilbert 22
Gottlieb, Andrew 305
Goz, Harry 27
Graceman, Anna 278
Graham, Andrea 117, 132
Graham, Scott 231
Graham, Stephen 102
Grames, Renny 43
Grammer, Camille 166
Grammer, Kelsey 166
Grand, Jayne 116
"La Grande Petite Fille" 262
Grandma Got Run Over by a Reindeer (film) 107–108, 322
"Grandma Got Run Over by a Reindeer" (song) 107
"Grandma's Killer Fruitcake" 107
"Grandma's Spending Christmas with the Superstars" 107
"Grandpa's Gonna Sue the Pants Off Santa" 107
Grant, Christopher, Jr. 3
The Grapes of Wrath 117
Grate, Brenda 296, 297
Graves, Mic 7
Gray, Christopher 210
Grazer, Brian 73
"A Great and Grumpy Holiday" 277
Great Flood 28
The Great Santa Claus Switch 25, 79, 105, 108–109, 148, 221, 272, 274, 285, 308, 322, 323, 324
The Great Santa Rescue 66
The Great Toy Robbery 110, 319
Greco, Azer 286
Green, Dorothy 212
Green, Seth 204
The Green Mile 281
Greer, Judy 111
Gresham, Catie 90
Grey, Joel 299
Grieg, Edvard 271
Griffin, Danél 303
Griffin, Eddie 316, 318
Griffin, Jennifer 44
Griffin, Lynne 215
Griffin, Nonnie 8
Griffith, Andy 51
Griffiths, Richard 171
Grillo, Gene 16
The Grim Adventures of Billy and Mandy 21, 42, 321
Grim and Evil 21, 42
Grimes, Scott 97, 181, 182
Grimes, Tammy 299
Grinch (character) 69–73, 124, 140, 161, 169, 283, 313
The Grinch (film) 71
Grisham, John 53
Gritz, Jennie Rothenberg 39
Groening, Matt 188, 189, 280, 310
Gross, Jurgen 65
Gross, Ken 290
Groundhog Day (Feb. 2) 124
Grove, Logan 7
Gruber, Franz 26, 27
Gruelle, Johnny 198
"Grumpy Kids" 291
Gudegast, Tatiana 235
Guerrero, Crissy 138
Guest, Nick 254
The Guild of Thespian Puppets 110
The Guild of Thespian Puppets Save Christmas 110–111, 319
Gumby Adventures 240, 257
The Gumby Show 240, 257, 324
Gumby: The Movie 240, 257
Gundersen, Chad 57
Gunnarsson, Sturla 156
Guttenberg, Steve 157, 263
Guy, Scott 306
Guyot, Paul 148
Guzelian, Eddie 165
Gwynne, Fred 170

Haas, Ed 171
Haase, Gary 213
Haberer, Kevin 43
Hadar, Ronnie 132
Haddad, Paul 8
Hagen, Daniel 91
Hague, Albert 70
Haigh, Michael 178
Haigney, Michael 116
Haikala, Antii 248
Halder, Ron 119
Hale, Jeffrey 110
Hale, Jennifer 146, 295
Halfpenny, John 140
Hall, Bug 170, 171
Hall, Michael 201
"Hallelujah" 90
"Hallelujah Chorus" 303
Hallmark Cards 122
Hallmark Channel 31, 157, 166, 186, 187, 233, 237, 263, 264

Halloween 22, 33, 40, 61, 74, 75, 76, 118, 152, 182, 221, 283, 284
Halmi, Robert, Sr. 182
Halvorson, Gary 84
Hamill, Dorothy 36
Hamill, Mark 146, 200, 246, 256
Hamilton, Jocelyn 140
Hamilton, Margaret 153
Hamilton, Patricia 165
Hamilton, Scott 184
Hamlin, Harry 150
Hammil, Elijha 197
Hammond, Darrell 100
Handley, Randy 29
Handy Manny 90, 91, 321
Hanna, Elizabeth 314
Hanna, William 46, 58, 95, 245
Hanna-Barbera Studios 45, 93, 273
Hannan, Peter 304, 305
Hannelius, G. 235
Hanrahan, Jack 135
Hanukkah 2, 19, 22, 111, 113, 124, 132, 173, 189, 205, 237, 251, 298, 302
"Happy Day" 90
"Happy Who-lidays" 72
Harary, Ronnen 198
Hardwick, Chris 16
Hardy, Carla 63
Hardy, G.H. 312
Hardy, Hagwood 293
Hardy, Oliver 27
Hardy-Ramanujan number 312
Hargreaves, Adam 56
Hargreaves, Roger 56
"Hark the Herald Angels Sing" 236, 278
Harman, Barry 27, 104
Harman, J. Boyce, Jr. 169
Harnage, Phil 142, 314
Harness, Jill 175, 275
Harnois, Elisabeth 193
Harper, Erick 107
Harper, Sam 131
Harrison, Audie 302
Harshman, Margo 80
Hart, Emily 234
Hart, Melissa Joan 234
Hartl, John 285
Hartley, Mariette 157
Hartman, Amy 90
Hartman, Butch 77, 87, 88, 160, 161
Hartman, Haven 17
Hartman, Phil 27
Hartnell, William 48
Hartwig, Gay 94
Harvey, Alfred 202
Harvey Comics 32, 39, 202
Harvey Films 32
Harveytoons 32
Hasbro Toys 104, 176, 295
Hashiguchi, Juli 22
Haskell, Mary Donnelly 191, 300
Hathaway, Anne 83
"Hava Nagila" 298
"Have Yourself a Merry Little Christmas" 29
"Havoc in Toyland" 262
Hawes, James 49
Hawker, Luke 143

Hawthorne, Nigel 28, 29
Hayes, Phil 234, 270
Hayes, Sean 124
Hayes, Steve L. 156, 166, 240
Hays, Erika 90
Hays, Robert 237
Haysbert, Dennis 124
"He Needs Me" 168
Healey, Barry 194
Healey, Michael 75
"Heart and Soul of Christmas" 213
Heat Miser 165, 314, 316, 317
"The Heat Miser Song" 314
Heaton, Patricia 289
Heavy Trevy (performer) 256
The Hebrew Hammer 2, 111–113, 321
Hedley, Glenne 242
Hefferon, Michael B. 142
Heffley, Lynne 28
Hegner, Michael 93
Heim, Carrie Kei 222
Heintz, Tim 191
Heit, Jonathan Morgan 119
Hel (goddess) 143
Hello Kitty's Furry Tale Theater 313, 320
Hellouin, Guillaume 101
Hemingway, Ernest 97
Henderschott, Adam 17
Henderson, A.J. 263
Henderson, Saffron 34, 234
Hendrikse, Maryke 26
Hendrix, Elaine 166, 170
Henley, Raphi 253
Hennessey, Dan 201
Henry, O. 312
Henson, Jim 81, 83, 108, 109, 171, 173
Hercules Saves Christmas 113–114, 230, 324
"Here Comes Santa Claus" 314
"Here We Come A-Caroling" 110, 278
Here's Love 220
Herman, David 281
Herman, Jerry 168
Herman, Joly 22, 122, 260, 296, 312
Hernandez, Noemi 82
Herrmann, Keith 27
Hershon, Marc 233
Hervey, Cheston 253
Heyward, Andy 272
Heyward, Michael 151
Hickey, William 284
Hickman, Sara 9
Hicks, Leonard 220, 221
Hidaka, Masamitsu 116
Higgins, John Michael 98
Higginson, Torri 296
Hightower, Edward 114
Higlen, David 265
Hill, Christopher 275
Hill, Dana 141
Hill, Eric 275, 276
Hillenburg, Stephen 137
Hillis, Ali 235
Hilton, Paris 75
Hinchey, Don 66
Hinckley, David 247
Hines, Gregory 213
His Dark Materials 97

"Histoires de Trolls" 261
Hitler, Adolf 295
Ho! Ho! Horrors! 255
Hobbs, Valerie 152
Hodkinson, Mark 93
Hoff, Dean 6
Hoffman, Chad S. 240
Hoffman, Dustin 309, 310
Hogan, Gabriel 145
Hohlfeld, Brian 175
Holden, Stephen 238
"Holiday for Thieves" 27
Holiday Hi-Jynx 114–116, 319, 324
Holiday Time 116–118, 319
Holidaze: The Christmas That Almost Didn't Happen 118–119, 320
Holland, Savage Steve 88, 139, 140
Holley, Addison 101
Holley, Kallan 197
Holley, Peter 252
Holloway, Sterling 310
Holly, Buddy 142
Holly, Lauren 232, 286
Holly and Hal Moose: Our Uplifting Christmas Adventure 119–120, 321
"A Holly Jolly Christmas" 122, 206
Holly Jolly Jimmy 120–122, 323
"Holman's Christmas Cookies" 236
Holmes, Jacelyn 8
Holmes, Jonathan 268
Holt, Bob 122, 123
Holt, David 55
Home Alone 73, 74, 75, 205, 237
"Home for the Holidays" 29
Hondo, Med 273
The Honeymooners 45, 93, 124
Hong, Jung Jin 55
Hood, Catherine 110
Hood, Gary 110
Hood, Lauren Elizabeth 231
Hooper 129
Hoops and Yoyo Ruin Christmas 122–123, 322, 324
"Hooray for Santy Claus" 220
Hootkins, William 150
"Hop Up, Jump In" 91
"Hope" (song) 58, 94
Hope, Barclay 296
Hope, Bob 204
Hopkins, Anthony 71
Hopkins, Josh 186
Hopper, Dennis 242
Hopper, Paul 264
Hopps, Kevin 209
Hornaday, Ann 10
Horne, Andrew 304
Horne, Erica 135
Horner, James 72
Horsley, Stewart 304
Horvitz, Richard 22
"Hot Fruitcake" 138
Houten, Jelka van 63
"How Great My Joy" 291
"How I Love Who-liday Shopping" 72
How Murray Saved Christmas (book) 123
How Murray Saved Christmas (film) 123–125, 323

Index

How the Grinch Stole Christmas! 69, 205
How the Toys Saved Christmas 46, 95, 125–126, 316, 323
Howard, Ron 73, 227
The Howdy Doody Show 126, 240, 257
Howdy Doody's Christmas 126–128, 324
Howe, Desson 285
Howells, William Dean 81, 83
Hübner, Charly 307
The Huckleberry Hound Show 124
Huddleston, David 222, 223, 224
Hudson, Jennifer 83
Hugh, Alex 47
Hughart, Ron 281
Hughes, Miko 288
Hughes, Robert 22
Hughes, Stuart 23
Hughes, Terri 132
Hughes, Terry 169
Humm, Clarissa 248
Humphrey, Rob 141
Hunka, Ryan 36
Hunt, Dawn 178
Hunt, Richard 109
Hunter, Bernice Thurman 23, 24
Hunter, Bruce 201
Hunts, Maggie 103
Hunziker, Peter 306
Hurd, Thacher 233
Hurley, Owen 33
Hutcheson, Jenny-Lynn 195
Hyatt, Pam 201
Hyland, Brian 211

"I Believe in Santa Claus" 314
"I Could Be Santa Claus" 314
"I Do Believe in Christmas" 259
"I Hate Christmas" 83
"I Hate Santa Claus" 211
I Know Why the Caged Bird Sings 81, 83
I Love Lucy 281
"I Saw Mommy Kissing Santa Claus" 129
I Saw Stroker Killing Santa Claus 128–129, 321
"I Saw Three Ships" 84
"I Stole Santa's Sack" 51
"I Want a Hippopotamus for Christmas" 84
"I Want a Snuffleupagus for Christmas" 83
"I Want to Help" 108
I Was a Teenage Werewolf 10
"I Wish I Could Be Santa Claus" 172
Ice Age 129, 130, 137
Ice Age: A Mammoth Christmas Special 129–131, 320
Ideal Toy Company 295
Idle, Eric 210, 211
"If We All Pull Together" 78
Igawa, Togo 44
"Iglora's Song" 306
I'm Dreaming of a White Ranger 2, 131–133, 324
"I'm Evil" 51

"In the Hall of the Mountain King" 271
In the Land of Magic 169
In the Nick of Time 133–134, 224, 322
"In the Woods" 78
Independence Day 48
Indiana Jones and the Last Crusade 200
Indiana Jones and the Temple of Doom 209, 248
Ingels, Marty 41
Ingham, Dave 55
Ingraham, Garrett 111
Insana, Tino 16, 141
Insolia, Marguerite 231
Inspector Gadget Saves Christmas 134–136, 324
Ireland, Kathy 191, 300
Irrera, Dom 16
Irvin, Brittney 26, 151
Irving, George S. 165, 314, 315
Irwin, Steve 304
Isaacs, Stanley 136
Iscariot, Judas 51
"The Island of Misfit Toys" 209
Iso, Beatriz 170
"It Could Be Worse" 211
It Nearly Wasn't Christmas (film) 81, 84, 136–137, 179, 198, 224, 319, 322
"It Nearly Wasn't Christmas" (song) 136
It's a SpongeBob Christmas! 137–139, 324
It's a Very Merry Eek's-Mas 139–140, 320, 322, 323
It's a Wonderful Leaf 140–142, 319
It's a Wonderful Life 16, 59, 82, 106, 107, 111, 193, 202, 218, 219, 228, 232, 256, 301
"It's All About" 104
"It's All about Heart" 172
"It's an Udderful Life" 15
"It's Beginning to Look a Lot Like Christmas" 143
"It's Christmas" 90
"It's Christmas Again" 82, 223
"It's Christmas Time" 108, 165
"It's Christmas Time of Year" 90
It's Fun to Learn with Spot 275
"It's Gonna Snow Right Here in Dixie" 314
"It's Not Easy Being Mean" 90
"It's Our Favorite Time of the Year" 94
"It's That Wonderful Time of the Year" 259
"It's the Most Wonderful Time of the Year" 29, 206
"It's Time to Be Brave" 104
"I've Got the Blues" 104
Iversen, Derek 139
Ives, Burl 206, 207
Ivory, Ed 284
Iwata, Keisuke 116

Jaas, Gardner 278
"Jack and Sally Montage" 284
Jack Frost 281

"Jack's Lament" 284
"Jack's Obsession" 284
Jackson, Phil 167
Jackson, Victoria 238
Jacobs, Danny 5, 159
Jacobs, Matthew 166
Jacobson, Eric 84, 172
Jacobson, Paul L. 222
Jacoby, Laura 181, 182
Jaffe, Michael 134
James, Caryn 86
James, Clayton 278
James, Danny 43
James, Jesse 116
James, Kevin 84
James, Vincent 167
James Bond (films) 77, 146, 189
Jane, Ian 171
Jankowski, Steve 237
Janson, Len 267
Jashni, Jon 144
Jaud, Janyse 176, 245
Jauregi, Kiko 170
Javits, Joan 213
Jay, Tony 146
Jefferies, LaShawn Tináh 3, 4
Jennings, Will 72
Jensen, Ashley 12
Jeralds, Scott 257
Jeremy Creek 287
Jesus Christ 2, 29, 34, 37, 44, 50, 51, 52, 57, 61, 66, 78, 103, 150, 169, 236, 251, 252, 253, 264, 265, 280, 290, 291
Jewel, Gary 263
Jewish Anti-Defamation League 111
Jimmy Neutron: Boy Genius 121, 238
"Jingle Bell Postcard" 236
Jingle Bell Rock (film) 142, 321
"Jingle Bell Rock" (song) 142
"Jingle Bells" 84, 110, 182, 254, 278
"Jingle, Jingle, Jingle" 206
"Job Switching" 281
Joens, Mike 105
Joey, Mongo 90
Johans, Jen 93, 254
Johanson, MaryAnn 189, 316
Johns, Alex 189
Johns, Cort 265
Johnson, Adam 43
Johnson, Amy Jo 131, 132
Johnson, Ashley 288
Johnson, Bailee 43
Johnson, David 132, 177
Johnson, Gerry 46
Johnson, Marguerite Annie 82
Johnston, Trevor 102
Johnstone, Nahanni 23
Joles, Bob 302
"Jolly Old St. Nicholas" 278
Jones, Chuck 70, 198
Jones, James Earl 184
Jones, Katherine Ann 303
Jones, Kivel 84
Jones, Morgan 92
Jones, Ron 204
Jones, Ruby 43
Jones, Shirley 51
Jones, Skip 310

Joosen, Leon 255
Le Journal de Spirou 13, 153, 266
"Joy to the World" 64, 278
Joyce, Michael R. 171
Joyner, Tom 213
Judovits, Danielle 282
Juhl, Jerry 108, 109
Julebukk 307
Julius Caesar 112
Jurwich, Don 154
"Just a Little Pinch of Sand" 270
Juster, Clive 276
Juusonen, Kari 93

Kahn, Harvey 293
Kaliban, Bob 47
Kamwa, Daniel 273
Kandel, Paul 27
Kane, Brad 47
Kane, Carol 22, 317
Kane, Christian 43, 147
Kane, Tom 295
Kapigian, Susan 20
Kaplan, Eric 281
Kappes, David R. 182
Karloff, Boris 70
Karvonen, Santtu 248
Kasem, Casey 66, 256
Kasha, Al 211
Kassir, John 21
Katagas, Anthony 173
Kattan, Chris 316
Katz, Claudia 125, 281, 313
Kauffman, Tom 302
Kay, Bernie 56
Kay, Dominic Scott 157, 264
Kaye, David 33, 210, 244
Keach, Stacy 237
Kearney, Barbara Jean 47
Keefe, Peter 184
Keenan, William 316
"Keep Christmas with You" 82
"Keep Your Chin Up" 209
Keeshan, Bob 127
Kelamis, Peter 26, 234
Kelleher, Terry 156
Kelley, David 66
Kelly, Casper 128, 129
Kelly, Karen 80
Kemner, Randy 58
Kempley, Rita 86, 225
Kennedy, Ellen 53, 234
Kennedy, Gordon 29
Kennedy, John F. 83
Kenny, Tom 91, 138, 190, 295, 304
Kent, Lisa 248
Keogh, Tom 98
Kerchner, Rob 202
Kermode, Mark 102
Kerrigan, Jonathan 231
Kerwin, Brian 302
Kesselman, Jonathan 112
Kesselman, Josh 112
Kevin and Bean (DJs) 204
Keyes, Douglas 111
Keys, Alicia 84
Kho, Nancy Davis 93, 268, 269, 299
Khouth, Sam 142
"Kidnap the Sandy Claws" 284
Kidsmas 4

Kim, Do Uk 55
Kim, Jin Yong 55
Kim, John 147
Kimball, John 154
Kind, Richard 216, 219, 235, 259
King, Cam 29
King, Kip 14
King, Larry 139
King, Shawn 209
King Features Syndicate 273
King Herod 252
Kingdom Under the Sea 103, 319
Kingston, Graeme 33
Kinney, Kathy 256
Kirk, James 191, 300
Kirk Cameron's Saving Christmas 251
Kirkpatrick, Wayne 29
Kitaen, Tawny 140
Kitt, Eartha 213, 251
Kitty Foiled 246
Klassen, Terry 33, 34, 210, 244, 245
Klebba, Martin 237
Kletter, Lenore 242
Kligman, Paul 206
Kline, B. 86
Kline, Jeff 175
Kline, Kevin 156, 157
Kling, Anja 63
"Kling, Glöckchen" 291
Kloss, Jeff 158
Kneitel, Seymour 39, 275
Knight, Andy 19, 20
Knight, Gail 303
Knight, Gladys 118
Knight, Peter 10
Knight, Wayne 117
Knight Rider 129
Knights, Christopher 159
Kobler, Flip 20
Koch, Ed 112
Koenig, Wolf 110
Kondelik, James 231
Koningsbrugge, Jeroen van 62
Konopelski, Steven 4
Kopp, Bill 139, 140
Kopp, Natasha 191
Koretsky, Rachel 17
Kouper, Corrine 101
Kowalchuk, Bill 209, 211
Kowalewski, Kyla Rae 7
Kraft, Scott 198
Krakowski, Jane 172
Kramer, Ryan 302
Krampus (film) 111, 142–144, 320
Krampus (mythical being) 142, 143, 144
Krampus Night 144
Krampusnacht 144
Kraus, Noah 307
Krause, Bernd 307
Kremer, Warren 202
Kressley, Carson 318
Krieg, Jim 256
Kristofferson, Kris 9
Kroesen, Chris 152
Krumholtz, David 224, 227
Ku Klux Klan 218
Kubiak, Walt 154
Kunis, Mila 204

Kurz, Joachim 307
Kusuhara, Eiji 44
Kwaitkowski, Tonia 36
Kwanzaa 2, 111, 113, 132, 251, 281
Kyoryu Sentai Zyuranger 132

LaBelle, Patti 213
LaBeouf, Shia 54
Ladd, Cheryl 234
LaDuca, Rob 162
Lafferty, Kevin 268, 297
LaFleur, Art 226, 228
LaFontaine, Don 238
Lageson, Lincoln 237
Lakin, Christine 264
LaLanne, Jack 318
LaMarche, Maurice 135, 281, 312
LaMarr, Phil 42, 281, 312
Lambert, Lynne 306
Lambo, Nicola 230
Lamont, James 7
Lamour, Dorothy 204
Lamoureux, Dylan 26
Lamport, Michael 304
Landon, Michael 205
Landry, Justin 30
Lane, Nathan 171
Lange, Ted 136
Langham Huntington Hotel and Spa 202
The Langoliers 65
Lansbury, Angela 19, 167, 168, 236
Lanskaya, Yelena 232
Lapland 102, 247, 248
Larroquette, John 147, 148
Last Chance for Christmas 145–146, 321, 323
The Last Christmas 146, 324
Latham, Jim 298
Latifah, Queen 130
Latino, Frank 149, 150
Latt, David Michal 231
Laurel, Stan 27
Laurie, Hugh 11
Lavin, Catherine 278
Lawley, Linda 236
Lawrence, Carolyn 121, 138
Lawrence, Joey 34, 76
Laws, Maury 165, 299, 314, 317
Lawson, Shannon 303
Lazar, Susan Miller 277
Leader, Hannah 38
Leary, Denis 130
Leave It to Beaver 122
Lechtenbrink, Volker 306
Lee, Brenda 200
Lee, Candace 37, 38, 57
Lee, Christopher Khayman 149
Lee, Danica 250, 251
Lee, Michelle 107
Lee, Teri 265
The Legend of Holly Boy 149
The Legend of Sleepy Hollow 256
Leguizamo, John 130
Lehn, Pam 220
Leigh, Katie 141, 164
Leigh, Susan K. 66
Leitch, Christopher 60
Le Mat, Paul 181
Lembeck, Michael 227, 229, 230

Index

lemurs 6
Lennaro, Daniel 45
Lennon, Terry 105
Lennox, Lisa 105
Leno, Jay 50
Leo, Armand 24
Leonardis, Tom 29
"Leon's Christmas" 261
Leopold, Glenn 288
Lepeniotis, Peter 106
LePrince de Beaumont, Jeanne-Marie 18, 19
Lesser, Elana 142
Lester, Robie 66
"Let It Snow! Let It Snow! Let It Snow!" 29
Levesque, John 281
Levine, Lauren 88
Levine, Stuart 195
Levitch, Speed 129
Levitin, Sonia 165
Levy, Eugene 202
Levy, Gilbert 273
Levy, Shuki 132
Lewis, Al 170
Lewis, Craig 296
Lewis, David 87, 88
Lewis, Marc Allen 308
Lewis, Morgan R. 33, 196, 249
Libman, Andrea 34, 151, 244
The Librarian 147
The Librarians 146, 147, 322, 323
The Librarians and Santa's Midnight Run 25, 79, 105, 109, 146–149, 221, 272, 274, 285, 308, 309, 322, 323
Liebmann, Norm 171
The Life and Adventures of Santa Claus 102, 223, 308
Liggieri, Allesandro 248
The Light in the Forest 149
A Light in the Forest: The Legend of Holly Boy 149–150, 320
Like Father, Like Santa 150–151, 320
Likes, Stephanie 103
Likomanova, Rossitza 302
Lillard, Matthew 178
Lillis, Rachel 116
Limousin, Odile 244, 245
Lincoln, Jim 297
Lind, Emily Alyn 196
Lint, Derek de 62
Lishman, Edna 195
List, Peyton 76
Liszt, Franz 154
Lithgow, John 222, 224
Litinsky, Irene 186, 187
Little, Cleavon 133
Little, Dwight H. 195
"Little Geniuses" 261
"The Little Match Girl" 35
Lively, Robyn 239
Livingston, Barry 79, 80
Ljoka, Quinn 231
Lloyd, Brooke 123
Lloyd, Christopher 216
Lloyd, Debby Lytton 211
Lloyd, Eric 224, 225, 226, 227, 228, 308
Lloyd, Michael 211
Lloyd, Robert 215
Lockhart, June 182
LoConti, Gary 150
Lodge, David 278
London, Robby 272
Long, Justin 236, 259
Long, Mike 177
Long, Shelley 76, 237
"The Longest Night" 262
Looney Tunes 198
Loos, Rob 28
Lopez, Mario 73, 75
Lord, Peter 13
Lord and Taylor (store) 312
Lorre, Peter 77, 104
Los Lobos (band) 297
Lost Horizon 309
Loughlin, Lori 186
Love, Ruby 55
"Love Is in Your Heart" 259
Lovelady, John 109
Lovett, Lyle 9
Lowenthal, Yuri 278
Lowry, Brian 7
Lubbock, Jeremy 278
Lucado, Max 37
Lucking, Bill 54
"The Lucky Charm" 261
Lurie, Evan 4
Lusk, Don 154
Lyde, John 44
Lynley, Carol 149
Lynn, Dina 66
Lynn, Sherry 164
Lyons, Ali 231

Maaginen kristalli 247
MacArthur, Sweeney 105
MacDonald, Norm 51, 92
MacFarlane, Rachael 97
MacFarlane, Ron 204
MacFarlane, Seth 95, 97, 203, 204
Mack, Allison 302
Mackasek, Andrew 82
Mackay, Frank 183
Mackay, Yvonne 179
MacKinnon, Don 175
Macleod, Lewis 44, 55
MacNeille, Tress 162, 188, 275, 281, 309, 312
MacNicol, Peter 188
MacWilliam, Keenan 173
Macy's Thanksgiving Day Parade 271
Madagascar (island) 6, 158, 159
Madagascar (series) 4, 159
Madagascar: Escape 2 Africa 159
Madeline 151
Madeline and Santa 151–152, 323
Madeline at the North Pole 151–152, 154, 180, 183, 184, 277, 297, 323
Madeline's Christmas 151, 152
Madeline's Christmas and Other Wintery Tales 152
Madinah, Shauna 278
Madison, Bailee 186, 187
Magasin des enfants 19
Magic Christmas Tree 152–153, 321
The Magic Crystal 247
"The Magic of Christmas" 176
"The Magic Pearl" 260
"Magic Sack" 4
The Magic Sack of Mr. Nicholas 3, 14, 51, 152, 153–155, 180, 183, 184, 277, 297, 323
"The Magic Wand" 261
The Magnificent Seven 309
Magnuson, Ann 170
Magon, Jymn 185
Maguire, George 113
Magwood, Robbie 193
Mahan, Kerrigan 132
Maher, Kaitlyn 216, 235, 259
Mahon, Barry 212
Mahoney, Michael 290
Makichuk, Jim 286
"Making Christmas" 284
"Making Toys" 223
Malek, Gabriella 3
Maliani, Michael 272, 314
Malkovich, John 242
Maloney, Patty 85
Mame 168
The Man Who Saved Christmas 155–156, 319
Manahan, Bob 132
Mancini, Henry 223
Mangano, Anthony 289
Mann, Danny 298
Mann, Larry 206
Mann, Rhoda 165, 314
Mann, Rich 80
Mann, Terrence 168
Mannheim Steamroller 36
Manville, Lesley 37
Manzano, Sonia 82
Maples, Marla 202
Mappin, Jefferson 296
Marcus, Cindy 20
Marcus, Rachel 23
Marcus, Russell 190, 191
Mareth, Glenville 222
Marianetti, Robert 129
Marienthal, Eli 302
Marin, Annette 136
Marin, Cheech 298
Marin, Sam 200
Marino, Umberto 126
Marks, Deborah 145
Marks, John D. (Johnny) 122, 206, 209, 211
Marks, Peter 296
Marlboro cigarettes 309
Marquez, Ramona 12
Marriott, Alan 119
Marsden, Jason 90
Marshal, Paul 16, 239
Marshall, Liza 102
Marshall, Rob 168
Marshall, Ron 314
Martin, Andrea 121
Martin, Jeff 256
Martin, Jesse L. 171
Martin, Linda 81
Martin, Meaghan 119
Martin, Tom 318
Marval, Rocky 36
Marvaud, Olivier 263
Mary Engelbreit's The Night Before Christmas 58, 156–157, 297, 321

"Mary Had a Little Lamb" 29
Mary Poppins 124
Masini, Patrice 273
Maslin, Janet 194
Mason, Owen 197
Mason-Dixon line 124
Massey, Christopher 259
Massey, Kyle 20
Matheson, Ali Marie 220
Matheson, Hans 37
Matheson, Tim 145
Mathews, Jack 99
Mattern, Anick 263
Matthews, Kevin 283, 300
Matthius, Gail 298
Mattson, James Iver 47
Mauney, Matt 252
Maurer, Joe 156
Mavis, Paul 138, 162, 200, 316, 318
May, Robert L. 206
Mazzarino, Joey 81, 83, 84
McAfee, Anndi 78
McAndrew, Stephen 58
McAvoy, James 11
McBain, Diane 54
McBroom, Amanda 14, 154
McCallum, David L. 10
McCanlies, Tim 10
McCann, Chuck 41
McCarthy, Cheryl 177
McCarthy, Emilia 23
McCarthy, Jenny 214, 215
McCarthy, John 46
McCarthy, Todd 73, 211
McCartney, Paul 211
McClure, Marc 114
McClurg, Edie 118, 246
McConaghy, Sean 231
McCorkle, Mark 118
McCoy, Matt 288
McCoy, Sylvester 37
McCracken, Craig 294, 295, 296
McCune, Ida Sue 58
McCusker, Eamonn 189
McCutcheon, Bill 220, 221
McDermott, Dean 60, 215
McDonagh, Maitland 112, 229
McDonald, Kevin 219
McDonald, Rodney 80
McDowall, Roddy 302
McDowell, Malcom 22
McDowell, Michael 285
McFadden, Robert (Bob) 299, 314
McFerrin, Bobby 242
McGill, Bruce 204
McGillis, Kelly 242
McGinley, Phyllis 315
McGinley, Ted 61
McGiver, John 299
McGovern, Terry 141
McGrath, Derek 145
McGrath, Tom 5, 159, 160
McIlvaine, P.J. 289
McInnis, Michael 306
McIntosh, Shannon 10
McIntyre, John 42
McKean, Michael 317
McKee, David 276
McKenna, Matt 97
McKennon, Dal 70

Mckillip, Britt 26
McKim, Dorothy 175, 196
McKinnon, Dallas 257
McKinnon, Danny 53
McLane, Colin 24
McLarty, Laurie 24
McLean, Ken 258
McLendon-Covey, Wendi 259
McLeod, Don 202
McMahon, Andrew 92
McMurray, Sam 170
McNamara, Mary 148, 186
McNeil, Craig 214, 215, 269
McNeil, Scott 33, 53, 209, 234
McRoberts, Anna 217, 236, 260
Meadows, Audrey 124
Meadows, Tim 188
Medford, Mark 305
Medley, Bill 211
Medrano, Joseph 278
Meehan, Thomas 193, 194
Meet the Santas 157–158, 264, 322
Mehler, Tobias 214
Meijer, Monica 63
Melendrez, Sonny 66
Méliès, Georges 35
Mella, Michel 273
"Les Mémoires du Père Noël" 261
Mena, Michael 248
Mende, Roger 150
Mendenhall, David 267
menorah 2, 19, 173, 189, 205, 302
Menville, Chuck 267
Mercer, Jack 39, 274
Mercer, Michael 183
Meredith, Burgess 222
Meroni, Gigi 256
Merrie Melodies 198
Merrill, Dan 306
Merritt, Pam 306
"Merry Christmas After All" 189
"Merry Christmas Day" 256
"Merry Christmas Is My Favorite
  Time of Year" 45
Merry Christmas, Mr. Moose 63
A Merry Little Christmas 288
Merry Madagascar 4, 7, 25, 158–
  160, 164, 180, 240, 259, 269, 322,
  323
Merry Wishmas 88, 160–162, 322
Mertens, Mark 248
"Message in a Bottle" 262
Messick, Don 14, 46, 58, 66, 154, 267
Messmer, Otto 89
Metzger, Kelly 119
MGM Studios 245
Miami Dolphins 201
Michaelangelo (performer) 278
Michele, Lea 27
Michelle, Julianne 308
Mickey Mouse 89, 162
Mickey Mouse Clubhouse 162, 324
Mickey Saves Santa 162–163, 324
Mickey's Once Upon a Christmas
  191
Mickey's Twice upon a Christmas
  300
Mickwee, Kelley 9
Micro-Games America Entertainment 25

Midden in De Winternacht 62
Middle of the Winter Night 62
Mighty Morphin' Power Rangers 131,
  132, 324
*Mighty Morphin' Power Rangers:
  The Movie* 131
Milbauer, Ron 132
Miller, Bridget 291
Miller, Chris 159
Miller, David B. 120
Miller, Fred 10
Miller, George 134
Miller, Glenn R. 231
Miller, Jennifer 278
Miller, Lara Jill 277
Miller, Larry 117
Miller, Randy 91
Miller, Randy III 274
Miller, Roger 293
Miller, Ryan 21
Miller, T.J. 130
Milligan, Deanna 174
Milne, Alan Alexander 174
Miloro, Andrea M. 131
Minkus, Barbara 41
Minnette, Dylan 316
Minow, Nell 73
Miracle at the 34th Precinct 7, 25,
  159, 163–164, 180, 240, 259, 269,
  322, 323
Le miracle de Noël 52
Miracle on 34th Street 31, 54, 59,
  102, 107, 164, 220, 280
"Miracles All Around" 37
Mirell, Gregory Scott 111
A Miser Brothers' Christmas 164–
  166, 315, 322, 323
Mission: Impossible 135
"Mr. Cuddles" 209
Mr. Lawrence (performer) 138, 139
Mr. Men and Little Miss 56
Mr. Men, Little Misses 55
The Mr. Men Show 56
Mr. St. Nick 166, 322
Mitchell, Elizabeth 226, 228
Mitchell, Mark 170
Mittenthal, Robert 45
Mochrie, Colin 303
Moffitt, John 109
Mohr, Jay 188
Mohr, Father Josef 26
Moloney, Jim 182
Momsen, Taylor 71, 72
Le Monde secret du Père Noël 260
mondegreens 189
Monet, Daniella 87, 88
Monken, Michael 123
Monrigal, A. 263
Monroe, Carol 177
A Monster Christmas 46, 53, 55,
  166–167, 207, 277, 323
A Monster Easter 167
A Monster Holiday 167
Monsters in the Closet 182
Montgomery, Grace 170
Montgomery Ward Company 206
Month, Chris 220, 221
Monti, Mary Elaine 306
Moon, Kate 205
Mooney, Paul 29

Moore, Dudley 222, 224
Moore, Joanne 258
Moore, Lon 47
Moore, Mary Tyler 126
Moore, Oscar 189
Moore, Tracy 8, 26, 59, 61, 76, 265, 304
A Moose Dropped In 62
Moranis, Richard 209
Morency, Pamela 123
Moreno, José Elías 217, 218
Moretz, Chloe 175
Morgan, Burke 80
Morgan, Frank 308
Morgan, Gavin 92
Mori, Takemoto 116
Morley, Vanessa 210
Morris, Andrew 243
Morris, Gary 184
Morris, Kat 200
Morris, Matt 184
Morris, Philip 66
Morris, Wesley 98
Morrow, Max 239, 240
Morteau, Laurent 273
Morton, Gig 216
Morton, Greg 314
Moses, Liz 47
Moss, Peter 24
Moss, Tegan 33
"The Most Wonderful Day of the Year" 206
Motz, Bill 20
Mount Korvatunturi 93, 247
Mt. Ruapehu 179
Mrs. Santa Claus (film) 167–169, 236, 321, 324
"Mrs. Santa Claus" (song) 168
Ms. Scrooge 28
Muir, E. Roger 126
Mule-Tide Christmas 169–170, 319
Mull, Martin 202
Mullen, Susan 232
Muller, Romeo 208
Mulroney, Dermot 187
Mumy, Liliana 216, 227, 228
Munroe, Gage 180, 197
The Munsters 170
The Munsters' Scary Little Christmas 170–171, 321
The Muppet Show 109
Muppets 81, 82, 83, 108, 109, 110, 171, 172
The Muppets 172
A Muppets Christmas: Letters to Santa 2, 82, 171–173, 321
Murdoch, Lachlan 194
Murdock, Colin 33, 209, 210, 234
Murietta, Peter 119
Murlowski, John 202
Murphy, Kevin 171
Murphy, Walter 124
Murray, Brian Doyle 305
Murray, K. Gordon 218
Murray, Michael J. 290, 293
Murray, Noel 144
Music, Lorenzo 104
Musical Mews 88
Musso, Mitchel 259
Must Be Santa 54, 173–174, 322

"My Best Christmas Yet" 172
"My Blue Christmas" 236, 314
My Friends Tigger and Pooh: Super Sleuth Christmas Movie 51, 174, 175, 323
My Little Pony 176, 295
My Little Pony: A Very Minty Christmas 176–177, 319
My Little Pony and Friends 104
Myers, Randy 302
Myrick, Ron 180
myrrh 252
Mystery Science Theater 3000 218, 221
Mysto Magic Exhibition Sets 155

"Nabbed" 284
Napel, Cameron Ten 57
Narrative Television Network 57
Nasfell, Andrea Gyertson 62
Nast, Thomas 148
National Lampoon's Christmas Vacation 75, 205, 317
The Naughty List 177–178, 323
Nawrocki, Mike 290, 291
Nearly No Christmas 136, 178–179, 321
Neeb, Martin J., Jr. 66
Nelson, Jerry 81, 84, 109
Nelson, Jessie 99
Nelson, Judd 30, 232
Nelson, Paul 67
Nelson, Willie 9, 236
Nemcova, Petra 37
Neumaier, Joe 37
Nevius, C.W. 227
The New Adventures of Madeline 151, 323
Newbern, George 234
Newhart, Bob 210
Newman, Andrew Hill 309
Newman, David 224
Newman, Eric 38
Newman, Fred 306
Newman, Leslie 224
Newman, Richard 34
Newman, Sydney 48
Newman, Tom 38
Newmyer, Robert F. 225, 227, 230
Newton, Sir Isaac 122
Newton-John, Olivia 36
Nicholas, Kim 212
Nichols, Charles A. 95
Nick Jr. 55, 249
Nick of Time 134
Nickelodeon 15, 55, 68, 77, 87, 121, 137, 138, 160, 197, 249, 276, 304
Nicktoons 77, 88, 121, 161
Nicodème, Daniel 116
Nicolai, Bruno 59
Nicolas, Olivier 263
Nicolet, Danielle 149
Nicoll, Kristina 105
Nielsen, Leo 276
Nielsen, Leslie 239
The Night B4 Christmas (film) 152, 154, 179–180, 184, 277, 297, 323
"Night B4 Christmas" (song) 180
"The Night Before Christmas" 156, 274

The Night Before the Night Before Christmas 7, 25, 159, 164, 180–181, 240, 259, 269, 322, 323
The Night They Saved Christmas 181–182, 321
Nighy, Bill 12
Nigro, Tony 97
Niko—Lentäjän poika 92
Niko—The Way to the Stars 92
Nilus the Sandman: The Boy Who Dreamed Christmas 182–183, 322, 324
Nine Dog Christmas 152, 154, 180, 183–184, 277, 297, 323
"Nine Dogs Out & Santa's In" 184
Nissen, Brian 279
Niven, David, Jr. 182
Nixon, Cynthia 194
Nixon, Richard M. 124
"No Santa, Just Me!" 165
Noah's Ark 28
The Nobelity Project 9
Noddy Goes to Toyland 185
Noddy Saves Christmas 184–185, 323
"Le Noël de Geignard" 262
"Un Noël pour Léon" 261
Norkin, Susan 178
Norman, Benjy 254
Norris, Daran 77, 88, 129, 161
North Pole 1, 2, 11, 14, 20–22, 24–26, 28, 29, 41–44, 46, 50, 54, 56, 58, 64, 77, 79–81, 87–89, 94, 95, 97–100, 104, 107, 108, 111–116, 118, 119, 121, 123, 126, 127, 130–136, 139, 140, 142, 145, 147, 150, 151, 152, 154, 159, 160, 162, 166, 169–188, 191, 193, 194, 195, 203, 204, 205, 209, 212, 214, 215, 216, 217, 219, 220, 223, 224, 225, 226, 228, 230, 231, 233, 235, 236, 237, 238, 240, 242, 243, 245, 249, 250, 253, 254, 261, 262, 267, 268, 269, 272, 276, 277, 280, 287, 293, 294, 297, 298, 300, 303, 306, 308, 314–317, 320, 321, 323, 324
Northern Lights (novel) 97
Northpole 185–186, 320
Northpole: Open for Christmas 186–187, 197, 320
"Nothing Says Christmas Like a New Pair of Socks" 176
Nottage, Antony 255
Novillo, Lisandro 283
"La Nuit la Plus Longue" 262
Nusair, David 20, 173, 216, 229
The Nutcracker 36, 205
The Nutcracker Suite 43, 84, 90
The Nutty Professor 238
Nye, Louis 66
Nyholm, Rick 11

"O Christmas Tree" 278
"O Hanukkah" 132
"O Holy Night" 235, 236
"O Little Town of Bethlehem" 29
Oates, Travis 175
Oberst, Bill, Jr. 282
O'Bray, Crystaleen 245
O'Brian, Peter 194
O'Brien, Conan 3, 312

O'Brien, Jane 312
O'Connor, Carroll 104
Odenkirk, Bill 281, 312
Odin (god) 143
O'Donahue, Ryan 275
Oedekerk, Steve 15, 16, 238, 239
Ogawa, Viviana 276
Ogle, Bob 70
"Oh Santa" 290, 291
O'Hanlon, Virginia 136
O'Hara, Catherine 284
O'Hara, Paige 19
Ohtani, Ikue 116
O'Hurley, John 118
Oldfield, Emily 167
Oldfield, Martin 167
Olding, Grant 254
Olentzero (mythical being) 169
Olentzero eta iratxoen jauntxoa 169
Olesker, Jack 34
Olive, the Other Reindeer 2, 187–190, 323
Oliver 220
Oliver, Christian 149
Oliver Twist 312
Olsen, Chris 291
Olsen, Jeffrey G. 128, 129
Olson, Brandon James 195
Olson, Erik 264
The Omen 112
"On A Volé Noël" 262
"On the Pulse of Morning" 83
On Whiskers, On Lola, On Cheryl and Meryl 190–191, 323
Once Upon a Christmas 191–192, 300, 319, 324
One Magic Christmas 54, 192–194, 320
O'Neal, Brian E. 180
O'Neal, Dink 79
"Oogie Boogie's Song" 284
Oppenheimer, Alan 14
oranges 49, 53
Orbach, Jerry 19
Ord, Murray 214, 215, 269
Orenstein, Janis 206
Oriolo, Don 90
Oriolo, Joe 32, 89
Orman, Roscoe 82
Orndorf, Brian 159, 217
Orr, James 180
Ortiz, Ana 166
Osment, Emily 118
Osment, Haley Joel 19
Osmond, James A. 136
Osmond, Marie 27
Osmond, Merrill 136
Osmond, Wayne 136
Osmond Brothers 136
Osowski, Douglas Lawrence 139
O'Sullivan, Michael 13, 253
"L'Ours en Peluche" 262
"Out of the Blue" 242
Outland 309
Overton, Teddy 103
Owen, Beverley 170
Owen, Rob 124
Owen, Stefania LaVie 143
Owens, Gerald 248
Owens, Tim 104

Oxley, Jennifer 251
Oz, Frank 82, 109
The Oz Kids 308

Pac-Man 40
Pac-Man's Christmas 41
Page, Ken 284
Paisley, Brad 84
Paley, Andy 91, 138
Palmer, Dave 4
Palmer, Mark 118
Panitz, Ty 216
Pantoliano, Joe 188
Papa's Angels 194–195, 320
Pappas, Valery 298
Pappenbrook, Bob 132
Pardi, Robert 166
Pardo, Ron 201
Paris, Frank 127
Parish, Richard C. "Dick" 152, 153
Parke, Dave 123
Parker, David Shaw 56
Parker, Justin 111
Parker, Noelle 86
Parkes, Gerard 173
Parkinson, David 192
Parnell, Chris 100
Parton, Dolly 302, 303
Pasanen, Petteri 93
Pasquin, John 225
Pasternak, Reagan 60
Pat Sullivan Studio 88, 89
Patch Adams 238
"Patch! Natch!" 223
Patrei, Michael 110, 111
Patrei, Nicholas 111
Patrick, Butch 170
Patterson, Ray 14, 41, 154
Patton 298
Patton, Chuck 135
Paul, Cinco 227
Paul, Ed 116
Paulsen, Rob 16, 77, 121, 298
PAW Patrol 197, 321
Payne, John 234
Pays, Amanda 237
PBS Kids 258
Peacock, Trevor 98
Peck, Josh 130
Pedersen, Aaron 304
Pedley, Heather 167
Peeler, Dan 270
Peer Gynt Suite No. 1 (Grieg) 271
"Peggy Sue" 142
Pegram, Steve 13
Pelfrey, Danny 236
Peltzman, Adam 4
Pemberton, Dave 201
penguins 5, 6, 84, 159, 178, 179, 188, 242, 272, 273, 276, 291, 309, 313
The Penguins of Madagascar 4, 5, 320
Pennington, Ty 84
Père Noël 52, 244
Le Père Noël et le magicien 245
Le Père Noël et les enfants du désert 244
Perez, Rosie 68
"La Perle Magique du Père Noël" 260

Perrichon, Annabelle 260
Perron, Michel 10
Perrotto, Sue 22
Perry, Lauren 51
Perry, Roger 79, 80
Perry, Ward 245
Peter Pan 81, 84, 136, 198
Peters, Bernadette 19
Peters, Blair 272
Petersen, Randy 191
Peterson, Jim 141
Peterson, Melinda 288
Petit, Leontine 64
"Les Petits Génies" 261
Pettis, Madison 171, 259
Pettus, Jerry, Jr. 47
Peyton, Marlowe 235
P.F. Volland Company 198
The Phantom of the Opera 36
Phillips, Betty 26
Phillips, Chris 306
Phillips, Colin 132
Phillips, Mackenzie 114
Phillips, Stan 152
Phillips-Oland, Pamela 78
photo-puppetry 250
Piano Concerto No. 1 (Liszt) 154
Picardo, Robert 20
Picheta, Andy 36
Pied Piper Playhouse 212
Pierce, Bradley 308
Pierce, Scott D. 97
Pike, Jim 304
Pilkington, Lorraine 44
Pillon, Jacqueline 304
Pinchot, Bronson 146
The Pink Panther (series) 135
Pinnock, Arnold 173
Piper, Billie 47, 48
Pipkin, Turk 9
Pirates World 212
Pirkle, Leonard 114
Pizzo, John 114
PJ Masks 100, 319
Platt, Phyllis 24
Playten, Alice 306
"Please Come Home for Christmas" 150
Pledge of Allegiance 189
Plener, Benji 8
Plummer, Christopher 151, 152
Plunlett, Gerald 34
Pocket Monsters 114
Podell, Rick 134
The Pointer Sisters 211
Pokémon 114
Poketto Monsuta 114
Pola, Eddie 206
The Polar Express 189
Pollak, Kevin 66, 226, 228
Poniewozik, James 70, 208
Pontac, Ken 297, 298
Poole, Duane 95
"Poor Jack" 284
Popeye the Sailor 273, 274, 320, 322
"Porte-Bonheur" 261
Portillo, Adolfo Torres 219
Portman, Rachel 19
Las Posadas 68
Posival, Marek 30, 31, 286

Pospisil, Eric 210
Post, Mikey 66
Postlewaite, Ashley 247
Potamkin, Buzz 28
Potter, Beatrix 276
Pottle, Sam 82
Poujol, Christophe 263
The Powerpuff Girls 294
The Powerpuff Girls Movie 295
Praytor, Jim 51, 247
Prechel, Greg 259
Precht, Bob 109
Predator 265
Predovic, Dennis 47
Preminger, Michael 134
Prep and Landing 196
Prep and Landing: Naughty vs. Nice 195–197, 320
"The Present" 184
"A Present for Santa" 261
"A Present for Two" 261
Prettige kerst, Mr. Moose 63
The Pretty Reckless (band) 72
Price, Connor 30
Price, Jeffrey 73
Price, Kent 277
Priest, Pat 170
Prince, Dennis 184
Prince, Jonathan 118, 119
Pritchard, Paul 232
Proctor, Phil 288
Professor Grampy 38, 39
"Prospects" 254
Prout, Kirsten 191, 300
Psalm 100 78
Puce Pop 222
Pucelli, Cristina 243
Pullman, Philip 97
Punsalan, Liz 36
Pups Save Christmas 197–198, 321, 322
Put a Helmet On 61
Putch, John 21, 25
Puttock, Heather 178
Les Pyjamasques 101

Questel, Mae 39, 274
Quezadas, Lupita 217
Quinn, Anthony Tyler 57
Quinn, Brandon 10
Quinn, Kevin 191
Quintel, J.G. 199, 200

Rabagliati, Alberto 58, 59
Rabb, Mike 92
Rabke, Kelli 306
Racioppo, Romuald 101
Rackstraw, Rob 167
Radice, Mark 84
Raggedy Andy Stories 198
Raggedy Ann and Andy in the Great Santa Claus Caper 81, 84, 136, 198–199, 324
Raggedy Ann Stories 198
Raichert, Lance 146
Raiders of the Lost Ark 298
Ralph, Toby 55
Ralston, Stuart 197
Ramadan 2, 189
Ramanujan, Srinivasa 312

Randall, Jordy 214, 215, 269
Randall, Tony 126
Randolph, Joyce 124
Rankin, Arthur, Jr. 208, 300, 316
Rankin, James 8
Rankin/Bass Productions 207, 208, 213, 315
Raposo, Joe 108
Rappoport, Fred A. 108
Rasmussen, Anna 231
Ratzenberger, John 124
Ravenscroft, Thurl 70
Raw Toonage 163
Reaves, Brynne Chandler 78
Rebollido, Steven 250
Recreation Corporation of America 212
Reed, Alan 45
Rees, A. 263
Regan, Peggy 310
Regular Show: The Christmas Special 199–201, 324
Reich, Uschi 307
Reid, R.D. 180
Reid, Stephen 104
Reilly, Brian 225, 227, 230
Reilly, Charles Nelson 66
Reilly, Judy 152
Reilly, Marc 103, 104
reindeer 1, 2, 7, 10, 11, 14, 20–22, 25, 26, 31, 33, 34, 37, 40–44, 46, 50, 55, 62, 64, 67–69, 77, 78, 81, 83, 85, 86, 88, 90, 92–94, 97, 98, 100, 101, 102, 104, 107, 108, 110, 111, 112, 116–119, 121–124, 128, 130, 135, 139, 145, 146, 154, 159, 160, 162, 165, 167, 168, 174, 175, 177, 179, 182–190, 197, 198, 200, 201, 204, 205, 212, 215, 216, 217, 219, 223, 224, 230, 231, 233, 234, 237–241, 243–250, 254, 260, 261, 263, 267, 268, 269, 270, 272, 273, 274, 275, 277, 280, 283, 293, 294, 296, 301, 303, 306, 307, 309, 311, 314, 316, 317, 320–323
The Reindeer Hunter 201, 273, 321
Reiner, Carl 5, 159
Reinhold, Judge 225, 227, 228
Reinsma, Dennis 62
Reisig, Joel Paul 265
Reiss, Mike 123, 124, 125, 131
Reit, Seymour 31, 32
"Le Retour du Père Noël" 262
The Return of Bruno 146
"The Return of Santa Claus" 262
Reubens, Paul 19, 284
Reverend, Alexandre 243
"La Révolte des Jouets" 262
Reynolds, Burt 129
Reynolds, Debbie 210
Rhea, Caroline 219
Rhodes, Kim 20
Rhymer, Don 227
Rice, Jonathan 256
Rice, Randy 184
Rich, Doris 220
Rich, Richard 279
Richards, Billie Mae 206, 293
Richards, Judi 58
Richardson, Derek 196

Richardson, Jake 202
Richardson, Kevin Michael 5, 16, 124, 161, 302
Richardson, Miranda 98
Richie Rich 202
Richie Rich's Christmas Wish 202–203, 324
Richmond, Randi 156
Richter, Andy 5, 159
Richter, Conrad 149
Riddle, Cynthia 306
Ridenour, Bridgette 252
Riehle, Richard 111, 202, 259, 282
RiffTrax 153, 212
Riggle, Rob 196
Rikert, Dustin 67
Ring, Bert 309
"Ring, Little Bells" 290, 291
Ripley, Jay 212
Rise of the Guardians 227, 228, 229
Rivera, Naya 178
Rivera, Theresa Sophia 82
Road to the North Pole 2, 95, 203–206, 323
Robbins, Dick 95
Roberge, Sean 314
Roberts, Bruce 209
Roberts, Emma 92
Roberts, Rick 180, 286, 289
Robertson, C.T. 212
Robertson, Meika 258
Robertson, Rob 258
Robey, Tim 102
Robinow, Tony 263
Robinson, Anthony 113, 114
Robinson, Douglas 24
Robinson, James G. 201
Robinson, Martin P. 81, 84
Robledo, S. Jhoanna 279
Robotboy 44, 324
Rock, Chris 159
"Rock Music" (song) 108
Rockettes 90
"Rockin' Around the Christmas Tree" 200
Rocky and His Friends 189
Rodari, Gianni 125
"Rodolphe A Disparu" 261
Rodriguez, Paul 118
Roe, Tommy 211
Roebuck, Daniel 51
Roemer, Larry 208
Rofé, Judy Rothman 152
Rogers, Amy Keating 296
Rogers, John 147, 148
Rolfe, Donna 24, 74, 75, 90, 104
Rolfe, Scott 231
Rolling Stone 312
Roman, Noel 108
Roman, Phil 108, 146
Roman, Susan 165
Romano, Jeanne 177
Romano, Ray 130
Romijn, Rebecca 147, 148
Romney, Clive 278
Rooney, Mickey 165, 314, 315
Root, Stephen 190
Roscoe, J.P. 41
Rose, Alexander J. 116
Rose, Charlie 270

Roseberry, Stephen 192, 301
Rosenberg, John M. 236, 259
Rosenmeyer, Grant 112
Rosman, Mark 269
Ross, Neilson 41
Rossen, Gregg 186, 187, 237
Rosser, Ankara 253
Rossi, Luigi "Shorty" 113, 114
Rossini, Gioachino 154
Roth, Bob 20
Roth, Mike 200
Rouse, Mitch 188
Roush, Matt 148
Roussel, Sarah 273
Roven, Glen 213
Rowan, Kelly 155
Rowe, Belinda 258
Rowe, Tom 166
Rowland, Beverly 136
Roxburgh, Ricky 255
Rubes, Jan 193
Rubiner, Mike 45
Rubino, Michael 272
Ruby, Cliff 142
Ruby, Joe 58
Rucker, Steve 78
Rudder, Michael 263
Rudman, David 84
Rudnick, Steve 225, 227, 230
Rudnicki, J.M. 263
Rudolph (reindeer character) 11, 22, 34, 41, 42, 69, 72, 89, 91, 104, 119, 120, 130, 162, 167, 184, 187, 201, 206–211, 216, 258, 260, 261, 263, 268, 277, 281, 283, 284, 296, 317, 320, 321
Rudolph and Frosty's Christmas in July 206
"Rudolph Is Missing" 261
Rudolph, the Red-Nosed Reindeer (film) 22, 69, 119, 206–208, 283, 317, 321
"Rudolph, the Red-Nosed Reindeer" (song) 119, 187, 206, 209, 211
Rudolph, the Red-Nosed Reindeer and the Island of Misfit Toys 206, 208–209, 320
Rudolph, the Red-Nosed Reindeer: The Movie 72, 207, 209–211, 321
Rudolph's Shiny New Year 206
Rukavina, Elizabeth 183
Russell, Brendan 304
Russell, Dan 7
Russo, Tom 13
Ryan, Will 204

Saban, Haim 132
Sabara, Daryl 256
Sadler, Marilyn 91, 92
Safadi, Talieh 150
Sagal, Katey 281, 311
Saint, Eva Marie 195
St. Germain, Tabitha 33, 119, 156, 176
St. John, Jill 186
St. John Publishing 32
St. Nicholas 28, 49, 53, 142, 143, 207, 252
St. Nicholas's Day 142, 144, 207, 233

Salisbury, Benjamin 308
Salkind, Ilya 224
"Sally's Song" 284
Saltzman, Mark 169
Salyers, William 200
Salzman, Bernard 54
Samerjan, George 60
Sampson, Tony 244
Samson, Andrew 173
Samuel, Tristan 197
Sanchez, Karen June 68
Sanchez, Ralph 164
Sand, Cole 243
Sanderson, Lisa 29
Sanrio 313
Sansom, Ken 175
Santa and the Desert Children 244
Santa and the Ice Cream Bunny 153, 211–213, 324
Santa and the Magician 245
Santa, Baby! (2001) 213, 214, 323
Santa Baby (2006) 213–214, 323
"Santa Baby" (song) 213
Santa Baby 2: Christmas Maybe 214–215, 324
Santa Buddies: The Legend of Santa Paws 216–217, 236, 259, 320
Santa Claus (character) 1–17, 19–26, 28–31, 33, 34, 37–48, 50, 51, 53–59, 61–70, 72, 77–102, 104–130, 132–143, 145–190, 191, 193, 194, 195, 196, 197, 198, 200, 201, 203, 204, 205, 206, 208, 209, 210–217, 219–232, 234, 236–250, 252, 253, 254, 257–265, 267–277, 280–291, 293–324
Santa Claus (1959) 117, 217–219, 220, 221, 324
The Santa Claus Brothers 219–220, 322, 324
Santa Claus Conquers the Martians 25, 79, 105, 109, 148, 153, 220–222, 272, 274, 285, 309, 319, 322
Santa Claus Defeats the Aliens 220
Santa Claus Is Comin' to Town 106, 138, 165, 223, 315
"Santa Claus Is Coming to Town" 143, 311, 316
"Santa Claus Is Gunning You Down" 311
"Santa Claus' Memoirs" 261
"Santa Claus, Santa Claus" 256
"Santa Claus' Secrets" 262
Santa Claus: The Movie 222–224, 324
The Santa Clause 30, 224–226, 227, 228, 229, 230, 234, 321
The Santa Clause 2: The Mrs. Clause 225, 226–228, 229, 264, 322
The Santa Clause 3: The Escape Clause 225, 227, 228–230, 324
Santa Claustrophobia 123
Santa Claws 225, 230–231, 322, 323
"Santa Has His Eyes on Me" 138
The Santa Incident 231–232, 322
Santa, Jr. 232–233, 322
Santa Mouse and the Ratdeer 233–234, 320, 322
Santa Paws 2: The Santa Pups 234–236, 259, 320

"The Santa Pups Are Coming" 236
Santa Switch 2, 236–237, 323
The Santa Trap 237–238, 322
Santa vs. the Snowman 238–239, 324
Santa vs. the Snowman 3D 238
Santa Who? 7, 24, 25, 159, 164, 180, 239–240, 259, 269, 273, 323
Santa-Witch 240–241, 257, 323
Santabear 241
Santabear's First Christmas 241
Santabear's High Flying Adventure 241–242, 320
SantApprentice 242
Santa's Apprentice 242–244, 322
Santa's Christmas Crash 244, 245, 322
Santa's Christmas Snooze 244, 245, 321
"Santa's Family" 211
Santa's Little Helpers 245–247, 320
Santa's Magic Crystal 247–248, 324
Santa's Magic Toy Bag 248–249, 323
Santomauro, Angelo 289
Sanz, Horatio 100
Saperstein, David 60
Sarandon, Chris 284
Sarbry, Jay 154
Satan 61, 111, 142, 295
Saturday Night Live 100
Savage, Fred 118
Savatage (band) 200
Save the Reindeer 2, 249–251, 281, 321
Savenkoff, Elizabeth Carol 209, 210
Saving Christmas 251–253, 319, 320
Saving Santa 253–255, 324
Savino, Chris 296
Sawyer, Brandon 6
Sawyer, Brian 186, 187, 237
"Say Goodbye to Christmas" 104
Scales, Crystal 121
Scaletta, Sante 30
Schaal, Wendy 97
Scharlach, Ed 256, 257
Scheck, Frank 38
Scheer, Alexander 307
Scheib, Richard 157, 264
Schellbach, Rich 249
Schenberg, Scott 170
Schenck, Jeffrey 74, 75, 76
Schickel, Erika 308
Schiffman, Risa 136
Schifrin, Will 78, 88
Schifter, David 170
Schirripa, Steve 84, 171
Schleppi, Helmut 62
Schlessinger, Laura 317
Schletter, Eban 138
Schmid, Rolf 126
Schoch, Cathy 54
Schonfeld, Renee 21, 186, 249, 254, 273, 283
Schooley, Robert 118
Les Schtroumpfs 13, 153, 266
Schubert, Franz 14, 267
Schultz, Bill 26
Schultz, Dwight 304
Schwab, Bill 196
Schwartz, Bill 47

Schwartz, David 78
Schwartz, Dennis 153
Schwartz, Elizabeth 157
Schwartz, Robert 240
Schwartz, W. Tyler 157
Schwartz, William J. 157
Schwarzenegger, Arnold 265
Schwimmer, David 159
Scolari, Peter 256
A Scooby-Doo! Christmas 255–257, 320
Scooby-Doo, Where Are You! 255, 256
Scopp, Alfie 207
Scott, Adam 143
Scott, A.O. 112, 144, 227
Scott, Bruce 153
Scott, Donovan 186, 236
Scott, George C. 298
Scott, Jeffrey 41
Scott, Michael 62, 150
Scott, Seann William 130
Scott, Tom Everett 235
Scott, Tony 168
Scrooge Loose 241, 257, 324
Seagren, Danny 109
Seale, Douglas 85, 86
Seaman, Peter S. 73
Search for Rudolph 258, 321
The Search for Santa Paws 7, 25, 159, 164, 180, 216, 224, 234, 240, 258–260, 269, 323
"Season of Love" 278
Second City Television 174
The Secret World of Santa Claus 260–263, 324
"Les Secrets du Père Noël" 262
Seelman, Aaron 255
Sega 270
Segar, Elzie Crisler 273
Seibert, Fred 161, 277
Seibold, J. Otto 187, 189
Seinfeld 124
Selick, Henry 285
Selig, Josh 249
Selness, Andy 61
Sergei, Ivan 214
Sesame Street 81, 82, 83
"Seven Days 'Til Christmas" 168
Severson, Charmaine 286, 288
Sevier, Corey 292
Sexton, Charlie 9
Sexton, Dale 34
Seymann, Scott B. 103
Shadix, Glenn 284
Shakespeare, William 112
Shannon, David 253
Shannon, Jeff 225
The Shapies 258, 321
Shapiro, Gary 66
Sharkey, Thomas 68
Sharples, Winston 90
Shatner, William 105, 140
Shawkey, Eric 103
Shawn, Dick 165, 314
The Shawshank Redemption 102
Shay, Alan 39
Shear, Michael 178
Shear, Samantha 178
Shee, Neil 126

Sheen, Charlie 122
Sheen, Martin 122
Sheetz, Chuck 257
Shekter, Mark 8
Shelley, Carla 13
Shelly, Bruce 272
Shelly, Reed 272
Shepherd, Laura 8
Shepherd, Sherri 190
Sheppard, W. Morgan 196
Shepphird, John 237
Sheridan, Chris 205
Sheridan, Kelly 176
Sherr, Lloyd 16
Sherrin, Robert 174
Shiel, Karin Young 83
Shields, Zach 144
Shilling, Jill 56
Shimerman, Armin 42, 157
Shimizu, Yuko 313
Shishido, Rhoydon 309
Shockley, William 67
"Shop, Shop, Shop" 103
Short, Martin 228, 229
"Show Me the Light (Love Theme)" 211
Showtime 249
Shropshire, Elmo 107, 108
"Silent Night" 9, 26, 27, 99, 132, 189, 236, 278
Silo, Susan 41
Silver, Jeffrey 225, 227, 230
Silver, Joel 99
"Silver and Gold" 206
"Silver Bells" 29
Silverman, Berkley 197
Silverman, Fred 13, 153, 266
Silverman, Melissa 13, 153, 266
Silvers, Phil 298
Silverstein, Keith 184
Sim, Alastair 143, 231
Simels, Steve 73
Simmons, Alexandria 309
Simmons, Jeffrey Scott 232
Simmons, Richard 210
Simon, Ben 159
Simonsen, Brad 64
Simotas, Nick 16
The Simpsons 189, 199
Simunek, Nick 255
Sinacori, Greg 4
Sinatra, Frank 237
Sindelar, Dave 35, 52
"Sing Hallelujah" 236
Single Santa Seeks Mrs. Claus 157, 263–264, 322
The Sinister Santa Claus Switch 109
Siracusa, Frank 60, 240
Sirico, Tony 84, 171
Sirois, Myriam 210
Skipping Christmas 53
Skye, Ione 231
Slam Dunk Ernest 86
"Sleigh Ride" 29, 314
Sloan, Douglas 132
Slott, Susan 92
Small Town Santa 264–265, 320, 322
Smith, Bob 126, 127
Smith, Christopher 102

Smith, Danny 10, 11, 204, 205
Smith, Hal 46, 58, 94, 164, 288
Smith, Jaclyn 181, 182
Smith, Jada Pinkett 159
Smith, Ken 218
Smith, Kurtwood 200
Smith, Robert O. 245
Smith, Roger 110
Smith, Sandra M. Levy 157
Smith, Sarah 13
Smith, Shannon 205
Smith, Willow 159
The Smurfs 3, 14, 153, 154, 265, 266, 267, 271, 321, 323
The Smurfs 2 14, 154, 266
The Smurfs: A Christmas Carol 267
The Smurfs and the Magic Flute 14, 154, 266
The Smurfs Christmas Special 14, 153, 265–267, 324
Smyrl, David 82
Snow (album) 61
Snow (film) 267–268, 321
Snow Miser 165, 314, 316, 317
"The Snow Miser Song" 165, 314, 317
Snow 2: Brain Freeze 7, 25, 159, 164, 180, 240, 259, 268–269, 323
"Snowball Fight" 4
"Snowkids Rock" 90
"Snowman Song" 175
Snuffy, the Elf Who Saved Christmas 81, 269–270, 323
"Snuffy's Goodbye Song" 270
"Snuffy's Theme" 270
Snukal, Sherman 8
Sogliuzzo, André 190
Soles, Paul 206, 293
Solomos, Steve 145, 180
"Some Kind of Miracle" 254
"Someone Like You" 184
Somerville, Bonnie 235, 259
Sommer, Paul 154
Sommers, Erik 97
Sondervan, Sofia 112
Song, Brenda 118
Song, Ka Moon 184
Sonic Christmas Blast 25, 79, 105, 109, 148, 221, 270–272, 274, 285, 320, 322
Sonic the Hedgehog 270
The Sopranos 84, 171
Soren, David 160
Sorich, Michael J. 132, 243
Sorvino, Paul 215
Sottnick, Mark 242
Soucie, Kath 19, 91, 146, 175, 227, 245
"Sounds of Christmas Day" 58, 94
South Pole 98, 159, 241, 242
Spacey, Kevin 98
Spadaro. F. Thom 79, 80
Spall, Rafe 102
Spano, Vincent 54
Sparber, Isadore 39
Spath, Tom 154
Spears, Aries 179
Spears, Ken 58
Spector, Irv 70
Spence, Rod 237

Spengler, Pierre 224
Sperakis, Constanza 68
Spike: The Elf That Saved Christmas 24, 240, 272–273, 321
Spinach Greetings 25, 79, 105, 109, 148, 221, 273–275, 285, 309, 320, 322
Spindt, Carla 114
Spingarn, Jed 122
Spinney, Caroll 81, 84
SpongeBob SquarePants 88, 137, 161, 324
The SpongeBob SquarePants Movie 137
Sporn, Michael 242
Spot the Dog 275
Spot's Magical Christmas 78, 275–276, 324
Spot's Musical Adventures 275
Springer, Philip 213
Springer, Tony 213
"The Sprites' Songs" 211
Sprouse, Cole 118
Sprouse, Dylan 118
Sproxton, David 13
Squires, Emily 83
Staahl, Jim 107, 108
Stabile, Nick 232
Stables, Kelly 215
Stack, Peter 73
Stadler, Krista 143
Stafford, Nancy 61
Stalin, Joseph 100
Stallone, Frank 98
Stallone, Sylvester 98
Stanfield, Byron 278
Stanford, Alan 92
Stanton, Harry Dean 193, 194
"The Star Child" 261
Star of Bethlehem 150
Star Trek 104, 105, 145
Star Wars 132
Star Wars: Episode V–The Empire Strikes Back 238
Stark, Avrill 244
Starsky and Hutch 129
Stassium, Ed 90
Statema, Jamie 61
Staunton, Imelda 12
Steele, Declan 258
Steenburgen, Mary 192, 193
Stefan, Dean 234
Stein, Ben 238
Steinbeck, John 117
Steinhöfel, Andreas 62, 63
Stell, Guillermo Calderón 219
Stelzer, Ali 103
Stephenson, John 38, 58, 94
Stephenson, Nathan 105
stereo-optical process 38
Sterling, Mindy 73
Stevens, Andrew 25, 80
Stevens, W.H., Jr. 294
Stevenson, Colette 8
Stewart, Catherine Mary 57
"Stick-to-It-Ive" 184
Stiers, David Ogden 19
Stiles, Victor 220, 221
Stiller, Ben 83, 159
Stiller, Jerry 124

Stine, Brad 61
Stinson, Donavon 87
Stipe, Michael 188, 189
Stockham, Benjamin 67
Stoddart, Alexandra 267
Stojko, Elvis 36
"Stolen Christmas" 262
Stoller, Fred 91
Stone, Dee Wallace 54
Stone, Doug 278
Stone, Jessica 149
Stone, Melanie 43
Stone, Terry 255
Stones, Tad 118
Stookey, Paul 112
"Stories" 19
Stormoen, Jake 43
The Story of Santa Claus 223
"The Story of the Trolls" 261
"Storytelling Song" 51
Stout, Austin 202
Stovall, Jim 57
Strand, Chantal 151
Strauss, John J. 227, 230
Strauss, Kurt 132
Stroker Ace 129
Stroker and Hoop 128, 321
Strong, Tara 88, 161, 175, 277, 294
Struthers, Sally 104
Stuart, Eric 116
Stuart, James Patrick 5
Studney, Dan 297
"Stuff!" (song) 103
Sturmer, Andy 175
"Suffragette March" 168
Sullivan, Ed 108, 109
Sullivan, Kevin 78, 161
Sullivan, Nicole 5, 117
Sullivan, Peter 75, 76
Sullivan, T.J. 16
Sullivan, Ursula Ziegler 198
"Super Lapin" 261
"Super Rabbit" 261
"Super Sleuths Theme" 175
The Super Special Gift 46, 53, 55, 152, 154, 167, 180, 184, 276–277, 297, 323
"Supercalifragilisticexpialidocious" 124
Supercinski, Lee 125
Suplee, Ethan 316, 318
Surridge, Jay 178
swaddling clothes 252
Swain, Bob 248
Swallow, Jerod 36
Swallow My Eggnog 204
Swan Lake 277
The Swan Princess 278, 279
The Swan Princess: A Royal Family Tale 278
The Swan Princess Christmas 277–280, 320
The Swan Princess: Escape from Castle Mountain 278
The Swan Princess: The Mystery of the Enchanted Kingdom 278
Sweeten, Madylin 54
Swift, Allen 299
"Swingle Bells" 254
Switzer, Michael 303

Sycorax 48, 49
Sykes, Bob 79, 81
Sykes, Wanda 16
Symphonie Fantastique (Berlioz) 267
Symphony No. 6 in B Minor (Tchaikovsky's "Pathetique") 267
Symphony No. 7 (Beethoven) 7
Symphony No. 8 in B Minor (Schubert's "Unfinished") 14, 267
Szalewski, Circus 123
Szeles, Sean 200
Sztopa, Veronica 151
Szwarc, Jeannot 224

T. Eaton Company 23
The Tail of Flopsy, Mopsy, and Ted 276
Tajiri, Satoshi 116
Takács, Tibor 192, 301
The Tale of Peter Rabbit 276
A Tale of Two Cities 281
A Tale of Two Santas 2, 280–282, 312, 321
"The Tall Little Girl" 262
Talley, Jill 138
Tambor, Jeffrey 64, 72, 175
"Tapis Volant" 261
Tarrach, Jürgen 63
Tataranowicz, Tom 180
Tate, Jennifer 254
Tatters, Wes 258
Tatum, Richard 243
"A Tavish Toy" 168
Taweel, George 28
Taylor, Harold Vaughn 153
Taylor, Matthew W. 64
Taylor, Robert 164
Taylor, Russi 41, 162, 184
Taylor, Veronica 116
Tchaikovsky, Pyotr 43, 90, 130, 267, 277
Teague, David 309
"The Teddy Bear" 262
Teen Wolf 10
Teeter, Lara 79
Telek, Ava 187
Teletoon 245
The Tempest 49
Tennant, David 47, 48
Terzo, Venus 34, 176
Tetley, Walter 58
"Thank You, Santa" 223
Thatcher, Kirk R. 173
"That's What I Love About Christmas" 176
"There's Always Tomorrow" 206
Thiessen, Tiffani 34, 186
Thiltges, Paul 126
Thimble Theater 273
"Things That I've Collected" 27
"Think Think Think" 175
"This Is Halloween" 284
Thomas, Brian 84
Thomas, Dave 78
Thomas, Dave Barton 165
Thomas, Jay 226, 228
Thomas, Jonathan Taylor 308
Thomas, Kevin 225
Thompson, Bobbe J. 268, 269

Thompson, Caroline 285
Thompson, Frank 86, 193
Thompson, Jay 90
Thomson, Desson 238, 285
Thor (god) 143, 307
Thorburn, Jim 292
Thorisson, Marteinn 93
Thorne, Alex 101, 197
The Three Dogateers 282–283, 320
The Three Dogateers Save Christmas 282
300 (film) 97
Three Musketeers 282
The Three Stooges 123
Thumbelina 212
Thurman, Annie 236
Thurman, Uma 171
Thyne, Tone 251
Tibbitt, Paul 138, 139
Tickety Toc 55, 322
Tickner, French 53, 151, 156, 244, 245
Tikvarovski, Bojan 119
Tillotson, Johnny 211
Tilly, Jennifer 204
Tim Burton's The Nightmare Before Christmas 21, 25, 33, 79, 105, 109, 148, 152, 221, 272, 274, 283–286, 309, 322
"Time to Celebrate Christmas" 236
"Time to Go (on a Trek Through the Snow)" 175
"Tinker Time" 259
'Tis the Season to Be Smurfy 267
Tisdale, Ashley 254
Tissier, Barbara 273
"To Fill the Sack for Santa" 4
"To the Rescue" 284
Toast of the Town 108
Tobocman, David 209
Tockar, Lee 33, 34, 156, 210
Tolsky, Susan 141
Tom, Lauren 281, 312
Tom and Jerry 245, 246
The Tom and Jerry Show 245, 247
Tomassian, Alexis 273
Tomlinson, Jeff 119
Tomlinson, William J. 120
Tongariro National Park 179
Tonight show 296
Toon Disney 190
Topsy, Prakash 263
Torres, Liz 191
Tosti, Eric 273
Tosti, Jean-François 273
Toth, Andy 26
The Town Christmas Forgot 286, 320
"Town Meeting Song" 284
The Town Santa Forgot 286–288, 320
The Town That Banned Christmas 288–289, 320
The Town That Forgot About Christmas 66
The Town That Santa Forgot 286
A Town Without Christmas 289–290, 320
Toy Story (series) 117
"The Toy Taker" 209

The Toy That Saved Christmas 290–292, 319
Toys "R" Us Family Theater 17
The Toys Who Saved Christmas 125
Traber, Vreni 126
Trachtenberg, Michelle 202
Trainor, Jerry 77
Trandahl, Paul 33
Trans-Siberian Orchestra 200
Travers, Mary 112
Travis, Randy 33
Traynor, Mark 258
Tree of Good and Evil 252
Tree of Life 252
The Tree That Saved Christmas 292–293, 320
Tremayne, Les 198
Treveiler, Robert C. 317
Trigg, Patsy 107
"Trim Up the Tree" 70
Tripp, Jenny 297
Tripp, Paul 59
The Trishas 9
troglodyte 293
The Trolls and the Christmas Express 293–294, 321, 324
"The Trolls' Song" 293
Trost, Tracy 57
True Boo 38, 39, 320
Trump, Donald 300
Tsai, Martin 38
Tubbe, Bruce 201
Tuber, Joel 242
Tubman, Harriet 112
Tucker, Ken 7, 134, 281
Tucker, Michael 133, 134
T.U.F.F. Puppy 77, 324
Tull, Thomas 144
Tuomainen, Hannu 93
Turner, Brad 174
Turner, Brian 214, 215
Turner, Christopher 244, 270
Turner, Ed 86
Turner, Marcus 244
Turner, Travis 88
Turner, William 84
Turoa Ski Fields 179
TVOKids 197
'Twas the Fight Before Christmas 294–296, 324
'Twas the Night 58, 152, 154, 157, 180, 183, 184, 277, 296–297, 323
'Twas the Night Before Bumpy 2, 297–298, 320, 322
'Twas the Night Before Christmas (film) 281, 299–300, 323
"'Twas the Night Before Christmas" (poem) 41, 58, 135, 295, 297, 299
"The 12 Days of Christmas" 4, 254, 278
"12 Days of Elevator Muzak" 254
"The 12 Labors of Santa" 261
Twice Upon a Christmas 191, 300, 324
Twillie, Carmen 211
Tylak, Paul 92
Tyler, Aisha 226, 228
Tyler, Ginny 241
Tyler, Steven 251
Tyng, Christopher 189

Tyson-Chew, Nerida 243
Tzachor, Jonathan 132

Ubach, Alana 190
U'Brien, Jane 258
Ulibarri, Amanda 4
"The Un-Christmas Song" 51
Uncle Grandpa 301, 323
Uncle Grandpa: Christmas Special 2, 301–302, 323
Underwood, Kianna 213
Underwood, Ron 214, 215, 318
Unlikely Angel (film) 193, 302–303, 320
"Unlikely Angel" (song) 303
"Up at the North Pole" 184
"Up on the Housetop" 111
Uranus 49
Urban, Andrew L. 243
Urban, Mitch 184
Urbano, Carl 14
Urbanski, Calla 36
Urretabizkaia, Itziar 170
Urspruch, Christine 307

Vaccaro, Brenda 154
Vahanian, Marc 25
Valderrama, Wilmer 91
Valdes, Leslie 162
Valdivia, Victor 298
Valenti, Mark 150
Valentine, Gary 73, 75, 76
Valentine, Steve 236
Vallance, Stephanie, Louise 151
Vallow, Kara 97, 205
Van Allsburg, Chris 189
Van Beuren Studios 89
Van Citters, Darrel 247
van der Bos, Michael 234
VandenBerghe, Maggie 114
Vander Pyl, Jean 45, 94
VanDerWerff, Todd 205
Van Dien, Casper 75
Van Dyke, Dick 162, 288
Van Gelder, Lawrence 211
Van Gogh, Vincent 43
VanHart, Loretta 304
Van Patten, Dick 43, 237
Van Peebles, Mario 111
Van Rijsselberge, Jan 44
Van Vleet, Richard 114
Varney, Jim 85, 86
Vasquez, Felix 187
Vaughn, Vince 98, 99
Vaughns, Byron 33
Vazquez, Gorka 170
VeggieTales 290
Ventress, Sib 180
Venuleth, Jacques 244
Verbong, Ben 63
Vernon, Steve 170
Verrall, Robert 110
A Very Barry Christmas 303–304, 323
A Very CatDog Christmas 304–305, 319
A Very Wompkee Christmas 305–306, 320
Viener, John 204
Vilanch, Bruce 136

Village of the Damned 112
Villela, Bernardo 63
Vince, Robert 217, 236, 260
Vincent, David 273
Vincent, Sam 33, 119, 156
Vinciguerra, Luc 244
Vischer, Lisa 291
Vischer, Phil 290, 291
Vischer, Shelby 291
"A Visit from St. Nicholas" 41, 58, 283
Vivanco, Karmelo 170
Vogel, Matt 84
Vox, Dylan 231
Vries, Joost de 64

Wachtenheim, David 129
Wade, Will 49
Waese, Jamie 106
Wagner, Lindsay 149
Wagner, Robert 186
Wahlforss, Mikael 248
Waldo, Janet 58
Walker, Angela 62
Walker, James T. 141
Walker, John 14
Walker, Matthew 300
Walker, Penny 253
Walker, Vince 254
Wallace, Betsy 161
Wallace, George 232
Wallace, Pamela 158, 264
Wallach, Eli 129
Walsh, M. Emmet 256
Walsh, Seamus 139
Walsh, Valerie 68
Walsh, Vivian 187, 189
Walt Disney World 212
The Waltons 106
"Waltz of the Flowers" 130
War of the Worlds 217
Warburton, Patrick 117, 204
Ward, B.J. 17, 22
Ward, Terry 56
Warmann, Amon 254
Warnat, Kimberley 194
Warner, Lynne 4
Warner, Paris 43
Warnes, Jennifer 211
Warren, Leslie Ann 202
Warren, Mary 66
Warzel, Matthew 170
Wasilewski, Audrey 235
Waskin, Mel 293
Waterhouse, Mary Anne 166
Watson, Dale 9
Watson, Muse 57
Watters, Mark 176
Waxman, Al 201
Wayne, John 56
WB Network 256
"We Are Santa's Elves" 206
"We Can Make It" 211
"We Don't Go Together At All" 168
"We Need a Little Christmas" 168
"We Wish You a Merry Christmas" 132, 278
"We Work Together" 91
Weaver, Beau 164
Webb, Andy 29, 31, 145, 157, 191, 209, 231, 286, 289
Webber, C.E. 48
Webster, Brian 27
Webster, Nicholas 222
Webster, Torri 286
Wedge, Chris 130
The Wee Winter Singers 299, 314
Weihnachtsmann 63
Weil, Cynthia 72
Weinstein, Phil 26
Weisz, Rachel 98
Weitzman, Matt 95
Welch, Savannah 9
"Welcome, Christmas" 70
Weldon, Kurt 248
Welker, Frank 14, 41, 42, 121, 135, 146, 154, 164, 256, 281, 309
Wells, Cassie 120
Wells, Dick 175
Welsh, Kenneth 23
Wendell, Pam 107
Wendt, George 214, 216
Wenger, Brahm 236, 259
Wenk, Sarah 256, 305
"We're a Couple of Misfits" 206
"We're Happy Little Christmas Elves" 108
"We're Not So Bad" 189
Wermers-Skelton, Stevie 196
Werner, Peter 29
Weseluck, Cathy 34, 119, 210
West, Adam 204
West, Billy 280, 304, 311
Westmoreland, Christie 269
Wetcher, Mathew 248
Whalen, Sean 112
"What About His Nose" 211
"What Makes Christmas Merry" 46
"What'cha Trying to Do to Me?" 303
What's New, Scooby-Doo? 255, 320
"What's This?" 284
Wheadon, Carrie R. 177
Wheeler, John 157, 263
When Angels Come to Town 290
When Angels Sing 9
"When I'm Home" 9
When Santa Fell to Earth 306–308, 319, 322, 324
"When Your Heart Is Ready" 306
"Where Are You Christmas?" 72
"Where Do You Go?" 270
"Where Do You Look for Santa?" 58
Where's Spot? 275
"Which One Is the Real Santa Claus?" 58, 94
"While by My Sheep" 290, 291
"Whistle" 168
White, Brian 258
White, Jaleel 270
White, Lari 184
White, Miss Lavelle 9
Whitestone, Steve 17
Whitmire, Steve 81, 84, 172
Whitney, Jamie 198
"Who Says There Ain't No Santa?" 67
Who Stole Santa? 25, 79, 105, 109, 148, 221, 272, 274, 285, 308–309, 322
"Who Stole Santa's Sack?" 51
"Who Will Sing to Me?" 259
"Who-bilation" 72
"Why Don't I Believe?" 259
"Wicked Little Me" 46
Wicksman, Dan 248
Wicksman, Nuria 248
Widmann, Benedikt 291
Wiesenfeld, Joe 24
Wilcox Paxton, Colin 194, 195
Wild Man (mythical being) 143
"Will I Ever See?" 51
Willard, Fred 118
William Tell 154
Williams, Ashley 268
Williams, Brad 114
Williams, Gary Anthony 129
Williams, Harland 118, 219
Williams, Hattie Mae 4
Williams, Paul 172, 173, 181
Williams, Phil 304
Williams, Rebecca 180
Williams, Rhys 296
Williams, R.J. 181, 182
Williams, Robin 309, 310
Williams, Stacy 86
Williams, Tyrel Jackson 3
Williams, Vanessa 213
Willis, Bruce 146
Willis, Miron 180
Willows, Alec 210
Willson, Meredith 220
Wilson, Dale 156
Wilson, Donald 48
Wilson, Jamie 9
Wilson, Larry 318
Wilson, Lee 79, 81
Wilson, Robert J. 150, 318
Wilson, Roy 164, 184
Wilton, Penelope 48
Winchell, April 164
Winchell, Paul 14, 58, 154, 267
Winding, Jai 234
Winer, R. 212
Wings (band) 211
Winks, Wendy 233
Winnie the Pooh 174
Winning, David 293
Winter, Christine 299, 314
Winter Solstice 251
"Winter Wonderland" 29
Winters, Jonathan 17, 238
Winthrop, Robert 177, 185
Wipf, Thomas 248
Wipp, Konrad 307
"The Wise Man's Journey" 29
Wise Men 252
Wiseman, Larisa 162, 277
A Wish for Wings That Work 309–310, 322
A Wish for Wings That Work: An Opus Christmas Story 309
The Witch Who Stole Santa Claus 109
Wittgens, Andrea 236
Wix, Katy 55
The Wizard of Oz 153, 218, 256, 306, 308

Index

Wolf "D" (performer) 180
Wolk, Andy 290
Wolverton, Jeff 64
Women's Army Corp 124
The Wompkee's First Grand Adventure 305
Wonder Pets! 249, 250, 251, 321
"Wonderful Christmastime" 211
The Wonderful Wizard of Oz 102
Wong, Miken 68
Wood, Bobby 29
Wood, Richard 132
Woodburn, Danny 216, 235, 259
Woodman, Danielle 227
Woods, Dana 24, 114
Woods, Mildred 178
Woods, Robert 79, 81
World War I 155
Worley, Jo Anne 79, 80
Wow! Wow! Wubbzy! 276, 323
Wright, Kay 41
Wright, Sean 278
Wright, Trevor 235
Wrights, B.J. 28
Wyle, George 206
Wyle, Noah 147
Wylie, Adam 78

Xmas Story 280, 310–313, 321

Yaeger, Mark 254
Yanagisawa, Takayuki 116
Yarrow, Peter 112
Yates, Gary 145
Yates, Jenny 29
The Year Scroogenip Swiped Christmas 313–314, 320
The Year Without a Santa Claus (1974) 46, 95, 126, 164, 165, 183, 314–316, 317, 323
The Year Without a Santa Claus (2006) 316–318, 319, 323
"The Year Without a Santa Claus" (song) 314
Yellen, Barry B. 59
Yentl 111
"Yes, Virginia, There Is a Santa Claus" 134, 136
Yogi's First Christmas 58, 94
Yorke, Wayne Thomas 191, 300
Yost, David 131, 132
"You Can Always Count on Santa" 91
"You Gotta Believe" 84, 124
Young, Alan 154
Young, Bryant 81, 84
Young, Carlson 75
Young, Mike 26
Young, Seldon O. 279
Young, Steve 189
Younts, Jay 252
"You're a Mean One, Mr. Grinch" 70
"You've Got Me, Honey" 51

Yule Goat 307
Yule log 195
Yule log cakes 151, 263
Yulies 74, 180, 216

Zachary, Noah 36
Zadora, Pia 220, 221
Zajac, Gord 42
Zamchick, Sofie 250
Zamm, Alex 268
Zamora, Rudy 14
Zann, Lenore 176
Zanni, Chiara 119, 156, 176
Zappia, Marco 51
Zappia, Robert 51, 247
Zappia, Rocco 51
"'Zat You, Santa Claus?" 29
Zelaya, Jose 68
Zelouf, Susan 92
Zembillas, Charles 78
Zemrak, Derek 114
Zieff, Rick 246
Zimmermen, Kris 146
Zipursky, Arnie 183
Zisk, Craig 166
Zuckerman, Alex 308
Zuckerman, Josh 296, 297
Zylberman, Noam 314